THE LOST DEBATE

THE
LOST
DEBATE

*German Socialist Intellectuals
and Totalitarianism*

William David Jones

UNIVERSITY OF ILLINOIS PRESS
URBANA AND CHICAGO

© 1999 by the Board of Trustees of the University of Illinois
Manufactured in the United States of America
I 2 3 4 5 C P 5 4 3 2 I

∞ This book is printed on acid-free paper.

Library of Congress Cataloging-in-Publication Data
Jones, William David, 1953–
The lost debate: German socialist intellectuals and
totalitarianism / William David Jones.
p.   cm.
Includes bibliographical references and index.
ISBN 0-252-02480-X (cloth: alk. paper)
ISBN 0-252-06796-7 (pbk.: alk. paper)
1. Socialism—Germany—History—20th century.
2. Socialists—Germany—History—20th century.
3. Intellectuals—Germany—History—20th century.
4. Totalitarianism—Germany—History—20th century.
5. Germany—Politics and government—20th century.
I. Title.
HX273.J66   1999
335'.00943'0904—dc21   98-58029
CIP

For Anne and David

Germany's special place in the history of this century is obvious: it is the only European country that has had to experience, suffer, and acknowledge responsibility for the devastating effects of both totalitarian movements of the twentieth century: Nazism and Bolshevism. I leave it to the learned professors of political science to point out or emphasize the indisputable specific differences between these two movements. . . . My point is that the same political experiences that have made the history of Germany a tragic history can also allow Germany to take its place in the forefront of a democratic and universalist expansion of the idea of Europe.

—Jorge Semprun, *Literature or Life*

CONTENTS

Preface
xi

Introduction
I

1. Strange Defeat: Leftist Intellectuals and Weimar's Collapse, 1928–33
21

2. Socialists in Dark Times: Perspectives from Exile, 1933–39
64

3. Varieties of Antitotalitarianism: Wartime Theories and Politics, 1939–45
108

4. Totalitarianism's Temptations: Into the Cold War
173

Notes
221

Bibliography
303

Index
347

PREFACE

Totalitarianism stands as one of the defining political ideas of this century, but precisely what the word *totalitarianism* indicates has long been at issue. The search for explanations of modern tyranny's origins and symptomatic features has proceeded for nearly eight decades, yielding various contested answers, and the search itself has now become an object of study. Yet accounts of totalitarianism as a type of regime or as a theory of dictatorship have all too often overlooked or unfairly slighted important left-wing critiques of modern tyranny—particularly those generated by independent or unorthodox Marxists in the years before the cold war. This book provides one of the elements that has been largely missing from historical studies of the various notions of totalitarianism: an account of their gradual and controversial emergence on the German left from the last years of the Weimar Republic to the first two decades of the cold war.

Any historical retracing of lesser-known concepts of totalitarianism must fight against a commonly held image of their origins. Because of the ideological dominance of one type of the concept during the cold war period, the debates about totalitarian dictatorship have often appeared to observers and participants alike as either a lamentable or praiseworthy product of the cold war itself. This picture is at once too simple and too politically convenient. As the arguments and evidence in the following chapters demonstrate, the comparative analysis of dictatorship in the twentieth century has a longer and more challenging history than the most outspoken critics and advocates of what has come to be called "totalitarian theory" have been willing to grant. Critiques of modern tyranny have emerged from a variety of political and philosophical perspectives, including conservative, religious, liberal, libertarian, and leftist. This book focuses on the interwar and wartime critiques of dictatorship produced by a group of leftist German intellectuals. Their writings offer one of the most compelling series of responses by an articulate and politically threatened group to that violent and decisive era.

The embattled political and theoretical positions of these intellectuals both enabled and compelled them to study the origins and character of modern dictatorship. During the early interwar years, they had supported a variety of socialist policies in Germany, and most of them were members of Marxist political parties. The defeat of both moderate and revolutionary socialism by the Nazis and their allies left these writers and activists personally and politically outcast. The fact that all of the German men and women whose lives and writings this book examines suffered exile, imprisonment, or death at the hands of a German state that systematically jailed or murdered hundreds of thousands of its native-born or naturalized citizens for the newly promulgated crime of being Jews (which several of these writers were, at least according to Nazi Germany's Nuremberg Laws) or socialists (which all of these writers were, at least some of the time) or both offers compelling evidence regarding the character of their history. Even those among them who had once hoped that the German Communist Party would lead a radical transformation of the nation and of Europe gradually became more critical of Communism and the Soviet Union. These writers soon became frustrated by the Communists' role in implementing several politically ineffective or even disastrous Comintern programs, and, as the consequences of Stalin's leadership quickly became clearer during the 1930s, they began to criticize the murderous domestic policies of the Soviet Union as well. Another important element of their history is that, during the years they spent living and writing outside Nazi Germany, these individuals helped shape and sometimes even led the scholarly discussion of modern dictatorship in their more or less uncomfortable havens in Czechoslovakia, France, the Netherlands, England, Mexico, and the United States. As exile scholars, policy analysts, and publicists, they labored for decades alongside or within the fractious community of the European and the American Left. Often forced to redirect their intellectual efforts to meet the demands of a daunting historical situation, they generated an extraordinary and divergent range of theoretical and practical writings on the crises of the 1930s and 1940s.

After World War II, as a kind of embodiment of "the return of the repressed," some of these individuals made their way to the Federal Republic of Germany, where they exerted an important and persistent influence on the emerging political culture. Even those writers who remained in England or the United States often found an ample German readership, for in the divided Germany of the postwar years, the problem of dictatorship—whether construed under the category of totalitarianism, fascism, or some other term—remained a constant and looming feature of public life. The very existence of two Germanies, clearly a legacy of both National Socialism and rising cold war tensions, served to heighten the controversy surrounding the idea of totalitarianism. As a result, the older, often neglected interwar studies on politics, economics, and society produced by this group of writers sometimes found an attentive audience, though the reception of their work was sharply mixed and selective. Controversies about their theoretical efforts intensified during the 1960s and continue to be replayed decades later in the work of an even younger generation of scholars and political writers. But by the time the Berlin Wall came down in 1989, only a tiny remnant of this older group of left-wing theorists remained on the scene to offer an analysis of the current upheavals in Germany.

The theoretical forays of these left-wing intellectuals into the terrain of contemporary politics and society may be read partly as the responses of an articulate and embattled band of dissidents to the kind of "everyday life" that had been forced on them as "unwanted" Germans and as exiles. Their writings also owed some vital element to their Marxist heritage—even in cases when they were explicitly and often noisily moving away from their earlier allegiance to Marxist notions of radical social transformation. They had entered politics and academic life as left-wing Weimar radicals who typically bucked party orthodoxy—whether Socialist or Communist—or at the very least attacked its shortcomings. In the exile and wartime intellectual battles over theoretical and practical tactics of resistance to dictatorship, however, they often ended up revising or even reviling what they regarded as "orthodox" Marxism. Yet for all their critical wrestling with Marxist historical concepts, they never quite escaped them entirely. Some of these thinkers continued to draw heavily on Marxist concepts and critical approaches and attempted to revitalize them, while others attempted to tear away at the Marxist theoretical apparatus. Rarely did they simply turn away from Marxism. They either attempted to revive it by some means or picked over what they took to be its remains even as its specter haunted them in return.

They quarreled among themselves about current leftist theory and practice as intensely as they had argued within and with the Marxist legacy itself. Only on rare occasions did all of these leftist intellectuals find common political or theoretical ground as Marxists or ex-Marxists, though pairs and small clusters of them did form lasting intellectual and personal alliances. The shared fund of allegiances, experiences, and ideas that informed their writings yielded no common judgment regarding the origins of modern dictatorship or even the best means of resistance to it. Consequently, no generalized theoretical formulation about totalitarianism gleaned from their efforts will be offered here. This book focuses instead on the provocative and seminal debate about the origins and character of modern dictatorship that these German socialist intellectuals generated—a many-sided series of critical explorations that never culminated in a consensus before or during the cold war and whose traces persist even after that singular conflict's end.

A few preliminary clarifications regarding the limits and intent of this project are in order. First, there is no attempt here to provide a systematic history of twentieth-century dictatorships. This is not, in other words, a book about Nazi Germany or Fascist Italy or the Soviet Union. It is a book about how a group of thinkers tried to understand the historical and social forces that had generated and shaped those regimes and others. Second, this book is not intended to defend the dominant cold war–era theories of totalitarianism. These comparative formulations, for all their indisputable interest and importance, have often proven to be as weak in their function as explanatory historical models as they have been potent for the purpose of political attack. I do, however, want to revisit a few of the totalitarian theories of the 1950s and 1960s in a somewhat different context—that is, as but one possible set of positions in a long-standing debate on the origins, actions, and consequences of twentieth-century dictatorships. As we shall see, some of the most provocative interwar and wartime writings of German left-wing intellectuals foreshadowed not only the cold war–era theories of totalitarianism but also some of the trenchant critical responses to them. My third initial point—which will be an obvious one to some readers—is that there is not just a single concept of totalitarianism but a variety of such concepts. This book is not an encyclopedic study of these various concepts, however. I am concerned here with only a few of them that German leftists generated in the interwar and wartime years.

These left-wing critiques of dictatorship have a renewed historical interest at the close of the twentieth century. Echoes of the arguments and issues that produced them still resound. The past decade has witnessed sharply disputed reassessments of the writings and lives of significant intellectual figures associated in some way with notions of totalitarianism, such as George Orwell, Hannah Arendt, and, in a distinct but related set of discussions, Martin Heidegger. The accounts historians offered over the past two decades to explain Nazi genocide against European Jews—one of the crucial issues that any historian attempting to describe or explain Nazi Germany must at some point address—have also provoked broad scholarly and public interest. Each of these scholarly conflicts—from the bitter intentionalist-functionalist debates on the importance of Hitler in the Nazi state to the *Historikerstreit* (historian's controversy) of the 1980s and the still more recent discussions of the complicity of "ordinary" Germans in violence against Jews—has touched on the totalitarianism debate in important ways.

At yet another level of scholarly discourse—but one still linked to the events and ideas that seized the attention of the thinkers this book examines—intellectual combat continues among theorists affiliated with Hegelian or Marxist notions of social "totality" or the Enlightenment project of a liberal, rationalized society (whose most important representative is the German philosopher Jürgen Habermas) and their postmodern critics (led in this particular debate by such figures as the French scholar Jean-François Lyotard), who charge that the rationalized social totality is inevitably a system of totalitarian oppression. This persisting debate has long since assumed an international character, and yet it often returns implicitly and explicitly to the terms and texts produced by intellectuals of the interwar German Left.

In more conventional popular debates on politics and policy, recent partisan struggles have revealed the surprising strength of some of the hastily renamed and reconfigured Communist parties in Eastern and Western Europe. The appeal of socialist politics has not been obliterated by the end of the cold war but may actually have been reinvigorated in particular national contexts. Even more dramatically (and certainly far more violently), the various neofascist movements in France, Italy, Russia, and Germany continue to offer dangerous challenges to the familiar social democratic-liberal-conservative partisan lineup typical of postwar Western European politics. Each of these moments of recent political and intellectual history bears some significant connection to the interwar and wartime debates about totalitarian dictatorship.

There are additional, perhaps even more compelling reasons to reconsider this old intraleft dispute. With startling speed, cold war certainties have crumbled, dulling the ideological sharpness of the predominantly anti-Communist versions of the totalitarian concept. But the problems of political violence and dictatorial repression have hardly disappeared. The moment of Communism's evident breakdown and retreat in Europe has already had numerous unexpected and unforeseeable consequences in this regard. Fifty years after the end of World War II, fascism has resurfaced not only as remembered violence but also as renewed violence. The vigorous resurgence of neofascist, overtly racist political movements in Eastern and Western Europe, some of them exhibiting both an anti-Semitic and an anti-Islamic character—the latter addition offering indirect evidence of the deadly effectiveness of the original varieties of fascism—raises the issue of political violence in the most urgent way.

The war in Bosnia and its challenge to international military and diplomatic systems invented in cold war times for cold war purposes has been the most disastrous result to date of the rapid shifts in the political and economic power alignments in Europe. The legacies of totalitarianism as unitary idea, murderous practice, political epithet, bogeyman, and self-immolating chaos in the course of the appalling violence in the former Yugoslavia are unmistakable. This was clearly not what had been hoped for after the cold war. The war in Bosnia marked a tendency toward ferocious, ideologically motivated violence in at least some parts of Europe—not to mention an occasional and regionally varying shift in political momentum not only away from Communism but also away from liberalism, social democracy, or traditionalist conservatism toward a fascistic, even genocidal nationalism that might reasonably be labeled "totalitarian." Whether the occasions of this kind of nationalism and their attendant international nonresponse renew themselves more frequently or rise up in some other region within or outside Europe (though not necessarily beyond European interests and influence, such as Rwanda), these bursts of political violence that display murderous popular rage and chillingly cynical opportunism will rightly gain the critical scrutiny of scholars and others. Familiarity with the investigations of European totalitarianism's earlier history might help sustain and instruct the opposition to such political movements.

Elsewhere, the residues of what the German historian and political scientist Karl Dietrich Bracher has labeled "the totalitarian experience" retain at least some of their cold war–era ideological pungency. In the United States, the Oklahoma City bombing atrocity of 1995 provoked the reflex in the national media of comparing and sometimes equating the murders and other crimes perpetrated by groups that emerged from the radical Left during the late 1960s and early 1970s with the violent acts of the radical rightist "militia" groups of the 1990s. The idea of totalitarianism certainly did not create these events and movements, but to a remarkable extent it has conditioned our responses to them, demonstrating the persistence of its power even in what may yet prove to be the period of its decline. The cold war's sobering aftermath ought to be the appropriate time for examining the terms and texts of a debate among a small but influential group of German socialist intellectuals on the problem of modern dictatorship that largely preceded the cold war. This book is an attempt to recover, reinterpret, and perhaps revitalize some of the fragments of that lost debate.

❧❧

I have had the good fortune to receive the generous assistance and support of many friends, relatives, colleagues, students, and institutions in the course of working on this project. The Claremont Graduate School (now the Claremont Graduate University), the Haynes Foundation, the Fulbright Commission, and the Council for European Studies at Columbia University provided funding crucial to my archival research. The History Program of the Claremont Graduate University also offered financial support for research assistants to help me complete some of the final preparations of the bibliography. During my work in the archives, I received the gracious and skillful assistance of Mieke Ijzermans and the rest of the staff of the International Institute of Social History in Amsterdam; Gunzelin Schmid Knoerr of the Horkheimer Archive at the Stadt- und Universitätsbibliothek Frankfurt am Main; Constance Cruickshank of the Faber and Faber Archive in London; the staff of the George Orwell Archive at University College in London; and the librarians of the Hoover Institution at Stanford. I am grateful for the patient and unfailing help offered by the staff at the Honnold Library of the Claremont Colleges, especially Martha Smith, Sheri Irvin, Meg Garrett, and Adam Rosenkranz. It is also my pleasure to acknowledge the cooperation of Peter Borkenau, the late Kay Boyle, and her attorney, Jerome Garchik, who granted me permission to examine and quote from private or previously classified documents related to Franz Borkenau.

As I began my explorations of the topic of left-wing antitotalitarianism a little over a decade ago, Richard Löwenthal and John E. Tashjean were extraordinarily helpful and encouraging. Our common interests as well as our disagreements on a number of issues generated a fruitful correspondence over the course of several years. This study owes a great deal to their generosity, and I know that I am but one of many scholars who have felt a personal sense of loss at their deaths. Lewis Coser, Elliott Eisenberg, Valeria

E. Russo, Russell Jacoby, Gerhard Bry, Götz Langkau, Stephen Eric Bronner, Rainer Erd, Ossip Flechtheim, Peter Lowe, Julla Rahmer, and the late Henry Schmidt provided me with extremely useful source materials or leads during the early stages of my research. A number of scholars and friends, including Michael Stanley-Jones, Charles Salas, Robin Walz, Tom Adams, William Smaldone, Martin Jay, Wolfgang Wippermann, Ian Kershaw, Alfons Söllner, Abbott Gleason, Elazar Barkan, Al Lindemann, David Large, Linda Sexson, Thomas Wessell, Michelle Maskiell, Billy G. Smith, Robert Rydell, Mary Murphy, Pierce Mullen, Susan Neel, Ray Mentzer, and James Allard, offered indispensable criticisms, suggestions, questions, and encouragement in response to parts of the manuscript, which they encountered in the form of articles, conference papers, or drafts of chapters. Several anonymous readers of the original manuscript suggested changes or additions that have found their way into the final version of this book. Sometimes readers' evaluations of the ideas and thinkers I discuss were quite different from mine, and in thanking these individuals, I do not want to give the impression that I am now enlisting them in my behalf. I do, however, greatly appreciate their thoughtful attention to my project. Three of my students at the Claremont Graduate University also offered timely and beneficial assistance. Peter Jana and Alexander Karn reviewed the manuscript and assisted me in preparing the bibliography. Matt Reed discussed with me some of the theoretical issues that appear in the final chapter. Janet Farrell Brodie and Elazar Barkan, chairs of the Claremont Graduate University's history and cultural studies departments, respectively, generously made funds available to support students who were assisting me in the final preparations of the manuscript. For their friendly interest in my work, I cannot say enough in the way of thanks to my friends and colleagues in the History, Political Science, and Geography Department at Mt. San Antonio College, the History Department of the Claremont Graduate University, the History Department of the California State Polytechnic University at Pomona, and the History and Philosophy Department at Montana State University. Sharing the challenges and rewards of teaching and scholarship with them has been one of the sustaining pleasures of the past decade. Working with the University of Illinois Press has been delightful. I wish to express my profound thanks to Dick Martin, who has been encouraging, patient, and prodding in just the right proportions since our first exchange of letters. Jane Mohraz gave the manuscript the great benefit of her thorough and knowledgeable attention.

For their patience and perceptive criticism over the years, I owe a special debt to four teachers with whom I studied at the Claremont Graduate School. Over the course of the past fifteen years, Robert Dawidoff has been an extraordinary teacher, mentor, and friend. His articles and books have reminded me not to forget the perspective of individuals or groups that have been persecuted, marginalized, or unjustly neglected. Harry Liebersohn has provided crucial advice on how to formulate and refine this project since its first incarnation as a seminar paper. His broad knowledge of European and German history, his meticulous comments on various drafts of the manuscript, and his generous support have been enormously helpful at every stage of my labor on this book. Working with Michael Roth has been both a revelation and a pleasure. In conversations going back over a decade now, he has given me more to think about—and a better model of how to do one's own thinking—than any student or colleague has a right to expect. Despite the demands of his teaching and administrative roles, Scott Warren offered to share with me his rich knowledge of political philosophy, challenging my conclusions about particular thinkers and offering alternative reconsiderations of their legacies. Over the course of a hectic, unpredictable, and yet productive decade, these four teachers have provided me with timely encouragement, and they have enriched my life with their friendship. All of the individuals I have mentioned here should take their portion of credit for whatever merits this book possesses. I bear the sole responsibility for its failures and omissions.

For their abiding love and support, I wish to thank my mother, Darlene Jones; my mother-in-law, Mary Rose Merten; and our families and friends. My father, Daryll Jones, died while I was completing the final version of the manuscript. I will always be grateful for his love and his example. Above all, I thank my wife, Anne Merten, and our son, David Merten-Jones, for their spirited and loving companionship. They have contributed to the completion of this book in more ways than I can count or name.

❧❧

Permission to use the following is gratefully acknowledged:

Excerpts from Max Horkheimer, "Autoritärer Staat," taken from *Gesammelte Schriften*, vol. 5. Copyright © 1987 S. Fischer Verlag GmbH, Frankfurt am Main.

Passages from Max Horkheimer, "The Authoritarian State," in *The Essential Frankfurt School Reader,* edited by Andrew Arato and Eike Gebhardt (New York: Continuum Publishing Company, 1993).

THE LOST DEBATE

INTRODUCTION

If there is any point in examining the conditions in which the representation of totalitarianism originally emerged and then developed during the course of several decades, it is because those conditions throw some light on the resistance of left-wing opinion. The new concept was regarded as a concept of the Right, forged to serve reactionary purposes. The struggle against totalitarianism seemed like a diversion whose aim was to obscure the reality of Western imperialism and to disarm the critique of the capitalist system. But we still have to ask why the non-communist Left, Marxist or quasi-Marxist, had left the initiative for formulating the totalitarian problem to conservatives or liberals, why analyses like those of Hannah Arendt found so little support.
—Claude Lefort, 1980

The most typical and influential concepts of totalitarianism have for decades focused on the comparison of Nazi Germany and the Soviet Union. Many scholars have contended that these were both "total" regimes, making absolute ideological, social, and economic demands on their citizens and exercising enormous coercive power against those who would not or could not conform. Given the extraordinary violence these two regimes perpetrated against civilians and their partly overlapping and intertwined historical careers as military powers, the reasons for investigating them as related or parallel phenomena might seem obvious enough. But the story of the origins and development of concepts of totalitarianism holds more interest and displays greater complexity than these comparisons can reveal. This book examines how German socialist intellectuals generated a series of writings on the problem of modern dictatorship before the advent of the cold war, leaving the legacy of a critical, left-wing alternative to the dominant discourse on the problem of totalitarianism. This diverse and extensive body of writings has not been neglected entirely, but it has generally received only partial and inconsistent attention.

Always a controversial notion, totalitarianism, considered as a political phenomenon and a conceptual model, became the object of study for a burgeoning academic subdiscipline during the initial period of the cold war. During these years, the emotions and events surrounding the defeat of the Nazi regime and the decisively established great power status of the Soviet Union mixed freely in a whirling and volatile political atmosphere. Scholars quickly took up the task of explaining these recent and continuing upheavals. Conferences, articles, and books on totalitarianism proliferated in the United States and Western Europe from the early 1950s through the 1960s, then tailed off for a few years. A new round of totalitarianism studies surged into view as détente waned during the late 1970s. With yet another renaissance after the fall of the Berlin Wall in 1989 and the collapse of the Soviet Union in 1991, the comparative notion of totalitarianism has now survived several premature burials.

Alongside the cold war deployment of this comparative analysis of the extreme Right (the Nazis) and the extreme Left (the Communists—the Soviet Union in particular) emerged a series of criticisms of these versions of the idea of totalitarianism. Challenges to the notion's accuracy and usefulness were launched by a number of scholars who were usually, though not always, on the political left themselves. The grounds for their rejection of the concept were rooted in political or interpretive considerations, or at times some measure of each. Local conditions influenced the specific nature and focus of these criticisms. In the Federal Republic of Germany, leftists often objected to the way the dominant version of totalitarian theory sanctioned the idea that the defeated totalitarians—the Nazis—were safely gone from the scene and that the surviving totalitarians representing a danger in the East—the Soviets and their Communist allies in the German Democratic Republic—should now be the primary focus of critical discussions of dictatorship. In Europe and the United States, debates raged among scholars over the issue of which regimes did or did not merit the label "totalitarian." In addition, alternatives to the totalitarianism concept, theories of dictatorship using such categories as fascism, Stalinism, Caesarism, or authoritarianism, among others, also generated their defenders and their controversies. But no idea or term so powerfully attracted advocates and opponents as *totalitarianism* did.

The fiery glow of the cold war–era debate on totalitarianism often cast its own origins into the shadows, and its crackling volume overwhelmed the diversity of voices that had long addressed the problem of the pervasive and oppressive power of the modern state. Indeed, many theoretical approaches to totalitarian dictatorship have appeared during the past seventy years, but their specifically left-wing formulations have so far gained less attention than their conservative and liberal versions. Left-wing attention to the problem of totalitarian dictatorship is precisely what the French political theorist Claude Lefort claimed was missing during the interwar, wartime, and postwar periods. He did allow that a few "isolated individuals or small revolutionary groups" on the left criticized not only fascist dictatorships but also Communist ones, yet he still contended that "most of them could not bring themselves to compare Stalinism and fascism and avoided speaking of a totalitarian state in the USSR."[1] Of course, when he referred to the theoretical projects of the non-Communist Left, Lefort was writing about his own activity as well as that of others. During the early years of the cold war, Lefort had been a member of one of those "small revolutionary groups," the unorthodox Marxist band known as Socialisme ou Barbarie, which also included Cornelius Castoriadis and Jean-François Lyotard. He became—following the earlier examples of Albert Camus, David Rousset, and Raymond Aron but differing from each of them in his political development and his conclusions—one of the relatively few prominent intellectuals with personal or political connections to the French Left who ventured to label the Soviet Union as "totalitarian" during the 1950s.[2]

Lefort pursued his own line of unorthodox leftist reasoning, which led him in the direction of a post-Marxian democratic radicalism, but once again local conditions channeled the discussion. Lefort's criticism of the lack of left-wing critiques of Soviet dictatorship strikes its mark far more squarely in the case of the French political Left than in that of the German Left, which is the focus of this study.[3] In Germany, the issue of totalitarianism was a "peculiar" one throughout the cold war. The superpower allies had mapped out the occupation "zones" for Germany even before the end of World War II. Allies quickly became enemies, and in the aftermath of the Berlin blockade and airlift, they sanctioned the creation of two Germanies in 1949. The concepts of totalitarianism in the West and fascism in the East gave added ideological force to each new German regime's efforts to manufacture a political consensus. These crucial national and historical distinctions as well as Lefort's remarks make clear that any consideration of the history of concepts of totalitarianism hauls us forcefully onto political as well as scholarly turf. In the light of this, the early cold

war era—the period of the totalitarianism debate's most intense politicization and ideological influence—is a good place to begin.

By the late twentieth century, a body of writings existed that could be
referred to as the "classical" versions of the cold war–era concept of totalitarianism. These would certainly include Hannah Arendt's *Origins of Totalitarianism* as well as the perhaps better-known fictional representations
of totalitarian dictatorship produced by Arthur Koestler, George Orwell,
and a host of Eastern European novelists, poets, playwrights, and essay-
ists, from Czeslaw Milosz and Alexander Solzhenitsyn to Václav Havel.
Some of these writings compared Nazism and Communism, but since
they appeared during the cold war (save for Koestler's *Darkness at Noon,*
first published in England in 1940 and then in the United States the following year), it is not surprising that most of them aimed their criticism
at the Soviet Union or some other East European regime. A few, such as
Orwell's *Nineteen Eighty-Four,* created indelible representations of future
or at any rate fictional totalitarian societies. These books on modern dictatorship and the controversies that arose at the time of their publication
also revealed that the notion of totalitarianism had quite different uses
and audiences in each half of a divided Europe. In Western Europe, it typically served the political interests of the Right, though many liberals made
ample use of it in both domestic and international politics, while in Eastern Europe, it became a serviceable weapon in the arsenal of protest
against Soviet hegemony in the region.[4]

The cold war–era version of the totalitarianism concept that had the
greatest influence on scholars specializing in the study of modern dictatorship, however, was not Arendt's, nor was it produced by a writer of
novels, poems, or plays. Carl J. Friedrich, a German-born political scientist who taught at Harvard University, formulated and advocated what
became the dominant version of totalitarian theory during the cold war.[5]
After his initial construction of a model of totalitarian regimes, he worked
on the concept in authorial partnership with Zbigniew Brzezinski, another European émigré who was also a Harvard political scientist.[6] The
often-cited totalitarian "syndrome" that this pair of scholars generated
and refined soon became a standard version of the theory, and in 1956,
on the eve of the Hungarian Revolution, it set forth the following characteristics:

> 1. an official ideology, consisting of an official body of doctrine cover-
> ing all vital aspects of man's existence to which everyone living in that
> society is supposed to adhere, at least passively . . . ;

2. a single mass party led typically by one man, the "dictator," and consisting of a relatively small percentage of the total population (up to 10 per cent) of men and women . . .;

3. A system of terroristic police control, supporting but also supervising the party for its leaders, and characteristically directed not only against demonstrable "enemies" of the regime, but against arbitrarily selected classes of the population; the terror of the secret police systematically exploiting modern science, and more especially scientific psychology;

4. a technologically conditioned near-complete monopoly of control, in the hands of the party and its subservient cadres, of all means of effective mass communication, such as the press, radio, motion pictures;

5. a similarly technologically conditioned near-complete monopoly of control (in the same hands) of all means of effective armed combat;

6. a central control and direction of the entire economy through the bureaucratic co-ordination of its formerly independent corporate entities, typically including most other associations and group activities.[7]

During the following years, many of the debates over the term's use focused on the relative strengths and weaknesses of some variation of Friedrich and Brzezinski's model or later modifications of it. Whatever its virtues and failures, the model clearly lent itself to comparative use. Also, in its generalizing, descriptive, and synchronic character—the political theorist Seyla Benhabib aptly describes this mode of research and presentation as "operationalized"—the model offered a succinctly formulated and altogether typical expression of early postwar political science. The book, however, did not please everyone. One of the early reviewers of Friedrich and Brzezinski's book, the historian Carl E. Schorske, criticized the book's institutional as opposed to historical approach. He persuasively insisted that the political dynamics and ideological appeal of such movements as fascism and Communism inevitably escaped the kind of analysis that the two Harvard scholars had provided. He also questioned a model that ruled out "Franco's Spain, Pilsudski's Poland, and other states that do not fully lend themselves to the a priori, taxonomic method of Friedrich and Brzezinski."[8]

Despite criticism, the Friedrich-Brzezinski model quickly assumed status as the paradigmatic scholarly incarnation of the totalitarian concept in the cold war period.[9] This model of the totalitarian regime not only gave some scholars an "ideal type"—a rough standard by which to measure a regime's relative levels of administrative control and oppressive harshness—but also proved its usefulness in the ideological battles of the early years of the cold war. Such a schematic comparison of Soviet, Nazi, or other regimes might have had reasonable scholarly uses, but this version of the theory has always also had enormous value as an intellectual weapon against Communism and as a tool for legitimating a variety of anti-Communist policies. Much cruder assertions of an imminent global leftist threat, however, provided a basis not only for an anti-Soviet foreign policy but also, especially in the United States, for domestic anti-Communism—or, what was more politically convenient for some, a shifting, nebulous, anti-"leftism" that might stamp a range of federal government policies from school integration to national health insurance as "creeping socialism." From this perspective, any identifiably left-wing or liberal-democratic policy pitched all its human cargo onto the slippery slope that swept downward into Communist totalitarianism.[10] Friedrich and Brzezinski were hardly responsible for all of the various uses and abuses of antitotalitarianism. Their work on the problem of totalitarianism remains in many respects a revealing and complex symptomatic expression of the tense and fearful political culture of that early postwar period. Because of the anti-Communist policies such theories helped legitimate, however, cold war–era concepts of totalitarianism, such as the one Friedrich and Brzezinski formulated, drew their bristling advocates and detractors from the start. As its central place in subsequent discussions of the comparative notion of totalitarianism shows, the Friedrich-Brzezinski "syndrome" became the most crowded point of arrival and departure for the ideologically dominant anti-Communist version of totalitarian theory. As such, it can at least serve as a provisional benchmark in the analysis of the idea's multistranded history without becoming the Procrustean measure or necessary endpoint of its development.[11]

The story of the various totalitarianism concepts begins over twenty years before the cold war, long before Friedrich's social scientific construction of one type of the concept. Use of the term *totalitarian* dates back to the rise of fascism in the 1920s. The Italian Fascists seized what had been a term of opprobrium and turned it into a propaganda boast. They first drew outraged criticism from Italian liberals for their "totalitarian" tactics in dismantling existing constitutional election procedures. But soon the Fascist leader Benito Mussolini made positive claims regarding the "violent totalitarian will" of his party.[12] According to scholarly accounts of the term's use, comparisons of fascism and Communism under the category of totalitarianism appeared by the late 1920s in journalistic writings.[13] This conceptual framework drew criticism nearly the moment it was ventured. As early as 1929, the sociologist Karl Mannheim discussed the tempting Bolshevik-fascist pairing in *Ideologie und Utopie* (*Ideology and Utopia*):

It has often been insisted that even Leninism contains a tinge of fascism. But it would be misleading to overlook the differences in emphasizing the similarities. The common element in the two views is confined merely to the activity of aggressive minorities. Only because Leninism was originally the theory of a minority uncompromisingly determined to seize power by revolutionary means did the theory of the significance of leading groups and of their decisive energy come to the fore. But this theory never took flight into a complete irrationalism. The Bolshevist group was only an active minority within a class movement of an increasingly self-conscious proletariat so that the irrational activistic aspects of its doctrines were constantly supported by the assumption of the rational intelligibility of the historical process.[14]

Mannheim, without using the term *totalitarianism,* offered a comparison of the two regimes, but he distinguished fascism from Bolshevism on the basis that the latter emphasized the principles of reason and class-consciousness. He also tended to criticize comparisons that stressed the role of force in both movements, which he viewed as a superficial similarity. But his arguments appeared in 1929, when Stalin was just beginning the most active and murderous phase of his policies of internal suppression and the Nazis had yet to win power in Germany. Nevertheless, his early critique of the "totalitarian comparison" suggests that as soon as the comparative approach to fascism and Communism appeared, it provoked important challenges. This continues to be the story of concepts of totalitarianism. Though much has happened since 1929 to make the fascist-Bolshevist comparison a compelling one for many scholars, Mannheim's critique, which sought to distinguish among political movements that were similarly repressive but proclaimed and pursued divergent goals, continues to find successors in some of the strenuous counterarguments to the cold war–era versions of totalitarianism theory.[15]

The prewar and wartime critiques of totalitarian dictatorship produced by leftist German intellectuals that are the primary focus of this book fit chronologically between Mannheim's *Ideologie und Utopie* (1929) and Hannah Arendt's *Origins of Totalitarianism* (1951). Conducted in the midst of a rapidly changing political landscape, these left-wing interwar and wartime critiques of dictatorship emerged in the writings of independent socialists, council Communists, radical Marxists, and disenchanted Social Democrats. They were attempting the difficult task of providing a theoretically grounded perspective on both quickly shifting events and long-developing crises. Fascism had succeeded in Italy in 1922, and Mussolini's "March on Rome" provided the National Socialists with a model for their own attempted coup in 1923.[16] The stormy career of the German Communist Party during the 1920s had alienated many radical intellectuals, and the Social Democrats appeared to them as politically too timid and tightly bound to the existing capitalist economic order. Even before the effects of the world economic crisis hit Germany, many Marxist intellectuals had cut off all connections to the two large socialist parties. When the Nazis seized power in 1933, leftist intellectuals often headed into exile with a sharply critical view of all of the new party movements and dictatorships—and with an urgent need to explain and resist them.

Even though they continued to see themselves as leftists, at least from late Weimar into the war years, several of these writers freely compared or equated fascism and Communism—though some of them favored comparison without necessarily wanting to imply equation. The writings of these leftist intellectuals would later be challenged, dismissed, or simply *missed* by many postwar leftists. Even Lefort, one of the most knowledgeable and incisive of the postwar, post-Marxian theorists on the left, minimized the scope and diversity of earlier leftist analyses of totalitarian dictatorship. His remarks asserting the relative absence of left-wing criticism of the Soviet Union as a "totalitarian" state find partial corroboration in the analysis of the British historian Ian Kershaw, who argues for the existence of a very limited version of the pre–cold war, left-wing critique of totalitarianism in his exhaustive and critical study of the scholarship on Nazi Germany, *The Nazi Dictatorship: Problems and Perspectives of Interpretation:* "In the 1930s and 1940s the concept [of totalitarianism] was applied by notable left-wing analysts of fascism such as Borkenau, Löwenthal, Hilferding, and Franz Neumann as a tool for characterizing what they saw as the new and specific in fascism (or Nazism) alone, without the comparative element of extension to Soviet Communism."[17] Kershaw mentions several key German socialist thinkers who fashioned critiques of fascism and Soviet Communism and whose work receives extensive analysis in the following pages. But the contention that Franz Borkenau, Richard Löwenthal, and Rudolf Hilferding shunned or neglected a comparative use of the totalitarianism concept in the 1930s and 1940s needs some revision, for each of these three writers made at least limited use of the notion in precisely this way by 1940.[18] Even Franz Neumann edged toward comparing Nazi Germany and the Soviet Union in some of his late 1940s writings, though he never seems simply to have equated the two regimes. Kershaw's assessment in *The Nazi Dictatorship,* a work rightly acknowledged as the most authoritative accounts of historians' various approaches to the study of Nazi Germany, indicates at least some scholarly consensus on the character and timing of the origins and development of antitotalitarian theory. But elements of this consensus need reexamination. Evidence from the prewar and wartime debate among independent writers on the German left demonstrates the emergence of at least provisional comparative discussions and occasionally even fairly detailed and systematic analyses of similarities between right-wing and left-wing forms of dictatorship.

Some scholars on the postwar Marxist left in Germany have also tended to reject or dismiss the importance of the left-wing tradition of antitotalitarianism, choosing instead to emphasize the use of fascism as the key comparative concept for the analysis of National Socialism.[19] For many intellectuals associated with the New Left, a totalitarian theory that lumped all Communist movements together with Nazism was sheer cold war ideology—or, as the British historian E. P. Thompson labeled it in "Inside *Which* Whale?" his polemical essay of 1960, "Natopolitan culture."[20] *Fascism* became the primary rubric for the study of dictatorship among younger intellectuals on the left, and it drew particular support within the German New Left for its political and theoretical virtues as a category bracketing Nazi Germany as well as Fascist Italy as movements concerned with the protection and intensification of capitalism. In postwar German scholarly discourse about National Socialism, the very words *Totalitarismus* and *Faschismus* often became terminological badges that identified, to some extent at least, the politics of speakers and writers.[21] In 1972, the Marxist political scientist Reinhard Kühnl raised the issue of conservative-liberal ideological hegemony in the course of condemning the influence of totalitarianism theory. In an introduction to a collection of essays by various left-wing scholars, entitled *Totalitarismus: Zur Problematik eines politischen Begriffs* (*Totalitarianism: Toward the Problematic of a Political Concept*), he offered the following hostile assessment:

> Investigating the journalistic and political effect of totalitarianism theory since 1945, one discovers at a glance—at least within the Federal Republic of Germany—an astonishing development: the rise to dominance of the version of totalitarian theory that represents National Socialism and Communism as identical. Around 1950, it was announced by the political parties, the government, and the majority of the press, and finally declared an obligatory ideology for school instruction. For nearly a decade and a half, its scholarly and politically dominant position was virtually uncontested, the weighty objections to its interpretations largely unnoticed.[22]

Kühnl offered a persuasive argument here, at least insofar as he described the powerful and politically useful hegemony of totalitarian theory in West Germany during the cold war. Another German scholar writing in the 1970s, Wolfgang Wippermann, described this comparative, cold war version of the concept of totalitarianism quite similarly—and convincingly—as "the quasi-official ideology of the State."[23]

In addition to Kühnl's general assault on what he took to be the political use and abuse of the theory of totalitarianism during the heyday of the cold war, he also discussed as examples of left-wing versions of the theory the writings of Herbert Marcuse and Franz Neumann, two theorists who for a time were affiliated with a group that came to be known as the Frankfurt School. The Frankfurt School refers to the core group of social theorists associated with the Institute of Social Research that began its work in Frankfurt am Main in 1923, fled to a series of provisional European "homes" after the Nazis gained power, relocated overseas to New York and Los Angeles (Santa Monica) during the late interwar and wartime years, and then returned to the Federal Republic of Germany after the war. The scholars associated with the Institute of Social Research had fairly diverse disciplinary backgrounds, but their common roots on the German political left for a time strongly influenced the institute's developing analyses of modern industrial capitalist society. In the postwar years, the group's small remnant of thinkers, led by Max Horkheimer and Theodor Adorno (the pair of thinkers whose writings represent the central nexus of the Frankfurt School's thought, along with the closely allied work of Friedrich Pollock, Leo Lowenthal, and, for a time, Herbert Marcuse), traveled more often within the territory of anti-Communism, however cautious and critical its political support for Western Europe and the United States may have been. By this time, however, Marcuse and Neumann were no longer affiliated with the institute. Even so, the work of this group of theorists has often been received by scholars as a product of a sort of shifting leftist collective of social analysts. The theoretical writings on dictatorship produced by a few of the central members or "fellow travelers" of the Institute of Social Research are central to this study.[24]

The New Left student movement of the 1960s responded to this older generation of theorists in a variety of ways, some young leftists finding in their work a guide to the critical study of the postwar world, others seeing it as a retreat from or even a betrayal of left-wing radical politics. Kühnl, an outspoken Marxist critic of *Totalitarismustheorie,* ranked among those young leftists more hostile to the work of the Institute of Social Research, and he cited only a few published writings by Marcuse and Neumann.

Furthermore, he was clearly skeptical about the value of these writings as political critique. Nevertheless, Kühnl offered a relatively rare example of critical analysis by a Marxist scholar on the topic of left-wing critiques of totalitarianism.[25] He remained, however, an adamant opponent of the theory and objected strongly to its redeployment during the *Historiker-streit* of the 1980s, the "historian's debate" that took up the issues of the "normalization" of German history and the causes of and responsibility for Nazi Germany's genocide against European Jews.[26]

Eike Hennig, a Marxist sociologist and political scientist also writing in the 1970s, shared much of Kühnl's criticism of the Frankfurt School on the idea of totalitarianism. In his remarks about this group of theorists, Hennig mentioned Franz Neumann as well as Herbert Marcuse, Max Horkheimer, and Friedrich Pollock as representative of a "left" (the quotation marks are Hennig's) version of the theory of totalitarianism, but he generally—and quite accurately—found the theory's most ardent supporters further to the right, among conservatives, liberals, and pro–cold war Social Democrats. Yet even so impressively thorough a researcher as Hennig did not trace in detail the origins or the impact of the "left" version of totalitarian theory in his densely packed Marxist critiques of research on German fascism and the *Historikerstreit.*[27]

Scholars on the left—and scholars in general—have rarely examined such intellectuals as Franz Neumann, Arthur Rosenberg, Herbert Marcuse, Ruth Fischer, Karl Korsch, Max Horkheimer, Franz Borkenau, Otto Rühle, Richard Löwenthal, Ernst Fraenkel, and Rudolf Hilferding as a group of writers with at least partly shared concerns about political regimes, ideologies, and practices that they would call "totalitarian." Along with this neglect of their work as part of a free-wheeling intraleft debate, there has been at times a misunderstanding of the comparative and critical thrust of some of their writings on totalitarian dictatorship. Cold war disputes over politics, policies, and theory helped bury some of the elements of their earlier critical effort. But the left-wing critique of totalitarian dictatorship was far more extensive than Lefort, Hennig, or Kühnl recognized, and it appeared several years earlier than Kershaw indicated in the 1993 edition of *The Nazi Dictatorship.*[28]

There are, however, good reasons why Lefort and Kershaw sound a somewhat similar note in their comments on the relative absence of left-wing uses of the totalitarian concept. First, there was the political problem of the Left during the cold war. Many cold war–era leftists had almost automatically distanced themselves from any version of totalitarian theory because of its usefulness as an omnibus anti-"Red" attack by conservatives against *any* faction on the left: Social Democrats, Communists, or independent Marxists. Working out theories of fascism and attacking the idea of totalitarianism were partly means of directing the criticism of modern dictatorship away from Soviet socialism and more directly against Western capitalism. Some people on the left wanted above all to resist attacks against "existing socialism" in the Soviet Union, and these groups and individuals are Lefort's primary targets. Second—and Lefort's and Kershaw's comments raise this issue as well, though indirectly—there was the problem of the lack of a systematic history of the Left's efforts to provide a critique of totalitarianism, as opposed to studies of the Left's (both old and new) analyses of fascism. There were exceptions to this rule, such as Berlin historian Wolfgang Wippermann's discussions of the development of theories of fascism, in which he also mentioned some early versions of the totalitarianism idea on the left and provided a brief account of their theoretical underpinnings. But these issues were not a central focus of Wippermann's monographs on theories of fascism, even though his books remain among the best starting points for the examination of left-wing ventures into the concept of totalitarianism.[29] For the most part, the left-wing debate on totalitarianism has been "lost" in a double sense: during the cold war it was generally surpassed and defeated as a conceptual framework for the analysis of dictatorship by liberal and conservative versions of antitotalitarian critique, such as Friedrich's and Brzezinski's, and at the same time its history suffered neglect. With the recent and noteworthy exceptions of Abbott Gleason's historical study of totalitarian theory and the collection of essays on totalitarianism edited by Alfons Söllner, Ralf Walkenhaus, and Karin Wieland, most accounts of the theory's origins contain only isolated or underdeveloped traces of the story of socialists' role in constructing concepts of totalitarianism.[30]

The career of the German historian Ernst Nolte offers a provocative and cautionary example of this relative lack of attention to the early socialist critiques of totalitarianism that emerged on the German left. In the early 1960s, Nolte gained attention by virtue of his unorthodox but widely praised (even by some leftists, at least initially) "phenomenological" study of fascism, *Der Faschismus in seiner Epoche* (translated into English under the title *Three Faces of Fascism*). The book briefly sketched some of the origins of theories of both fascism and totalitarianism and even explained in a brief appendix some of the methodological and philosophical issues at stake in the debate between advocates of the two competing theoretical categories. These historical sections on the critiques of dictatorship, however, descended into Nolte's account as appropriate but only briefly glimpsed scenery behind the revised discussion of fascism he wished to stage. He provided an idiosyncratic, philosophical analysis of fascist movements, but it was not part of his project to present a systematic historical account of the writings in which the critical analysis of fascism took shape—a discussion that might have led him to consider early descriptions of totalitarianism as well.[31] A few years later, however, he edited a widely used collection of some of these writings, but even the editorial introductions in this book contained a brief background essay rather than a systematic discussion. Nolte's apparent lack of interest in a sustained analysis of the origins of totalitarian theory can be attributed at least partly to the fact that one of the foremost purposes of his writings in the 1960s was to highlight his theory of fascism as *opposed* to—or at least as a serviceable alternative to—the theory of totalitarianism. By the 1980s, Nolte had reversed himself, at least in terms of his theoretical model of choice, and would revise and revive his singular version of the theory of totalitarianism (or, as he himself put it in a radio-television dialogue with the German historian Hans Mommsen—one of the chief opponents of totalitarian theory—"historicize" or "deepen" the theory) in a series of books and articles that sparked and stoked the so-called historians' debate.[32]

Another example of how the story of totalitarianism as a problem of theory and practice for left-wing theorists has often been missed emerges in the work of a far less controversial scholar, the French historian Pierre Ayçoberry. His lucid and shrewdly structured study *The Nazi Question* offered an extended historiographical essay that summarized and judged various writings on Nazism—including several produced by the left-wing theorists whose work gains our attention here. But Ayçoberry's focus on discussions of National Socialism and fascism ignored some of these writers' most innovative contributions to a comparative theory of totalitarianism.[33]

Another case of partial attention to left-wing writers on totalitarian dictatorship is the work of the German scholar Walter Schlangen, author of two encyclopedic studies: *Die Totalitarismus-Theorie: Entwicklung und Probleme* (*The Theory of Totalitarianism: Development and Problems*) and *Theorie und Ideologie des Totalitarismus: Möglichkeiten und Grenzen einer liberalen Kritik politischer Herrschaft* (*Theory and Ideology of Totalitarianism: Possibilities and Limits of a Liberal Critique of Political Power*). Schlangen did include many references to the published writings on dictatorship by European and American leftists, but he emphasized those writings that could be seen as way stations along the road to the dominant cold war–era totalitarian theory.[34] Admittedly, this gave Schlangen's monograph a necessary frame of reference, but by focusing on the cold war version of the theory as the presumed endpoint of *Totalitarismustheorie,* he missed a number of key texts that had presented left-wing criticisms of fascist and Communist dictatorships, such as Otto Rühle's "Brauner und Roter Faschismus" ("Brown and Red Fascism") and Franz Borkenau's *Pareto.* Moreover, by relying almost exclusively on accessible published sources, his analysis could not attend to a variety of pertinent but little-known correspondence, exile publications, and manuscripts. Finally, an essential point of Schlangen's work, which was clearly intended as a response to the revival of the fascism concept sparked by Nolte's *Der Faschismus in seiner Epoche* as well as the writings of some Marxists and other scholars associated with the New Left (including Reinhard Kühnl), was to discredit the theory of fascism (*Faschismustheorie*) and to reassert the validity and relevance of the theory of totalitarianism (*Totalitarismustheorie*).

Schlangen was aided in his efforts by a formidable scholar who had by this time assumed Carl Friedrich's place as the chief defender of the concept of totalitarianism: Karl Dietrich Bracher. This prolific Bonn historian and political scientist, whose influence derives primarily from his magisterial and massively documented accounts of the disintegration of the Weimar Republic and the structure and policies of the Nazi regime, wrote the foreword to Schlangen's *Theorie und Ideologie des Totalitarismus,* published in 1972.[35] Bracher described *Totalitarismustheorie* as a necessary bulwark against both the right-wing authoritarianism of the "Carl Schmitt School" and the "Marxist polemic" against the idea of the democratic state.[36] This was Bracher's sharply phrased way of bringing one of the dominant conceptions of the totalitarian problem—specifically, the claim that right-wing extremism and left-wing extremism were equally threatening to parliamentary democracy—out of its historical origins in late Weimar and into discussions of the violent and radical Red Army Fraction and the neo-Nazi groups that troubled the Bonn government during the late 1960s and the 1970s.

Bracher's stress on the debate between advocates of *Faschismustheorie* and *Totalitarismustheorie* was quite timely. By the early 1980s, scholars in the United States and Europe had generated a great number and variety of articles and books on this very issue. The crux of the matter was whether it was more accurate to bracket Nazi Germany as one of several right-wing *fascist* movements in Europe or to class it with the Soviet Union as one of the two great *totalitarian* regimes of this century, in which the conventional categories of "right" and "left" are rendered moot and the issues of state terror and single-party control supersede other factors.[37] In an essay he wrote in 1987, Bracher continued to defend the idea of totalitarianism vigorously: "All justifications for getting rid of the concept of totalitarianism are inadequate, so long as we do not come up with a better word for this phenomenon: to call it authoritarian or fascist does not quite capture it and is even more vague and general. The rejection of the concept comes primarily from those to whom it may very well apply—just as, conversely, we hear talk of 'democracy' especially where no such thing exists."[38] The agenda of these two statements is telling. The first asserts a passionate but at least ostensibly scholarly opinion. The second is a rather scatter-shot political blast. This mix of motives and targets captures nicely the typical character of discussions of the idea of totalitarianism. Bracher's defense of the idea has remained consistent and passionate throughout its long, bumpy travels from the 1950s to the present. Certainly this has not been an easy chore. Over the past three decades, the concept of totalitarianism was attacked during the period of swiftly rising opposition to the Vietnam War in the late 1960s, mostly neglected in the brief mid-1970s interlude of détente, and then revived in France, Germany, and the United States during the conservative resurgence of the late 1970s and early 1980s.[39] Somewhat paradoxically, the end of the cold war has not completely dampened the idea's popularity, as might have been expected, but has appeared to give it a renewed purchase. A recent translation into English of several of Bracher's essays from the years of totalitarianism theory's "comeback" testifies to the idea's continuing role in scholarship and political debate.[40]

Still more recently, Abbott Gleason, in his perceptive and wide-ranging account, *Totalitarianism: The Inner History of the Cold War* (1995), has undertaken the difficult task of tracking the history of the concept across seven decades and around the globe. He discusses the work of several of the German leftists who wrote about totalitarianism, but the sheer scope of his lively and copiously documented book necessarily prevents a close tracking of the career of the totalitarian concept among such a small community of thinkers as the one examined here. Moreover, Gleason restates a typical assessment of the Left's characteristic rejection of the notion of totalitarianism in terms similar to the criticisms lodged by Lefort: "Most people on the Left have been highly resistant, until recently at least, to any suggestion that the classification of the Soviet Union as totalitarian is more than a conservative canard. The deeper reason for this is that to do so calls into question whether or not Marx's philosophy, the predominant idiom of the Left in the twentieth century, was really liberating. That idea is under heavy siege now in the Western world."[41] Gleason's remarks may be accurate enough about many leftists, especially those for whom rejection of the concept of totalitarianism has been an essential part of a left-wing political identity. He is certainly right about the embattled state of Marxism. Yet in the face of the resistance of many interwar and wartime leftists and their postwar heirs, a relatively small but significant group of left-wing writers criticized the Soviet Union as "totalitarian" over five decades ago—sometimes cautiously, in other cases quite openly—and their arguments have received little systematic scholarly attention.

The German Left during the period under discussion here shared with other large political groups the characteristics of internal schism and conflict, and thus it continues to demand differentiated historical reconstruction. I have therefore marked off the scope of this study of German socialist intellectuals according to several considerations. Only a tiny fragment of the larger German Left receives primary attention in this study—a group of roughly a dozen intellectuals. I have included discussions of individuals whose writings and careers show common political experiences or affiliations and some degree of attention to the work of other writers in the group. As for my claims for their socialism, I simply intend to indicate their (at least temporary) commitment to Marxian notions of class conflict, the exploitive and self-contradictory nature of capitalism, and radical social revolution. I do not limit the term *socialist* to only those with some kind of party affiliation, nor do I belabor the issue of whether individuals who were Communists or Social Democrats can reasonably be lumped together under a common "socialist" label. There is also the question of just how "German" these intellectuals were, an issue whose pursuit could become needlessly complicated and analytically obtuse. I have chosen an open and flexible notion of "German" in applying the designation "German socialist intellectual" throughout this book, using it to indicate anyone who was German by birth, who took German citizenship as an adult, or whose personal involvement with organizations of the German Left was prolonged and significant. Some cases are simple enough: well over half of the writers I discuss were German-born nationals. Several others were Austrian-born leftists who became German citizens during the Weimar Republic. Less numerous, but exercising a strong influence in German Social Democratic circles, were several Russian Menshevik exiles who had moved to Germany during Weimar and then shared yet another bitter exile after the Nazi takeover. Over half of the writers discussed in the following pages were ethnic Jews, which made them the special targets of National Socialist "racial" policies, regardless of the extent of their personal, religious, or cultural identity with Judaism.[42] Nearly all of these writers lost their German citizenship for a time because of Nazi policies against those classed as Jews or active leftists. The members of this group of theorists were for the most part leftist exemplars of Nietzsche's idea of the "good European"—cosmopolitans, atheists, and internationalists of an independent cast of mind who therefore could never have been Hitler's kind of "good Germans." But they were Germans in another sense—that is, in their cultural identity. Even in exile, even "in translation," this typically revealed itself. This group distinguishes itself in yet another way: these writers can continue to provoke interest today because their writings—a sizable portion of them, at any rate—remain a compelling archive of the interwar and wartime era that is at the same time remarkably timely. Several of these German socialist intellectuals generated historical and philosophical accounts of their time that still command scholarly attention, and they constructed theoretical perspectives and methods of critique that remain vital tools in the study of history, politics, society, ideology, and culture.

The left-wing notions of totalitarianism examined in this study were elements of a debate that has been lost or at best sporadically alluded to in historical accounts of the political writing of the interwar and wartime period. One reason for the neglect or misunderstanding of left-wing antitotalitarianism is that interwar leftists' use of the term *totalitarian* was tentative, experimental, and ambivalent.[43] Precisely because the Left's critiques grew up alongside the liberal and conservative analyses of fascism and totalitarianism, their partly shared terminology sometimes blurred crucial theoretical and political distinctions. To complicate matters further, the critique of totalitarianism paved the way to an acceptance of political liberalism or even conservatism for a number of thinkers who began their intellectual careers on the revolutionary or the social democratic German left. In short, the interwar and wartime appraisal of totalitarian dictatorships forced many leftists toward a critical rethinking and even rejection of Marxism, an exercise that appeared to many younger leftists as catastrophic retreat, passive accommodation, or at best vacillation in the context of cold war polarization. These personal and political consequences of the "lost debate" receive substantial attention in the following pages.

The choice of a narrower range of historical evidence offers some advantages. In contrast to the daunting array of theoretical writings examined in Abbott Gleason's and Walter Schlangen's surveys of the concept of totalitarianism, this book will provide a fresh account of the concept's historical development by means of a selective, historical reconsideration of the writings of a few German leftists from the late 1920s to the cold war era. If this project is successful, the concept of totalitarianism may shed the heavy methodological and ideological armor that often encapsulated it in the 1950s and 1960s, if only provisionally, and may appear once more as a limber, loose-jointed, unfinished, varying, and occasionally quite radical and innovative notion. Moreover, a historical approach to left-wing versions of the theory of totalitarianism may be able to avoid one of the most serious shortcomings of the Friedrich-Brzezinski model of totalitarianism itself: its tendency to pay insufficient attention to the historical development of political movements and ideas and other contingent social, psychological, and economic factors in dictatorships.

This account of left-wing antitotalitarianism focuses on the developing analysis of fascism and the roughly simultaneous appearance of the Nazi-Soviet comparison. It examines four key phases of the history of antitotalitarian thinking and writing on the German left. Chapter 1 discusses the early critiques of fascism and Bolshevism generated prior to the Nazi takeover of Germany. The considerations on the emergence and the appeal of fascism in particular would provide an important basis for later comparative studies of dictatorships. Chapter 2 examines the early exile period, when German socialist intellectuals were attempting to understand and explain their defeat at the hands of the Nazis as well as to offer tactics and strategies of resistance. At the same time, they observed in many of the domestic and foreign policies of the Soviet Union a clear danger to democratic principles and socialist ideals. Chapter 3 discusses the crucial wartime years, during which several of the most influential and controversial left-wing writings on totalitarianism appeared. The concluding chapter briefly takes up the cold war careers of these German leftists—though by 1949, *former* leftists would sometimes be a more appropriate description—including an exploratory investigation of the legacies of their interwar and wartime debates about totalitarian dictatorship.

Labeling these thinkers' efforts a "lost" debate requires one final bit of clarification. The adjectives *neglected* or *misunderstood* might be used as well. But some writings produced in the course of this debate certainly have not been ignored, while many others included in this study have received only scant attention. One of the reasons for the obscurity of some of the pre–cold war writings on totalitarian dictatorship produced by the German Left is the historical situation of flight and exile in which their authors worked. Several of these books and essays appeared in non-German language publications, émigré journals, or even typewritten manuscripts that circulated among only a few friends and colleagues. Some of

the telling moments of these discussions turn up only in private correspondence or organizational position papers that have received little attention. This study makes fairly extensive use of such sources and therefore provides new evidence of left-wing intellectuals' approach to the
problem of totalitarian dictatorship. Another reason for the marginalized
status of some of these writings is more directly political: these writers
often used the style and vocabulary of Marxian socialism just when that
outlook was undergoing yet another period of crisis, schism, and disloca-
tion. The early postwar period also brought Marxism or indeed any type
of socialist outlook under suspicion or even persecution in the United
States and other nations of the anti-Soviet NATO alliance, where nearly
all of these writers lived and worked. That most of these writers had long
since abandoned hope for a humane state or society in the Soviet Union
under Stalin did not lead them always to embrace the cold war policies and
ideologies of the West, though as we shall see, several of them did so. In
any case, their socialist past and sometimes socialist present could brand
them as false messengers, whose words of criticism against Communist
political regimes now encountered a skeptical, if not outright hostile,
audience.

An event that took place early in the cold war reveals something of the
odd and even precarious political situation of the leftist antitotalitarian
writer. In 1947, a first-term congressional representative from California,
Richard Nixon, came face-to-face with a former leader of the German
Communist Party, Ruth Fischer. By that time, the cold war was taking
shape, and Fischer, who had been a Weimar-era leftist and then a refugee
from the Nazis, pursued a career as a fervently anti-Communist writer. She
appeared before the House Committee on Un-American Activities as a
witness against one of her brothers, Gerhart Eisler, who was a member of
the Communist Party.[44] Nixon acknowledged the force of her opposition
to Communist "methods," but he also inquired about her current attitudes toward the philosophical and political outlook of Marxism. Fischer
proceeded to attack both her brother Gerhart and Stalinism vigorously
and in detail, but she never answered the congressman's question about
her Marxism. She knew all too well the dangers such a discussion might
pose, and Nixon had not yet perfected his unrelenting style of political
attack. Or perhaps he simply did not want to risk calling into question the
credibility of so useful and friendly a witness as Fischer. In any event, her
cupful of media fame would evaporate quickly, while the young congressman was about to tap an apparently eternal source.[45]

This brief episode, with its vivid display of the provocative and symbolic historical links between the political battles and personalities of one era and those of another, offers an initial glimpse into the complicated legacy of the German leftist opposition to totalitarian dictatorship. Looking into the contested and many-stranded development of left-wing considerations of the problem of totalitarianism places the broader debate on modern dictatorship in a different historical light—a light that may now accentuate certain writers and specific elements of their theories that have for too long remained obscure. Such an investigation may do little more than help restore some of these thinkers and texts to our historical field of vision. This is certainly one of its immediate goals. But this study might also help renew the debate on the origins and character of modern dictatorships in ways that force a reconsideration of the discussions of the totalitarian state that emerged on the German left before the cold war.

1

Strange Defeat: Leftist Intellectuals and Weimar's Collapse, 1928–33

The disastrous rôle of the Communist Party is well known. They hoped to create a revolutionary situation by destroying parliamentary democracy and then creating a Bolshevist dictatorship. In fact, they were the allies of the National Socialists in their struggle against the "Social Fascists," in other words Social Democrats and Trade Unions.

—Franz Neumann, 1933

The birth, troubled career, and ultimate collapse of Germany's first republic have rightly attracted the attention of numerous scholars.[1] Because the Weimar Republic's demise ushered in the violently destructive Nazi dictatorship, its history holds a special poignance and horror. The dynamic cultural and intellectual life of Weimar exhibited both adventurous experimentation and an intense self-consciousness. The political character of the Weimar Republic showed similar features but also offered exaggerated displays of caution and recklessness, meticulous parliamentary coalition-building and a deadly, autocratic intolerance. Not surprisingly, given its origins in military defeat and political compromise, the Weimar Republic's political order drew intense criticism as soon as its constitution took effect in 1919. The regime's prolonged crisis and ultimate capitulation to the Nazis in 1933 set off a long series of controversies on the causes of its failure.

One of the fairly typical elements of this story, as the labor lawyer Franz Neumann analyzed it in 1933 and as historians have often constructed it since, has been the argument that the Weimar Republic succumbed to a combination of pressures from the extreme Left (the German Communist Party) and the extreme Right (the Nazi Party).[2] This interpretation has its merits, particularly from the standpoint of liberal constitutional history, which has told in a variety of ways the story of the deadly transition during late Weimar, from legislative deadlock to executive rule to state-party dictatorship. Such a perspective also often tends to equate the significance of the pressures against the constitutional "center" from each end of Weimar's deadly earnest and active political lineup, and thus it helps to legitimate the kind of comparison of fascism and Communism that became so essential to the dominant cold war idea of totalitarianism. Since the Social Democrats had been the most reliable and effective political supporters of the Weimar Constitution, the strong involvement of some of the theorists associated with this party in the formulation of an outlook that condemned the antiparliamentary extremes of the Right and Left is hardly surprising. For these historical and political reasons, the traumatic period of the Weimar Republic remains an essential starting point for the analysis of German leftists' attention to the theoretical and practical problem of dictatorship.

The German Left and the New Dictatorships

The nominally Marxist but tactically reformist and parliamentary German Social Democratic Party (Sozialdemokratische Partei Deutschlands—SPD) spent the entire period of the Weimar Republic (1919 to 1933) pinned down between the sporadic but well-aimed criticisms of the more antibourgeois and politically oppositional German Communist Party (Kommunistische Partei Deutschlands—KPD) and the constant hostility of the conservative and far right parties—expressed most aggressively during Weimar's closing years in the violent words and deeds of the National Socialist German Workers' Party (Nationalsozialistische Deutsche Arbeiterpartei—NSDAP), better known as the Nazi Party. The uneasy and conflicted position of the Social Democrats, betwixt and between other political movements that viewed the moderate socialists as a primary enemy, had been established even before the constitutional regime of the Weimar Republic itself; indeed, it became the party's fate from the close of World War I to the Nazi seizure of power.[3]

The choices and failures of the SPD were crucial components of the era's politics, but there is blame enough to parcel out among several of the various political parties of the Weimar Republic. It is arguable, for example, that the parties of the German Right—regardless of their level of electoral support and even though they might have been alternatively supported or brought up short by their tacit partners in the German military elite—were always more powerful than the Communists ever were during the entire Weimar period. Moreover, the parties of the Right had the electorally useful habit of equating the Social Democrats and the Communists as twin Marxist dangers to the national order.[4] Even so, the Communists had certainly been no friends whatsoever of the "bourgeois republic" or its beleaguered Social Democratic guardians. By 1931, for example, some representatives of the German Communist Party voted along with the Nazi faction in the Prussian regional parliament to dump the lawfully elected Social Democratic government of Prussia from power. They failed to gain their immediate goal, but the desired result came about under different circumstances the following year, with disastrous consequences.[5] For their part, the Social Democrats had blocked their opponents on the radical left—and given them political ammunition for future use—over a decade earlier, during the interlude between the end of the empire and the establishment of the Weimar Republic. The prowar SPD faction, led by Friedrich Ebert and Philipp Scheidemann, gained power by cooperating with the reactionary and authoritarian German Military High Command in the weeks following the end of World War I, not only helping disarm and dismantle any revolutionary threat but also presiding over the crackdown that led to the murders of several prominent leftists. As the Weimar Republic experienced the shock of the world economic crisis in the early 1930s, the leaders of that same moderate socialist party acquiesced to presidential rule by executive decree, doing more than any other German party would do to preserve parliamentarism but, as it horribly turned out, also buying time for its enemies to demolish the Weimar Republic. These actions—and inactions—typified the crucial relationships between the two great left-wing German parties as well as their shifting stance toward opponents on the political right.

It would be but one of the era's surplus of ironies that two prominent former Social Democrats who had broken angrily with the party for its cooperation with the German government during World War I had also laid the theoretical groundwork for criticism of the radical new political factions of the 1920s that would pose the biggest right- and left-wing threat to the Weimar-era SPD. The significant critical attacks against fascism and Bolshevism by members of the German Left began with the tactical expressions of two of its seasoned and most radical leaders: Clara Zetkin and Rosa Luxemburg—though to be sure this attack did not initially link the two parties as comparable "totalitarian" movements. These two women had risen to prominent roles in the SPD during the prewar years. Luxemburg, who had gained a position of intellectual leadership in the German socialist movement despite her sex, her Jewish ethnicity, and her Polish national origins, possessed a commanding voice on the European left. She often intimidated other leading socialists by virtue of the fearsome intelligence and deftly aimed sharpness of her written and spoken arguments.[6] Zetkin had long played a crucial role in attempting to bridge the concerns of socialism and feminism, though she was less intellectually original and assertive than her younger friend Luxemburg.[7] Their courageous and principled antiwar stance in 1914 set them apart from a number of more accommodating and opportunistic leaders of the SPD. They had both participated actively and at great personal cost in the opposition to the war—Luxemburg spent many months in prison for her defiance of the government—and in the wartime band of radical socialists called the Spartacus Group (later the Spartacus League). Its members opposed the war, condemned the majority SPD, and remained for a time an autonomous radical group within the larger, newly formed Independent German Social Democratic Party (Unabhängige Sozialdemokratische Partei Deutschlands—USPD). Luxemburg took a leading role at the congress of various radical factions that created yet another left-wing party, the German Communist Party, in late December 1918, a few weeks after the end of the war.[8]

The wartime and early postwar writings and speeches of Luxemburg and Zetkin contributed powerfully to the 1920s socialist debates on the problem of dictatorship and the necessity of a left-wing response and were as important as those produced by any European Marxists of the period. An example of this contribution was Clara Zetkin's speech at the meeting of the Communist Party International Executive Committee of 1923 in Moscow, where she raised the issue of fascism in Italy as an immediate threat to the Left globally.[9] Zetkin, then recovering from an illness, was carried into the meeting and spoke from a seat placed in the midst of her comrades. The cogency of her words more than matched the drama of her entry. Her discussion made a crucial contribution to an intensified and theoretically unblinkered Marxist analysis of fascism, claiming that fascism was *not* "simply bourgeois terror" but a complex and dynamic movement that "exercises a stirring and overpowering influence on broad masses of the population."[10] Her attempt to emphasize the reality of a highly differentiated working class within which fascism might make real political gains marked at least a preliminary step away from the simplistic equation of class and consciousness that plagued all too many Marxists. This speech was arguably her most important contribution to the critical interwar debates about socialist theory and tactics.[11]

Zetkin's reflections on the problem of fascism, for all their stress on the need for new perceptions of the radical Right's appeal, took place within an accepted left-wing discourse. She had not repudiated any key element of the Comintern's particular variety of the Marxist outlook, nor had she in this speech launched the slightest attack on the new bearer of radical socialist hopes: the Soviet Union. Despite growing tensions in the Communist movement, the political leaders on the scene in Moscow in 1923 still included Vladimir Lenin, Leon Trotsky, Lev Kamenev, Alexandra Kollontai, and Nikolai Bukharin, as well as Joseph Stalin. The Soviet revolutionary regime had somehow survived. The terrible violence of the civil war had subsided. It would be succeeded by other bloody events, to be sure, but with a suddenness and on a scale as yet unforeseeable. For many European Marxists, the moment contained both great hopes and, in the wake of Mussolini's successful "March on Rome" the preceding October, great dangers.[12] At this moment, when a new range of political possibilities had taken shape, Zetkin remained an admirable but aging figure from the past for the Comintern as well as for the leading members of the German Communist Party—who were about to be replaced by a still younger group. The immediate fate of her remarks on fascism is a case in point.

According to ex-Communist Ruth Fischer's account of the Moscow meeting where Zetkin gave her innovative speech on fascism, Karl Radek, the mercurial and brilliant apparatchik who became the most important representative of the Comintern in Germany for a few years, took his turn at the speaker's rostrum immediately after Zetkin. Radek acknowledged Zetkin's discussion of fascism but confessed that he "could not even follow it clearly."[13] He then moved on to what he thought was a much more urgent matter: the nationalist protest campaign in Germany against the execution of a violent German right-wing extremist, Leo Schlageter, by the French army that was then occupying the Ruhr Valley as punishment for German nonpayment of war reparations. Reading Fischer's fairly detailed description of these speeches and their policy outcome, one must bear in mind that she eventually joined the KPD faction opposed to Radek, and her account of these events—written twenty-five years later—at times tends to make him look excessively foolish. This Schlageter policy of extreme appeals to nationalism can be traced to Radek's skills at altering his course—if not his claimed destination—with the shifting winds. However risky and ultimately ineffective the new course may have been, it can also be interpreted as a practical fulfillment of Zetkin's urgings for a flexible approach in appealing to the interests and needs of working-class Germans. The so-called Schlageter line also reveals, however, that even the interwar Comintern could conclude that, under certain circumstances, the distance between the politics of the extreme Right and the extreme Left could be spanned with no great trouble, a conclusion that, shorn of careful attention to contingent historical factors, would stand as one of the pillars of some of the later cold war versions of totalitarian theory.

In any case, the Schlageter episode, which took its place in the historical landscape of the period as one more bloody moment of the early postwar years, also captures the unsettled and portentous qualities of events in Germany in 1923. The unrelenting inflation of the German mark, which accelerated even more furiously in the wake of the French-Belgian occupation of the Ruhr in January, threatened to shatter the economy and knock the liberal and antirevolutionary Weimar Republic off its feet. The death of Schlageter, who had committed acts of violence against the French occupation, provoked a popular outrage against France as well as the Weimar government's passivity. From the perspective of oppositionist groups, nationalist appeals offered the opening for a timely additional shove that might topple the German Republic. The National Socialists made skillful propaganda use of the occupation and its attendant deadly episodes, such as the Schlageter incident, for their own purposes of delegitimating the fragile new German state. Starting with Radek's speech, which was the opening maneuver in a series of skirmishes intended to undermine the Weimar Republic and also to peel away working-class support from the extreme nationalist Right, so did the Communists. The campaign gained broad support among KPD leaders (including Fischer, who went so far as to encourage street violence against "Jewish capitalists" in one of her speeches), local groups, and newspapers. The summer of 1923 witnessed the Communists undertaking both an Anti-Fascist Day protest and the so-called Schlageter line, honoring the right-wing extremist. An abortive uprising by Communists in several German cities during October 1923 crowned their ideological zigzags and tactical opportunism with disastrous political defeat. Zetkin's promising start on an innovative theoretical and practical response to fascism nearly got lost in the mess.[14]

The results of the 1923 debacle proved significant to the fate of the KPD. Ruth Fischer and her allies in the party and the Comintern picked up the pieces in the aftermath of defeat. They quickly received the blessings of the Comintern and Stalin to revise policy in the direction of even sharper criticism of the Social Democrats. Thus began one of the several careers of the so-called social fascism propaganda line on the Communist left—that is, bracketing Social Democrats with fascists as partners against the working class. Fischer also shucked off the legacy of a humanist and Marxist internationalism that had been shared by such figures as Zetkin, Luxemburg, and, in his more devious and idiosyncratic way, Radek. For a time, Fischer would move the KPD along the path laid out by the Comintern during Gregory Zinoviev's brief period of leadership—until she was ousted from the leadership and then expelled from the party in 1925. By that time, Radek had already gone tumbling down, along with the leaders of the KPD "right" of 1923, led by Heinrich Brandler and his old friend August Thalheimer, initiating the steady decline that led to Radek's victimization by Stalin in the purges of the 1930s.[15] It would be years, however, before these notorious defeats and disappearances emerged. For the moment, even in their failures of 1923, the Communists of all factions were to be outdone by the Nazis. The Nazis staged their attempted coup in November—the violent and ludicrous "Beer Hall Putsch" in Munich—and the trial of Adolf Hitler that followed gave the National Socialists tremendously helpful national publicity.[16]

The Communists would eventually recover from their losses of membership and voter appeal, but never during Weimar would they be able to match the National Socialists in either the rhetoric or the practice of fanatical nationalism. Nevertheless, the Schlageter campaign and the left-right coup attempts of the fall of 1923 became additional examples of parallel Communist-Nazi policies from the Weimar period that, years later, would later help reinforce the totalitarian models that asserted a rough radical left–radical right equivalence. For her part, Clara Zetkin continued to be useful to the Communist Party as an icon who had parted with the legacy of the bad old days of social democracy. Despite her impressive theoretical leadership on the phenomenon of fascism, she wielded little practical influence in the Communist Party by the time the constitutional order of the Weimar Republic began to disintegrate. In the summer of 1932, she achieved her last public moment. By virtue of her status as the oldest member of the Reichstag, she chaired the opening of its final session prior to the accession of Hitler to the chancellorship in 1933. She died in exile in the Soviet Union later that year.[17]

If the left-wing analysis of fascism in Weimar Germany moved at first by fits and starts in the shadow of other, more urgent issues, the left-wing critique of the Bolshevist type of dictatorship appeared as an even more controversial undertaking. This project had begun several years before Zetkin's speech on fascism, with Rosa Luxemburg's powerful essay on the Russian Revolution. Luxemburg's article on Lenin and the Bolsheviks had been written during the fall of 1918. She would be murdered in Berlin by a paramilitary squad on 15 January 1919 at the time of the failed Spartacist uprising, which she had supported. Whether she would eventually have chosen to publish her critique of Lenin and the Bolsheviks therefore cannot be known. In any case, the document was not published right away— but neither was it buried for long. The essay was published posthumously by one of Luxemburg's surviving partners and political heirs, the embattled German Communist critic of the Comintern, Paul Levi. In the early years of the Weimar Republic, he had grown increasingly hostile to the steadily growing Comintern domination of the KPD, and he loosed Luxemburg's words on the vanguard of international revolution in 1922, soon after his departure from the party.[18]

Luxemburg's assessment of the Russian Revolution under Lenin's leadership was harsh, though as one of her recent editors and biographers, Stephen Eric Bronner, has argued, it was clearly *not* an outright dismissal of the Bolsheviks. She admired their audacity, their willingness to risk all as an example to working-class movements in other nations.[19] Nevertheless, the force of her criticism of the Revolution's suppression of dissent remains impressive eight decades later: "Without general elections, without unrestricted freedom of press and assembly, without a free struggle of opinion, life dies out in every public institution, becomes a mere semblance of life, in which only the bureaucracy remains as the active element. Public life gradually falls asleep, a few dozen party leaders of inexhaustible energy and boundless experience direct and rule."[20] With her list of freedoms of the kind associated by some on the left with "bourgeois" parliamentary republican government, Luxemburg anticipated in detail the arguments of some later left-wing critics within and outside the Soviet Union who did not want to throw out all of the squawking, feisty, and yet very much newborn liberal civil rights with the bourgeois, capitalist bathwater.[21] What is important here—in addition to the specific kinds of criticism Luxemburg expressed—is that the two strands of critique Zetkin and Luxemburg fashioned, the antifascist and the guardedly anti-Bolshevist, which appeared in the first years of the Weimar Republic, were not often spliced together by any writers on the left until several years later. Understanding how and why this theoretical enterprise came about requires looking at historical and political factors.

There were two overriding historical impulses that helped generate a socialist attack on both the Soviet model of socialism and the German fascist party of National Socialism. First, there was the division of the German Left into two major parties—the Communist and Social Democratic—as well as numerous splinter groups. Second, there were the events and shifting alliances that produced the defeat of the parliamentary German Left and the ultimate destruction of republican government itself at the hands of the Nazis. In these years of the late Weimar period, the analysis of fascism and the problem of left-wing schism had acquired much more than theoretical interest. The goal for moderate leftists was political victory and the achievement of working-class social and economic transformations, while revolutionaries of the Left sought to intensify and exploit the crises of the early 1930s. As the situation of all elements of the Left in the Republic grew more tenuous and the Nazi movement swiftly and shockingly emerged as the largest single political party in Germany, sheer survival often superseded other goals. The political writings of these years offer ample evidence that the German Left generated a variety of theoretical approaches that marked crucial stages in the development of the left-wing critiques of fascist movements and dictatorships as well as occasional ventures in the direction of a comparative theory of totalitarianism.

The German Left Divided

In the years leading up to World War I, fissures had begun to appear in the giant edifice of the German Social Democratic Party, the organization that had represented the German workers' movement since the 1870s. The war blasted it into fragments. These internal divisions over party organization and support for the war ultimately resulted in the formation of a significant though short-lived dissident splinter party: the USPD, or Independent German Social Democratic Party. Soon after the end of the war, another large radical party of the Left appeared: the KPD, or German Communist Party.[22] Throughout the Weimar Republic, the SPD and the KPD played what was perceived then and now as a zero-sum game in electoral politics—that is, a battle for votes among the working-class electorate in which the gains of one party marked the losses of the other. Despite its sizable electoral support, the KPD remained an outsider organization, while the reformist SPD became either an essential component of government under the Weimar Constitution or its reliably loyal opposition. From 1919 until 1932, the SPD was the largest party in Germany and served as the bulwark of the Weimar Republic.[23] Social Democratic cabinet ministers participated in several national ruling coalitions with Gustav Stresemann's liberals and the Catholic Center Party. At the same time, the KPD assumed the role of a radical protest party, attacking the capitalist character of Weimar society. It adopted neither a consistently legalist nor a steadfastly revolutionary program, sometimes participating in city or regional governments but also engaging in dramatic but abortive attempts at revolution.[24]

The bitter and persistent conflict between these two parties of the divided Weimar Left was the seedbed for the emergence of new critiques of the policies of Lenin and the Bolsheviks, the KPD, and the Comintern by moderate socialists or by radicals who grew to despise central party authority. These critiques helped establish the basis for the secondary and gradual development of theories of totalitarianism—or at least the use of a notion of the total state—among both orthodox Social Democratic and independent writers on the German left. Ironically, some of the most effective attacks of both the Social Democrats and the Communists against each other invoked the ideas and the career of the same person: Rosa Luxemburg.

In her intelligent and unsparingly critical analysis of the parties and policies of Marxian socialism, Luxemburg had no peer. For the theoretical and practical shortcomings of both Social Democratic reformism and Bolshevism, she cherished an unflagging but carefully focused hostility. Luxemburg's brutal murder by members of the right-wing paramilitary Freikorps, acting as forces for "order" with tacit government approval, had placed the SPD (which controlled the government's executive faction at the time) out-of-bounds for many leftists. The course of the KPD, which soon became a Comintern affiliated party, in exactly the direction Luxemburg had feared, made it almost equally unattractive. To put it simply, the SPD's toleration of the attack against the Spartacist soldiers' and workers' rebellion in Berlin and its leaders' passive response to the murders of Luxemburg, Karl Liebknecht, and others made the party anathema among the most radical leftists. Moreover, the radicals who joined the Communists had no leaders with the intellectual gifts or the polemical ferocity to replace Luxemburg.

Judgments about Luxemburg's potential value to the Weimar Left have proliferated over the decades. Years after he had become a bitter anti-Communist, the sociologist and historian Franz Borkenau could still write the following appraisal of Luxemburg's value to the German workers' movement:

> With the destruction of Luxemburg and her personal circle German communism lost the one capable set of leaders it had. . . . Looking backward

upon her role and attitude, one finds it difficult to believe that anything but a break could have been the end of her relations with the Comintern. But in the meantime she would have been the one person able to balance and withstand the influence of the Russians. She alone might have had the authority and strength to carry those she had persuaded to co-operate with the Bolsheviks with her when she broke with them. All the others who later took that step were officers without troops. She might have left at the head of an army; which would have been of incalculable consequence for the unity of the German workers when they attempted to withstand Hitler.[25]

Some of the older German Marxists, including both Communists and former Communists, offered a different view, scorning Luxemburg's "utopian" vision of working-class spontaneity. Nevertheless, the historian Arthur Rosenberg, who had been a leading Communist for several years during Weimar, acknowledged the force of her personality, the great loss that workers had suffered by her murder, and the potency of her criticism of Lenin's Bolshevik Party.[26]

During the Weimar period and after, Luxemburg's political and intellectual legacy was claimed by some of her old comrades, such as Clara Zetkin and Paul Levi—who ultimately diverged in their understanding of just what actions that legacy should inspire—and her example found a special place in the thought and writings of a younger generation of German Marxists.[27] Moreover, some of the intellectuals who left or were driven from the KPD during the 1920s became, as Luxemburg had been, vocal and troublesome heretics, but they were not necessarily her disciples. Among these nettlesome former leading party members were Arthur Rosenberg, Karl Korsch, and Ruth Fischer. Fischer, born in Germany but reared in Austria, had been a cofounder of the Austrian Communist Party and soon joined forces with the Weimar KPD, where, as we have already seen, she played an important role. She belonged to the generation that reached adulthood at the time of World War I and the Russian Revolution, and for a time she tended to admire Leninist-style organization and tactics as more realistic and effective than Luxemburg's democratic and humanistic revolutionary notions. During her career with the Communist Party, Fischer mocked and disparaged the theories and tactics of the older generation of Social Democrats, with Luxemburg as her special target. Her brief stint as a leader of the KPD marked an intensively "Bolshevizing" phase, in opposition to the political style and theoretical position of Luxemburg and Levi. Years later, as an anti-Communist historian of the KPD, Fischer would offer a rather more sympathetic portrait of Luxemburg as a tragic figure of the Left, but she would still characterize Luxemburg's influence in the upheavals of late 1918 and early 1919 as baneful.[28]

In contrast, the Marxist philosopher Karl Korsch, whose written comments on Luxemburg were a mix of both critical and positive evaluations, would remark in a letter to his friend Paul Mattick that "one's position towards Rosa always appears to me to still be the best proof-stone for revolutionaries."[29] For some other left-wing critics of state-party dictatorship—Max Horkheimer and Otto Kirchheimer, in particular—she remained an important theorist, a model revolutionary, and compelling and powerful writer. Horkheimer, for instance, writing from exile in the United States just as the military violence of World War II reached its peak, borrowed Luxemburg's famous formulation that the modern world was faced with the choice between "barbarism or freedom."[30]

The legacy and fate of Rosa Luxemburg were also important factors in the constriction of possibilities for party allegiance among left-wing intellectuals in Weimar Germany. By the late 1920s, the rival orthodoxies of revolutionary centralism in the service of the Comintern and parliamentary social democracy in the service of the Weimar Republic proved unsatisfactory to a number of independent-minded radical leftists. The alternatives for the dissenting German leftists in terms of party affiliation were to remain within the left-wing of the SPD, join the short-lived USPD, move over to the KPDO (German Communist Party Opposition), or, by the end of the Weimar Republic, link up with one of the other small organizations formed most often by outcasts of the KPD. In short, left-wing intellectuals found it increasingly difficult to follow the example of Rosa Luxemburg. She had been able for a time to remain relatively independent within a large party of the working class. For the generation of German socialist intellectuals who followed her into the Communist Party, the alternatives were soon reduced to party orthodoxy or political marginalization. Even at the time of renewed left-wing electoral success in the late 1920s, there was a steady drain of scholars and intellectuals away from the KPD.[31]

Despite the divisions within the German Left and the tendency of party bureaucrats to alienate potential allies among the intelligentsia, there were some hopeful signs for German working-class politics. After the national economy revived in the mid-1920s, the working-class parties appeared to regain an important role in the Reichstag. In May 1928, the two major left-wing parties of Germany elected the highest combined number of Reichstag representatives they had yet gained under the Weimar Republic. The Social Democrats retained their status as the largest delegation in the Reichstag, increasing their total from 131 (at the last election in 1924) to 153. Only in the election of January 1919 had they ever gained more representatives. The number of Communists in the Reichstag jumped from 45 to 54 representatives. This resurgence of the left-wing parties after the accession of General Paul von Hindenburg to the presidency in 1925 stood out clearly in the electoral results. There never was an alliance of the KPD and the SPD at the national level, however. Moreover, the electoral gains of 1928 would produce little practical impact on national policy, and the SPD's revival would prove illusory.[32]

The intricate twists and turns of developing policy within the SPD and KPD of the 1920s led them through both internal crises and continuing battles with each other.[33] By the late 1920s, the KPD had moved decisively away from its "left" phase of 1924–25, when the policies of party leader Ruth Fischer and her supporters in the Comintern, chiefly Zinoviev, had taken the German Communists in a putatively revolutionary direction and away from the "united front" tactics urged by the party's right.[34] This period also marked the decisive ascent of Stalin to leadership in the Soviet Union, which had portentous consequences for the German Communist Party—or at least for its national leaders. On top of their tactical differences, Fischer was apparently too independent-minded for Stalin's liking, and when he was able to take stronger control of Comintern policy, he coolly rid the party of Fischer and her partner, Arkadij Maslow, and he finally destroyed their erstwhile Comintern protector, Zinoviev. Under the new leadership of the intellectually plodding but tractable Ernst Thälmann and the other apparatchiks who met the approval of the Moscow-based Comintern bureaucracy, the KPD's Central Committee initiated a series of policy and personnel changes in 1926, expelling leading left oppositionists and insisting on loyalty oaths from middle- and lower-ranking party members. Though never absolute, the bureaucratic centralization of the KPD and its policy subordination to the Comintern were reaching a climax by 1928. During the remaining years of the Weimar Republic, the Comintern continued to play a central role in articulating the KPD's national policies and official doctrine and selecting its executive personnel.[35] But innovative and persuasive research published over the past two decades indicates that the KPD's politics—however internally authoritarian—were often "homegrown" and even regionalized to a significant extent. Opposition and autonomy regarding policy matters often existed at the local level, even if strong Soviet influence on the KPD's leadership ranks lasted for decades. Yet in spite of the more nuanced picture of the Weimar KPD that has been emerging, the new research has not substantiality altered the older view that the deeply hostile rivalry between the SPD and the KPD remained a crucial feature of national electoral politics.[36]

If the KPD often seemed to be a tightly unified and militantly revolutionary party, the SPD appeared as a polyglot alliance of various left-wing groups that agreed above all on the importance and feasibility of parliamentary reformism in behalf of working-class objectives. Yet the specific content of those moderate socialist objectives, in 1928 at least, became a point of conflict. Old divisions over "reform versus revolution" had never entirely disappeared, and the success of the SPD in the elections of 1928 brought the issue of a positive socialist program into sharp relief.[37] Since the revolution of 1918–19, the SPD had oscillated between its post-Wilhelmine role as a crucial guarantor of constitutional legitimacy and its original prewar role as the political representative of working-class aspirations and dissent. When its few opportunities for institutional leadership arose, the moderately socialist SPD failed to assert itself as a party in power with clearly articulated goals of social transformation, let alone decisively pursue such goals. Rudolf Hilferding, the SPD theoretician and finance minister, articulated the party's priorities in May 1928 as "the maintenance of democracy" in order to provide "the indispensable precondition for the realization of socialism."[38]

Hilferding, an economist and the author of *Finanzkapital* (1910), the most important attempt to bring Marxist economics to bear on the conditions of capitalism in the early twentieth century, was a native Austrian and had trained as a physician. Choosing to enter into active political life, he began publishing articles on economics, moved to Berlin at the invitation of the SPD theoretician Karl Kautsky, and became an adviser to the SPD leadership and a teacher at its party school (along with Rosa Luxemburg, with whom he was never particularly close personally or politically) before World War I. Drafted into service by Austria in 1915, Hilferding served as a physician behind the lines. He was able to return to Germany during November 1918, soon after the kaiser's flight and the proclamation of the German Republic. After a brief affiliation with the dissident USPD, Hilferding resumed his role as the most important journalist and theorist for the Weimar SPD.[39]

In the mid-1920s, Hilferding had good reason to focus on the need to ensure institutional reforms, but he also provided a rationale for the Social Democrats' cautious economic policies, which had begun to frustrate even the decidedly nonrevolutionary trade unions affiliated with the party. The unions now found themselves fighting to maintain previous gains instead of moving to reach new ones. As a result of the unions' increasing militancy, the delicate coalitions between liberals and moderate socialists on economic policy envisioned by Hilferding and Foreign Minister Gustav Stresemann, a politically flexible nationalist, met resistance. Both radical trade unionists and conservative business interests balked at the prospect of compromise. Stresemann's death in 1929 brought these maneuvers to a halt. Policy stalemate and increasing acrimony among the German parties preceded the global economic collapse of 1929, which only worsened existing hostilities within and against the Weimar government.[40]

In short, the electoral successes of the Social Democrats in 1928 and the continued hold of the Communists on a large minority of working-class voters served to emphasize the apparent political strength of the German Left and to intensify its internal weaknesses and divisions.[41] By the late Weimar period, the hostility between the German Social Democrats and German Communists reached a high point, which persisted into the exile years, complicating and ultimately nullifying efforts to form a common front against the Nazis, even after Hitler's accession to dictatorial power.

One event in particular vividly displayed the hostility between the Social Democrats and the Communists and drove them even further from any possibility of coalition: the May Day demonstrations of 1929 in Berlin. For a few days, complex institutional and ideological conflicts within the Left achieved austere and brutal form, taking on a terrible symbolism for many of those caught up in the struggle. At the heart of the bloody events of May 1929 lay the inability of a party in power—the SPD—to control the actions of public functionaries nominally under the direction of its elected officials. In this case, the SPD government in Prussia—typically far more assertive and canny than the national SPD leadership—loosed an unreliable police force on pugnacious but unarmed KPD demonstrators, who had defied a ban on May Day parades declared by Berlin police chief Karl Zörgiebel, an SPD member. Zörgiebel's ban on parades was clearly directed against the street activism of the KPD, but it was at least partly an attempt to avoid even uglier incidents in the growing public violence between right- and left-wing groups in Berlin. The KPD's defiance of the ban brought on a police riot instead. Innocent bystanders in the area of the demonstrations were shot down. Apartments in the working-class districts of Wedding and Neukölln were searched and ransacked. Local residents responded with bitter verbal and physical assaults on the police. Over a period of three days, the police escalated their violence, which resulted in some forty deaths and dozens more injuries and a bitter legacy of KPD hostility toward the SPD leadership.[42]

Among those who responded angrily to this fiasco was the radical Marxist theoretician and journalist Karl Korsch, who, though no longer a member of the KPD, also had no love whatsoever for the SPD. Korsch is well known to scholars of the European Left as the author of *Marxismus und Philosophie* (*Marxism and Philosophy*), which along with Georg Lukács's *Geschichte und Klassenbewußtsein* (*History and Class Consciousness*) and Antonio Gramsci's *Quaderni del Carcere* (*Prison Notebooks*), has had a lasting influence as one of the innovative post–World War I investigations of the importance of Hegel to Marxism. Korsch and Lukács had been linked as objects of condemnation by the Comintern and were joined as well in the minds of many Marxists, who found in their writings of the early 1920s a bracing philosophical resistance to the ossified Marxism of both social democracy and Communism.[43]

Born near Hamburg in 1886, Korsch had studied law, economics, and philosophy at several German universities. Completing his doctorate in law at Jena in 1910, Korsch pursued legal studies in England from 1912 to 1914. During this time, he also had extensive contacts with the Fabians, ultimately joining the group. He returned to Germany at the outbreak of World War I and served in the infantry. Fred Halliday, a Korsch scholar and translator, mentions that Korsch's opposition to the war led to the loss of his status as a reserve officer and a temporary demotion to corporal. This act would appear to be consistent with some of Korsch's later political decisions and directions in its willfulness, its romantic and symbolic solidarity, and its ultimately questionable effectiveness. He was twice awarded the Iron Cross for bravery. Identifying his politics with those of the wartime oppositionists and postwar revolutionists, however, he joined the USPD in 1919. In any case, during the volatile weeks and months that followed the declarations of a German Republic on 9 November 1918, he expressed his real enthusiasm not for any of the organized socialist parties but for the workers' and soldiers' councils (*Räte*). In their behalf, he participated in the debates on "socialization" of the economy in Berlin during the early months of the Weimar Republic. Soon after the breakup of the councils during the consolidation of the new German government under the military and the right-wing of the SPD, Korsch renewed his oppositionist politics from within the KPD.[44]

Korsch's early Weimar career was tumultuous and productive, a mix of political and intellectual activities. He was a German Communist Party member from 1920 to 1926, and he served as a Reichstag delegate for the party. He also was involved peripherally in the activities of the Weimar-era Institute of Social Research, in whose journals—*Archiv für die Geschichte des Sozialismus und der Arbeiterbewegung* (*Archive for the History of Socialism and the Workers' Movement*) and its successor, *Zeitschrift für Sozialforschung* (*Journal of Social Research*)—he often published review articles. He met with the political and literary theorist Georg Lukács at a seminar on Marxism held in Thuringia in 1923. Photographs of Korsch on that occasion show him dapper and smilingly confident. In these years, his range of activities was remarkable. He even taught part-time in a school for working-class students (the Karl Marx Schule, formerly the Kaiser Wilhelms Gymnasium) in Berlin run by his wife, Hedda Korsch, who was in her own right an active socialist educational reformer and teacher. Characteristically, he openly voiced his objections to KPD policy and the party's endless round of leadership changes. As a result, he was forced out of the KPD in 1926. He then began a series of involvements with small, marginal left-wing groups. He eventually became a friend and "political teacher" to Bertolt Brecht, Weimar Germany's most important playwright and poet.[45]

By 1929, he had taken up his permanent position as a left-wing critic of the Left, and the appalling May Day killings by Berlin police offered him an occasion to condemn both major left-wing parties. In an article published in *Die Aktion* in May 1929, Korsch bitterly observed that "if the worker does not shoot, the police shoot for him. Evidence: the dozens of murdered workers and uninvolved passers-by, men, women, and children!" He further declared that "the interest of the German bourgeoisie is increasingly the same as that of the German Social Democracy."[46] He also aimed his passionate scorn at the Communists for calling for the demonstration in defiance of the police ban and then failing to provide leadership once the street fighting began. Moreover, he argued, the real crime of the Communists was that they overlooked the true revolutionary potential of the working class shown during the bloody May days. The KPD used the event merely for propaganda gain without actually wanting a revolutionary conflict. Korsch concluded that the only positive result of the street fighting was the demonstration of tough defiance on the part of the working class, and the repetition of the old and difficult lesson that it must become its own master.[47] Korsch's attitude of "a plague on both your houses" regarding the two major parties on the left had already become a common one among Weimar's left-wing intellectuals, and it characterized his writings for the rest of his life.

For many voters on the German left, the events in Berlin in 1929 had the effect of granting increased legitimacy to the now renewed and ultimately disastrous Communist Party policy that labeled the Social Democrats "social fascists."[48] This hostile verbal turn (*Sozialfaschismus* was a crude word play on the term *Sozialdemokratie*) gave a shorthand propaganda formulation to the Communists' claim that the SPD posed a greater threat to the working class than did the Nazis or other right-wing and nationalist groups. The police attacks of May were a perfect moment to exploit this argument, and the Communists hoped to gain votes among angry workers who had previously voted for SPD candidates. For the SPD leadership in Prussia, however, the May 1929 riots were an ugly and distressing reminder of the party's inability to transform electoral strength into a transforming social and economic policy—and of the depth and persistence of divisions on the left.

The German Left, still feeling the effects of the wartime and revolutionary period, now experienced a new round of intensified conflicts, which took on added urgency in the light of crises all over Europe. The fate of the Soviet Russian regime under the new leadership of Joseph Stalin became an especially compelling spectacle. Within limits, the Soviets also influenced the German Communists through their financial sponsorship of and doctrinal hold on the Communist International. Despite the grotesque distortion of political realities and terminology it represented, the Comintern's critique of "social fascism" hit the SPD at its point of greatest theoretical ambivalence and political inconsistency: the problem of reconciling its revolutionary rhetoric with its acceptance of the Weimar legal system and the administrative imperatives demanded by participation in government coalitions with nonsocialist and antisocialist (and, of course, antirevolutionary) parties.

The resurgence of the doctrine of "social fascism" met with fierce criticism from former Communists of significant international stature, including Leon Trotsky and August Thalheimer.[49] Even though the doctrine also faced some resistance within the rank and file of the KPD, the party leadership and its publications droned the "social fascist" line virtually up to the moment of the Nazi seizure of power.[50] Clearly, the SPD had sacrificed much of its credibility among significant portions of the working-class constituency it claimed as its base. At the next Reichstag election in September 1930, the SPD suffered a nationwide loss of roughly 600,000 votes, while the KPD gained some 1,300,000.[51] In the Neukölln district of Berlin—traditionally an important SPD stronghold, but the scene of some of the bloody fighting of the previous year—the KPD outpolled all other parties, receiving 70,344 votes to the SPD's 65,783.[52] *Blutmai* (Bloody May) was surely not the sole cause of this electoral turnabout—debates about unemployment insurance, which were sharpened because of the rapid rise in working-class unemployment, were key in the election of September

1930—but the May disaster was perhaps the most traumatic and public reminder of intraleft political conflict since the murders of Rosa Luxemburg and Karl Liebknecht.

The Left's divisions had deepened by 1932, when Korsch made one of the most emphatic of his many comparisons between fascism and Bolshevism as deceivers of the working class. His criticisms of the similarities between the behavior of the regimes in Italy and the Soviet Union and the fascist movement in Germany appeared in the context of general remarks about the degeneracy of the postrevolutionary period in Europe. In the following passage from "The Marxist Ideology in Russia," Korsch began with a sharp attack on Lenin:[53]

It was the orthodox Marxist Lenin who in opposition to all his earlier declarations first set up the new Marxist myth of the inherently socialist character of the Soviet state and of the thereby basically guaranteed possibility of a complete realization of socialist society in an isolated Soviet Russia.

This degeneration of the Marxian doctrine to a mere ideological justification of what in its actual tendency is a capitalist state and thus, inevitably, a state based on the suppression of the progressive revolutionary movement of the proletarian class, closes the first phase of the history of the Marxist ideology in Russia. . . . In spite of appearances and of many real differences caused by the specific conditions prevailing at different times in different countries, the historical development of *Russian Marxism* (inclusive of its last Leninist and Stalinist stages) is essentially the same as that of so-called *Western* (or *Social Democratic*) *Marxism* of which it really was and still is an integrating, though at present outwardly detached, component. . . . The *bourgeois degeneration of Marxism in Russia today* is in no way essentially different from the outcome of the series of ideological transformations which, during the war and post-war periods and, even more visibly, after the ultimate annihilation of all former Marxist strongholds by the unopposed advent of fascism and nazism, befell the various currents of so-called Western Marxism. Just as the "national socialism" of Herr Hitler and the "corporative state" of Mussolini vie with the "Marxism" of Stalin in an attempt to invade, by the use of a pseudo-socialist ideology, the very brains and souls of their workers as well as their physical and social existence, so does the democratic regime of a people's front government presided by the "Marxist" Leon Blum or for that matter, by Mr. Chautemps himself, differ from the present-day Soviet state not in substance, but only by a less efficient exploitation of the Marxist ideology. Less than at any previous time does Marxism today serve as a theoretical weapon in an independent struggle of the proletariat, for the proletariat, and by the proletariat.[54]

This passage shows Korsch's utter disillusionment with "the Soviet experiment" and his equally deep pessimism about the state of working-class politics in Europe. His equation of the methods of fascism and Stalinist Marxism was quite bluntly put for a leftist of that time, but other critics were following a similar path.

Max Horkheimer was a thinker much further removed from the political activities of the left-wing parties than Korsch was. The son of a wealthy businessman, Horkheimer was nearly a decade younger than Korsch and, though he had been drafted into the wartime army, he saw no active military service because of his ill health. He sympathized with the failed German revolution of 1918–19 and turned to scholarship of an oppositionist character. A philosopher by training, Horkheimer increasingly conceived of his discipline in social and historical terms. In 1930, he was named as the new director of the Institute of Social Research. Early the following year, he proposed a broad program of social analysis that would make use of a variety of disciplinary perspectives, though with a continuation of the institute's strong Marxist orientation. The splintering and ultimate destruction of the Weimar government by the Nazis voided the institute's future in Germany.[55]

In the closing years of the Weimar Republic, Horkheimer offered an increasingly pessimistic picture of the political fate of the German working class comparable in some of its conclusions to Korsch's 1932 essay "The Marxist Ideology in Russia." Horkheimer recorded his misgivings in a short book entitled *Dämmerung: Notizen in Deutschland* (*Twilight: Notes on Germany*). The book, constructed from Horkheimer's occasional short writings from 1926 to 1931, was published in 1934 under the pseudonym Heinrich Regius. Its radical outspokenness has forced a second look at the earlier work of Horkheimer, whose postwar distance from the more politically engaged and Marxian theory of old friends, such as Herbert Marcuse, has been well documented.[56] *Dämmerung* is a provocative mix of political observations and occasionally lengthier philosophical reflections, along with a sampling of critical appraisals of the behavior of groups and individuals around him. At many points of its fascinating yet fragmentary discourse, the book gives evidence of the attenuation of Horkheimer's faith—which was always limited—in the value of institutional political action.

The most important of his considerations of the division of the German Left was a handful of pages entitled "Die Ohnmacht der deutschen Arbeiterklasse" ("The Powerlessness of the German Working Class"). According to Horkheimer, the German working class was divided in terms of both revolutionary consciousness and its actual social and economic conditions. Reformist socialism's relative success made employed workers leery of the risks that revolution would bring. The unemployed workers, however, were frustrated by the SPD's caution and, in Horkheimer's perception of things, shifted back and forth between the Communist Party and the National Socialists. The factional politics on the left, Horkheimer concluded, "condemns the workers to actual powerlessness."[57]

Each of the workers' parties received Horkheimer's unforgiving verdict. First, Horkheimer scraped away the KPD's facade of radicalism to uncover the antitheoretical sloganeering that served as the expression of its policy: "In the intellectual realm, the impatience of the unemployed finds itself repeated in the slogans of the Communist Party. Principles do not take form in a timely fashion from a store of theoretically manufactured materials, but are instead seized undialectically."[58] Then he turned to the Social Democrats:

> In contrast to Communism, the reformist wing of the workers' movement has forgotten that effective improvement in human relations is impossible under capitalism. It has lost its hold on all elements of theory. Its leadership is the precise image of the most secure party members: many try to keep their jobs by all means available, even the abandonment of basic loyalties; the fear of losing their positions increasingly becomes the only rationale for their actions. The ever present need to repress what remains of their better consciousness requires the continual preparation of these reformist German politicians to angrily abandon Marxism as an outdated error. Any precise theoretical point of view is more hateful to them than the bourgeoisie itself.[59]

Workers without parties representing their collective interests, parties without theoretical consideration of or faith in self-conscious working-class radicalism, and intellectuals like Horkheimer himself, increasingly at odds with both working-class and socialist party allegiances, all entered a period of crisis and defeat for which the term *disillusionment* is entirely inadequate.

The personal fates of Korsch and Horkheimer would be closely connected with the events of the early 1930s that scarred the history of Germany and the rest of Europe, though in strikingly divergent ways. Korsch was becoming a politically and intellectually isolated figure even before Weimar's demise. The heady atmosphere of the early 1920s, when Korsch, Georg Lukács, and a corps of young leftist intellectuals—several of whom would later play important roles in the Institute of Social Research under Horkheimer's leadership—could meet in a stimulating and productive week of discussion at Thüringen was long gone. For Korsch personally, the end of Weimar meant the beginning of a series of moves that would eventually lead him and his wife into exile in the United States. These years were marked by false starts on theoretical books, the energy-sapping frustration of sporadic and short-term teaching positions, and—the final cruelty of fate—a long illness and mental disability.[60] For Max Horkheimer, a career of scholarly and publishing productivity and the remarkably successful leadership of a significant research institute in exile and in postwar Germany lay in store. But in 1932, such futures were still unimaginable, and the overriding crisis of the moment was the fate of Germany under the conditions of deep and increasingly violent internal division that accompanied the world economic collapse.

The German Left Defeated

The failure of the divided German Left to defend itself effectively against the advance of a right-wing coalition that eventually awarded leadership to the National Socialists remains one of the most disturbing features of the late Weimar period. German leftists had not ignored the problem of domestic fascism, which was most clearly evident in the rise of National Socialism. By early 1933, German socialists across a wide spectrum of opinion had formulated a variety of theoretical and practical responses to fascism, but the inadequacy of those responses and the Left's ultimate defeat have occasionally threatened to eclipse the Left's legacy of resistance, which, for all its ineffectiveness, contrasts sharply with the behavior of the traditionally conservative political factions and parties. From the early 1920s, the phenomenon of National Socialism provided German leftists with ample evidence of fascism's domestic appeal—and even occasional alliances between the SPD and KPD were still possible in the crisis year of 1923.[61] Through the rest of the 1920s, however, the appeal of fascism in Germany appeared to have reached its limit. Nevertheless, the experience of the Italian Left had provided an important cautionary example for the Germans. Other fascist or similarly dictatorial rightist regimes in Europe also offered themselves as substantive warnings to thoughtful opponents.[62] The quality and number of German socialists' systematic efforts to articulate a critical understanding of fascism and its unique German variant—National Socialism—as opposed to considerations of possible alliances with this new political force, set them apart from other political parties and groups, particularly during the years 1930 to 1933.[63]

One response typical of an organization or a movement in crisis ap-

peared in due course among socialists in late Weimar: the return to canon-
ized master texts as a guide to action or understanding in the present. In
one variation, the Left's response to National Socialism took the form of a
more or less simplistic "class agent" theory derived nominally—and quite
crudely—from Marx or Lenin. The standard version of this analysis characterized the Nazis as the errand-boys of monopoly capital. As early as 1924,
Stalin enlarged this analysis to include attacks on social democracy and
fascism as "twins"—a correlate of the "social fascism" propaganda.[64] Another approach, one far more fruitful, came from one of the dissenting
KPDO theorists, the former KPD Central Committee member August
Thalheimer. He sought a way to gain a theoretical lever on the present by
refashioning the tools Marx and Engels bequeathed to socialism.

Thalheimer had entered left-wing politics as a journalist for the SPD
press. He joined the Spartacist faction during World War I and was elected
to the Central Committee of the KPD in 1919. Along with Heinrich Brandler, he became a leader of the so-called right-wing faction of the KPD until
the failure of the 1923 insurrection in Germany, which had been undertaken at the insistence of the Comintern leadership. Thereafter he traveled,
taught, and served on the program committee of the Comintern, but his
opposition to the Comintern's official position on fascism that had been
developed at the Sixth World Congress in 1928 led him actively to oppose
KPD policy. With Brandler, he edited the KPDO newspaper, *Gegen den Strom*
(*Against the Current*), which routinely published articles by Leon Trotsky
and others who had been cast out of the Communist Party.[65]

Thalheimer's most significant contribution to left-wing political
theory was a critical analysis of fascism in 1928, produced while he was
still a member of the KPD.[66] After his expulsion from the party, however,
the articles remained unpublished until January 1930, when they appeared in *Gegen den Strom* under the title "Ueber den Faschismus" ("On
Fascism"). His provocative discussion took as its touchstone Karl Marx's
Eighteenth Brumaire of Louis Bonaparte. In response to the defeat of the
French Revolution of 1848, Marx had constructed his famous and ferocious indictment-cum-analysis of the dictator Louis-Napoleon Bonaparte
and the social forces that had yielded up the second French Republic to
this execrable nephew and his supporters. Thalheimer's purposes were
similar to Marx's—that is, criticism and analysis—but instead of referring
to the threat of National Socialism in Germany, his remarks focused on
Italian Fascism. This is not surprising. In 1928, Germany's distinctive form
of fascism had yet to make much of a political dent in the institutional
structure of the Weimar Republic.

For Thalheimer, Bonapartism and fascism were not the same thing, but they were related.[67] Within limits, Thalheimer asserted, Marx's study of France in the mid-nineteenth century could still provide the kind of understanding crucial to the defeat of fascism. With its combination of nuanced political perceptiveness and careful yet flexible attentiveness to Marx's writings, "Ueber den Faschismus" contributed greatly to the Left's array of theoretical approaches to state-party dictatorship.[68]

One of the first conditions of Bonapartism that Thalheimer linked to his own times was a "severe defeat of the proletariat at a time of deep social crisis."[69] A struggle without victory created a heightened awareness of the threat of civil conflict and social revolution. From that point on, the class groups in power would be more alert. In Thalheimer's account, the revolutionary ferment in Europe after the armistice took the place of the June days of 1848, which Marx had described so vividly. Ultimately, in the face of a politically activated working class, increased executive power appeared to the bourgeoisie as the savior of its interests.[70] Despite the differences in details, Thalheimer argued, Bonaparte's coup found its historical echo in Mussolini's takeover of the Italian state.[71] Marx's powerfully expressed analysis of the failed French Revolution of 1848 would serve not only Thalheimer but also numerous left-wing critics of the degeneration of democratic republics into dictatorships.[72] In a similar manner, Thalheimer's own essay served as the fundamental model/opponent for several of the German socialist critiques of fascism.

Among the points of Thalheimer's analysis that would soon show up in the work of other left-wing theorists of fascism was his description of such movements as the association of déclassé elements from *all* classes.[73] By allowing greater attention to the complex political expression of underlying social conflicts, Thalheimer made possible a methodological shift away from the simplistic economic determinism of the Comintern scribes. That is, Thalheimer effectively challenged the political morality plays sanctioned by the Communist Party's official Diamat-based (*Diamat* was shorthand for *dialectical materialism*) "agent" theories of fascism in which certain classes, or their "agents," played scripted roles in every major social conflict. He did not ignore class conflict any more than Marx had, but he understood, as Marx certainly did, that party politics, the relation between state power and various economic interests, and, most important for Thalheimer, the developing conditions for right-wing dictatorship offered a more complicated and shifting set of conflicts and alliances than could be expressed in the "clarity" of a two-class model. As a result of his fairly successful heresy, Thalheimer became one of the most cited references among those German leftists who wished to distance themselves or their analysis of fascism from the Comintern and its "agent-of-the-bourgeoisie" or "social fascism" lines. Moreover, Bonapartism theory would soon find its way into a variety of analyses of both fascism and Communism.[74]

Thalheimer had mentioned in passing a comparison that would eventually become a staple of many discussions of interwar politics: "The 'December gang' of Louis Napoleon was the counterpart of the small, revolutionary secret organization of the French working class of that time. The Fascist party is the counterrevolutionary counterpart of the Communist Party of Soviet Russia."[75] These remarks stand as evidence of a broadly comparative perspective on dictatorship, but Thalheimer clearly intended to praise the achievement of the Russian Revolution. The comparison of single-party dominance in Italian and Soviet state operations later became a method by which to label both states, along with Nazi Germany, as totalitarian dictatorships. Thalheimer's Leninist outlook of course had nothing to do with such an open condemnation of the Soviet Union, but several younger writers on the subject of totalitarianism, who had also been originally Leninist in their political orientation, would not hesitate to offer such damning comparisons.

In 1928, when Thalheimer began writing his path-breaking revision of the Bonapartism thesis, the Left was still preoccupied with its internal divisions, and the threat of fascism seemed slight. The NSDAP vote had actually declined by nearly 100,000 in the May elections of that year. The party lost two deputies as a result, placing only twelve deputies in the new Reichstag—fewer than the Bavarian People's Party.[76] The collapse of the world economy that began in 1929, however, created conditions that would grant the movement new life, although it was not immediately evident that the Nazis would come to dominate the broad right-wing opposition to the Weimar Republic. A more traditional conservative organization, the German National People's Party (Deutschnationale Volkspartei—DNVP), led by industrialist Alfred Hugenberg, might have seemed at the time far more likely to provide the strongest and most appealing right-wing leadership.

But from 1930 to 1933, Hugenberg and his party remained stuck in a regional and electoral dead end, while the brash and violently dynamic National Socialists registered swift gains. The NSDAP's electoral platform was an inchoate mix of anti-Semitism, anti-Left hysteria, militarism, contradictory economic promises tailored to various local or regional audiences with incompatible interests, and irrational *völkisch* appeals, all expressed in violent rhetoric and wrapped in the most visually striking public displays that Joseph Goebbels and local Nazi propagandists could muster. Even more blatantly than any of its political rivals, the Nazi movement never had a consistently rational central doctrine. For several years, particularly in the context of economic disaster and parliamentary deadlock of the early 1930s, this proved no disadvantage.[77]

In the Reichstag elections of 14 September 1930 the Nazis received over 6.41 million votes—second only to the SPD's 8.58 million.[78] With this stunning electoral success, the National Socialist German Workers' Party had not gained mere legitimacy but had attained real political ascendancy within the ranks of the opposition to the evanescent Weimar coalition of liberals, the Center Party, and the SPD. Fascism was no longer a mere threat; it had become the chief political rival to the two great socialist parties. At the level of left-wing theory, Thalheimer's preelection analysis clearly required extension and revision. Also placed on the left-wing theorists' urgent agenda was the exploration of the possibility of a united front against the National Socialists. This was not to be.

The lack of cooperation between German Communists and Social Democrats has long been one explanation of the Nazis' successful takeover of Germany.[79] But as late as the fall of 1932, one former Communist who had gone over to the SPD in 1929, Henry Pachter (then known by his German name, Heinz Pächter), declared that the breach between the two parties marked irreconcilable conceptions of working-class democracy and that a united front would arise only out of desperate opposition to a mutual enemy. Pachter's article "Kommunismus und Klasse" ("Communism and Class") appeared in Rudolf Hilferding's journal, *Die Gesellschaft,* in October 1932. In its depiction of two opposing concepts of dictatorship—bourgeois and proletarian—it attempted to explain the lack of a common left-wing front against National Socialism and at times anticipated the theory of totalitarian convergence between Nazism and Communism. He also contributed to one of the most important genres of political writing of this century: the anti-Communist polemic written by an ex-Communist.

Pachter, born in Berlin in 1907, entered socialist politics from an upper-middle-class, German-Jewish background. As a young man, he had participated in one of the hiking and singing youth groups described under the general heading of *Wandervögel* (birds of passage). Sometimes seen by historical and sociological commentators primarily as forerunners of the Hitler Youth, many of these groups diverged sharply from that pattern, attracting young leftists who later became Marxian socialists. In his late teens, Pachter switched his affiliation to the youth league of the KPD at the urging of his friend Karl August Wittfogel. Wittfogel was fast becoming a leading German Communist intellectual, and as a scholar of Asian history and society, he generated a voluminous body of work, capped by his post–World War II study, *Oriental Despotism*. Since the early 1920s, he had been an important member of the group affiliated with the Institute of Social Research, though his particular brand of Marxism and his KPD membership kept him always at a theoretical and political distance from its leading members. Like Pachter, Ruth Fischer, and Franz Borkenau, Wittfogel eventually became a cold war critic of Soviet totalitarianism. In addition to his political friendships and connections, Pachter also met Hannah Arendt while they were university students at Freiburg, and the two would remain friends during the years of exile. Pachter's studies in Freiburg and Berlin focused on history and philosophy, and among his professors were the Marxist historian Arthur Rosenberg and the philosophers Edmund Husserl and Karl Korsch.[80] As Korsch's writings often did, Pachter's article on the state of the German Left in 1932 indicated a willingness to stake out an iconoclastic position. As a young writer on politics, then, Pachter was a radical even within the camp of dissenting left Social Democrats.

In "Communism and Class," Pachter cut through all the hopeful cant about the possibilities for unity on the left. He declared flatly that a union of the German Left was an illusory goal:

> A proletarian united front against fascism is possible whenever there is a specific goal that demands struggle: in most cases just a human life or a house to be defended—any action of simple solidarity whose initial political impact is only minimal. A proletarian united front becomes impossible as soon as it is conceived in political terms, as soon as it requires a concrete notion of joint actions, as soon as the workers' parties are to conclude even a mere truce (*Burgfriede*) regarding agitation and theory. This is not very surprising.[81]

It might in fact have appeared surprising to some on the left who viewed a united socialist front as the most effective weapon against fascism. But Pachter quoted an authoritative source to bolster his argument about the undesirability of such a bloc: Ernst Thälmann, the head of the KPD. Thälmann had argued, also in 1932, that he opposed cooperation with the SPD "in defending the present system of bourgeois rule."[82]

Pachter drew several political conclusions from the peculiar situation of the KPD in 1932 and from Thälmann's remarks. The KPD, Pachter offered, was vulnerable to repression by the conservative coalition that held effective power in Germany, but it could not see its way to forming a necessary alliance with the SPD. Why? Practical and ideological confusion. By continuing to call for the dictatorship of the proletariat—meaning the dictatorship of the party—and ridiculing the parliamentary forms of Weimar, the Communists tore up the ground on which they stood. The Nazis also spoke of dictatorship, but more persuasively. By idealizing the role of the party as the representative of the masses and by virtually dispensing with any need for the working class except for its numbers, the Communists encouraged the desperate frustration and swiftly changing political loyalties that characterized the behavior of many unemployed and discontented workers. For the KPD, Pachter asserted, *any* mass support for radical change would suffice so long as the party remained in the vanguard of the revolution: "If . . . the masses—as seen by the party—fill a vacuum that any other mass could fill just as well, then the party leadership—as seen by the masses—is a vacuum that any other party could fill as long as it meets their quasi-religious desires. A party that bases its propaganda on this principle, therefore, runs a clear risk of actually working for another party. That is why lately we have so often seen those moves back and forth between Communists and Nazis. . . ."[83] Pachter was articulating the observation common on the non-Communist Weimar left that many voters in the late Weimar period sought "salvation" in their support for divergent extremist parties, a kind of desperate and inconsistent political behavior: if the Nazis could not deliver, then perhaps the Communists could, and vice versa.[84]

Because of the dangers that a politicized irrationalism presented, there could be no way of joining up with a party that had become a "church," as Pachter termed the KPD.[85] The appeal of irrational devotion to the "theology" of the movement, he implied, would be as likely to work in favor of fascism as to aid in proletarian revolution. Without claiming that the KPD worked in frequent collusion with Nazism—as some KPD leaders continued to say of the SPD—Pachter pointed out the dangerous folly of KPD policy. Moreover, he argued, the KPD had actively assisted the NSDAP in its attempt to overthrow the SPD in Prussia, and its open joy in response to SPD defeat belied the claim to a sincere desire for a left-wing united front.[86]

In the second half of his essay, Pachter traced the history of efforts to create a united German Left since the World War. None of these attempts had resulted in lasting cooperation. Only desperate circumstances and clear, limited goals could produce a KPD-SPD alliance, he concluded. Even in the crisis of 1932, "a united front cannot be 'manufactured' but will, in practical terms, be formed whenever the class enemy tries to strike both his enemies with one blow."[87] Just as Pachter seemed to intimate, that blow was not long in coming, and it struck at both of its left-wing targets with manifest power and effectiveness.

With dispassionate skepticism, Pachter had analyzed the persisting division of the German Left. In the same demythologizing spirit, another former German Communist—and Pachter's teacher—Arthur Rosenberg, produced a study of Bolshevism that attempted to explain the split in the international Left: *Geschichte des Bolschewismus* (*A History of Bolshevism*). Pachter had cited Rosenberg's book approvingly in his own essay.[88] Like Pachter's hard-headed commentary on the division of the German workers' movement, this book, the most important Weimar-era historical account of the effect of the Russian Revolution and Bolshevism on the international workers' movement, also appeared in the crisis year of 1932.

Arthur Rosenberg was a university instructor of politics and history and a veteran of numerous conflicts on the radical German left. In his capacity as a scholar, Rosenberg had written striking reinterpretations of ancient history and taught university courses in Berlin—though he never attained regular faculty status. He had also been a member of the Reichstag delegation of the KPD, but as a result of the increasing Comintern control over policy at the national level, Rosenberg had left the Communist Party in May 1927 and retired from his seat in the Reichstag the following year.[89] From 1928 to 1938, he wrote and published a series of books that have held their place among the best works on European politics and history produced during the interwar period.[90] Rosenberg's account of the rise of the Bolshevist faction to power in Russia—and the importance of this fact to the entire European workers' movement—remains one of the most important documents of the confrontation between the once-dominant tradition of German revolutionary socialism and its dynamic and successful rival, Bolshevism. *Geschichte des Bolschewismus* unfolds a narrative of political Marxism's transition away from the beliefs of the founding generation of theorists and activists to Leninist Bolshevism. After having spent much of the 1920s as a Leninist and active KPD leader, Rosenberg had become sharply critical of the Soviet Union. He now argued that it was opposed to the concept of true socialism: "The full freedom of the mind that belongs to a true socialist society is certainly not available in Soviet Russia, because the ruling party dictatorship cannot live without a rigid, dogmatic doctrine—obligatory for all—the so-called Leninism."[91] This passage captures precisely both the tone and the substance of Rosenberg's disdain for the Soviet regime in the early 1930s, but his criticisms were not limited to Soviet failures to provide for individual and intellectual freedom. According to Rosenberg, the Soviet system had also failed to achieve its most important self-declared goals: socialist economic transformation and international working-class revolution.

Rosenberg announced his critical opinion of the kind of economic system that had developed in the Soviet Union, and like many other leftist critics of the Soviet Communists, he called this system *Staatskapitalismus*—state capitalism. This particular choice of terminology is important, for it could sometimes be used to deny implicitly the Bolsheviks' claim to have completed an economic revolution and to have established socialism. The term is a controversial one that has appeared in the analyses of a diverse range of writers, but it also had impeccable origins on the revolutionary left: Lenin himself had developed the concept of state capitalism to help explain the New Economic Policy (NEP) of limited capitalism that the Soviet Union adopted in the early 1920s to recover more rapidly from the effects of wartime economic devastation. Lenin claimed, however, that a "proletarian state" would ensure that the benefits of this type of capitalist development would not be limited to the bourgeoisie.[92] Even so, use of the term *state capitalism* by other socialists would soon indicate an intent more hostile than explanatory.

Rosenberg argued that the state capitalism policy led the Soviet Communists to assert absolute dictatorial control to prevent local economic enterprise from slipping away from governmental authority. In effect, he claimed that NEP was the economic equivalent (and predecessor) of Stalin's doctrine of "revolution in one country": "State capitalist Russia no longer depended on the irresistible advance of the world revolution. It could exist peacefully within the capitalist world."[93] Clearly, Rosenberg now took his place as one of the most critical participants in the continuing debates about how to characterize the Soviet economy: was it truly socialist, or was it really a variant of capitalism that used the state instead of private ownership as the means of capital accumulation? If the latter were the case, how could the Soviet Union serve as a model for a new socialist society in the already industrialized nations? This specifically economic question, with its decisive political implications, would reappear in later discussions of both the Soviet and the Nazi regimes.

Rosenberg condemned even more sharply the political, cultural, and intellectual state of the new regime in Russia compared with those of the working class of Western Europe, and his concluding verdict on the twin phenomena of the Russian Revolution and the Comintern made the point more specific:

The Bolshevist doctrine and method were terrifically progressive for the Russia of the Czars. But they were reactionary in the western industrialized states, where the bourgeois revolution has been completed, where the peasants are no longer the greatest portion of the population, and where the proletariat has already learned to build and govern its own organizations....

... The shadows of the great Russian Revolution still cover the rest of the international working class. But the Communist International has no more influence over the active movement of the world proletariat. What the Bolsheviks accomplished in the course of the Russian Revolution remains an immortal historic deed. But insofar as the international bourgeoisie still fears Bolshevism, it is mistaken. It has reason to fear the international Marxist proletariat and world revolution, but "Bolshevism" is not identical with these things.[94]

Rosenberg's *Geschichte des Bolschewismus* and his histories of the Weimar Republic were important sources for several of the other writers discussed in this study. For example, Franz Borkenau, like Rosenberg an ex-Communist, acknowledged the acuity of Rosenberg's analysis of Bolshevism.[95] But Borkenau's praise appeared several years after the publication of *Geschichte des Bolschewismus,* when the consequences of fascist victory had momentarily overshadowed the debates on the left that Pachter and Rosenberg had described. As it happened, in the closing months of 1932, it fell not to Rosenberg or Pachter but to Borkenau to write one of the last critical analyses of fascism to be published in Germany after the Nazi takeover.

The shocking electoral successes of the National Socialists, which after the balloting of July 1932 enabled the Nazis to become the most numerous party faction in the Reichstag, stimulated further reconsideration of the origins and class roots of fascism on the part of its left-wing critics.[96] One of the individuals who took up this effort was the scholar-journalist Franz Borkenau. Born and reared in Vienna, Borkenau studied at the University of Leipzig and joined the KPD in 1921—at a time when party membership was declining.[97] He served for several years in Berlin as a leader of the party's student organization, and he also performed research for the Comintern under the direction of the economist Eugen Varga. After he left the Communist Party in 1929 in a dispute over his opposition to the "social fascism" line (along with his younger friend Richard Löwenthal), he remained an independent Marxist for several years before beginning a decisive move away from revolutionary socialism toward an unorthodox political liberalism. He worked as a researcher with the Frankfurt Institute of Social Research from the late 1920s until 1932, but he took up free-lance political writing as an additional means of support and as an outlet for expressing his distinctive views on European events.[98]

Borkenau's revision of left-wing thinking about fascism confronted the anomalous appearance of National Socialism in an industrially advanced country, when many socialist analyses of fascism had described such movements as a function of economic *under*development taking the form of a party dedicated to accelerated capital accumulation on behalf of a weak bourgeoisie. The case of Germany confounded this hypothesis. Borkenau, writing in the *Archiv für Sozialwissenschaft und Sozialpolitik*, attempted a revised "sociology of fascism" in the light of events in Germany. But by the time his article was published, in February 1933, even Borkenau's revisionist conclusions lagged behind the rapid course of political developments. Nevertheless, his analysis deserves attention because of its attempt to describe fascism as a possible political correlate of industrial modernization, one of the first of many such efforts.[99]

"Zur Soziologie des Faschismus" ("Toward a Sociology of Fascism") began by placing German fascism in the foreground of the argument. Nazism was the first fascist movement to gain strength in a fully industrialized nation, and Borkenau raised the question of whether fascism was "a manifestation specific to capitalistically underdeveloped nations or a worldwide developmental tendency of the present period."[100] Borkenau mentioned in passing the writings of August Thalheimer and the Austrian Social Democrat Otto Bauer on the subject, but he quickly proceeded to offer a description of fascism that diverged sharply from theirs at several points.[101] Most important, he attempted to move away from the model of Italy as the "ideal type" of fascism, stressing the growing number and the local characteristics of similar movements that had appeared in Europe during the postwar period, regardless of their success at seizing state power.

In this essay, Borkenau used the word *totalitarian* to describe the character of Italy's reigning political movement. He argued that Italian Fascism had emerged as the consequence of a unique set of circumstances: a weak bourgeoisie, a strong working class, and the consequent lack of an adequate means of capital accumulation. In 1922, Mussolini had taken control of the Italian state, which he then used to force radically modernizing policies on the nation, including concentration of state power and acceleration of private industrial growth, all under the control of an "exclusive dictatorship of a totalitarian Party."[102] Italy's relative backwardness and working-class resistance to the rationalizing and therefore socially disruptive introduction of capitalist production had created an opening for Fascism. The Fascists had usurped the special historical role of the bourgeois class in carrying out capitalization while successfully claiming to advance only national interests. In other words, the Fascists would use the Italian state to transform the economic and social relations of its civil society.

Borkenau also joined the attack launched by unorthodox leftists against the crude economism of some Marxist theories of fascism by insisting that the fascist totalitarian party was not simply the agent of the bourgeoisie and that the fascists exerted power over the economy through a state apparatus that did not derive its legitimacy from one class alone.[103] The class origins of fascism were more complex than that: the fascists drew their most zealous followers from the déclassés of all classes of society, Borkenau argued, following Thalheimer. He concluded (with uncharacteristic optimism) that the German bourgeoisie would not allow itself to be ruled by the National Socialists. He would survive to revise his analysis still further in exile.

Another writer who participated in the debates among socialists about the rise of fascism was the labor lawyer and scholar Franz Neumann, born in Kattowitz (now Katowice, Poland) in 1900. He also fits squarely into the generation of German socialists whose careers as political analysts carried over into the postwar years. He is best known for his wartime study of the Nazi state, *Behemoth,* but his prewar and postwar writings have recently become the focus of renewed debate. He is also known as an important member of the Institute of Social Research, though he cannot be regarded as a member of the Frankfurt School's "inner circle." A veteran of World War I, who apparently entered service late in the conflict and saw far more action as a supporter of the abortive revolution of 1918–19 than he did at the front, he became an extremely active and effective Weimar-era labor lawyer associated with the moderate wing of the SPD. He studied with one of the most important legal theorists and practitioners of the day, the controversial Carl Schmitt, who joined the Nazi Party in 1933. But Neumann also studied with or worked alongside socialist and trade union legal experts, including Hermann Heller, Otto Kahn-Freund, and Ernst Fraenkel. Because of his identities as a prominent Social Democrat and as a Jew, he was one of the first Germans to be stripped of his citizenship under Nazi rule. The destruction of his career in Germany forced him into exile in England, where he studied with the influential scholar and left-wing activist Harold Laski. His years in the United States are certainly far more important phases of his intellectual career, but it is useful to recall his Weimar years, for they alert us to the origins of his more directly political and legal interests, which set him in contrast with the core group of institute theorists, including Theodor Adorno, Max Horkheimer, and Herbert Marcuse, who were more involved with the analysis of culture and philosophy.[104]

Unlike several of his politically active generational peers, Neumann in exile initially moved away from his position as a moderate Social Democrat toward a more radical and critical stance on the legacy of Weimar, eventually turning even further from party activism than they would. Examples of thinkers whose paths briefly paralleled Neumann's were Borkenau, Pachter, and Löwenthal. But they were all former members of the KPD, a party that had openly opposed and even despised the compromise structure of Weimar. In exile, they moved steadily toward parliamentary and anti-Soviet reformist socialism. They were also even less closely connected with the Institute of Social Research than Neumann would be. Only Borkenau performed research and published books and articles under its auspices in the early 1930s, during the course of an increasingly distant relationship with the institute's new leading group.[105] As a labor lawyer, teacher, and SPD activist, Neumann stood apart from both former Communists and the institute's leading theoreticians. He had witnessed the destruction of the Weimar Republic from the perspective of the organized labor movement. The objects of his political and intellectual commitments had failed and suffered destruction. After the utter defeat of the German Left in 1933, he would never recover much faith in the ability of the working class either to achieve social revolution or to defeat fascism without external aid. His political transformation and disillusionment reveal with poignant clarity the intensity of the pressures that defeat and exile brought to bear on many members of the German Left.

In the spring of 1933, Neumann was briefly taken into police custody and then "visited" by the paramilitary SA (Sturmabteilung—Storm Troopers) a few weeks later at his law office. He left Germany soon thereafter.[106] From exile in England, Neumann indicated the change in his political outlook that the Nazi's success had engendered when he published his first epitaph for the Weimar Republic (the first, that is, of several versions he would write over the next twenty years): "The Decay of German Democracy," in the October–December 1933 issue of the *Political Quarterly*.[107] Neumann's harshest criticism in this summary was his judgment on the Weimar Constitution. He declared that the National Socialist Revolution (his term) succeeded because of the "Anti-State which the democratic State tolerated though it was born to destroy democracy."[108] In short, the German Parliament could never channel the influence of German parties but instead became their hapless creature. Neumann went so far as to argue that "German Parties were—apart from one unimportant exception [unnamed]—based on a totalitarian philosophy (*Weltanschauungs-Parteien*). They laid claim to the whole of the individual. They were totalitarian parties."[109]

By this use of the term *totalitarian,* Neumann apparently intended to point out that the parties attempted to control as many aspects of their members' lives as possible. For example, he described how each party developed its own clubs not only for political discussion and action but also for music, sports, youth, professions, and various types of laborers. Moreover, Neumann argued, such parties did "not suit parliamentary democracy and in the second place the radical totalitarian parties did not recognise the rules of the parliamentary game."[110] At this juncture, Neumann's critique of "totalitarian parties" did not incorporate a critique of the totalitarian state, but that was not long in coming. His blanket use of the term, without the previously common quotation marks, perhaps merely indicated the spread of the word's use to describe a range of intolerant and oppressive political movements. But his description of "totalitarian parties" left little doubt that he included the SPD as well as the KPD under this label. For the moment, however, he focused not on the problem of dictatorship but on the circumstances in liberal Weimar that had permitted the capture of the state by its least tolerant and most anticonstitutional party.

Neumann also repudiated the suicidal political tolerance and fastidious representativeness of the Weimar government. Under the Weimar Constitution, strictly proportional representation guaranteed even relatively tiny parties a voice in the Reichstag. To be sure, this was a more democratic apportionment of political representation than was common among the world's republics, but it carried the risk of granting legitimacy to extreme and even openly antirepublican parties. The Nazis, for example, had placed a dozen brown-shirted deputies on the floor of the Reichstag in 1928 with a mere 2.6 percent of the national vote. Ten or more parties routinely elected delegates to the Reichstag, making the formation of a ruling government coalition an extremely difficult and delicate project.[111]

Even the working class and its trade unions, which Neumann had served as a legal adviser for some years, did not escape his wrath. The apparent guarantee of a legal and independent role in society granted to the trade unions by the Weimar Constitution did not secure such a position in practice. Once the economy began to fail, wages were fixed by the state instead of by collective bargaining. As a result, strikes diminished in number and strength, shifting from offensive to defensive actions. The ultimate demise of German trade unionism came about after Hitler's appointment to the chancellorship, when the leadership of some labor organizations desperately attempted to cut loose from the SPD and adopt a quasi-fascist program in order to salvage some independent status under the Nazis. Neumann argued that this tactic gained nothing and surrendered a great deal in terms of socialist principles and that the naked opportunism it demonstrated may have further sapped traditionally left-wing workers' ability to retain a sense of ideological difference from the National Socialists.[112]

Neumann's attack on totalitarian parties in 1933 was but one element of his general argument about the collapse of Weimar, but the clearest targets of his critique were easy to identify: the Nazi Party and the German Communist Party, which had both aimed to destroy parliamentary democracy in Neumann's opinion.[113] As mentioned at the beginning of the chapter, this particular line of argument has become one of the durable explanations for the demise of Weimar, and it has also provided one path to the model of totalitarianism so common among cold war political theorists. Here and there in his writings on dictatorship, Neumann would continue to appropriate this analytical pairing of Nazism and Communism, but he made systematic use of it only after World War II. Yet in his deep involvement in the labor politics of the first German Republic as well as his drift from one kind of orthodox party Marxism—Social Democratic in his case—toward a critically independent leftism increasingly skeptical about Marxist notions of social change, he stands as a representative figure. Neumann's early critique of totalitarianism, however, remained firmly rooted in Marxist class categories, and his opposition always took the form of advocacy of democratic socialism, one of the distinguishing features of his use of a version of the concept of totalitarianism that persisted until his death in 1954.[114] Discussions of some of his seminal writings on the workings of the Nazi state appear in later chapters.

Even before Neumann wrote his hostile epitaph for Weimar, another young Social Democrat who would later become Neumann's friend and collaborator, Otto Kirchheimer, had been dissecting the problematic character of the Weimar constitutional order, but with an initially far more developed interest in the problem of dictatorship. Born and reared in Heilbronn, Kirchheimer studied law and politics in Münster, Cologne, Berlin, and Bonn. In Bonn, he wrote his dissertation for Carl Schmitt in 1928 on the topic of the divergent doctrines of the state advocated by the socialists and the Bolsheviks.[115] He published an article in *Zeitschrift für Politik* that same year synthesizing arguments drawn from his longer academic treatise.[116] His most important early manuscript, *Weimar—und Was Dann? Entstehung und Gegenwart der Weimarer Verfassung* (*Weimar and What Then? The Origin and Present Status of the Weimar Constitution*), was published in 1930. It was a remarkably prescient analysis of Germany's political predicament and remains one of the most perceptive of the left-wing studies of the Weimar constitutional regime. In 1932, he analyzed the constitutional theory of Carl Schmitt's *Legalität und Legitimität* (*Legality and Legitimacy*), arriving at a critical perspective on the book but admiring Schmitt's clear statements on the constitutional issues the Weimar regime could not resolve. Continuing to focus his research on the political and institutional crises of the moment, he also contributed analyses of the Prussian SPD's debacle of 1932 and the national constitutional upheavals of that same year. It is worth noting that, despite their sharply critical tone toward official SPD policy, all of these late Weimar articles appeared in the SPD's theoretical journal, *Die Gesellschaft*.[117] The primary interest of Kirchheimer's early articles lies in their increasing reliance on Luxemburgist notions of radical socialist democracy to criticize both the practices of the Soviet Union and the increasingly authoritarian Weimar government.

Kirchheimer's 1928 article, "Zur Staatslehre des Sozialismus und Bolschewismus" ("Toward a Doctrine of the State in Socialism and Bolshevism"), still shows the strong disdain for liberal constitutional ideology and practice that typified the work of his one-time mentor, Carl Schmitt. He relied heavily on Schmitt's famous dictum that sovereignty belongs to the individual or institution capable of deciding what an "emergency" situation is and acting outside of tightly demarcated—but ultimately breachable—liberalist bounds.[118] His characterization of the Soviet system of rule shows, however, that Kirchheimer was interested in radical revolutionary responses to the weaknesses of liberal theory and practice—not Schmitt's authoritarian conservative responses.

Kirchheimer was particularly intrigued by and skeptical of the possibilities represented by the Bolshevik notion of dictatorship of the proletariat, as we see in the following passages: "The Bolshevik dictatorship does not embody an organic process of transition; its exceptional quality as an emergency situation consists in the fact that in order to establish the socialist state of social equality it must first create the prerequisite conditions. This leads to a number of political measures which reveal the characteristic trait of every dictatorship: in order to realize its cherished ideals it is forced to resort to measures that *ipso facto* contradict the ideal to be realized."[119] This contradiction did not force Kirchheimer's rejection of the Soviet form of dictatorship at this time, however, for at least the "Bolshevik concept" of proletarian dictatorship had not yet been hitched to traditionally liberal constitutional forms—mere "legal mechanisms," in Kirchheimer's view at that time—and the Soviet Union defied categorization as a traditional state because it replaced state sovereignty with class sovereignty: "The Bolshevik prophets of the political myth of world revolution—who consider Russia merely as the launching pad—are the sworn, irreconcilable enemies of the powers that are lined up behind the facade of 'the state,' that is on the one hand, the capitalist power groups with their imperialist policies and, on the other, the holders of the theory of twofold progress, the wardens of the legal mechanism, namely, Social Democracy and the petty bourgeoisie."[120] The attitudes and assumptions of Kirchheimer in 1928 about the value of Bolshevist theory and practice would undergo a swift transformation under the pressures of the next five years. Turning from Leninism and the neo-Hobbesianism of Schmitt, he soon discovered in the writings of Marx and Rosa Luxemburg a series of quite different ideas on political legitimacy.

Weimar—and What Then? published in 1930, reveals the beginning of the shift in Kirchheimer's thinking. Opening with a quotation from Rosa Luxemburg's *Sozialreform oder Revolution* (*Social Reform or Revolution*) in which she emphasized that constitutions can only mark—but not extend—the limits of the revolutions that precede them, Kirchheimer's pamphlet presented a brilliantly argued and critical dissection of the Weimar Constitution. On the specific issue of the appearance of dictatorship in Germany, Kirchheimer claimed that Germany's current situation presented a "bourgeois political democracy," quite limited in its rearrangement of prewar political and social power, that was in transition toward a bourgeois dictatorship along the lines of Italian Fascism. The boundary between the two kinds of bourgeois regimes was unclear, he continued, but it was a mistake to believe, as many moderate socialists did, that the constitution could be salvaged for the purpose of socialist transformation: "This constitution of a bourgeois value system in the process of dissolution can be nothing more than the servant of whoever is momentarily the more powerful."[121] He was, as events demonstrated, remarkably accurate in this component of his analysis.[122] Neumann, however, responded to Kirchheimer's article in a critical review that answered the question "Weimar and What Then?" by urging "first try Weimar!"—indicating clearly that in 1930 Neumann still felt the constitutional opportunity offered by the fragile Weimar Republic should not be written off so quickly.[123] Unhappily for both men, though in confirmation of Kirchheimer's prediction, the conservative parties, dominated by the wealthiest sectors of the agrarian and business classes, at first attempted to rule under the aegis of Hindenburg's emergency decrees from 1930 to 1932— with the SPD's "toleration" of this makeshift (though constitutional) arrangement.[124] The following year, however, the ruling conservative groups felt compelled to seek a broader popular base and risked an alliance with the one mass party whose program was most like theirs: the National Socialist German Workers' Party. With the conclusion of this agreement in the cabinet of January 1933, fascist-style dictatorship in Germany was about to become an accomplished fact.

Only weeks after Hitler's appointment to the chancellorship, Kirchheimer published an article that once more returned to the theme of dictatorship, "Marxismus, Diktatur, und Organisationsformen des Proletariats" ("Marxism, Dictatorship, and the Organizational Forms of the Proletariat").[125] Here, Kirchheimer placed himself more clearly than ever in the tradition of Rosa Luxemburg and other left-wing critics of Bolshevism and at the same time offered a perspective on the need for a proletarian revolution that seems as remarkably optimistic about actual possibilities as *Weimar—and What Then?* had been accurate and pessimistic in its appraisal of them three years earlier.

The article emphasized the importance of the relationship between the revolutionary proletariat and both party and state institutions of democracy, stressing that the Bolshevist regime of the Soviet Union served as a cautionary model—not an ideal type—of working-class democracy:

> When the civil war with its dire need for the centralization of all energies was over, the structure of the state practically coincided with that of the party. The soviets had become empty shells and Lenin's theory of the state with its dialectical contradiction between authoritarian revolution and primitive democracy had been definitively transformed to conform to his unequivocally authoritarian theory of the party. And the authoritarian party had found its linear continuation in the actual structure of the state.
>
> . . . The Russian example is classic for that narrowing of the governmental basis which most gravely jeopardizes the chances of a proletarian democracy, as Rosa Luxemburg, as well as Martov and Dan, showed again and again.[126]

The purpose of Kirchheimer's critical appraisal of Leninism was clearly to restate the need for the German working class to "bring about the final victory of proletarian democracy."[127]

In the course of his article, Kirchheimer favorably cited both Borkenau's analysis of fascism and Rosenberg's analysis of Bolshevism—as well as the work of Luxemburg and the Mensheviks Yulii Martov and Fyodor Dan.[128] Moreover, he seemed to conclude that avoiding the first of these two developments—fascism—would be a violent process: "We are probably facing the situation expressly foreseen as possible in the Linz Program of the Austrian Socialist party, namely, that the working class can conquer executive political power only by a civil war which has thus been forced upon it."[129] Avoiding the second fate, a Bolshevist regime in Germany depended on democracy within the revolutionary movement and democratic state institutions. As a strategy for the conditions prevailing in early 1933, Kirchheimer's article, so full of revolutionary hopes and plans, now seems to be an easy target. Yet as a restatement of democratic socialist ideals for a mass political movement in a time of extraordinary crisis, the essay offered a reasonable formula for a radical democratic politics of resistance. Kirchheimer's essay had also touched on the left-wing dilemma of seeking a way to combat a fascist or Bolshevist dictatorship and yet avoiding a retreat to conservative or liberal positions. Like Borkenau and Neumann, Kirchheimer would live to theorize and write another day.

At the same time, another group of writers, generally more experienced in the benefits and costs of participating in the exercise of governmental power than such younger radicals as Kirchheimer, Borkenau, or Neumann, attempted to judge the next stage of political change in Germany. Unlike some of the younger radicals, they successfully avoided the conclusion that violence was either imminent or necessary. From 1924 until just after the Nazi seizure of power, the main journal of Social Democratic intellectuals was *Die Gesellschaft*. Rudolf Hilferding, whom we have already encountered in his roles as SPD theorist and Weimar finance minister, was the journal's editor. Through it, he was party publicist and leading thinker. He also gathered about him a group of writers who helped perform many of the hands-on chores of editing and writing. A high percentage of this core group consisted of exiled Mensheviks who had settled in Berlin during the 1920s.[130]

Criticism of the KPD was a common theme of articles in *Die Gesellschaft* up to and shortly after the Nazi *Machtergreifung* (seizure of power). These articles were the work of not just the Menshevik contingent but also other writers across the spectrum of the Social Democratic Party. The issue-by-issue contents of *Die Gesellschaft* offer a revealing, though hardly conclusive, portrait of the concerns of the SPD's moderate intellectuals during the crisis months from the July 1932 ouster of the SPD regime in Prussia by Chancellor Franz von Papen to the appointment of Adolf Hitler to the chancellorship early the following year. If the substance of the articles in *Die Gesellschaft* is any guide, it is not too much to say that in late 1932 and early 1933, the SPD's leading intellectuals remained almost as concerned about the Communists as they were about the Nazis. One of the last issues of *Die Gesellschaft* began with Hilferding's appraisal of the November 1932 election, "Zwischen den Entscheidungen" ("Between Decisions"). The article emphasized the caution that the SPD must show in its dealings with the KPD. Hilferding's piece was followed by Alexander Schifrin's hostile evaluation of the recent political role of the KPD entitled "Wege aus der Spaltung" ("Routes out of the Schism"), and later in the same issue Walter Biehahn's friendly review of Arthur Rosenberg's *Geschichte des Bolschewismus* appeared. There was no major assessment of the continuing threat of National Socialism in this issue.[131]

The moderate SPD's preoccupation with the Communists had at least some logical basis, though. The November 1932 elections had shown a marked and rapid drop in the level of support for the NSDAP—a loss of roughly 2 million votes since the July elections. Meanwhile, the KPD had made major gains—nearly 700,000 votes above its July total. In addition to its electoral gains, the KPD had recently gone to new extremes in its struggle for working-class votes by joining the NSDAP in support of a wildcat transport workers' strike in Berlin, which also occurred in November 1932.[132] The level of voter support for the liberal parties and the Center Party showed little change. The weakened liberals of the German Democratic Party (DDP), for example, had not recovered from their debacle of July 1932 and thus would hold no effective power in the negotiations for a new parliamentary coalition. In view of these facts, the SPD's shift in attention toward the KPD appears less foolish and spitefully factional than it might at first glance. The Nazis' electoral support had apparently crested and begun to wane, while the KPD—which drew more directly from the SPD's traditional constituency in the working class—showed a steady increase.[133] The extreme dangers presented by both the Communists and the Nazis troubled the SPD leadership as it waited for the Hindenburg clique to attempt to form yet another government with SPD "toleration" but without SPD participation. As Rudolf Hilferding wrote to Karl Kautsky, an SPD elder, on 1 December 1932: "The situation is certainly unpleasant. The fascist danger still threatens and the increase [in support] for the Communists disturbs our people even more. Indeed, a further advance in this direction would certainly bring the greatest danger that the attraction of the

Communists would increase powerfully as soon as they surpassed our numbers. It is not a pretty scene, but adventurist stupidities would only make things worse."[134] The day after this letter was written, Hindenburg dismissed Papen as chancellor and appointed General Kurt von Schleicher in his place. Even so knowledgeable and uneasy an observer of these maneuvers as Hilferding could hardly have suspected that, within two months, President Hindenburg would be persuaded by his conservative advisers to dump Schleicher, name Hitler chancellor of Germany, and thereby give the Nazis the opportunity to seize power, which the voters had denied them twice in 1932.[135] But the political and social defeat of the working-class parties at the hands of the Nazis and their allies in 1933 would be as swift as it was strange.

By mid-1933, German leftists had assembled a battery of analytical tools for the study of state-party dictatorships. These theoretical analyses of the new regimes in Italy, the Soviet Union, and Germany approached but, with only a few rare exceptions, did not yet embrace the terminology or the comparative analytical framework of "totalitarianism theory." More important, left-wing opposition to National Socialism suffered terrible defeats even as the theoretical insights of German leftists grew suppler and more differentiated. The gap between theory and practice has rarely if ever had such a high cost. Defeat in early 1933 and the flight into exile during the following months were due to forces that were quickly beyond the reach of those who might have been in possession of a "correct analysis." The German Left was divided, overwhelmed, baffled. No effective armed resistance took place. Such "adventurist stupidities" would have been entirely out of character for the SPD. The Nazis, assessing the relative dangers on the left accurately, turned their attention first to the less numerous but more physically formidable Communists. The SPD met its fate shortly thereafter. Soon, the German Left that could never share a political platform shared instead political dismemberment and destruction.[136]

When the days and weeks of decisive action came, left-wing resistance to the Nazis' *Gleichschaltung* (coordination) was fragmentary and pathetically inadequate. Despite all the faults of the German Left, it bears repeating that among the most important elements in the National Socialists' initial success in seizing control of the state apparatus was the cooperation offered—however grudgingly and with whatever levels of suspicion— by President von Hindenburg, the police, the army, and several key leaders of the conservative parties. A careful review of the events in Germany and elsewhere in Europe that followed the appointment of the leader of the National Socialist Party to the chancellorship yields examples of missed historical opportunities as well as the power of contingent factors.[137] As it happened, Henry Pachter's pessimistic verdict on the possibilities for a united Left in the fall of 1932 turned out to be correct. Even so, the shocking collapse in 1933 and the political division and defeat of the German Left did not preclude its further analytical productivity, for even in exile, several intellectuals associated with the German Left continued their analysis of "fascist," "Bolshevist," "Stalinist," or "totalitarian" dictatorship as independent writers and scholars or as party-affiliated theorists.

SOCIALISTS IN DARK TIMES:
PERSPECTIVES FROM EXILE, 1933–39

The political antithesis of fascism is not Bolshevism, from which fascism has simply taken over its political methods and its contempt for personal rights and intellectual freedom; the antithesis is revolutionary democratic socialism.

—Alexander Schifrin, 1933

Ten different cliques of German émigrés squat in ten different Prague cafés attempting to discover ten different ways of rebuilding the ruined German workers' movement. In Vienna and Zürich, Strasbourg and Paris, Amsterdam and Copenhagen, the same picture presents itself. The German proletariat has many saviors. But it will receive no salvation in socialism from these saviors.

—Otto Rühle, 1934[?]

The period from 1933 to 1939 was a disastrous time for the European Left generally and for the German Left in particular. Within months of the Nazi *Machtergreifung,* both the KPD and the SPD lay in scattered fragments. Many of their leaders were in jail, on the run, or already in exile. Rank-and-file party members remaining in Germany retreated into what remained of private life or engaged in courageous but often tragically isolated and uncoordinated acts of resistance. By 1934, fascist movements or parties aping fascism in many important respects controlled or threatened the governments of several European nations. Italy and now Germany set the models for fascist rule. Austria and Spain would soon follow this trend.[1] Compounding the political and theoretical difficulties confronting leftists was the fact that, throughout this period, the domestic policies of the Soviet Union under the leadership of Joseph Stalin often showed a brutality that rivaled or even surpassed that of the fascists. Even so, from the perspective of the democratic, antifascist Left, there were genuinely hopeful moments in the decade as well—the workers' rising in Austria in 1934, the French socialists' electoral victory in 1936, and the leftist revolution in Spain touched off by the right-wing military rising in July of that same year. Nevertheless, as the potential for greater resistance to fascism succumbed in each particular case to the contingencies of international political and military conditions, policy choices that went awry, leftist groups at odds with their leadership, and the rapidly shifting configurations of power in those times and places, these moments sooner or later brought with them new causes for dismay.[2]

For German leftists in exile, as for tens of thousands of others during the 1930s, the loss of home and citizenship brought additional sources of stress: denial or restriction of civil rights, personal isolation, cultural marginalization, ruined careers, poverty, and a sense of political powerlessness that may have gradually appeared to acquire permanence. Nevertheless, for some of the left-wing German intellectuals who survived and found the ability to make ends meet, the years 1933 to 1939 marked a remarkably productive period, at least from the standpoint of theory. The feisty assertiveness of Alexander Schifrin and the cynicism of Otto Rühle in the epigraphs above indicate the opposite poles of political attitudes among the exiled Left by which its theoretical enterprises were oriented. Forced to sense the direction of political developments in their homeland from greater or lesser distances, these German exiles entered unfamiliar terrain, in both literal and figurative terms. As socialist intellectuals, they labored to increase in their new home countries the understanding and awareness of the real threat of National Socialism and also to strengthen the theoretical capacity of Marxism and the socialist movement generally to aid in the practical and political resistance to fascist dictatorship.

The theoretical and organizational responses of a number of German socialist intellectuals to the ascendancy of fascism in Germany and, though to a lesser extent, to Stalin's dictatorship in the Soviet Union acquired added force and focus during the early exile period. These writers made increasing uses of theories of fascism, as well as theories using various notions of totalitarianism. Contrary to the limited scholarly acknowledgment of the emergence of totalitarian theory on the left, the comparison of the two regimes began to appear in the years just *before* the Hitler-Stalin pact, particularly in connection with the Spanish civil war and the "show trials" in the Soviet Union. During these years, the term *totalitarian* began to appear frequently in the writings of several dissenting socialists of international reputation, Trotsky being the most famous example.[3] The term's referents during the last few years of the interwar period would more often include the Soviet Union as well as Italy and Germany. But there was no uniformity to this change in the categorization and analysis of dictatorial regimes. The turn to comparative models of totalitarianism on the left was gradual, partial, tentative, and contested, which is, of course, one of the reasons it has been so difficult to recognize.

In addition to the impact of significant political differences within its ranks, the very scattering of the German Left across Europe—from the Soviet Union to Czechoslovakia, France, and England, and, even beyond, to the United States, Cuba, Panama, and Mexico—helped give rise to dozens of divergent interpretations of the political crises of the moment.[4] Rival theoretical constructions of the problem of dictatorship, as well as different organizational and political experiences with actual regimes, also played a role. In these writings of the period from the Nazi takeover to the outbreak of another general European war in 1939, the terms *fascist* and *totalitarian* were often used almost interchangeably. In part, the willingness of German socialists, particularly Social Democrats, to employ the "totalitarian analogy" of damning Communism as exhibiting much in common with fascism had been provoked by the Communists' attack on "social fascism" in the Weimar period. The polemical and ideological usefulness of the accusation of "totalitarian" practices had led such Social Democratic writers as Curt Geyer and Alexander Schifrin to condemn the Soviet Union along with fascist movements as dictatorial organizations from the early 1930s.[5] Now, however, the hostile adjectives proliferated freely, and one of the tasks facing socialist intellectuals writing about dictatorship was to try to give the terms *fascist* and *totalitarian* more precise meaning.

New Perspectives on Fascism

For a number of months after the Nazi takeover, the critique of the Soviet Union faded somewhat into the background, while the victories of fascism in Germany in 1933 and then in Austria the following year gained the attention of many intellectuals of the German Left in exile. In short, the focus of the analysis of dictatorship shifted rapidly under the fearsome pressure of events. Several innovative and "revisionist" discussions of fascism soon appeared that focused on German fascism or the German "total state"—or both.

In 1934, Herbert Marcuse, a writer whose work had a more critical and philosophical radicalism than that of his more directly political left-wing peers, gave his assessment of German fascism from exile.[6] Like most of the intellectuals discussed in this study, Marcuse came from a prosperous family. He was born and reared in Berlin, which, as one of Marcuse's biographers, Barry Katz, has pointed out, had transformed itself into a center of German culture as well as politics and commerce. Marcuse's own development was symptomatic of the possibilities available to a young man of the bourgeoisie, and his growing cultural interests and politically oppositional stance showed themselves early. He attended a gymnasium in the Charlottenburg district of Berlin. There, as well as at home, he was introduced to the historical and literary heritage of the German past, and he joined one of the numerous *Wandervögel* hiking and social groups. He served in the army during World War I, but not at the front. Instead, he found himself in Berlin during the weeks of revolutionary tumult following the mutiny of the sailors at Kiel and elsewhere. He participated in the Berlin rising and was actually elected to one of the soldiers' councils, but he apparently cherished a far greater sympathy for the revolution in the South, the Munich revolution led by Kurt Eisner. These revolutionary movements failed bravely but horribly, and Marcuse turned his back on party politics forever after the murders of Rosa Luxemburg and Karl Liebknecht.[7]

During the 1920s, Marcuse took up the study of literature and philosophy in Freiburg with, among others, the influential phenomenologist Edmund Husserl. In 1922, he completed his doctoral dissertation on the *Künstlerroman* (the novel of the artist) in the department of literature. After a spell of working and writing in Berlin, Marcuse turned his energies once more to the study of philosophy. Under the impact of his close reading of Martin Heidegger's *Sein und Zeit* (*Being and Time*), he returned to Freiburg as a member of Heidegger's advanced seminar. His connection with Heidegger, who later joined the Nazi Party, had a great impact on Marcuse's early philosophical interest in the categories of historicity, being, social renewal, and social totality. Despite some shared philosophical concerns and methodologies, in several vital respects Marcuse adamantly and unequivocally rejected Heidegger's political conclusions, particularly his allegiance to the Nazis.[8] Marcuse had already fled Freiburg—and Germany—by 26 May 1933, when Heidegger issued one of his first public statements to the students and faculty after assuming the post of rector of the university: a passionately worded commemoration of the tenth anniversary of the execution of "a young German hero," Leo Schlageter, who had once been a student at Freiburg.[9]

In the course of his studies with Heidegger, Marcuse had completed a long manuscript entitled *Hegels Ontologie und die Grundlegung einer Theorie der Geschichtlichkeit* (*Hegel's Ontology and the Foundation of a Theory of Historicity*), published in 1932. Apparently, it was to have been his *Habilitationsschrift*, the postdoctoral work that would open the possibility of a tenured academic career. But even before the Nazi takeover in January of the following year, Marcuse lost hope for gaining a university chair. He accepted an offer from the Institute of Social Research, now led by Max Horkheimer, to take a position at its branch in Geneva. Marcuse's move to Geneva marked the beginning of a theoretically fruitful period for both him and the institute. In the late fall of 1932, however, the project of immediate importance was flight, and Marcuse left Germany with his family weeks before Hitler was named chancellor. Marcuse would remain in Switzerland for less than two years before immigrating to the United States.[10]

Marcuse's first important published contribution to the institute's work on authoritarian politics and society was the article "Der Kampf gegen den Liberalismus in der totalitären Staatsauffassung" ("The Struggle against Liberalism in the Totalitarian View of the State"), which appeared in 1934 in the *Zeitschrift für Sozialforschung* (*Journal of Social Research*). The article is important in understanding Marcuse's life and work in several ways. First, despite the momentary end of his hopes for a traditional academic career, the article offered evidence that Marcuse had found an ideal institutional home. His work clearly fit into the institute's overall project of analyzing modern society from a variety of disciplinary perspectives, which included examining the ideological workings of fascism, and Marcuse's arrival significantly strengthened the philosophical component of this undertaking. Second, and crucial to an examination of notions of totalitarianism in the work of the exile German Left, Marcuse's analysis of fascism as a kind of totalitarianism derived from intensified and distorted aspects of liberalism devoted little attention to class analysis and economistic argumentation and hence constituted something of a break with previous left-wing writings on fascism, especially in its emphasis and style of presentation.[11] Third, and also important in the context of this study, Marcuse's 1934 article established some of the philosophical basis for his distinctive and deeply controversial postwar attacks on the totalitarianism of *all* developed societies, whether capitalist or Communist.[12]

Marcuse opened his argument with a catalogue of the characteristics of fascist ideology: the "heroizing" of man, the philosophical valorization of life itself as a primal given, irrational naturalism, and universalism. But he proceeded to show that the "current theory" of the total state drew these principles from certain aspects of the liberalism it ostensibly loathed. Moreover, Marcuse contended, "liberalism is entirely at one [*'ganz einig ist'*] with the new worldview [of totalitarian fascism] in its fight with Marxian socialism."[13] At the very least, then, in Marcuse's reading of the problem, fascism and liberalism were linked in their hostility to socialism. The remainder of his article attempted to specify the complex and dialectical nature of the ideological and economic relationship between liberalism and fascism that he had described in the first few pages of his analysis. As Pierre Ayçoberry has argued, according to Marcuse "one had to read the texts [that expressed the totalitarian outlook] on several levels, and this is why his article unfolded as a kind of spiral."[14]

Central to Marcuse's argument was the fact that liberalism was historically related to European industrial capitalism and imperialism in the nineteenth century, not just to the hopeful slogans and constitutional forms defending individual rights produced during the revolutionary era of the late eighteenth century. Fascism had only contempt for the liberal social and political agenda of rights, but fascists did not wish to disturb the capitalist economic basis of modern society that was part of the liberal achievement.[15] Moreover, fascism did not perpetuate only the economic base of monopoly capitalism that had been created under the conditions of the presumably moribund liberal society. According to Marcuse, the uses that the new totalitarian outlook could make of the remains of liberalism extended beyond the merely economic, for even the liberal terminology of equality and natural rights finds its echo—though certainly a distorted one—in fascist ideology. Marcuse bolstered this argument by citing the fascists and protofascists Moeller van den Bruck, Benito Mussolini, and Hans J. Wolff on the eternal character of Nature, the equality of social interests and powers, and the appearance (in the 1930s) of "a new epoch of natural law."[16] The old, familiar wineskins of liberal language could indeed be filled with the new totalitarian wine, even if, as Marcuse might have noted at the time, the old skins must inevitably burst. He speculated that the connections between fascism and the liberal economic basis of modern society might reproduce not an authoritarian bourgeois state but something entirely new. This new kind of political regime, the totalitarian state, made use of the economic order created under liberalism and the terminology of liberal philosophy, but it aimed beyond their old limits toward a new kind of state organization whose structure and operations could not yet be glimpsed.

In the concluding section of the article, entitled "Der Existentialismus," Marcuse turned from his campaign against liberalism and aimed his sharpest attack on the connection between the new order and the "political configuration" of existentialism, which he was still careful to separate from its "philosophical form."[17] That is, he wished to defend the critical and still useful elements of existentialist philosophy against the contamination resulting from their popularization in Nazi propaganda and the politicization of existentialism performed by such individual philosophers as his former teacher Martin Heidegger. The fate of existentialism and philosophy in general under the Nazi regime was, however, manifest. Marcuse lamented that existentialism, initially conceived in opposition to liberalism's faith in the victory of reason and its preoccupation with universal principles, had now attached itself politically to fascism. Existentialism's service to fascism betrayed all great philosophy. The Kantian tradition of the free, self-determined individual had been negated. Heidegger, whom Marcuse quoted in this concluding passage, now contended that "the Führer himself and alone is for today and the future the German reality and its law."[18] As a consequence of its opportunism, existentialism had transformed itself into an ideological gargoyle for the hulking edifice of the new regime. Marcuse concluded that the fate of the workers' movement, inextricably bound up with the crippled and now violently upended German philosophical tradition of idealism from Kant and Hegel through Heideggerian existentialism, remained in doubt.

This article, originally conceived as a response to one of Hitler's own speeches and written during the first months of exile, established the basis for Marcuse's unique perspective on fascism and totalitarianism, one that, despite its changing focus over the course of the next several decades, continued to emphasize the philosophical and ideological foundations of the modern "total-state" as they were put into practice in class relationships.[19] Marcuse's analysis differed from most of his peers' analyses in that he muted the discussion of class per se, in favor of exploring the origins and manifestations of ideologies, collective perceptions, and the unreflective behavior of groups. This was not necessarily un-Marxian, but it certainly constituted a different kind of radical perspective, one typical of the leading thinkers associated with the Institute of Social Research.[20] The primary strength of the kind of ideological analysis Marcuse could offer in 1934 was its ability at least to indicate the complex character of the historical, economic, and philosophical relationship between fascism and liberal capitalism without relying on "agent" theories or blaming a selected group (the petty bourgeoisie, the industrialists, the Social Democrats, the Communists, etc.).

The essay's most important omission, which would persist in much of

Marcuse's later work, was its failure to investigate and articulate more clearly the issue of why fascism targeted both liberalism and socialism. In short, Marcuse often denied political, parliamentary liberalism the careful historical analysis that he could muster quite effectively in discussing the effects of the capitalist economies rationalized under the aegis of economic liberalism, the ideological development of fascist totalitarianism, or the transformations of radical theory.[21] The actual and potential connections—whether historical, political, or ethical—between liberalism and socialism found little place in the theoretical apparatus sketched out in "Der Kampf gegen den Liberalismus in der totalitären Staatsauffassung."[22]

Nevertheless, considered in the light of events occurring shortly before its appearance—Heidegger's acceptance of the rectorship of Freiburg University under the auspices of the Nazi regime, his membership (however brief its "active" phase) in the Nazi Party, Carl Schmitt's helpful service as a legal practitioner and theorist for the "new order"—Marcuse's article on the ideological support of political existentialism for totalitarianism remains one of the most provocative and forceful expressions of rage the philosopher ever produced.[23] His analysis, however, was as narrow in its focus as most other early critiques of fascism were general.

The same year that Marcuse published his article, 1934, the German historian Arthur Rosenberg offered a revised interpretation of fascism that emphasized above all some of the factors the younger social theorist had not attended to in any detail: the political deformations of party and class allegiances that had made the Nazi victory possible. Shortly after the Nazi takeover in 1933, Rosenberg had fled with his family into exile in Zurich and then Liverpool, where he obtained a fellowship at the university.[24] Despite the considerable demands of his teaching load and his family's difficult financial circumstances, he continued to write about the political and economic crisis in Europe, often using the pseudonym "Historicus." The pseudonym drawn from the past belied the fact that Rosenberg had become fundamentally a historian of and for the present. Having recently written his bold and still valuable interpretations of the history of the German Empire and Bolshevism, Rosenberg now turned his attention to the analysis of German fascism. He insisted on the importance of this project in the opening pages of *Der Faschismus als Massenbewegung* (*Fascism as a Mass Movement*):

> The conflict over the theory of fascism is not just a pastime for people who sit at their desks and speculate about sociology. It is in reality a bitterly earnest matter of extraordinary practical and political meaning for the

working class. Whoever wants to defeat his opponent must know him precisely. The fantastic and logic-defying explanations of fascism that have
spread far and wide have produced among democrats and socialists the
conviction that their present greatest enemy is something thoroughly irrational and invincible by reasonable means. From this perspective, fascism appears as an act of Nature, like an earthquake, a primal force that
bursts forth from the hearts of people and suffers no resistance. The fascists themselves often support these sentiments, especially in Germany,
when they affirm that the rule of reason and mechanistic logic is over, and
that the emotions, the original instincts of the people, have now returned
to power.[25]

Rosenberg's declaration of the need for a more precise analysis of fascism
was not just hortatory wind, as so many such protestations had been and
would be. He backed up his criticism by presenting a remarkably sophisticated and path-breaking account of fascism that drew on a variety of
empirical evidence, including systematic examination of Nazi electoral
support—precisely the kind of evidence that many leftists and other observers had neglected.

First, Rosenberg debunked the common leftist myth that fascism was
simply the party of the petty bourgeoisie. He insisted that fascism could
succeed only with the cooperation of elements of the wealthy capitalist
class.[26] Looking at the case of the Fascist Party in Italy, Rosenberg observed
that the class status of members who attended the party congress of November 1921 could in no way be described as predominantly "petty bourgeois": "Till the end of 1921, Mussolini led a typical bourgeois party, with
a particularly strong component of intellectuals and academics and with
a certain working-class following. The Fascist program transformed itself
with unusual speed and thoroughness in the years from 1919 to 1922. The
tactics of holding power were all important to Mussolini. The points of the
program were, by contrast, completely secondary."[27] By emphasizing Mussolini's opportunism and the diversity of his party's constituency, Rosenberg avoided two of the pitfalls that have entrapped many analysts of fascism down to the present: a simplistic attribution of class attitudes,
loyalties, and divisions, on the one hand, and, on the other, the attempt
to grant fascist ideology the status of a coherent and developed philosophical system that stood apart from the influence of developing historical events and political conflicts.[28]

The theoretical suppleness and empirical thoroughness of Rosenberg's
Faschismus als Massenbewegung showed themselves even more clearly in
his discussion of fascism's record in Germany. One of the great strengths

of his analysis was that he insisted on and explained the differences between the class makeup of Germany and that of Italy, as Borkenau had done in his brief essay on the sociology of fascism—though there is no direct evidence that Rosenberg had read Borkenau's analysis. Above all, Germany had a much higher concentration of wage workers (including nonfactory wage workers) than Italy did. Italian Fascism would be—and here again, Rosenberg agreed with Borkenau—a kind of modernizing dictatorship, in contrast to German fascism, which had now succeeded in an already industrialized nation.

Tracing the shifting patterns of voter loyalty to the Weimar Republic and the consequent fates of the various parties, which also offered variable levels of support for or enmity against the government, Rosenberg developed a rudimentary but effective electoral sociology in the course of *Der Faschismus als Massenbewegung.*[29] That is, like the Marx of *The Eighteenth Brumaire,* Rosenberg carefully attended to such factors as intraclass divisions, malleable political alliances, and the challenges to institutional politics brought on by changing national or regional economic circumstances as well as by more persisting class divisions. His focus on empirical detail within a Marxian theoretical framework raised the persuasiveness and explanatory power of his work well above the "class agent" theories of Communist orthodoxy, and at the same time it marked him off from the philosophically based critique of such writers as Marcuse. Moreover, Rosenberg's insistence on the critical importance of specific historical developments and distinctions prevented him from theorizing on the basis of undifferentiated, unhistorical conceptions of fascism, capitalism, liberalism, or class conflict.

Breaking free of the categories common to many analyses of German fascism produced on the left, Rosenberg pointed beyond economic explanations to two of the party's many sources of popular political appeal: anti-Semitism and the "socialist" component of National Socialism. Rosenberg insisted, as relatively few leftists of the 1930s would do, on the crucial and distinctive importance of anti-Semitism to the core Nazi membership and outlook. But he did not write only on anti-Semitism's usefulness in mobilizing segments of the petty bourgeoisie. Here, he left behind the tendency of many Marxists of the day to focus almost solely on class and economic issues and pay less heed to other cultural, social, and psychological factors. Knowing from personal experience the deeply conservative, antirepublican, and anti-Semitic subculture of the German academy, Rosenberg aptly described the postwar support among faculty and students from wealthy families for notions of "racial purity" that renewed and intensified the anti-Semitism of the Imperial period.[30] This new anti-Semitism not only cemented the support for Nazism in some universities but also had a useful propaganda effect in electoral politics: the Nazi identification of Jews with "big capital" served as an alternative to the Marxian anticapitalism of the Social Democratic or Communist kind, which were in any case also "Jewish," according to the Nazi doctrine.[31] As for the "socialist" element of National Socialism—its declared opposition to capitalism and the rule of wealth and tradition, a propagandistic appeal articulated largely in cities and areas of high unemployment—this "radical" aspect of Nazi ideology attracted to the party a corps of brutal and adventurous veterans and the bitter unemployed. During the Weimar years, however, many other German voters also sought a means of supplanting the existing order, invigorating the nation, and increasing their personal wealth or power. These observations have sometimes found a place in the arguments of scholarly analysts of Nazi Germany, but Rosenberg was the only one of the group of German socialists included in this study who emphasized them prior to the Nuremberg Laws of 1935 and the *Kristallnacht* pogrom of 1938.[32]

In his concluding remarks on German fascism, Rosenberg sketched the analysis of late Weimar that he would elaborate the following year in *Geschichte der Deutschen Republik (History of the German Republic)*. The key components of this interpretation can be stated briefly. In the face of the autocratic methods of Chancellor Brüning and his successors, the Social Democrats became first the prisoners and then the victims of their policy of legal opposition and "tolerance" for the minority coalition cabinets. Meanwhile, the Communists made a left coalition impossible, but they could not gain the trust of more than a limited sector of the working class. While the other great parties foundered, the "catch-all" strategy of the Nazis, remarkably successful so long as they were in opposition, made them at last the indispensable ally of the traditional conservatives and *völkisch* parties. They provided a mass base for the counterrevolutionary politics of Papen and Hindenburg, who finally assented to a cabinet headed by Hitler. But the "double character" of Nazism, as Rosenberg labeled the simultaneous role of the party as real bulwark and ostensible critic of capitalism, created a dilemma for the party: "The Nazis [in contrast to the Italian Fascists] are a party of dying capitalism, and they must disguise their capitalist character from the masses in order to succeed in proletarian Germany. Thus Hitler's dictatorship was from the beginning burdened with an insoluble contradiction, which did not exist for Mussolini."[33] Rosenberg wanted to conclude that the new German regime could not last because of internal rivalries that would shatter the Nazis' seeming unity, a hypothesis the recent Night of the Long Knives massacre bore out in Rosenberg's too optimistic view.[34] That he was wrong in some of his short-term predictions—obviously capitalism and liberalism have both proven far more durable than many observers of the 1930s imagined they could be—does not diminish the clear superiority of Rosenberg's analysis to so many others that claimed a Marxian foundation. Few could foresee, in the months just before and after the Night of the Long Knives in June 1934—which was a brief period of crisis for the new regime—that the Nazis could so quickly and successfully dismember and then reconfigure the units belonging to the *"alte Kämpfer"* (old fighters) of the paramilitary SA by forging an alliance with the German army and then, after militarizing both the economy and society, send the nation to war.[35]

In spite of the evident differences in Rosenberg's and Marcuse's disciplinary method and focus, they shared the insight that while fascism was opposed to the parliamentarism and legalism of the liberal order, at the same time it could thrive in a crisis-ridden capitalist society marked by increasing monopolization and dominated, though somewhat uneasily, by the representatives of the most antiparliamentary elements of the bourgeoisie—who were no liberals, as both Rosenberg and Marcuse indicated. In this way, as both theorists also argued, the representatives of capital did not "create" fascism as the Stalinists claimed but would certainly make compromises with it, and not with socialism. Most important, the two agreed that fascism did not shatter but actually perpetuated the class character of bourgeois society. Both of them also emphasized the utter isolation of the German working class in 1934, and Rosenberg explicitly warned against precipitous alliances with liberals or "benevolent" conservatives.[36] But while Marcuse had at least hinted that the new totalitarian order contained something unprecedented in terms of social organization, Rosenberg saw little practical difference between National Socialism and the conservative antiparliamentarism of Brüning. For Rosenberg, the decisive collapse of the Weimar Republic occurred in 1930, not 1933, which would probably seem an odd line of demarcation to most present-day scholars of Nazism. Yet from the standpoint of working-class individuals and groups and their need to mobilize political resistance to the destruction of the fragile achievements they had registered during the Weimar regime—the concerns of an activist-scholar—Rosenberg's periodization made good sense.

In a final bow toward the resilience and continuing reliability of Marxism, Rosenberg insisted that "fascism has brought nothing new to the picture of modern class struggle. Above all, it has introduced nothing that would somehow lead to a revision of any of the fundamental perceptions of Marx."[37] Some sixty years later, Rosenberg's confidence may seem tragically outdated, simply outrageous, or, like Rosenberg's Marx, in need of no revision. Such affirmations of the undiminished authority of Marx would became increasingly rare among the group of exiles discussed in this study. But even for those socialists moving away from Marxism by way of a revision or outright rejection of Marx's image of historical progress, their attention to class conflict and to the political character of economics would remain for the most part undiminished for the next few years. In 1934, a younger writer, who a decade later would become one of the new, post-Marxian revisionists, was already at work on his own analysis of fascism that constituted yet another attempt to demonstrate the validity of the theoretical perspectives inherited from Marx.

Richard Löwenthal was the youngest of the antitotalitarian writers included in this study. He was born in Berlin in 1908 to a middle-class family involved, like Marcuse's, in business. Pursuing his university studies in Berlin, he joined the KPD in 1926 and remained a party member till 1929. Along with his friend and mentor Franz Borkenau, he broke with the party over the "social fascism" policy. Löwenthal, however, did not keep his distance from party politics, as Borkenau would do. Instead, he remained affiliated for about two years with the KPDO, then took a leading role in the exile and wartime resistance group Neu Beginnen (Neu Beginning), and finally joined the SPD.[38]

In view of Löwenthal's and Neu Beginnen's importance to the formulation of left-wing criticism of the Soviet Union as well as Nazi Germany, some background on this group and his role in it needs to be provided here.[39] The left-wing socialists and former Communists associated with Neu Beginnen represented one of the few efforts to bring together leftists with different party affiliations—though within a few years the group became essentially a left-wing tendency associated with the SPD. To aid in conversational secrecy, Neu Beginnen began as group called the ORG, or LO, or simply O (its full name was Gruppe Leninistische Organisation, roughly translatable as Leninist Organization Group). Initially formed as a self-consciously elite cell of activists, the ORG started operations in Berlin during the late 1920s. The ability of its diverse membership to carry out low-level, but effective information-gathering and propaganda work and to formulate innovative theories of dictatorship resulted in its record as one of the most productive German socialist underground or exile opposition groups. Several members and friends of this group were essential to the wartime and postwar critique of totalitarianism.

The ORG/Neu Beginnen's political tendencies straddled the border between social democracy and Communism, and its origins and membership reflected this ideological heterogeneity.[40] Initially led by Walter Löwenheim, a former German Communist, the ORG expanded its membership carefully during the late Weimar period, as the central leadership anticipated greater political turmoil. In the year after the Nazi *Machtergreifung*, differences within the group about tactics and outlook developed into irreconcilable factions. Some favored an active and broad-based resistance policy, while Löwenheim and his faction argued that a core of the ORG's elite leadership should go into exile and that those remaining behind should exercise caution and go into temporary retreat.[41] For a time, the group's relative diversity set it apart from other left-wing organizations—even the apostate Franz Borkenau remained for a few years a "fellow traveler" of Neu Beginnen, and in early 1934 he urged his old friends in the Austrian Social Democratic Party to imitate its leadership's retreat-and-survive tactics.[42]

Finally, in 1935, many of the group's younger members, including Richard Löwenthal and Karl Frank, broke with Löwenheim and his followers in the ORG, and for a time they continued a more activist program of "in-country" work. Ironically, the title of a book Löwenheim had written two years earlier describing the group and its aims, *Neu Beginnen,* now became the name associated with the group led by Frank. Like Löwenthal, Karl Frank was a former member of the KPD. Reared in Vienna, he participated, along with Ruth Fischer, in the group of Austrian Communists who formed a party organization after the war. He joined the KPD in 1920, when he moved to Berlin. Before his expulsion from the party in 1928, he served as an editor of *Die Rote Fahne* and *Die Internationale,* important Communist Party publications.[43] The bitterness of the split between the Löwenheim faction and the somewhat larger faction that sided with Frank may be glimpsed in the writings by and about those who participated in the ORG or Neu Beginnen groups. In any case, while Neu Beginnen's membership included several young former Communists who would become well-known antitotalitarian writers (including Löwenthal), the ORG faction led by Löwenheim, which included Arkadij Gurland, later a researcher and writer with the Institute of Social Research, also made noteworthy efforts to explain and oppose totalitarianism.[44]

Even after the internal split, Neu Beginnen contained within its ranks an outstanding group of scholars and activists. Its intellectual leader was

Richard Löwenthal, though several others made important practical and theoretical contributions as well. One brilliant young radical, Liesel Paxmann, played a particularly important and dangerous role for the group. She served as a courier until her death in 1935—likely by suicide—while in Gestapo custody. As the example of Paxmann shows, the role played by women in Neu Beginnen was crucial. Some were leading theoreticians and policymakers, among them Evelyn Anderson, Edith Schumann, and Vera Franke, and others worked as rank-and-file information gatherers and couriers. Ossip Flechtheim was another young member of the group. His exile career would include work as an assistant to Franz Neumann at the Institute of Social Research and as a professor of political science at universities in the United States. The group's politically heterogeneous character persisted even in exile. For example, prominent former Communists, including Ruth Fischer and Otto Rühle, were on the group's "key list" of overseas supporters and contacts.[45]

Both as the ORG and as Neu Beginnen, however, the group's factions remained objects of controversy on the exile left. Walter Löwenheim used the pseudonym Miles, and the ORG had quickly become known as the Miles Group or, to outsiders at least, as Neu Beginnen, the title of Löwenheim's controversial book announcing the group's outlook and goals.[46] The group and the book drew immediate hostile criticism from the SPD's older generation of party intellectuals, particularly Karl Kautsky.[47] Most of the details of Kautsky's criticism, though interesting as a document of the strife within the interwar German Left, are not pertinent here. What does stand out is Kautsky's rejection of Löwenheim's apparent desire to erect a new state in Germany that would be dominated by the (revolutionary) Social Democrats. The Miles Group, Kautsky contended, sought to replace one dictatorial regime with another without proper emphasis on democratic freedoms. Here Kautsky was in part accusing the group of a Leninist strategy, which the ORG had openly embraced from the start.[48]

Coming to Löwenheim's defense in the period just before the ORG/Neu Beginnen split was Franz Borkenau, writing under the pseudonym of Ludwig Neureither. Borkenau argued that the role of the revolutionary "Avantgarde," as he termed it, was essential in active underground opposition, such as that advocated by Löwenheim. Leninist principles of organizational discipline and centralism simply made sense under existing circumstances.[49] As Richard Löwenthal recalled it years later, however, Borkenau's strong defense of Löwenheim was already out of date. Löwenheim/Miles represented a position that a majority faction of the group now rejected.[50] Once more, in other words, one of Borkenau's articles had already been outpaced by events. Nevertheless, the quarrel involving Löwenheim, Kautsky, and Borkenau showed the sharpness of the internal debate over tactics and strategy on the exile democratic left. The ages of the participants in this particular dispute also suggest a generational element in the controversy that should not be ignored. Kautsky certainly held a place of honor—if not power—as the chief representative of an older generation of SPD leadership. Löwenheim, the domineering and now displaced "father" of the ORG, was not yet forty; Borkenau was barely thirty-three; Karl Frank was just forty; and Richard Löwenthal, Evelyn Anderson, and Erich Schmidt, more typical of the generation of the leaders of the reconstituted Neu Beginnen faction of the ORG, were still in their twenties.[51]

Socialist theory, resistance strategies, and organizational structure were important issues for the exile German Left, but there were also other matters at stake in the frequent intraleft disputes. Members of the old Social Democratic Party leadership living in exile (Sozialdemokratische Partei Deutschlands im Exil—SOPADE) controlled monies vital to the survival of the party and to the success of any resistance efforts. Gaining (or losing) the support of well-connected and well-financed groups such as SOPADE, not to mention British, French, or other international socialists and trade unions, marked an important stage in the life of any opposition group, and the ORG/Neu Beginnen was no exception. After spending many frustrating months seeking greater SOPADE assistance, the post-split Neu Beginnen leadership, though it continued to work for better relations with the exile SPD leadership, also began more actively to seek other potential allies—including the German Communist Party in exile.[52] This strategy, strenuously debated within Neu Beginnen, ultimately resulted in a reconsideration of the Communist Left—at least in terms of the actions of its leadership—that began to approach the later totalitarian theorists' analogy between fascism and Bolshevism, Communism, or Stalinism. More often than not, the key figure in these interwar debates was Richard Löwenthal.

From late Weimar till his death in 1991, Löwenthal remained the most politically active of any of the writers discussed in this book. In the early 1930s, his commitment to resistance against the Nazi regime left him in a dangerous situation. As a former Communist and an ethnic Jew, he undertook his practical and theoretical work of opposition in Germany at tremendous personal risk. He remained in Berlin for over two years after the Nazi takeover, and he continued to coordinate actions of the "in-country" members of the Neu Beginnen resistance group, which included both young workers and university-trained leftist scholars. In the fall of 1935, the Gestapo's arrest of a Neu Beginnen comrade from the Düsseldorf group led to forced confessions and the disclosure of the identities of many of the group's members throughout Germany. By the end of November, a series of arrests had decimated this left opposition faction. Many of those taken into police custody were couriers and informants in their late teens or early twenties who lived in the working-class Berlin districts of Wedding and Neukölln. The "in-country" operation did not completely disband in the face of this horrible crisis—in fact, the group reconstituted itself in a few locations—but it would never recover its former strength in Berlin. Because of the imminent danger of his own arrest, Löwenthal had little choice but to leave Germany.[53] But in the months before these events, while he was still gathering information and organizing small groups of workers into resistance cells, he wrote critiques of fascism that appeared in the exile journal *Zeitschrift für Sozialismus,* the successor to Hilferding's *Die Gesellschaft,* whose publishing operation had moved to Karlsbad, Czechoslovakia.

These antifascist writings, published in 1935, were foundation stones of a Marxian critique of state-party dictatorship, but they differed from Marcuse's, Borkenau's, and even Rosenberg's work in that Löwenthal focused more sharply than the others on the relationship between economic crisis and class politics in Germany. These complex and tightly argued essays were the product of Löwenthal's solitary reflections on the problem of fascism, he later stated, and were not the residue of conversations with his friend Borkenau or even his Neu Beginnen comrades in Berlin.[54] The editor's brief introduction to the first installment of the series announced that its author was "a comrade living in *Germany*"—which must have been a heartening fact for most of the journal's readers.

The first article appeared in the July/August 1935 edition of *Zeitschrift für Sozialismus* and was entitled "Die Wandlungen des Kapitalismus" ("The Transformations of Capitalism"). The two later sections, both bearing the title "Der Faschismus," were published in the September/October and November/December issues of the same journal.[55] Löwenthal began "Die Wandlungen des Kapitalismus" with a detailed explanation of the development, function, and consequences of monopoly capitalism from the turn of the century to the current world economic crisis—a phenomenon central to the arguments of both Marcuse and Rosenberg, as we have seen.

Focusing on the economic factors that played a key role in the rise of fascism but leaving the crude formulations of such Comintern lights as Stalin and Ernst Thälmann far behind, Löwenthal systematically analyzed the effects of monopolization in both the economic and the political spheres. Monopolization, a dominant but never uniform process in the first part of the century, raised the level of social organization, but in a contradictory fashion that left outmoded, unmonopolized sectors of production in the lurch. As Löwenthal put it, "Organizational rationality becomes the engine of economic irrationality."[56] The uneven development of the capitalist economy threatened social disruption and thus required an instrument for distributing both capital and the products of capitalism: state interventionism, or "the subventionist state," in Löwenthal's parlance.

According to Löwenthal, the state's role in the economy had become greater in the postwar period, but it developed even more decisively in the face of the economic collapse of the early 1930s. The individual state's ability to keep the contradictions of capitalist development from spilling out into the specific sectors of the economy affected most directly by international developments, such as the banking sector, was sharply limited, however.[57] Every new crisis created a new set of relationships for the state to manage, so that its efforts became like those of a juggler with a steadily increasing number of fragile objects to keep aloft and in motion—and whose performance would determine the audience's fate. Sooner or later, the inevitable breakage would frustrate and anger and, by analogy, damage the political legitimacy of the state.

The economic collapse exerted its impact in the political sphere by intensifying conflicts in the "interest party" parliamentary system. One of Löwenthal's essential points about the economic collapse was that conflicts and contradictions within the capitalist camp had both produced the current crisis and tended to prevent its resolution. This was because, he argued, the world economic crisis had generated destructive vertical fissures *within* the capitalist class, indeed within all classes, in addition to having worsened the existing horizontal class divisions. The crisis also politicized the supporters of the various class parties and tended to exaggerate the parties' class character. In desperate attempts to protect their own sectors of the society, the parties, representing these various classes, portions of classes, or regional subgroups, lost their ability to form coalitions. At the same time, no single party was strong enough to subjugate the others, so the political crisis tended to mimic the economic one: intensification without resolution.[58]

The consequences of parliamentary deadlock were especially bad for the labor movement, in Löwenthal's judgment. The parties most supportive of parliamentary democracy (in the German case, the SPD) became the scapegoats for the collapse of the state's ability to relieve the real economic distress of the electorate: "The less it [the labor movement] can exert a Marxist dominance of the situation, the more the dominance of Marxism will be declared responsible for every misery."[59] The Left's political appeals to class could not outpace the National Socialists' potent mixture of appeals to nationalism and "democracy" and their demonization of "liberal chaos," Jews, and the Left. Driving directly against the class character of the workers' movement in its slogans if not its actual considerations of political alliances, the National Socialists drew support from a variety of classes—a "people's community [*Volksgemeinschaft*] of the bankrupt"—as Löwenthal put it.[60] The National Socialists further outflanked the socialists, and other parties as well, by offering no specific economic proposals that might have to be rationally elaborated and practically tested.

Löwenthal's descriptive sections on "the fascist revolution" and "the fascist state" explained the means and the consequences of the fascist seizure of power as a generalizable model, but his examples drew primarily from the German case and added little to the picture Rosenberg had provided earlier. But Löwenthal, unlike many others on the left who saw fascism as merely the concentration of reactionary forces, allowed that the fascist movement was, in a limited sense at least, revolutionary:

> The fascist revolution is thus a true revolution insofar as it represents a necessary turning point in the evolution of bourgeois society, conditional on economic development and taking place in a revolutionary form. Its typical results show:
>
> 1. a new higher form of state organization;
> 2. a new reactionary form of social organization;
> 3. a growing state check on economic development by reactionary powers that have seized control of the state.
>
> While the growing political and social weight of the parasitic and reactionary strata stabilizes, the reactionary role of the state locks in. At the same time, the power of the unified and better organized state is strengthened, while the organizations of the progressive classes, above all, are annihilated. A situation arises in which the dynamic of the forces of production is only able to carry through its work—and is forced to carry it through—against the pressure of the political system.[61]

The last of these three "results" of the fascist revolution that were specified in Löwenthal's model would be challenged by the bourgeoisie, however. In this argument, Löwenthal anticipated the work of such writers as Franz Neumann, who would push the argument about the relationship between the Nazi state and capitalism even further by contending that the new regime not only avoided becoming a barrier to capitalist economic development but sometimes became its ally.[62] By introducing the issue of the degree of political control of the revolutionary Nazi state *over* the economy, Löwenthal also entered into the long debates among leftists over the relative importance or "autonomy" of the two spheres of politics and the economy and the putative role of fascism as a "modernizing" movement. For the moment, however, he would conclude that the "primacy of politics" to which he alluded was but the deceptive facade of the fascist order. Löwenthal's analysis remained within the framework of a Marxism that understood political events and transactions as variables that were still configured and ultimately determined by economic relations. The issue of the relationship between economic and political factors remained a problematic one for many leftists, however, because any theoretical discussions about this relationship had the potential of calling into question notions inherited from three generations of Marxian writing about capitalist society—including some of Marx's own writings.[63]

In his third article, Löwenthal attempted to construct a scenario whereby the fascist revolution's success in achieving the "total state" generated the conditions for its own destruction. Here, he qualified the provisional notion of the all-controlling state that he had articulated in his previous article. He conceded that, more than any previous form of the state, the fascist state removed the bourgeoisie from direct power over the economy. But the position that the fascist party transcended all classes was a sham: "All the contradictions of the regime find their concentrated expression in an economic policy in which nothing persists except change. The form, in which all activity emanates from a centralized, all-powerful apparatus, contradicts the content, which shows that this apparatus is the plaything of various interests in conflict with each other, the object of their shifting strengths."[64] The economic power of the bourgeoisie as a whole never yielded entirely to the fascist state. Partly because of its inability to establish rational policies (and here fascist antirationalism proved deadly), the total state was not able to impose itself on a capitalist economy whose productive process was the object of constant pressures for rationalization. The fascist party and the state would then proceed in a zigzag fashion, responding first to one set of priorities, then another, but finding no way out of the need to constrict development in some areas of the economy at the expense of producing armaments. The oscillations in economic policy did not produce benefits across class lines but distributed them primarily among the various sections of the propertied class. According to Löwenthal's hypothesis, longer working hours for less pay and a decline in the standard of living of the masses would be the ultimate consequences of this process, setting in motion a new economic crisis in which the fascist state itself would be delegitimated. The Nazi regime's only way out of this dilemma (and here Löwenthal's prediction turned out to be accurate enough) was imperialistic aggression.[65]

Decades later, Löwenthal did not reject his early essays on fascism but called them "immature" and preferred the analysis in his 1946 book, *Jenseits des Kapitalismus (Beyond Capitalism)*.[66] It is not necessary to share Löwenthal's judgment about his own writings, though. Moreover, Löwenthal's economically oriented Marxist analysis of fascism of the mid-1930s cannot be dismissed as merely impressionistic, reductionist, or nonempirical. At the time of their appearance, the articles he wrote for the *Zeitschrift für Sozialismus* offered as thoughtful and many-sided a critique as any thinker on the left had constructed to that time.

After leaving Germany, Löwenthal lived in Paris and then in London, where he became one of the most active members of Neu Beginnen's foreign bureau, which attempted to direct overall operations of the group's local affiliates, obtain financial support, revive the radical tradition of the SPD, and secure a place for the party in postwar Germany. Löwenthal took part in each of these activities to such an extent that he had little time for his own theoretical projects until after the war. He continued to publish in the *Zeitschrift für Sozialismus* for the rest of its brief existence, but increasingly his time was devoted to composing Neu Beginnen correspondence, programs, and theoretical position papers.[67]

The critiques of fascism proposed by these three independent leftists extended into issues related to ideology formation (Marcuse), the political mobilization of a mass movement that sanctioned the destruction of individual and group rights (Rosenberg), and the complex play of forces among the "totalitarian party," the economy, and the "total state" (Löwenthal). These writings provided a theoretical basis for later and broader critiques of "totalitarianism," which would occasionally include the Soviet Union. But to recall a point made earlier, the careers of individual writers followed this general development from *Faschismustheorie* to *Totalitarismustheorie* only unevenly, and sometimes not at all. By the mid-1930s, Rosenberg was already an outspoken critic of the Soviet Union, but he never explicitly formulated a systematic comparison of Communism and fascism. To a certain extent, Marcuse would make use of similar comparisons, but only insofar as he included *all* industrially developed societies—including (and, at times, especially) capitalist ones—under the "totalitarian" label. In the mid-1930s, Löwenthal still insisted on the importance of fundamental differences between the Communist and the fascist party dictatorships.[68] His reliance on an empirical analysis, grounded in economic and historical understanding, showed only slight and temporary modifications over the course of the next five decades. This methodological inclination gives his interwar speculations on the crucial role of the political sphere lasting interest, and it also indicated Löwenthal's deep indebtedness to his Marxist intellectual background. Other thinkers, however, were about to make their comparisons between Nazi Germany and the Soviet Union even more directly and polemically.

Charting Theories of the Totalitarian State

Several early left-wing formulations of the concept of totalitarianism and the analysis of the totalitarian state appeared between 1933 and 1939. Two groups of left-wing intellectuals produced some of the most provocative and practically oriented efforts at new theories of dictatorship based on living models. The first group, the chief writers and editors associated with the Social Democratic journal *Zeitschrift für Sozialismus,* responded in various ways to the Nazis' claims to have created a "total state." The second group, the resistance activists of Neu Beginnen, also had practical concerns that generated explorations of a comparative theory criticizing both the fascists and the Communists. A third example of these tentative notions of totalitarianism emerged in the writings of a very independent leftist, a loner really, Franz Borkenau, who fashioned an idiosyncratic comparative model of dictatorship by using components of theory from Marx and the Italian sociologist Vilfredo Pareto.

As even leftist "outsiders" like Franz Borkenau and Richard Löwenthal understood, one of the most important organs of publication for German socialist writers in exile was the relocated and reassembled *Die Gesellschaft,* now published in Czechoslovakian exile under the name *Zeitschrift für Sozialismus.*[69] Its pages were open to the usual cast of characters from the leading ranks of the Weimar SPD, but among its writers now appeared younger leftists, including the ex-Communists Borkenau and Löwenthal as well as such SPD activists as Franz Neumann. Despite the new location, the new name, and a burst of revolutionary intensity and rhetoric in the period immediately after the Nazi takeover, much of the old, reformist *Die Gesellschaft* spirit remained intact. It would be, as the months of exile wore on, a noticeably chastened spirit as well. Articles representing a fairly broad range of left-wing political opinion continued to appear—excluding party

Communists, of course. The Menshevik exiles—Iurii Denicke (who used the pseudonym Georg Decker), Gregor Bienstock, and Alexander Schifrin in particular—continued to dominate the pages and editorial policy of the journal, though Rudolf Hilferding remained as editor.[70]

The debates that played out in the *Zeitschrift für Sozialismus* show that the isolation and weakness of German socialists in the mid-1930s had not blunted the edge of internal debate. On the contrary, many of the cracks that lay beneath the semblance of SPD unity in late Weimar opened into rifts and even chasms under the pressures of the Nazi earthquake. During its brief existence, *Zeitschrift für Sozialismus* became one of the most important paper and ink battlegrounds of the various tendencies among German socialist exiles.

One of the issues debated in the *Zeitschrift für Sozialismus* was the exiled SPD's relationship with other groups on the left, including the KPD, the Comintern, various tiny splinter parties and organizations, and the socialist parties of France and Great Britain, where many German leftists now lived. The Nazi dictatorship in Germany—its character and the means of overthrowing it—was of course another frequent topic of articles appearing in *Zeitschrift für Sozialismus*. Often the terms *totalitarian, totalitarianism,* and the *total state* appeared in discussions of these issues. What these terms meant, however, was not always readily apparent.

In fact, the first article of the first number, written by Hilferding, optimistically announced the revolutionary character of the moment and then immediately turned to the discussion of "the *total state,* as the Fascists and National Socialists call their dictatorship."[71] He described the importance of the takeover of all independent organizations by the National Socialist state, the proscription against discussing fundamental social questions, and the consequent depoliticization and atomization of the people: "The citizens of the state were transformed into the slaves of the state."[72] The Nazis achieved this transformation, Hilferding continued, on the basis of mass support even stronger than that of the Bolshevik and Italian Fascist dictatorships. The totalitarian comparison was mentioned only briefly here.[73] At this time, the "total state" of Hilferding's analysis remained primarily the *fascist* state—not the Bolshevik one—and he ventured no systematic comparison of the Nazi and Soviet regimes. In the concluding paragraphs of his 1933 article, Hilferding returned to the imagery of "the total state": "The struggle against the total state can be only a total revolution."[74] For the dean of orthodox Social Democratic intellectuals, the vocabulary of "totalitarianism" and the "total state" remained for the time being largely a set of catchwords—political epithets rather than political epistemology. By 1940, however, Hilferding's perspective and his use of the category of "totalitarianism" would become more theoretically precise and critical, particularly with regard to the Soviet Union.

Even in 1933, Hilferding's mention of the "total state" was hardly novel. References to the "total state" and "total dictatorship" quickly became routine in the vocabulary of *Zeitschrift für Sozialismus* writers. The widespread use of such terminology was apparently at first a critical response to the "claims to totality" (*Totalitätsanspruch*) made by the fascist regimes themselves. Sometimes the socialist writers offered a self-conscious theoretical or empirical analysis of the various "total" systems, but often the word received no clarification beyond the immediate context of its appearance as a pejorative adjective. Soon, however, somewhat more carefully specified uses of the category of "totalitarian" states appeared, as in the following examples from early issues of the *Zeitschrift für Sozialismus:* "It was the triumph of the dark, destructive powers of war, the corruption of the delusory idea of humanity, when Hitler's dictatorship instituted, in the 'total state,' the preparation of the whole people for the purely abstract goal of power without regard for the welfare of individuals or the society."[75] For Max Klinger—the pseudonym of Curt Geyer, a former USPD radical of the *Räte* movement of 1918–19 and later the editor of *Vorwärts,* the SPD newspaper—the new "total state" was a consequence of old ideals of state power and the practical political experiences of mobilization and control during World War I.[76] The unprecedented forces gathered and exercised by the state at that time served as the fulfillment of reactionary dreams and as a model for future imitators. This argument soon became a standard feature of historically oriented critiques of totalitarianism, such as Franz Borkenau's and Hannah Arendt's. For the moment, however, it was but an aperçu in Geyer's more general attack on the fascists.

Another author, Franz Wegner, insisted that the "total state" and the "totalitarian party" remained largely verbal achievements and that the attempt to realize them would fall short:

> The "totality" has only one chance of realization: if the state succeeds in getting all the decisive social groups back on their feet, not only economically, but in the sense of controlling the formation of their will as an all-class, all-encompassing state party, that is, precisely to create a fascist party. The totalitarian party is the necessary correlate of the authoritarian state during the period of revolutionary turmoil in the economy and the

attendant, spontaneous upheaval in the relative powers of the masses. But it is an insufficient correlate.[77]

Wegner tied the rise of the "totalitarian party" to the revolutionary period that accompanied and immediately followed the war. He emphasized the "totality" of the state as a function of the totalitarian party's ability to coordinate all social groups, including their economic activities and their emotional energies. Yet he considered the party ultimately insufficient to this gigantic task. Class struggle would stubbornly resurface, despite all of the propaganda and policy efforts to drown it. In short, the "total state" was an impossible ideal. Wegner's hypothesis holds particular interest because it bears a fairly close resemblance to the far more systematic and empirically grounded analysis of Nazism that Franz Neumann later developed in *Behemoth* and that more recent historians, the so-called structuralists, have expanded: the *lack* of seamless unity in the National Socialist regime, its fundamental character as an "un-state" in perpetual chaos that bore within itself the class structures and conflicts of capitalist society. In 1942, when *Behemoth* was published, Neumann would also share to a limited extent Wegner's faith in the possibility that internal conflict could significantly disrupt the Nazi state.[78]

A few months later, Max Seydewitz offered yet another gloss on the "totality" of the fascist state as he conceded its short-term gains: "The victory of fascism in Germany is complete. In the short span of a year Hitler has been able to produce the totality of the fascist state and to overcome all resistance."[79] Seydewitz, in contrast to Wegner, emphasized the *success* of Hitler in establishing a total state.[80] His article emphasized the difficulties of penetrating and breaking apart the unitary force of the new state. Seydewitz meant to indicate the need for an exclusively proletarian revolt to smash the Nazi hegemony, but the claim of successful and absolute Nazi "totality" would also serve those who, from exile (where there was at least relative safety), urged intraclass cooperation or international war against Hitler and those who, in Germany, disliked the new order but kept quiet about it.[81] Focus on a pyramidal structure of power in the Third Reich— the realized "total state," with Hitler as the uncontested dictator at its summit—has been another feature of much of the postwar historical writing about the Nazi period (though it has come under substantial attack from the structuralists). In Wegner's and Seydewitz's articles, we see that the bold outlines, if not the empirical details, of this later interpretive debate over the degree of "totality" achieved by the Nazi state and the importance of Hitler's role within it were already in place as early as 1934.[82]

Zeitschrift für Sozialismus ceased publication nearly two years before Czechoslovakia was taken over by Nazi Germany. The community of German socialists in Prague disbanded to seek other places of refuge, and the journal was not revived. As the historian André Liebich has argued persuasively, Hilferding's contact with Denicke and Schifrin had played a key role in the development of antitotalitarian themes in some of Hilferding's last essays on the Soviet Union—essays that would first appear in a Russian-language Menshevik publication and then percolate among the leftist intellectuals of the German refugee community with great effect.[83] Even though Hilferding and others had yet to give it precision, the use of the term *totalitarian* proliferated from the mid-1930s. It would be a simple matter to multiply examples of references to the "total state" and "totalitarian parties" from the *Zeitschrift für Sozialismus* and from other SPD and left-socialist journals as well.[84] What many of these writings share is a focus on the fascist regimes—Nazi Germany in particular—as "total states." As the examples demonstrate, the functions of these uses of *total* were varied and even conflicting, but there was no necessary contradiction for these writers in their use of both *fascism* and *totalitarianism* as labels for the Nazi state. Complicating searches for "fascism as totalitarianism" arguments is the simultaneous appearance of forerunners of the comparative model of totalitarian theory, which also found their place in the essays and books of the early exile period.

At roughly the same time, the group of left-wing intellectuals, journalists, and scholars belonging to Neu Beginnen took up a far more direct and active resistance role than the Hilferding circle or Max Horkheimer's Institute of Social Research. Though all of these groups were propelled by events and experience in the direction of new theories of dictatorship, Neu Beginnen's members waged a particularly difficult and complex fight both against fascism and for their acceptance as a "loyal opposition" on the non-Communist left. Its practical and theoretical attempt to position itself as a bridge between the SPD and the KPD in the mid- to late 1930s offers a unique example of the freewheeling and bitter discussions that marked the appearance of a left-wing antitotalitarian outlook.

The debates within Neu Beginnen over its relations with the exile KPD and the Comintern reached their greatest intensity from 1936 to 1939, the period that began with the Moscow show trials of old Bolsheviks and the Soviet involvement in the Spanish civil war and ended with the Hitler-Stalin Pact and the outbreak of war. The call for a "Popular Front" uniting socialists, Communists, and socially progressive liberals, initiated in France during the fall of 1935, was designed to draw a group like Neu Beginnen into a broad antifascist alliance.[85] One of the earliest documented discussions of this policy within Neu Beginnen took place in May 1936. Although an opening to the KPD seemed desirable, a policy of remaining independent of the KPD apparatus also received support.[86] Within ten weeks, the Spanish civil war and the Moscow trials had begun, heightening the group's ambivalence about joining forces with the Communists.

The various contacts, personal experiences of individual members, and policies attempted by Neu Beginnen from the mid-1930s through the early years of World War II constitute a fascinating history. The most important issues in the context of antitotalitarianism on the left, however, are the theoretical and practical problems of Neu Beginnen's perceptions of the KPD and the Soviet Union thrashed out by Löwenthal and others in the group up to the beginning of World War II. Some events and issues provoked little or no internal debate. Support for the republican side in the Spanish civil war was automatic. The group also swiftly generated a draft letter opposing the executions that followed the first round of show trials in Moscow.[87] But there was no end to disagreement about how precisely to characterize the Soviet state regime.

One discussion within Neu Beginnen about the Soviet Union echoed some of the controversies of late Weimar theoretical disputes: the adequacy of the Bonapartism theory to describe twentieth-century dictatorships. When Thalheimer had helped reintroduce this approach, the subject of investigation was fascism; within Neu Beginnen, the subject was the Soviet Union. In January 1937, one of the group's members, "Landau" (Max Blatt), wrote an essay on the Soviet Union as an example of Bonapartism.[88] "Mary" (Evelyn Anderson) and "Ernst" (Richard Löwenthal) responded weeks later, unequivocally rejecting Blatt's application of the "Bonapartism thesis."[89] The pair acknowledged the damage done by the show trials but insisted that Spain offered a new test for the Soviet Union: the issue was not yet closed. The exasperated Blatt responded in a letter asking, "What crime does one have to wait for in order to characterize the Soviet Union as Bonapartist?"[90] The debate would continue for months, but events in Spain turned the group's leadership fairly steadily toward criticism of the Soviet Union.[91]

While Neu Beginnen continued its early practical and theoretical responses to dictatorship, an important theoretical effort by Franz Borkenau appeared in 1936. Borkenau's efforts would lead him away from Marxism, but until the end of the decade he remained in the camp of unorthodox socialists who were attempting to fashion a theory of dictatorship that moved beyond orthodox Marxian analysis without surrendering all of its potential for generating essential perspectives. In the mid-1930s, he made several significant contributions to the development of critiques of totalitarian dictatorship. His best-known writings on politics and dictatorship, *The Spanish Cockpit* (1937) and *The Communist International* (1938), appeared toward the end of the decade, but they were preceded by several years of intensive analysis of the current political scene and the historical past.

Early in the decade, Borkenau had been associated with the Institute of Social Research (most likely, he first came to the institute when it was still under the direction of Carl Grünberg, who was succeeded by Max Horkheimer). His first book—a study of sixteenth- and seventeenth-century philosophy and its ideological relation to the rise of capitalism—was published in 1934 with the institute's sponsorship. By that time, however, Borkenau's effort drew only the coolest support from Horkheimer, Friedrich Pollock, and the rest at the institute. He was also associated with key Austro-Marxists in the group close to Otto Bauer, but he was almost certainly absent from the scene at the time of the failed socialist rising in Vienna, choosing survival over heroics.[92] From 1933 to 1935, he devoted his energies to a series of essays on political topics in which he blended historical and sociological concerns. Among the topics he took up were fascism (1933), trade unions (1934), and the European Left (1935). These essays displayed the emerging persona of Borkenau the independent journalist-scholar: blunt, iconoclastic, intense, didactic. But Borkenau had yet to place his analyses of fascism and Bolshevism in the framework of a general and comparative theoretical argument. He would soon discover a perspective congenial to this project.[93]

In his apparent attempt to formulate an alternative to strictly Marxist models of social change that he now accepted only in part, Borkenau took as his subject a writer far removed from any socialist perspective: Vilfredo Pareto (1848–1923). This Italian sociologist and economist had detested democracy and lamented the participation of the "masses" in national political life. Pareto was a seemingly odd choice of subjects for a left-wing activist and writer such as Borkenau. Most likely, though, Pareto's ideological affiliation with fascism recommended study of his thought to Borkenau.[94] Despite his claims for Pareto's significance, Borkenau made no secret of his scorn for the Italian's highblown geometrical formulations and his hypotheses of "residues" and "derivations."[95] But he defended a version of Pareto's theory of the circulation of elites, which he used as a means of analyzing the political developments of Italy, Germany, and the Soviet Union.

Briefly stated, Pareto's theory of the circulation of elites posits a hierarchical model of society characterized by significant differences in the economic and political abilities of its various social strata. Elites, Pareto contended, can be found in all the various classes and in vocational and social groups. The political elite, which includes the wielders of national power, is typically the most important. But there is also a process Pareto called the "circulation of elites," whereby elites are both replenished and eventually replaced. Individuals possessed of innate biological superiority in intelligence, will, or leadership will rise into the higher classes of society, while those of inferior gifts, regardless of their status at birth, will tend to sink. Only free competition can guarantee this result, however. In the absence of free circulation, new elites will arise under less than ideal conditions. Pareto was unable to conceive of a balance between the need for regeneration and the destructive forces required to accomplish it. He concluded that the best possibility, a free market capitalist competition, could not survive the demands of the masses for economic security. Pareto finally arrived at a pessimistic vision of the cyclic recurrence of the degeneration, destruction, and regeneration of elites.[96]

Borkenau argued that Pareto's admiration for liberalism and his contempt for democracy had resulted in a sociology that was at least as polemical as it was scientific:

> It is as the precursor of an attitude to social life becoming more powerful every day that Pareto is of the greatest interest to us, whatever the objective value of this attitude as to its content of scientific truth may be. In Pareto's work for the first time, the powerful tendency towards a change of political machinery and social organization since embodied in Bolshevism, Fascism, National Socialism and a score of similar movements has found clear expression: clearer here than in the work of Georges Sorel, who alone could be ranked with Pareto as a precursor of the political and social changes we behold in our days.[97]

Though he had not provided a sufficiently convincing analysis of Italy's past social development, Pareto had accurately formulated the key components of fascist propaganda techniques and ideology: the lions would subdue the foxes; sheer force and repetition of slogans would replace the appeal to reason; the decadent old liberal world would give way to a vital new elite.[98]

In formulating his own arguments regarding elites, which was evidently the purpose behind his study of Pareto, Borkenau rescued a revised theory of elites, which he put to use in his closing chapters, "Bolshevism" and "Fascism."[99] Borkenau's discussion emphasized the impact of the economic disruptions that had followed World War I. To explain the rise of the new mass movements of fascism and Bolshevism, he established a schematic portrait of the political-economic context of their appearance. He hypothesized that free competition would lead and indeed had led to concentration of production in the hands of the ablest capitalists and that a more or less "natural" economic elite had arisen.[100] But as larger and larger enterprises collapsed when competition continued at higher levels of concentration, as they had after the crash of 1929, great numbers of workers and investors felt the harmful effects. An increasingly destructive competition ensued. At some point, depending on particular national circumstances and the relative power of economic classes, political parties, and other social groups, the state was forced to intervene with laws that established some limited control over the distributive rewards of industrial production. By virtue of its new role in a period of crisis, "the state becomes important for the very life of every one of its citizens, who fight a desperate battle for the domination over it, in order to preserve their existence and make the others perish. Theoretically the struggle may lead to the complete victory of one group of citizens over all the other groups, ending in a complete unification of society."[101] Borkenau's model of social change revealed a Marxian theory of capitalist economic crisis and state intervention and a revised Paretoan notion of the emergence of new political elites. The result of the process Borkenau described—the "complete unification of society"—would not be a true unity but a hierarchical order under the authority of a state controlled by a new elite, and here he cited the case of the Bolsheviks.[102] A linchpin of this analysis (and one that stands out even more clearly decades later) was Borkenau's emphatic shift of focus from the economic to the political in his description of the essential workings of the twentieth-century state. In his subsequent writings, Borkenau would describe such a new order as a "totalitarian state."

In the chapters entitled "Bolshevism" and "Fascism," Borkenau specified how the new elites had gained and, as of 1936, retained power. Here Borkenau made his closest comparisons between the Soviet Union and Nazi Germany, revealing their similarities and differences in the light of Pareto's political sociology. He observed that Bolshevist socialism "puts Pareto's theory to its strongest test."[103] The radically egalitarian social theory of Bolshevism declared not only that economic elites were bound to disappear but also that the state apparatus eventually would have to vanish as well. Only then could all forms of domination be abolished. Pareto's insistence on the inevitability of natural domination was utterly incompatible with Bolshevism—or at least with Bolshevist ideology. Borkenau, however, drew a distinction between ideological appeals for revolution to achieve a classless society and the actual practices of Leninism. The latter rested not on unbending principle but on the political needs of the moment as determined by the party leadership: "At every important moment of the Russian revolution Marxism had to be abandoned. . . . It was a belief and not a scientific guide. In reality, Lenin acted by ingenious intuitions, based on close knowledge of facts, as all great political leaders of all times have done. And the main function of Marxism was to hold the elite together. . . ."[104] Borkenau claimed that the Bolsheviks were not the vanguard of the classless society but the creators of a new and oppressive hierarchy. By emphasizing the elitism of the Bolsheviks' theoretical standpoint and policy decisions, Borkenau could apply his Paretoan revisionism to the study of the Soviet Union.[105] He had completed the construction of a conceptual road that would lead him to the discovery of other "totalitarian affinities" between fascism and Bolshevism.

Borkenau next examined the formation of the Bolshevik and fascist elites. He pointed out that they had arisen as responses to divergent economic and political conditions and enunciated, radically opposed goals. He also noted the clear differences in the parties' primary class appeal, arguing that "National-socialism at the moment of its advent was more of a victorious regime of the upper classes than Italian Fascism had been, not to mention Bolshevism."[106] He also found some significant similarities, though. Each of the three parties (Italian Fascist, German National Socialist, and Soviet Communist) appealed to an elite of some kind—nationalist, racial, and, in the rather complicated case of the Bolsheviks, both a class (the proletariat) and a political vanguard acting in behalf of that class (the party).[107] Moreover, in each of these parties, a single individual served as the official articulator of ideology and policy and as the paternal symbol of authority. Hitler and Mussolini had assumed this role in the early days of their respective parties. Borkenau argued that Stalin's ascent reflected a bureaucratization and ossification of the Russian Revolution, accompanied by an intense struggle for power within the party elite, carried out over a period of years in the wake of Lenin's brilliant successes. All three men, however, had succeeded by being "able manager[s] of the party machine."[108] Each of these recent elite party movements had achieved a fairly high level of cohesiveness before its successful revolution and seizure of the state. The formation of elites prior to the overthrow of the old state meant that, in the event of revolutionary success, reconstruction of a new state apparatus by the elite party would be swift and decisive.

Among the new elite's vital tasks was the organization of collective displays of nationalism to stimulate fanatical allegiance to the new order. On this point, Borkenau again found Pareto's writings pertinent to the events of the 1930s. The Paretoan categories of "non-logical action," which Borkenau had dismissed as poor sociological theory, found their home in both fascist and Bolshevist ideology:

> Sentiments uncontrolled by reason *have* really played an enormous rôle in the ascendancy of Fascism, and in addition, in the later developments of Bolshevism the same sentiments came to the forefront, though in the official Bolshevist theory this trend is neglected or rejected. Bolshevism of course has to take over many elements of the age of enlightenment, and of rationalism as an ideology, in order to fit the Russian population for a modern industrial order. The common trend, however, the acceptance of authority instead of rational consideration, the eulogy of activity in the place of thought, the unconsidered acceptance of a few metaphysical principles taken for granted and the rejection of any "problems" not solved by these official axioms, is conspicuous. In Fascism as well as in Bolshevism, rationalism is banned from the most important spheres of human life and relegated to matters of pure technique. One may doubt whether, in the long run, a rationalistic technique can coexist with thoroughly anti-rationalist habits of life.[109]

This damning analysis might be broadened to include any number of regimes that are not usually dubbed "totalitarian," but Borkenau's prescient remarks on the role of irrational propaganda in fascism and Bolshevism indicated his grounding in Marxian theories of ideology and his willingness now to apply such theories to a self-declared Marxist regime.

Rounding out his comparative analysis, Borkenau briefly discussed the internal policies common to the state-party dictatorships of the 1930s: institutionalized violence and party monopolization of economic and political power.[110] He had mentioned these as characteristics of fascism in his articles of 1933 and 1934, but he now understood them as integral to Soviet Communist policies as well. By the closing chapter of *Pareto*, Borkenau had outlined a theory of totalitarian convergence: "It has often been observed that in Fascism and Bolshevism along with an evident antagonism in social policy, there goes a surprising similarity in political institutions. From the point of view of the theory of domination and of elites, Bolshevism and Fascism can only really be treated as slightly different specimens of the same species of dictatorship."[111] For the moment joining Trotsky and other dissenting or unorthodox leftists in his analytical bracketing of the two most important dictatorial regimes in Europe, Borkenau was about to embark on yet another decisive step in his journey away from the camp of revolutionary Marxism.

The same year *Pareto* was published, 1936, Borkenau would turn from exploring and modifying theoretical models of revolution and dictatorship to examining a contemporary test case: Spain. The revolution and civil war in Spain were the final events in Borkenau's political move away from Marxian socialism. Probably more than any other moment in the long retreat of the exiled German Left up to the outbreak of war in 1939, the Spanish civil war intensified the impassioned and yet also mixed responses of antifascism and anti-Communism that would sometimes culminate in varieties of left-wing antitotalitarian theory.

Spain and the Hitler-Stalin Pact

The impact of the Spanish civil war on the hopes of the German Left in exile would be hard to overestimate.[112] The war, which broke out in July 1936, pitted an antiparliamentary coalition that included the *falange* (Spain's brand of fascism), the military, the Catholic church, and conservatives against the Loyalist alliance of liberal republicans, a huge and active contingent of revolutionary anarchists, and Marxian socialists of every stripe.[113] This intense and bloody conflict, which lasted from 1936 to 1939, offered European leftists the first real opportunity to take up arms against fascism since the Austrian workers' rising of 1934, and many exiled German leftists went to Spain to assist in the defense of the Republic. The group of writers discussed in this book was divided in its responses to the war only in terms of how and to what degree to become involved in support of the Republic and the Spanish Left, not in terms of where their sympathies in the conflict lay. Some offered organizational support, some helped find homes for refugees, others went to Spain to participate in or to observe the conflict and write about it.

The individual writer of this group of left intellectuals most directly involved in the war was Henry Pachter, who went to Spain and supported the extreme leftist and vociferously anti-Communist Workers' Party of Marxist Unification (Partido Obrero de Unificación Marxista—POUM), the party whose militia George Orwell would join in 1937, more or less by chance. Pachter spent several months in Spain and wrote a book, *Espagne: Creuset politique,* under the pseudonym Henri Rabasseire (a rough translation of his name into French). The book, published in 1938 in Paris, was a typical product of the moment—impassioned, polemical, and desperate in tone. Nevertheless, it is superior to many books of those years because of its political shrewdness and historical insights. As his 1932 essay on the KPD demonstrated, Pachter had dispensed with the party's practical and theoretical positions several years earlier, and he retained few of the illusions about the chances for left-wing unity that many British and American volunteers brought with them to Spain. Like his POUM comrades, he was outspokenly critical of the Spanish Communist Party and its increasingly important role in the restructured republican government. He referred to the period of terror behind republican lines that followed in the aftermath of the defeat of the POUM and the anarchists in the intraleft fighting during the spring and summer of 1937 as "the hour of the Jacobins." Nonetheless, he found the civil war and especially the popular revolution that it had set in motion worthy of his commitment, and, at the conclusion of his book, he held out the hope that "the Spanish people have not yet had their last word."[114]

Karl Korsch also found the Spanish Revolution compelling, but from the standpoint of the scholar and theorist more than the participating activist. He wrote articles on the process of socializing the economy, which had begun so quickly in the revolutionary region of Catalonia after the war broke out. Like many others on the left, Korsch viewed Spain as a scene of important socialist experiments in economic reorganization. The extent to which workers could run the economy for their own benefit and under the control of their own elected councils was of particular importance and interest to Korsch. The possibilities for a transformation of the economy disappeared, however, under the pressures of the war at the front and the emergence of an antirevolutionary alliance of the Spanish Communist Party (Partido Comunista de España—PCE) and moderate liberals that dominated politics behind the front. Korsch soon became aware of this.[115] The two articles he wrote, "Economics and Politics in Revolutionary Spain" and "Collectivization in Spain," were originally intended for the journal of the Institute of Social Research, *Zeitschrift für Sozialforschung*. But as Korsch's biographer Douglas Kellner has described this particular disagreement between Korsch and the institute, he "ended up publishing them in *Living Marxism*, a journal edited by Paul Mattick, after the *Zeitschrift*'s editors 'politically castrated' them and 'distorted their form.'"[116]

The articles were sharply political. In "Economics and Politics in Revolutionary Spain," in particular, Korsch spent as much time criticizing the Communists in Spain and the Stalinist regime in the Soviet Union as he did explaining the significance of the efforts of the Spanish workers in

Catalonia—and lamenting the likely defeat of their revolution. By 1939, *before* the announcement of the Hitler-Stalin Pact, he would ask, "What is the reason for the particularly close resemblance between the Communist dictatorship in Russia and its nominal opponents, the fascist dictatorships in Italy and Germany?" He concluded that "it ceases to be inconceivable that the Russian state in its present structure should act as a powerful lever in the fascization of Europe."[117] Clearly, the disillusioning effect on Korsch of this period of the Moscow trials and the defeat of the Spanish Revolution was profound, as evidenced not only by his attacks on the Soviet Union but also by the ambivalence of his critical positions on Marxism in his writings of these and subsequent years. At times, as in *Karl Marx* (1938), he could still appear as an orthodox Marxist to the letter, but, in his essays, he sometimes dismissed Marxism as irredeemably compromised or historically surpassed.[118]

For their part, the writers and researchers of the Institute of Social Research in New York had just completed their massive and remarkable compilation of essays in 1936, *Studien über Autorität und Familie* (*Studies on Authority and the Family*), and they were engaged in a variety of other research projects related to fascism and mass culture.[119] Not surprisingly, in view of the institute's research interests instead of activist concerns, Horkheimer and his colleagues appear to have been as far removed from the Spanish civil war intellectually as they were physically. There is almost no mention of the conflict in the institute's correspondence or published writings of the years 1936 to 1939. But Herbert Marcuse did describe the war's impact on his own thinking years later in the foreword to the first volume of *Kultur und Gesellschaft:* "The last struggle for freedom, solidarity, and humanity in the revolutionary sense took place on the battlefields of the Spanish Civil War. Even today the songs sung for and in this struggle are the single remaining reflection of a possible revolution for the younger generation. Here was the end of an historical period, and the terrors of the coming age announced themselves in the simultaneity of the Civil War in Spain and the Trials in Moscow."[120] There is no reason to think that Marcuse's judgments regarding the war in Spain were altered after the fact. Moreover, despite how little the institute involved itself in discussions of or writings on the war, its leader, Max Horkheimer, offered what support he could muster for refugees from Spain and other countries under fascist threat or actual control. The daunting and time-consuming humanitarian work Horkheimer and his colleague Friedrich Pollock performed in helping many left-wing scholars, party activists, and their families to find homes and work in exile during the 1930s constitutes a little-known chapter in the history of the Institute of Social Research.

It was, in any case, Franz Borkenau who wrote, after his connection with the Institute of Social Research had ended, the most important book about the war in Spain produced by a German exile.[121] *The Spanish Cockpit*, Borkenau's account of the Spanish civil war, discussed the war's first year in terms of the social and political alignments within Spain and openly disputed the position common among European leftists that the civil war was just a local version of the larger struggle against fascism. Based on the observations he made during two visits to Spain (in August 1936 and January 1937), Borkenau insisted that Spain was unique among European nations and that its fate, despite the involvement of outsiders of all political persuasions, would be to continue its rather solitary path at the periphery of Western European civilization.

Of greater moment to the analysis of totalitarianism, however, were Borkenau's observations about the decline of the revolutionary aspects of the civil war—radical changes evident in people's hopes, public speech, demands for institutional change, and social behavior, changes that were so prominent in the summer of 1936—into a kind of bureaucratic terrorism only months later. Borrowing heavily from the theoretical perspectives he had articulated a year earlier in his study of Vilfredo Pareto, Borkenau described the development and behavior of a new revolutionary elite in republican Spain: "Every revolution seems to undergo, in its course, this transformation from mass terrorism to police terrorism. The transformation was cut short in France by the fall of Robespierre, not before having made considerable progress. It came to full strength in Russia in the years after the end of the civil war. In Spain, where the properly revolutionary processes have been so quickly superseded by something entirely different, it has made great strides in the few months since the beginning of the civil war."[122] Borkenau's model of revolutionary transformation from "mass terrorism" to "police terrorism" aimed to explain how the anarchists, who had provided the truly revolutionary impetus of the early weeks of the revolution against the military attack led by General Franco and his fascist allies against the fragile Republic, steadily lost power to a coalition of Communists and liberals who wanted to stifle the revolution. It also provided a useful point of reference for the comparative study of modern revolutionary movements generally.

The transition from mass revolution to police control gradually left the anarchists on the outside looking in among the powerful forces on the republican side. The anarchists' refusal to take an active part in the new regime, while consistent with their doctrines, proved disastrous politically. The Spanish Communists in particular, a small and insignificant party in Spain at the start of the war, used the temporary disruption of order and the hasty process of organizational restoration in the wartime Republic to gain vital positions of power in the police and the military—and to conduct extralegal terror behind the lines. They accomplished all this with a bit of help from the NKVD—the notorious Soviet secret police.[123] Borkenau had personal experience with these new forces of order. As a result of his journalistic nosiness, Borkenau was interrogated and spent a night in jail. But this was before the intensive intraleft purges of May and June 1937, and he was released unharmed. Unwilling to risk further incidents of this kind, Borkenau returned to England to complete his book.

The most controversial and unorthodox opinion Borkenau delivered in the course of his narrative was that the revolution in Spain was halted, not helped, by the active intervention of the Comintern and the Soviet Union: "As it was, and as it had to be, because the failure of the Spanish Left coincided with fascist intervention, republican Spain was at the mercy of the force which brought help. . . . For it was force with a revolutionary past, not with a revolutionary present, which had come to help the Spaniards. The communists put an end to revolutionary social activity, and enforced their view that this ought not to be a revolution but simply the defence of a legal government."[124] As he, George Orwell, Henry Pachter, and a minority of others on the left contended, the Communists were on the right wing of the revolutionary movement in Spain, and their leadership constantly pushed the policy of "war first, revolution later," in contrast to the anarchist (CNT-FAI) and POUM factions, which refused to separate the two struggles. Intraleft tensions grew into open hostility, especially behind the lines in the province of Catalonia, where the anarchists remained powerful. In the spring of 1937, the POUM and its reluctant allies among the anarchists suffered a bitter defeat at the hands of government police supported by the Communists. Borkenau's assessment had proven remarkably prescient.[125]

One of Borkenau's readers, who had just returned from Spain in the spring of 1937, was George Orwell. Orwell had witnessed the intraleft May fighting in the Catalonian capital of Barcelona, and, for the moment at least, his outlook coincided with Borkenau's. The Englishman, who had been reading every book on Spain he could get hold of, undertook to publish a favorable review of *The Spanish Cockpit* in the *New Statesman*. It was refused on political grounds, and Orwell hit the roof. He had to condense the review article and publish it in *Time and Tide*.[126] The episode led to Orwell's increased hostility to what he now called "the Communism-racket" and initiated a friendship with Borkenau. Borkenau wrote to Orwell less than a week after the review appeared and asked to meet with him.[127] This first exchange of views on Spain led to further meetings and correspondence. In 1938, after reading Orwell's newly published *Homage to Catalonia*, Borkenau offered his bluntly stated version of the "totalitarian comparison" in a letter of congratulations: "To me your book is a further confirmation of my conviction that it is possible to be perfectly honest with one's facts quite irrespective of one's political convictions. And this, to me, seems a much more important issue at present, than any problem of a more directly social and political character. Fascism, both of the brown and of the red sort, is drowning us in lies; the best way to oppose it, is simple truth."[128] Whether Orwell agreed strictly with the formulation "red and brown fascism" is hard to say. But Orwell and Borkenau shared common ground politically for a time, and one result of their friendship was that Eileen O'Shaughnessy Blair, the novelist's intelligent, able, and generous spouse, would give Borkenau useful editorial assistance with his English-language manuscripts.[129] The two men remained on friendly terms until Orwell's death in 1950. By then, they would be counted among the ranks of the early cold war critics of totalitarianism. In 1937, however, their writings represented a minority point of view even on the marginalized anti-Stalinist intellectual left.

Borkenau's unhappy experiences with the Communist Party, first in Germany and then in Spain, left him deeply hostile to the romanticization of the party and its role in Spain, which had quickly become a staple of Popular Front propaganda.[130] Nevertheless, Borkenau proudly described the role of the Communist-led and Moscow-funded International Brigades—especially the German units—that fought on the republican side.[131] *The Spanish Cockpit,* in its idiosyncratic way a passionate statement about the character of the war, expressed little optimism about the Republic's chances for survival. The book also stands as the epitaph for Borkenau's hopes about the revolutionary success of even such a radical and populist group as the Spanish anarchists, with whom he clearly sympathized.

In his concluding remarks, Borkenau analyzed the peculiar case of Spain. He found the civil war essentially a local affair into which foreign forces and ideologies had intruded. The war was not, in Borkenau's view, simply an episode in the larger battle between fascism and antifascism. In a passage that elaborated his earlier discussions of fascism as a modernizing dictatorship, he even denied that the Franco forces were significantly fascist:

Fascism, classically represented in the present German and Italian régimes, means something quite definite. It means, first of all, a dictator who is recognized as the "leader"; it means, secondly, a one-party system; it means, thirdly, the "totalitarian state," in the sense that the régime dictates not only in matters of politics in the proper sense, but in every aspect of public and private life; it means, in the fourth place, that no force independent of the central party is tolerated in any field whatsoever; it means, moreover, that the party, by means both of conviction and violence, tries to get the unified consent of the nation and succeeds, to a large degree, in this attempt. It means, finally, that the totalitarian power is used in order to achieve a higher degree of co-ordination and efficiency in every branch of public life; fascism is the most powerful political agent of "modernization" that we know of.

Hardly any of these features have their counterpart in the Franco régime.[132]

This passage is striking, and the path Borkenau carved with this attempt to list the defining characteristics of fascism deserves emphasis here. Simply substitute the word *totalitarianism* for *fascism,* and this schematic definition could have come from the pen of Carl J. Friedrich in the 1950s— including not only its systematic description but also its deeply pessimistic character. There were, however, essential differences in the historical situation as well in method that must be taken into account when comparing the approaches of Borkenau and Friedrich as theorists of totalitarianism. Most important, in the case of *The Spanish Cockpit,* Borkenau did not include any mention of the Soviet Union in his remarks on the fascist state, and even Franco's regime did not measure up to Borkenau's definition of "classical" fascism, so the theoretical outlook of this work remained largely within the sphere of *Faschismustheorie.* For Borkenau, only the forces from outside Spain—Italy and Germany—represented true fascism. The nationalists in Spain were not a fascist movement as such, but merely included fascists as one component of a mix of modernizing and antimodernizing authoritarian groups.

Borkenau's description of fascist dictatorship and the "totalitarian state" as agents of modernization stood out as a succinct and boldly stated model—as formulaic (and therefore potentially comparative) a set of categories as any that had yet appeared. In Borkenau's view, the generous and romantic solidarity represented by such movements as Spanish anarchism would certainly not survive the revolutionary onslaught of the modern industrializing dictatorship if it succeeded in seizing control of the Spanish state in either its fascist or Communist incarnations.

Borkenau clarified these ideas in an article he published in the British journal *Sociological Review* in 1937. This article, "State and Revolution in the Paris Commune, the Russian Revolution, and the Spanish Civil War," revealed the extent to which Borkenau had broken not only with Communism but also with any Marxian theory of democratic, working-class revolution. The article was written during the hiatus between Borkenau's two visits to Spain that preceded the publication of *The Spanish Cockpit*. As the article shows, he understood Spanish anarchism as a genuinely revolutionary working-class movement, but one caught between its purist ideology of equality among workers and peasants in a stateless society, on the one hand, and the practical need to consolidate and institutionalize revolutionary gains, on the other.[133] In Spain, Borkenau argued, the Communists gained power at the expense of the anarchists precisely because they understood the need to take up quarters within the apparatus of the state during its wartime reorganization. The conclusion he drew from his observations in Spain was that all revolutions are condemned to reconstitute the state after destroying it—and that under the conditions prevailing after World War I and the Russian Revolution, the new state would in all likelihood be a totalitarian state-party dictatorship. In his utter rejection of a Marxian notion of working-class revolution that he previously had held, Borkenau now appeared as not only heretical but scarcely revolutionary at all. In a handful of years, he would be demanding an antitotalitarian "counter-revolution."[134] Only a few of the leftist German exile intellectuals—Ruth Fischer and Karl August Wittfogel, for example—would join Borkenau in his particular kind of ferocious, occasionally reckless, and yet at moments oddly despairing anti-Communism. But even those who balked at the image he would soon develop of a totalitarian state that overcame all its historical obstacles, smashed all political alternatives, and escaped or effectively suppressed internal contradictions often shared his hatred and distrust of the Communist Party leadership.

One incident of the Spanish civil war that involved the fate of a German émigré socialist helps illustrate how the war deepened the hostility of many Social Democrats and independent radicals like the Neu Beginnen group toward the Comintern in Spain and the exile leadership of the German Communist Party: the disappearance and death of Mark Rein. Rein was the son of the prominent Menshevik exile Rafael Abramovitsch. Reared in Berlin, Rein had been active in German Social Democratic youth organizations and later became a member of Neu Beginnen. He volunteered to offer his skills as a radio electronics specialist to the republican side in Spain soon after the civil war broke out. In April 1937, he was invited to a meeting with some acquaintances. He soon disappeared from his room at the Hotel Continental in Barcelona, and members of his unit were unable to find him. His father, believing that Rein had been abducted and murdered, possibly by Soviet agents, sought the help of German left-wing organizations in locating his son or at least learning his fate. All the efforts of father and friends, including Richard Löwenthal and Willy Brandt, the future mayor of West Berlin and chancellor of the Federal Republic of Germany, produced no results.[135] Rein's body was never found, and no documented explanation for his death emerged. Neu Beginnen's contacts with the German Communists in exile regarding Rein's disappearance produced only an evasive and disappointing letter from "Walter" (Walter Ulbricht, later head of the Communist Party in the German Democratic Republic). He could offer no leads on Rein but took the opportunity to denounce the "Trotskyists" in the POUM and to suggest that they were responsible for the kind of intraleft conflicts that had so enraged Neu Beginnen.[136]

Rein's disappearance was but one tragic case among thousands in Spain, but even so, the attempt to discover his whereabouts had involved many leaders of the German or at any rate SPD-affiliated Left in exile, and the sad episode served to reinforce the existing mistrust of the Communists. The preeminent historian of the German Left's involvement in Spain, Patrik von zur Mühlen, mentions the account of Julius Deutsch, an Austrian socialist who served on the republican side. Deutsch surmised that Rein was forced or lured onto a boat in the Barcelona harbor and then killed somewhere off the coast of Spain, but no definitive corroboration of this has ever come to light.[137] Years later, Richard Löwenthal would remark that even the Hitler-Stalin Pact of August 1939, so shocking to many leftists in Europe and to leftists worldwide, was no great surprise to him in the light of the conduct of the Communists behind the lines during Spanish civil war.[138] In many ways, the two events can hardly be separated politically or chronologically, for only five months after Franco's forces defeated the Republic, the Hitler-Stalin Pact was announced.

Neu Beginnen responded swiftly to the German-Soviet agreement in a discussion that took place at the end of August 1939, just prior to the outbreak of war in Europe. The group condemned the division of Eastern Europe into "spheres of influence" and expressed outrage over the demoralizing and dangerous effect the pact would have on the socialist movement in Germany as well as on Communists under imminent danger of attack in such countries as France. They understood that the realpolitik security needs of the Soviet Union were hardly a factor to be ignored but that, from the standpoint of the interests of socialism, the pact must be condemned as reactionary. The "Soviet-fascist pact" indicated once and for all that the interests of the Russian state and the interests of the socialist movement were not necessarily congruent and could even be in conflict. Poland was soon invaded, first from the west, then some three weeks later, from the east.[139]

The war intensified the crisis of the exile Left even more sharply. With its customary responsiveness, however, Neu Beginnen quickly took up the issue of how the war and German-Soviet cooperation would present both dangers and opportunities for socialist organizations. The KPD's and the Comintern's support for the Soviet agreement with Germany posed a serious problem for any common antifascist front, the group concluded, but it was equally true that the continuation of the partnership posed political problems for both signatories to the pact.[140] Moreover, in Löwenthal's words, "fascism remains the primary strength of the world reaction and the chief enemy. . . . It is only the Stalin regime that has ceased to be a factor in the socialist movement."[141] In other words, despite his willingness now to characterize the Soviet Union as "totalitarian," Löwenthal still emphasized the important differences between the two regimes, and he refused to use the opportunity offered so temptingly by the German-Soviet Boundary and Friendship Treaty simply to replay the tone and revise the content of the old "social fascism" slogan for use against the Communists by labeling Germany and the Soviet Union as "identical twins." Cheap propaganda points were of no importance at that moment. The overwhelming present need was to reinvigorate an international socialist opposition to fascism— without Stalin and the Soviet Union, if need be.[142]

Another revealing example of the group's efforts to join forces with the non-Communist Left in the countries of exile was Karl Frank's address to the Fabian Society in October 1939, entitled "The War Aims of the German Opposition." Frank expressed Neu Beginnen's criticism of the Hitler-Stalin Pact and likewise condemned the Red-Brown alliance that had helped oust the SPD from power in Prussia in 1932. Arguing for a "planned socialist society," Frank concluded by expressing the desire of the radical Left "to transform this war into the revolution." Over the course of months, this vision of socialist radicalism ultimately lost out to strategies of coalition-building—a political style that Frank's London audience knew quite well. Frank himself eventually immigrated to the United States, where he continued to raise funds and establish useful contacts for the group.[143]

The remainder of the group's core in London, including Richard

Löwenthal, finally chose to integrate Neu Beginnen into the SPD during the war.[144] Even as its political star rose during the wartime years, the group's radicalism declined, leaving in retrospect less the legacy of a fundamental rethinking of SPD reformist policies and tactics than that of a more or less ordinary but protracted generational succession to party leadership conducted under the extraordinary conditions of exile and war. Perhaps this is too hasty a judgment, though. The appearance of several Neu Beginnen veterans in key postwar academic and political positions in Berlin and the Federal Republic indicates the lasting impact of the group's members on German public life, long after the group as such had ceased to exist.[145] Moreover, many former Neu Beginnen members—though not all, to be sure—gave some measure of support for the cold war political and military opposition to the Soviet Union.[146] This is evidence for the general point that these German socialist intellectuals—including the members of Neu Beginnen—who had either been members of the Weimar KPD or who had attempted work in coalitions with the Comintern during the exile years would often later become the most outspoken of the Social Democratic anti-Communists.

The theoretical and practical activities of Neu Beginnen during the early Nazi period show that underground opposition was a dangerous, if disappointingly unsuccessful, undertaking. The secret meetings, the constant fear of informers, unexpected visits from the police or the Gestapo, the danger of establishing contacts outside one's own small circle were all part of Neu Beginnen's operations. But the group represented, if only for a short time, the kind of vital alliance of intellectuals and workers that socialists have so often solicited. The leadership of the group reflected this heterogeneity, and the active rank and file were quite often young radicals who came from the *Mietskaserne* (rent barracks) of the industrial districts and whose activities in opposition to the Nazis, however modest in their effects, at least testify to organized German socialist working-class resistance to Nazism. The far better known resistance efforts of the Kreisau Circle (and the July 1944 assassination plot against Hitler) and the White Rose student group took shape several years after the *Machtergreifung* and represented the heroic but belated and also tragically ineffective opposition of traditionally educated conservatives and upper-middle-class socialists—a partnership with a diverse array of additional political allies to be sure—to the ruinous policies of the reckless and murderous Nazis.[147] The ultimate futility of the opposition offered by Neu Beginnen must also be acknowledged, but the group's origins in Weimar radicalism and its spirited socialist character in the face of Nazi tyranny deserve broader recognition than they have generally received.

At the time, however, the fact of failure was paramount. Not only were the various efforts at resistance unable to dislodge or even seriously challenge the Nazi regime, but the prewar period of exile had brought the divisions within the German Left into the open, just as Otto Rühle's sardonic observation on the émigré scene indicated. Nonetheless, as the writings discussed in this chapter demonstrate, the analysis of dictatorship, if not the actual battle for its defeat, had made significant progress. Attention to the ideological, political, and economic reasons for the Nazis' success had led to more carefully differentiated concepts of fascism. Study of the rise of new dictatorial elites in several European countries had generated unorthodox and provocative theoretical perspectives on state-party regimes. Most important for the development of socialist perspectives on right- and left-wing dictatorships, political events in the Soviet Union and Spain required clearer assessments of the dangers and complexities of broad left-wing alliances. What remained of Marxian socialism in these various enterprises, however, would become a problematic issue, as Rühle had guessed it would. These efforts at formulating left-wing critiques of totalitarian dictatorship during wartime resulted in a multitude of perspectives—several of them resting on revitalized efforts at Marxist political analysis, some characterized by a rejection of Marxism, and some revealing an utter abandonment of the revolutionary Left.

VARIETIES OF ANTITOTALITARIANISM:
WARTIME THEORIES AND POLITICS, 1939–45

This European war is an "ideological war." It is a fight of the liberal powers of Europe against the biggest "totalitarian" power, Germany. And Germany, in this war, is cooperating, though in an ambiguous manner, with Russia, the other big totalitarian power of the world. . . . The division could not be more clear-cut; liberal powers here, totalitarian powers there.

—Franz Borkenau, 1940

"Totalitarian" is a word of many meanings too often inadequately defined.

—Ernst Fraenkel, 1941

The period from 1939 to 1945, coinciding with the war in Europe, saw the appearance of several of the most important left-wing writings on totalitarian state-party dictatorship. Some of these critiques anticipated the dominant cold war–era concept of totalitarianism, while others departed from that type of concept considerably or even challenged its legitimacy. These writers' widely divergent viewpoints on totalitarianism hardly exhausted the range of explanations of the dictatorships in Germany and the Soviet Union that were offered during the interwar and wartime years, but they were among the most systematic and innovative analyses of that time.[1] This chapter approaches these writings in the context of the wartime debates on the exile German left about the comparability (and compatibility) of dictatorial regimes, the correct framework and terminology to use in analyzing and categorizing them, and the relative importance of the economic, political, and cultural roots of modern dictatorship.

German leftists' comparative analysis of the movements and regimes of fascism and Communism took on a sharper edge during the period of the Hitler-Stalin Pact. The disastrous course of the war for the beleaguered anti-Axis coalition, from the invasion of Poland in September 1939 through mid-1941—with the heartening exception of the Battle of Britain—gave antifascists in exile genuine cause for despair. Several analyses produced by German socialists offered hostile comparisons of the regimes in Germany and the Soviet Union—even after the beginning of the German army's Operation Barbarossa (the surprise invasion of Soviet territory on 22 June 1941) that would advance with shocking speed to the outskirts of Leningrad and Moscow by the first week of December 1941. Two events, Japan's attack on Pearl Harbor that same week and Hitler's precipitous declaration of war on the United States, would transform the scope and character of the conflict. The U.S. entry into the war gave at least some hope for an eventual halt to Axis gains, but the ultimate results were not immediately foreseeable—nor was the unprecedented violence that was about to be unleashed on the civilian populations of Europe and Asia.[2]

Despite the desperate straits of the anti-Axis alliance, in whose countries most of these writers had taken refuge, German socialists sometimes included criticism of the Western capitalist powers in their writings on dictatorship, and some of them continued to define *totalitarianism* as an essential characteristic of all the powerful nation-states of the period, whether capitalist or not. Not surprisingly, most of the writings discussed here initially found a small audience, several of them went unpublished for years, and a number of others remain available only in research archives. The difficulty in accessing some of these writings has certainly been one of the reasons for the dearth of scholarly works on the phenomenon of left-wing antitotalitarianism. Their political incompatibility with consensus views of totalitarianism during the cold war was likely another strike against them. Even the pairing of Nazism and Stalinism as "red and brown fascism," for instance, could not save a manuscript from the neglectful condescension of posterity.

Brown and Red Fascism

Of the handful of leading Weimar-era Communists included in this study, Otto Rühle is today probably the least known. He also had the longest history as a left-wing political activist and intellectual in Germany. In 1914, Rühle joined Karl Liebknecht and a dozen others in the SPD's Reichstag delegation in opposing the granting of war funds.[3] Never personally close to Liebknecht, Rosa Luxemburg, or Clara Zetkin, Rühle nevertheless hooked up with a variety of groups that opposed the SPD from the left. He joined a leftist group, the German International Communists (Internationale Kommunisten Deutschlands—IKD), at the end of the war; participated in the workers' and soldiers' councils (*Räte*) movement; and served on the executive board of the Spartacists—the predecessor of the KPD. His career with the KPD was quite brief, however, though he had been a member of its founding conference. After his expulsion from the Communist Party in late 1919, he linked up with various Weimar-era leftist opposition groups and wrote on education, psychology, family relations, and Karl Marx. Never so important an oppositionist as August Thalheimer or Heinrich Brandler, Rühle nonetheless wrote stinging criticisms of the KPD leadership and policy for a decade into the exile period—though several of his longer manuscripts were not published until after his death.[4]

In 1936, Otto Rühle settled in Mexico along with his energetic spouse, Alice Gerstel-Rühle, who also had a considerable publication record in socialist education and child psychology. Rühle had been invited by the Mexican government to serve as an educational adviser. There, the couple took up a turbulent yet apparently affectionate friendship with their neighbors, Leon Trotsky and Natalya Sedova. Gerstel-Rühle reported that Trotsky and her husband had frequent battles over long-lost issues of party-versus-democracy or the precise moment at which Stalin had gained control of the apparatus of the Communist movement. These discussions sometimes led to bitter shouting matches and abrupt departures, followed days or even hours later by renewed overtures of friendship. Rühle also participated in the public "tribunal" led by the American philosopher John Dewey that examined Trotsky's alleged crimes against the Soviet Union.[5] It would be interesting to know if Rühle ever showed Trotsky his unpublished manuscript, "Brauner und Roter Faschismus" ("Brown and Red Fascism"); Trotsky might well have been outraged by the historical details but might have agreed with his political interpretation of the current status of the dictatorships in Germany and the Soviet Union.

"Brauner und Roter Faschismus" is an example of a genre at which Trotsky himself excelled: history as polemic. The text begins with a curt, pointed synopsis that indicates the tone and substance of the rest of the analysis:

> The character of the present world situation is in the first instance determined by European factors, at whose apex stand [conditions in] Germany and Russia.

These factors, embodied in Germany by Nazism and in Russia by Bolshevism, are the results of a development which shaped the contents of the postwar European economy and politics.

Economically, this postwar period is anchored in ultraimperialist monopoly capitalism, which tends to a system of state capitalism. Politically, it paved the way for a totalitarian state order, which culminated in a system of dictatorship.[6]

In his characteristically blunt manner, Rühle had begun his argument with the kind of comparison of the Soviet Union and Nazi Germany that flourished briefly during the period of the Hitler-Stalin Pact and then reappeared in the late 1940s. Rühle gave further specificity to this analogy in his next passage, which referred to "the inner congruence of the tendencies of German and Russian state capitalism, and the structural, organizational, dynamic, and tactical identity, which is a necessary consequence of the political pact and the unity of military action."[7] The rest of his text, which was not published during Rühle's lifetime, continues this analogy in a caustic indictment of the dictatorial regimes in Germany and the Soviet Union, freely drawing comparisons between the two states.

Starting with an analysis of the period beginning with World War I, Rühle explained the war itself as the inevitable result of the competition among national "trusts."[8] Wartime crisis never allowed the economies of the leading industrial nations to recover their former vigor, and the European collapse appeared to mark a chaotic "decline of the West." The revolutionary opportunity that presented itself in Germany lapsed because of the caution and the outright hostility toward revolution shown by the Social Democrats at the top and among the masses, Rühle maintained. Rudolf Hilferding received Rühle's special attention as the author of the "masterpiece of bagatellization and sabotage of the work of socialization" begun in the German Revolution of November 1918.[9] Hilferding had attempted to rationalize the process of socialization of the economy, insisting that capitalism needed rebuilding before successful socialization could take place. Rühle's rage against the "charlatanry" of Hilferding's policies and their "laughable dilettantism" was equaled only by his anger at "the masses" for putting up with the situation: "Instead of being freed from capitalism, the masses were plunged into still worse slavery. Nevertheless, they did not chase their leaders to the devil. Betrayer and betrayed were worthy of one another. . . . People learn nothing from history. Not even the workers."[10] Rühle's cranky and embittered message was not an unusual one for the intellectuals associated with the working-class movement to pass along. Franz Borkenau and Arthur Rosenberg had also concluded that the bulk of the German working class of 1918–19 was not interested in or able to carry out a revolution—even with the example of Russia before it.[11]

Rühle's verdict on the Russian Revolution was equally harsh. In his view, the revolution had never brought the majority of people together with the principles of socialism. Bureaucratization came about quickly, Rühle argued, beginning with the civil war period. Unlike many writers who have blamed either Lenin or Stalin for the ossification of the Russian revolutionary movement, Rühle offered this assessment: "Trotsky, who does not want to admit that he himself is one of the chief founders of the Russian bureaucracy, inaugurated this change in the Army. . . ."[12] Rühle's readiness to dismiss Trotsky's claim to leadership of the Oppositional Communists is remarkable. According to Rühle, Stalin simply brought to bureaucratic and terroristic fruition the harsh policies that Trotsky had practiced as leader of the Red Army.

Even for the founder of the Bolshevik Party, Lenin, there was no place of honor in Rühle's account. Rühle declared that Lenin had been theoretically and practically unprepared to lead a proletarian movement,[13] that Lenin was "no dialectician, but only an opportunist," and that the Bolshevik leader was an "unconditional admirer of Kautsky"—which was perhaps the nastiest criticism Rühle could imagine. The fate of a revolution left to the management of such a backwards thinker was foreordained, so far as Rühle was concerned. Lenin's narrow conception of the revolution could not accept the independent and democratic dynamism of soviets, and he replaced them with an autocratic structure even as the name "soviet" was retained as a false label for the new party-state apparatus.[14]

The fate of the soviets was especially disastrous, for their death ended the possibility of a real socialist revolution. Rühle, like others who had witnessed the birth and death of the German Revolution of 1918–19, held to the view that the workers' and soldiers' councils of those days—roughly the German equivalent of the Russian soviets—were the only political form through which a true revolution could be expressed. That is, the councils, unlike the party apparatus of either the Bolshevik or Social Democratic type, constituted a localized and democratic movement led by the most spirited and class-conscious sections of the proletariat. Rühle angrily toppled the heroic figures of the Left. Lenin failed as a revolutionary because he destroyed the soviets to ensure Bolshevik supremacy. Luxemburg failed as a revolutionary because she would not venture a complete and decisive break from all party structure to serve the new revolutionary synthesis that the councils represented.[15]

Rühle also blamed the two major parties of the European Left, the German Social Democrats and the Russian Bolsheviks, for the victories of fascism in the interwar years. He labeled the Soviet Union a fascist state, as the title of his text indicated. Such episodes as the Social Democrats' willingness to throw in with the German High Command in 1918 and Lenin's flirtations with capitalism in the early 1920s were equally catastrophic: "What began as the compromise of the Social Democrats, ended with Fascism. What began as Lenin's theory of compromise, ended in practice with Stalinism."[16] Stalin in turn would make the final compromise with Hitler: "The only thing lacking for a complete harmony between Berlin and Moscow is a military and wartime alliance against socialist revolution. The day will come when even this will become historical reality."[17] In short, for Rühle, the path to totalitarianism lay across the corpses of the workers' councils in Russia and Germany. Just as Rühle had predicted, this path led further to a pact between the dictatorial regimes in these same two nations that had as their common goal the destruction of even the possibility of socialist revolution.

The old-fashioned radicalism of Rühle's outlook today looks like an eccentric exception to the dominant view of the problem of totalitarianism, but perhaps it is one worth remembering in this fin-de-siècle period of the rapid deformation of European political and military institutions under the violent pressures of an array of popular movements and capitalist "reforms" set on sweeping away or refashioning the old state structures and economic policies in the former Soviet Union, the former Yugoslavia, and other nations recently departed from Communism. Even the passion and spleen of his rhetoric find voice again these days. Rühle's cautionary tale of how the victories of "the people" can rapidly turn into horrible defeats remains a powerful restatement of a typical and troubling political scenario of the past two centuries. At the moment of Europe's descent once again into war, his dissenting critique of totalitarianism was an old radical Marxist's blow aimed at the forces that had stilled the collective song of comradely revolution. His attack on state-party dictatorship concluded with a hopeful restatement of the possibility for the creation of a socialist society that embodied the most democratic and humane of Marx's visions: "Only if it [the labor movement] proceeds to throw into the balance the complete deployment of its great numbers, its decisive role in the process of production, the emancipation from a bourgeoisified leadership and the freedom of its own initiative and autonomy by means of workers' councils, will it succeed in attaining a socialism 'where the freedom of each is the condition for the free development of all.'"[18]

At about the time Rühle wrote "Brauner und Roter Faschismus," Karl Korsch was patiently trying to aid the cantankerous and often rather haughty Rühle in his writing and publishing efforts. Rühle and his intermediaries had no luck with American publishers, though. One of them, John Day Company, declined Rühle's manuscript on the grounds that it already had Peter Drucker's *End of Economic Man* on its list. Even Max Eastman's intervention with another publisher met with failure. Korsch's friend Paul Mattick, the editor and Marxist theorist, offered to publish some of Rühle's essays, but the manuscript of "Brauner und Roter Faschismus" languished for years.[19] Despite Korsch's sympathy for some of Rühle's political views, he offered Mattick the following assessment: "I agree with you about Rühle. He belongs too much to the old world, to which he stands opposed. But where do we stand? A French skeptic said, 'On est toujours le réactionnaire de quelqu'un,' which means, 'One is always someone else's reactionary.' So Trotsky, for Rühle, belongs to the dead past, Rühle for us, we for . . . others of whom we now know nothing."[20]

Political Strategies of Antitotalitarianism

Among those others of whom Korsch and Mattick probably knew nothing, or certainly very little, was the surviving band of radicals in Neu Beginnen. The previous chapter related how Richard Löwenthal and his colleagues in the group were quick to respond to the Hitler-Stalin Pact and the invasion of Poland. In the position paper issued on 1 October 1939, entitled "Zur Einschätzung der deutsch-russischen Zusammenarbeit" ("Toward an Assessment of German-Russian Cooperation"), Löwenthal had not only suggested the need for revised organizational tactics but also offered terse and unpromising conclusions. He stated that (1) the Soviet Union's nonaggression pact with Germany had made the invasion of Poland secure and easier for Germany; (2) Soviet troops had occupied much of eastern Poland and also the Ukraine not to prevent their capture by German troops but as an aggressive act of annexation; (3) the Soviet Union had a common interest with "Hitler Germany" in the recognition of the new boundaries (eliminating an independent Poland); and (4) these facts were hidden by sections of the West European Communist parties that were now pushing for neutrality.[21]

In view of these facts, Löwenthal continued, it was essential to be clear about the possible fate of the workers' movement. A choice between "capitalist imperialism" and a system of "totalitarian oppression" was no choice.[22] This situation of two undesirable extremes had not yet arisen, but its possibility had to be reckoned with: "Their [the workers's] path, the path to a higher organization of the economy through the free activity of working people, the path of democratic socialism, would be blocked by the movement of history."[23] As prose, this was about as close to exalted rhetoric as the hard-headed Löwenthal would ever come. As policy, it represented the attempt to convey an understanding of the disastrous potential of the present configurations of power. Comparing the closing paragraphs of Rühle's book with Löwenthal's essay, one finds, despite the generational, temperamental, stylistic, and strategic differences between the two men, a similar tenderness about the working classes in whose interests they endeavored to speak and act. For the democratic German Left, late 1939 was a horrible moment: its two most powerful enemies in Europe had joined forces.

Even though the Soviet Union had ceased (for the time being) to offer diplomatic or military opposition to National Socialist Germany—working in effect, if not formally, as an ally of the Nazis in some instances—Neu Beginnen did not resort to equating the two regimes, but it did make frequent use of the term *totalitarian* to describe the character of their policies. The group's ambivalence toward the Soviet Union was manifest in another position paper, "Russland und die deutsche Revolution" ("Russia and the German Revolution"), written sometime in 1940, possibly 1941, which indicates the persistence of a differentiated and remarkably open-minded critique of the Soviet Union within the leadership of Neu Beginnen.[24] The essay poses and answers a series of questions about the nature of the Soviet Union, its role in the war, and its likely response to any socialist revolution in Germany. The Soviet Union, the paper begins, exhibits a "bureaucratically organized planned economy" in a relatively backward nation and would offer a good example of socialist development "if it were bound up with a suitable political regime." The document also describes the Soviet Union quite straightforwardly (and repeatedly) as "a totalitarian party dictatorship."[25] The discussion of *how* this dictatorship came to be bears closer examination: "The party dictatorship, originating under the pressure of the civil war, was brought to a lasting totalitarian system in order to win the masses for the material sacrifices necessary for industrialization and collectivization. The combination of the monopoly position of the party with the plebiscitary fiction of democracy led to the destruction of factual discussion and criticism by totalitarian demagogy."[26] This paper identifies the historical source of "totalitarian" Soviet developments as the policies necessitated by the extraordinary internal disruptions of the civil war of 1918 to 1921—*not* the inherent nature of Leninism or Bolshevism—that Stalin carried forward and intensified under the "peacetime" conditions of forced economic modernization. This explanation would be the basis for Löwenthal's only partly changing position on the origins of Soviet totalitarianism over the course of the next five decades.[27] In 1940 and early 1941, such a position avoided the temptation to write off the Soviet Union and opened the way for a historical understanding of its internal and external policies.

The estimate of the Soviet Union's role in the war was equally nuanced and clear-eyed. The propaganda image of the Soviet Union as a "peaceful nation in an imperialistic world" was not taken at all seriously. Instead, Neu Beginnen characterized Stalin's foreign policy as one of weakening the great powers and avoiding war with its ambitious neighbors, Germany and Japan. The group also declared that the Soviet Union was no longer a revolutionary force, as its behavior with respect to popular uprisings in China and Spain had demonstrated. The Bonapartist thesis was dismissed yet again, however, and the Soviet Union's annexation policy was described as—at least partly—the creation of a "security zone" against the Nazis in the event that the mutual nonaggression agreement turned sour. The paper also noted that, so far, the Soviet Union had seized only territories that did not bring it into direct conflict with other great powers. The entire policy demonstrated not the strength but the weakness and fragility of the Stalin regime.[28] The paper's argument implied that the totalitarian Soviet state was subject to change, even though for the present and in "the coming European revolutions" that Neu Beginnen presumed would follow or bring to an end the current war, "totalitarian Russia" would attempt to force areas under its control to mimic its structure.[29]

Neu Beginnen did not have to stand by this relatively gloomy outlook after the Nazis attacked the Soviet Union in 1941. Clear Soviet allegiance to the Allied camp now renewed the opportunity for greater cooperation with the German Communists and the Soviet Union in practical matters. Indeed, Löwenthal understood this as a necessity, for in 1942, he was already speculating about the possible alignments of political and military forces in postwar Europe. In a brief position paper dated 6 June 1942, Löwenthal suggested that the best chance of a free socialist Europe lay in the "liquidation" of the Comintern and an agreement between the Soviets and Anglo-Americans about Europe's future. This would mean that a united German workers' party could link up with both the British Labour

Party and the Soviet Communists. "Only such a party," Löwenthal contended, "would have a serious chance of carrying out a social revolution
without establishing a lasting totalitarian dictatorship."[30]

Löwenthal reckoned that such a development was not mere specula-
tion. The Comintern was as good as dead, the possibility of mutual Brit-
ish-Soviet accommodation in Europe real, and the popular desire for a
united German socialist party strong. On the other side of the coin, however, U.S.-Soviet tensions were troublesome, and the relative strength of
the three major allies was uncertain. In view of this, the Soviets were un-
likely to agree to any plans for Europe right away. Moreover, the Comintern might still play a role and would remain an enormous danger. The
policy of Neu Beginnen would be extremely difficult: "This generates for
us the dilemma that our behavior with regard to the Communists must
simultaneously serve as the preparation for unity in the best case and for
struggle against the totalitarian danger in the worst case. And for an in-
determinate period during the course of events we shall not know which
case will arise."[31] The practical consideration of this dilemma led him to
the following policy recommendations: (1) Neu Beginnen should engage
the Communists in dealing with current practical issues and indicate an
interest in protecting the Soviet Union; (2) the group must not treat the
Communists now as they had during the Soviet-German pact of 1939–41
but must instead show willingness to cooperate; (3) Neu Beginnen should
not refuse "party-to-party" activities with the KPD because of its own inferior size but should remain cautious in any such undertaking; and (4)
such a tactic would succeed because of the group's "organizational discipline" and clear understanding of the basis and dangers of such a tactic.[32]

Löwenthal's proposed response to the problem of state-party dictatorship offers a compelling example of the bold theoretical and practical
character of some variants of left-wing antitotalitarianism. Here was an
organization, Neu Beginnen, that had been founded on Leninist principles of internal organization but was increasingly committed to developing a democratic and pluralist socialist movement in postwar Germany.
The group's willingness to seek contact with the Communists in 1942
clearly set it apart from the far more cautious old guard of SOPADE. The
postwar SPD, especially in Berlin, soon drew much of its leadership from
younger socialists who had been affiliated with Neu Beginnen and had
attempted, throughout the exile period, to steer a middle course between
Soviet Communism and Anglo-American capitalism. That this tactic ultimately failed must be admitted, but even this failure shows the accuracy
of Löwenthal's assessment of 1939—that is, that the workers' movement

could be blocked and would have to await a better historical moment to achieve its aims. Nevertheless, Löwenthal's essays demonstrate that, even during wartime, his brand of left-wing antitotalitarianism did not prevent great flexibility in practical political alliances and did not produce a static view of the Communist opposition as an irredeemable and unchanging enemy. His friend Borkenau's wartime version of antitotalitarianism revealed quite a different theoretical and policy direction.

Totalitarian Enemies

Franz Borkenau's opposition to totalitarianism was nothing if not distinctive and unreserved. He shared much of Rühle's critical view of the two powerful dictatorial states, but he drew political conclusions quite opposed to Rühle's. He had also abandoned the activist's role that guided the flexible judgments on the Soviet Union and the German Communists put forth by his friend Richard Löwenthal. Most important, Borkenau now had a provocative prehistory of World War II to offer, and he published it in *The Totalitarian Enemy*. Although the text was disappointing because of its awkward structure and the details of some of its arguments, it represented a path-breaking venture into a comparative analysis of dictatorship based on the theory of revolutionary totalitarian elites that Borkenau had been using since he wrote *Pareto* in 1936.

Borkenau wrote *The Totalitarian Enemy* over the course of a few months in late 1939, after the invasion of Poland by Germany and the Soviet Union. The book's timely appearance gave immediacy to his criticism of "the view commonly held that Fascism and Communism were deadly enemies, and that their hostility was the crux of world politics to-day."[33] This commonplace assumption of the past decade had left its possessors in a quandary, and it demanded revision, if not complete replacement. In place of the old outlook, Borkenau provided his own fundamental assumption: "the essential similarity between the German and the Russian systems."[34] Armed with this revision of typical left-wing analysis (if not of his own or Otto Rühle's, with whom Borkenau had apparently had no contact whatever), he conducted his examination of the "totalitarian enemy."

The rush to publication had its cost, though. *The Totalitarian Enemy* is a loosely structured book, a hurried series of assertions held together by the occasional force of particular arguments and the urgency of Borkenau's message. Propaganda often overwhelms scholarship, more so than in the other writings discussed in this chapter. Borkenau, more clearly than any other of the writers included in this study, had anticipated, indeed almost welcomed, "the conflict between the democratic and the totalitarian types of régime,"[35] for he believed it gave the conflict a political and ideological clarity that made possible greater popular support for decisive military action. In a letter to his publisher, Geoffrey Faber, dated 3 October 1939, Borkenau announced that he had begun to write a new book, and he declared that, in addition to its scholarly intent, its purpose was to provide support for the war effort.[36] In the text that resulted from Borkenau's swift and ferocious writing effort appears the outlines of a cold war–era antitotalitarianism taking shape years before the cold war itself had begun. The result is by turns uncannily foresighted and disappointingly rough in its presentation, offering exaggerated examples of Borkenau's strengths and weaknesses as a writer.

Borkenau's text is a particularly problematic one in the context of this study, because it is difficult to describe it as socialist in any sense. Borkenau's writings from 1939 on can be fairly classified as liberal in their political assumptions and intent.[37] He was perhaps referring indirectly to his own mixed views when he stated in *The Totalitarian Enemy* that "in our present state, there are a Liberal and a Socialist fighting within the soul of every one of us."[38] Moreover, Borkenau remained a "fellow traveler" of social democracy for some years—through approximately the late 1940s. Even though the traces of his Marxist vocabulary and the Weimar political veteran's slashing style of argumentation show in his anti-Communist writings, he repeatedly made the point that he was interested only in reporting the truth insofar as he could grasp it. Let us examine then the truth Borkenau wished to report in 1940.

Borkenau began his book with a chapter entitled "An Ideological War," for this is how he understood World War II: liberalism versus totalitarianism. The pact between Germany and Russia (and in this book, Borkenau hardly used the term *Soviet Union*) had made ideological clarity and political amicability easier for Britain and France, but it had complicated the position of Western socialists who wanted to hold to an ideal of economic transformation *and* an ideal of liberty. Borkenau argued one must conclude either that both Russia and Germany were socialist (in the economic sense) or that neither was: "A position such as this ought to give grounds for the most searching inquiries and revision of all views, both on the Right and on the Left."[39] He hoped to make plain the terms of this apparent conundrum by analyzing Nazi Germany's economic system.

Nazi economics, Borkenau concluded, drew on no coherent theory and involved swiftly changing, even contradictory policies. But a few trends were clear to him: the development of a system of state slavery (for subject peoples, to be sure, but also for many Germans themselves); a military economy that strictly controlled working hours, wages, and prices; and—most question from a socialist perspective—the suppression of class struggle for the purposes of the Nazi elite (Borkenau's arguments from *Pareto* reappeared here, stated in precisely the same terms). Borkenau, apparently anticipating the hostility this last point would provoke among the socialist and Labour Party readers he still valued, explained his position in this way:

> It has become apparent that the Nazi economic régime is directed against the interests of every class of the German population, with the exception of the Nazi bodyguard itself. That is the reality behind the boast of the régime that it is in the service of no class. The Nazis boast that they have suppressed the class struggle, but in reality it was always their game to stir up the consciousness of every class. They came into power in alliance with the most reactionary group of capitalists, promising them that they would wipe out the Labour movement, and they actually did wipe it out. But at the same time they spoke the language of revolutionary extremism to the unemployed, promising the destruction of the capitalists, and in fact they are destroying them. They have continued that game in the international sphere. . . .[40]

In other words, the Nazis simply played one class against another to secure power, for power was more important to them than mere profit or control of the means of production. The "logic" of Nazi economics led to both collectivism and war.[41]

Borkenau concluded this section with remarks aimed at his socialist audience. He acknowledged that his characterization of Nazi economics as "socialist" begged the question of the relation between the socialist labor movement and the horror of National Socialism: "Yet we cannot be content with the simple statement that this society of slaves and slave-drivers is in many respects the exact contrary of the ideals of democratic Socialists. . . . [B]ut so much is clear, that it has certain points in common with the society Socialists were aiming at. And the question remains: how far can the desirable features of the system, if there are any, materialize without its abhorrent features?"[42] Fear of controversial positions was not part of Borkenau's style. He plunged forward to a discussion of what he understood as the inexorable modern trend toward "collectivism," which he also characterized as "socialism."

Paying homage to Marx's accurate prediction that economic competition would lead to larger and larger corporations—the trend toward "collectivism"—and disruption on a mass scale whenever one of these huge enterprises went under, Borkenau dismissed virtually all other vital components of the Marxian theoretical apparatus: the labor theory of value, the proletarian-bourgeois class struggle, the end of capitalism and private property as the result of economic crisis and a climactic revolutionary struggle.[43] Borkenau claimed that the Nazis had pushed toward a Marxian-type economic collectivism even more rapidly than had socialists— even though the National Socialists had pursued their policies in a brutal manner at odds with the humanistic ideals of socialism. This reversal of roles Borkenau saw as yet another of the bitter "dialectical" ironies of history.[44] That is, in Borkenau's view, the Nazis were a revolutionary force acting to speed the economic collectivism envisioned as a positive goal by their most prominent ideological enemy: Karl Marx.[45]

Interestingly, even as Borkenau set forth his idiosyncratic analysis and described the paradoxes of Nazi economics, he held no hope for a return to what he called "orthodox Liberalism." Borkenau also understood the trend toward centrally organized and planned economies as a generally desirable and necessary one. The dogma of free markets and competition, carried into full practice under the conditions prevailing in the twentieth century, would result in horrendous social disruption:

> The orthodox Liberal argument far surpasses in ruthlessness anything ever conceived by Nazis and Bolsheviks. Supposing no economic unit were protected, and no doles were given to the unemployed, most of the victims of the slump would probably not find new employment before they starved. The argument is in substance identical with the Bolshevik argument that a few tens of millions of people killed in a world revolution do not matter, if only the killing brings about social progress. The only difference is, that the murderous effects of unrestricted competition would be infinitely more cruel, in our present stage of industrial development, than the most cruel world revolution.[46]

Just when Borkenau seemed, in the vehemence of his attacks on "the collectivists," to have joined forces with Ludwig von Mises, Friedrich Hayek, et al. in championing the free market system of classical liberalism, he made statements such as this, which show how much he had accepted the notion common among intellectuals of the Left—including Löwenthal, Marcuse, Horkheimer, and Korsch—that the world economic crisis and the war that followed represented the absolute and final end of free market capitalism as both theory and practice.[47] He was also extremely interested in imagining what would follow the current crisis. The new economic order, in Borkenau's view, could only be some kind of "collectivism." The remaining question—and by far the more important one to Borkenau—had to do with the nature of the new political order: would it be a totalitarian dictatorship or a democratic system?

Most of the following three chapters, "Nazi Mentality and Its Background," "The New Tyranny," and "The Nazi War," consist of fairly typical anti-Nazi writing of the wartime period. They contain a lengthy and largely unremarkable historical interpretation of Nazi ideology, the political origins of the movement, and the personal degeneracy of its leaders. But they also contain, in some brief passages of this particularly rambling and poorly organized section of the book, Borkenau's thoughts on the political question alluded to in the previous paragraph: did a transformed and "collectivized" economic system such as the Nazis had introduced—which Borkenau called "State Socialism of the Nazi type"—inevitably lead to state-party dictatorship, or were other alternative political orders possible?[48]

Fascism, Borkenau concluded, was not inevitable, but the stalemate or collapse of parliamentary systems in the face of crisis did inevitably invite a return to a "paternal government." If *that* solution failed, as it had in Germany from 1930 to 1933, the way would be open for a coalition of déclassés—an observation that once again echoed the arguments of Thalheimer's essay of 1930 as well as Löwenthal's writings on fascism: "In the Nazi Party there met landowners and industrialists threatened with bankruptcy, young people from the universities who had never a hope of finding jobs, workers from decaying industries, or unemployed, peasants threatened with eviction owing to their inability to pay taxes."[49] The only hope for parliamentary systems rested with the ability of the elected leadership to resolve crises within the institutional framework of that particular state. Failing this, the old elite, and indeed the entire state apparatus, would fall prey to an opportunistic fascist movement like National Socialism.[50] The Nazis made swift electoral gains because they offered some promise of relief for virtually everyone—except, of course, Jews. As yet, however, Borkenau had little to say about Nazi anti-Semitism.

This passage on the fluid and heterogeneous composition of the Nazi *Volksgemeinschaft* reminds us that it was crucial to Borkenau's analysis of state-party dictatorship, from the mid-thirties on, to avoid a class analysis of the support for fascism that did not account for the way in which economic crisis led to great differences in the vulnerabilities of people who occupied the same class. In his view, mass voter support for fascist parties could be understood only by attending to the complexity of divisions within as well as between classes. For all the occasional bombast of his arguments, Borkenau never relied on the capitalist "agent" theories so endearing to the Comintern's spokesmen, nor did he blame the "petty bourgeoisie" or the "Lumpenproletariat" for the advent of fascism. According to Borkenau, the totalitarian state-party inevitably tried to draw from as broad a constituency of support as its momentary needs would allow or require. This resulted in a labile internal politics that turned cynical opportunism into the highest campaign-time virtue.

The Hitler-Stalin Pact was an example of this same opportunistic principle carried into the realm of foreign policy.[51] Borkenau saw the military nonaggression agreement between Germany and the Soviet Union as an act of desperation rather than calculation on the part of the Nazis. Internal conditions of labor and production in Germany had worsened, and the popular euphoria of the early years of the Nazi regime had dissipated, leaving aggression as the sole means of reinvigorating the movement. Nazi Germany consented only reluctantly (Hitler most reluctantly of all, Borkenau speculated) to the sacrifice of its most cherished plans to expand eastward. War could simply wait no longer, and Hitler and the military wanted at least a relatively secure eastern front. Despite his emphasis on the similarities between the two regimes, Borkenau never went so far as to claim that this alliance was a natural and inevitable one between the "brother" totalitarians Hitler and Stalin.

The chief totalitarian movement, in Borkenau's account of the advent of war, remained the Communist Party of the Soviet Union. Like the rest of the book, this section of the text shows the unevenness of an extremely hasty job. Nevertheless, these final pages contain Borkenau's unequivocal indictment of the Soviet Union: "Russia is the totalitarian country *par excellence;* Communism the purest and most logical form of totalitarianism."[52] Borkenau offered evidence for this blistering condemnation in his discussion of the Bolshevik Revolution and Soviet developments during the 1920s. Unlike Rühle, who had aimed much of the fury of his attack on totalitarianism at Lenin, Borkenau directed his sharpest attacks at Stalin: "The year 1929, when the first Five-Year plan was launched, marks the final emergence of totalitarianism in Russia."[53] But like Rühle, Borkenau leveled sharp criticism at Trotsky as well, whom Borkenau labeled the "arch-Fascist." In Borkenau's opinion, Stalin's ascendancy culminated a process initiated primarily under Trotsky's "War Communism," whereby "economics were subordinated to politics, which is one of the most distinctive features of a totalitarian régime."[54] Borkenau admired rather than decried Lenin's flexibility in policy matters, as Rühle had.

Lenin, despite his ruthlessness, was moved by serious ideals and pursued clear goals, as Borkenau saw it, and he described the collapse of the old Bolshevik movement in the face of miserable and unyielding economic and political conditions and the social and political violence that resulted as the "tragedy" of those who pursued the illusion of a global proletarian revolution.[55] Borkenau also argued that the totalitarian dictatorship in the Soviet Union under Stalin was more advanced—in some respects even more structurally ossified—than the fascist regimes in Italy and Germany. But the leaders of Nazi Germany, Borkenau warned, were quickly attaining the levels of totalitarian control present in the Soviet Union and were already advancing even more rapidly in their oppressive internal policies and aggressive territorial conquests.[56]

The concluding propaganda point of the book can be expressed simply: defeat Germany. Borkenau's peroration called for England to "save the world from Nazi barbarism."[57] There was at this point in Borkenau's text no mention whatever of the Soviet Union as one of the "totalitarian enemies." On the one hand, the book presented a remarkable foretaste of the cold war antitotalitarianism to come, yet, on the other hand, its inconsistencies and oversimplifications make it an inferior example of Borkenau's thinking and writing. *The Totalitarian Enemy* might be fairly described as the anticipation of an issue, the barest outlines of an antitotalitarian theory, all couched in a wartime exhortation aimed at that reader whose political outlook rested on the shifting frontier between liberalism and socialism—which was where Borkenau seems to have found himself at the time.

During 1940, Borkenau continued his friendly chats with George Orwell about current wartime events and strategies, but soon he was interned as an "enemy alien."[58] As his friend Richard Löwenthal remembered the episode, Borkenau was given the choice to remain in Great Britain or go to Australia. He chose the latter because he thought England would be defeated. At least one of Borkenau's leftist acquaintances from Weimar days could not contain his sarcasm. In a review of one of Borkenau's several books on global events, Karl Korsch noted Borkenau's recent internment in a hostile swipe at his faith in the tolerance and goodwill of parliamentary regimes. The decision to accept internment in Australia did not endear him to some of his non-Marxist acquaintances in England either, and upon his return, Borkenau looked for ways to leave England for the United States or the Continent, where better opportunities might await him.[59] In the meantime, Korsch would have to work out his own theoretical position on the new events in Europe.

The Totalitarian Counterrevolution

Karl Korsch's fragmentary exile oeuvre yields some of the most controversial contributions to the debate on the similarities and differences between the dictatorships in Germany and the Soviet Union. During late 1939, for example, he began to formulate his own theory of "counter-revolution." Korsch had briefly mentioned the Hitler-Stalin Pact and the outbreak of war in a letter to Max Horkheimer, describing both events as symptoms of a powerfully antirevolutionary tendency in the current period.[60] In three brief articles, published in *Modern Quarterly* and *Living Marxism,* Korsch explained his view that the "counter-revolution" was the main movement of the moment—and at the same time he pointed out "orthodox" Marxism's inability to figure a theoretical or practical way out of the situation.[61]

In "State and Counter-Revolution," Korsch described the counterrevolution as the variety of efforts in several nations—including nations politically and even militarily opposed to one another—to nullify the "independent movement of the European working class."[62] The leading party in this process that Korsch identified was the Soviet Union, which had "degenerated" (Korsch's term) steadily since it became isolated at the end of the last war: "The Russian state has abandoned more and more its original revolutionary and proletarian features. Through the comprehensiveness of its anti-democratic and totalitarian development it has often anticipated the so-called fascist characteristics of the openly counterrevolutionary states of Europe and Asia. . . . The leading bureaucracy of the so-called workers' state has become irretrievably enmeshed in the counterrevolutionary aspects of present-day European politics."[63] Thus far, Korsch sounded quite like Borkenau in his writings of the early 1940s. For a solution to this threatening historical problem, however, Korsch returned swiftly to his faith in the radical working-class camp that Borkenau had abandoned:

> Russian and non-Russian workers today cannot confine themselves to experiencing the steadily advancing counterrevolution without making every effort to interpret its significance. By a careful examination of the past they must find out both the objective and the subjective causes for the victory of fascist state capitalism. . . . Finally they must find out a practical way to resist, as a class, the further encroachments of the counterrevolution and later to pass from an active resistance to an even more active counteroffensive in order to overthrow both the particular state capitalist form recently adopted and the general principle of exploitation inherent in all old and new forms of bourgeois society and its state power.[64]

Unfortunately for the working class, according to Korsch, Marx had failed to study counterrevolution adequately. Even *The Eighteenth Brumaire* offered only a botched and partial effort at such analysis, in Korsch's view. Korsch would therefore try to supply the necessary theory.

Korsch began this section of the article by dismissing the Bonapartism explanation of dictatorship. The Bonapartist theory's emphasis on the role of charismatic leaders and aggressive militarism did not convince Korsch of the theory's applicability in the current situation.[65] The key to his own notion of counterrevolution lay in the properly Marxist examination of the economic development of class conflict—not in the study of the epiphenomena of politics that were the province of such Bonapartism theorists as Thalheimer, who was an old political and theoretical opponent of Korsch's in any case.[66] The beginnings of the socialist economic structure of the Soviet Union, artificially developed and protected during the period of "War Communism," were overwhelmed by the contradictions that the Soviet state, serving as a kind of "transmission belt," inevitably imported into it in the course of the capitalist economic crises of the next decade. These ideas were but the outline of a theory, as Korsch acknowledged, but he would return to it over the course of the following year.[67]

"The Fascist Counter-Revolution" continued almost exactly where "State and Counter-Revolution" had left off: with the attempt to articulate a general theory of the counterrevolution, since Marx had failed to do so. Korsch announced what he described as the *"law of the fully developed fascist counterrevolution of our time."* Its tenets were few: "After the complete exhaustion and defeat of the revolutionary forces, the fascist counterrevolution attempts to fulfill, by new revolutionary methods and in widely different form, those social and political tasks which the so-called reformistic parties and trade unions had promised to achieve but in which they could no longer succeed under the given historical conditions."[68] Korsch, in attempting to offer a Marxian improvement on Marx by explaining the counterrevolution, returned to a touchstone of Marxian theory (without bothering to cite it): the preface to *A Contribution to the Critique of Political Economy.*[69] Korsch explained the success of fascism in the postwar period by stating that capitalism "had not, in fact, developed all the forces of production."[70] In both peace and war, fascism had continued to revolutionize the capitalist forces of production, despite its anticapitalistic propaganda and its claims to put an end to class conflict. This continued development of the capitalist forces of production should not, Korsch warned, be transformed in the thinking of socialists into a "preparation stage" for the inevitable revolution. Fascism actually represented the danger of a more or less permanent defeat of the working class.[71] The only way out of this impasse, Korsch concluded, was though a working-class revolution that would also be a confirmation of fundamental Marxian insights: "Total mobilization of the productive forces presupposes total mobilization of that greatest productive force which is the revolutionary working class itself."[72] Once again, and in this he seldom varied, Korsch placed his hopes on the revolutionary capacity of the working class. As closely as he would at times approach some of the radical revisionism of Horkheimer or the bitterly anti-Soviet rhetoric of Borkenau or Rühle, Korsch continued to apply—in fact increasingly turned to—Marxian categories that he apparently continued to believe would provide a reliable guide to the criticism of capitalist society. His protests about the inadequacy of "Marxism" (his quotation marks) had to do with the distortions wrought by the revisionists and Bolshevist epigones, not the original work of Marx and Engels (and sometimes Luxemburg and Lenin as well) as critics of capitalism.

"Democracy" and the capitalism of the nonfascist, and non-"socialist" countries were the targets of Korsch's next article on the theme of counterrevolution, "The Workers' Fight against Fascism" (1942). Korsch began this article, in which disdainful quotation marks abounded, with the statement that the working class was not interested in defending the "democracy" represented by the Western capitalist nations: "The 'secret' underlying the verbal battles between 'totalitarianism' and 'anti-totalitarianism' and the more important diplomatic and military struggle between the Axis and the Anglo-American group of imperialist powers is the historical fact that the worst, and the most intimate foe of democracy today is not Herr Hitler, but 'democracy' itself."[73] "Democracy" meant the political order in the capitalist nations, their "nostalgia" for individual rights, free trade, and constitutional forms, all of which Korsch viewed as a mask for persisting class conflict. For the workers, there was no desirable choice between Hitler and "democracy."

Indeed, more than any other of the leftist opponents of totalitarianism, Korsch refused to acknowledge any overriding difference between the two sets of wartime combatants or any practical need for the working class to choose allegiance to one over the other. His overarching theory of counterrevolution subsumed both "totalitarian" fascism and "democratic" fascism—"two equally capitalistic parts of that one big capitalist power that rules the world today."[74]

Korsch's verdict on "democracy" in the Western capitalist nations further indicated a potential for the increased similarity of the two types of totalitarian order. The criticism of Nazism in these lands—particularly the United States—was specious, he declared, for while fascist ruthlessness drew fire, fascist economic efficiency and civil order were secretly envied.[75] In the West, "sentimentality" about democratic and liberal political traditions steadily gave ground to the need for an administratively rationalized capitalist economy to compete with those of the openly fascist nations. The resort to outright fascism was not unimaginable. Market capitalism was on its way out; a new form of highly concentrated monopoly capitalism had emerged. The "End of Economic Man" was at least a half truth, Korsch insisted.[76]

What to call this new form of capitalism, which was the economic basis of the continuing counterrevolution, posed an interesting but not especially troublesome issue for Korsch:

> It does not matter so much whether we describe the new system that has replaced it in terms of "monopoly capitalism," "state capitalism," or "a corporate state." The last term seems most appropriate to the writer for the reason that it recalls at once the name that was given to the new totalitarian form of society after the rise of fascism in Italy twenty years ago. There is, however, a difference. The corporate community of the US represents as yet only the "economic basis" of a full-fledged totalitarian system, and not its political and ideological superstructure. On the other hand, one might say that in backward countries like Italy and Spain there exists as yet only the totalitarian superstructure, without a fully developed economic basis.[77]

What the passage shows above all is that Korsch's notion of counterrevolutionary totalitarianism could now be applied to the study of virtually any nation's economic or political modernization. His model of mid-century historical change now took on a quality of inevitability and decisiveness: a final battle between revolution and counterrevolution was afoot, Korsch intimated. In addition to its apocalyptic tone—quite understandable for an essay written by a leftist (or anyone, for that matter) in 1941—Korsch's theory of totalitarian base and superstructure could be manipulated quite freely. For all its apparent Marxian orthodoxy, the model he offered identified neither base nor superstructure as the determining or conditioning social factor. This flexibility of theory may have been an advance over the "vulgar" models of other theorists, but it seemed to indicate even more the unfinished character of Korsch's own notion. His concept of totalitarian counterrevolution functioned for him as a kind of analytical adjustable wrench with which he could grasp the economic development of any nation—even if in the course of the analysis the sharp corners of historical situations were rounded off a bit because of the imprecision of the tool.

Korsch's "counter-revolutionary totalitarianism" was finally too broad and generalized to have persuasive explanatory power. The one consistent point in Korsch's suggestive but underdeveloped analysis of counterrevolution was the call for the workers to overthrow both the "democratic" and the "totalitarian" forms of capitalism and to institute socialism. Even as his isolation increased and his defense of Marxian analysis alternately waxed and waned, his close attention to class struggle and his genuine hopes for proletarian revolution never disappeared. After the war, Korsch continued to hope that the working class could ride out the long "Kondratieff Wave" of counterrevolution that had yet to subside.[78]

Responding to the New Authoritarian State

In 1940, at about the same time Korsch was writing about the "totalitarian counter-revolution" and Hilferding was developing his essay on the "totalitarian state economy," Max Horkheimer, who did not often write about politics as such, generated perhaps his most radical and provocative essay on the current dictatorial regimes in Europe. He labeled the various kinds of regimes he discussed as versions or special types under the general rubric of the "authoritarian state." He had apparently had some difficulty deciding on the appropriate term to use in describing the new dictatorships. A letter from Karl Korsch, which takes up a discussion of the relative applicability of the terms *Staatssozialismus, Staatskapitalismus, autoritärer Staat,* and *Faschismus,* may indicate that Horkheimer wanted to sound out Korsch not only on the content of the essay but also on the issue of nomenclature.[79] These are hardly fundamentally significant matters in the larger context and course of Horkheimer's scholarly career, but they are intriguing faint traces of his role in the subsequent "state capitalism" debate that took place within the institute.

Horkheimer's 1940 essay "Autoritärer Staat" constitutes far more than a faint trace of his developing social theory, however. As the most outspoken political *cri de coeur* to be found among Horkheimer's writings of the wartime period, the essay has gained the well-deserved attention of scholars. Apparently he began to write it about the time he was initiating plans to move from New York to the Los Angeles area, a change that resulted in a division and eventual reorganization of the institute. However, the essay circulated for the first time among only a very small group in 1942 as part of a mimeographed collection of writings dedicated to the memory of Walter Benjamin, the brilliant essayist, critic, and former associate of the institute who had died tragically during his flight from France to Spain after the German occupation of Paris.[80] The article shows Horkheimer's reliance on the concept of state capitalism but also indicates the ways in which he attended to the differences and similarities between the Soviet Union and the fascist states. At the same time, the article cleared a space to differentiate his own thoughts on dictatorship from those of Korsch, Hilferding, and his colleagues at the institute, Friedrich Pollock and Franz Neumann.

With the term *authoritarian state,* Horkheimer indicated the regimes and economic systems of both National Socialist fascism (which he called "state capitalism" or simply "fascism") and the Soviet Union (which he did not call by name but instead labeled as "integral statism" or "state socialism").[81] His terminology, which bracketed the Soviet and German states as different species of the genus "authoritarian state," approximated arguments that Hilferding was raising against the concept of state capitalism yet also avoided some of the oversimplifications of Korsch's "counterrevolution" thesis. That Horkheimer was familiar with the ideas of both thinkers can be inferred by his continuing correspondence with Korsch at the time of writing and revising the essay and by the attention of his colleagues Friedrich Pollock and Franz Neumann to Rudolf Hilferding's argument about the Soviet "totalitarian state economy" in their own writings of 1941–42.

Horkheimer did not abandon the term *state capitalism,* even as he put forth his somewhat different and broader concept of the authoritarian state, asserting in his opening paragraph that "state capitalism is the authoritarian state of the present."[82] The problem that Horkheimer addressed initially was that the end of capitalism that Marxism foretold—crisis, collapse, and revolution—had been forestalled by the advent of state capitalism, which replaced the free market and attempted to circumvent its manifest weaknesses. Unfortunately, as a part of the monopolization and centralization process that resulted in state capitalism, the workers' organizations themselves had been integrated into the bureaucratic apparatus of the transformed but still capitalist economy.[83] He warned that "adaptation is the price that individuals and organizations must pay in order to prosper under capitalism."[84] Horkheimer found the symbolic historical origins of this process in Germany adumbrated in "the shadowy relationship between Lassalle, the founder of the German Socialist mass party, and Bismarck, the father of German state capitalism."[85] Some type of authoritarian state waited in the wings from the time of these nineteenth-century events, for it was clear that the bureaucracies of both the government and its "opposition" had a mutual interest in expanding and rationalizing state control. The question would be: which kind of authoritarian state would emerge?

At this point, Horkheimer introduced the Soviet model, under the pseudonym of "integral statism" or "state socialism," which he said was "the most consistent form of the authoritarian state."[86] Its capacity to accelerate accumulation and production was extraordinary (Stalin's five-year plans were clearly the uncited evidence here). The Soviet bureaucratic state regimented and regulated the entire society directly, and despite claims to the contrary, the proletariat remained in a position of powerlessness under "integral statism." Horkheimer argued that the Soviet working class "will be trapped in a vicious circle of poverty, domination, war, and poverty until they break through it themselves."[87] Horkheimer summed up his views on the Soviet Union, what it was, and what it might have meant to the working-class movement as follows: "Only the bad in history is irrevocable: the unrealized possibilities, missed chances, murder with and without juridical procedures, and that which domination inflicts on human beings."[88] However delicately Horkheimer had danced around the issue of what to call the Soviet Union, his verdict on the performance of "integral statism" was clear enough.

In contrast to the more unitary form of the Soviet regime, the fascist model of the authoritarian state showed a mixed form, Horkheimer insisted. Fascism approached the style of "integral statism" in some respects, but it left much of the process of capital accumulation in private hands. In their economic policies, however, both forms of the authoritarian state tended to reduce economic questions to issues of technique. Power and control would lose all rational basis beyond the "legitimacy" sustained by their own momentum. Terror and the authoritarian state were identical, and therefore no "progress" out of the authoritarian state should be imagined. Historical escape from the authoritarian state demanded the radical action of the working class: the only way out of either of the two forms was revolution. Horkheimer perceived "the system of workers' councils [*das Rätesystem*]" as the only kind of force that could lead a revolution. A revolution led by a party would quickly turn into a new order of domination.[89] With such dire predictions and formulas for action, Horkheimer's politics quite closely approached Korsch's and even Rühle's at that time— he simply did not express himself so directly and polemically as they did.

But even as he professed his belief in the need for radical praxis, Horkheimer insisted, more than Korsch would at this time, on the validity of a radical theory that refused to become part of any new order of command—even a self-proclaimed revolutionary order—and would make its solitary way through the ruins of the present:

> The readiness to obey, even when it sets out to think, is of no use to theory. Despite all the urgency with which theory attempts to illuminate the movement of the social totality even in its minutest details, it is unable to prescribe to individuals an effective form of resistance to injustice. Thought itself is already a sign of resistance, the effort to keep oneself from being deceived any more. Thought does not simply stand opposed to command and obedience, but sets them for the time being in relationship to the realization of freedom. This relationship is in danger.[90]

"For the time being" has often become a permanent exhibition in the museum of false political expectations in this century, and Horkheimer's next major project, taken up in collaboration with Theodor Adorno, would assert far more emphatically the necessity of theory's divorce from practice. His 1940 call for a momentary holding action later began to appear as the beginning of a slow, steady retreat.

He did not, however, close the essay with this appeal to and for theory. Horkheimer spent his last paragraph in a response to those who, like Borkenau and to a certain extent his friend Friedrich Pollock as well, argued for adapting to the imperatives of state capitalism. Horkheimer paraphrased this position in a passage that conveys at once a sense of irony, restrained rage, and a battle against resignation:

> If there is no return to liberalism, the correct form of activity appears to be the extension of state capitalism. To work with it, expand it, and extend it everywhere to advanced forms appears to offer the advantage of progress and all the security of success, which one can only wish for *politique scientifique*. Because the proletariat has nothing more to expect from the old powers, there is nothing left but union with the new. . . . It would be sentimental to remain opposed to state capitalism merely on account of the slain. It could be said that the Jews were mostly capitalists, after all, and that the small nations have no right to exist. State capitalism is simply what is possible today. . . . But the historical outlook of such reasoning recognizes only the dimension in which progress and regression take place; it ignores human intervention. It values people only for what they are under capitalism: as social quantities, as things. As long as world history follows its logical course, it fails to fulfill its human destiny.[91]

Poised between radical thought and revolutionary act, the argument of Horkheimer's "Autoritärer Staat" could be fairly described as the sublimation of his wartime political and theoretical ambivalence. Appropriately enough, Horkheimer's essay stands also as a kind of extended commentary on the last phrase of Walter Benjamin's "Theses on the Philosophy of History," which asserts that "every second of time was the strait gate through which the Messiah might enter."[92] That is, the moment for the necessary revolutionary response to the authoritarian state is the perpetual now: *Jetztzeit.*

In terms of his general understanding of the "authoritarian state," Horkheimer had held to a notion of state capitalism but had not made its defense or definition the centerpiece of his presentation. He agreed with Rudolf Hilferding's conclusion during the early months of the war that the state now assumed a new role as the manager of the economy and the distributor of its rewards, but he continued to use the "state capitalist" designation that Hilferding had by then rejected. Horkheimer had avoided, or at least put off for the moment, the kind of revision or direct refutation of Marxian theory for which Hilferding seemed headed. As it happened, Horkheimer's colleagues Friedrich Pollock and Franz Neumann were about to have it out over the notion of state capitalism, and each of these institute colleagues cited Hilferding (not Horkheimer) prominently in the course of their arguments. It would be mistaken to read too much into this "neglect," however. Horkheimer's essay had perhaps not yet circulated at that time, and, in any case, it had to attend to business other than the concept of state capitalism. Instead of discussing the approach that critique of dictatorship should take—the proper weighting of political and economic factors in the analysis of totalitarian states—Horkheimer had been more interested in asserting the urgent need for radical theory that did not bind itself in advance to a party position.

In leftist programmatic terms, Horkheimer had also approximated Korsch's insistence on the need for revolution to overturn both fascist and "integral" states, but more as the understanding of an unrealized moment of history than as the direct call for action. Horkheimer's "authoritarian state" differed also from Korsch's idea of "counter-revolution" in that Horkheimer's understanding of dictatorial regimes led him to focus more sharply on Nazi Germany as the primary danger to the working class and to critical thought itself. Korsch's outspoken and evenhanded condemnation of both "totalitarian" and "antitotalitarian" powers did not find a direct equivalent in Horkheimer's subtler and more cautious analysis. Horkheimer's next major analysis of the "totalitarian" order would lead him still further from the social/historical categories and notions of praxis associated with Marxian critique.

Totalitarianism and the State Capitalism Debate

German leftist intellectuals' use of the notion of state capitalism in debates about dictatorship arose from the need to explain the apparently new kinds of economies in several European nations now under single-party rule. The term *state capitalism* would appear in a number of books and articles in addition to Arthur Rosenberg's book on Bolshevism and Horkheimer's essay on the authoritarian state. Rosenberg's formulation of the notion of state capitalism in relation to the Soviet Union was an explicitly critical one. Later in the 1930s, however, defining the term *state capitalism*—which had apparently been a relatively routine matter for some thinkers, including Korsch and Horkheimer—became an ever more controversial issue for several German leftists writing on the problem of dictatorship. In view of the importance of this concept in the writings of several thinkers whose ideas about dictatorship tended in the direction of totalitarian theory, a few of these essays and debates on state capitalism merit particular attention. Some formulations of the concept of state capitalism closely accompanied the use of comparative notions of totalitarianism. In this group of writings, the key issue at stake was the relative importance theorists granted to, on the one hand, the agency of the political state in the totalitarian dictatorship or, on the other hand, to the ultimately determining forces of the capitalist economy that continued to be a source of contradiction and crisis. For theorists who still considered themselves part of a Marxist tradition, interpretive questions regarding economic determination "in the last analysis," the relative or absolute autonomy of the new political dictatorships, and the issue of whether capitalism in its free market or monopolistic forms was embodied or surpassed in these new dictatorships were of critical importance. The mechanism of crisis, if any, that these authors hypothesized and whether they argued that the working class would play a role in overthrowing dictatorships were also crucial.

A touchstone for this discussion of the economic and political character of the new dictatorships was an essay written in 1940 by Rudolf Hilferding. His analysis of the relative usefulness of the rival models of state capitalism and totalitarianism was unique among writings of the German exiles in that it focused almost exclusively on the Soviet Union instead of on Fascist Italy or Nazi Germany. In addition, of the German socialists who developed a critique of totalitarianism that closely compared Nazi Germany with the Soviet Union, Rudolf Hilferding possessed the greatest international stature. As André Liebich has argued, Hilferding likely drew inspiration and perhaps specific ideas regarding the formulation of such a critique of Soviet totalitarianism from his close friends in the circle of Mensheviks-in-exile who staffed *Die Gesellschaft* and the later *Zeitschrift für Sozialismus*.[93] Indeed, Hilferding's article on the Soviet totalitarian system first appeared in the exile Menshevik publication *Sotsialisticheskii Vestnik*.[94] Unlike other socialist writers who focused primarily on the state-party and its relation to individuals and national institutions, and who described the Soviet economy, as well as fascist ones, as particular forms of "state capitalism," Hilferding used his economic expertise to fashion an analysis of the dictatorial state's new position on the production and distribution of goods as the decisive factor. He claimed that the development of the "totalitarian state economy" in the Soviet Union marked the appearance of an unprecedented form of social organization: the "first *totalitarian state*—even before the name was invented."[95]

Hilferding declared that "the concept of 'state capitalism' can hardly pass the test of economic analysis." It not only was inadequate to describe the new kind of regime represented by the Stalinist dictatorship but was actually misleading. State capitalism could be understood even by some socialists as a transitional stage toward socialism, but such was not the case. The notion of state capitalism implied that the market continued to operate and that something resembling a traditional state apparatus now took over the bourgeoisie's previous role of enforcing capital accumulation. Both notions were certainly false, Hilferding stated, at least with respect to the Soviet Union.[96]

The "totalitarian state economy," as Hilferding labeled the Soviet system, was not governed by the rules of competition that characterize a market system, nor did "profit" exist, at least in the capitalist sense of private accumulation and "ownership" of surplus production. Accumulation in the Soviet economy, Hilferding continued, had nothing to do with the accumulation of capital in a system of capitalist *production* but instead constituted the fuel for a *consumption*-based economy organized by the bureaucracy but controlled by the Communist party leadership. The party, through the state's bureaucratic apparatus, allocated the "rewards" of economic production. In short, politics had gained control over economics and subjected it to the decisions of the party elite. The idea of the primacy of politics that Löwenthal had mentioned in his analysis of economics in

National Socialist Germany now became central to the new notion of totalitarianism in the Soviet Union propounded by Hilferding: "A state economy . . . eliminates precisely the autonomy of economic laws. It represents not a market but a consumers' economy. It is no longer price but rather a state planning commission that now determines what is produced and how. Formally, prices and wages still exist, but their function is no longer the same; they no longer determine the process of production which is now controlled by a central power that fixes prices and wages."[97] Moreover, Hilferding insisted, the system that had developed in the Soviet Union during the twenties and thirties was neither properly capitalist nor socialist: "It represents a *totalitarian state* economy, i.e., a system to which the economies of Germany and Italy are drawing closer and closer."[98]

The implications of his analysis for traditional Marxism seemed clear, and Hilferding did not shy away from the need for a thoroughgoing reconsideration of inherited socialist doctrine. Marxist Social Democrats had been unable to imagine that "the political form of that 'managed economy' which was to replace capitalist production for a free market could be unrestricted absolutism."[99] Whether Hilferding would have merely refashioned Marxism or would have finally rejected it cannot be known with absolute certainty, for he did not live to pursue the provocative line of analysis that he had initiated. His essay "Das historische Problem" indicates that he was moving toward an argument for the "primacy of the political" of the type that Löwenthal had mentioned in the mid-1930s and that was about to embroil the Institute of Social Research in one of its liveliest internal disputes.[100] Unlike most of these writers, who by the beginning of the war had fled to England or North America, Hilferding remained in Paris. Some months after the German army defeated France, Hilferding was arrested in the southern part of the country, where he was waiting for an exit visa, taken back to Paris, and died—evidently a suicide—while in the brutal custody of the Gestapo. Even after his death, Hilferding's essays on the totalitarian state economy and "the historical problem" circulated widely among émigré socialists. But his comparative economic analysis of the "totalitarian state economy" would not be published in English until 1947, when it appeared in *Modern Review,* a journal of democratic socialism. As further testimony to the ways in which the fate of German social democracy was bound up with the fate of the Mensheviks, one of that journal's editors was Hilferding's old friend and comrade Iurii Denicke (Georg Decker), and its operations were supported by Raphael Abramovitsch, the father of Mark Rein, the missing volunteer for Republican Spain.[101]

As Hilferding fitfully but forthrightly revised and rethought his theoretical outlook during the 1930s and early 1940s, several younger intellectuals were paying close attention to his work and generating their own bold revisions and innovations. Horkheimer's essay on the authoritarian state was but one of many discussions of dictatorship he and his colleagues in the Institute of Social Research generated. Collectively and individually, the members of the institute were responsible for several of the best-researched and most theoretically sophisticated studies of dictatorship produced during the wartime period. It is equally clear that by the 1930s, the institute's leading figures held no illusions about the direction of the Soviet Union under Stalin. Moreover, attempts to explain the oppressive character of the Soviet dictatorship often appeared in connection with the analysis of the Nazi regime, making possible a careful but critical comparisons of the two systems.[102] But as Helmut Dubiel has noted, the heterogeneity of these various writings has caused them to be forgotten as a group of critiques—a collective body of research and writing that approached many aspects of the new dictatorships, the National Socialist regime in particular, from a variety of angles.[103] One of the central issues that divided the institute's writers in their appraisal of state-party regimes was the notion of state capitalism and its corollary, the idea of the primacy of the political.

Within the Institute of Social Research, the debate over the influence and importance of the economic as opposed to the political aspects of the modern dictatorships took an increasingly sharp, even personal form in a controversy over the applicability of the concept of state capitalism. Some of the key arguments in this debate were responses to the theory that Hilferding had articulated in 1940, and his essay became an important source of evidence for both parties to the debate. The following section summarizes the terms of this debate as they appeared in the writings of the key antagonists and looks at the ways in which this event not only revealed conflicts within the Institute of Social Research over theories of dictatorship but also connected with wider debates on the exile German left.[104]

The kernel of the "state capitalism" controversy within the institute was Franz Neumann's response to Friedrich Pollock's position on the subject as articulated in his article "State Capitalism: Its Possibilities and Limitations." Pollock had a stronger academic training in economics than most of the other members of the institute had. Max Horkheimer had entrusted to Pollock, his friend from school days, control of the business affairs of the institute, and therefore, despite the importance of his work to the group as a whole, Pollock was left with less time than the others had for research and writing.[105]

The article, one of the few publications that Pollock contributed during the New York exile period of the institute, showed that Pollock, like Horkheimer, continued to rely on the concept of state capitalism. Even though he shared many of the economic assumptions of Rudolf Hilferding, who had *rejected* the concept, Pollock kept the term *state capitalism* and did not follow Horkheimer's alternative "authoritarian state" typology. He instead arrived at his own set of categories for the modern state regimes. He referred now to "democratic" and "totalitarian" forms of state capitalism. Both types of state capitalism had replaced the free market with a "system of direct controls." The state now regulated both production and consumption through these controls. Under the "totalitarian" form of state capitalism, a party elite directed the economy in collaboration with the state bureaucracy (Pollock included the military here) and the "top ranking personnel" of the industrial and business sectors.[106]

Pollock's "totalitarian" state capitalist regimes were Nazi Germany and the Soviet Union, and in the article he gave far more attention to the former regime than to the latter.[107] His "democratic" state capitalist regimes were the industrialized Western European and American nations. Pollock described that form of state capitalism as democratic without using Korsch's scornful quotation marks and without repeating Horkheimer's criticism of the working-class parties as being integrated into the state capitalist regime: "Under a democratic form of state capitalism the state has the same controlling functions but is itself controlled by the people. It is based on institutions which prevent the bureaucracy from transforming its administrative position into an instrument of power and thus laying the basis for transshaping the democratic system into a totalitarian one."[108] Even if we grant that he was describing democratic state capitalism as an ideal type, Pollock's uncritical and optimistic comments on the performance of the Western capitalist, constitutional states stand out in contrast to the more critical analyses of Korsch and Horkheimer. His analysis of totalitarian state capitalism, however, would approximate theirs more closely.

Pollock's description of the general model of state capitalism offered almost precisely the same menu of characteristics that Hilferding had assembled in his article of 1940: a central plan; controlled prices, production, and consumption; the gradual disappearance of "profit" as traditionally understood (although Pollock allowed for the preservation of the "profit motive" in performance); and application of principles of scientific management.[109] He even cited Hilferding to support the argument that under state capitalism, commodity production for the market is replaced by a state-mandated production for use.[110] But Hilferding had focused on the Soviet Union, not Nazi Germany, and he also denied that the Soviet economy could be adequately defined as capitalist or socialist. While Hilferding decisively rejected the notion of state capitalism as he formulated it and saw the greatest fulfillment of the new and noncapitalist totalitarian state tendencies in the Soviet Union, Pollock kept the term *state capitalism* and some of its component concepts, and he did not go far to specify their operation beyond the example of Nazi Germany. That is, even though he implied that there was a global tendency toward state capitalism, in Pollock's view the National Socialist regime was clearly the most compelling case.[111] In further contrast to Hilferding's open insistence on the primacy of politics under the Soviet "totalitarian state economy," Pollock seemed almost to have backed into a similar concept of the primacy of politics in his own version of the state capitalism thesis, without following up to any great extent on the theoretical and practical implications of this line of argument. Franz Neumann believed that he understood these implications quite clearly, and he rejected Pollock's state capitalism concept, especially insofar as it was intended to be a theory that might explain the economy of Nazi Germany.

At about the time Pollock's essay was published, Neumann demonstrated his adamant opposition to the state capitalism thesis in a letter to Max Horkheimer, declaring that the state capitalism essay marked an unequivocal farewell to Marxism.[112] Neumann sharpened and elaborated his objections later in 1941 as he completed his manuscript for the first edition of *Behemoth*. His criticism of Pollock's state capitalism model arose from three major weaknesses that he perceived in this concept: (1) it did not clearly identify an inherent tendency to crisis in state capitalist economies, (2) it replaced the analysis of class struggle with an examination of administrative-terroristic imperatives of managerial control, and (3) it contended that economic relations in Nazi Germany were entirely subordinate to political ones. Quite soon, in his wartime book, *Behemoth*, Neumann would dismiss the theory outright: "The very term 'state capitalism' is a *contradictio in adiecto*."[113] At the opening of his section entitled "An Economy without Economics?" he cited Pollock's article in a footnote, but the writer who had offered "the best formulation of this type of theory," in Neumann's view, was one of the most outspoken opponents of state capitalism terminology: Rudolf Hilferding.[114] After restating Hilferding's arguments on the Soviet economy and noting the efforts of others to apply them to Germany, Neumann—who did not pause to directly refute or even address the applicability of the state capitalism concept to the Soviet Union—launched into his own criticism of the concept.

To a very limited extent, Neumann would agree with Hilferding and Pollock at the level of theory. That is, the kind of regime both Hilferding and Pollock described (though their terminology and conclusions diverged), in which the economy had been subordinated to political decisions, would do away with the contradictions inherent in capitalism. What Neumann denied was that such an "ideal type" had been realized in Germany. Moreover, he rejected the deep pessimism that a theory resting on the primacy of politics legitimated:

> If we share this view, we must also conclude that nothing but a series of accidents can destroy such systems. If the systems are held together only by political ties and not by any inescapable economic necessity, only political mistakes can destroy them. But why should political errors occur? Politics divorced from economics is a mere technique, an art. In the era of state capitalism it is a technique of mass domination, a technique that has indeed been highly developed. . . . So skilful a system of mass domination may secure the stability of the system for a thousand years. That is, indeed, the promise that Hitler holds out to his people.[115]

Neumann could not, at least not in 1941, consider the rejection of what was to him such a fundamental notion: Germany remained a class society, and its capitalism, regardless of its deviations from the "classic" market model, carried within itself the same social contradictions and inherent tendencies toward crisis endemic to both market and monopoly capitalism. He called his own theoretical model of the German economy a "totalitarian monopolistic economy."

Neumann's concept of the totalitarian monopolistic economy attempted to hold to Marxian categories in the analysis of what he admitted was in some ways a hybrid system, but one without a coherent political center. First, he asserted, the Nazis had no economic theory worthy of the name, and their policies were ad hoc attempts to achieve short-term goals. That did not, however, imply that the economy itself could not be explained.[116] In fact, Neumann argued, much of the old system remained in place, for monopoly capitalism had survived from the Weimar period into the Third Reich.[117] The new form he perceived, totalitarian monopoly capitalism, "is a monopolistic economy—*and* a command economy. It is a private capitalistic economy, regimented by the totalitarian state."[118] This new form of capitalism showed a few primary tendencies under the Nazi regime (and here I have condensed quite radically the sweep and detail of Neumann's argument): to accelerate cartelization and rescue it from the negative impact of the world economic crisis, largely by means of military production; to lower unemployment through a variety of state commanded projects administered under private or Nazi party leadership and quite often for private profit; to sustain and even to maximize profit itself, which had not only *not* disappeared, as it was supposed to under the state capitalism model, but had not even been properly regulated; to engage in military aggression, because the scarcity of resources and labor in Germany could not be made up through trade; to subject labor to a system of accelerated production and stabilized wages at the same time; and to sustain and even intensify the economic effects of antagonistic class relations while it denied these relations in propaganda, atomized the working class, and prevented autonomous workers' organizations. What Neumann contended in his massively documented account was that such coherence as the Nazi regime possessed resided foremost in the persisting elements of capitalism and not in its chaotic political realm, which he denied constituted a state, properly speaking, at all.[119] With this verdict, Neumann had not simply rejected the state capitalism concept, he had turned it on its head—or put it on its feet, depending on one's point of view.

The importance of the state capitalism debate to the development of left-wing concepts of totalitarianism can be summarized in the following observations. Hilferding's rejection of the state capitalism concept led him to the formulation of the totalitarian state economy theory, which pointed to the Soviet Union as its prototype, with Italy and Germany following close on its heels. If the economic basis of these three regimes was similar, as his argument implied, it was but a short theoretical step, however one judges its validity, to insist that the political form of these regimes was bound to be similar as well. Some theorists, such as Hilferding, also perceived contradictions in the concept of state capitalism that inclined them toward a rejection of the more orthodox Marxist base-superstructure model in which the economic relations of the mode of production were the most fundamental factor conditioning other aspects of the social totality. The political practice likely to arise from Hilferding's theory— that is, the potentially swift passage from Marxian orthodoxy to apostasy—included the likelihood of acceptance of mixed economies and the end of appeals to revolutionary action in favor of unmixed devotion to parliamentarism. The wartime political transformations of Franz Borkenau—who had already sketched his own notion of the primacy of politics in *The Totalitarian Enemy*—and Richard Löwenthal—who had put off his reckoning with the same notion only for a few years—could serve as the clearest examples of this transition.[120]

Pollock's adherence to the state capitalist concept had quite a different political and theoretical outcome than Borkenau's did. Helmut Dubiel speculates that Pollock's largely non-Marxian revision of the notion of state-party dictatorship helped Horkheimer and Adorno free themselves from even the somewhat ambivalent and increasingly muted Marxian focus on economics, class relations, and revolution that had appeared in Horkheimer's "Autoritärer Staat."[121] Adorno, whose use of Marxian concepts was always selective, seems to have been somewhat less in need of such a liberation than Horkheimer was. In any case, Pollock had chopped away at the brambles of economic analysis that might have blocked the path for the kind of cultural and philosophical critique that Horkheimer and Adorno soon ventured in *Dialektik der Aufklärung* (*Dialectic of Enlightenment*). In terms of the theory-practice dialectic, Pollock's version of the theory of the primacy of politics had helped sanction a further retreat from practical politics.

For all its assertiveness, Neumann's dismissal of the state capitalist concept and the accompanying notion of the primacy of politics constituted a Marxian holding action as much as a critical advance. *Behemoth* offered a kind of Marxist critique of the Nazi regime, but even some of its admirers glimpsed ambiguity and ambivalence lurking within its formidable scholarly apparatus. The Marxism that Neumann was prepared to use in *Behemoth* did not please the politically more pessimistic Horkheimer or pass muster with Korsch in his early 1940s *enragé* phase. It would, however, be lavishly praised by Rosenberg, who was in the midst of a transition to social democracy—Franz Neumann's now-rejected point of origin. Even the practical political component and the class subject of Neumann's Marxism were becoming more than a little murky. In his totalitarian monopoly capitalism model, Neumann emphasized the contradictions in the administrative and accumulation needs of the Nazi regime far more than he did any overt manifestations of class conflict, though these, too, could be glimpsed. Nonetheless, the fact remained that issues of class consciousness and proletarian revolution, though not absent, were not central to his analysis. They appeared most clearly at the end of the first section of the book and in the book's conclusion, a series of speculations about the "conscious political action of the oppressed masses, which will utilize the breaks in the system."[122] But these "breaks in the system," to the extent that they actually existed, did not allow for the kind of internal revolt against the Nazis that Neumann at times envisioned.

Perhaps because a united working-class response was absent, the tensions within Neumann's Marxist outlook would become more apparent in the postwar period.[123] At the time of *Behemoth*'s first publication, however, Neumann's ambivalence about the working class remained a subtle gap in the Marxist orientation of his remarkable presentation. Despite acknowledging the overwhelming danger and difficulty of radical praxis in Nazi Germany, he still insisted on its possibility. With such theoretical and political stakes as these, the state capitalism debate within the institute's circle was, at the time, something more than the "conflict about words" that Rolf Wiggershaus, a leading historian of the Institute of Social Research, has labeled it.[124]

The conflict over the issue of state capitalism did not prevent Neumann from serving as a fund-seeking ambassador in the institute's behalf, however. Just three weeks after Neumann had blasted Pollock's article, he reported once more to Horkheimer on a meeting he had held with an administrator from the amply-funded Council for Democracy regarding financial support for some of the institute's research on anti-Semitism. The official admitted skepticism about the institute's project because he perceived the group as Marxist and therefore incapable of offering an unbiased perspective. Neumann wrote Horkheimer that he had explained to the official that some institute scholars were Marxists but that no member of the group was a member of the Communist Party. Persuaded by Neumann's arguments, the council official—a Harvard professor named Carl J. Friedrich, who was to play such an important role in the formulation of postwar totalitarian theory—promised to assist the institute in securing funds for its project.[125]

Also in 1941, another theorist with a professional and scholarly background remarkably like Neumann's offered his assessment of the German dictatorship. The author, Ernst Fraenkel, had not had access to the economic statistics that fueled Neumann's analysis in *Behemoth,* but he had five years' experience as a labor lawyer under the Nazi regime. The book Fraenkel wrote was quite well received at the time of its publication. Fraenkel's brief discussions of the concept of the totalitarian state merit careful consideration because of their unique angle on the problem of state-party dictatorship and totalitarian theory.

Case Study of a Totalitarian Legal System

One of the difficulties in identifying the left-wing versions of anti-totalitarianism produced by German intellectuals and scholars is that most of the pertinent documents were written and published in exile—if they were published at all. Ernst Fraenkel's book *The Dual State: A Contribution to the Theory of Dictatorship* is exceptional in this regard, for it was mostly written in Nazi Germany. From 1933 to 1938, Fraenkel continued to practice law in Berlin. As a result of this unique experience, he had access to published sources related to Nazi law, and he could observe juristic practices firsthand. Fraenkel had been a law partner of Franz Neumann in the Weimar period, when both were active in behalf of trade unions and SPD political causes. Their books on Nazi political, legal, and economic behavior stand as two of the best-informed and most lasting contributions to scholarship on Nazi Germany that were published during the war.

Unlike Borkenau's *Totalitarian Enemy,* which was clearly aimed at a popular reading audience, Fraenkel's *Dual State* had more scholarly intentions, as evidenced by his financial and research supporters, described in the preface. Fraenkel had received help of one kind or another from the New School for Social Research and its rival, Horkheimer's Institute of Social Research, as well as the aid of numerous individuals, including Frederick Pollock, Franz Neumann, and Carl J. Friedrich. In other words, though he had been isolated personally and politically during his years in Nazi Germany, Fraenkel had very quickly resumed contact with the German exile groups and individuals in the United States to whose work his own bore some resemblance.[126] The preface was written in Chicago and dated 15 June 1940, just a week before the signing of the armistice that concluded the German army's shockingly easy defeat of France. The regime that now controlled or intimidated nearly all of continental Europe now held even greater significance for its opponents.

Yet, unlike most of the other books and essays discussed in this chapter, *The Dual State* did not attempt a grand interpretation of National Socialism that compared it to other regimes or examined it as a symptom of larger developments in Western civilization. Fraenkel's analysis focused almost exclusively on legal systems and practices under the Nazi regime: "'Totalitarian' is a word of many meanings too often inadequately defined. In this treatise we have tried to isolate one important characteristic of the totalitarian state in Germany, and by studying this fundamental aspect of the National-Socialist regime we hope to make clearer the legal reality of the Third Reich."[127] Fraenkel worked from no particular general model or menu of characteristics that designated the totalitarian state, as Borkenau tended to do, but instead proceeded in a more rigorously inductive fashion, from concrete details to general conclusions.

Indeed, Fraenkel was leery of the one general model of the totalitarian state that he described, and he took some pains to explain his decision to make only limited use of such a model. His reasons for rejecting the totalitarian state model in 1940 bear closer examination:

> The concept of the "totalitarian state" is not unambiguous. The ambiguity in the term "totalitarian state" may be explained by the fact that there are two types of states with totalitarian tendencies. The common character of the totalitarian tendencies is the subordination of all activities to the ends of the state. This may be done on the one hand in the name of the masses. . . . On the other hand a state may be called totalitarian because of its absolute exercise of power in order to strengthen the state in its external relationships.[128]

Such states would displease conservatives because of their political appeals to the masses and would anger liberals because of their denial of guaranteed rights. This model offered the options of yet another kind of emphasis in the effort to understand the totalitarian state—study of its internal and external political policies. Fraenkel placed his emphasis almost entirely on the former and arrived at an encyclopedic and critical survey of the Nazi legal system that challenged the model of the totalitarian state" a "catchword," as Fraenkel called it, that was already coming into vogue.[129]

In addition to the "ambiguities" Fraenkel located in the totalitarian state concept, he cited problems with one of its formulations taken from Carl Schmitt:

> We have avoided using the term "totalitarian state" because of its complex connotations. Its use in Germany goes back to Carl Schmitt's book *Der Hüter der Verfassung* [The Guardian of the Constitution] where the term totalitarian state was used for the first time in connection with Ernst Jünger's concept of "total mobilization." Carl Schmitt refused to accept a definition of the "totalitarian state" as one which controls every aspect of social and economic life. He distinguished between two types of totalitarianism, the qualitative and the quantitative type.[130]

Schmitt had called the Weimar Republic a "quantitatively totalitarian state," a form that was the sum total of its weaknesses, in his critical view. Fascism, however, represented for Schmitt a "qualitatively totalitarian state." Schmitt's *qualitative* totalitarianism did not attempt to control all aspects of the society and economy—a claim that stood in direct opposition to the typical postwar definition of totalitarianism—but left some room for "a free individual business enterprise and for a public sphere that does not overlap the sphere of the state."[131] Fraenkel offered the opinion that Schmitt's remarks on the qualitative totalitarian state, taken from a speech to an industrial employers' group in November 1932, differed little from the notion of the totalitarian state expressed by a Nazi legal official.[132]

The appearance of Schmitt's ideas in a discussion of totalitarianism by a member of the German Left should by now be no surprise. Like Marcuse and Neumann, Fraenkel gave Schmitt's formulations due attention, but the qualitative totalitarian state theory served for the most part as an occasional reference point, for Fraenkel did not simply accept Schmitt's categories of totalitarianism even though he felt compelled to restate them and made limited use of them. The gap between the Schmittian ideal type of the qualitative totalitarian state and the institutional and practical reality Fraenkel had observed was finally the most compelling reason for his extremely qualified use of the concept. The freedom that the Nazi regime allowed to private enterprise and corporatist "estates," sometimes actually denying the state and police apparatus power over them, indicated that even Schmitt's revision of the totalitarian state concept marked an untenable retreat. Under National Socialism, capitalism remained sacrosanct. A totalitarian state that limited the scope of its own police and regulatory powers and deferred in some cases to the decisions of private groups and individuals was, one might reasonably conclude, a political entity unconcerned about contradictions between its advertised aims of "total" control and the practical means of generating greater wealth and power.[133]

In his denial that the National Socialist state regulated all aspects of the economy, Fraenkel also rejected, by definition, Pollock's concept of state capitalism. As Neumann would do in *Behemoth,* Fraenkel insisted on the close and even cooperative relationship between capitalism and National Socialism: "Faced with the choice between substantial rationality and substantial irrationality, German capitalism casts its vote for the latter. It will accommodate itself to any substantial irrationality if only the necessary pre-requisites for its technically rational order are preserved. . . . This symbiosis of capitalism and National-Socialism finds its institutional form in the Dual State."[134] The persisting anticapitalism of *The Dual State* stands out all the more boldly in the context of Fraenkel's low-key and tightly argued presentation. His simultaneous rejection of both the actual Nazi dictatorship and too simple or too benign theoretical models of dictatorship, such as Schmitt's notion of the totalitarian state, demonstrates the self-conscious attention to theoretical and empirical analysis that marked the best wartime writing by leftists on state-party dictatorship.

In terms of its methodology and its outlook on the behavior of modern dictatorships, Fraenkel's book contributed greatly to the empirical analysis of the Nazi dictatorship. Its detailed arguments about specific laws continue to offer a point of departure for research into the fate of the German legal and governmental systems under Nazi rule.[135] More important, the broad framework of Fraenkel's "dual state" argument, in which he distinguished between the coexisting "prerogative state" and "normative state," has also left its mark on subsequent study of the Nazi regime, as well other totalitarian regimes. The "prerogative state" he identified as the "arbitrary measures (*Massnahmen*), in which the dominant officials exercise their discretionary prerogatives" and in which principles of justice, legal rights, jurisdictional limits, and regulation of politics or government played no role. The aims of the "prerogative state" were overwhelmingly political—and in Nazi Germany "there is nothing which cannot be classified as 'political.'"[136] If the Nazi state were absolutely totalitarian, he argued, the so-called normative state of jurisdictional procedures and protections would have been entirely superseded and absorbed because of the demands of the "prerogative state." Why had this not occurred? Fraenkel claimed that the Nazis' desire to preserve and foster a productive capitalist economy had allowed elements of the "normative state" to survive:

> In spite of the existing legal possibilities for intervention by the Prerogative State where and whenever it desires, the legal foundations of the capitalistic economic order have been maintained. . . .
>
> The courts are responsible for seeing that the principles of the capitalist order are maintained—even though the Prerogative State occasionally exercises its right to deal with individual cases in the light of expediency and the special nature of the case at hand. The decisions show that the courts have successfully maintained the legal system necessary for the functioning of private capitalism. The legal institutions essential to private capitalism, such as freedom of enterprise, sanctity of contracts, private property, the right of the entrepreneur to control labor, regulation of unfair competition, regulation of patent, trade-mark rights, etc., legal protection for interest agreements, property and transfer for purposes of security, still exist in Germany. To this extent the courts have striven to maintain the supremacy of the law. In order that we may not complicate our analysis, we are not considering cases touching on the Jewish problem.[137]

The claim that the normative state's most important role was the protection of capitalism was an essential part of Fraenkel's project of radically qualifying Schmitt's notion of the totalitarian state while simultaneously condemning German capitalism. Such claims about the relationship between the Nazi regime and capitalism have continued for over fifty years now to serve as a focus for important and impassioned debates about the ideological and practical character of German fascism, the relative autonomy of Nazi rule, and, by comparative extension, the similarities and differences between Nazi and Soviet economic policy. Since Fraenkel had extensive knowledge of Nazi legal practice, his readers in the present can only rue the fact that he chose not to discuss in any detail the effects of the "dual state" on the legal status of German Jews.[138]

The broadly Marxian outlook that informed Fraenkel's wartime study stood in contrast to the procapitalist or pro-"mixed economy" arguments that characterized much of the postwar writing on totalitarian dictatorship produced in the Federal Republic. But the questions and issues Fraenkel raised have attracted scholars representing a wide range of methodological and political perspectives. He stands as a key figure in the moderately socialist political science tradition that arose—with important rivals to its right, to be sure—in the postwar period. Indeed, three of these interwar leftists, Fraenkel, Richard Löwenthal, and Ossip Flechtheim, would by the 1960s become professors of political science at the same institution—the Free University of Berlin.

Interestingly, the leftist legal perspective on dictatorship and capitalism common to the work of Fraenkel, Kirchheimer, and Neumann would experience a notable revival during the late 1960s and early 1970s in such journals as *Politische Justiz,* whose very title came from one of Kirchheimer's later books.[139] But while several of Kirchheimer's and Neumann's books of the exile period were republished in German during the 1960s, Fraenkel's book on the Nazi legal system was not available in German until 1974. As evidence of the difficulties that return as well as exile posed even to such successful scholars as Fraenkel, he and Manuela Schöps had to translate *The Dual State* back into German (as *Der Doppelstaat*) from the English version of 1941, because the final version of the German-language manuscript that had been used for that wartime English translation was not preserved.[140] Eagerly received by many young scholars of the German New Left, Fraenkel's book remains a major text in the tradition of democratic socialist critique of the law.

Another key significance of the book in terms of the political and theoretical status of left-wing antitotalitarianism is that Fraenkel's highly qualified and critical use of the idea of totalitarianism alerts us to the ambivalence with which the term was often brought into play in the analysis of actual regimes. As we shall see, Franz Neumann's approach to and use of the related notion of the totalitarian state in *Behemoth* was at once even more critical, more theoretical, and more broadly aimed in its use of empirical evidence than Fraenkel's few references to the notion in his monograph on the Nazi legal system.

Nazism as "Totalitarianism"?

Franz Neumann's *Behemoth* quickly took its place as one of the most authoritative studies of the Nazi regime. Its use of empirical data appealed to an Anglo-American scholarly audience that was more attuned to social scientific argumentation than to the type of philosophical writings produced during the war by Neumann's former institute colleagues, such as Marcuse in *Reason and Revolution* or Horkheimer and Adorno in *Dialectic of Enlightenment*. Neumann's legal expertise as well as his studies with the British social scientist Harold Laski in the early exile years had given him an extraordinary foundation for such a comprehensive study of Germany under Nazi rule.[141] First published in 1942 and revised two years later in a second edition, *Behemoth* was the only one of the wartime texts that attempted systematically to consider several other theoretical approaches to the Nazi order and to provide a corrective to their perceived weaknesses. From the standpoint of a theory of dictatorship that accounts for its own origins and situates itself with respect to other approaches, Neumann's remains a work clearly superior to the others of its day and type. Along with Fraenkel's *Dual State*, *Behemoth* has long served as a model for a social scientific approach that grows out of Marxist theory. As we have seen earlier in this chapter, the book's position in the state capitalism debate was central. This section focuses primarily on *Behemoth*'s various responses to and tentative uses of a notion of the totalitarian state.

Chronologically as well as theoretically, *Behemoth* fell mostly outside the kind of cold war–era perspective on *Totalitarismustheorie* identified with Carl J. Friedrich and Karl Dietrich Bracher, but Neumann's masterful use of empirical evidence and his leftist historical perspective gave his work a unique status. *Behemoth* influenced both Friedrich and Bracher in their investigations of the problem of totalitarian dictatorship.[142] A number of Marxist scholars of the postwar Left have also cautiously approved of Neumann's book. As mentioned in the introduction, Reinhard Kühnl's discussion of Neumann's work in an essay on left-wing versions of totalitarian theory and Eike Hennig's attention to Neumann's atypical "left" version of *Totalitarismustheorie* stand as examples of this approval.[143] Kühnl, in particular, praised Neumann's *Behemoth* and mentioned his limited and nuanced (and Marxian) use of a notion of totalitarianism. But none of these writers analyzed Neumann's actual use of the concept in any detail. Apart from political scientist Alfons Söllner's perceptive discussion of Neumann's distinctive position in the development of theories of totalitarianism, the secondary literature virtually ignores the subject.[144] This neglect of Neumann's approach to and ultimate rejection of the notion of the totalitarian state in *Behemoth* is unfortunate, for such an analytical focus reveals not only his reservations about the term *totalitarian* and its cluster of meanings but also the effort of an important leftist scholar to define an alternative to or at least a correction of the totalitarian state model.

Neumann began his book by redefining the nature of the society he intended to explain. He said that Nazi Germany was becoming a "nonstate," a chaotic social amalgam devoid of a rational basis of order in political theory or governmental practice. With this bold argument, Neumann began, in a sense, with Fraenkel's conclusion. Borrowing from the writings of the Jewish eschatological tradition (with a nod to Hobbes), Neumann labeled the Nazi system "The Behemoth"—the name of the monster who would rule the land just before the end of the world, as Leviathan ruled the sea.[145] A redoubtable rationalist, Neumann undertook an ordered portrait of a system that seemed to spin itself into greater and greater magnitudes of disorder. Although the internal tensions of this project left their traces in the text, Neumann still demonstrated admirable skill at isolating the key elements of the Nazi regime that would make possible a coherent interpretation.

He divided his book into five sections: an introduction that sketched the collapse of the Weimar regime, a study of the political and ideological basis of the Third Reich, an analysis of the German economy under the Nazis, a description of the class character of German society, and a brief summary containing predictions about the likely development of National Socialism. As Ernst Fraenkel had done, Neumann generated a perspective on developments under Nazi totalitarianism that stressed the lack of a rational legal order, but he went far beyond the scope of Fraenkel's work in discussing matters of economic practice and class relations in Nazi Germany.[146] A few sections of the book presented Neumann's distinctive contributions to the critique of totalitarian practice and the concept of totalitarianism that showed an even more emphatic engagement with these problems than Fraenkel's *Dual State*.

Expansions of or revisions of his earlier writings on totalitarian dictatorship emerged early in the text. Neumann's historical section on the collapse of the Weimar Republic showed that he had not pursued the comparative possibilities of his earlier bracketing of the Nazis and Communists as "totalitarian" parties in the 1933 essay, "The Decay of German Democracy." Neumann now qualified the argument that the Weimar Republic fell victim to the combined antidemocratic forces of the Left (Communism) and the Right (National Socialism). Instead, Neumann repeated and intensified his hostility to the leadership and the decisions of the Social Democratic Party. He wrote, for instance, with unconcealed scorn of the deal the Social Democratic Party leader Friedrich Ebert had cut with the German Army High Command in November 1918, and he made a point of disputing, though with respectful delicacy, Arthur Rosenberg's dismissal of General Wilhelm Groener's later testimony that substantiated Ebert's hostility to revolution ("Bolshevism") at the time.[147] At times, Neumann seemed to lay the blame for the demise of the Weimar Republic at the feet of the Social Democrats, dismissing the view of the Prussian Social Democrat Otto Braun that Versailles and Moscow were to blame: "That the Social Democratic party failed remains the crucial fact, regardless of any official explanation. It failed because it did not see that the central problem was the imperialism of German monopoly capital, becoming ever more urgent with the continued growth of the process of monopolization. The more monopoly grew, the more incompatible it became with the political democracy."[148] No text we have discussed placed such heavy emphasis on the responsibility of the Social Democrats for the collapse of Weimar democracy, and this is one element of Neumann's book that makes it a controversial text even today.

Other portions of the text attended more directly to the theoretical and practical issue of the totalitarian state. But Neumann had no comparative model to articulate or Red-Brown fascism argument to make, à la Borkenau or Rühle. Instead, Neumann measured the totalitarianism concept as formulated by the Nazis themselves against his assessment of the Nazi regime's actual practices: "The idea of the totalitarian state grew out of the demand that all power be concentrated in the hands of the president. Immediately after Hitler's accession to power, political theorists began to make much of the totalitarian idea as elaborated by the constitutional lawyers. All power was to be vested in the state; anything less was sabotage of the National Socialist revolution. The totalitarian state was described as an order of domination and a form of people's community."[149] But this ideal, expressed by such leading figures in the party as Hitler, Goebbels, and Frick, could not be realized.[150] It had to be revised to fit with the existing economic and political conditions.

Entering the scene just before the Nazi takeover with a more flexible version of the totalitarian state argument was Carl Schmitt. Neumann cited precisely the same theoretical distinction articulated in the 1932 speech by Schmitt to the industrialists' group that Fraenkel had, but the tone of his remarks was far less neutral and respectful:

> A special twist given the totalitarian doctrine by Carl Schmitt, the most intelligent and reliable of all National Socialist constitutional lawyers, helped greatly. He made it palatable even to big industry, something he had set out to do as early as 1932. . . . He invented a distinction between two kinds of totality, the Roman and the Germanic. Roman totality was quantitative; the Germanic qualitative. The former regimented all spheres of life, interfering with every human activity. In sharp contrast, the Germanic remained content with a strong and powerful state that demanded full political control but left economic activities unrestricted. Schmitt's doctrine is, of course, no more Germanic than its opposite is Roman.[151]

Schmitt's formula, Neumann offered, was simply a second-rate reformulation of the ideas of the authoritarian liberal theorist Vilfredo Pareto. As propaganda, however, it had served quite well.[152]

For a brief time, according to Neumann, the totalitarian state notion—as revised by Schmitt and Hitler as well, to allow for the continued existence of capitalism—served the practical needs of the more cautious and savvy Hitler faction of the NSDAP in the weeks and months after the *Machtergreifung*. The Hitler faction was interested in maintaining its newly won and fragile internal and international legitimacy in the face of the unrestrained desires of Ernst Röhm's SA faction to "clean house" and seize as much wealth and power as it could. Hitler and his secretary Rudolf Hess, claiming as justification for their actions the need to maintain the necessary conditions for achieving the totalitarian state, declared the army, the civil service, and business sacrosanct. Other institutions and groups—the Reichstag, unions, Jews, social "undesirables," left-wing parties, and the like—were not so fortunate, and again the totalitarian theory of the state was invoked, but this time as a justification for the brutal "synchronization" of all public institutions and activities.[153] Soon the legal basis of the state, the constitution, was so quickly and repeatedly mutilated by various Nazi policies that much of the need for a traditionally legitimate "state" vanished. Nazi success provided its own kind of "legitimacy," and the project of the totalitarian state faded into the background.[154]

As the totalitarian "ideal" diminished in importance, however, the actual development of the German state in the Nazi period exhibited a more complex pattern. Indeed, Neumann argued, tendencies toward the totalitarian state in bureaucratic and military matters accelerated, particularly under the pressures of economic mobilization and war.[155] But these events would simultaneously extend the power of the state and bring it into further conflict with the Nazi Party bureaucracy. Overlapping responsibilities and barely circumscribed spheres of authority constantly plagued state-party relations in Germany. Ultimately, Neumann would hypothesize a kind of stalemate: "The state and the party stand side by side. Legally neither controls the other, each is sovereign in its own field—a constitutional situation which is self-contradictory."[156] The "un-state," or Behemoth, was at its most important and fundamental level a result of the contradiction between, on the one hand, the tendencies toward realization of totalitarian state model and, on the other hand, the resistance to those trends embodied in the irrationality of the Nazi Party movement that had, initially at least, declared the totalitarian state model as its goal and professed to have realized it. Neumann attempted to describe the result of the breakdown or, better put, the inability to achieve this seamless totality of power: "I venture to suggest that we are confronted with a form of society in which the ruling groups control the rest of the population directly, without the mediation of that rational though coercive apparatus hitherto known as the state. This new social form is not yet fully realized, but the trend exists which defines the very essence of the regime."[157] That this new social form was oppressive and brutal was an obvious fact for Neumann, but he did not make a point of calling it "totalitarian" in his conclusion. He had applied the adjective *totalitarian* here and there throughout the text. In his analysis of the economic system of Nazi Germany, he had even found a place of prominence for the term: Totalitarian Monopolistic Economy. But in his discussion of the totalitarian state, his focus narrowed to considerations of its theoretical and propaganda model and the evidence he had assembled regarding the regime's actual behavior. Neumann's research disconfirmed the realization of the totalitarian state model, and he did not attempt, in the Schmittian fashion, to qualify or improve the totalitarian state concept or to replace it under the same heading to make it fit his conclusions. He also diverged from Fraenkel's notion of the dual state, finding in Nazi Germany a structure of rule but not a state.

Behemoth drew favorable notices immediately after its publication. In one of the last review articles he would write before his death, Arthur Rosenberg described Neumann's book on Nazi Germany as an analysis that would be of lasting value for a renewal of political science in the aftermath of liberalism's defeat: "It is a most important part of our fight against Fascism to develop a new theory that fits into the changed world and defeats Fascism on its own field. It is the greatest merit of Neumann's book that it helps to clear the ground for the necessary new political science of our time."[158] Rosenberg's estimation of *Behemoth* as a work that would outlast other contemporary writings on dictatorship proved correct. It remains one of the handful of books written during the war that continues to serve as a major interpretation of Nazi Germany.[159] Even among this handful, only Ernst Fraenkel's *Dual State* and Sigmund Neumann's *Permanent Revolution* approach its importance.[160] The book's role in clearing the way for a "new political science" is another matter, however, since Franz Neumann's blend of historical and systematic analysis represented a waning more than a burgeoning tradition in political science. Nevertheless, no other book of his would have such a lasting impact on scholarship. Despite *Behemoth*'s qualification and ultimate rejection of the theoretical notion of the totalitarian state, this concept would be one to which Neumann would return, with all appropriate ambiguity and skepticism, in the postwar period. In that quite different context, Neumann would sometimes find the totalitarian analogy much more useful and legitimate.

Arthur Rosenberg's old comrade Karl Korsch agreed that Neumann's book was of great importance as a description of National Socialism, but he offered a sharply different appraisal of *Behemoth*'s value as a contribution to political theory. Korsch welcomed Neumann's effort to fill a "deplorable gap in the current anti-totalitarian literature," but he made no secret of his disagreement with Neumann's moderate and parliamentary socialist perspective.[161] For example, Korsch criticized Neumann's "legal mind" insofar as Neumann concerned himself too greatly with constitutional traditions, rational positive law, and the fate of the German state with or without the Nazis.[162]

Even more puzzling to Korsch were Neumann's efforts to unravel the twists and turns of Nazi ideology even as Neumann protested that no consistent Nazi ideology could be isolated and analyzed, only a series of makeshift slogans and programs that had been thrown aside as soon as they were no longer serviceable. Korsch complained that Neumann's assertion that Nazi ideology "offers the best clue to its ultimate aims" was not only distracting but also dangerous, and he claimed that "quite often" Neumann "himself inadvertently falls for an outright fascist idea."[163] Just which fascist ideas Neumann "fell for," Korsch did not mention, however.

Korsch next took Neumann to task for failing to reconcile his critique of those who characterized the Nazi economy as state capitalism with his own inability to conceive of the state itself as "an instrument of the ruling industrial class." In other words, according to Korsch, Neumann retained both a Marxian view of the Nazi economy and a non-Marxian (though from Korsch's perspective, annoyingly Social Democratic) regard for the ability of the Weimar state and some future German parliamentary state to mitigate or control monopoly capitalism: "If the main cause of the present unsatisfactory state of affairs is the collapse of that system of checks and balances by which the wild and insatiable forces of monopoly capitalism were controlled and restrained at the time when there was still a real 'state,' the first thing that is required after victory to destroy the scourge of Nazism is to restore the genuine political democracy of the Weimar Republic."[164] Korsch's ironic intent with these remarks was quite clear, for he found this conclusion derived from Neumann's thinking about the role of the state particularly weak. At least, he concluded, Neumann himself provided evidence that he knew a return to Weimar would not be desirable even if it were possible.[165]

Almost certainly Korsch's harsh and sometimes unfounded criticisms of Neumann's book were aimed also at Korsch's old nemesis, the SPD, and perhaps also, though indirectly, at the Institute of Social Research. Korsch had described the personnel of the institute in coolly hostile terms a few years before the review article, and he had been recently disappointed when he was approached for an article for the institute's journal (published in the United States as *Studies in Social Science and Philosophy*) only to be put off sometime later.[166] Neumann's former affiliation with the SPD made him a particularly splendid target for Korsch's wrath against what he regarded as the sloppy theory of reformists—hence the article's draft title identifying Neumann as an SPD spokesman ("A Social Democrat Looks at Totalitarianism") when this was certainly no longer the case— and Korsch's incorrect presumption of Neumann's continuing close relationship with the Horkheimer circle also set Neumann up as a scapegoat in the matter of Korsch's own unhappy relationship with the institute. Perhaps unfortunately, the review did not lead to any documented exchange between Korsch and Neumann. In fact, *Behemoth*'s author might never have seen Korsch's review, for it was eventually published under a different title ("The Structure and Practice of Totalitarianism") in the small circulation journal *New Essays*.[167]

For all his carping about Neumann's book, however, Korsch himself soon arrived at some quite similar conclusions about the Nazi regime in a 1943 lecture he gave to a group of scholars in Seattle. He insisted on the capitalist character of the German economy, he listed virtually the same groups that Neumann had—the party, the business elite, and the state bureaucracy—as the "ruling class" of Germany, and he figured that external military defeat (not an internal workers' revolt) would be the end of "totalitarian Germany."[168]

Korsch did stress the importance of the connection between Hitler and the military elite far more than Neumann had done. In fact, their arguments on this single point were strongly at odds. Here is Neumann's judgment on the role of the army in the Nazi regime:

> The German army leadership, like the ministerial bureaucracy, is probably not National Socialist, strictly speaking. No one really knows anything about the exact relation between the party and the armed forces. One guess is as good as another. . . .
>
> It is not true that the army rules Germany. It has never done so and does not now. In fact, it does so less today than in any previous war. At the same time, the army is the sole body in present-day Germany that has known how to keep itself organizationally free from party interference. Through its economic generals, in fact, the army has encroached upon the party and the civil bureaucracies.[169]

Korsch offered a markedly different assessment, emphasizing the powerful role of the German army in shaping the Nazi regime: "that comparatively small number of the officers [*sic*] caste of the old imperial army who maintained their supreme control over the foreign as well as the domestic politics of Germany through the whole interlude of the Weimar republic and oppenly [*sic*] reasserted it with the advent of the new Nazi-Empire."[170] Perhaps Korsch's much longer and more distressing involvement in World War I fueled his wrath against the German military. Korsch even warned that the officer corps of "totalitarian Germany" would continue to pose the gravest of postwar dangers.[171] Clearly there was a great distance between the two men's views on the role of the military in Nazi Germany.

A more important difference in the two thinkers' attitudes from the standpoint of theory is that Neumann was far more interested in a class-based analysis of the Nazi regime that stressed the direct role of capitalist economics, while Korsch was, in this essay at least, willing to see the power of economic status and capitalist production mediated in crucial ways by the military institutions and individuals who had acted to preserve capitalist class relations but were not necessarily themselves capitalists. Korsch's 1943 presentation does not fit well with the ultraorthodoxy of his essays of 1939–41 on counterrevolution or his hostility to Neumann's *Behemoth*, a book that was for the most part straightforwardly Marxist.

Korsch also alluded to the possibilities of future collaboration between "totalitarian and anti-progressive forces everywhere," with a déclassé military elite forming the nucleus of such a coalition. He also stressed the connection between both world wars in a fashion that partially antici- pated the claims about German expansionism put forth by the historian Fritz Fischer in the 1960s. In sketching this picture of postwar dangers, Korsch indicated that portions of the German and Italian military elites were an even greater danger to "the anti-totalitarian alliance," as he called it, than Hitler and the Nazis themselves—or their industrial-capitalist fel- low travelers. He also discussed the differential effects of the Nazi takeover on a variety of classes and groups, emphasizing the role of the lower middle classes as supporters of Nazism, as in most typical Marxist analy- ses of that time, but he did not leave the complicated matter of partial working-class support for and involvement in Nazism out of the picture. Though he continued to emphasize the tendencies of economic produc- tion as central to the development of Nazi Germany, it must be said that Korsch was not one to stick to orthodox formulas when he glimpsed ana- lytical problems that a reductively economistic or "vulgar Marxist" type of class analysis could not solve.[172] The oscillation between orthodoxy and heterodoxy that marked his later writings lies at the heart of the ambiva- lent character and the mixed reception of that work. But in his wartime essays, Korsch only occasionally exhibited the tendency to veer away from a Marxist class-based critique of dictatorship, or "totalitarian fascism," that became typical of others in this group of German socialists.

In his insistence on the progressive (and at least potentially revolu- tionary) character of the German working class, Korsch remained unre- servedly Marxist. This again stands in marked contrast to Neumann, who persisted in a more traditionally Marxist theoretical model of Nazi economics in *Behemoth* but had already retreated from the notion of the inherently progressive and revolutionary potential of the workers. In view of the deep tensions in their theoretical and their political out- looks, it is no wonder that the two men remained alienated to some extent from both American liberalism and the Marxist Left during the 1950s. The marginalization of Korsch, in particular, both on the left and in the nation of his exile (the United States), a fate that Lukács noted and used to legitimate his own rather more tactful behavior toward the Com- munist Party apparatus, finds ample substantiation in the desultory character of his career during and after the wartime period.[173] Korsch moved from one short-term professorship to another, never finding permanent academic employment, and his fragmentary critical writings on the problem of "counterrevolutionary totalitarianism" have not gained much attention.[174]

Perhaps it was as he surveyed his own meager prospects in 1941 that Korsch was at last moved to grudging praise for the Horkheimer circle (though his personal animosity never flagged) in a letter to a friend: "[T]hey have done better than I should have expected. It is a sad fact that one may have to acknowledge today what one would have despised some years ago but the gods are with those who do something whatever might have been done but has not been done in fact by others."[175] As Korsch wrote this rueful assessment of the work of the Institute of Social Research, two of its leading figures, Horkheimer and Adorno, were about to take up a project that would result in one of the most important books of philosophy written during the wartime years.

The Critique of Totalitarian Reason

Members of the Institute of Social Research underwent yet another series of moves and political transformations during and immediately after the war. Horkheimer's relocation from New York to California led to a cutback in the staff of the institute. In the face of these changes and in order to support their families, Marcuse and Neumann took up work with the U.S. military's Office of Strategic Services (OSS). Two other institute colleagues, Arkadij Gurland and Otto Kirchheimer, soon joined them. Neumann and Kirchheimer in turn helped Henry Pachter acquire a position with the Office of European Economic Research, which was affiliated with the OSS. Friedrich Pollock served as a consultant to the antitrust division of the U.S. Department of Justice, and another member of the institute, Leo Lowenthal, worked with the Office of War Information. But the group's research and writing efforts continued, even as the institute experienced the disruptions and reconfigured political orientations of the wartime years. One of the institute's research associates, the ex-Communist Paul Massing, was working on a study of anti-Semitism in Imperial Germany, *Rehearsal for Destruction*. At the same time, his wife, Hede Massing—Ruth Fischer's former sister-in-law—was reaching the end of her involvement with Communism. Another institute affiliate, Karl Wittfogel, had also broken with the Communist Party, at the time of the Hitler-Stalin Pact, and, throughout the exile years, he produced numerous articles and papers that drew on the research he had been pursuing on Chinese civilization. By the end of the war, however, he was at a great intellectual and personal distance from Horkheimer. Wittfogel's role with the institute had long been a marginal one, but his final break with the group was another symptomatic shift that augured the political and ideological battles of the cold war.

Institute publications as well as personal careers underwent a change in focus and direction. A broadly conceived project on anti-Semitism clearly demonstrated Horkheimer's concern about analyzing this crucial element of Nazi propaganda and policy in its historical, psychological, and cultural origins and manifestations. But by the end of 1941, the *Zeitschrift für Sozialforschung* and its American version, *Studies in Philosophy and Social Science,* had ceased publication. Even so, the intellectual productivity of the institute's members—old and new, marginal contributors and "inner circle" members—reached a pitch of collective intensity and quality during the wartime years. At about the time that Marcuse's *Reason and Revolution* and Neumann's *Behemoth* were published, Horkheimer began work with his longtime institute colleague Theodor Adorno on another major book project.[176]

Adorno's work has been neglected or marginalized in the history of concepts of totalitarianism, yet his contribution is discernible and distinctive.[177] This neglect emerges from the contested and often highly politicized response to totalitarian theories. Scholars on the left would tend to separate Adorno from what they regard as cold war ideology (or to criticize his near approach to it), while liberal or conservative scholars might not see how Adorno's writings have anything in common with the work of such people as Friedrich, Arendt, or Bracher.[178] The institute's brilliant polymath, Adorno initially gained a reputation for his writings on music and philosophy. Born in Frankfurt am Main in 1903, Theodor Wiesengrund-Adorno grew up in an atmosphere of material comfort and cultural attainment, provided by his father's successful business and his mother's and aunt's strong musical talents. A precocious member of the circle around composer Arnold Schoenberg, Adorno pursued his university education at the Goethe University in Frankfurt, completing a dissertation on the phenomenologist Edmund Husserl, but he also studied Kant with a family friend, the prolific and independent-minded scholar of culture Siegfried Kracauer. By the mid-1920s, Adorno's circle of friends and acquaintances included the composers Ernst Krenek, Hanns Eisler, and Kurt Weill; the singer-actress Lotte Lenya; the poet-playwright Bertolt Brecht; the essayist Walter Benjamin; the philosopher Ernst Bloch, and, of course, Max Horkheimer. Most of these individuals were decidedly to the left politically, and Adorno himself joined in the reconsiderations of philosophical Marxism inspired by the writings of Georg Lukács, especially *History and Class Consciousness.* During the early exile years, which he spent largely in London, Adorno wrote for the *Zeitschrift für Sozialforschung* and joined the institute in the United States only in 1938. For several years, his work stood sharply apart from the economic and political studies of Neumann and Kirchheimer, and he tended to have less to say about political issues than either Horkheimer or Marcuse. But Adorno's intellectual influence on Horkheimer grew during the exile years, and he followed Horkheimer and Pollock soon after they moved to Santa Monica, California. There, the convergence of some of Adorno's and Horkheimer's ideas on the crises of contemporary culture and their roots in the oppressive and rapidly multiplying power of instrumental reason and "enlightened" civilization led to a path-breaking collaboration. They began work on the components of a manuscript, originally entitled *Philosophische Fragmente,* analyzing the roots of the contemporary crisis of civilization in the early 1940s, completed the draft in 1944, and published it with an additional section on anti-Semitism three years later in Amsterdam.[179]

The book that resulted from this authorial partnership, *Dialektik der Aufklärung (Dialectic of Enlightenment),* veered away from the path of virtually all other left-wing critiques of totalitarianism. It clearly parted company even with those texts of other institute thinkers that focused on the origins and the character of the state-party dictatorship, even though it bears an identifiable relation to that type of critique. The filigree net of its theoretical apparatus caught and held some Marxian concepts—the irrationality of market capitalism, the alienation of the human subject, reification, the role of ideology in structures of culture and power—but it let others, such as the primacy of class conflict, the necessary and inevitable proletarian revolution, and the model of historically progressive economic development, slip on through. Of the books that participated in the left-wing antitotalitarian discussions that took place during wartime, only Marcuse's *Reason and Revolution* demonstrated a similarly strong philosophical orientation.[180] Yet even Marcuse did not venture so broad an argument—in either its historical or its conceptual scope—as the one that Horkheimer and Adorno attempted. Because of its assertions about totalitarianism and the manner in which it strove to transcend traditional Marxist categories of social analysis even as it acknowledged some of their lasting power, the book requires consideration in this study. The project of this section is not to analyze the book's arguments in all their detail but to define and interpret its unusual construction of the problem of totalitarianism.

In *Dialectic of Enlightenment,* Horkheimer and Adorno did not expressly locate the origins of totalitarianism primarily in economic crisis, fascism, Bolshevism, or the ideology of Nazism. They certainly referred directly and indirectly to this related cluster of factors in the course of their arguments, but they viewed them as intensified recent moments in the development of technically oriented rationality in the West, which was to them the chief culpable historical process. Stated as boldly and provocatively as possible, the thesis of their book was "Enlightenment is totalitarian."[181] But the arguments that followed were subtle and complex. The book remains in some ways the most troubling of all the critiques of an intractable problem identified as "totalitarianism" that has yet appeared, precisely because of its radical character and its authors' only partial hope of finding political or cultural solutions to the pervasive problem of totalitarian reason.

In a fashion markedly different from Borkenau's and with a different audience in mind, Adorno and Horkheimer were also undertaking a clear departure from Marxism to offer a critical history of the current world crisis. Martin Jay has aptly characterized this aspect of Horkheimer and Adorno's intellectual project:

> In calling Horkheimer's and Adorno's critique "radical," the word should be understood in its etymological sense of going to the roots of the problem. This is especially important to grasp in view of the Frankfurt School's growing distrust of what passed for "radical" politics in later years. Paradoxically, as the theory became more radical, the Institut found itself decreasingly capable of finding a connection to radical praxis. The desperate hopes of Horkheimer's wartime essay on the "Authoritarian State" soon gave way to a deepening gloom about the chances for meaningful change. Disillusioned with the Soviet Union, no longer even marginally sanguine about the working classes of the West, appalled by the integrative power of mass culture, the Frankfurt School traveled the last leg of its long march away from orthodox Marxism.[182]

To Jay's succinct account of the development of Horkheimer's and Adorno's thought during the 1940s, one might add that *Dialectic of Enlightenment* can also be read as yet another text in the heterogeneous tradition of German socialist antitotalitarian writings, which, as we have seen, often served as avenues away from orthodox Marxism—Borkenau's, Löwenthal's, Hilferding's, perhaps even Korsch's, as well as those of several others who had been at one time associated with the Frankfurt Institute.

In Adorno and Horkheimer's critique, the terms *fascism* and the *totalitarian state* were used interchangeably. In this terminological matter, their work did not differ much from that of other left-wing writers of the period. But in the long-range historical perspective of their work, which understood the totalitarian state as an inherent potential of Western rational culture, they stood apart from all other writers. They broadened the historical boundaries of their investigations, but it was clear that their approach had no aspiration to be a systematic, narrative historical investigation of the process of enlightenment. They focused on only a few crucial cultural moments in the long epoch of Western civilization: the Homeric tale of Odysseus (the epic of self-repression), the *Juliette* of Sade (the story of efficient brutality), the modern "culture industry" (the administration of mass deception), and anti-Semitism (the social mechanism of paranoia). Their remarks on fascism and the totalitarian state were scattered and do not constitute an attempt at the kind of comparison and empirical analysis favored by Borkenau, Löwenthal, and especially Neumann. Nevertheless, Horkheimer and Adorno portrayed the dangers posed by "totalitarian reason" as fundamental, and it is therefore necessary to piece together some of the elements of this problematic as it appears in the text.

The adjective *totalitarian* emerged in the vocabulary of Adorno and Horkheimer not as an all-purpose term describing state-party regimes but as a label the two theorists had attached to the unifying and flattening character of an instrumentalized reason that did not tolerate anything it could not organize. Opposition to totalitarianism in their conception of the problem rested on a philosophical resistance to the Hegelian notion of totality, which merged the subject and the object of philosophical understanding into a single, seamless conceptual entity. In other words, they rejected the totalitarian world that permitted no gap between the concept of social totality and its realization. Totalitarian states were, to these thinkers, a disastrous outcome of this "identity theory" as it was realized in the sphere of political and economic behavior.[183] As Martin Jay has argued, "In this view, totality became little more than a synonym for totalitarianism."[184] Insisting on "difference" and "negation" of the social totality as essential principles and performances of critical philosophy and as social and political values as well, Horkheimer and Adorno attacked the Western cultural tradition for generating the technological means of repression and the intolerant ideology of power as its own reward that culminated in the destruction of all space in which individuals might develop and preserve their uniqueness. The "base" of their theoretical model now replaced conflicts involving Marxian class struggle with a broadly conceived dialectic of civilizing processes stressing conflicts between humans and nature (the technological dimension of organized society), within humans themselves (the psychological dimension of individuals in society), and between reason's program of enlightenment and its program of control (which became manifest in both technology and political repression—the totalitarian state).

A few of the book's many references to political theory and practice indicate the accuracy of Jay's remarks about the pair's pessimism. A reference from the "Notes and Drafts" section entitled "On the Critique of the Philosophy of History"—"the philosophy of history" was the authors' coded term for Marxism—shows how deeply their disappointment ran:

> The authors [of the philosophy of history] identified themselves against their own will with the suppression which they wanted to abolish. The philosophy of history repeats a process which occurred in Christianity: the goodness which in reality remains at the mercy of suffering is concealed as the force which determines the course of history and ultimately triumphs. It is idolized as the spirit of the world or as an immanent law. In this way, however, history is transformed directly into its opposite, and the idea itself (which wanted to arrest the logical course of events) is distorted. . . . Christianity, idealism, and materialism, which in themselves contain truth, are therefore also responsible for the barbaric acts perpetrated in their name. As representatives of power—even if of power for good—they themselves became historical forces which could be organized, and as such played a bloody role in the true history of the human race: that of the instruments of organization.[185]

Marxism, in other words, could not be trusted to correct itself. It might do so, but its paradoxically transhistorical claims to truth and its commitment to praxis left the matter in doubt, to say the least. The political point that Horkheimer and Adorno advanced here bespoke a fastidious caution. The authors had delicately rested their critique of Marxism (under an alias) on the evidence (uncited and unexplained) of the Soviet Union's violent new society (unmentioned).

Fascism offered to Horkheimer and Adorno even more horrifying and identifiable examples of the perverse workings of civilization, in which only the worst potentials of historical development were realized and reason and resistance eventually were bent to serve primal impulses of unreason and violent oppression:

> The carefully thought out symbols (which are proper to every counterrevolutionary movement), the skulls and disguises, the barbaric drum beats, the monotonous repetition of words and gestures, are simply the organized imitation of magic practices, the mimesis of mimesis. The leader with his contorted face and the charisma of approaching hysteria take command.

The leader acts as a representative; he portrays what is forbidden to every-one else in actual life. Hitler can gesticulate like a clown, Mussolini strike false notes like a provincial tenor, Goebbels talk endlessly like a Jewish agent whom he wants murdered, and Coughlin preach love like the sav-ior whose crucifixion he portrays—all for the sake of still more bloodshed. Fascism is also totalitarian in that it seeks to make the rebellion of sup-pressed nature against domination directly useful to domination.

This machinery needs the Jews. Their artificially heightened promi-nence acts on the legitimate son of the gentile civilization like a magnetic field. The gentile sees equality, humanity, in his difference from the Jew, but this induces a feeling of antagonism and alien being. And so impulses which are normally taboo and conflict with the requirements of the pre-vailing form of labor are transformed into conforming idiosyncrasies.[186]

The spectacular success of fascism in this project of securing the totalitar-ian entrapment of reason and rebellion in the logic of their own impera-tives simply multiplied the skepticism and pessimism to which the book gave voice. The rationalized unleashing of violence relied on the indi-vidual willing to obey in order to gain permission to "return to the mi-metic practice of sacrifice."[187] In the culminating realization of their in-tent, the Nazis' propaganda and ceremonial imagery of death sanctioned murder.

Only Wilhelm Reich's *Mass Psychology of Fascism* (1933) and Erich Fromm's *Escape from Freedom* (1941) can be compared with *Dialectic of Enlightenment* as contemporary left-wing attempts to reveal the psycho-logical elements of the violent new totalitarian movements.[188] But in ad-dition to this passage's powerful effort to explain the appeal and the ef-fects of the Nazi dictatorship, it shows how Adorno and Horkheimer had begun to link their critique of totalitarian domination more closely to a critique of anti-Semitism. A few years earlier, in 1939, even after exposure to abundant evidence of Nazi attacks on German Jews and other European Jews, their property, and their rights, Horkheimer's analysis of anti-Semitism in the essay "Die Juden und Europa" ("The Jews and Europe") showed little advance on the typically economistic explanations of anti-Semitism offered by orthodox Marxists (starting with Marx himself), though it did attend to some of the historical transformations of anti-Semitism that had appeared in the context of political crisis and economic change since World War I. As several historians have argued, anti-Semitism was central to Nazi ideology but was not the Nazis' sole or most effective propaganda vehicle even in the late Weimar years. As the Nazis gained political supporters, anti-Semitism certainly persisted in Nazi speeches but not always at the same level of intensity. Moreover, while there was active German participation in the so-called *Kristallnacht* anti-Jewish pogrom in November 1938, there was also widespread criticism. In short, the route from the Nazi seizure of power in 1933 to the genocide of the war years appears not to have been so direct as some scholars argue.[189]

There is, then, a plausible explanation for Horkheimer's apparent inattention to the deadly character of Nazi anti-Semitism in his prewar writings. As the historians Dan Diner and Christopher Browning have pointed out in different contexts, even in 1939 the mass murder of Jewish Germans and other European Jews was months away. The Nazi policy of genocide accelerated its murderous operations as the war itself exploded into greater levels of violence, starting in 1941. Diner maintains that the famous sentence in Horkheimer's essay, "Whoever refuses to speak of capitalism should also remain silent on fascism," must be read in terms of its prewar context. "Die Juden und Europa" also argued that anti-Semitism and National Socialism were tightly bound together; indeed, the essay opened with that assertion. But Horkheimer clearly did not view anti-Semitism as a given historical entity of an unvarying and inevitably murderous intensity. In Horkheimer's view, Jews functioned for the Nazis as a personified (and, because of long-standing anti-Semitic prejudices among Christians, readily available) target for their rage against the economic and social relations of the liberal, bourgeois order.[190]

To an extent, such an interpretation could be seen as an updated version of the critique of anti-Semitism as "the socialism of fools," to borrow the German Social Democrat August Bebel's phrase. But Horkheimer's statements also clearly relied on Pollock's notion of state capitalism, which argued that the state had usurped the traditional capitalizing and profit-making roles of corporations and financial institutions. Horkheimer's use of this premise led him to conclude that the recent shift toward state capitalism had nullified the role of Jews in those segments of the economy in which they had been particularly important.[191] Horkheimer's argument clearly attacked fascism, but it also aimed at liberal capitalism as the system that had spawned the Nazi regime. In "Die Juden und Europa," which Horkheimer completed on 1 September 1939, according to his own statement at the end of the article—the day Germany invaded Poland—Central European Jews, in their everyday reality as an internally diverse religious and ethnic community that had been swiftly and brutally disenfranchised during the 1930s and now stood under dire threat, held virtually no place. Jews served as a kind of functional category in the service of what remained an analysis based primarily on economic considerations. Horkheimer and Adorno's mode of understanding and explaining anti-Semitism soon began to change, however.[192]

In *Dialectic of Enlightenment,* Horkheimer and Adorno attended far more carefully to the psychological and cultural components of Nazi anti-Semitism as well as to the more frequently noted economic elements of this ideology. As Dan Diner and Martin Jay have both argued, the discussion of anti-Semitism in the book gathered fragmentary insights and suggested possible routes toward a more systematic critique. It is true that for all the persisting traces of an economistic type of Marxist treatment of the topic, the authors' insights into anti-Semitism continued to develop in the direction of a more nuanced and revealing Marxian critique of ideology that such essays as Marcuse's critique of the totalitarian view of the state had mapped out a decade earlier.[193] But these densely packed and suggestive passages—none longer than a dozen or so pages, the last added in 1947—cannot be described as a full-blown theory of anti-Semitism. Moreover, no politics emerged from this theorizing about anti-Semitism. The "powerlessness of the working class" that Horkheimer had described at the end of the Weimar Republic now seemed transformed into the authors' intriguing but also politically marooned notion of the powerlessness of theory. In their discussion of anti-Semitism, the authors at least began to probe the elements of Nazi race hatred in terms of their psychological, behavioral, and ideological effects on individuals and society at large. This step marked a significant interpretive advance for a critical approach that continued to show at least tentative connections to the Marxian Left, even when compared with the earlier efforts at a critique of dictatorship developed by such scrupulous analysts as Fraenkel and Neumann, for instance, whose efforts at understanding Nazism offered cautious and limited attention to anti-Semitism. Along with this gain in the analytical force of critical theory, however, came the dismaying political implications of *Dialectic of Enlightenment.*

The book contains one of the most provocative and far-reaching critiques of Western civilization ever constructed, though it can also be interpreted as a kind of desperate rescue operation on that same civilization. By thrusting before the reader the contradiction between the claims to progress and the actual barbaric state of the world, Adorno and Horkheimer could at least hope for a critical reevaluation of modernity. But their book offered little hope for cultural remedies, let alone political ones. Its authors concluded that a lack of formulas for action was hardly the most demanding problem at that moment. In a knotty concluding passage at the end of the final section, "Elements of Anti-Semitism," a portion of the text that first appeared in the 1947 edition of the book, Adorno and Horkheimer offer one last tempting possibility (couched in a verbal and conceptual hedging of bets) of resistance against the overwhelming tendency toward totalitarian administration that German fascism represented:

> If the progressive ticket strives for something which is worse than its own content, the content of the Fascist program is so meaningless that, as a substitute for something better, it can only be upheld by the desperate efforts of the deluded. Its horror lies in the fact that the lie is obvious but persists. Though this deception allows of no truth against which it could be measured, the truth appears negatively in [the] very extent of the contradiction; and the undiscerning can be permanently kept from that truth only if they are wholly deprived of the faculty of thought. Enlightenment which is in possession of itself and coming to power can break the bounds [*Grenzen*] of enlightenment.[194]

A radical critique of the totalitarian order, yes, but note how far it lies from the stubbornly Marxist basis of Rühle's and Korsch's theories of revolutionary proletarian praxis. Its political agnosticism also shared little with the perspectives of such thinkers as Borkenau and Löwenthal, who spent the war years as activists and publicists frequently offering specific programmatic recommendations. "The undiscerning" are not a class but a mass without character, thus far incapable of or prevented from critical reason, let alone political revolt. Yet, to be fair, the thesis of *Dialectic of Enlightenment* also lies at a remove from the kind of antirationalist assertions associated with Heideggerian *Existenzphilosophie*.[195] As has often been said of the Horkheimer circle, its critique had no known addressee, save perhaps other theorists. Adorno himself once stated that it was a kind of message in a bottle.[196]

At the time Horkheimer and Adorno were writing *Dialectic of Enlightenment,* their opposition to totalitarianism clearly did not lead to formulas for mass or individual political action; nor was such a project their goal. They had offered an analysis of totalitarianism without projecting any sort of antitotalitarian politics. This distinguished their approach from those of other intellectuals on the left, certainly from Marxists, but also from traditional liberals and conservatives (who often have been very effective in linking theory and practice). The lack of an identifiable positive political argument is perhaps another reason why *Dialectic of Enlightenment* has never made it into the "canon" of antitotalitarian writings. The uncoupling of theory from practice, however useful and justifiable a move it might have been to protect thought from the predations of practical implementation, left Horkheimer and Adorno open to a variety of political and philosophical criticisms from both the Right and the Left. Yet under the conditions of the mid-1940s, political action—even the demand for it—indicated to Horkheimer and Adorno the surrender of theory to practice, the loss of the particular in the universal, and it served to accelerate tendencies toward centralized and totalitarian social administration. In fact, leading members of the institute always feared the possibility of totalitarian repression in their place of exile, the United States. As even one of the more sympathetic historians of their efforts has pointed out, they never looked closely for the reasons why this trend toward totalitarianism did not manifest itself in the United States to the extent that it had in Europe.[197] Given the traumatic experiences and understandings that were accumulated by German leftist exiles during the dozen years of the Nazi dictatorship, such fears about the possibility of oppression or even attack are not too surprising. Arguably the events that ended the war in 1945 also confirmed some of their worst fears: the use of atomic weapons represented yet another example of instrumentalized reason in the service of violence.

Even so, the political despair and passivity to which Adorno and Horkheimer's analysis led have long generated criticism from a variety of perspectives, especially from the Left.[198] To a limited extent, Horkheimer can be answered even from the perspective of his own earlier writings. As the Weimar Republic careened to its end, Horkheimer had argued that the powerlessness of the working class had resulted from, among other things, the lack of theory. Now Horkheimer and Adorno could be accused of acquiescing in a similar powerlessness, but lack of theory was hardly the problem. There was an overabundance of theory—but an asymmetrical version of it. *Dialectic of Enlightenment* had generated an indelible image of Enlightenment's instrumentalized reason as inexorably oppressive, a dynamic, omnivorous system, yet a system guided by fixed imperatives. By the close of World War II, however, a too selective field of historical vision had blinded Horkheimer and Adorno to a more nuanced view of "Enlightenment" itself as both an historical moment and as an historical process (not, of course, to be confused with simplistic, linear notions of historical "progress"). Stephen Bronner has pointed out that the values that grounded the effective practical and philosophical *opposition* to fascism in the West (not to mention Communism in the East)—limits on state power, openness to alternative explanations of natural or social reality, and the emancipatory traditions of "republicanism, socialism, and internationalism" could all be traced to the liberal legacy of the Enlightenment.[199] It is not necessary to champion such values as the unfailing antidote to "totalitarian reason," but their evident persistence represented the possibility of retaining (or regaining) precisely that crucial space that lay between the idea of social totality and its realization—a gap that could be used for the consideration or enaction of emancipatory ideas and politics. Horkheimer and Adorno had come quite close to declaring such a possibility dead. The theorists who had so tellingly criticized "the philosophy of history" at last omitted too much history—both past and present—from their account of philosophy. But in a move typical of this pair of thinkers, they appear to have anticipated this kind of criticism in their critique of Kantian ethics, a critique that historicized the efforts of "bourgeois" philosophy to construct a barricade against the consequences of its own corrosive power: "The moral teachings of the Enlightenment bear witness to a hopeless attempt to replace enfeebled religion with some reason for persisting in society when interest is absent. . . . It is the conventional attempt of bourgeois thought to ground respect, without which civilization cannot exist, upon something other than material interest and force; it is more sublime and paradoxical than, yet as ephemeral as, any previous attempt."[200] Leaving no privileged position—or even a hiding place—for liberal optimism and ethical appeals to reason, Horkheimer and Adorno held to an image of reason as the inevitable, even if unwilling, servant of power. The totalitarian state was not a deviation or detour away from the advance of reason; it was reason's political apotheosis. This passage also hinted at Horkheimer's later retreat back to the terrain of cautious bourgeois convention and the reconsideration of religious yearnings, however "enfeebled." Certainly no unproblematic return to Marxism could now be undertaken.[201] Adorno continued to appropriate Marxian analytical tools in the analysis of culture, but the situation of culture and society appeared to him as it did to Horkheimer: a Marxist politics simply perpetuated some of the most dangerous notions of progress and totality. Adorno's later writings on culture insisted on particularity, dissonance, and discrete aesthetic moments—missed or realized. His friendship with Horkheimer persisted throughout the remainder of their lives, but their projects tended to diverge.[202] *Dialectic of Enlightenment* remained their one significant collaboration. Emanating from a strangely and only partially sheltered place in an alien land during the most violent decade in human history, it represented a timely and fundamental reappraisal of civilization and of the prospects for its "improvement." For the sheer discomforting boldness of its critique, the book continues to demand attention. But in its refusal of politics, *Dialectic of Enlightenment* offered at best a temporary place of refuge for social theory.

The political pressures of the early postwar era had yet to gain their full force when further splits among the members of the antitotalitarian Left began to appear. The postwar fate of the Institute of Social Research is a case in point. While Marcuse kept trying to discover theoretical and practical ways to reverse the long retreat of radical politics, Horkheimer and Adorno remained unconvinced of the possibility for societal change in the direction of freedom. In 1946, Marcuse urged Horkheimer to reestablish the *Zeitschrift,* but Horkheimer refused. Economic circumstances and his wife's illness compelled Marcuse to continue to work in U.S. government service until the early 1950s, when he was at last able to secure a teaching job.[203] His subsequent experiments in radical theory had increasingly less in common politically with Horkheimer's and Adorno's writings, though his arguments often rested on similar theoretical foundations. Even after they reestablished the institute in Frankfurt, Horkheimer and Adorno pursued their projects in relative isolation, for in their view, the primary item on the postwar social agenda was the refinement of technologically assisted administrative capacity, with all the horrors such bland language concealed: the totalitarian rationalization of unreason.

It should be quite clear by now that there was no developed left-wing "school of thought" on totalitarianism. The examples of antitotalitarian theory examined in this chapter formed no single, cohesive outlook and were not, to say the least, stages on the way to a left-wing consensus on the problem of "totalitarian dictatorship," "state capitalism," or the role of "totalitarian enlightenment." But the revivals, revisions, and even the rejections of Marxian theory, particularly the left-wing theories of dictatorship, do indicate at least the common understanding of most of these thinkers that both the remnants of Second International Marxism and its primary intraleft opponent, Leninism, had proven utterly incapable of meeting the theoretical and practical challenges posed by the modern totalitarian state. The left-wing opponents of state-party dictatorship were also alike in their evident understanding of the need for careful choices in the method and object of their analyses and in their attention to the likely political consequences of those choices. Moreover, apart from Adorno and Horkheimer, they often attempted to follow the Marxist tradition of unifying theory and practice, however ineffective these efforts may have been in terms of their political results. During the war and immediately afterward, several of these thinkers became directly active in military intelligence or occupation efforts that took them far from their earlier careers and political commitments. Borkenau served with a press service attached to the U.S. Army's occupation forces in 1945–46. In 1944, Fraenkel produced a book on the occupation of Germany after World War I that clearly anticipated the occupation of Germany once again in the near future. Kirchheimer, Neumann, and Marcuse continued to work for the OSS during the war—Marcuse stayed on for several years more with the State Department. What the relative success or failure of these activities can teach about the Left's desire for the unity of theory and practice, however, remains open to debate.[204]

Whatever their wartime fates and commitments, by the end of World War II, German socialist intellectuals had constructed several important approaches to the problem of totalitarian dictatorship. By 1940, Franz Borkenau had already assembled most of the components for the "classic" model-building tradition of cold war antitotalitarianism that linked Nazi Germany and the Soviet Union. During the war years, Richard Löwenthal and his colleagues in Neu Beginnen cautiously used a rudimentary totalitarian theory as a rationale for policy decisions—another precursor of cold war uses of the notion. Rudolf Hilferding constructed a broad version of totalitarian theory that focused on economic policy in the course of a reformist condemnation of Nazi Germany and the Soviet Union, while Karl Korsch and Otto Rühle aimed their radical revolutionary notions of "totalitarian counterrevolution" and "brown and red fascism" as broadsides against these same two regimes as well as the Western capitalist allies. Scholars associated for a time with the Institute of Social Research—in particular Franz Neumann and Otto Kirchheimer—along with Ernst Fraenkel established the basis for a critical left-wing social science that made only cautious and methodologically limited use of schematic models of totalitarian dictatorship, and they subordinated that project to the analysis of empirical evidence from specific case studies and the articulation of a socialist perspective. The surviving core members of the institute, led by Max Horkheimer, Friedrich Pollock, and Theodor Adorno, continued to focus on the ideological manifestations of totalitarianism in terms of its continual rationalization of culture and social control. Herbert Marcuse's postwar work would draw on both of these strands of the institute's theorizing, the social scientific and the philosophical-cultural, but he would attempt to argue in behalf of a more radical politics than would either camp of the interwar and wartime branches of the institute's researchers. In short, the attraction of a comparative analysis of fascist and Communist (and sometime also capitalist) regimes proved irresistible for several German socialist intellectuals, but others extended the range of left-wing theory by creating alternative means of explaining the new systems of power—the Nazi and Stalinist regimes above all.

The concluding chapter of this book traces a few selected examples of the historical transformation of these various conceptual strategies of left-wing antitotalitarianism into the cold war period. It also provides a look at some of the effects of these hard-won perspectives on the work of individual theorists of totalitarianism and other more recent strains of postwar political theory. But the conclusion of this study cannot complete the history of the fate of left-wing antitotalitarianism, for that history continues into the present. As is perhaps all too obvious, elements of each of the antitotalitarian outlooks examined here survived or were reinvented during the postwar period under radically different historical circumstances. Under the pressures of the cold war, left-wing antitotalitarianism would fracture still further, generating a variety of opposed perspectives: ideological justifications for anti-Communist policy and social scientific models of totalitarianism, on the one hand, and radical critiques of both cold war bipolarism and its affiliated versions of the theory of totalitarianism, on the other.

4

TOTALITARIANISM'S TEMPTATIONS: INTO THE COLD WAR

These days, the espousal of Marxism is considered a symptom of national and human degeneracy. At the same time public discussion to a large extent now adopts a concept of dictatorship that was decisively molded by Marxist thought.
—Otto Kirchheimer, 1933

I find it a shame that Professors Marcuse and Löwenthal, with various differences, have used the notion of totalitarianism as a comprehensive concept for different systems. With such a notion the historical dimension gets lost....
—Rudi Dutschke, 1967

The closer one looks at the developing notions of totalitarianism, the more one sees theoretical diversity, methodological controversy, and, above all, the intellectual and rhetorical effort to gain control over contested political terrain. Yet, for these intellectuals of the German Left, this absence of consensus did not indicate that totalitarianism appeared as a theoretical and political problem only "in the eye of the beholder." There were at least two significant points of agreement among this group of writers. First, they unequivocally rejected the models of social and political organization embodied in the regimes of both the Soviet Union and Nazi Germany. Second, all of them persisted, to some extent at least, in expressing a critical attitude toward free market capitalism. In addition, several of them continued to support a fundamental transformation of society—through either reform or revolution—that could reasonably be labeled "socialist." What was often lost or was retained only with a fiercely

173

combative persistence in the cold war years was the articulation of just such a perspective, one that simultaneously challenged the legacy of Nazism, the persistence of the Soviet dictatorship, and the ideological, economic, and political dominance of the Western capitalist powers.

It did not take long for the cold war to produce the characteristic ideological and political formations that, despite a series of challenges, would remain in place for the next four decades. Left-wing antitotalitarianism did not completely disappear, but it became a politically marginalized outlook in both Europe and the United States until the 1960s. Its ambivalent, fragmentary, and yet stubbornly socialist character held relatively little political or theoretical appeal in a time when bipolarism seemed to offer the only "realistic" choices—at least in the Western Allied Zones of Germany and in the United States. In a more politically fluid postwar setting, such as France, for example, where republican traditions had deeper roots than in Germany and where there was a stronger and more oppositional Left dominated by the presence of a large Communist Party, the nuanced political tactics accompanying the search for a "third path"— one that might avoid both the bipolar power grid and the espousal of a Stalinist brand of Marxism—remained options for several years. The celebrated Sartre-Camus debate of 1952 in France departed from both the tone and the form of postwar intellectual politics just across the border.[1] But even the Camus-Sartre exchange marked the end of the most public phase of the "third path" debate, not a significant advance or renewal, and left-wing criticism of the Soviet Union continued to receive hostile responses from the French Communist Left. The French leftist opposition to Soviet policy—even when it also criticized the policies of the United States—remained politically and theoretically isolated for years, as the fate of the Socialisme ou Barbarie group led by Claude Lefort and Cornelius Castoriadis during the 1950s would reveal. The French Communist Party remained the primary institutional voice of the political Left, largely crowding out the moderate Socialist Party and other groups until after the upheavals of 1968.

In the case of the two cold war Germanies, by contrast, the same intraleft conflict took place across as well as within national borders, and the debates over notions of totalitarianism and fascism became even more intensely political battlefields than they would be for years in France. By 1949, the former anti-Nazi Allies and their supporters in each sector sanctioned the creation of two client German states following the dramatic Berlin airlift that foiled the Soviet blockade of the city's western sectors. The forced unification of the Social Democratic and Communist parties in the Socialist Unity Party of Germany (Sozialistische Einheitspartei Deutschlands—SED) of the Soviet sector had embittered many of those who had hoped for some other resolution to the bitter left-wing party battles. Some left-wing intellectuals, however, sensed that the possibility of generating a radical and democratic socialist political movement was at least temporarily moribund even before the creation of the two separate Germanies.[2]

German Socialist Intellectuals after the War

In September 1947, a group of old friends and acquaintances met to discuss the current state of democratic socialism in Germany. Among those in attendance were Franz Neumann and two of his former colleagues from the Institute of Social Research, Arkadij Gurland and Paul Massing. Gurland had been associated with the old Weimar-era ORG led by Walter Löwenheim, and Massing, as previously mentioned, was yet another Weimar Communist who had eventually left the party to embrace parliamentarism and liberal politics.[3] They agreed that since there had been no socialist movement in Germany since 1933, there had been no socialist intellectuals either. They also had nothing but complaints to register about the postwar revival of the SPD. The party had lost touch with any truly democratic impulse, they argued, and its leader, Kurt Schumacher, was content to preside over a remnant of the party's faithful supporters.[4] A cluster of left-wing German intellectuals thus dismissed the party whose tactics, in their view, continued to ratify the impossibility of a socialist transformation of Germany, at the very moment when the nation experienced the painful process of shaping itself anew. The harsh verdicts on the SPD are not surprising, Neumann's in particular. This group's insistence on socialist intellectual work as a function of the existence of a socialist mass movement simply echoed the tradition of generations of German Marxists. Nevertheless, the judgment that there were no German socialist intellectuals can be challenged.

To have said that there was often little common ground among intellectual adherents of the German socialist movement—or any large political movement—would have been to say that things were entirely typical. To say that from 1933 there was no socialist movement in Germany may also true in an important but very specific sense. In Nazi Germany, Marxian socialism "existed" largely in prison, in subversion, in secret, or in silence. But to say there had been, therefore, no socialist intellectuals since 1933 is simply inaccurate. There had always been an international network of socialist parties, unions, and intellectuals—supported by, among other things, mass political organizations, research institutions and universities, and national governments. Even Borkenau, with his new emphasis on nationalism, did not deny the persistent international solidarity among socialists—even if he insisted that it had shown at best a primarily defensive character.[5] This socialist solidarity is precisely what had sustained the individuals who issued their opinions in the dismal fall of 1947—enabled to be sure, by other political traditions that some members of this group of intellectuals had begun to reconsider: liberal constitutionalism, individual rights, and the granting of sanctuary to political refugees—however institutionally fragile and horribly undercut by anti-Semitism and anti-Communism these practices often were.

What the record of this meeting reveals above all is the depth of pessimism among these particular left-wing writers, who had been part of the Weimar SPD or KPD, had later joined the staff of the Institute of Social Research, and then at last had found posts in U.S. military or academic institutions. It may also indicate a self-conscious unhappiness about their present lack of any other than academic, bureaucratic, or military affiliation. Their earlier, more directly political commitments had atrophied owing to historical and personal factors largely beyond their control. But in this sense, their criticism of the SPD, however valid, also had a kind of "sour grapes" quality to it. The party, after all, had once been the political home of Neumann and Gurland, too, though they had often despised the work of its elders. The fate of the postwar SPD remained, for the time being at least, in the hands of older, deeply committed, but somewhat inflexible leaders, such as Kurt Schumacher.[6] But it was about to be taken over by a corps of younger, more pragmatic figures associated with the Ernst Reuter circle—including several former Neu Beginnen members. Under different historical circumstances, Franz Neumann, Arkadij Gurland, and perhaps Otto Kirchheimer might have become leading party intellectuals—a role that it is impossible to imagine for such personalities as Max Horkheimer, Theodor Adorno, Herbert Marcuse, or Friedrich Pollock. In 1947, however, they were most definitely on the outside looking in, and it was not at all difficult for them to find fault with what they saw.

The verdicts of these alumni of the Institute of Social Research did not reflect the opinion of several other survivors from the Weimar-era intellectual Left, who were almost exhilarated by the political prospects of postwar Germany—and by their own revived fortunes as well. In Germany and the United States, some of these other survivors of the wartime period played an active role in journalism, academic institutions, government service, or all three—just as Neumann and Kirchheimer had and would. In brief, the postwar careers of these writers followed a variety of paths, but their common background as critics of dictatorship persisted as one of the most important factors in the kind of professional and theoretical work they undertook.

Three of the German left-wing antitotalitarians—Rudolf Hilferding, Otto Rühle, and Arthur Rosenberg—did not survive the war years. As discussed in the previous chapter, Hilferding died while in the hands of the Gestapo. The other two men died of natural causes during 1943 while in exile.[7] The contributions that these veterans of pre–World War I strife on the German left might have made to the postwar discussions of totalitarianism can only be surmised. The direction of Hilferding's thinking about the Soviet Union would likely have led him to remain in the postwar SPD and to advocate at least limited support for the NATO alliance. Even had he lived, however, it is somewhat difficult to imagine his taking more than a marginal, elder statesman's role in the reconstruction of the SPD. Arthur's Rosenberg's later writings, particularly *Demokratie und Sozialismus,* indicate that he would have been a likely candidate for membership in one of the unorthodox socialist groups of the European or American Left seeking a third path. Or, perhaps he might have joined his old friend and student Henry Pachter, who as a member of the circle associated with the American journal *Dissent,* supported the United States against the Soviet Union but never minced his criticism of American politics. Pachter also served as a cantankerous yet avuncular mentor to young scholars interested in the interwar Left.[8] Otto Rühle, however, would likely have remained what he had become after 1933—an unhappy exile, with only his abiding faith in the proletariat and the memories of a few brief moments of political glory to brighten his political isolation. Had he survived the war years, one can even imagine him considering a return to East Germany—with plenty of rancor but perhaps without irony.

The younger survivors of the interwar and wartime German Left faced quite a different series of intellectual and political challenges in the postwar period. Particularly after 1949, left-wing scholars and intellectuals from (and in) Germany had little room in which to maneuver. For those who assumed public political roles, choices of cold war allegiance were almost inevitable—and quickly the readily available sides were the United States and the Soviet Union and their respective sets of allies in NATO and the Warsaw Pact. But for this group of German socialists, such choosing produced a wide variety of allegiances. Some, such as Franz Borkenau and Ruth Fischer, who together helped found the anti-Communist Congress for Cultural Freedom, enthusiastically embraced the cause of the cold war. Others, such as Richard Löwenthal and Ernst Fraenkel, also supported the cold war and remained affiliated with the SPD in the postwar period. Over the following decades, they argued for the need to support the capitalist powers of NATO in foreign policy matters—but without abandoning progressive, albeit cautiously reformist working class–oriented domestic policies. Franz Neumann often traveled to Germany in the early postwar years, but he retained his Columbia University professorship and avoided direct political party involvement. Nevertheless, he, too, came down strongly on the side of the Western Allies during and after the Berlin blockade, declaring that strong support for the western zones of Berlin was absolutely vital: "no sacrifice can be great enough to make the city viable—economically and politically."[9]

Even for those who maintained a deep skepticism about the Western powers and the cultures they had bred, Max Horkheimer, Theodor Adorno, and Friedrich Pollock, for instance, the perspectives of orthodox Marxism and class struggle proved mostly or entirely disposable, and by the late 1960s—even before the invasion of Czechoslovakia in 1968—the Soviet Union became the target of their most damning pronouncements.[10] It was more than a bit ironic that the German exile radical who managed to gain the most attention in the postwar United States was an advocate of the "great refusal," a writer openly and unceasingly hostile to the culture and politics of the cold war: Herbert Marcuse.

This concluding chapter offers a brief look at some of the issues that marked the most influential considerations on totalitarianism among leftist German intellectuals in the cold war era: postwar revisions or rejections of Marxism, divergent theoretical and practical responses to cold war politics, and the impact of totalitarian theory on the study of politics and society in postwar Germany. The course of the several notions of totalitarianism offers peculiar insights into the fates of ideas. Along with liberalism and socialism, but with even more malleable political identity attached to it, the concept of totalitarianism has served as both an oppositional and a ruling idea. In terms of the significance of its historical context, opposition to totalitarianism carried a far different set of commitments and risks in the interwar and wartime years than it did in the West during the cold war. This book closes with an assessment of the influential perspectives and theoretical issues that remain as legacies of the work of these individuals and a reconsideration of the relative value that some concepts of totalitarianism might still possess.

On Marx and Marxism: Further Revisions

Several of these intellectuals found themselves both professionally and politically adrift during the early cold war period, trying in their forties and fifties to secure academic careers in the United States or the Federal Republic of Germany. Not entirely comfortable either in or out of the political activist's role, they were keepers of the thin flame of socialist unorthodoxy, fellow travelers of liberalism who could not completely embrace it or its policies. Marxism had become for several members of this group either one of many historically surpassed critical perspectives or a trusty but outmoded tool that required radical refashioning. This group of thinkers would include Franz Neumann and Otto Kirchheimer. Others, among them Franz Borkenau and Richard Löwenthal, sooner or later rejected all but the most schematic elements of their earlier theoretical Marxism. They now shunned and even scorned a Marxist political perspective.[11]

Karl Korsch, however, appears never to have abandoned Marxism altogether, despite his severe criticisms of what it had become as institutionalized practice. His postwar work suffered because he never found long-term employment in the United States. During the war, he had taught at the State College of Washington in Pullman (later Washington State University) and at Tulane University in New Orleans, but he did not gain a teaching position thereafter.[12] In the early cold war years, he reestablished contact with his old KPD comrade Ruth Fischer, who, after a series of involvements in left-wing splinter groups, had survived exile as a social worker and journalist in the United States. She even became a favorite of the fiercely anti-Communist Luce publications. She consulted with Korsch on the manuscript of her lengthy and bitterly polemical history of the Weimar KPD, *Stalin and German Communism*—yet another important example of ex-Communist anti-Communism. Their correspondence was friendly and topical. She disagreed with Korsch on the prospects for the revolution in China, in which he placed great hopes, and joked with him about the likely outcome of the 1952 presidential election. Their personal connections with other antitotalitarian intellectuals also emerge in these letters. Korsch asked Fischer to get copies of a review from Franz Borkenau's journal, *Ost-Probleme,* and an article by Richard Löwenthal in *Der Monat.* He told her of his admiration for Milovan Djilas, the former member of Tito's Communist government in Yugoslavia who was beginning to formulate the ideas that led to his dismissal from the party and culminated in his famous critical appraisal of Communism in power, *The*

New Class. They discussed the personal and political ups and downs of "Karl August" (Wittfogel), their mutual friend from the old days. The record of Korsch's correspondence with Fischer breaks off in 1957, and it is apparent that his tragic and prolonged illness soon made intellectual work impossible.[13]

Korsch's various comments on the place of Marxism in the revolutionary movements of the century remain a somewhat controversial topic for some leftist scholars, but his continuing interest in the fate of Marxism is undeniable. In 1952, Korsch issued one of his oracular and wistfully hopeful pronouncements on Marxism: "The broader development of Marxism during the last 150 years, of which 'Soviet Marxism' will perhaps in a future time appear as only 'a short and somewhat disreputable episode,' has not received due attention . . . because from 1917 to this day a disproportionate part of the general interest as well as that of the scholars has been absorbed by the sensational drama that unfolded itself on the Russian scene."[14] Little would occur over the next generation to change the circumstances that gave rise to this judgment. He would also insist, in his correspondence with Bertolt Brecht, that condemnation of the Soviet Union served reactionary purposes.[15]

Korsch did not specify the role that might remain for Marxism as a foundation for political or philosophical critique. Though he had chosen not to publish it, he had written "Ten Theses on Marxism," which sketched only the possibility of such a continuing use for Marxian theory and even declared flatly that "the first step in re-establishing a revolutionary theory and practice consists in breaking with the monopolistic claim of Marxism to revolutionary initiative and to theoretical and practical leadership."[16] Debates persist as to whether these remarks were intended as a conclusion or simply as a provocation to further Marxian investigations. In what was apparently his last letter to Ruth Fischer, dated 4 July 1957, he had signed himself "your old friend, co-Marxist and -Leninist."[17]

Some forty years later, it is certainly possible to imagine that the apparent transformation and at least temporary decline of the Communist Party of the former Soviet Union may lead to a revival of Marxist theory and politics in some parts of the world. That the fate of Marxism has for so long been intertwined with the status of Soviet Communism need not lead to the conclusion that the future course of either is a short route to oblivion. In both Russia and Poland, for example, revised versions of the Communist Party have managed to survive. These parties are no longer claiming to be the engines of radical social transformation but instead exist primarily as creaky political vehicles for the defense of workers' interests in retaining jobs and public services in the face of a headlong rush to privatization and free market capitalism. Communism's future appears even less assured, to say the least, in several of the other European nations where "official" Marxism survived primarily as the ideological justification for oppressive regimes. It is possible to identify ways in which Korsch's specific criticisms of the lopsided, oppressive, and mechanistic Marxism of the Soviet Union, criticisms that varied little in their essential points from the late 1920s onward, have been at least partly vindicated by the events of the past decade. The proletarian revolution he desired has not materialized, however, at least not as Korsch seems to have imagined it.

Franz Neumann's postwar revision of Marxism was perhaps even more personally and intellectually traumatic than Korsch's or Fischer's. In any case, he offered even less in the way of utopian political hopes than Korsch did. His bitterness or resignation about the collapse of the link between Marxist theory and practice often emerged indirectly, as in his increasing reliance on liberal thinkers to ground his discussions of politics and law.[18] Occasionally, however, he articulated his harsh views on the fate of Marxism quite directly. In two radio broadcasts delivered in Berlin as part of a 1950 series on Marxism aired by the "Radio University" program of station RIAS and sponsored by the newly established Freie Universität Berlin (Free University of Berlin), Neumann offered his appraisal of the transformations of Marxism and the relationship between Marxism and intellectuals. He linked the unhappy fate of Marxism to the historical succession from Marx's democratic theory, to Lenin's "aristocratic" political revolution, and finally to Stalin's "caesaristic and total dictatorship," whose most important constituent element, Neumann insisted, was terror.

Neumann traced the relationship between Marxism and intellectuals in a similarly declining arc. He listed four main types of Marxism: social reformist, revolutionary, Bolshevist, and purely academic. It was starkly evident that in 1950 none of them held much appeal for Neumann. Revolutionary Marxism, best represented by Trotskyism, Neumann dismissed as both shadowy and quite out of touch with reality. Academic Marxism that sundered praxis from theory was no kind of Marxism at all. The field was left to social reformism and Bolshevism (which Neumann clearly equated with Communism). But social reformism no longer needed Marx, Neumann contended. Kantian notions of human autonomy and mutual regard supplied the moral basis for a reformist politics. For social democratic theory, Marxism had become simply a theoretical reflex disconnected from any truly revolutionary outlook or intent. In practice, defense of the Social Democratic Party and allied trade union organizations led to a defense of "invested interests" and the integration of the working-class organizations into capitalist society. These were the same developments that had enraged Neumann at the time of the Weimar Republic's destruction. In his view, intellectuals connected with social reformism tended to become conformist functionaries until new conflicts arose. Only then could intellectuals once again take up their proper role as critics of society.

Neumann aimed his sharpest criticism at Bolshevist intellectuals. They were quite simply the functionaries of a terrorist system. He noted national differences: the shocking ignorance of American Communist intellectuals and the conformity of French Communist intellectuals. He acknowledged that Marxism's all-embracing theory of society had a particularly seductive appeal for scholars and writers. Moreover, the power of the Soviet Union had transfixed intellectuals in many nations who failed to understand that Bolshevist Marxism had nothing to do with the original notion of freedom embodied in Marxism. Since 1927, Neumann insisted, Bolshevist intellectuals had been the instruments of an apparatus of terror.[19]

Not only did Neumann see a diminished role for Marxism in the postwar period, he also tacitly accepted the broad historical and theoretical consequences of Hilferding's notion of the totalitarian state economy in the case of the Soviet Union. That is, by the early 1950s, Neumann had become convinced of the primacy of politics that he had only allowed as a slim and likely disastrous possibility at the time he wrote *Behemoth*. In a speech delivered at the Berlin Hochschule für Politik in 1951, he emphasized his new position: "The domination of politics over economics is clear. But difficult questions arise here: if politics is thus predominant, can the domination of totalitarian politics be overthrown? Or are there inherent laws in accord with which total politics must collapse? My answer to this is, *No!*"[20] Neumann now concluded that Marxian theories of class conflict and inherent tendencies toward capitalist crisis, such as the one he had attempted to articulate in the case of the "un-state" of Nazi Germany, were inoperative. This speech indicates that Neumann had finally abandoned the very position from which he had criticized Pollock ten years earlier. The theoretical difficulties created by the success of the various separate careers of modern totalitarian states became for Neumann a hindrance that even his renewed interest in liberal theory could not entirely overcome before his untimely death.[21]

Neumann's example indicates that the complex and dismaying challenges to left-wing theory launched by the interwar and wartime totalitarian dictatorships could threaten and even sunder an attachment to

Marxism. In the case of several of these antitotalitarian writers, earlier optimism regarding the future of revolutionary socialism vanished. They adjusted, rearranged, or abandoned their Marxism in response to their new conclusions on the active and even determining role of politics in society. The philosopher Judith Shklar wrote perceptively of this dilemma in reference to Franz Neumann's postwar turn:

> History for him was not just a meaningless struggle for power but also a purposeful development of ideas. This, in fact, is as far as socialism today can go, apparently. The new recognition of the autonomy of politics in history need not end in Machiavellism, but it does not seem to lead to a new radicalism. Though it implies that men are free to determine their fate, it has simply not stirred socialists to new hope. But, since pure power was revealed to socialists for the first time in its most abhorrent, totalitarian form, this is only natural.[22]

Neumann's postwar theoretical development, signified at one level by his decisive move away from Marxism, showed the effects of the previous two decades that Shklar, also writing in the 1950s, described so ably and sympathetically.

Despite his frequent revisions and retreats, however, the theoretical and intellectual legacy of Neumann continues in at least two traditions of social critique. Those who wish to hold to a relatively flexible Marxism that still insists on the ultimately determining power of class relationships will find in *Behemoth* and Neumann's prewar essays a model of Marxian scholarship that demonstrates a mastery of the available evidence of current economic and political developments and a tenaciously rationalist presentation of both evidence and conclusions. The Marxist historian Timothy Mason skillfully built on this portion of Neumann's legacy in his provocative essay on the primacy of politics in National Socialism and a variety of his other writings.[23] The questions the Marxist Neumann posed about the economic policies characteristic of modern capitalist parliamentary systems or one-party "revolutionary" states, the sources of power in these regimes, the role of their political practices and ideologies, their beneficiaries, and the fate of the working classes within these systems remain crucially important questions for historians and political analysts.

The liberal Neumann produced extremely lucid but less dynamic examples of scholarship. Yet even this portion of his legacy still resounds in discussions of the rule of law and the dilemmas of democratic politics in modern times. His postwar essays were brilliant and learned considerations of political concepts—natural law, freedom, federalism, and totalitarian dictatorship—as well as political thinkers—Hobbes, Locke, Montesquieu, and Bodin, among others. Unfortunately for the reception of Neumann's thoughtful and critical new line of analysis, these writings were broadly historical in scope and conception and therefore at odds with the growing trend of political science toward quantification and synchronic models.[24] In this "liberal" phase of his work, Neumann had recourse to more traditionally left-wing perspectives than the fashionable jet age formulas of "interest group politics" and "the end of ideology." His late essay "Anxiety and Politics," which shows Neumann's increasing turn to the psychology of collective social and political behavior that had long interested his former Institute colleagues Marcuse, Horkheimer, and Adorno, at the same time reveals him once more in the guise of the Weimar SPD labor lawyer, pleading for more vigorous public speaking and writing, democratic reformism, and "the humanization of politics."[25] Neumann, despite his disillusionment with Marxism, would always be pulled toward radical social criticism and an active endorsement of popular movements for democracy and human rights.

The postwar writings of Neumann's former colleagues also serve as evidence of the mixed fate of their Marxism. Marcuse's *Eros and Civilization* and *One-Dimensional Man* were, most importantly, attempts to renew the possibility of utopian theory and praxis. In the case of Horkheimer, by contrast, the abandonment of the Marxian utopia ultimately separated political radicalism from theoretical radicalism. For each of these theorists, left-wing antitotalitarianism, whether expressed as an eclectic liberalism (Neumann), a type of neo-utopianism (Marcuse), or a politically abstinent critical theory (Horkheimer and Adorno), had represented a kind of defensive reaction and appeared at last as an impoverished political substitute for the revolutionary project of Marxism, regardless of the theoretical contributions this group of thinkers achieved.

Even Borkenau, who had traveled the furthest from Marxism, continued to return to Marx's writings, not only to testify to their continuing international importance but also to come to a clearer understanding of why the social theorist's ideas had once been so appealing. Borkenau's last book project, completed the year before his death, was a one-volume collection of Marx's writings. In a long introductory essay, "Praxis und Utopie," he compared Marx's theoretical adventure to the mythical flight of Icarus—a glorious ambition and a determined inventiveness resulting in disaster.[26] That Borkenau was still poking among the fragments of the wreck spoke to the persistently compelling nature of what he himself had labeled as the abortive journey of revolutionary Marxism.

Responding to the Cold War: Pro and Con

Of the writers examined in this book, Borkenau became perhaps the most important and prolific publicist for an antitotalitarianism that focused almost solely on the Soviet Union. After the war, he returned to Germany with a press service attached to the U.S. Army, but he soon accepted the rather surprising offer of a position as professor of history at the University of Marburg. During the years of exile, his book on the development of the "bourgeois image of the world" apparently found an audience of which he had been unaware.[27] He quickly found himself dissatisfied with academe, however. He left Marburg in 1949 to engage actively once more in political journalism. For a few years, he edited a journal on Eastern European affairs, *Ost-Probleme,* which received funding from the U.S. government. His brief moment of fame among circles of policy analysts in the West came in 1953 when he accurately indicated that Stalin was either dead or seriously ill, because the Soviet newspapers gave unusual space to some of his rivals and because, on certain public occasions, Stalin was neither present nor mentioned so prominently as had been customary. Borkenau thus became one of the founding practitioners of the approach to Soviet studies known as Kremlinology—discussed in Germany under the rather less respectful term *Kreml-Astrologie* (Kremlin astrology).[28]

Borkenau's work as a journalist yielded dozens of publications in journals with a fairly broad circulation, such as *Der Monat, Commentary, Twentieth Century, Neues Abendland,* and *Rheinische Merkur.*[29] He wrote mostly articles of political commentary, and his work showed a quality of insight and expertise that raised it well above the general run of cold war–era journalism. On at least one occasion, however, Borkenau became reckless in his anti-Communist zeal. In 1951, he testified against a U.S. officer of the occupation period, accusing the man of "Communist sympathies." The target of this testimony was Joseph von Franckenstein, a courageous wartime spy for the Allies and the husband of the writer Kay Boyle. He soon lost his State Department job. Years of court appeals followed. A decision in April 1957 reversed Franckenstein's dismissal, in behalf of which Borkenau had clearly been a crucial witness. Tragically, Franckenstein died soon after his reinstatement.[30]

Borkenau also played an important part, along with Ruth Fischer and Melvin J. Lasky, in creating the Congress for Cultural Freedom. This organization sought to provide a platform for moderate socialist and liberal anti-Communist intellectuals during the tumultuous early years of the cold war. In June 1950, Borkenau served as a fiery and controversial speaker at the congress's inaugural public meeting in Berlin. Borkenau's speech, praising U.N. intervention in the Korean War, struck a British participant at the congress, the historian Hugh Trevor-Roper, as an inflammatory display, and the audience response to the speech reminded him of the Nazi fanaticism of recent memory.[31] In 1952, Borkenau published a new study of Communism, *Der Europäische Kommunismus* (issued in English the following year as *European Communism*), which he dedicated to his late friend George Orwell, but it was inferior to his earlier book on the subject, *The Communist International* (1938). Both of these books, along with Ruth Fischer's *Stalin and German Communism*, became influential formulations of the so-called Stalinization thesis on the development of the KPD.[32] Although he gained a larger audience with his new book on Communism, his writing now descended frequently into the bitterest polemics. The anti-Communist passions of the fifties sometimes overwhelmed Borkenau's true gift for unorthodox yet insightful analysis, the very quality that had been the source of some brilliant historical and sociological writings in the thirties. Also, during the postwar years, he made no further forays in the direction of refining or extending his pioneering theoretical work on the problem of totalitarianism, leaving such work to the academic social science community. Only in his posthumously collected and edited historical essays of the postwar years do we encounter once again the bold surveyor of the human landscape whose writings are worth reading for their spirit of intellectual and scholarly adventure.[33] But it was his unrelenting postwar anti-Communism, his voluminous journalism, and his occasional book-editing and translating efforts that made him a well-known figure to those interested in the study of international politics and political theory.

Borkenau's Weimar comrade Ruth Fischer pursued a similar cold war career as publicist and ex-Communist. As discussed in the introduction, Fischer gained media publicity in the United States during the early postwar years for publicly denouncing her brother, Communist Party member Gerhart Eisler. She also maintained contacts with a number of her acquaintances on the German left. Her correspondents included such former antagonists as Heinrich Brandler as well as such old friends as Korsch, but she also met with somewhat more cautious allies, including Borkenau and Richard Löwenthal. The book she had shared with Karl Korsch in manuscript form, *Stalin and German Communism*, struck precisely the right cold war note at the time of its publication in 1948, especially for those intellectuals who were seeking a means of explaining and validating the developing power alignments. Its insider's perspective and vivid characterizations of personalities and events added to the book's political appeal. Stalin hovered over the narrative as a pernicious yet somehow elusive presence, the embodiment of the "state party." Fischer also emphasized the totalitarian character of the KPD and its postwar successor, the Socialist Unity Party in the most provocative fashion, concluding that "the Socialist Unity Party . . . unites the features of its two totalitarian predecessors, the Communists and the Nazis."[34] Fischer offered no comparative model, however, nor did she have much at all to say about the National Socialists, save for a concluding passage that asserted the strong influence of Stalin on Nazi organization, propaganda, and methods of social control.[35] Her story was the tale of the defeat of the true revolution (Lenin's) by the false one (Stalin's), a message whose boldness of anti-Communist sentiment likely obscured the persistence of its leftist politics for many readers in the United States.

The reception of the book among her old and new friends on the left reveals the intense and mixed response that Fischer so often evoked. She sent a copy of *Stalin and German Communism* to one of her old antagonists of the Weimar KPD's "Right," Heinrich Brandler, with whom she had managed to establish fairly cordial relations in exile. Brandler wrote to her that "apart from a series of inaccurate details," the book presented a "not unimportant piece of history," but he also called its style that of a "red conspiracy," provocatively comparing it with the fraudulent and viciously anti-Semitic tract *Protocols of the Learned Elders of Zion*. Curt Geyer also wrote to Fischer in the fall of 1948, telling her that he had reviewed the book. He also corrected several of her errors and disputed a number of her interpretations, continuing this discussion in a second, lengthy letter. George Orwell, by contrast, soon registered his great enthusiasm for her effort (though he also offered a gentle correction, namely that Bertolt Brecht was living in Germany, not in the United States, as she had claimed), and he mentioned that a forthcoming novel of his might interest her, though he did not reveal its title—*Nineteen Eighty-Four*.[36] Fischer's English admirer was about to become a far more famous and influential— and arguably even more deeply misunderstood—leftist anti-Communist than she would be.

Karl August Wittfogel also participated in the anti-Communist denunciations of the early cold war, though in his own work he continued to draw on portions of Marx's theoretical legacy. Having burned his bridges to the Communist Party after the Hitler-Stalin Pact and to the Institute of Social Research by the early cold war years, Wittfogel also became one of the important scholarly critics of Communist China, citing the new regime as yet another major example of totalitarian dictatorship. During the war, Wittfogel had secured a permanent teaching position at the University of Washington. In addition to his research and publication efforts, he now offered his political expertise in the service of national efforts to combat Communism. Wittfogel's testimony before congressional committees involved accusing major scholars in his field of Communist Party affiliation or challenging their professional standing. His actions and statements were and rightly remain a controversial episode in the history of postwar anti-Communism. Nevertheless, his long-awaited book on China, *Oriental Despotism,* received generally positive notices upon its publication in 1957, despite his fears about organized Communist opposition.[37] Its examination of what Marx and other scholars had called the "Asiatic mode of production" has, to be sure, found its way into some studies of China. But because of the immense range of his arguments and evidence, Wittfogel's influence crossed disciplinary boundaries as well. His ideas on "hydraulic societies" have found a place in, for instance, the work of a younger generation of innovative historians of the American West.[38]

In addition to its comprehensive model of historical development, *Oriental Despotism* offered several anti-Communist diatribes. The introduction, for example, contains Wittfogel's claim that the "Asiatic mode of production" concept of civilization that he planned to explore had been marginalized and even censored under Soviet authority: "The campaign against the Asiatic concept shows the master minds of the Communist camp unable to bolster their rejection with rational arguments. This in turn explains the oblique and primarily negative methods with which the friends of Communist totalitarianism in the non-Communist world oppose the outlawed concept."[39] The point here is not to enter into the debate about the adequacy of the concept of the Asiatic mode of production or Wittfogel's investigations of "hydraulic societies" but simply to indicate the extent to which his scholarship on the ancient past had become intertwined with the anti-Communist struggle of the present. Hostile references to the domestic terror in the Soviet Union and images of a systematic Communist attack against him and his work appear at several junctures in the book.[40]

Just as Fischer's embrace of anti-Soviet policy held no interest for Korsch, Borkenau's and Wittfogel's enthusiastic acceptance of the cold war alignment initially found few imitators among their former colleagues and acquaintances from the Institute of Social Research. For several of them, cold war politics offered no more appeal than Weimar's politics had. But the work of the institute itself steadily gained a place in postwar intellectual discussions in both Europe and the United States, cold war or no. Indeed, in addition to the inherent interest of many of his philosophical writings, a striking element of Max Horkheimer's career was his ability to thrive as the head of a research institute dedicated to projects outside the academic and political mainstream. His skills as an organizational leader were formidable. He pared down the institute during wartime and then swiftly rebuilt it—back in Germany, no less—by the mid-1950s.

The hardening of his views on the issue of totalitarianism, however, marked Horkheimer's gradual and uneasy truce with the cold war. Despite his everlasting dislike for the United States and its culture, he became an even more outspoken critic of the Marxism of the Soviet Union. Even in *The Eclipse of Reason,* published in 1947, Horkheimer made explicitly political the kind of philosophical criticism of the Soviet Union that had appeared earlier in *Dialectic of Enlightenment* and some of his essays: "Theories embodying critical insight into historical processes, when used for panaceas, have often turned into repressive doctrines. As recent history teaches, this holds true for radical as well as for conservative doctrines."[41] Horkheimer did not name names, but the target of these remarks is clear enough. In the spirit of such writers as Hannah Arendt, Leo Strauss, Dante Germino, and Michael Oakeshott, Horkheimer labored to preserve for political philosophy a sphere "beyond ideology" and partisan political battles.[42] The point of Horkheimer's unwillingness to participate more directly in politics was not only or primarily, as a few of his Marxist critics have argued, just to indulge a reactionary and "existential" politics, or even simply to avoid getting his hands dirty with partisan issues, but also to preserve a standpoint from which to criticize the very character and concerns of contemporary political culture.[43] In the context of the early postwar period, this goal allowed a more open rejection of not only Western capitalism but Soviet Communism as well (if not always of Marxism per se). Horkheimer and Adorno's critique of "totalitarian reason" addressed Western civilization's inherent tendencies toward domination that neither the great cold war powers nor their most influential political intellectuals paid much attention to in the first decade after the war.

In 1968, two long decades after the beginning of the cold war, Horkheimer wrote a new preface for some old essays, the collection issued in English as *Critical Theory.* In this preface, written at the height of student protests in the Federal Republic, he condemned both Soviet totalitarianism and the New Left. As if to close the circle of his youthful radicalism and his later skepticism, he attended to both chores by referring to the words of Rosa Luxemburg—managing at the same time to put in a good word, if not exactly a hurrah, for "the so-called free world":

> Despite her adherence to the Russian Revolution, Rosa Luxemburg, whom so many students venerate, said fifty years ago that "the remedy which Trotsky and Lenin have found, the elimination of democracy as such, is worse than the disease it is supposed to cure." To protect, preserve, and, where possible, extend the limited and ephemeral freedom of the individual in the face of the growing threat to it is far more urgent a task than to issue abstract denunciations of it or to endanger it by actions that have no hope of success. In totalitarian countries youth is struggling precisely for that autonomy which is under permanent threat in nontotalitarian countries. Whatever the reasons offered in justification, for the left to help the advance of a totalitarian bureaucracy is a pseudorevolutionary act, and for the right to support the tendency to terrorism is a pseudoconservative act. As recent history proves, both tendencies are really more closely related to each other than to the ideas to which they appeal for support. . . . To judge the so-called free world by its own concept of itself, to take a critical attitude towards it and yet to stand by its ideas, and to defend it against fascism, Stalinist, Hitlerian, or any other, is the right and duty of every thinking man. Despite its dangerous potential, despite all the injustice that marks its course both at home and abroad, the free world is at the moment still an island in space and time, and its destruction in the ocean of rule by violence would also mean the destruction of the culture of which the critical theory is a part. To link these essays with my own current position on these matters is one motive for their reissue.[44]

Here we find not only the equating of the Left's and the Right's hostility to a critical and rational Western tradition—one philosopher's only partly qualified support for the cold war antitotalitarian outlook—but also a hint of the durable "both ends against the middle" explanation for the collapse of the Weimar Republic. In this preface, Horkheimer was not so distant in his thinking, or the tone of his expression of it, from the early postwar writings of Franz Borkenau. The difficult strategy of theoretical critique and political distance he and Adorno had attempted to practice proved increasingly untenable during the volatile 1960s. Yet to dismiss their project out of hand as insufficiently radical is to beg the question of what exactly constitutes a post-Marxian radical politics.[45] Horkheimer's former colleague Herbert Marcuse would choose a different path, one that led in the direction of answering precisely that question.

From the mid-1930s on, Marcuse had consistently held to some type of antitotalitarian critique, though the nature and focus of that critique changed somewhat over time. The cold war, however, remained for him a primary target. His postwar writings, which made him one of the important theoretical sources for adherents of the New Left in the United States, France, and Germany, have become as widely known as those of any of the intellectuals of the German Left discussed in this book. In the light of this fact, a few of those instances when his singular brand of antitotalitarianism made its appearance need emphasis here, for however one judges its strengths and weaknesses, Marcuse's philosophical project constituted at least an attempt to generate new currents of radical thinking and politics in the midst of what he perceived as cold war stagnation.[46]

His first major postwar book was *Eros and Civilization.* Of all of his books, this one indicated most clearly his aptitude for developing innovative philosophical constructions. Marcuse freely borrowed critical theoretical notions and terminology from Marx and Freud, but he did not simply repeat the pattern of their conceptual architecture. In the dynamic character of his philosophical work, he had few peers among those who continued to call themselves Marxists during the cold war. Also during this period, his critique of totalitarianism, for all its challengeable assumptions and occasional political naïveté, retained a provocative idiosyncrasy that—for some New Leftists, at least—posed a tactically useful counterargument to hegemonic cold war ideology. His 1958 study, *Soviet Marxism,* for example, must be read as a gutsy though at times necessarily awkward attempt to discuss the subject named in the title without "playing into the hands of" either party to the cold war.[47] Most important, Marcuse's analysis of totalitarianism insisted on the complex and historical character of political developments and intellectual traditions, and he refused to model the Soviet Union as a fixed and implacable social order. The very word *totalitarianism,* Marcuse argued, sometimes blocked an effective investigation into the nature of the twentieth century: "The usage of the word 'totalitarianism' as a catchall for the Platonic, Hegelian, Fascist, and Marxian philosophies readily serves to cover up the historical link between totalitarianism and its opposite, and the historical reasons which caused classical humanism to turn into its negation."[48] The book challenged a host of cold war terms and conclusions, and the most important passages of *Soviet Marxism* are those that attempt to highlight and evaluate the fragmentary evidence of the transition away from the totalitarian terror of the Stalinist era. Marcuse was also unique among those who referred to the Soviet Union as "totalitarian" in that he argued that a fundamental difference between that regime and Nazi Germany was the former's historical roots in Marxist rationality and the latter's utterly destructive (though instrumentally rationalized) irrationality. In his view, Soviet Marxism contained at least the possibility that its irrational components of exploitation and oppression would be eroded by the persistent demands of its rational social goals.[49]

He explicitly mentioned the problem of totalitarianism only rarely in his renewal and redirection of Freudian social criticism, *Eros and Civilization.* But when discussion of this issue appeared in the text, it indicated the general target of his postwar writings, even though the angle of attack would change from work to work: "Totalitarianism spreads over late industrial civilization wherever the interests of domination prevail upon productivity, arresting and diverting its potentialities. The people have to be kept in a state of permanent mobilization, internal and external. The rationality of domination has progressed to the point where it threatens to invalidate its foundations; therefore it must be reaffirmed more effectively than ever before."[50] The target was "late industrial civilization"— often simply called, rather hopefully, "late capitalism"—and Marcuse wanted to expose its oppressive character, particularly in the United States. In a critique that he shared with the authors of *Dialectic of Enlightenment,* Horkheimer and Adorno, Marcuse pointed to the "rationality of domination" as the ideology undergirding the immense structure of the modern military-industrial state. These arguments were to become staples of New Left critique—with the term *totalitarianism* typically omitted because of its association with pro-Western anti-Communism. In his continued use of the terms *totalitarian* and *totalitarianism,* Marcuse stood virtually alone among radical leftist thinkers. Hence, the sharply hostile response of the German student radical Rudi Dutschke in 1967 to Marcuse's use of the term *totalitarian* to describe the Soviet Union, and Marxist historian Reinhard Kühnl's sarcastic quotation marks when he discussed Marcuse's "left" version of the theory of totalitarianism.[51]

By using the term *totalitarian,* though, Marcuse did not intend merely to disparage certain objectionable political-state regimes. Instead, he referred to *all* "overdeveloped" societies (as he called them in *Eros and Civilization*) that denied the possibilities of freedom in the name of efficiency and order. This unorthodox use of the term certainly served to anger those who would never imagine bracketing the United States and the Soviet Union as commonly "totalitarian" regimes. Moreover, as the historian Christopher Lasch would argue some years later in *The Minimal Self,* Marcuse's provocative use of the term risked dissipating the force of the word that had once been reserved as a label for the most murderously violent regimes and practices of the century. In this sense, Lasch continued, the work of Orwell and Arendt on the problem of totalitarianism was far superior to *all* the variations on the theme that followed during the 1950s, for, in spite of the questions that could be raised about elements of their work and their politics, Orwell and Arendt had been right in insisting on both the horror and the novelty of Nazi and Stalinist totalitarianism, though Arendt would later blunt the force of this critique somewhat with her famous formulation on the Nazi "banality of evil." Cold war totalitarian theory typologists and left-wing critics of totalitarianism alike had too often missed, ignored, or occasionally even "trivialized" these issues. Lasch's points in this discussion are largely on the mark. For all its philosophical and political radicalism, Marcuse's antitotalitarian critique of the interwar years gradually lost its edge in the postwar period. His defiant resistance to postwar intellectual accommodationism remained appealing to many individuals in the younger generation of students and scholars, but his political conclusions sometimes rang false, particularly when they attempted to stretch a comparative model of totalitarianism to suit an embattled anti–cold war perspective. It must be mentioned, however, that in their blurring of political and historical distinctions in the service of politics or policies quite at odds with Marcuse's perspective, the dominant cold war versions of totalitarian theory were often no better.

The most interesting and successful of Marcuse's considerations of totalitarianism deflects at least partially the kind of criticisms Lasch raised. *One-Dimensional Man* also risked trivializing or at least diminishing the terror and oppression of the totalitarian states of the 1930s and 1940s, but anyone who uses the term *totalitarian* in a comparative sense risks this. *One-Dimensional Man* argued that the brutally violent techniques of the crude and horrible Nazi and Stalinist totalitarian regimes may no longer be necessary. The diversity of ideological instruments by which industrial civilization sustains itself has created a different kind of totalitarianism. It generates support and subverts criticism without the need to apply random or systematic terror and open threats of physical coercion. In short, Marcuse maintained, the success of "the empire of civilization" has become so complete that "one is willing to admit economic and political madness—and one buys it."[52] Totalitarianism, Marcuse intimated, is now in your head, so to speak, a psychologically imposed force of "repressive desublimation" in the service of the needs of dominant institutions to deny individual liberation and happiness. His perspective on the problem of totalitarian authority closely paralleled the concerns of Horkheimer and Adorno. But instead of accepting their pessimistic political conclusions, Marcuse focused, for a time at least, on the role of radical political action as at least a possible point of collective resistance to the new totalitarianism. The shifting topical emphasis and diverse rhetorical tones of Marcuse's philosophical writings may be interpreted as effectively through the grid of his persisting antitotalitarianism as they are by means of his more obvious focus on liberation, for whether he discussed them in terms of political ideology, idealist philosophy, social and individual psychology, or utopian revolution, totalitarianism and liberation—as he defined them—remained the essential polar stars by which Marcuse navigated his evolving philosophical project for over four decades.[53]

The manifest strengths and weaknesses of Marcuse's work raise the question of whether *any* concept of totalitarianism is really required to provide the basis of struggles for "liberation" or "containment," for this is what these theories are ultimately about, in practical political and ideological terms: conflict, oppression, resistance, and liberation. The "great refusal" of cold war bipolarism advocated by Marcuse offered at least a theoretical means of holding to a kind of radicalism (and the question of whether his was a Marxist radicalism is unimportant to my specific point here) and at the same time subverting both the terminology and the assumptions of the cold war. As a strategy, the "great refusal" demanded a degree of critical tenacity and an acceptance of personal isolation for which only a very few members of Marcuse's younger audience had sufficient patience. As some of his socialist critics would argue, this strategy still left open the question of whether such a "refusal" constituted an effective radical politics. At the same time, some of his even more hostile and vociferous conservative and liberal opponents would insist that his political position simply registered the discontent of a defeated philosophical-utopian elite.[54] Marcuse's writings stand as a paradoxical and contested remnant of the heterodox leftist tradition of antitotalitarian critique.

The Long March Through the Institutions

One of the most important intellectual and cultural consequences of left-wing antitotalitarianism in the postwar period was its impact on the postwar German academy. The return of Horkheimer and the institute to Frankfurt and the subsequent careers of both constitute important episodes, but the institute's retreat from politics was strongly evident until the emergence of Jürgen Habermas as the leading figure in a new generation of institute scholars.[55] Another academic institution became a much more vital scene of the creation and reception of political and scholarly antitotalitarianism: the Freie Universität Berlin. Founded in 1948 during the Berlin blockade as an alternative to the Humboldt Universität in the Soviet sector of Berlin, the Free University was certainly the quintessential cold war institution of higher education in postwar Germany. Franz Neumann had been one of the most important advocates of a new university in the American zone of the city. Another founding figure of the Free University and a key on-site adviser to the American general Lucius Clay was Carl J. Friedrich, the Harvard professor who soon became the leading theorist of totalitarianism in the United States.[56] Other scholars associated with totalitarian theory who taught at the Free University in the cold war period included Richard Löwenthal and Ernst Fraenkel. Ossip Flechtheim, who had been an Institute of Social Research assistant to Franz Neumann and who was also an old Neu Beginnen comrade of Löwenthal, was another left antitotalitarian who eventually joined the political science faculty in Berlin.[57]

Ernst Fraenkel's postwar approach to political science shows even more clearly than Neumann's how Marxism was abandoned and antitotalitarianism and parliamentary interest-group theory took its place. In his relatively rapid integration into the postwar academic scene, Fraenkel was an atypical example of those left-wing antitotalitarians who found places in the German academy. He moved perhaps the furthest away from connections with even the "purely academic" Marxism that Neumann had described in his Berlin radio lecture of 1950, and his work did not often sound the same notes of irritation and dissent that frequently emerged in the writings of both Neumann and Otto Kirchheimer.[58] Fraenkel became known for a party and institutional approach to politics that meshed neatly with the social scientific methods then dominant in the United States. His long and productive tenure at the Free University, which he capped, appropriately enough, as director of the school's center for American studies (expanded under the name John F. Kennedy Institut starting in late 1963), was marked by an initially calm period of political moderation and methodological orthodoxy, later shattered by the student movement of the late 1960s.[59] Cold war–era adherence to the social scientific model of totalitarianism was one of the issues that would provoke the indignation of some of the New Left's more theoretically adept members.

Another of the left-wing antitotalitarians who taught politics at the Free University during the 1960s, Richard Löwenthal, had concluded the wartime period working as a correspondent for the BBC but then returned to Germany, where he participated in the reorganization of the SPD. He became friendly with one of the other young returning exiles who gathered in Berlin: Willy Brandt. In 1946, he also authored an important study of economics and politics entitled *Jenseits des Kapitalismus* (*Beyond Capitalism*).[60] After several years of work as a journalist in Europe and as a scholar in the United States, Löwenthal eventually gained a chair on the faculty of the Institut für Politikwissenschaft (Institute of Political Science) at the Free University.[61] There he became known as an expert on Soviet and Asian political developments. He also involved himself as Rudi Dutschke's antagonist during debates in connection with the Socialist German Students' League (Sozialistische Deutsche Studenten—SDS) protests of 1967 and 1968 against the shah of Iran and the war policy of the United States in Vietnam.[62]

Dutschke was one of the most brilliant and certainly the most charismatic of the young intellectuals of the German New Left (Neue Linke). After barely surviving a brutal assassination attempt in 1968, Dutschke would produce his own reinterpretation of Marxism, one that drew heavily on the writings of Lenin and Georg Lukács—the intellectual revolutionary and the revolutionary intellectual—who had been so markedly influential on the young German leftists of Löwenthal's generation. Dutschke's book, *Ein Versuch Lenin auf die Füße zu stellen* (*An Attempt to Stand Lenin on His Feet*), explored the legacy of the Russian Revolution in search of a foundation for the kind of Marxist revolutionary politics that Löwenthal had long since abandoned. Even their shared emphasis on the role of avant-garde leftist groups and their admiration for Lenin could not bridge the political gap regarding U.S. foreign policy, university issues, and the SPD itself that lay between them. Their confrontation during the height of leftist activism against the politics and policies of the Federal Republic thus offered a powerful distillation of intraleft generational conflict: the radical student leader of the late Weimar years took on the radical student leader of the sixties.[63]

Herbert Marcuse's visit to the Free University in the summer of 1967 served as the catalyst for their public dispute. During this debate in the crowded Audimax on the Free University campus, Dutschke made his critical statement about Marcuse's and Löwenthal's use of the term *totalitarian* in their remarks. Dutschke condemned *Totalitarismustheorie* as an ideological apparatus that flattened and distorted the past: "I find it a shame that Professors Marcuse and Löwenthal, with various differences, have used the notion of totalitarianism as a comprehensive concept for different systems. With such a notion the historical dimension gets lost. . . ."[64] Dutschke's targets in 1967 were two veterans of these earlier discussions of totalitarian dictatorship, individuals who were each other's political and intellectual opponents, men who had for over twenty years been contesting the meaning and function of totalitarianism *and* socialism in the postwar world. It seems reasonable to call such a moment both a typical and ironic example of the fate of left-wing antitotalitarianism in Germany. The divergent and combative views of Löwenthal and Marcuse on the problem of totalitarianism were at least partly lost on the younger Dutschke, who rejected the term's use out of hand. The most logical target of Dutschke's remarks—the Friedrich-Brzezinski model of totalitarianism—was at best only partly represented by Löwenthal's position in the debate, but no matter. In addition to the other sparks that were struck that day—and there were apparently many—the old antagonism between Löwenthal and Marcuse was one that flared quickly. As significant "elder statesmen" in the battles between the German New Left and the SPD, Marcuse and Löwenthal each took up the role of representative combatant. The philosopher defended his revolutionary and anticapitalist antitotalitarianism, and the political scientist defended his reformist and anti-Communist antitotalitarianism. In his remaining years, Dutschke would attempt to carve his own path, but he inevitably passed over some of the same political and theoretical terrain that Marcuse and Löwenthal had trodden decades earlier.[65]

Löwenthal's activities in Berlin were hardly limited to the campus. He also contributed mightily to the intellectual and policy debates within the SPD, remaining an important figure in the party's intelligentsia through the 1980s. Despite his willingness to maintain a dialogue with the Socialist Unity Party, his antipathy to Communism never flagged. Löwenthal's publications of the 1950s and 1960s bore such titles as *World Communism: The Disintegration of a Secular Faith.*[66] In 1960, he published an essay that placed him squarely among the defenders of a version of cold war antitotalitarianism, and for several years thereafter Löwenthal's books continued to rely to some extent on the cold war totalitarianism model.[67]

By the 1970s and 1980s, however, as if in belated response to Dutschke's sharp words about the urgent need to retain "the historical dimension," Löwenthal began to insist that the notion of totalitarianism had outlived its proper historical context because the Soviet Union had undergone fundamental changes since Stalin's death. He began to argue that only the Hitler and Stalin dictatorships of the 1929–53 period merited the label "totalitarian." Its continued use, Löwenthal concluded, was more polemical than scientific. The world had entered a perplexing and still dangerous era, but one rich with possibilities for cooperation or at least tolerance, which he labeled "post-totalitarian." Responses to Löwenthal's newest revisionism were not always positive, even among some of his longtime admirers, but his shrewd and forthright redefinitions of the problems of dictatorship and revolution in his writings of the 1980s were characteristic moves for this relentlessly skeptical political thinker.[68]

From the Weimar Communist Party through Neu Beginnen to the postwar SPD, Löwenthal's political and intellectual career characteristically revealed a dispassionate sense of the possibilities of the given moment and the unstinting defense of reason in politics. He also remained, in marked contrast to his old friend Franz Borkenau, a successful "organization man," an outspoken and independent-minded one to be sure but one who sought to exert influence through his role in the SPD, as a member of academic committees and institutions, and as an adviser on public policies as well as through his writings. These strategies and the organizational "insider style," if one can call it that, were typical of very few other intellectuals discussed in this book, perhaps only Franz Neumann (with whom Löwenthal had apparently had little or no personal contact). In Löwenthal's consistent adherence to this strategy—and also in his formidable ability to pull it off—he stands out among the thinkers of this group. His antitotalitarianism, with its roots in the Weimar period, was always theoretically and practically tactical, and it served primarily as a means of disassociating his cautious and institutionally oriented democratic socialism from what he considered to be the disastrous legacy of Communism.

The role of antitotalitarian theory in the postwar German academy has not disappeared since Löwenthal and Fraenkel were leading figures at the Free University, but it has certainly waned, at least as a concern of political scientists. Historians, however, have continued to discuss and debate the origins, adequacy, and purposes of *Totalitarismustheorie*. A small number of scholars, particularly the controversial Ernst Nolte, wished to reinvigorate the cold war version of the notion, but others have discussed it mostly to condemn it as either a reductive model of limited use or the ideological tool of German and American neoconservatism. In late 1988, a lecture took place at the Free University during its fortieth anniversary celebration that revealed something of the mixed fate of *Totalitarismustheorie* at that institution and the ways in which the conflicts over the concept dating back to the 1960s continued to be replayed there.[69] In a discussion of the topic "Die FU—ein Bollwerk der Totalitarismustheorie?" ("The FU—A Bulwark of Totalitarianism Theory?"), the historian Wolfgang Wippermann, a specialist on fascism and Nazism and a veteran of the student political disputes of the 1960s, argued that the premises of the theory of totalitarianism were false but that it survived because it had long proven politically convenient for conservatives. Furthermore, he argued, the Free University had served as a bastion of the theory from 1948 to the present.

In the course of his remarks, which were quite well received by the several dozen students in attendance, Wippermann cited Neumann, Löwenthal, Fraenkel, and Flechtheim as examples of leftist antifascists who had later become antitotalitarians, for reasons he did not attack. His sharpest criticisms were aimed at the slavophobic scholars working on topics related to Eastern Europe (*Ostforschung*) and at "race" researchers at the university, including some professors who had been holdovers from the Nazi period. In his response to Wippermann's remarks, Gert-Joachim Glaeßner, a political scientist, did not disagree with his historian colleague but concluded simply that few political scientists even cared much about *Totalitarismustheorie* any longer. His criticism of the theory limited itself to totalitarianism's weaknesses as an empirical concept and downplayed its political basis or implications.

Before closing remarks or rebuttals could be offered, a lively, loud, and assertive group of student protesters entered the lecture hall, requested and received the attention of those assembled, and denounced proposed changes in the university's Latin American Institute, one of the last strongholds of leftist faculty radicalism. The demonstration gained notable numerical strength by the addition of students from the audience for this critical discussion of *Totalitarismustheorie,* which then came to an abrupt halt. The protest action continued that evening and led to a universitywide strike that eventually spread to the downtown campus of the Technische Universität and lasted the remainder of the winter semester. A course on *Faschismustheorie* was among the better attended student-run seminars of the *"Streiksemester."* One of the students' demands (which, to the surprise of few, ultimately went unheeded) was to rename the Otto Suhr Institut—the university's Department of Political Science—the Rudi Dutschke Institut. As this minor episode seemed to indicate, a truly "post–cold war" Free University could be some years in the making, despite the fall of the Berlin Wall that occurred roughly a year later. More important for the concerns of this study, the theory of totalitarianism proved once more to be an outcast notion for many younger German leftists. In short, the ghosts of the Neue Linke and Neu Beginnen continued to engage in a bitter and earnest debate.

Legacies of the "Lost Debate"

The repetition and fetishization of the cold war concept of totalitarianism by political intellectuals and politicians on the right in Western Europe and the United States during the 1980s shrewdly took advantage of the utter rejection of the concept by many political intellectuals on the left. The forgetfulness of many leftists, liberals, and conservatives regarding the varied but substantial historical legacy of left-wing criticism of totalitarian regimes served the political interests of conservatives and cold war liberals most effectively. Many among the postwar generation of left-wing or liberal intellectuals in the United States and Europe often could neither entirely embrace nor reject the predominant comparative model of totalitarian theory that was deployed with varying effectiveness over the years to attack the Soviet Union and, by extension, to explain the need for the cold war. It was, after all, a model that often helped marginalize or even attack their scholarly and political activity.[70] Even so, any failure to condemn avowedly left-wing dictatorial regimes because of the political proximity of the target to one's own beliefs and ideas risked the kind of muddled avoidance, political duplicity, and intellectual cowardice condemned by such Marxist and non-Marxist radicals as Karl Korsch and Claude Lefort. One leftist scholar has argued the point this way: "The phenomenon called 'totalitarianism' can neither be explained away by 'circumstances,' nor denied simply because it serves 'the enemies of socialism.'"[71] This is a crucial theoretical and political issue for any reconsideration of socialism in the late twentieth century.

That many leftists continued to embrace the "Soviet model" or to explain away its various "flaws" is undeniable, but there were other voices on the left as well. It is important to recall two related but distinct features of the history of the production and reception of totalitarian theory. First, criticism of dictatorship and the abuse of state power in regimes claiming a Marxist or socialist basis simply was not neglected by a number of thinkers on the left in Germany or other nations before, during, or after the cold war. Some German leftists had begun such a broadly comparative and politically focused critique of the Soviet Union and Nazi Germany before the end of Weimar. Second, willingness to criticize the Soviet Union—particularly its long Stalinist phase—did not at the same time license the conclusion that any and all versions of the totalitarianism thesis were equally valid. Even into the 1980s, the various cold war–era versions of totalitarian theory were alternatively accepted, qualified, revised, or rejected—and for historically specific and identifiable reasons—by some of the same German socialist intellectuals who had helped construct concepts of totalitarianism in the first place. These thinkers generally left behind neither a handy policy formula nor an all-purpose comparative model but instead offered questions and alternatives, which, despite the passage of decades, the fall of the Berlin Wall, the end of the cold war, and perhaps even the "end of history"—which already appears to have been temporary—have not been entirely surpassed.[72]

What Jürgen Habermas wrote a decade ago in response to the attempt by Ernst Nolte and others to write histories of the Nazi dictatorship that would "normalize" the past and provide a shared historical identity might also be said of debates about the history of concepts of totalitarianism:

> The inevitable pluralism of readings, which is by no means unmonitored but on the contrary rendered transparent, only reflects the structure of open societies. It provides an opportunity to clarify one's own identity-forming traditions in their ambivalences. This is precisely what is needed for the critical appropriation of ambiguous traditions, that is, for the development of a historical consciousness that is equally incompatible with closed images of history that have a secondary quasi-natural character and with all forms of conventional, that is, prereflexively *shared* identity.[73]

As Habermas wrote with reference to the continuing debates about the German historical past, it is equally clear that the role of the "ambiguous tradition" of antitotalitarianism in that very history will remain bitterly contested. Obviously, the problems associated with the battles over the nature of modern dictatorship and the place of these debates in the convoluted and often tragic history of the German Left in the twentieth century have not been resolved in the course of this study—nor was such a resolution my intent. As of this writing, these problems have already reappeared but not in the terms common in 1933 or 1945. The political terrain of Germany looks familiar only to those who are eternally prepared to issue an answer to "the German Question." This landscape has probably changed irreversibly, and the ideological boundaries of a new German political culture remain in considerable flux, even though German geographical boundaries are now likely to remain in place for some time. German and other leftists may well continue to conclude that none of the past antitotalitarian outlooks of the sort discussed here is sufficient to the requirements of socialist theory or action in the present. But at least some traces of the various theoretical debates I have reconstructed in the foregoing pages remained visible in later considerations on totalitarianism. What follows is intended as a selective survey of these connections, not as an exhaustive critique of all their numerous ramifications.

First, some important ideas growing out of German left-wing critiques of dictatorship were evident in the work of the two most famous writers on the topic of totalitarianism: Hannah Arendt and George Orwell. Five decades after their first publication, *The Origins of Totalitarianism* and

Nineteen Eighty-Four continue to be the most influential interpretations of totalitarianism. Examining their relation to earlier leftist critiques is a means of articulating connections that are easily ignored. Both writers were familiar with some of the books and essays of these German intellectuals of the Left. Arendt's knowledge of many of these writings was particularly extensive, as a perusal of her notes and references in *The Origins of Totalitarianism* reveals. In the course of her massive and complex argument, she cited favorably the writings of Rosa Luxemburg, Rudolf Hilferding, Franz Borkenau, Arthur Rosenberg, Franz Neumann, Ernst Fraenkel, and Richard Löwenthal. Her chapter "Totalitarianism in Power" reveals the influence of the debates among interwar and wartime left-wing theorists of dictatorship most clearly: "What strikes the observer of the totalitarian state is certainly not its monolithic structure. On the contrary, all serious students of the subject agree at least on the co-existence (or the conflict) of a dual authority, the party and the state. Many, moreover, have stressed the peculiar 'shapelessness' of the totalitarian government."[74] Quite appropriately, Arendt cited Franz Neumann—one of those "serious students of the subject"—as an authoritative source for this central conclusion about the character of the totalitarian Nazi regime. For Arendt, Neumann's *Behemoth* had been essential reading, though she might with equal logic have given Ernst Fraenkel credit for his related notion of the dual state. But the personal, historical, and theoretical connections between Arendt and the German socialist intellectuals who preceded her in their analysis of dictatorship do not begin and end with footnote citations. She was married successively to two men who had been closely involved with the German Communist Party, Günther Stern and Heinrich Blücher. Blücher had been affiliated for a time with the Spartacists even before the founding of the KPD. This makes Arendt herself no kind of Marxist, of course, but Marxism was a world of discourse and politics with which she was quite familiar.[75] Along with the generation of German socialist writers examined here, but in her own distinctive fashion, she continued to engage Marx and Marxism in her philosophical writings. One of her most provocative books, *On Revolution,* argued for the vitality and spontaneity of revolutionary councils, citing among others the case of Munich in 1918–19—a revolutionary example also favored by Marcuse, Horkheimer, and Korsch. Her review essay on Rosa Luxemburg, which is as much a tribute as a critique, has long served as the introduction to J. P. Nettl's standard biography of this radical German Marxist.[76] In a nod toward the internationalist strain in the socialist tradition, which was also a typical position of the thinkers examined here, she also had high regard for Rosa Luxemburg's critique of imperialism as well as her courageous defense of democratic political participation and the principle of social justice. *The Origins of Totalitarianism* and Arendt's later philosophical study *The Human Condition* also deserve to be read as important evidence of her continuing critical dialogue with the Marxist tradition, as Seyla Benhabib has argued in *The Reluctant Modernism of Hannah Arendt*.[77]

Orwell's connections to this body of theoretical writing are perhaps less obvious than Arendt's, but his participation in the left-wing opposition to Nazi and Stalinist dictatorships was perhaps even more direct in a political sense. His passionately prorevolutionary memoir of the Spanish civil war, *Homage to Catalonia* (which Lionel Trilling quickly assimilated into cold war anti-Communism in the United States in his well-known introduction of 1952), was in many respects a continuation of Borkenau's criticism—which also emanated at that time from a left-wing perspective—of the Spanish Communist leadership and the Comintern in *The Spanish Cockpit*. Borkenau himself mentioned in a friendly letter to Orwell that their books were really two halves of an extended commentary on "the revolutionary phase of the Spanish war." It is also significant that in *Homage to Catalonia* Orwell favorably cited only Borkenau's book among the numerous recent writings on the Spanish civil war he had read and reviewed, and yet the importance of his friendship and intellectual exchanges with Borkenau is still little known, misunderstood, or misrepresented.[78]

There is another related point regarding the impact of the cold war on the reception of socialist opposition to dictatorship: Arendt's and Orwell's powerful (though not especially Marxist) criticisms of imperialism and capitalism. Even imperialism's role as a historical forerunner of totalitarianism—an essential argument in Arendt's *Origins of Totalitarianism* and an easily neglected element of Orwell's *Nineteen Eighty-Four*—had been briefly and pointedly elaborated years earlier by one of the most radical of the leftist German critics of totalitarian dictatorship—Karl Korsch: "The novelty of totalitarian politics in this respect is simply that the Nazis have extended to 'civilized' European peoples the methods hitherto reserved for the 'natives' or 'savages' living outside so-called civilization."[79] Arendt makes a similar argument in her section on imperialism in *The Origins of Totalitarianism,* and it is not at all difficult to imagine Orwell agreeing entirely with both the tone and the content of these remarks.[80] But Arendt's extensive sympathies with leftist notions of anti-imperialism and a democratic, participatory council communism—along with Orwell's consistent and outspoken advocacy of democratic socialism—continue to gain less attention than their opposition to Soviet-style Communism.[81]

It would, however, be a denial of their important differences to fit together the approaches and conclusions of these writers too neatly. Orwell and Arendt discussed the problem of totalitarian dictatorship in quite divergent ways. Orwell evoked the subjective experience of totalitarianism in *Nineteen Eighty-Four,* while Arendt evaluated its broad historical-philosophical nexus in *The Origins of Totalitarianism.* The heterogenous theoretical and historical writings of the German socialist intellectuals typically remained at a level somewhere between these two approaches to the totalitarian experience. Marcuse, Adorno, and Horkheimer offered subtly reasoned insights into the means by which individuals were subordinated to totalitarian civilization, but generally their writings, for all their persisting interest, lacked the immediacy and claustrophobic intensity of Orwell's dystopian novel.[82] Neumann and Borkenau, to cite a scarcely compatible pair of thinkers with significant socialist pasts, both analyzed totalitarianism with the goal of explaining its political and economic operations but did not construct an intellectual or historical framework comparable in its generalizing capacity to Arendt's distinctive philosophical approach. The writings that most closely attend to Arendt's philosophical concerns, but from a more clearly leftist political perspective, are the essays and books of Claude Lefort. Perhaps because of the very proximity of Lefort's ideas to her prodigious work on totalitarianism (though it is important to state here that Lefort's arguments are much more than a mere "revision" of Arendt), he has apparently been unable to see much evidence of leftist participation in antitotalitarian discourse. It is possible that Arendt's and Orwell's books have cast such a deep shadow over the antitotalitarian arguments that paralleled or preceded theirs that the occasionally quite similar arguments of Korsch, Borkenau, and Löwenthal, for instance, have remained relatively little known to such thinkers as Lefort, who later offered their own leftist criticisms of totalitarian dictatorship.

The New Left's condemnations of both capitalism and Soviet Communism also contained at least some elements of the critiques of totalitarian dictatorships produced by the members of the "older" Left. In 1967, Rudi Dutschke impishly and tellingly quoted the words of the younger, more radical Löwenthal to the older, more conservative Löwenthal. But as their exchange revealed, the very term *totalitarianism* had by then become something of an obsession for both generations of political theorists, and it stood as a barrier to discussion.[83] For a few members of the older generation of socialists, its use signified a willingness to criticize the "Communist East." For many politically active leftists of the younger generation, however, its use signified the desire to demonize Communism as equivalent to Nazism in order to short-circuit criticism of the "capitalist West." During the 1960s and 1970s, these two positions were ultimately irreconcilable, with consequences that continue to play out on the German political scene and elsewhere.

Even a provisional judgment on the conceptual and practical usefulness of antitotalitarian theories can reasonably separate itself from an insistence on their political and historical significance. Arguably, each of the theoretical perspectives developed on the German left brought with it some insights, as well as potential interpretive and political liabilities. The project of tracing the philosophical impact of German leftist antitotalitarianism—particularly that generated by Horkheimer and Adorno in *Dialectic of Enlightenment*—offers significant possibilities for a revised understanding of the "prereflexively" familiar history of the recent past. The philosophical critique of "totalitarian reason" developed by these two thinkers, and in a different fashion by Herbert Marcuse, for all its power to compel a rethinking of the project of civilization, still leaves us in the midst of that project with no other point of departure (regardless of where we might be headed). I state this with a daunting awareness of how critical theory and some of the similar positions elaborated under the category of poststructuralism have armed themselves against such obvious complaints and against being incorporated into any kind of status quo or programmatic politics. Yet at the same time, another thinker with connections to the legacy of critical theory has sought means by which we might judge the project of civilization without shunning political involvement. Among their many other projects, the writings of Jürgen Habermas have encompassed both a continuation of the interdisciplinary work that typified the approach of the Institute of Social Research and a rejection of the retreat from politics that marked the later work of Max Horkheimer and Theodor Adorno.[84] Habermas's defense of the Enlightenment project of reason in the service of a chastened but persistent notion of progress has also included the strenuous conceptual effort to preserve multiple perspectives in the interpretation and articulation of political choices. Such efforts can be legitimately understood as a component of the need to oppose totalitarianism. His theories relying on a pluralistic and discursive search for solutions to social and political problems can be read, in other words, as the basis of an antitotalitarian practice.[85]

Other philosophers, notably the French poststructuralists, whose intellectual kinship to Horkheimer and even more clearly to Adorno has now been elaborated in some detail, have objected to Habermas's discourse theory.[86] They distrust its reliance on a universal political ideal: an "ideal speech situation," in which political decisions emerge in the course of a discussion carried out among equals. Some of the poststructuralists have followed (or, in some cases, arrived independently at) the conclusions of the later strain of critical theory—adopting a position similar to the political skepticism announced in *Dialectic of Enlightenment*. Jean-François Lyotard's *Postmodern Condition: A Report on Knowledge*, published in 1979, offers a useful example. In this book, Lyotard sarcastically rebuked Habermas for discourse theory's insufficient inoculation against the notion of social totality and universal ideas, whose presence threatened to reproduce the oppressive "idea of a unitary end of history"—the totalitarian legacy of the Enlightenment (and Hegel and Marx).[87] But the intense philosophical debates among these innovative theorists that have continued over the past two decades still appear to leave social philosophy at an impasse on the matters of political practice and the dangers of totality: critique of power does not enable or allow escape from it. In view of this, Habermas and some of his poststructuralist critics frequently counsel and enact similar practices: local action, open discussions, and democratic participation. I do not mean to argue that their efforts to construct responses to the overwhelming and all-too-familiar dangers of a uniform social totality (could we call it totalitarianism?) are the same; rather, some ways of reading their respective positions permit the conclusion that they are not always diametrically opposed to one another, as sometimes might appear to be the case.

Discussions of another issue central to modern political theory and policy, human rights, offer additional fragmentary evidence of the presence of the totalitarianism concept. Claude Lefort, for example, has criticized the leftist neglect of not only totalitarian dictatorship but also the issue of rights. He has pointed out that Marxist discussions of dictatorship have to their detriment often ignored or diminished the importance of the ideas and practices of human rights.[88] The Enlightenment tradition of human rights, developed both implicitly and explicitly by Lefort, Habermas, and other contemporary scholars working in the same general direction, offers both an alternative to the political failures of Marxism and a continuing discussion about the nature, limits, and uses of power. Here, too, however, the persistently optimistic impulse of Habermasian democratic thinking confronts the poststructuralist rejection of any putative individual "subject" of rights (whether presupposed or imposed) or "social totality" (whether of a Marxist or liberal-Enlightenment theoretical foundation) that might claim to grant or represent rights. Despite continuing differences between these sets of intellectual antagonists, the battle lines on the issue of human rights are less clearly drawn. During an interview that took place in 1984, Michel Foucault himself acknowledged the persisting power of the idea and practice of rights inherent in a "dialogue situation."[89] Indeed, the considerations on democratic participation and public life, law and constitutionalism, civil society, and human rights developed by not only Lefort, Habermas, and Foucault but also several contemporary American theorists and scholars, including Seyla Benhabib, Lisa Jane Disch, Jeffrey C. Isaac, Jean Cohen, and Andrew Arato, demonstrate the extent to which the many-sided discussion among the disunited heirs of such antitotalitarian theorists as Horkheimer and Adorno, as well as Hannah Arendt, has remained a crucial presence in broader philosophical debates about politics over the past three decades.[90]

The historical configurations and philosophical oppositions that mark poststructuralist participation in antitotalitarian theorizing merit further attention in this context. Shadowing the efforts of Habermas, the work of Foucault, Lyotard, and other poststructuralist thinkers has offered to the continuing debates on totalitarianism a deep suspicion—rooted in a particular reading of the historical experiences of this century—regarding the totalitarian potential of traditionally leftist or liberal "universals," such as the state, the individual subject, and the philosophical, scientific, and political pursuit of truth. Foucault's distinctive antitotalitarianism focused on the relationship between Enlightenment thinking and the controlled order of the Benthamite Panopticon, or "carceral society" as he labeled it in *Discipline and Punish*. This approach to the problem of power circumvented the preoccupation with particular state regimes that Foucault himself argued was a mark of a distorting and tendentious cold war discourse. In short, totalitarianism could always be condemned too easily as the technique of rule performed by the "other." Foucault refused this particular language game.[91] In addition, Foucault's focus on the human body as the object of punishment, normalization, and surveillance brought to philosophical investigation an eloquent and unremitting protest against violence, a protest that sought no "really existing" regime (such as the Soviet Union) or "universal" and transhistorical standard (such as Habermas's discourse theory offers) as the ground for its legitimacy. The multifarious but related philosophical stances of poststructuralism and deconstructionism often aimed their political critiques at the intellectual and political legacy of Communism, and they located the rationalizing imperative of the Enlightenment inheritance as the origin of totalitarian dangers.[92] In the light of this, Foucault's writings, along with some of those produced by Jacques Derrida, Jean-François Lyotard, and the so-called New Philosophers, could be understood as warnings about totalitarian control (both fascist and Marxist) and assertions of "difference" in a world of actual and potential "totalities." Even so, Foucault's philosophical arguments struck some of his liberal and leftist critics as dangerously untethered in political and ethical terms. When Habermas referred to Foucault disparagingly as a "young conservative," it was partly because of his own historically based suspicions about the possible political direction in which the voluntarist and antirationalist elements of the Frenchman's philosophy might lead: totalitarian (specifically fascist or neofascist) unfreedom. Even though Foucault's death over a decade ago cut short his provocative dialogue with Habermas, interest in the issues raised in the course of their various disputes has scarcely diminished.[93]

As an alternative philosophical and political stance, the much older radical position of such leftist antitotalitarian "council Communist" theorists as Korsch and Rühle could hardly pass muster with either Habermasian discourse theory or Foucauldian skepticism regarding such total philosophical systems as Marxism. The council Communist ideal did allow for a consistently radical and revolutionary Marxist critique of capitalism, dictatorship, and Soviet-style "existing socialism," but this outlook could quickly become disengaged from all but the most marginalized or sectarian Marxist politics in the cold war period. It has also had the capacity to perform the dubious chore of shielding Marxism against any responsibility for the form and content of Soviet Communism or other movements claiming a Marxist inspiration. In terms of its own program, at least the radical leftist version of antitotalitarian theory refuses to accept the permanent victory of "counterrevolution" in either its capitalist or its Communist form. Korsch and Rühle also maintained that working-class people would have to be the chief political agents of and the democratic participants in any fundamental social change—a position abandoned by most of the key members of the Institute of Social Research as well as the younger generation of such ex-Communists as Borkenau, whose consistent focus on elites as the agents of historical change indicates that he had never believed much in the revolutionary character of the proletariat in the first place. Council Marxism's neglect or even rejection of the less spectacular—and, as we learn all too frequently, partial and tenuous—gains of liberalism in terms of the ideas and institutions of constitutional checks on state power, parliamentary democracy, tolerance for diverse opinions, practices, and beliefs, specified civil rights for individuals, and the ideal of the rule of law, however, leaves this ultraleft position a dubiously one-sided one in terms of political practice.[94] The idea of a reengagement of radically Marxist antitotalitarianism with democratic revolution—a goal that calls Marcuse as well as Korsch and Rühle to mind—testifies at least as much to stubborn Marxist hopes as to the current viability of a Marxist political project. For all but a tiny remnant of its former following, the kind of "scientific" Marxism that possessed all the answers is long gone. But as Korsch himself insisted, Marxism could be only a developing critical position *within* capitalist society, not the platform for a fixed, transhistorical, and omniscient socialist theory. That portion of the Marxian tradition that is still capable of posing essential and as yet unanswered questions to capitalist societies—or fascist or totalitarian socialist ones—may yet have a considerable future.[95]

The predominant type of cold war totalitarian model that views Nazism and Soviet Communism as rough equivalents, however, bears its own interpretive and political burdens even as it justifiably pleads for attention to the similarities between these two regimes in terms of their means of control and the incredible violence they inflicted. The model's comparative equation has certainly helped to undermine—at times usefully—absolute Left-Right dichotomies. More important, it provides a means by which to call the bluff of regimes that have claimed to be "progressive" because they advertise a Marxist or socialist foundation. So long as this comparative model does not ignore fundamental historical changes in the character and policy of regimes and focuses on mechanisms of rule in diverse state systems, its strengths are manifest. But for all its power to call critical attention to nations and policies, the totalitarianism concept too easily serves as a substitute for a differentiated and historical analysis of state-party political movements and ideologies. Its continued validity in the critique of regimes in the present can be sustained most effectively and persuasively when the concept is utilized, for example, as a bulwark against the denial of human freedom, as in Lefort's arguments, where the category of totalitarianism serves as a kind of negative standard by which to gauge efforts to expand democratic participation and to protect a public forum for the discussion of rights.[96]

Even when writing in behalf of such projects, however, comparative totalitarian theory's adherents can still easily slip into customary cold war modes. Some of the recent writings of a widely admired German historian and political scientist, Karl Dietrich Bracher, offer an example of this problem. In one of the more persuasive of his essays on totalitarianism and democracy, "Revolution against Totalitarianism," Bracher argued that a "reconstructed Europe" must offer federal structures of cooperation and integration "with protection for human and civil rights." This hopeful image of a nontotalitarian future was in itself unobjectionable, especially since it was accompanied by Bracher's lament (in 1992) about the "bloody civil wars that have been raging in Yugoslavia." But Bracher's brief analysis of contemporary Europe showed how even a stubborn advocate of the comparative totalitarian model could miss what might have been one of the more interesting opportunities to put it to use. Bracher cast the blame for violence in the Balkans primarily on "the Communist legacy."[97] This is an argument worth examining, if only in a preliminary fashion, while bearing in mind the perspective of comparative totalitarian theory.

First, looking for historical factors that might help explain the bloody events in the Balkan region during this century is a reasonable undertaking. Some explanations are far too simple: the region's history is not just an unbroken series of ethnic conflicts. Bosnia and its capital of Sarajevo have been the settings for a rich cosmopolitan culture. Nevertheless, religious and ethnic battles are a significant part of the region's history, as Bracher himself noted. But their episodic appearances long predated the arrival of Communism in the region. Moreover, the political boundaries of Yugoslavia that drew together "a diversity and intermingling of nationalities" were not simply a legacy of the Ottomans or Hapsburgs. Nor were they initially drawn by Stalin or Tito; they were generated primarily by means of complex and contested diplomacy under the aegis of the Western Allies after World War I. Perhaps because Bracher needed to be brief in what was, admittedly, a topical essay and not a historical monograph, he did not mention these particular facts. To be sure, Communism and Communists are, in a variety of ways that bear looking into, deeply implicated in the events that shattered the former Yugoslavia, as Bracher claimed. But Bracher missed almost entirely the comparative perspective that might have emerged by taking into account not only the "Communist legacy" but also the legacy of the interwar and wartime fascist nationalisms—including German National Socialism—that have sanctioned unspeakable violence in the Balkans. Instead of such a comparison, he omitted any specific mention of the impact of World War II in Yugoslavia. This gap in the narrative made even less sense since the essay's stated theme was the "revolution against totalitarianism." The massacres perpetrated by German troops in the Balkans and the Nazis' sponsorship of the deadly Croatian Ustasha also constitute part of the region's history. It was, after all, the recently reunified Federal Republic of Germany that hastily recognized the independence of Slovenia and Croatia in 1991, accelerating the breakup of Yugoslavia, sanctioning the revival of memories of previous German interventions in the region, and, not least of all, making it easier to activate nationalist fears and hatreds among the Serbs. Bracher struck a little closer to the mark when he linked the most recent Balkan war to the efforts of some powerful Serbian factions in the government and military in the oppression of other groups, most notably the Albanians in Kosovo, but even this formulation oversimplifies the matter. He also warned, accurately, that the European Community and the United Nations appeared unprepared to act decisively in the interests of peace. Even so, Bracher's lament in the article's conclusion about the Balkan region's aggressive nationalisms (which he avoided labeling as "fascism") just briefly mentioned the role of Nazism and omitted entirely the actions of Imperial Germany and the reunified Federal Republic as possible factors in the historical background of the recent Bosnian war.[98]

Simply put, Bracher is far more persuasive when he investigates the elements of a specific historical situation and leaves the totalitarian model to one side than he is when he uses it as the basis for arguments about the recent past. Bracher's authoritative writings on the collapse of the Weimar Republic and the Nazi state remain extremely valuable additions to our historical understanding of those events and regimes, but the importance of his books is tied more closely to his extensive research and his undeniable skills as a writer than to his specific advocacy of totalitarian theory. His condemnations of the Nazi regime have for decades been admirably clear and unequivocal, but his remarks on the effects of Communist totalitarian rule in the postwar era, though not without merit, are at times lamentably reductionist and so one-sided as to be of limited value for historical understanding, let alone political policy.[99]

In addition to the intensified politicization that has accompanied the models of totalitarianism produced during the early and late cold war years, there are methodological problems. If the totalitarian concept has certain strengths and usefulness for initial levels of political and historical comparison, the Friedrich-Brzezinski model also implicitly insists that two such brutal regimes as Nazi Germany and the Soviet Union not only must be condemned but also must somehow be bracketed conceptually. This is a position that, like many of Borkenau's arguments in *The Totalitarian Enemy*, energizes certain kinds of political opposition but also at times relies too heavily on formulaic explanations for contingent and conditioned historical changes. In place of official Marxism-Leninism's blindly hopeful scenarios of future socialist glories, some of the cold war antitotalitarian arguments have also often indulged in a kind of gratuitous political despair, as if the Soviet regime could be understood only as an eternal and unchanging entity from Stalin (or Lenin) down. My point here is not to succumb to the grotesque and false dilemma that either left- or right-wing dictatorships are to be automatically "preferred" but instead to insist that the comparative models of totalitarianism, like other models generated by much of cold war–era social science, could all too readily assume a static and unhistorical character, which would then be attributed to the object under investigation. Of the many weaknesses of the cold war formulations of totalitarian theory that have often been criticized, one of the most important is insufficient attention to the actual and potential changes that take place in political regimes and the details and functions of their policies.[100] When, for instance, Friedrich's and Brzezinski's classic cold war–era model—so close in spirit and content to Franz Borkenau's interwar notions of fascist totalitarianism—describes the terror of totalitarian regimes as being launched against "arbitrarily selected" groups, there is a danger that the violent anti-Semitism and antileftism that ought to be essential topics for understanding the ideological and practical components of National Socialism move to the periphery of the analysis in order to make Nazism comparable to Soviet Communism, whose policies of domestic terror ran more broadly in a social sense and, especially under Stalin, less predictably than Nazi terror. Neither dictatorship's system of terror can be adequately explained as "arbitrary" or random, however. The party-state dictatorships have often chosen their human targets carefully, or they certainly had at least some fairly definite social and political effects in mind with the violence they inflicted. More to the point, these regimes invented and imposed the categories of people who would be "disappeared," however different from each other the victims may have been under each regime or at different times in the contingent historical development of each regime.[101]

In any case, for many historians, the crucial ideological and historical differences between the political movements and conditions that produced Hitler's regime and those that generated Lenin's and Stalin's—differences that often make the dominant cold war version of totalitarianism theory so problematic and Procrustean—offer another set of problems to bedevil totalitarian theory. These problems, related to both historical interpretation and politics, have been persuasively enumerated by scholars for over thirty years.[102] What Tim Mason declared in a discussion of the structuralist-intentionalist debates of the 1970s could often be applied with equal logic to many of the uses of comparative theories of totalitarianism: "If historians do have a public responsibility, if hating is part of their method and warning part of their task, it is necessary that they should hate precisely."[103]

Another closely related objection to totalitarian theory is that, all too often, the dominant totalitarian model of the cold war era presumed as a counter example an always successful liberal model of legitimate parliamentarism, legal guarantees of personal rights and freedoms, and progressive capitalist development. For at least the first two decades of the cold war, if not well beyond that period, this was hardly the political reality in a number of Western nations, including the United States.[104] The role of totalitarian theory in helping to legitimate U.S. military interventions in Vietnam, Cuba, and Nicaragua that, whatever else they were intended to accomplish, also perpetuated a troubling heritage of overseas imperialism and the domestic repression of dissent has made the task of separating the postwar idea of totalitarianism from a legion of deeply controversial and antidemocratic political practices next to impossible.[105]

Current uses of some forms of totalitarian theory to analyze and describe non-Western societies, such as Islamic states or China, face similar objections. Totalitarian theories should not necessarily be abandoned altogether for current analytical purposes, but such undertakings will offer substantial intellectual and political challenges to those scholars or policymakers who would attempt to avoid the self-serving ideological simplifications of an "us-versus-them" schema that reproduces, albeit in a renovated, post–cold war antitotalitarian discourse, the imperialist mentalities and misunderstandings of previous decades and centuries. Moreover, the implied reference to the examples of past "totalitarian" dictatorships that occurs any time the term itself is invoked can no longer be so easily contained and manipulated as it was during the cold war. The selective uses of such comparisons drawn from history to provide an ideological sanction for foreign policy in the decade since the fall of the Berlin Wall are not especially encouraging evidence of the continued viability of totalitarian theory as a tool for the clarification of public issues. Asserting that Saddam Hussein of Iraq is "worse than Hitler" may help legitimate a war, but at the same time such a comparison creates extraordinary public expectations about the necessary outcome of the war. The gradual disappearance of the "totalitarian" label in particular cases can be equally revealing evidence of its limitations. During the 1980s, the adjective some Western leaders used to describe the Chinese government and its policies shifted from *totalitarian* to *authoritarian,* reflecting the impact of expanding international trade relations more than any marked relaxation of the oppressiveness of China's domestic policies.[106] The very term *totalitarian* might eventually be dumped from official policy statements in some countries as excess historical and ideological baggage.

If changing foreign policy needs represent one danger to the survival of totalitarian theory, its lack of attention to labor and other class-related issues ought to be another. The cold war model of totalitarianism often tended to shove the role of class in the origin and persistence of modern dictatorships to the periphery of scholarly discussion. Neglecting class and class conflict is undoubtedly one of the central reasons why traditional Marxists and some members of the New Left objected not only to the Friedrich-Brzezinski model but also to some of the wartime and postwar formulations of theorists with roots on the left, including Horkheimer, Adorno, and Marcuse. Theories of fascism have at the very least kept considerations of class and social organization under dictatorship from dissolving into static historical or political models of total control, pervasive social atomization, and an undifferentiated mass society. The shift toward totalitarian theory and away from the analysis of fascism entailed the near disappearance of discussions of class from the work of several of the German theorists discussed in this book, most notably Borkenau, Horkheimer, and Adorno. Franz Neumann's postwar work resisted this shift to some extent, but he still showed a diminished interest in class-based interpretation of politics.[107] Given the defeat or capture of independent working-class organizations by the Nazi and Stalinist states, this reduced attention to class conflicts in the postwar period is not too surprising, but it was another example of the pernicious dehistoricization sanctioned by postwar totalitarian theory: the working class, once unsuccessful (as in 1933), was in the postwar period mere social clay to be molded by governments, political parties, or trade union bosses. Marcuse, for example, raised the issue of class in his postwar writings mostly to show that the working class was now fully integrated into the totalitarian order and therefore could not be considered a potential source of social or political transformation.[108] Despite such dramatic examples as the Solidarity movement in Poland, the issue of class continues to receive muted attention in some recent books about the development of totalitarian theory or histories rooted in the theory of totalitarianism. Likewise, issues related to the construction of gender roles or sexual identity under modern dictatorships—topics that have received extensive and valuable attention for roughly three decades—have appeared only fairly recently in the work of historians or political theorists who continue to rely on the cold war to-talitarianism paradigm. Not surprisingly, the historians who advocate totalitarian theory the most strenuously are usually linked to an older historiographical tradition that emphasizes the political history of lead-ers, parties, and regimes.[109] There is no overriding methodological reason for these omissions or marginalizations, however. These differences of approach and focus emerge, more likely, out of the political and norma-tive engagements of scholars, with generational shifts in research inter-ests and approaches also playing a role. But the loss of the ideas of class and social conflict, which are of course fundamental to any theories rooted in Marxism but are hardly any longer its exclusive property, was not the only danger posed by the turn to the Soviet-Nazi comparative version of totalitarian theory.

The issue of the relationships between history, historiography, and politics has also dogged concepts of totalitarianism. The comparative cold war version of the theory, which offered a means of condemning Nazism and Communism at one stroke, could also—in the hands of some schol-ars—have the effect of relativizing the violence of these regimes. The *Historikerstreit,* or "historian's controversy," of the late 1980s offered a particularly clear example of how long-standing debates about totalitari-anism could continue to play a dubious role in scholarly and public dis-course about these two particular state-party dictatorships. The *Historiker-streit* emerged in the charged political atmosphere of what turned out to be the last years of the cold war. A series of controversies in the Federal Republic about the structuralist and intentionalist interpretations of the Nazi regime, the emotional response of Germans to the airing of the U.S. television series *The Holocaust,* and the calls by conservative politicians and historians for a "normalization" of German history stirred public dis-cussion of the Nazi era from the late 1970s through the mid-1980s. In 1985, West German chancellor Helmut Kohl invited U.S. president Ronald Reagan to visit a cemetery in Bitburg, Germany, where the remains of both Holocaust victims and Waffen SS troops were buried. The growing contro-versy in both nations about the symbolic (and in Reagan's remarks, literal) equation of both groups of wartime dead as "victims" brought public debate about the past to new levels of intensity. Then the Berlin historian Ernst Nolte—yet another of Heidegger's former students—set off an even more acrimonious series of exchanges among scholars and journalists when he suggested that Nazi genocide against European Jews was mod-eled on Soviet terror and in some sense justified by alleged Zionist threats of violence against Germany.[110]

Nolte's claims relied on a version of the notion of totalitarianism that "explained" and relativized Nazi violence not only by equating it with Soviet violence but also by suggesting a causal relationship in which Hitler was provoked to genocide by tales of Communist terror. This egregious use of a totalitarianism concept threatened to sink—or in Nolte's phrase, "deepen"—the explanatory usefulness of the totalitarian idea clear out of sight.[111] Jürgen Habermas led the critical response to Nolte's argument and extended his condemnation to the efforts of other German historians, including Michael Stürmer and Andreas Hillgruber, who were generating accounts of the past that also served neoconservative political ends, though their writings did not simply echo Nolte's work.[112] A series of bitterly polemical books and articles about the German past poured forth, and the question of how the story of twentieth-century Germany might acceptably be narrated and understood eventually elicited the opinions of dozens of scholars and intellectuals in Europe and the United States. The relationship between Nolte's expressed views and the controversial notion of totalitarianism was not the central focus of this dramatic and very public exchange, but the connection was unmistakable.[113]

Karl Dietrich Bracher's efforts to separate his own generally more empirical, traditionally liberal, and clearly articulated version of a totalitarianism concept from Nolte's vague speculations and tendentious use of a comparative totalitarian notion for the purpose of historical "normalization" of the Nazi era offer evidence of Bracher's fears about the possible damage the *Historikerstreit* could do to the very idea of totalitarianism. Bracher quickly took his stance above the polemics of the *Historikerstreit* by dismissing both of its chief antagonists, Nolte and Habermas, for their past role in "tabooing the concept of totalitarianism and inflating the formula for fascism."[114] Once again, Bracher's concerns about saving his version of the concept were timely. Within a handful of years, the fall of the Berlin Wall and the swift decline of Communism in the former Soviet bloc had granted legitimacy to the comparative study of the consequences of the right- and left-wing dictatorships in Central and Eastern Europe in this century—not to mention greatly increased access to archives. Undoubtedly, there will be some significant historical scholarship to emerge from this research, though two of the most innovative and knowledgeable non-German historians who have specialized in the topics of German Communism and Nazi Germany—respectively, Eric Weitz and Ian Kershaw—urge caution.[115] Kershaw's remarks on the usefulness and applicability of the concept of totalitarianism are more persuasive than is Bracher's polemical defense of the concept: "The demise of the Soviet

Empire and German unification have focused new attention on the concept of totalitarianism and opened up opportunities for comparative research on an empirical basis. Empirical findings have not, however, necessitated a major revision of the totalitarianism concept. Nor is it easy to see how they might do so. The theoretical basis of the concept is largely unaltered. Its limitations remain considerable."[116] Kershaw's criticisms of the totalitarianism concept are aimed primarily and with great effectiveness at the cold war version of the Nazi-Soviet comparative model that tried to extend the use of the concept to post-Stalinist regimes. His carefully wrought arguments against this static, predictable, and highly politicized version of the concept do not dismiss out of hand the usefulness of all formulations of the concept of totalitarianism. Kershaw tries instead to mark out reasonable limits to its applicability in comparative historical studies, and he sees its most important value as a means of "highlighting the singularity of each system."[117]

Stalinism and Nazism: Dictatorships in Comparison, a collection of essays edited by Kershaw and Moshe Lewin, an historian of the Soviet Union, offers powerful evidence that important comparative scholarship on these two regimes can proceed without any reliance whatsoever on the concept of totalitarianism. Kershaw's contribution to the book, an essay on Hitler and Stalin entitled "Working towards the Führer," pursues this very methodological and conceptual issue, though at times indirectly. He argues for the retention of concepts of fascism and targets the simple equation of the Hitlerist and Stalinist regimes as a misleading analytical focus on "superficial similarities." His analysis of the two dictators and their styles of leadership leads to a discussion of Hitler's role in the Nazi regime that is authoritative, empirical, and systematically critical of any simple equation of Nazi political dynamics with those of the Stalinist system of rule in the Soviet state. It must be also be noted here that in his concluding arguments, Kershaw cites Franz Neumann's *Behemoth* as a key statement on the nature of Nazi "governmental disorder."[118] Kershaw's essay, along with several others in *Stalin and Nazism,* demonstrates the value of a comparative approach to the study of dictatorship and at the same time goes far to render "the totalitarianism concept" an analytical relic in the field of historical studies. Indeed, the book offers perhaps the most effective scholarly argument yet lodged against the continued use of totalitarian theory, without making that argument its primary task.

Kershaw's critique of the concept of totalitarianism in its cold war guise has now been joined by several recent historical studies of dictatorship that simply do without concepts of totalitarianism.[119] But as Kershaw's discussions of the issue acknowledge, even the criticisms do not negate the need for the study of the concepts of totalitarianism. I have argued here that a longer historical perspective on several of these concepts and considerations of totalitarianism must be offered, one that takes into account the explorations of the totalitarian analytical schema that preceded the cold war. As this chapter has shown, German leftist antitotalitarianism has been varied and ambiguous in its effects, but it has also been of considerable importance to the postwar intellectual exchanges in Europe and the United States. This mixed fate of the concepts of totalitarianism even enters into Kershaw's critique: as he persuades us of the weakness of one version of the totalitarian concept, he cites the central interpretation of Nazism formulated by Franz Neumann, one of totalitarianism theory's most important left-wing investigators. In addition, even if the role of totalitarianism concepts in historical studies has entered a final decline—a conclusion that is, for better or worse, not yet warranted—concepts of totalitarianism may have other valid uses. As mentioned previously, they continue to appear as effective critical elements in a contemporary political philosophy of rights, sustaining the heterogeneous postwar tradition that runs from Arendt to Lefort, Habermas, and others. At present, such a use of totalitarian concepts shows more life and promise than the persistence of these concepts in historical or foreign policy-oriented scholarship; however, any speculations ventured here about the relative worth of particular concepts of totalitarianism will neither settle nor direct their future. If the experience of the past five decades is any guide, scholars will continue to praise or condemn concepts of totalitarianism, but they will not be able to bury them. For all their motley conceptual and historical baggage, the term *totalitarianism* and the numerous comparative analytical concepts and polemical arguments mustered under its banner will likely survive.[120]

Finally, yet another outcome of interwar and wartime thinking about totalitarianism may persist, though in a less obvious way. One of the most important scholarly legacies of the left-wing tradition of antitotalitarianism has been the critical and historically oriented social scientific analysis of dictatorship generated by such writers as Franz Neumann, Otto Kirchheimer, Ernst Fraenkel, and Richard Löwenthal. Since their lives and understandings were so deeply marked by historical crises, it is not surprising that their work has been most influential in the field of historical studies. The work of such historians as Tim Mason, Jane Caplan, Detlev Peukert, and Ian Kershaw, to cite but four notable examples, arguably carries forward some of the most important results and approaches of those earlier scholars of dictatorship, though with a much larger store of archival material at hand. Although they may not form a "school" of historical writing, with all of the personal, institutional, and methodological connections that such a term implies, they have often acknowledged the important influence of the earlier generation of leftist German scholars on the study of dictatorship.[121]

Ideas about the internally conflicted structure of the Nazi regime and the primacy of the political in modern dictatorships, which emerged most clearly in Franz Neumann's work, were a significant advance for left-oriented historical approaches in need of alternatives to economistic and reductive types of Marxism and traditionalist scholarly emphasis on the most obvious political manifestations of rule, such as the person and personality of the dictator. Attention to developing class relations and the social and cultural tensions inherent in modern dictatorships were evident in the most valuable writings produced by Arthur Rosenberg, Richard Löwenthal, and Franz Borkenau as well as the intellectuals mostly closely associated with the Institute of Social Research. Moreover, for all their frequent conceptual shifts away from a formal reliance on Marxism, these scholars of totalitarian dictatorship did not lose sight of the historical development of both ideology and policy, and they were willing to revise or jettison models and assumptions—including some formulations of the concept of totalitarianism itself—that failed to explain the political phenomena they observed. Although their wartime analytical strategies and conclusions may be dismissed by some Marxists or other critical radicals as "positivist" or even "defeatist" or by liberal and conservative scholars as politically "biased" toward Marxian formulations, these theorists consistently opposed state-party dictatorships—both Nazi and Soviet—without subscribing quietly to all of the policies and ideological claims of the West during the cold war.[122] Their sustained advocacy of democratic political institutions and at least moderately socialist public policies indicates that these thinkers were as clear about which political practices they favored—even under the postwar conditions of "existing capitalism"—as they were about those they opposed. The results of their efforts were not at all revolutionary, as if the work of intellectuals alone could have manufactured such a result, but compared with the remains of other intellectual and political tendencies of this century, theirs is not such a poor legacy.

A few essential conclusions about the importance of these traces of left-wing antitotalitarianism may be stated more simply and unequivocally: German socialists were some of the most important thinkers and writers who originated and sustained a debate about the causes and character of totalitarian dictatorships. Within the German Left of the interwar and wartime years, there was bitter disagreement about the definition of, origins of, nature of, and means of overcoming totalitarianism, and for some, the term was but an occasional substitute for *fascism.* Those who identified themselves as leftists might deploy or reject the term *totalitarianism* as they chose, and in using it they could draw on an array of possible definitions, some of them rooted in the tradition of revolutionary Marxism, some not. But as the examples in this study have shown, the term's use or nonuse by intellectuals on the German left from the Weimar Republic to the Bonn and Berlin republics did not always constitute a litmus test of socialist radicalism. Likewise, those who regarded themselves as liberals or conservatives did not exercise sole claim to use of the word totalitarian.

Regardless of who has used or still uses concepts of totalitarianism, it should be clear by now that for a time such notions were held by members of the Marxist or quasi-Marxist German Left as well as liberals and the Right. It is equally evident that left-wing opposition to fascism did not preclude theoretical or practical opposition to Bolshevism, Communism, or Stalinism—before, during, or after World War II. In fact, for a number of German intellectuals who engaged in political and scholarly debates from the end of the Weimar Republic to the beginning of the cold war, and sometimes even later, opposing totalitarianism could also mean working in defense of socialism.

NOTES

Introduction

1. Claude Lefort, *The Political Forms of Modern Society: Bureaucracy, Democracy, Totalitarianism,* ed. and trans. John B. Thompson (Cambridge, Mass.: MIT Press, 1986), 274–75. Unless otherwise cited, all translations from foreign-language sources into English are my own.

2. Several of Lefort's books and essays, notably the writings collected in *The Political Forms of Modern Society,* offer some of the most provocative and systematic critical readings of Marx by a former Marxist that have appeared in the postwar period. Other pertinent writings by Lefort include *Éléments d'une critique de la bureaucratie* (Geneva: Droz, 1971); *Un homme en trop: Réflections sur "L'Archipel du Goulag"* (Paris: Seuil, 1976); *Sur une colonne absente: Écrits autour de Merleau-Ponty* (Paris: Gallimard, 1978); *L'invention démocratique: Les limites de la domination totalitaire* (Paris: Fayard, 1981); and *Essais sur le politique* (Paris: Seuil, 1986), translated by David Macey as *Democracy and Political Theory* (Minneapolis: University of Minnesota Press, 1988). See also Cornelius Castoriadis, *La société bureaucratique* (Paris: Union générale d'éditions, 1973); *L'experience du mouvement ouvrier,* 2 vols. (Paris: Union générale d'éditions, 1974); *L'institution imaginaire de la société* (Paris: Seuil, 1975); *La société française* (Paris: Union générale d'éditions, 1979); *Capitalisme moderne et révolution* (Paris: Union générale d'éditions, 1979); *Political and Social Writings,* 2 vols., trans. and ed. David Ames Curtis (Minneapolis: University of Minnesota Press, 1988); *Philosophy, Politics, Autonomy: Essays in Political Philosophy,* ed. David Ames Curtis (New York: Oxford University Press, 1991); "Power, Politics, Autonomy," in *Cultural-Political Interventions in the Unfinished Project of Enlightenment,* ed. Axel Honneth et al. (Cambridge, Mass.: MIT Press, 1992), 269–97; and *The*

Castoriadis Reader, trans. David Ames Curtis (Oxford: Blackwell, 1997). The best analysis in English of the work of Lefort and Castoriadis is Dick Howard, *The Marxian Legacy,* 2d ed. (Minneapolis: University of Minnesota Press, 1988). Among the writings of Jean-François Lyotard that are most pertinent to the history of the critiques of totalitarianism are *La condition postmoderne: Rapport sur la savoir* (Paris: Éditions de Minuit, 1979) and *Le postmoderne expliqué aux enfants* (Paris: Éditions Galilée, 1988). Important writings on politics and totalitarian dictatorship by the others mentioned here include David Rousset, *L'univers concentrationnaire* (Paris: Éditions du Pavois, 1946); Albert Camus, *L'homme révolté* (Paris: Gallimard, 1951); and Raymond Aron, *L'opium des intellectuels* (Paris: Calmann-Lévy, 1955) and *Démocratie et totalitarisme* (Paris: Gallimard, 1965). Aron was a liberal, not a socialist, but for a time he had friends on the intellectual left, including Jean-Paul Sartre and Simone de Beauvoir.

3. On the postwar left in France, see David Caute, *The Fellow-Travellers: A Postscript to the Enlightenment* (New York: Macmillan, 1973); Tony Judt, *Marxism and the French Left: Studies on Labour and Politics in France, 1830–1981* (Oxford: Clarendon, 1989) and *Past Imperfect: French Intellectuals, 1944–1956* (Berkeley: University of California Press, 1992); and Sudhir Hazareesingh, *Intellectuals and the French Communist Party: Disillusion and Decline* (New York: Oxford University Press, 1992). See also the discussions of the Communist Left and the problem of totalitarianism in François Furet, *Le passé d'une illusion: Essai sur l'idée communiste au XXe siècle* (Paris: Laffont/Calmann-Lévy, 1995).

4. A short list of the best-known, or at any rate most influential, cold war–era writings (apart from Koestler's wartime *Darkness as Noon*) that attempted to analyze or portray the nature of totalitarian regimes includes Arthur Koestler, *Darkness at Noon* (New York: Macmillan, 1941); George Orwell, *Nineteen Eighty-Four* (London: Secker and Warburg, 1949); Hannah Arendt, *The Origins of Totalitarianism* (1951; reprint, New York: Harcourt Brace Jovanovich, 1979); Jacob L. Talmon, *The Origins of Totalitarian Democracy* (Boston: Beacon, 1952); Czeslaw Milosz, *The Captive Mind,* trans. Jane Zielonko (New York: Knopf, 1953); Carl J. Friedrich and Zbigniew Brzezinski, *Totalitarian Dictatorship and Autocracy* (Cambridge, Mass.: Harvard University Press, 1956; 2d ed., 1965); Barrington Moore Jr., *Social Origins of Dictatorship and Democracy: Lord and Peasant in the Making of the Modern World* (Boston: Beacon, 1967); and Karl Dietrich Bracher, *Die Auflösung der Weimarer Republik: Eine Studie zum Problem des Machtverfalls in der Demokratie* (Stuttgart: Ring, 1955), *Die deutsche Diktatur: Entstehung, Struktur, Folgen des Nationalsozialismus* (Berlin: Kiepenheuer und Witsch, 1969), *Zeitgeschichtliche Kontroversen: Um Faschismus, Totalitarismus, Demokratie* (Munich: Piper, 1984), and *Die totalitäre Erfahrung* (Munich: Piper, 1987). See also the voluminous fictional, autobiographical, and historical writings of Alexander Solzhenitsyn, Primo Levi, Jorge Semprun, Ignazio Silone, Victor Serge, Elie Wiesel, Margarete Buber-Neumann, Milan Kundera, Václav Havel, Danilo Kis, Nicola Chiaramonte, Milovan Djilas, and Roy Medvedev, among others. In the spirit of George Orwell's imaginative construction of a night-

marish social order, Margaret Atwood's *Handmaid's Tale* (Boston: Houghton Mifflin, 1986) offers a vivid and powerful feminist perspective on the problem of totalitarian power.

The issue of East European uses of the totalitarianism idea has emerged more clearly since 1989. For an unconventional example of the use of antitotalitarian critique in Eastern Europe, see Václav Havel, "The Velvet Hangover," trans. Káca Poláčková Henley, *Harper's* 281 (October 1990): 18–21. In this translation of a speech given in July 1990, Havel referred to "the shattering of the totalitarian system" and to "the new totalitarianism of consumption, commerce, and money." As we shall see, Havel to some extent followed the usage of such earlier German leftist writers as Karl Korsch and Herbert Marcuse in describing both communism and capitalism as exhibiting "totalitarian" characteristics. A timely and provocative collection of anti-Communist writings with a generally Eastern European focus is Ellen Frankel Paul, ed., *Totalitarianism at the Crossroads* (New Brunswick, N.J.: Transaction Books, 1990). Essays by Vladimir Bukovsky, Andrzej Walicki, and Zbigniew Rau offer various perspectives of Eastern European émigrés from the months just before the fall of the Berlin Wall. Still better is Andrzej Walicki, *Marxism and the Leap to the Kingdom of Freedom: The Rise and Fall of the Communist Utopia* (Stanford, Calif.: Stanford University Press, 1995).

Even former Communist Party apparatchiks have gotten into the act. For example, Alexander N. Yakovlev, a Soviet-Russian reformist and a survivor of regimes from Stalin through Yeltsin, has argued that "the totalitarian, Stalinist regime in Russia had to be exploded from within the totalitarian party" (quoted in Carol J. Williams, "World Report Profile: Alexander N. Yakovlev," *Los Angeles Times,* May 23, 1995, H5). See also Abbott Gleason's discussion of some of the term's new advocates in *Totalitarianism: The Inner History of the Cold War* (New York: Oxford University Press, 1995), 211–16.

Former Western Communists have continued to turn out ferocious condemnations of their earlier politics. One of the most important of the recent books of this type is Furet's *Le passé d'une illusion.* See also Tim Snyder's review of Furet's, Walicki's, and Gleason's books on totalitarianism: "'Coming to Terms with the Charm and Power of Soviet Communism,'" *Contemporary European History* 6, no. 1 (1997): 133–44. Snyder shrewdly elucidates each author's personal relationship to the history of Communism while at the same time avoiding a reductive biographical interpretation.

5. Friedrich, who ranked as a formidable historian and political scientist before the advent of the cold war, first publicly discussed his systematic model of totalitarianism at a conference he organized on the subject. See the book that resulted from this gathering of influential scholars from diverse fields: Carl J. Friedrich, ed., *Totalitarianism: Proceedings of a Conference Held at the American Academy of Arts and Sciences, March 1953* (Cambridge, Mass.: Harvard University Press, 1954). In this context, it is also worth noting that the controversial German historian Ernst Nolte has stated that "the well-known form of the theory [of totalitarianism] was devel-

oped by German or German-Jewish immigrants to the United States such as Franz Borkenau, Hannah Arendt, and Carl J. Friedrich." See Nolte, *Streitpunkte: Heutige und künftige Kontroversen um den Nationalsozialismus* (Berlin: Propyläen, 1993), 28. I would add that Borkenau and Arendt might reasonably be described in some respects and for some purposes as both German and German-Jewish. Borkenau's case is rather complicated, for he was also at times Austrian, Christian, Communist, and anti-Communist. Nolte is the only scholar I know of who mentions Borkenau's innovative work on the concept of totalitarianism alongside that of Arendt and Friedrich. Borkenau's numerous writings of the interwar years are an important focus of this book.

6. During the 1960s, Brzezinski gradually abandoned use of the totalitarian model in his own work. Abbott Gleason, the author of a recent history of totalitarianism, has speculated that this shift away from the model likely occurred as a result of Brzezinski's involvement in policy-making during the Kennedy administration and later as national security adviser to President Carter. Friedrich, however, continued to defend the notion against its various critics during the crucial cold war years from the early 1950s to the late 1960s. See Gleason, *Totalitarianism*, 202. Brzezinski had apparently ceased to rely on the totalitarianism paradigm before the 1970s, since Friedrich lamented his former ally's departure from the model, citing an article Brzezinski had published in 1966. See Carl J. Friedrich, "The Evolving Theory and Practice of Totalitarian Regimes," in *Totalitarianism in Perspective: Three Views*, by Carl J. Friedrich, Michael Curtis, and Benjamin R. Barber (New York: Praeger, 1969), 123–64; and Carl J. Friedrich, "Fascism versus Totalitarianism: Ernst Nolte's Views Reexamined," *Central European History* 4, no. 3 (1971): 271–84. The article Friedrich criticized was Zbigniew Brzezinski, "The Soviet Political System: Transformation or Degeneration?" *Problems of Communism* 15, no. 1 (1966): 1–15. On Friedrich's career and the development of his version of totalitarian theory, see Hans J. Lietzmann, "Von der konstitutionellen zur totalitären Diktatur: Carl Joachim Friedrichs Totalitarismustheorie," in *Totalitarismus: Eine Ideengeschichte des 20. Jahrhunderts*, ed. Alfons Söllner, Ralf Walkenhaus, and Karin Wieland (Berlin: Akademie, 1997), 174–92.

7. Friedrich and Brzezinski, *Totalitarian Dictatorship and Autocracy,* 1st ed., 9–10.

8. Seyla Benhabib, *The Reluctant Modernism of Hannah Arendt* (Thousand Oaks, Calif.: Sage Publications, 1996), 67; Carl E. Schorske, Review of *Totalitarian Dictatorship and Autocracy,* by Carl J. Friedrich and Zbigniew Brzezinski, *American Historical Review* 63, no. 2 (1957): 367–68.

I use *fascism* to indicate such political movements and ideas collectively and uppercase it only when discussing the Fascist Party of Italy. Likewise, the term *socialism* refers to leftist movements and ideas generally, and *Socialist* or *Social Democrat* refers to specific parties and their members. Since the terms *Communist* and *Communism* most often refer to a party and its members, theories, or policies in this book and since they are somewhat less generic than the others, I leave them capitalized. The authors I discuss, however, generally did not adhere to such distinctions, and I have not altered their spelling or terminology to fit mine.

9. Gleason also mentions the dominant influence of the Friedrich-Brzezinski model in *Totalitarianism*, 125. The model's career is hardly over. One recent and widely praised study, Klaus P. Fischer's *Nazi Germany: A New History* (New York: Continuum, 1995), opens with a chapter entitled "The Origins of Totalitarianism" that cites the Friedrich-Brzezinski model as a basis of the book's analysis (17–18).

10. A wide-ranging discussion of the domestic political and ideological effects of anti-Soviet foreign policy and anti-Communist domestic policy in the United States appears in Stephen J. Whitfield, *The Culture of the Cold War* (Baltimore: Johns Hopkins University Press, 1991). See also Whitfield's comments on the decline of the idea of totalitarianism during the period of detente in "'Totalitarianism' in Eclipse: The Recent Fate of an Idea," in *Images and Ideas in American Culture: Essays in Memory of Philip Rahv*, ed. Arthur Edelstein (Hanover, N.H.: University Press of New England, 1979), 60–95.

11. Even some conservative and liberal social scientists remained unsatisfied with the Friedrich-Brzezinski model of totalitarian regimes. Leonard Schapiro, a specialist in Soviet studies, presented his own model in *Totalitarianism* (New York: Praeger, 1972). Other essential discussions of totalitarianism and totalitarian theory include Hans Buchheim, *Totalitäre Herrschaft: Wesen und Merkmale* (Munich: Kösel, 1962); Konrad Löw, ed., *Totalitarismus* (Berlin: Duncker und Humblot, 1988); Michael Curtis, *Totalitarianism* (New Brunswick, N.J.: Transaction Books, 1979); Manfred Funke, ed., *Totalitarismus: Ein Studien-Reader zur Herrschaftsanalyse modernen Diktaturen* (Düsseldorf: Droste, 1978); Martin Jänicke, *Totalitäre Herrschaft: Anatomie eines politischen Begriffs* (Berlin: Duncker und Humblot, 1971); Aryeh L. Unger, *The Totalitarian Party: Party and People in Nazi Germany and Soviet Russia* (Cambridge: Cambridge University Press, 1974); and Bruno Seidel and Siegfried Jenker, eds, *Wege Der Totalitarismusforschung* (Darmstadt: Wissenschaftliche Buchgesellschaft, 1974). Bracher has also articulated his own more historically oriented version of totalitarian theory in *Zeitgeschichtliche Kontroversen*, 43–44. Yet another scholar, Herbert Spiro, found totalitarian theory wanting for both political and methodological reasons. He suggested in his definition of the term *totalitarianism* in the second edition of the *International Encyclopedia of the Social Sciences* that "a third encyclopedia of the social sciences, like the first one, will not list 'totalitarianism.'" See Spiro, "Totalitarianism," in *International Encyclopedia of the Social Sciences*, 2d ed., vol. 16 (New York: Macmillan, 1968), 112.

12. Quoted in Karl Dietrich Bracher, "Totalitarianism," in *Dictionary of the History of Ideas*, vol. 4, ed. Philip P. Wiener (New York: Scribner, 1974), 408.

13. For the history of these early uses of the term *totalitarian*, see Jens Peterson, "Die Entstehung des Totalitarismusbegriffs," in *Totalitarismus*, ed. Funke, 105–28; and Ian Kershaw, *The Nazi Dictatorship: Problems and Perspectives of Interpretation*, 3d ed. (London: Edward Arnold, 1993), 19–22.

14. Karl Mannheim, *Ideology and Utopia*, trans. Louis Wirth and Edward Shils (San Diego: Harcourt Brace Jovanovich, 1985), 145–46. The source of this translated passage is Karl Mannheim, *Ideologie und Utopie* (Bonn: Cohen, 1929), 111–12.

15. The objections to the comparison (*Vergleich*) of Nazism and Soviet Communism registered by postwar scholarly writers are partly similar to those raised by Mannheim over sixty years ago. See, for instance, Hans Mommsen, "The Concept of Totalitarian Dictatorship vs. the Comparative Theory of Fascism: The Case of National Socialism," in *Totalitarianism Reconsidered,* ed. Ernest Menze (Port Washington, N.Y.: Kennikat, 1981), 146–65; Benjamin Barber, "Conceptual Foundations of Totalitarianism," in *Totalitarianism in Perspective,* by Friedrich, Curtis, and Barber, 3–39; and Wolfgang Wippermann, *Faschismustheorien: Zum Stand der gegenwärtigen Diskussion,* 5th ed. (Darmstadt: Wissenschaftliche Buchgesellschaft, 1989), 96–101.

16. The strong connections between the two movements receive a brief and vigorous reappraisal in Tim Mason, "Whatever Happened to 'Fascism?'" in *Nazism, Fascism and the Working Class: Essays by Tim Mason,* ed. Jane Caplan (Cambridge: Cambridge University Press, 1995), 323–31. See also the excellent discussions of the two regimes by Tobias Abse, Tilla Siegel, Michael Geyer, and others in Richard Bessel, ed., *Fascist Italy and Nazi Germany: Comparisons and Contrasts* (Cambridge: Cambridge University Press, 1996). Fittingly, this collection of essays emerged as the result of a conference held at St. Peter's College, Oxford, in 1993 to honor the memory of Tim Mason. Fascism studies are in the midst of a renaissance these days, marked by the appearance of several important books on the topic written from diverse perspectives, including Mason, *Nazism, Fascism and the Working Class;* Roger Eatwell, *Fascism: A History* (New York: Penguin Books, 1996); Roger Griffin, *The Nature of Fascism* (New York: St. Martin's, 1991); Stanley G. Payne, *A History of Fascism, 1914–1945* (Madison: University of Wisconsin Press, 1995); Walter Laqueur, *Fascism: Past, Present, Future* (New York: Oxford University Press, 1996); and Mark Neocleous, *Fascism* (Minneapolis: University of Minnesota Press, 1997). This proliferation of important work on fascism has occurred partly because rightist movements have returned to political prominence in Europe. The innovative work of one scholar, Zeev Sternhell, who has argued that France was the most important source of fascist ideas, has also played a significant role. See Sternhell, *Ni droite, ni gauche* (Paris: Édition du Seuil, 1983); "The 'Anti-Materialist' Revision of Marxism as an Aspect of the Rise of Fascist Ideology," *Journal of Contemporary History* 22, no. 3 (1987): 379–400; and Sternhell, Z. Sznajder, and M. Asheri, eds., *The Birth of Fascist Ideology* (Princeton, N.J.: Princeton University Press, 1994). For a carefully argued discussion of fascism and the "New Radical Right" in Europe, see Diethelm Prowe, "'Classic' Fascism and the New Radical Right in Western Europe: Comparisons and Contrasts," *Contemporary European History* 3, no. 3 (1994): 289–313.

17. Kershaw, *The Nazi Dictatorship,* 20.

18. Kershaw responded quite generously to an earlier version of one of this book's chapters and acknowledged my arguments regarding Franz Borkenau's for-

mulation of a comparative totalitarianism concept in the late 1930s. See William David Jones, "Toward a Theory of Totalitarianism: Franz Borkenau's *Pareto*," *Journal of the History of Ideas* 53, no. 3 (1992): 455–66. For discussions of Hilferding's version of the idea of totalitarianism, see André Liebich, "Marxism and Totalitarianism: Rudolf Hilferding and the Mensheviks," *Dissent* 34 (Spring 1987): 223–40; and William Smaldone, "Rudolf Hilferding and the Total State," *Historian* 56 (August 1994): 97–112. Richard Löwenthal's earliest uses of the totalitarian comparison appeared in some of his unpublished writings from the wartime period, which are discussed later in this book.

19. For excellent accounts of the German Left's analyses of fascism, with emphasis on the postwar era, see Wolfgang Wippermann, "The Post-War German Left and Fascism," *Journal of Contemporary History* 11, no. 4 (1976): 185–219; and Wolfgang Wippermann, "Faschismus—nur ein Schlagwort?" in *Tel Aviver Jahrbuch für deutsche Geschichte*, vol. 16 (Gerlingen: Bleicher, 1987): 346–66.

20. E. P. Thompson, "Inside *Which* Whale?" in *George Orwell: A Collection of Critical Essays,* ed. Raymond Williams (Englewood Cliffs, N.J.: Prentice-Hall, 1974), 87. The title of Thompson's essay—and much of its content as well—was a hostile rejoinder to Orwell's "Inside the Whale," in *Inside the Whale and Other Essays* (Harmondsworth, England: Penguin Books, 1982), 9–50.

21. Alfons Söllner elaborates a perspective on the politicization of the terms similar to the one I argue here in his introductory essay, "Das Totalitarismuskonzept in der Ideengeschichte des 20. Jahrhunderts," in *Totalitarismus,* ed. Söllner, Walkenhaus, and Wieland, 10–21. Juan Linz aptly points out that the dispute over the relative valuation of *fascism* and *totalitarianism* as analytical categories was important, but he adds that this issue does not entirely explain the debates on dictatorship of the 1960s. See Linz, "Totalitarianism and Authoritarianism: My Recollections on the Development of Comparative Politics," in *Totalitarismus,* ed. Söllner, Walkenhaus, and Wieland, 151–53. See also Wolfgang Sauer, "National Socialism: Totalitarianism or Fascism?" *American Historical Review* 73, no. 2 (1967): 404–24. By the late 1970s, scholars were discussing the apparent decline of *both* concepts. See Whitfield, "'Totalitarianism' in Eclipse"; and Gilbert Allardyce, "What Fascism Is Not: Thoughts on the Deflation of a Concept," *American Historical Review* 84, no. 2 (1979): 367–88. The end of détente brought them both roaring back—especially totalitarianism.

22. Reinhard Kühnl, "Zur politischen Funktion der Totalitarismustheorien in der BRD," in *Totalitarismus: Zur Problematik eines politischen Begriffs,* ed. M. Greiffenhagen, R. Kühnl, and J. B. Müller (Munich: List, 1972), 7.

23. Wippermann, "The Post-War German Left and Fascism," 193.

24. The most important sources on the history of the Institute of Social Research and the Frankfurt School are Martin Jay, *The Dialectical Imagination: A History of the Frankfurt School and the Institute of Social Research* (Boston: Little, Brown, 1973); and Rolf Wiggershaus, *Die Frankfurter Schule: Geschichte, Theoretische Entwicklung, Politische Bedeutung* (Munich: Deutscher Taschenbuch, 1988), translated by

Michael Robertson as *The Frankfurt School: Its History, Theories, and Political Significance* (Cambridge, Mass.: MIT Press, 1994). On the group's theoretical background and development, see also David Held, *Introduction to Critical Theory: Horkheimer to Habermas* (Berkeley: University of California Press, 1980); Judith Marcus and Zoltán Tar, eds., *Foundations of the Frankfurt School of Social Research* (New Brunswick, N.J.: Transaction Books, 1984); Thomas Bottomore, *The Frankfurt School* (Sussex: Ellis Horwood, 1984); Seyla Benhabib, *Critique, Norm, and Utopia: A Study of the Foundations of Critical Theory* (New York: Columbia University Press, 1986); Douglas Kellner, *Critical Theory, Marxism, and Modernity* (Baltimore: Johns Hopkins University Press, 1989); and Stephen Eric Bronner, *Of Critical Theory and Its Theorists* (Cambridge, Mass.: Blackwell, 1994).

25. See also Andreas Wildt, "Totalitarian State Capitalism," *Telos*, no. 41 (Fall 1979): 33–57.

26. Reinhard Kühnl, "'Linke' Totalitarismusversionen," in *Totalitarismus*, ed. Greiffenhagen, Kühnl, and Müller, 97–119, 141–44 (notes). Other critical Marxist discussions of the theories of totalitarianism and fascism in the writings of Horkheimer and his institute collegues appear in Zoltán Tar, *The Frankfurt School: The Critical Theories of Max Horkheimer and Theodor W. Adorno* (New York: John Wiley and Sons, 1977), 113–15; Phil Slater, *Origin and Significance of the Frankfurt School: A Marxist Perspective* (London: Routledge and Kegan Paul, 1977), 59–62; and Michael Löwy, "Partisan Truth: Knowledge and Social Classes in Critical Theory," in *Foundations of the Frankfurt School of Social Research*, ed. Marcus and Tar, 289–304. These books and Löwy's article, along with Perry Anderson's *Considerations on Western Marxism* (London: New Left Books, 1976), still offer the most systematic, forceful, and clearly stated Marxist critiques of the Frankfurt School.

For an English-language collection of the key documents in the *Historikerstreit*, see *Forever in the Shadow of Hitler? Original Documents of the Historikerstreit, the Controversy concerning the Singularity of the Holocaust*, trans. James Knowlton and Truett Cates (Atlantic Highlands, N.J.: Humanities, 1993). A brief discussion of the *Historikerstreit* also appears in the final chapter of this book. For a controversial volume of writings on the *Historikerstreit*, see Reinhard Kühnl, *Vergangenheit, die nicht vergeht: Die "Historiker-Debatte"; Darstellung, Dokumentation, Kritik* (Cologne: Pahl-Rugenstein, 1987).

27. Eike Hennig, *Zum Historikerstreit: Was heißt und zu welchem Ende studiert man Faschismus?* (Frankfurt am Main: Athenäum, 1988), 69; Eike Hennig, "Zur Theorie der Totalitarismustheorien oder Anmerkungen zum Nimbus eines politischen Begriffs," *Neue Politische Literatur* 21, no. 1 (1976): 1–25. Some of Hennig's appraisals of both the cold war–era theory and the various left-wing versions of the theory among scholars affiliated with the Frankfurt Institute of Social Research are found in *Thesen zur deutschen Sozial- und Wirtschaftsgeschichte, 1933 bis 1938* (Frankfurt am Main: Suhrkamp, 1973), 245–48; and *Bürgerliche Gesellschaft und Faschismus in Deutschland: Ein Forschungsbericht* (Frankfurt am Main: Suhrkamp, 1982), 29–31, 56–63.

28. Kershaw has offered some of the most thoughtful and persuasive recent criticisms of the revival of totalitarian theory following the collapse of the Soviet Union. See his "'Working towards the Führer': Reflections on the Nature of the Hitler Dictatorship," *Contemporary European History* 2, no. 2 (1993): 103–18; and "Totalitarianism Revisited: Nazism and Stalinism in Comparative Perspective," in *Tel Aviver Jahrbuch für deutsche Geschichte*, vol. 23 (Gerlingen: Bleicher, 1994), 23–40. For a wide-ranging collection of essays on the Nazi-Soviet comparison, see Ian Kershaw and Moshe Lewin, eds., *Stalinism and Nazism: Dictatorships in Comparison* (Cambridge: Cambridge University Press, 1997).

29. See Wolfgang Wippermann's compact and thoroughly documented *Faschismustheorien* and *Zur Analyse des Faschismus: Die sozialistische und kommunistischen Faschismustheorien, 1921–1945* (Frankfurt am Main: Verlag Moritz Diesterweg, 1981). Another helpful book on the topic of left-wing critiques of fascism is David Beetham's excellent collection of primary source texts, *Marxists in Face of Fascism: Writings by Marxists on Fascism from the Inter-War Period* (Totowa, N.J.: Barnes and Noble Books, 1984).

30. Gleason's *Totalitarianism* offers numerous useful discussions of Menshevik, German leftist, and other socialist arguments against totalitarian dictatorship. See also Liebich, "Marxism and Totaltarianism," as well as the brief discussion of the issue in André Liebich, *From the Other Shore: Russian Social Democracy after 1921* (Cambridge, Mass.: Harvard University Press, 1997), 238–42. For essays that discuss the part leftists, including such former Communists as Arthur Koestler, Margarete Buber-Neumann, Cornelius Castoriadis, Ruth Fischer, and Franz Borkenau, played in developing notions of totalitarianism, see Söllner, Walkenhaus, and Wieland, eds., *Totalitarismus*.

31. Ernst Nolte, *Three Faces of Fascism*, trans. Leila Vennewitz (1963; reprint, New York: New American Library, 1969), 17–47, 569–72. The original German edition of the book was entitled *Der Faschismus in seiner Epoche* (Munich: Piper, 1963). See also Nolte's *Marxismus-Faschismus-Kalter Krieg: Vorträge und Aufsätze, 1964–1976* (Stuttgart: Deutsche Verlagsanstalt, 1977); *Deutschland und der Kalte Krieg* (Munich: Piper, 1974); and *Der europäische Bürgerkrieg, 1917–1945: Nationalsozialismus und Bolschewismus* (Frankfurt am Main: Propyläen, 1987). This last book was Nolte's weightiest utterance in the *Historikerstreit*. See also the collection of essays on fascism edited by Nolte, *Theorien über den Faschismus* (Cologne: Kiepenheuer und Witsch, 1967).

32. Ernst Nolte, "Fernsegespräch zwischen Hans Mommsen und Ernst Nolte vom 7. Februar 1987," in *Das Vergehen der Vergangenheit: Antwort an meine Kritiker im sogenannten Historikerstreit* (Berlin: Verlag Ullstein, 1987), 84–85. See also Ernst Nolte, "Die historisch-genetisch Version der Totalitarismustheorie: Ärgernis oder Einsicht?" *Zeitschrift für Politik* 43 (1996): 111–22. On the historians' debate, see *Forever in the Shadow of Hitler?* A more extensive discussion of this controversy, with a focus on Nolte's singular use of the totalitarian comparison, appears in the concluding chapter.

33. Pierre Ayçoberry, *The Nazi Question: An Essay on the Interpretations of National Socialism (1922–1975)*, trans. Robert Hurley (London: Routledge and Kegan Paul, 1981).

34. Walter Schlangen, *Theorie und Ideologie des Totalitarismus: Möglichkeiten und Grenzen einer liberalen Kritik politischer Herrschaft* (Bonn: Bundeszentrale fur politische Bildung, 1972); Walter Schlangen, *Die Totalitarismus-Theorie: Entwicklung und Probleme* (Stuttgart: W. Kohlhammer, 1976). Writing at about the same time, Leszek Kolakowski, a Polish émigré philosopher, offered a massive and systematic historical-philosophical critique of Marxism that included several brief comments on leftist antitotalitarian writings. His observations were generally more knowledgeable and even more hostile toward Marxism than Schlangen's. But as with Ayçoberry's *Nazi Question*, this critique was not the central focus of the book. See Kolakowski, *Main Currents of Marxism*, 3 vols. (Oxford: Oxford University Press, 1978). Stephen Eric Bronner has persuasively refuted some of Kolakowski's remarks on Karl Korsch. See Bronner, *Of Critical Theory and Its Theorists*, 30, notes 49 and 57.

35. Bracher's most important books are *Die Auflösung der Weimarer Republik* and *Die deutsche Diktatur*.

36. Karl Dietrich Bracher, foreword to *Theorie and Ideologie des Totalitarismus*, by Schlangen, 7. For a more elaborate and systematic defense of *Totalitarismustheorie*, see Bracher, *Zeitgeschichtliche Kontroversen*, 34–62. See also his emphatic restatement of support for totalitarianism theory, *Turning Points in Modern Times: Essays on German and European History*, trans. Thomas Dunlap (Cambridge, Mass.: Harvard University Press, 1995). For a powerful account—and persuasive refutation—of the various attempts (as in Bracher's brief remarks in the foreword to Schlangen's book) to bracket as closely and consistently similar the political theories of the right-wing jurist of the Weimar period, Carl Schmitt, who eventually joined the Nazi Party, and those of some of his Marxist students, such as Otto Kirchheimer and Franz Neumann, see William Scheuerman, *Between the Norm and the Exception: The Frankfurt School and the Rule of Law* (Cambridge, Mass.: MIT Press, 1994). Several books on Schmitt have appeared over the past two decades, including Joseph Bendersky, *Carl Schmitt: Theorist for the Reich* (Princeton, N.J.: Princeton University Press, 1983); and John P. McCormick, *Carl Schmitt's Critique of Liberalism: Against Politics as Technology* (Cambridge: Cambridge University Press, 1997). McCormick makes numerous references to Kirchheimer and Neumann and asserts that Schmitt's leftist students actually "have done as much to obfuscate as to clarify" their teacher's ideas through misinterpretations of his writings (125, note 5). Chapter 3 discusses some of Schmitt's ideas on the totalitarian state more extensively.

37. A compact and lucid survey of this debate, with references to the pertinent literature in both English and German, appears in Kershaw, *The Nazi Dictatorship*, 17–34. See also the representative collection of essays in Menze, ed., *Totalitarianism Reconsidered*.

38. Bracher, *Turning Points in Modern Times*, 151. The article's first, German-language version is dated 1987 in the "notes on sources," 332.

39. For a detailed account of these events, see Gleason, *Totalitarianism*. Some of the most influential books in the revival of the concept were Jean-François Revel, *La tentation totalitaire* (Paris: Éditions Robert Laffont, 1976), translated by David Hapgood as *The Totalitarian Temptation* (New York: Doubleday, 1977); Bernard-Henri Lévy, *La barbarie a visage humain* (Paris: Éditions Grasset and Fasquelle, 1977), translated by George Holoch as *Barbarism with a Human Face* (New York: Harper and Row, 1979); Bracher (see the books cited in notes 4 and 36); and Jeane Kirkpatrick, *Dictatorships and Double Standards* (New York: Simon and Schuster, 1982).

40. Bracher, *Turning Points in Modern Times*. See also Kershaw, "Totalitarianism Revisited"; and Christopher Hitchens, "How Neoconservatives Perish: Good-bye to 'Totalitarianism' and All That," *Harper's* 281 (July 1990): 65–70. Hitchens's article is reprinted in *For the Sake of Argument: Essays and Minority Reports* (London: Verso, 1993), 140–48. Hitchens offered a brief, incisive account of the term's uses and gave the hegemonic cold war version of the concept and its admirers a swift and gleeful political burial. He rightly criticized the attitude of political despair the concept has often legitimated, and he particularly objected to Jeane Kirkpatrick's Reagan-era refashioning of the totalitarian notion as a handy rationale for an anti-Left foreign policy. Despite clear signs of wear and tear, the concept functioned nicely during the 1980s to prop up an anti-Left domestic policy as well. Since the collapse of the Soviet Union in 1991, the idea seems to have returned to the political discourse in Europe to some extent, and its career in the United States may not yet be over. But it is rather difficult to see how the dominant anti-Communist totalitarian model—especially the version revived by neoconservatives during the 1970s and 1980s—could be of much further policy use when it had not been especially helpful in explaining how or why the supposedly monolithic, implacable, totalitarian Soviet regime could collapse politically and then officially dismantle itself with a minimum of bloodshed. See Kirkpatrick, *Dictatorships and Double Standards*, 23–52, 96–138. See also Jeane Kirkpatrick, *The Withering Away of the Totalitarian State and Other Surprises* (New York: American Enterprise Institute, 1991).

41. Gleason, *Totalitarianism*, 9.

42. A representative collection of writings by several of the Austrian Left's important theoreticians, who were so influential in German socialist circles, appears in Thomas Bottomore and Patrick Goode, eds., *Austro-Marxism* (Oxford: Oxford University Press, 1978). On the Menshevik exiles, see Liebich's definitive study, *From the Other Shore*. On the possible connection between the left-wing, theoretically critical outlook and the Jewish backgrounds common to several of these thinkers, see Jay, *The Dialectical Imagination*, 31–35.

43. See Liebich, "Marxism and Totalitarianism," 223–40. Liebich accurately points out that the adjective *totalitarian* (often set in quotation marks, in whatever

language it appeared) preceded the noun *totalitarianism* and that both terms were at first used by leftists in an imprecise way (232).

44. Such appearances were to become part of the legend of the Eisler family. Ruth Fischer's other brother, Hanns Eisler, also a Communist, was a composer who wrote a variety of orchestral pieces, including the national anthem of the German Democratic Republic. He faced a hostile House Committee on Un-American Activities months later. For a helpful capsule biography of Hanns Eisler, see Anton Kaes, Martin Jay, and Edward Dimendberg, eds., *The Weimar Republic Sourcebook* (Berkeley: University of California Press, 1994), 746.

45. Sabine Hering and Kurt Schilde, *Kampfname Ruth Fischer: Wandlungen einer deutschen Kommunistin* (Frankfurt am Main: Dipa, 1995), 276–78. For accounts of the tribulations of the brothers Eisler before the House Committee on Un-American Activities, see Anthony Heilbut, *Exiled in Paradise: German Refugee Artists and Intellectuals in America from the 1930's to the Present* (New York: Viking, 1983), 370–74; and David Caute, *The Great Fear: The Anti-Communist Purge under Truman and Eisenhower* (New York: Touchstone Books, 1979), 233–34, 495–96.

Chapter 1: Strange Defeat

1. The following books constitute only a sampling of the massive scholarship on the subject of Weimar Germany: Bracher, *Die Auflösing der Weimarer Republik;* Martin Broszat, *Hitler and the Collapse of the Weimar Republic,* trans. V. R. Berghahn (Leamington Spa: Berg, 1987); Eberhard Kolb, *The Weimar Republic,* trans. P. S. Falla (London: Routledge, 1992); Gordon Craig, *Germany, 1866–1945* (New York: Oxford University Press, 1978); Detlev Peukert, *The Weimar Republic: The Crisis of Classical Modernity,* trans. Richard Deveson (New York: Hill and Wang, 1992); and Heinrich August Winkler, *Weimar: 1918–1933: Die Geschichte der ersten deutschen Demokratie* (Munich: Beck, 1993). See also Kaes, Jay, and Dimendberg, eds., *The Weimar Republic Sourcebook.* For an excellent critical discussion of recent scholarship on the Weimar period, see Peter Fritzsche, "Did Weimar Fail?" *Journal of Modern History* 68 (September 1996): 629–56. Fritzsche has recently offered his own bold reinterpretation of this period in *Germans into Nazis* (Cambridge, Mass.: Harvard University Press, 1998).

2. Franz Neumann, "The Decay of German Democracy," *Political Quarterly* 4, no. 4 (1933): 525–43.

3. The literature on the SPD from the outbreak of World War I to early Weimar is voluminous. Some of the most useful surveys and monographs are Richard Breitman, *German Socialism and Weimar Democracy* (Chapel Hill: University of North Carolina Press, 1981); W. L. Guttsman, *The German Social Democratic Party, 1875–1933: From Ghetto to Government* (London: Allen and Unwin, 1981); Donna Harsch, *German Social Democracy and the Rise of Nazism* (Chapel Hill: University of North Carolina Press, 1993); Susanne Miller, *Die Bürde der Macht: Die deutsche Sozialdemokratie 1918–1920,* Beiträge zur geschichte des Parlamentarismus und der politischen Parteien, vol. 63 (Düsseldorf: Droste, 1978); David W. Morgan, *The So-*

cialist Left and the German Revolution: A History of the German Independent Social Democratic Party, 1917–1922 (Ithaca, N.Y.: Cornell University Press, 1975); and A. J. Ryder, *The German Revolution of 1918: A Study of German Socialism in War and Revolt* (Cambridge: Cambridge University Press, 1967). Essential background on the SPD of this period can be found in one older "classic" study and two more recent ones: Robert Michels, *Political Parties,* trans. Eden and Cedar Paul (New York: Dover, 1959); Carl E. Schorske, *German Social Democracy, 1905–1917: The Development of the Great Schism* (1955; reprint, Cambridge, Mass.: Harvard University Press, 1983); and Guenther Roth, *The Social Democrats in Imperial Germany* (Totowa, N.J.: Bedminster, 1963).

4. Bracher, *Die Auflösung der Weimarer Republik,* 578. On the military's role in Weimar politics, see also Gordon Craig, *The Politics of the Prussian Army, 1640–1945* (Oxford: Oxford University Press, 1955).

5. On the Communists' murky role in this parliamentary maneuvering that led to the so-called Red referendum of 1931, see Ben Fowkes, *Communism in Germany under the Weimar Republic* (London: Macmillan, 1984); 163–71; and Ossip K. Flechtheim, *Die KPD in der Weimarer Republik* (1948; reprint, Hamburg: Junius, 1986), 219–20. On the Social Democratic Party's response and their ouster in 1932, see Harsch, *German Social Democracy and the Rise of Nazism,* 127–31; and Breitman, *German Socialism and Weimar Democracy,* 169–88.

6. On Luxemburg (1871–1919), see J. P. Nettl, *Rosa Luxemburg,* 2 vols. (New York: Oxford University Press, 1966); Hannah Arendt, *Men in Dark Times* (New York: Harcourt, Brace and World, 1968), 33–56; Norman Geras, *The Legacy of Rosa Luxemburg* (London: New Left Books, 1976); Ossip K. Flechtheim, *Rosa Luxemburg: Zur Einführung* (Hamburg: Junius, 1986); and Stephen Eric Bronner, *Rosa Luxemburg: A Revolutionary for Our Times* (New York: Columbia University Press, 1987). Excellent recent interpretations are Bronner's introductory essay, "Reflections on Rosa," in *The Letters of Rosa Luxemburg,* ed. and trans. Stephen Eric Bronner (Atlantic Highlands, N.J.: Humanities, 1993); and Eric D. Weitz, "'Rosa Luxemburg Belongs to Us!': German Communism and the Luxemburg Legacy," *Central European History* 27, no. 1 (1994): 27–64. Schorske's *German Social Democracy* discusses Luxemburg's vital contribution to the radical critique of social democratic theory and practice in the years of her greatest activity in Germany.

7. On Zetkin (1857–1933), see the biographical accounts of Karen Honeycutt, "Clara Zetkin and the Women's Social Democratic Movement in Germany" (Ph.D. diss., Columbia University, 1976); and Karen Honeycutt, "Clara Zetkin: A Socialist Approach to the Problem of Women's Oppression," *Feminist Studies* 3, nos. 3/4 (1976): 131–44. See also the numerous references to Zetkin in Jean Quataert, *Reluctant Feminists in German Social Democracy, 1885–1917* (Princeton, N.J.: Princeton University Press, 1979); Schorske, *German Social Democracy;* Ruth Fischer, *Stalin and German Communism: A Study in the Origins of the State Party* (1948; reprint, New Brunswick, N.J.: Transaction Books, 1982); Fowkes, *Communism in Germany under the Weimar Republic;* and Flechtheim, *Die KPD in der Weimarer Republik.*

8. The congress met from 30 December 1918 to 1 January 1919 and declared the founding of the KPD on the last day of its deliberations. See Hermann Weber, ed., *Der Gründungsparteitag der KPD: Protokoll und Materialien* (Frankfurt am Main: Europäische Verlagsanstalt, 1969); Eric D. Weitz, *Creating German Communism, 1890–1990: From Popular Protests to Socialist State* (Princeton, N.J.: Princeton University Press, 1997), 78–99; and Fowkes, *Communism in Germany under the Weimar Republic,* 19–23. On the opportunism and antirevolutionary actions of some SPD leaders, such as Philipp Scheidemann and Friedrich Ebert, see Schorske, *German Social Democracy.*

9. Clara Zetkin, "The Struggle against Fascism," in *Marxists in Face of Fascism,* ed. Beetham, 102–13. For a brief discussion of Zetkin's analysis of fascism, see Wippermann, *Faschismustheorien,* 14–16.

10. Zetkin, "The Struggle against Fascism," 103–4.

11. Some scholars of fascist theory, most notably A. James Gregor, emphasize Zetkin's apparent borrowing of key ideas and entire phrases from the arguments of Gyula Sas, who wrote under the pseudonym of Aquila. See Gregor, *Interpretations of Fascism* (New Brunswick, N.J.: Transaction, 1997), 137–38. See also Gyula Sas, "The Nature and Historical Significance of Fascism," in *Marxists in Face of Fascism,* ed. Beetham, 113–21. While Sas's originality no doubt deserves more attention than it has received, Zetkin's speech had the greater impact on the leftist discussion of fascism.

12. On the events of this volatile postwar period, see Francis Carsten's authoritative studies, *Revolution in Central Europe, 1918–1919* (Berkeley: University of California Press, 1972) and *The Rise of Fascism* (Berkeley: University of California Press, 1982).

13. Quoted in Ruth Fischer, *Stalin and German Communism,* 271. The German text of the speech is reprinted in Dietrich Möller, *Revolutionär, Intrigant, Diplomat: Karl Radek in Deutschland* (Cologne: Verlag Wissenschaft und Politik, 1976), 245–49, and translated in Kaes, Jay, Dimendberg, eds. *The Weimar Republic Sourcebook,* 312–14. Fischer, the former Elfriede Eisler (1895–1961), was a member of the German Communist Party at the time, and she was about to take over a leading role in the party. By the time she described these events in 1948, Fischer had become an embittered opponent of Stalinism. Her history of the Weimar KPD deserves to be consulted, but it must be used with caution, since many sections consist of partial and self-serving recollections. For a thoughtful and largely sympathetic discussion of Ruth Fischer's role in the Weimar KPD and her subsequent activity in the development of postwar *Totalitarismustheorie,* see Karin Wieland, "'Totalitarismus' als Rache: Ruth Fischer und ihr Buch 'Stalin and German Communism,'" in *Totalitarismus,* ed. Söllner, Walkenhaus, and Wieland, 117–38.

14. On Fischer's antipathy to Radek and his important role in both the Schlageter campaign and the failed rising of October 1923—which Radek had initially opposed but was then ordered by the Politburo to guide—see Warren Lerner, *Karl Radek: The Last Internationalist* (Stanford, Calif.: Stanford University Press, 1970),

117–25. Fischer's anti-Semitic and inflammatory speech is cited in Werner T. Angress, *Stillborn Revolution: The Communist Bid for Power, 1921–1923* (Princeton, N.J.: Princeton University Press, 1963), 340. Fischer was an ethnic Jew, though with Moscow's prodding the KPD would steadily divest itself of its Jewish leaders by the end of the 1920s. Stefan Heym's compelling biographical novel, *Radek* (Munich: Bertelsmann, 1995), offers an imaginative historical reconstruction of these events and personalities. See also Fowkes, *Communism in Germany under the Weimar Republic*, 91–99; Flechtheim, *Die KPD in der Weimarer Republik*, 136–50; and Kolb, *The Weimar Republic*, 45–50.

15. Lerner, *Karl Radek*, 126–34; Fowkes, *Communism in Germany under the Weimar Republic*, 107–41; G. L. Ulmen, *The Science of Society: Toward an Understanding of the Life and Work of Karl August Wittfogel* (The Hague: Mouton, 1978), 143–44. According to J. P. Nettl, Fischer would characterize the influence of Luxemburg's politics, which included a commitment to democracy, as "syphilitic." See Nettl, *Rosa Luxemburg*, 751, 800, 805–6. On Radek's decline and fate under Stalin, see Möller, *Revolutionär, Intrigant, Diplomat*, 48–51. Radek's official explanation of the failed rising of 1923 appears in the same volume (258–68).

16. On the Communist's debacle, see the different perspectives offered in Angress, *Stillborn Revolution*; Fowkes, *Communism in Germany under the Weimar Republic*, 95–109; and Ruth Fischer, *Stalin and German Communism*, 282–347. Influential accounts of these events of 1923 set in broader national and international contexts are also found in Craig, *Germany, 1866–1945*, 434–68; and Franz Borkenau, *The Communist International* (London: Faber and Faber, 1938), 243–56.

17. Bracher, *Die Auflösung der Weimarer Republik*, 624; David Beetham, "Biographical Notes," in *Marxists in Face of Fascism*, ed. Beetham, 365. Zetkin authored one more book in the service of her new political allies: *Trotzkis Verbannung und die Sozialdemokratie* (Berlin: Internationaler Arbeiter, 1928).

18. Rosa Luxemburg, *The Russian Revolution, and Leninism or Marxism?* trans. and ed. Bertram Wolfe (Ann Arbor: University of Michigan Press, 1961), 25–80. On the controversial publication of the essay, see Nettl, *Rosa Luxemburg*, 783, 792–94. On Levi's role as opponent of Russian dominance in the policy and leadership disputes of the German Communist Party, see Albert S. Lindemann, *The "Red Years": European Socialism versus Bolshevism, 1919–1921* (Berkeley: University of California Press, 1974); and Richard Löwenthal's detailed treatment of this period in "The Bolshevisation of the Spartacus League," in *International Communism*, St. Antony's Papers, no. 9, ed. David Footman (London: Chatto and Windus, 1960), 23–71. Löwenthal is particularly critical of Radek, whom he viewed as negotiating a twisting, opportunistic course among various factions in the KPD as well as between the Comintern and the Soviet Politburo, groups that were by no means in consistent alignment on foreign policy issues. For a brief summary of Levi's career and political affiliations, see Jan Foitzik, *Zwischen den Fronten: Zur Politik, Organisation und Funktion linker politischer Kleinorganisationen im Widerstand, 1933 bis 1939/40* (Bonn: Verlag Neue Gesellschaft, 1986), 296.

19. On this essential point, see Bronner, *Rosa Luxemburg,* 62–67.

20. Quoted in ibid., 65.

21. On the complications—and frequent sloppiness—that attend using the terms *bourgeois* and *liberal* interchangeably to indicate a particular set of political and class relations, see Geoff Eley and David Blackbourn, *The Peculiarities of German History: Bourgeois Society and Politics in Nineteenth-Century Germany* (Oxford: Oxford University Press, 1984). For instance, Eley offers this cautionary remark: "There is often a great deal of conceptual slippage from 'bourgeois' to 'liberal' in the writings of German historians, confusing the two terms' legitimate application, with a tendential reduction of politics to class" (56).

22. On the origins of the SPD's split into various hostile factions prior to the war and to the abortive revolution of 1918–19 (which led to the founding of the KPD), see Schorske, *German Social Democracy.* On the short-lived but vitally important USPD, see Morgan, *The Socialist Left and the German Revolution.*

23. Breitman, *German Socialism and Weimar Democracy.*

24. For general accounts of the KPD during Weimar, see Volker Berghahn, *Modern Germany: Society, Economy and Politics in the Twentieth Century* (Cambridge: Cambridge University Press, 1987), 82–128, passim; and Craig, *Germany, 1866–1945,* 460–68. More detailed studies include Flechtheim, *Die KPD in der Weimarer Republik;* Fowkes, *Communism in Germany under the Weimar Republic;* Hermann Weber, *Die Wandlung des deutschen Kommunismus,* 2 vols. (Frankfurt am Main: Europäische Verlagsanstalt, 1969); and Klaus-Michael Mallmann, *Kommunisten in der Weimarer Republik: Sozialgeschichte einer revolutionären Bewegung* (Darmstadt: Wissenschaftliche Buchgesellschaft, 1996).

25. Borkenau, *The Communist International,* 147–48.

26. Arthur Rosenberg, *Geschichte des Bolschewismus* (1932; reprint, Frankfurt am Main: Athenäum, 1987), 104–5, 156–59. In his account, first published in 1932, Rosenberg (1889–1943) praised Luxemburg's critique of Lenin but also pointed out the resemblence between Trotsky's and Luxemburg's notions of party centralism, nationalism, and the spontaneity of the workers' revolutionary efforts. This may partly explain his clear distance from each of these leaders' outlooks. For Rosenberg and many other German Marxists, the more democratic and worker-dominated *Räte* (Councils) of 1918–19 remained the best model for revolutionary practice.

27. See the discussions of Levi's postwar role as a bearer of Luxemburg's ideas about party organization in Lindemann, *The "Red Years,"* 123–25; and Richard Löwenthal, "The Bolshevisation of the Spartacus League." Both of these writers are generally sympathetic to Levi, whom they see as a principled, even if ultimately unsuccessful, opponent of party centralism.

28. Rosenberg's assessment of Luxemburg is mentioned earlier and in note 26. Fischer's later discussions of the KPD and her own role in it would play down the degree to which her own attitudes and policies of the 1920s helped generate the kind of party she later condemned in the 1940s. Fischer (see notes 13–15) led the KPD briefly during Weimar Republic, and she would also become one of the im-

portant left-wing antitotalitarians of the early cold war period. Her theoretical contributions to theories of fascism or totalitarianism prior to that time had but little influence on debates within the Left, however. On her political career and writings, see Hering and Schilde, *Kampfname Ruth Fischer;* and Ruth Fischer and Arkadij Maslow, *Abtrünnig wider Willen: Aus Briefen und Manuskripten des Exils,* ed. Peter Lübbe (Munich: R. Oldernbourg, 1990). As for Fischer's judgments on Luxemburg, in *Stalin and German Communism,* Fischer would portray the "atmosphere" of the Spartacist Convention as one "of confusion, of disintegration" owing largely to Luxemburg's interventions, and Fischer also asserted that Karl Liebknecht saw Luxemburg's perspective on events in Germany as "dangerously unrealistic" (76). Fischer herself was not in Berlin during these events, and thus her dismissal of the thoughts and actions of virtually all of those present on the scene warrants a skeptical reading. J. P. Nettl notes the variety—and effectively challenges the veracity—of some of Fischer's anti-Luxemburg remarks and criticisms of *Spartakusbund* policies in his biography, *Rosa Luxemburg,* 533, 747, note 2, 751, 767, note 2.

29. Quoted in Douglas Kellner, ed., *Karl Korsch: Revolutionary Theory* (Austin: University of Texas Press, 1977), 68, note 70. See Kellner's discussion of Korsch's shifting views on Luxemburg and translations of Korsch's pertinent writings on Luxemburg in chapter 2, "Korsch and Communism," and chapter 6, "The Crisis of Marxism." Nevertheless, as Martin Jay maintains, Korsch generally distanced himself from Luxemburg, despite his claims for her value as a "touchstone." See Jay, *Marxism and Totality: The Adventures of a Concept from Lukács to Habermas* (Berkeley: University of California Press, 1984), 142.

30. Max Horkheimer, "Vernunft und Selbsterhaltung" (Reason and self-preservation), in *Gesammelte Schriften,* vol. 5, *"Dialektik der Aufklärung" und Schriften, 1940–1950* (Frankfurt am Main: Fischer, 1987), 350. His words as translated from the German differed from hers only slightly: "At the end of the progress of reason's self-negation, nothing more remains but the relapse into barbarism or the beginning of history." His English-language version of the essay echoed precisely Luxemburg's antitheses of "barbarism or freedom." See Horkheimer, "The End of Reason," *Studies in Philosophy and Social Science* 9, no. 3 (1941): 388. Otto Kirchheimer was yet another admiring and self-conscious inheritor of the Luxemburg legacy. See his "Marxismus, Diktatur, und Organisationsformen des Proletariats," *Die Gesellschaft* 10 (1933): 230–39.

31. Of the writers who are the focus of this study, Karl Korsch, Arthur Rosenberg, Ruth Fischer, Franz Borkenau, Henry Pachter, and Richard Löwenthal all left or were expelled from the KPD from 1925 through 1929.

32. The electoral statistics are from Breitman, *German Socialism and Weimar Democracy,* 198–99.

33. On the Weimar SPD, see ibid.; Harsch, *German Social Democracy and the Rise of Nazism;* and William H. Maehl, *The German Socialist Party: Champion of the First Republic, 1918–1933* (Philadelphia: American Philosophical Society, 1986). On the

KPD, see Fowkes, *Communism in Germany under the Weimar Republic;* Hermann Weber, *Die Wandlung des deutschen Kommunismus;* and Weitz, *Creating German Communism,* 100–279. Weitz's extensive analysis of rank-and-file party culture of the Weimar period ranks as one of the most important recent contributions to the history of the KPD.

34. Flechtheim, *Die KPD in der Weimarer Republik,* 151–95; Fowkes, *Communism in Germany under the Weimar Republic,* 110–37; Borkenau, *The Communist International,* 265–68. On the "united front" and "popular front" tactics of the Comintern, see the thoughtful and innovative analysis of Gerd-Rainer Horn, *European Socialists Respond to Fascism: Ideology, Activism and Contingency in the 1930s* (Oxford: Oxford University Press, 1996), 26–36.

35. Borkenau, *The Communist International,* 268–70; Fowkes, *Communism in Germany under the Weimar Republic,* 140–41; Weitz, *Creating German Communism,* 278–301. Weitz points out that the Comintern's directives to the KPD were sometimes defied or badly carried out. In short, the relationship between the two groups was often far from harmonious. On the anti-Semitism evident in the KPD's personnel changes of the period, as well as those of other parties, see Saul Friedländer, *Nazi Germany and the Jews,* vol. 1, *The Years of Persecution, 1933–1939* (New York: Harper Collins, 1997), 106.

36. The role of such former KPD insiders as Franz Borkenau, Ruth Fischer, and Richard Löwenthal in generating and sustaining the "Stalinization thesis" regarding the German Communist Party—a notion that often supported the acceptance of the dominant totalitarian theory of the cold war period—is examined in the closing chapter. Important examples of the revisionist scholarship on the Weimar-era KPD that challenges or modifies this traditional view includes Weitz, *Creating German Communism;* Mallmann, *Kommunisten in der Weimarer Republik;* Eve Rosenhaft, *Beating the Fascists? The German Communists and Political Violence, 1929–1933* (Cambridge: Cambridge University Press, 1983); James Wickham, "Social Fascism and the Division of the Working-Class Movement," *Capital and Class* 7, no. 1 (1979): 1–65; Eva Cornelia Schöck, *Arbeitslosigkeit und Rationalisierung: Die Lage der Arbeiter und die kommunistiche Gewerkschaftspolitik, 1920–1928* (Frankfurt am Main: Campus, 1977); and Atina Grossman, "Abortion and Economic Crisis: The 1931 Campaign against §218 in Germany," *New German Critique* 14 (Spring 1978): 119–38.

37. Breitman, *German Socialism and Weimar Democracy,* 144–47.

38. Quoted in ibid., 146–47. See also the excellent critical discussion of the SPD's inability to build on the 1928 election results that appears in Harsch, *German Social Democracy and the Rise of Nazism,* chapter 2.

39. The life and work of Rudolf Hilferding (1871–1941) were mostly neglected from the mid-1960s to the mid-1980s, but this appears to be changing. William Smaldone's new biography, *Rudolf Hilferding: The Tragedy of a German Social Democrat* (De Kalb: Northern Illinois University Press, 1998), offers a broadly conceived and thoughtful reconsideration of the intellectual and political importance of this crucial figure. Another notable recent study is F. Peter Wagner, *Rudolf Hilferding:*

Theory and Politics of Democratic Socialism (Atlantic Highlands, N.J.: Humanities, 1996). Still valuable is Wilhelm Gottschalch, *Strukturveränderungen der Gesellschaft und politisches Handeln in der Lehre von Rudolf Hilferding* (Berlin: Duncker und Humblot, 1962). Brief assessments of Hilferding's Weimar years include William Smaldone, "Rudolf Hilferding and the Theoretical Foundations of German Social Democracy, 1902–33," *Central European History* 21, no. 3 (1988): 267–99; and Breitman, *German Socialism and Weimar Democracy,* 116–30, passim.

40. On the fracturing of political support for the Weimar Republic, see Peter Fritzsche, *Rehearsals for Fascism: Populism and Political Mobilization in Weimar Germany* (New York: Oxford University Press, 1990); Bracher, *Die Auflösung der Weimarer Republik;* Thomas Childers, *The Nazi Voter: The Social Foundations of Fascism in Germany, 1919–1933* (Chapel Hill: University of North Carolina Press, 1983); Peukert, *The Weimar Republic,* 222–46; and Craig, *Germany, 1866–1945,* 534–68. On Stresemann's important role, see Henry A. Turner, *Stresemann and the Politics of the Weimar Republic* (Princeton, N.J.: Princeton University Press, 1963).

41. See Breitman, *German Socialism and Weimar Democracy,* 144–45; and Harsch, *German Social Democracy and the Rise of Nazism,* 42–43.

42. Breitman, *German Socialism and Weimar Democracy,* chapter 8, offers a succinct analysis of the Prussian SPD's greater independence and political savvy compared with the national party's. For accounts of the May Day violence in 1929, see Thomas Kurz, *"Blutmai": Sozialdemokraten und Kommunisten im Brennpunkt der Berliner Ereignisse von 1929* (Berlin: Dietz, 1988); Flechtheim, *Die KPD in der Weimarer Republik,* 201–3; and John Willett, *The New Sobriety: Art and Politics in the Weimar Period, 1917–1933* (1978; reprint, London: Thames and Hudson, 1987), 178–80.

43. Sources on Korsch (1886–1961) include Hedda Korsch, "Memories of Karl Korsch," *New Left Review,* no. 76 (November/December 1972): 35–45; Michael Buckmiller, ed. *Zur Aktualität von Karl Korsch* (Frankfurt am Main: Europäische Verlagsanstalt, 1981); Patrick Goode, *Karl Korsch: A Study in Western Marxism* (London: Macmillan, 1979); Gian Enrico Rusconi, "Korsch's Political Development," *Telos,* no. 27 (Spring 1976): 61–78; Russell Jacoby, *Dialectic of Defeat: Contours of Western Marxism* (Cambridge: Cambridge University Press, 1981), 92–99; Kellner, ed. *Karl Korsch;* Hans-Jürgen Kornder, *Konterrevolution und Faschismus: Zur Analyse von Nationalsozialimus, Faschismus und Totalitarismus in Werk von Karl Korsch* (Frankfurt am Main: Peter Lang, 1987); Jay, *Marxism and Totality,* 128–49; and Paul Breines, "Korsch's Road to Marx," *Telos,* no. 26 (Winter 1975–76): 42–56. See also Paul Breines, "Praxis and Its Theorists: The Impact of Lukács and Korsch in the 1920s," *Telos,* no. 11 (Spring 1972): 67–103; and Fred Halliday, "Karl Korsch: An Introduction," in Karl Korsch, *Marxism and Philosophy* (New York: Monthly Review Press, 1970), 7–26.

In 1924, Gregory Zinoviev, director of the Comintern, named Korsch, Lukács, and several others as special offenders in the matter of Communist unorthodoxy. See Jay, *Marxism and Totality,* 129, note 4. Subsequently, these thinkers gained attention as some of the most innovative Marxist thinkers of this century. The original German-language version of Korsch's book was entitled *Marxismus und Philosophie* (1923; reprint, Frankfurt am Main: Europäische Verlagsanstalt, 1966). The book with which it is so often paired and compared, Georg Lukács's *Geschichte und Klassenbewußtsein* (Berlin: Malik, 1923)—the original edition of *History and Class Consciousness*—had a strong and immediate impact on Marxist intellectuals in the 1920s, despite its author's long-term and peculiar attempt simultaneously to claim at least parts of it and to distance himself from some of the consequences of its "highly contradictory amalgam of theories." Lukács's collected works and various autobiographical writings (see the references in the bibliography) offer the record of one of the most influential and controversial Marxist intellectuals of this century. See also Lukács's 1967 preface to *History and Class Consciousness,* trans. Rodney Livingstone (Cambridge, Mass.: MIT Press, 1971), x. Antonio Gramsci's *Quaderni del carcere: Edizione critica,* 4 vols., ed. Valentino Gerratana (Turin: Giulio Einaudi Editore, 1975)—known in various English-language editions as *Prison Notebooks*—though originally published piecemeal over the course of decades has also had a far more attentive and important reception than Korsch's work. More recently available in English are Gramsci's *Prison Letters,* ed. Frank Rosengarten, trans. Raymond Rosenthal (New York: Columbia University Press, 1994).

Regardless of how one views its results, the recovery of the tradition of Hegelian thought in Marxism stands as one of the seminal developments in West European intellectual life in this century. The secondary literature on this general phenomenon—and on the books and careers of Korsch, Lukács, and Gramsci, in particular—is by now an archive unto itself, though its growth appears to be slowing over the past decade. Important considerations on the career and influence of Lukács are found in the books by Michael Löwy, Harry Liebersohn, Agnes Heller, Lee Congdon, and Georg Lichtheim that are listed in the bibliography. For a clearly presented guide to the complexities and shifting terms of this historical development in philosophical Marxism as well as the work of its interested critics, not to mention the immense secondary literature on the topic as of the mid-1980s, see Jay, *Marxism and Totality.* For a study of the course and impact of the turn to Hegelian thought in France, one of the most significant scenes of this development, see Michael S. Roth, *Knowing and History: Appropriations of Hegel in Twentieth-Century France* (Ithaca, N.Y.: Cornell University Press, 1988). The key figure in Roth's study is Alexandre Kojève, the innovative philosopher and influential author of *Introduction to the Reading of Hegel,* ed. Allan Bloom, trans. James H. Nichols (Ithaca, N.Y.: Cornell University Press, 1980).

44. Halliday, "Karl Korsch," 7–9. See also Paul Breines, introduction to *Three Essays on Marxism,* by Karl Korsch (New York: Monthly Review Press, 1971), 3–10.

45. Halliday, "Karl Korsch," 7–26; Foitzik, *Zwischen den Fronten,* 291. On the extent of Korsch's influence on Brecht, see Eugene Lunn, *Marxism and Modernism: An Historical Study of Lukács, Brecht, Benjamin, and Adorno* (Berkeley: University of California Press, 1982), 108–9, 130–32. Brecht, for instance, criticized the "social

fascism" line but never repudiated the Soviet Union, as Korsch did unequivocally. On the 1923 meeting of the leading German speaking Marxist theoreticians, which Hedda Korsch (1890–1982) also attended, see Michael Buckmiller, "Die 'Marxistische Arbeitswoche' 1923 und die Gründung des 'Instituts für Sozialforschung,'" in *Grand Hotel Abgrund: Eine Photobiographie der Kritischen Theorie,* ed. Gunzelin Schmid Noerr and Willem van Reijen (Hamburg: Junius, 1988), 141–82.

46. Karl Korsch, "Blutiger Mai in Berlin," *Die Aktion* 19, nos. 3/4 (1929): 92.

47. Ibid., 93–94.

48. See Wickham, "Social Fascism and the Division of the Working-Class Movement," 1–65.

49. Trotsky clearly despised the SPD leadership, including Rudolf Hilferding, but in 1931 he urged the KPD to seek practical alliances with the SPD rank and file. See Leon Trotsky, "For a Workers' United Front against Fascism," in *Marxists in Face of Fascism,* ed. Beetham, 208–11. In 1937, however, Trotsky would still refer to "the historic crime of reformism" in a reference to the SPD's role in 1918–19. See Leon Trotsky, *The Revolution Betrayed,* trans. Max Eastman (1932; reprint, New York: Pathfinder, 1972), 8–9. See also August Thalheimer, "So-called Social-fascism," in *Marxists in Face of Fascism,* ed. Beetham, 195–97.

50. See, for example, Ernst Thälmann's speech to the KPD Central Committee of February 1932 in *Marxists in Face of Fascism,* ed. Beetham, 161–67.

51. Statistics from Breitman, *German Socialism and Weimar Democracy,* 198–99.

52. Felix Escher, *Neukölln* (Berlin: Colloquium, 1988), 75.

53. Korsch's changing perspective on Lenin and the timing of his disillusionment with the founder and leader of Bolshevism has become a point of controversy among some Korsch scholars. Douglas Kellner claims that Korsch strongly admired Lenin until he saw the consequences of his policies after the mid-1920s (which places this moment after Lenin's death). Other writers, including Henry Pachter, who studied with Korsch during this period, and Russell Jacoby, who has also written about Korsch, argue that the Weimar Marxist theoretician joined Lenin's critics much sooner. See Douglas Kellner, "Korsch's Revolutionary Historicism," *Telos,* no. 26 (Winter 1975–76): 70–93; Henri Rabasseire [Pachter], "Kellner on Korsch," *Telos,* no. 28 (Summer 1976): 195–98. Russell Jacoby, *Dialectic of Defeat,* notes Korsch's critical remarks about Lenin in 1924 and argues that the Comintern's attack on Korsch was no mistake but was consistent with its attempt to control discussions of Marxism (96, 175–76, note 71). Jay mentions the debate about Korsch and Lenin, with references, in *Marxism and Totality,* 131, note 10.

54. Quoted in Kellner, ed., *Karl Korsch,* 163–64. Léon Blum and Camille Chautemps were political leaders of the moderate Left in France.

55. See Horkheimer's inaugural address as head of the institute, in Max Horkheimer, *Between Philosophy and Social Science: Selected Early Writings,* trans. G. Frederick Hunter, Matthew S. Kramer, and John Torpey (Cambridge, Mass.: MIT Press, 1993), 1–14. For a brief summary of Horkheimer's life and career, see John McCole, Seyla Benhabib, and Wolfgang Bonß, "Introduction, Max Horkheimer:

Between Philosophy and Social Science," in *On Max Horkheimer: New Perspectives,* ed. Seyla Benhabib, Wolfgang Bonß, and John McCole (Cambridge, Mass.: MIT Press, 1993), 1-22. In addition to the essays collected in *On Max Horkheimer,* the most important secondary sources on Horkheimer (1895-1973) and his career with the Institute of Social Research are Jay, *The Dialectical Imagination;* and Wiggershaus, *Die Frankfurter Schule.* Wiggershaus emphasizes that the institute's focus changed even before the Nazi takeover when the leadership shifted from Carl Grünberg to Horkheimer and social theory superseded social history as a focus of research and writing (40). For divergent perspectives on the role and significance of Horkheimer's and the institute's "critical theory" in the tradition of socialist thought, see Scott Warren, *The Emergence of Dialectical Theory* (Chicago: University of Chicago Press, 1984), 144-76; and Kolakowski, *Main Currents of Marxism,* vol. 3, 341-95. Warren praises critical theory's insistence that Marxism was an "open-ended critique" but laments its eventual sundering of theory from practice. Kolakowski emphatically condemns the various critical theorists in turn, objecting to both their politics and their philosophy.

56. The issue of the Institute of Social Research and its distance from Marxist orthodoxy has received a good deal of attention. See Jay, *Marxism and Totality,* 196-219; Slater, *Origin and Significance of the Frankfurt School,* 89, 165; Tar, *The Frankfurt School,* 42-43; Douglas Kellner, *Herbert Marcuse and the Crisis of Marxism* (Berkeley: University of California Press, 1984), 416, note 85; and Barry Katz, *Herbert Marcuse and the Art of Liberation: An Intellectual Biography* (London: Verso, 1982), 160. Slater and Tar generally emphasize the non-Marxist character of critical theory—Horkheimer's version of it in particular. All of these authors see Marcuse as the theorist of this group who remained closest to the Marxist tradition, though they disagree on how close to that tradition he was in his later work.

57. Max Horkheimer, "Die Ohnmacht der deutschen Arbeiterklasse," in *Gesammelte Schriften,* vol. 2, *Philosophische Frühschriften, 1922-1932,* ed. Gunzelin Schmid Noerr (Frankfurt am Main: Fischer, 1987), 375.

58. Ibid., 375-76.

59. Ibid., 376.

60. On Korsch's Weimar and exile career, including his clash with the KPD and Comintern leadership, see Hedda Korsch, "Memories of Karl Korsch"; and Kellner, ed., *Karl Korsch,* 30-113. See also the sympathetic appraisal of Korsch in Russell Jacoby, *Dialectic of Defeat,* 92-99. Jacoby also emphasizes Korsch's isolation and laments the scholarly neglect of his writings.

61. Breitman, *German Socialism and Weimar Democracy,* 103-4.

62. For a survey of the complicated and ultimately failed politics of leftist European antifascism, see Larry Ceplair, *Under the Shadow of War: Fascism, Anti-Fascism, and Marxists, 1918-1939* (New York: Columbia University Press, 1987).

63. An exhaustive study of the Social Democrat's opposition to the Nazis during the Weimar period both summarizes and reinterprets the record of this period: Wolfram Pyta, *Gegen Hitler und für die Republik: Die Auseinandersetzung der deutschen*

Sozialdemokratie mit der NSDAP in der Weimarer Republik. (Düsseldorf: Droste, 1989). Pyta's conclusion echoes the long-standing analysis of the collapse of Weimar as the result of the forces of right-wing (NSDAP) and left-wing (KPD) extremism, which ruined any hope for the SPD's parliamentary efforts to save the Weimar Republic. Unlike some other historians who draw this same conclusion, however, Pyta also highlights the role played by traditional conservatives in bringing Hitler to power. Rejecting the formula that Weimar Germany was a "republic without republicans," he argues that, in its period of crisis, Germany was a "republic without republicans in positions of power," a verbally small but politically decisive distinction (515).

64. Joseph Stalin, "The Period of Bourgeois-Democratic Pacifism," in *Marxists in Face of Fascism,* ed. Beetham, 154.

65. Frank Adler, "Thalheimer, Bonapartism and Fascism," *Telos,* no. 40 (Summer 1979): 101. Adler's biographical essay on Thalheimer (1884–1948) provides useful background for study of the work of this important figure of the German Left. See also Martin Kitchen, "August Thalheimer's Theory of Fascism," *Journal of the History of Ideas* 34, no. 1 (1973): 67–78; Jost Dülffer, "Bonapartism, Fascism and National Socialism," *Journal of Contemporary History* 11, no. 4 (1976): 109–28; Ruth Fischer, *Stalin and German Communism,* 198, 207–10, 216, 278–82; Flechtheim, *Die KPD in der Weimarer Republik,* 125–38, 154–62, 174, 200–201; and Fowkes, *Communism in Germany under the Weimar Republic,* 147–52. Thalheimer's later career holds little significance for this study. After the Nazi victory in Germany, Thalheimer went to France and eventually settled in Cuba, where he died in 1948. A more recent and highly controversial assessment of Weimar, David Abraham, *The Collapse of the Weimar Republic,* 2d ed. (Princeton, N.J.: Princeton University Press, 1987), made limited use of Bonapartism theory in its critical and innovative Marxist analysis of German fascism. The scathing professional and public attacks on Abraham's work, which focused on methods, methodologies, use of evidence, and (not least) the politics of historical interpretation are ably recounted in Robert Novick, *That Noble Dream: The "Objectivity Question" and the American Historical Profession* (Cambridge: Cambridge University Press, 1988), 612–21. For the final major round of arguments from two of the principals in the debate, David Abraham and Gerald D. Feldman, see *Central European History* 17, nos. 2/3 (1984): 159–293.

66. David Beetham, introduction to *Marxists in Face of Fascism,* ed. Beetham, 27.

67. August Thalheimer, "Ueber den Faschismus," parts 1/2, *Gegen den Strom,* 11 January 1930: 32. Translated by Judy Joseph as "On Fascism," *Telos,* no. 40 (Summer 1979): 109–22. I have consulted Joseph's translation but have offered my own translation here.

68. Beetham, introduction to *Marxists in Face of Fascism,* ed. Beetham, 25–39. Beetham's discussion of the theoretical approaches to fascism generated by Thalheimer, Leon Trotsky, and Ignazio Silone merits careful study in this context.

On Marx's notion of Bonapartism and its influence on the work of theorists, see Wolfgang Wippermann, *Die Bonapartismustheorie von Marx und Engels* (Stuttgart: Klett-Cotta, 1983).

69. Thalheimer, "Ueber den Faschimus," parts 1/2, 32.

70. Ibid., 32.

71. Thalheimer, "Ueber den Faschismus," part 4, *Gegen den Strom*, 25 January 1930: 66.

72. See Wippermann, *Die Bonapartismustheorie von Marx und Engels*.

73. Thalheimer, "Ueber den Faschimus," parts 1/2, 33.

74. Wippermann, *Die Bonapartismustheorie von Marx und Engels*, 205–15. Wippermann notes the innovations of Thalheimer's theorizing even as he argues that it did not differentiate clearly enough between modern fascism and the Bonapartism of the previous century. Wippermann has argued elsewhere that Bonapartism theory was the crucial bridge toward the notion of the "primacy of the political" (and away from putatively more orthodox Marxist notions of the "primacy of the economic") for such thinkers as Rudolf Hilferding, Otto Bauer, Arkadij Gurland, and Franz Neumann. See Wippermann, *Zur Analyse des Faschismus*, 44–50.

75. Thalheimer, "Ueber den Faschismus," part 4, 66.

76. Statistics from Breitman, *German Socialism and Democracy*, 198–99.

77. Several excellent analyses of the Nazi electoral strategies are in Thomas Childers, ed. *The Formation of the Nazi Constituency, 1919–1933* (Totowa, N.J.: Barnes and Noble Books, 1986).

78. Statistics in Breitman, *German Socialism and Democracy*, 198–99.

79. See, for instance, Arthur Rosenberg, *Entstehung und Geschichte der Weimarer Republik* (Frankfurt am Main: Europäische Verlagsanstalt, 1984), 210. This volume is a combined reprint edition of two books, *Die Entstehung der Deutschen Republik* (Berlin: Rowohlt, 1928) and *Geschichte der Deutschen Republik* (Karlsbad: Graphia, 1935).

80. The most complete biographical sketch of Pachter (1907–80) is Stephen Eric Bronner's helpful introduction to Henry Pachter, *Socialism in History: Political Essays of Henry Pachter*, ed. Stephen Eric Bronner (New York: Columbia University Press, 1984), xi–xxx. Pachter left his own accounts in "On Being an Exile," in *The Legacy of the German Refugee Intellectuals*, ed. Robert Boyers (New York: Schocken, 1972), 12–51, and "Empire and Republic: Autobiographical Fragments," in *Weimar Etudes*, edited by Stephen Eric Bronner (New York: Columbia University Press, 1982), 3–92. See also Martin Jay, "Remembering Henry Pachter," in *Permanent Exiles: Essays on the Intellectual Migration from Germany to America* (New York: Columbia University Press, 1986), 257–61. On Wittfogel (1896–1988), see especially Ulmen, *The Science of Society*, plus the numerous references in Jay, *The Dialectical Imagination*, and Wiggershaus, *Die Frankfurter Schule*. Ulmen's detailed account indicates that Wittfogel was also a friend of Georg Lukács during the Weimar years. A brief discussion of Wittfogel's cold war anti-Communism and his contributions to leftist conceptions of totalitarianism appears in the final chapter of Ulmen's book. See

also Karl August Wittfogel, *Oriental Despotism* (New Haven, Conn.: Yale University Press, 1957).

81. Pachter, "Communism and Class," in *Socialism and History,* 89.

82. Quoted in ibid., 90–91.

83. Ibid., 97.

84. On the volatile late Weimar electorate, see Childers, *The Nazi Voter,* 192–269, and Richard F. Hamilton, *Who Voted for Hitler?* (Princeton, N.J.: Princeton University Press, 1982). See also Thomas Childers, "The Limits of National Socialist Mobilisation," in *The Formation of the Nazi Constituency,* ed. Childers, 238–41; and Jürgen Falter, "The Two Hindenburg Elections of 1925 and 1932: A Total Reversal of Voter Coalitions," *Central European History* 23, nos. 2/3 (1990): 225–41.

85. Pachter, "Communism and Class," 97.

86. Ibid., 102, 105. In 1932, the Papen government succeeded in ousting the SPD from power in Prussia under the provisions of the notorious Article 48 of the Weimar Constitution, which granted the national government broad emergency powers. Otto Braun's SPD government in Prussia, the party's last stronghold of effective power, submitted weakly to what amounted to a coup. On these events and their disastrous consequences, see Breitman, *German Socialism and Weimar Democracy,* 178–88; and Broszat, *Hitler and the Collapse of Weimar Germany,* 120–22. Harsch discusses the coup, the ineffective SPD and working-class response to it, and its important place in the historiography of the period in *German Social Democracy and the Rise of Nazism,* 193–202.

87. Pachter, "Communism and Class," 109.

88. Ibid., 92–93, 104.

89. On Rosenberg (1889–1943), see Helmut Berding, "Arthur Rosenberg," in *Deutsche Historiker,* vol. 4, ed. Hans-Ulrich Wehler (Göttingen: Vondenhoeck and Ruprecht, 1972), 81–96; and Rudolf Wolfgang Müller and Gert Schäfer, editors' introduction to *Arthur Rosenberg zwischen Alter Geschichte und Zeitgeschichte, Politk und politischer Bildung,* ed. Rudolf Wolfgang Müller and Gert Schäfer (Göttingen: Muster-Schmidt, 1986), 7–33; Francis Carsten, "Arthur Rosenberg: Ancient Historian into Leading Communist," *Journal of Contemporary History* 8, no. 1 (1973): 63–75; Hans-Ulrich Wehler, introduction to *Demokratie und Klassenkampf: Ausgewählte Studien,* by Arthur Rosenberg, ed. Hans-Ulrich Wehler (Frankfurt am Main: Verlag Ullstein, 1974), 5–15; Michael Kater, "Refugee Historians in America: Preemigration Germany to 1939," in *An Interrupted Past: German-Speaking Refugee Historians in the United States after 1933,* ed. Hartmut Lehmann and James J. Sheehan (Washington, D.C., and Cambridge: German Historical Institute and Cambridge University Press, 1991), 89–90; and Wolfgang J. Mommsen, "German Historiography during the Weimar Republic and the Émigré Historians," in *An Interrupted Past,* ed. Lehmann and Sheehan, 47–48.

90. The titles are *Die Entstehung der Deutschen Republik* (1928), *Geschichte des Bolschewismus* (1932), *Der Faschismus als Massenbewegung* (1934), *Geschichte der Deutschen Republik* (1935), and *Demokratie und Sozialismus* (1938). For a discussion

of these books in relation to Rosenberg's career, see Gert Schäfer, "Geschichts-schreibung und politische Erfahrung bei Arthur Rosenberg," in *Arthur Rosenberg zwischen Alter Geschichte und Zeitgeschichte,* ed. Müller and Schäfer, 115–34.

91. Rosenberg, *Geschichte des Bolschewismus,* 252.

92. Quoted in ibid., 182–84.

93. Ibid., 184.

94. Ibid., 254–55.

95. Borkenau, *The Communist International,* 430–31, 433.

96. See, for example, Hans Speier, *German White-Collar Workers and the Rise of Hitler* (New Haven, Conn.: Yale University Press, 1986 [manuscript written in 1932]). Speier's methodologically innovative and politically prescient book was nearly completed before Hitler's ascension to the chancellorship. One final section on the fate of the trade unions under Nazi rule was added in 1933. Speier was a student and associate of Emil Lederer, the prominent Social Democratic antifascist. Both men immigrated to the United States, where Lederer became an important figure at the New School for Social Research in New York. See Lederer's contribution to the literature of antitotalitarianism, *State of the Masses: The Threat of the Classless Society* (New York: Norton, 1940).

97. Fowkes, *Communism in Germany under the Weimar Republic,* 205.

98. Biographical sources on Borkenau (1900–1957) include Richard Löwenthal, editor's introduction to *End and Beginning: On the Generations of Cultures and the Origins of the West,* by Franz Borkenau (New York: Columbia University Press, 1981), 1–29; Valeria E. Russo, "Profilo di Franz Borkenau," *Revista di filosofia* 20 (June 1981): 293–94; and John E. Tashjean, "Borkenau: The Rediscovery of a Thinker," *Partisan Review* 55, no. 2 (1984): 289–300.

99. Mihály Vajda, *Fascism as a Mass Movement* (New York: St. Martin's, 1976), 63, credited Borkenau as being one of the first (along with Antonio Gramsci) to advance this point. Bernt Hagtvet and Reinhard Kühnl go even further, declaring simply that "the first writer to apply the modernization thesis to fascism was surely Franz Borkenau." See Hagtvet and Kühnl, "Contemporary Approaches to Fascism: A Survey of Paradigms," in *Who Were the Fascists? Social Roots of European Fascism,* ed. Stein Ugelvik Larsen, Bernt Hagtvet, and Jan Petter Myklebust (Bergen: Universitetsforlaget, 1980), 50, note 82. This is not necessarily a point of praise, however, for the so-called modernization thesis has received a great deal of criticism from the Left as well as from other analytical perspectives. See also the discussion of this element of Borkenau's analysis of fascism in Gregor, *Interpretations of Fascism,* 160–62, 167, 172.

100. Franz Borkenau, "Zur Soziologie des Faschismus," *Archiv für Sozialwissenschaft und Sozialpolitik* 68, no. 5 (1933): 513.

101. Ibid., 515–16. See also Gregor, *Interpretations of Fascism,* 159–60.

102. Borkenau, "Zur Soziologie des Faschismus," 540.

103. For an example of the "agent" or "instrument" theories of the Comintern,

see Dmitrii Manuilski, "On Fascism," in *Marxists in Face of Fascism,* ed. Beetham, 157–61. Manuilski was the chief Soviet delegate to the Comintern.

104. Sources on Franz Neumann (1900–1954) include Rainer Erd, ed., *Reform und Resignation: Gespräche über Franz L. Neumann* (Frankfurt am Main: Suhrkamp, 1985); Alfons Söllner, "Franz L. Neumann—Skizzen zu einer intellektuellen und politischen Biographie," in *Wirtschaft, Staat, Demokratie: Aufsätze, 1930–1954,* by Franz L. Neumann (Frankfurt am Main: Suhrkamp, 1978), 7–56; Joachim Perels, ed., *Recht, Demokratie und Kapitalismus: Aktualität und Probleme der Theorie Franz L. Neumanns* (Baden-Baden: Nomos, 1984); Jay, *The Dialectical Imagination,* 144–48, 161–65; and Wiggershaus, *Die Frankfurter Schule,* 251–58. For personal reminiscences as well as assessments of Neumann's work, see Otto Kirchheimer, "Franz Neumann: An Appreciation," *Dissent* 4 (Fall 1957): 382–86; Herbert Marcuse, preface to *The Democratic and the Authoritarian State: Essays in Political and Legal Theory,* by Franz Neumann, ed. Herbert Marcuse (Glencoe, Ill.: Free Press, 1957), vii–x; and Helge Pross, introduction to *Demokratischer und autoritärer Staat,* by Franz Neumann (Frankfurt am Main: Fischer, 1986), 9–27. Among Neumann's circle of friends and colleagues, Heller, Kahn-Freund, and Fraenkel also voiced antifascist political opinions. See Hermann Heller, *Europa und der Faschismus* (Berlin: W. de Gruyter, 1931); and Otto Kahn-Freund, *Labour Law and Politics in the Weimar Republic,* ed. Roy Lewis and Jon Clark (Oxford: Blackwell, 1981). A more extended discussion of Ernst Fraenkel appears in the following chapter. For a general account of these thinkers and their approach to legal theory, see Wolfgang Luthardt, *Sozialdemokratische Verfassungstheorie in der Weimarer Republik* (Opladen: Westdeutscher, 1986).

105. There are, of course, several other figures who could be mentioned here as Communists or ex-Communists who had more or less close connections to the Institute of Social Research during Weimar and the early exile years, including Karl Korsch, Karl August Wittfogel, and Henryk Grossmann. See Jay, *The Dialectical Imagination,* 5–20.

106. Marcuse, preface to *The Democratic and the Authoritarian State,* by Franz Neumann, vii; Pross, introduction to *Demokratischer und autoritärer Staat,* by Franz Neumann, 11.

107. Franz Neumann, "The Decay of German Democracy," 524–43.

108. Ibid., 526.

109. Ibid., 528.

110. Ibid., 529.

111. Breitman, *German Socialism and Weimar Democracy,* 198–99.

112. Franz Neumann, "The Decay of German Democracy," 536. On the general topic of the fate of the working class under Nazism, see Tim Mason, *Social Policy in the Third Reich: The Working Class and the National Community* (Providence, R.I.: Berg, 1993); Alf Lüdtke, "What Happened to the 'Fiery Red Glow'?" in *The History of Everyday Life,* ed. Alf Lüdtke, trans. William Templer (Princeton, N.J.: Princeton

University Press, 1995), 198–251; and Francis Carsten, *The German Workers and the Nazis* (Aldershot, England: Scolar, 1995).

113. Franz Neumann, "The Decay of German Democracy," 538.

114. On the distinctive and precise character of Neumann's use of *totalitarianism*, see H. Stuart Hughes, *The Sea Change: The Migration of Social Thought, 1930–1965* (New York: Harper and Row, 1975), 120–21.

115. A recently published collection indicates a renewed interest in Kirchheimer and Neumann. See Franz Neumann and Otto Kirchheimer, *The Rule of Law under Siege: Selected Essays of Franz L. Neumann and Otto Kirchheimer,* ed. William E. Scheuerman (Berkeley: University of California Press, 1996). See also the numerous biographical references to Kirchheimer (1905–65) in Jay, *The Dialectical Imagination;* and Wiggershaus, *Die Frankfurter Schule.* A brief biographical sketch of Kirchheimer and Neumann also appears in Scheuerman, *Between the Norm and the Exception,* 3–6. In both books mentioned here, Scheuerman attempts to restore some elements of Kirchheimer's and Neumann's work to the current debates among political and legal theorists. Scheuerman also takes up the prickly subject of Kirchheimer's association with Carl Schmitt. This issue had reemerged during debates in the 1980s about the degree of Schmitt's influence on some of the thinkers associated with the Institute of Social Research, or Frankfurt School. Schmitt was a conservative legal scholar, political theorist, and critic of Weimar who later became a Nazi Party member. See *Telos,* no. 71 (Spring 1987) and no. 72 (Summer 1987). The inspiration for the exchange on Schmitt and the Frankfurt School was Ellen Kennedy's insistence that Marcuse, Kirchheimer, and Franz Neumann had brought a crucial reliance on Schmittian concepts with them when they joined the Institute of Social Research. The responses of Martin Jay, Alfons Söllner, and Ulrich K. Preuss persuasively and severely limited the force and scope of Kennedy's argument. See Ellen Kennedy, "Carl Schmitt and the Frankfurt School," *Telos,* no. 71 (Spring 1987): 37–66; Martin Jay, "Reconciling the Irreconcilable? Rejoinder to Kennedy," *Telos,* no. 71 (Spring 1987): 67–80; Alfons Söllner, "Beyond Carl Schmitt: Political Theory in the Frankfurt School," *Telos,* no. 71 (Spring 1987): 81–96; Ulrich K. Preuss, "The Critique of German Liberalism: Reply to Kennedy," *Telos,* no. 71 (Spring 1987): 97–109; and Ellen Kennedy, "Carl Schmitt and the Frankfurt School: A Rejoinder," *Telos,* no. 73 (Fall 1987): 101–16. For a thorough general account of Schmitt's career, see Joseph W. Bendersky, *Carl Schmitt: Theorist for the Reich* (Princeton, N.J.: Princeton University Press, 1983). Bendersky's effort to provide a biography that avoids the extremes of apology and attack is largely successful, though he sometimes strains to deemphasize the extent of Schmitt's complicity with the Nazi Party. Other scholars offer a far more critical analysis of Schmitt's legal and theoretical support for the antirepublican Weimar conservatives and later for the Nazis. See, for example, William E. Scheuerman, "Legal Indeterminacy and the Origins of Nazi Legal Thought: The Case of Carl Schmitt," *History of Political Thought* 17, no. 4 (1996): 571–90; Richard Wolin, "Carl Schmitt, Political Existen-

tialism, and the Total State," *Theory and Society* 19, no. 4 (1990): 389–416; and Richard Wolin, *Labyrinths: Explorations in the Critical History of Ideas* (Amherst: University of Massachusetts Press, 1995), 103–22. Schmitt's importance to twentieth-century political theory is indisputable, but given the sponsors and causes Schmitt served with his formidable intellectual powers during and after Weimar, his career and his ideas will rightly remain enmeshed in controversies similar in their intensity and importance to those involving Martin Heidegger and his writings.

116. Otto Kirchheimer, "Zur Staatslehre des Sozialismus und Bolschewismus," *Zeitschrift für Politik* 17 (1928): 593–611. See also Frederic S. Burin and Kurt L. Shell, preface to *Politics, Law, and Social Change: Selected Essays of Otto Kirchheimer*, by Otto Kirchheimer, ed. Frederic S. Burin and Kurt L. Shell (New York: Columbia University Press, 1969), x–xi; Jay, *The Dialectical Imagination*, 148–50; and Wiggershaus, *Die Frankfurter Schule*, 258–61.

117. Otto Kirchheimer, "Legalität und Legitimität," *Die Gesellschaft* 9 (1932): 8–20; "Die Verfassungslehre des Preußenkonfliktes," *Die Gesellschaft* 9 (1932): 194–209; "Verfassungsreaktion 1932," *Die Gesellschaft* 9 (1932): 415–27; "Verfassungsreform und Sozialdemokratie," *Die Gesellschaft* 10 (1933): 20–35; "Marxismus, Diktatur, und Organisationsformen des Proletariats."

118. See Carl Schmitt, *Political Theology*, trans. George Schwab (Cambridge, Mass.: MIT Press, 1985). Chapter 1, "The Definition of Sovereignty," begins with the well-known sentence: "Sovereign is he who decides on the exception." Kirchheimer would always be skeptical of liberal constitutionalism's claims to have liberated individuals and to have protected them from the state, but he did not launch his later criticism from a consistently Schmittian perspective.

119. Kirchheimer, "The Socialist and Bolshevik Theory of the State," in *Politics, Law, and Social Change*, 15.

120. Ibid., 21. By the term *twofold progress,* Kirchheimer meant the reformist socialist notion that progress in capitalist development takes place alongside progress in the development of humanity.

121. Kirchheimer, "Weimar—and What Then?" in *Politics, Law, and Social Change,* 74.

122. The extent to which Kirchheimer was "naive" in his conclusions of 1930 and the SPD moderates more "realistic" has been a point of some debate. As Martin Jay contended years ago in a review of Istvan Deak's *Weimar's Left-Wing Intellectuals,* the radicalism of positions such as Kirchheimer's was quite defensible. For the text of the review, see *Commentary* 48, no. 4 (1969): 94–98. Jay repeated this judgment in *The Dialectical Imagination* (327, note 23), disagreeing with John Herz and Erich Hula's verdict that Kirchheimer "underestimated the advantages which even an authoritarian rule . . . entailed as contrasted with what was to come: Nazi totalitarianism" (Herz and Hula, "Otto Kirchheimer: An Introduction to His Life and Work," in *Politics, Law, and Social Change,* xvi). I share Jay's view that "what was to come"—though not necessarily inevitable—was bound up inextricably

with the "authoritarian rule" of the Brüning, Papen, and Schleicher cabinets and that attempts to see them as separate developments from among which one might have selected the "lesser evil" is (and was, tragically) mistaken.

123. Franz Neumann, "Die soziale Bedeutung der Grundrechte in der Weimarer Verfassung," in *Wirtschaft, Staat, Demokratie*, 56.

124. Breitman, *German Socialism and Weimar Democracy*, 161–73. On the shifting political allegiances of the period, see Falter, "The Two Hindenburg Elections of 1925 and 1932," 225–41.

125. Kirchheimer, "Marxism, Dictatorship, and the Organization of the Proletariat," in *Politics, Law, and Social Change*, 22–32.

126. Ibid., 30–31. Kirchheimer's attention to the Menshevik political leaders and the theorists Yulii (Yuri) Martov and Fyodor (Theodore) Dan reflected the strong involvement of these Russian exiles and their comrades with the German Social Democratic Party. On this topic, see Liebich, *From the Other Shore*.

127. Kirchheimer, "Marxism, Dictatorship, and the Organization of the Proletariat," 32.

128. Ibid., 26, 30.

129. Ibid., 27–28.

130. Liebich, "Marxism and Totalitarianism."

131. Rudolf Hilferding, "Zwischen den Entscheidungen," *Die Gesellschaft* 10, no. 1 (1933): 1–9. In the same issue of *Die Gesellschaft*, see Alexander Schifrin, "Wege aus der Spaltung," 10–19; and Walter Biehahn, "Zur Geschichte des Bolschewismus," 36–52.

132. There are numerous references to this strike in the literature on late Weimar. The Berlin transport (Berliner Verkehrsgesellschaft—BVG) strike of November 1932 has long served some historians as evidence for the thesis that a combination of right- and left-wing antiparliamentarism killed the Weimar Republic. For a small sampling of these hostile accounts of the BVG strike, see Flechtheim, *Die KPD in der Weimarer Republik*, 225–26; Borkenau, *The Communist International*, 376; and Craig, *Germany, 1866–1945*, 564.

133. Childers, "The Limits of National Socialist Mobilisation." On the decline of the liberal parties, see Larry Eugene Jones, *German Liberalism and the Dissolution of the Weimar Party System, 1918–1933* (Chapel Hill: University of North Carolina, 1988).

134. Rudolf Hilferding to Karl Kautsky, 1 December 1932, Nachlaß Karl Kautsky, D, XII, 658, 1–2, Internationaal Instituut voor Sociale Geschiedenis (hereafter IISH), Amsterdam.

135. Broszat, *Hitler and the Collapse of Weimar Germany*, 133–49.

136. On the ideological predisposition of the SPD to inertia in just such a crisis, see the concise analysis in Harsch, *German Social Democracy and the Rise of Nazism*, 239–40. See also Robert A. Gates, "German Socialism and the Crisis of 1929–33," *Central European History* 7, no. 4 (1974): 332–59; and Heinrich August Winkler, "Choosing the Lesser Evil: The German Social Democrats and the Fall of the Wei-

mar Republic," *Journal of Contemporary History* 25, nos. 2–3 (1990): 205–25. For a brief accounting of the high cost of KPD resistance, including the devastating number of arrests and executions of KPD members under the Nazis, see Weitz, *Creating German Communism,* 280–81. Weitz's source for the number of victims is Horst Duhnke, *Die KPD von 1933 bis 1945* (Cologne: Kiepenheuer und Witsch, 1972).

137. A similar argument about the destruction of the Weimar Republic appears in Hans Mommsen, *From Weimar to Auschwitz,* trans. Philip O'Connor (Princeton, N.J.: Princeton University Press, 1991), 60–61. For an innovative and painstaking reappraisal of this period in the history of the European Left, see Horn, *European Socialists Respond to Fascism.* Important analytical perspectives on this era are also in Heinrich August Winkler, ed., *Die Krise des europäischen Sozialismus in der Zwischenkriegszeit* (Göttingen: Vandenhoeck und Ruprecht, 1991); Ceplair, *Under the Shadow of War;* and Gregory Luebbert, *Liberalism, Fascism, or Social Democracy* (New York: Oxford University Press, 1991). For a broader perspective on the interwar Left, see Albert S. Lindemann, *A History of European Socialism* (New Haven, Conn.: Yale University Press, 1983).

Chapter 2: Socialists in Dark Times

1. The question of which regimes merit the label fascist and which do not has long engaged historians and political scientists in a debate that often intersects the one over totalitarianism. The concept of fascism remains in many ways an even more vital and useful approach to the study of dictatorships past and present than the idea of totalitarianism, though I reject the various arguments that the embrace of one of these two terms necessitates absolute and hostile abandonment of the other. I agree with those who are willing to apply the fascist label to the later interwar and wartime states in Germany and Austria as well as Italy. Spain's dictatorship presents a more complicated case, but fascism was an important ideological and social component of Franco's movement and the regime it established, and applying the fascist label to Spain is far from being the most questionable use of the term. But those who argue that Nazi Germany represented in many respects a unique regime whose extraordinarily murderous and racist character at times eludes generalized and comparative notions of fascism raise a point that merits attention. On this issue, see Kershaw, *The Nazi Dictatorship,* 17–39; Neocleous, *Fascism,* ix–xii, 22–30, 38–58; and Mason, "Whatever Happened to 'Fascism?'" 323–31. See also Michael Burleigh and Wolfgang Wippermann, *The Racial State: Germany, 1933–1945* (Cambridge: Cambridge University Press, 1991), 7–22, 304–7. Burleigh and Wippermann finally distance themselves from the inherited theoretical models of modernization, fascism, and totalitarianism, concluding that Nazi Germany "was a singular regime without precedent or parallel" (307) that consequently must be studied as a unique historical entity. Kershaw agrees with some of Burleigh and Wippermann's conclusions about the crucial importance of racialism to the Nazi regime, but he wishes to retain some elements of the com-

parative perspectives they reject. See Kershaw, *The Nazi Dictatorship*, 39, note 63, 148, note 61.

On fascism, see the recent books by Payne, Neocleous, Griffin, Eatwell, and Sternhell mentioned in the introduction. Other essential surveys and national studies include Renzo De Felice, *Interpretations of Fascism*, trans. Brenda Huff Everett (Cambridge, Mass.: Harvard University Press, 1977); Emilio Gentile, *Le origini dell'ideologia fascista* (Cremona: Cremona Nuova, 1975); Emilio Gentile, "Fascism in Italian Historiography," *Journal of Contemporary History* 21, no. 2 (1986): 179–208; A. James Gregor, *The Ideology of Fascism: The Rationale of Totalitarianism* (New York: Free Press, 1969); A. James Gregor, *Italian Fascism and Developmental Dictatorship* (Princeton, N.J.: Princeton University Press, 1979); Dante Germino, *The Italian Fascist Party in Power* (Minneapolis: University of Minnesota Press, 1959); Martin Kitchen, *Fascism* (London: Macmillan, 1975); Martin Kitchen, *The Coming of Austrian Fascism* (London: Croom Helm, 1980); Reinhard Kühnl, *Formen bürgerlichen Herrschaft: Liberalismus-Faschismus* (Reinbek: Rowohlt, 1974); Stanley G. Payne, *Falange: A History of Spanish Fascism* (Stanford, Calif.: Stanford University Press, 1961); Eugen Weber, *Action Française* (Stanford, Calif.: Stanford University Press, 1962); Eugen Weber, *Varieties of Fascism: Doctrines of Revolution in the Twentieth Century* (New York: Van Nostrand, 1964); Roberto Vivarelli, "Interpretations of the Origins of Fascism," *Journal of Modern History* 63 (March 1991): 29–43; and Hans Rogger, "Was There a Russian Fascism?" *Journal of Modern History* 36 (December 1964): 398–415. Valuable comparative perspectives on Italian and German fascism are in Wolfgang Schieder, *Faschismus als soziale Bewegung: Deutschland und Italien im Vergleich* (Göttingen: Vandenhoeck und Ruprecht, 1983); and Bessel, ed., *Fascist Italy and Nazi Germany*. The complex and crucial relationship between fascism and traditional conservatism is explored in Hans Rogger and Eugen Weber, eds., *The European Right: A Historical Profile* (Berkeley: University of California Press, 1965); and Martin Blinkhorn, ed., *Fascists and Conservatives* (London: Unwin Hyman, 1990).

2. Horn's *European Socialists Respond to Fascism* attempts to break out of the gloomy, "always already understood" narrative pattern that these events often receive.

3. See, for example, Leon Trotsky, "Why They Confessed Crimes They Had Not Committed," in *Writings of Leon Trotsky (1936–37)*, ed. Naomi Allen and George Breitman (New York: Pathfinder, 1978), 56–63. In a comment on the show trials orchestrated by Stalin, Trotsky wrote, "The first capitulation [of the accused] was to be only the beginning. The regime became increasingly totalitarian, the struggle against the Opposition fiercer, the accusations increasingly monstrous" (58). In 1937, Trotsky also compared Stalin's regime with fascism: "Stalinism and fascism, in spite of a deep difference in social foundations, are symmetrical phenomena. In many of their features they show a deadly similarity. A victorious revolutionary movement in Europe would immediately shake not only fascism, but Soviet Bonapartism" (Trotsky, *The Revolution Betrayed*, 278–79). For a critique of Trotsky's

views on fascist political movements, see Robert S. Wistrich, "Leon Trotsky's Theory of Fascism," *Journal of Contemporary History* 11, no. 4 (1976): 157–84. Other important leftist critics of the Soviet Union—as well as Italian Fascism and National Socialism—included at this time Otto Bauer, Gaetano Salvemini, C. L. R. James, Pietro Nenni, Ignazio Silone, Victor Serge, and a large contingent of exiled Mensheviks. Their books and articles are among the most important documents of the tradition of radical socialist dissent against both Stalinism and fascism in this period.

4. A few examples will suffice here: Ruth Fischer and Arkakij Maslow escaped Berlin on a motorcycle, fled to Prague, then landed in Paris for a time. There Fischer came into contact with Trotsky and his son, Leon Sedov, who were both later murdered by Stalinists. Fischer ended up in New York. Maslow died under murky circumstances in Cuba. Meanwhile, Borkenau moved from Vienna to Amsterdam, then to Paris, then London, with a year's sojourn in Panama. The core members of the Institute of Social Research and their families immigrated to the United States. So did Karl and Hedda Korsch. Otto Rühle and his wife, Alice Gerstel-Rühle, ended up in Mexico and became neighbors of Leon Trotsky and Natalya Sedova, who had been compelled to leave Paris. Mindful of the constantly disrupted working conditions of intellectuals like these, Ayçoberry remarks that the authors of the various writings on fascism that bear so many similarities may have been largely ignorant of one another's work. See Ayçoberry, *The Nazi Question*, 86–87.

5. Wippermann has also traced many of the appearances of the "totalitarian analogy" in the writings of Social Democrats in *Zur Analyse des Faschismus*, 24–25, 32–33, 42–45, 54–58.

6. General sources on the life and work of Marcuse (1898–1975) include Kellner, *Herbert Marcuse and the Crisis of Marxism;* Katz, *Herbert Marcuse and the Art of Liberation;* Lucien Goldmann, *Das Denken Herbert Marcuses: Kritik und Interpretation der kritischen Theorie* (Munich: TWA Reprints, 1970); and Alasdair MacIntyre, *Herbert Marcuse: An Exposition and a Polemic* (New York: Viking, 1970). See also the extensive discussions of Marcuse in Jay, *The Dialectical Imagination;* Jay, *Marxism and Totality;* and Wiggershaus, *Die Frankfurter Schule.*

7. Katz, *Herbert Marcuse and the Art of Liberation*, 15–31.

8. The necessary note here regarding Marcuse's relationship with Martin Heidegger and the highly charged issue of Heidegger's role in National Socialism could run to extraordinary length, but I will try to be brief. A useful introductory text for those unfamiliar with the discussions of Heidegger's complicity with Nazism is Richard Wolin, ed., *The Heidegger Controversy: A Critical Reader* (Cambridge, Mass.: MIT Press, 1993). Wolin's book offers a selection of texts by Heidegger, the responses of some of his contemporaries—including Marcuse—to his involvement with the Nazis, and the judgments of more recent commentators. It also includes a selected bibliography drawn from the massive secondary literature. Marcuse's relationship with his former mentor is also discussed in the books by Jay, Katz, Kellner, and MacIntyre cited in note 6.

9. Martin Heidegger, "Schlageter," reprinted in Wolin, ed., *The Heidegger Controversy*, 42. Heidegger's public statements as rector of Freiburg University are collected in Guido Schneeberger, *Nachlese zu Heidegger: Dokumenten zu seinem Leben und Denken* (Bern: Suhr, 1962). See the discussion of the KPD's "Schlageter line" in the previous chapter.

10. Katz, *Herbert Marcuse and the Art of Liberation*, 37–87. See Herbert Marcuse, *Hegel's Ontology and the Theory of Historicity*, trans. Seyla Benhabib (Cambridge, Mass.: MIT Press, 1987).

11. Martin Jay stresses the essay's importance as a foreshadowing of the work that the institute would undertake in the following years. He also sees the limitations of a perspective that ignored the achievements of parliamentary liberalism in its traditions and practices—however imperfect—of civil rights. See Jay, *The Dialectical Imagination*, 121–24.

12. Marcuse's later attempts to argue that the repression in the West and the East had similar effects—though he did not argue that they were identical—exasperated not only American liberals and conservatives but also some of his generational peers with roots on the German left. One of these, Henry Pachter, also mocked the universality of Marcuse's revolutionary prescriptions as abandoning Marxism for romanticism and having substituted himself for Hegel's "World Spirit" insofar as Marcuse marked out the wants and needs of a socialist without apparent desire for a popular debate on the matter. See Pachter, "The Idea of Progress in Marxism," in *Socialism in History*, 83–84. Richard Löwenthal offered a similarly critical view of Marcuse's political conclusions while indicating an interest in his philosophical writings (Richard Löwenthal, interview with author, Berlin, 3 August 1987). Perhaps the most scathing and systematic attack on Marcuse's later writings appears in Kolakowski, *Main Currents of Marxism*, vol. 3, 396–420. A clearly stated renewal of the typical liberal and conservative criticisms of Marcuse's views on totalitarianism appears in Simon Tormey, *Making Sense of Tyranny: Interpretations of Totalitarianism* (Manchester, England: Manchester University Press, 1995), 100–132.

13. Herbert Marcuse, "Der Kampf gegen den Liberalismus in der totalitären Staatsauffassung," *Zeitschrift für Sozialforschung* 3, no. 2 (1934): 167. The article is translated as "The Struggle against Liberalism in the Totalitarian View of the State," in Herbert Marcuse, *Negations: Essays in Critical Theory*, trans. Jeremy J. Shapiro (Boston: Beacon, 1968), 3–42.

14. Ayçoberry, *The Nazi Question*, 63. Ayçoberry's comments on "Der Kampf gegen den Liberalismus in der totalitären Staatsauffassung" rightly stress the originality of Marcuse's essay as well as the predominance of its philosophical (as opposed to political) agenda. Ayçoberry's dismissal of Marcuse's discussions of class as differing little from "vulgar" Marxism is off the mark, however. Another historian, Abbott Gleason, refers to the "thin and abstract quality" of Marcuse's discussion in the article and, rather like Ayçoberry, sees it as primarily derived from the antifascist critiques formulated by other Marxists during the 1920s. See Gleason,

Totalitarianism, 34. I find Martin Jay's judgments on "The Struggle against Liberalism" (explained in note 11) more persuasive.

15. Marcuse, "Der Kampf gegen den Liberalismus in der totalitären Staatsauffassung," 165–68.

16. Ibid., 169–70.

17. Ibid., 185.

18. Quoted in ibid., 194.

19. Marcuse stated years later that the article took its inspiration from "a speech by Hitler, a speech at the industrial club in Düsseldorf" (quoted in Kellner, *Herbert Marcuse and the Crisis of Marxism,* 96).

20. Detailed discussion of the theoretical writings on fascism and dictatorship that institute thinkers produced during the 1930s appears in the previously cited books and articles of Martin Jay, Rolf Wiggershaus, Douglas Kellner, Alfons Söllner, Helmut Dubiel, Russell Jacoby, and Barry Katz. See also Leo Lowenthal, *An Unmastered Past: The Autobiographical Reflections of Leo Lowenthal,* ed. Martin Jay (Berkeley: University of California Press, 1987); and Michael Wilson, *Das Institut für Sozialforschung und seine Faschismusanalysen* (Frankfurt am Main: Campus, 1982).

21. Alfons Söllner rightly emphasizes the use Marcuse and the other central thinkers of the Institute of Social Research made of "a sociohistorical and ultimately economic framework," but this framework was often so deeply imbedded (or assumed) in the discussion of cultural and ideological developments that its outlines are sometimes hard to discern. Nevertheless, I agree with the point that Söllner makes in connection with these remarks, namely, that Marcuse's view of liberalism was more nuanced than at least one of his critics, Ellen Kennedy, contends. See Söllner, "Beyond Carl Schmitt: Political Theory in the Frankfurt School," *Telos,* no. 71 (Spring 1987): 88–89.

22. These very connections would, however, find a central place in Marcuse's wartime study of the history of social philosophy since Hegel, *Reason and Revolution: Hegel and the Rise of Social Theory* (1941; reprint, Boston: Beacon, 1960). Marcuse offered the following formulation in the course of a discussion of Hobhouse and Hegel: "The principles of liberalism are valid, the common interest cannot be other in the last analysis than the product of the multitude of freely developing individual selves in society. But the concrete forms of society that have developed since the nineteenth century have increasingly frustrated the freedom to which liberalism counsels allegiance" (397).

23. In his superb account of the formation of the racial policies of the Nazi regime, Saul Friedländer mentions that Heidegger and Schmitt both joined the Nazi Party on the same day: May 1, 1933. It is conceivable that the symbolic significance of the date was not lost on two such brilliant thinkers. See Friedländer, *Nazi Germany and the Jews,* vol. 1, 54–55.

24. Wehler, introduction to *Demokratie und Klassenkampf: Ausgewählte Studien,* by Arthur Rosenberg, 9–10.

25. Arthur Rosenberg [Historicus], *Der Faschismus als Massenbewegung*, in ibid., 223.

26. Ibid., 236–37.

27. Ibid., 258.

28. Each of these questionable procedures was in evidence during the revival of *Faschismustheorien* in the 1960s. Some Marxists were guilty of advocating a reductive class analysis, while abler historians, such as Tim Mason, put concepts of class to use in a more differentiated and illuminating fashion. See Mason, "The Primacy of Politics: Politics and Economics in National Socialist Germany," in *Nazism, Fascism, and the Working Class*, 53–76. Mason's essay first appeared in the leftist German journal *Das Argument* in 1966. The other tendency of this revival period, the discussions of fascist ideology, though quite revealing in particular points, sometimes attributed great intellectual depth and philosophical significance to the violent and opportunistic pronouncements of fascist leaders that had much more to do with immediate issues of politics and power than they did with "transcendence." Ernst Nolte's *Der Faschismus in seinen Epoche* offers an example of this approach.

29. Rosenberg [Historicus], *Der Faschismus als Massenbewegung*, in *Demokratie und Klassenkampf*, 262–64, 266–68, 280–89. See in particular his use of the voting statistics of various representative Berlin districts from the Reichstag election of March 1933.

30. See also Arthur Rosenberg, "Treitschke und die Juden: Zur Soziologie der deutschen akademischen Reaktion," *Die Gesellschaft* 2 (1930): 78–83. One of the most important books of the period written by a leftist and focusing on the history of German anti-Semitism was Paul Massing, *Rehearsal for Destruction: A Study of Political Anti-Semitism in Imperial Germany* (New York: Harper and Brothers, 1949). The book was produced as part of a series sponsored by the Institute of Social Research. For excellent examples of scholarship on late Imperial and Weimarera anti-Semitism in the academy, see Rudy Koshar, *Social Life, Local Politics, and Nazism: Marburg, 1880–1935* (Chapel Hill: University of North Carolina Press, 1986); and Konrad Jarausch, *Students, Society, and Politics in Imperial Germany: The Rise of Academic Illiberalism* (Princeton, N.J.: Princeton University Press, 1982). See also Peter Pulzer's durable general study, *The Rise of Political Anti-Semitism in Germany and Austria* (New York: John Wiley and Sons, 1964).

31. Rosenberg [Historicus], *Der Faschismus als Massenbewegung*, in *Demokratie und Klassenkampf*, 273–74.

32. Ibid., 277–78. On this point, see also Fritzsche, *Germans into Nazis*, 195–214. Fritzsche sees the Nazi appeal to a broad spectrum of voters in late Weimar arising more from their radically anti-status quo and antileftist politics than from their extreme expressions of anti-Semitism.

33. Rosenberg [Historicus], *Der Faschismus als Massenbewegung*, in *Demokratie und Klassenkampf*, 289.

34. Ibid., 299.

35. The so-called Night of the Long Knives was part of Hitler's bid to seal the loyalty of the German army by means of a swift terrorist campaign against the leadership of the SA, his own paramilitary force, whose leader Ernst Röhm cherished plans of absorbing the traditional military into the SA under his authority. The army and the SS (Schutzstaffel—Hitler's elite bodyguard organized under Heinrich Himmler, who was Röhm's bitterest rival in the Nazi Party) cooperated in carrying out these murders. Among those killed in the course of this bloody purge were Röhm, many of his officers, a substantial number of low-ranking SA men, and a few leftover rivals from the Weimar years, including conservative former chancellor Kurt von Schleicher. For an excellent narrative account of the events of the purge, see David Clay Large, "The Night of the Long Knives: Nazi Germany and the Blood Purge," in *Between Two Fires: Europe's Path in the 1930s* (New York: Norton, 1990), 101–37. On the causes and consequences of this event, see Dietrich Orlow, *The History of the Nazi Party: 1933–1945* (Pittsburgh, Pa.: University of Pittsburgh Press, 1969), 56–192.

36. Rosenberg [Historicus], *Der Faschismus als Massenbewegung*, in *Demokratie und Klassenkampf*, 303.

37. Ibid.

38. For biographical information on Richard Löwenthal (1908–91), see his preface to *End and Beginning*, by Borkenau, vii–ix. Additional biographical information on Löwenthal is taken from an interview with the author, Berlin, 3 August 1987. See also Foitzik, *Zwischen den Fronten*, 298.

39. Until quite recently, the best source in English on this group—though it was openly skeptical about some of Neu Beginnen's policies and theoretical positions—was Lewis J. Edinger, *German Exile Politics: The Social Democratic Executive Committee in the Nazi Era* (Berkeley: University of California Press, 1956). Arguably Edinger's study on the exile German socialists has not been altogether surpassed but rather usefully supplemented or disputed by more recent work, such as Johannes Klotz, *Das "kommende Deutschland": Vorstellungen und Konzeptionen des sozialistischen Parteivorstandes im Exil 1933–1945 zu Staat und Wirtschaft* (Cologne: Pahl Rugenstein, 1983). Two of the best English-language books on German resistance to Hitler are typical of the relative neglect of ORG/Neu Beginnen. The authors of the excellent group of essays in David Clay Large, ed., *Contending with Hitler: Varieties of German Resistance in the Third Reich* (New York: German Historical Institute and Cambridge University Press, 1991), make no mention of Neu Beginnen. Klemens von Klemperer's *German Resistance against Hitler: The Search for Allies Abroad, 1938–1945* (New York: Oxford University Press, 1992) contains a few scattered references to Neu Beginnen but mostly limits these to the overseas organizational activities of Richard Löwenthal and Karl Frank that took place after the Nazi takeover. Recent examples of German scholarship on Neu Beginnen are Hartmut Mehringer's exhaustive biography of one of the group's key members, *Waldemar von Knoeringen: Der Weg vom revolutionären Sozialismus zur sozialen Demokratie* (Munich: Saur, 1989); and Hartmut Mehringer, "New Beginning," in

Encyclopedia of German Resistance to the Nazi Movement, ed. Wolfgang Benz and Walter H. Pehle, trans. Lance W. Garmer (New York: Continuum, 1997), 213–16. The recently published *Encyclopedia of German Resistance to the Nazi Movement* offers more information than any other recent English-language source on the history of the group, and it also includes brief biographical sketches of several individual members of ORG/Neu Beginnen.

40. Much of the information in this section is, except as otherwise cited, from Richard Löwenthal, *Die Widerstandsgruppe "Neu Beginnen,"* Beiträge zum Thema Widerstand, 20 (Berlin: Informationszentrum Berlin, 1982); and Mehringer, "New Beginning."

41. Foitzik, *Zwischen den Fronten,* 78–80; Edinger, *German Exile Politics,* 163–68. Walter Löwenheim (1896–1977) wrote a history of the ORG that has only recently been made available: *Geschichte der Org (Neu Beginnen), 1929–1935: Eine zeitgenössische Analyse,* ed. Jan Foitzik (Berlin: Edition Hentrich, 1995). Foitzik's introduction is the best brief account of the ORG's formation and early activity. The privately published memoir of Gerhard Bry, *Resistance: Recollections from the Nazi Years* (West Orange, N.J., 1979), also offers a vivid story of the group as well as an alternative explanation of the reasons for the split and its enaction from the perspective of a member of the Frank-Löwenthal-Erler faction. Professor Bry generously sent me a copy of his book.

42. Anson Rabinbach, *The Crisis of Austrian Socialism: From Red Vienna to Civil War, 1927–1934* (Chicago: University of Chicago Press, 1983), 115–16.

43. A capsule biography of Karl Frank (1893–1969) appears in Foitzik, *Zwischen den Fronten,* 270–71. Foitzik contends that it had been Frank who was largely responsible for the slogan *"neu beginnen"* in the first place. For more information on the group, see Foitzik, *Zwischen den Fronten,* 70–85, 130–40, 202, 341. Foitzik's study is the best readily available survey source on the history and structure of ORG/Neu Beginnen, as well as other small opposition groups. Kurt Kliem's "Der sozialistische Widerstand gegen das Dritte Reich, dargestellt an der Gruppe 'Neu Beginnen'" (Ph.D. diss., Marburg, 1957) is also excellent, and it is richer in detail than Foitzik's necessarily briefer treatment of the group, which is only part of a larger study of many organizations. Some of Walter Löwenheim's defenders take issue with portions of Kliem's work as favoring the Frank-led Neu Beginnen group. In my research into the history of the group, I received helpful assistance from discussion or correspondence with former members of or descendents of members of each of the old ORG/NB factions, including Gerhard Bry, Ossip Flechtheim, Richard Löwenthal, Peter Lowe, Julla Rahmer, and Henry Schmidt.

44. Walter Löwenheim's nephew, Peter Lowe, also made available to me some excerpts from the writings of his father, Ernst Löwenheim (1898–1984), also a key member of the ORG. These indicate clearly that a theoretically grounded critique of the Soviet Union as an example of totalitarian dictatorship was one common feature of both the ORG and Neu Beginnen factions. On Gurland's role with the ORG, see Bry, *Resistance,* 131.

45. At Neumann's suggestion, Flechtheim wrote his splendid history of Weimar Communism, *Die KPD in der Weimarer Republik*. On Paxmann, see Foitzik, *Zwischen den Fronten*, 308. The group's more directly political influence was carried forward by, among others, Fritz Erler (1913-67), an activist who served as a leading member of the group for years and then played a key role in the resurgence of the Social Democrats in the early postwar period. The group's list of actual or potential supporters is the "Schlüsselliste," Neu Beginnen Archiv, 2, [1937], IISH, Amsterdam. See Foitzik, *Zwischen den Fronten*, 268, 270, 309. On the important role of women in the group, see Mehringer, "New Beginning." Further information on Neu Beginnen was provided by Ossip K. Flechtheim in an interview with the author, Berlin, 18 July 1989.

46. Miles [Walter Löwenheim], *Neu Beginnen: Faschismus oder Sozialismus Als Diskussionsgrundlage der Sozialisten Deutschlands* (Karlsbad: Graphia, 1933).

47. Karl Kautsky, "Eine Diskussionsgrundlage," *Zeitschrift für Sozialismus* 1, no. 2 (1933): 50-58.

48. Ibid., 58.

49. Ludwig Neureither [Franz Borkenau], "Klassenbewußtsein," *Zeitschrift für Sozialismus* 1, no. 5 (1934): 152-59. Borkenau followed up this discussion with two more articles published under the name Ludwig Neureither: "Staat und Revolution," *Zeitschrift für Sozialismus* 1, no. 6 (1934): 181-85; and "Noch einmal 'Klassenbewußtsein,'" *Zeitschrift für Sozialismus* 1, no. 10 (1934): 325-29.

50. Richard Löwenthal, interview with author, Berlin, 3 August 1987.

51. Edinger has also called attention to this generational element of Neu Beginnen's quarrel with the SOPADE leadership. See Edinger, *German Exile Politics*, 96-98.

52. SOPADE leader Otto Wels claimed that the exile leadership was in no position to aid the Miles Group and denied it financial support in 1935 on account of "disloyalty." See Otto Wels to Karl Frank, 30 January 1935, Neu Beginnen Archiv, 6, IISH, Amsterdam. See also Foitzik, *Zwischen den Fronten*, 137.

53. Richard Löwenthal, interview with author, Berlin, 3 August 1987. See also the Neu Beginnen Archiv, 59/2, IISH, Amsterdam, which contains some partial records of the November arrests.

54. Richard Löwenthal, interview with author, Berlin, 3 August 1987.

55. Paul Sering [Richard Löwenthal], "Die Wandlungen des Kapitalismus," *Zeitschrift für Sozialismus* 2, nos. 22/23 (1935): 704-25; "Der Faschismus," *Zeitschrift für Sozialismus* 2, nos. 24/25 (1935): 765-87; and "Der Faschismus," *Zeitschrift für Sozialismus* 2, nos. 26/27 (1935): 839-56.

56. Sering [Richard Löwenthal], "Die Wandlungen des Kapitalismus," 713.

57. Ibid., 724.

58. Sering [Richard Löwenthal], "Der Faschismus," 777-78.

59. Ibid., 780.

60. Ibid., 781.

61. Ibid., 787. One of the more interesting interpretations of Nazism that tries

to explain its complex dynamic of traditionalist and technophile elements is Jeffrey Herf's *Reactionary Modernism: Technology, Culture, and Politics in Weimar and the Third Reich* (Cambridge: Cambridge University Press, 1984).

62. Franz Neumann's argument, stated in his wartime book, *Behemoth: The Structure and Practice of National Socialism* (New York: Oxford University Press, 1942), 220–361, is not, to say the least, without its critics. In recent decades, a far more nuanced picture of the relations between the Nazi state and big industry has emerged—one that confirms some of the broad outlines of Neumann's argument but qualifies it in case-by-case studies of various industrial sectors. See, for example, John R. Gillingham, *Industry and Politics in the Third Reich: Ruhr Coal, Hitler and Europe* (New York: Columbia University Press, 1985). I have cited the first edition (1942) of *Behemoth* in subsequent notes unless the second edition (1944) is specifically mentioned.

63. The complexities and innovations of Marx's historical, political, and philosophical essays, as well as his economic writings—whatever their limitations and weaknesses—render crude assertions about the inescapable "determinism" of Marxism unpersuasive, however. See, for example, Kolakowski's discussions of this issue in his descriptions of the Marxism of Antonio Gramsci and the postwar East European "revisionists" (a group that once included Kolakowski) in *Main Currents of Marxism*, vol. 3, 231–36, 462–66. Admittedly, the work of some publicists and theorists of the Second International and the Third International has frequently served to give a dubious legitimacy to such views of Marx's outlook.

Some of the wartime discussions of the controversial issue of the "primacy of politics" in modern capitalist societies are examined in greater detail in the following chapter. Wippermann has analyzed the course of this debate among Social Democrats of the 1930s in *Faschismustheorien*, 39–42. Franz Neumann took up the issue in *Behemoth* (1942 and 1944) and in some of his later writings. See also the revival of this issue on the left in the late 1960s and early 1970s, especially Mason, "The Primacy of Politics," 53–76. See also Nicos Poulantzas, *Political Power and Social Classes* (London: New Left Books, 1973); Jane Caplan, "Theories of Fascism: Nicos Poulantzas as Historian," *History Workshop Journal*, no. 3 (Spring 1977): 83–100; and Kershaw, *The Nazi Dictatorship*, 40–58.

64. Sering [Richard Löwenthal], "Der Faschismus," 843.

65. Ibid., 848. An argument that was in some respects quite similar to Löwenthal's—namely, the contention that internal economic factors and crises significantly influenced Nazi foreign policy, including the timing of the invasion of Poland—would appear years later in the work of some Marxist scholars. See, for example, Mason, "Internal Crisis and Wars of Aggression, 1938–39," in *Nazism, Fascism and the Working Class*, 104–30; and Tim Mason, "The Domestic Dynamics of Nazi Conquests: A Response to Critics," in *Reevaluating the Third Reich*, ed. Childers and Caplan, 161–89.

66. Richard Löwenthal, interview with author, Berlin, 3 August 1987; Paul

Sering [Richard Löwenthal], *Jenseits des Kapitalismus: Ein Beitrag zur sozialistischen Neuorientierung* (Nuremburg: Nest, 1946).

67. See the following articles in the *Zeitschrift für Sozialismus* by Paul Sering [Richard Löwenthal], "Historische Voraussetzungen des deutschen Nationalsozialismus," 3, no. 30 (1936): 959–75; "Die Aufgaben der deutschen Revolution," 3, no. 33 (1936): 1041–49; "Was ist der Volkssozialismus?" 3, no. 36 (1936): 1105–36. Sering's [Löwenthal's] long essay on folk socialism took up the entire final issue (no. 36) of *Zeitschrift für Sozialismus*.

68. Sering [Richard Löwenthal], "Der Faschismus," 843.

69. The first number, published in October 1933, bore the title *Sozialistische Revolution: Monatsschrift für die Probleme des Sozialismus*. Thereafter, the journal bore the simpler and somewhat less provocative name *Zeitschrift für Sozialismus*. The Czech government censors had blocked further use of the "Socialist Revolution" title for the journal. See Wagner, *Rudolf Hilferding*, 166, 181, note 46; and Edinger, *German Exile Politics*, 101.

70. Liebich, "Marxism and Totalitarianism." Richard Löwenthal maintained that Hilferding had little to do with the hands-on work of editing the journal (interview with author, Berlin, 3 August 1987). William Smaldone's biography of Hilferding offers a detailed portrait of Hilferding's continuing role as editor. See Smaldone, *Rudolf Hilferding*, 179–92.

71. Rudolf Hilferding, "Die Zeit und die Aufgabe," *Sozialistische Revolution* 1, no. 1 (1933): 1–11.

72. Ibid., 6.

73. Ibid.

74. Ibid., 10.

75. Max Klinger [Curt Geyer], "Der Rückfall in den Machtstaat," *Sozialistische Revolution* 1, no. 1 (1933): 16.

76. On the life and career of Geyer (1891–1967), see Curt Geyer, *Die revolutionäre Illusion: Zur Geschichte des linken Flügels der USPD; Erinnerungen von Curt Geyer*, ed. Wolfgang Benz and Hermann Graml (Stuttgart: Deutsche Verlagsanstalt, 1976); Curt Geyer, *Die Partei der Freiheit* (Paris: Graphia, 1939); and numerous references to Geyer in Morgan, *The Socialist Left and the German Revolution*.

77. Franz Wegner, "Koporativstaat," *Zeitschrift für Sozialismus* 1, no. 2 (1933): 105.

78. The structuralists (also called functionalists) are those historians who generally emphasize the contingent and improvised character of the Nazi apparatus of rule. Their interpretive opponents, labeled the intentionalists, see the role of Hitler as central to the character and actions of a responsive Nazi hierarchy. One key focus of this intense debate is the analysis of the Holocaust. Hans Mommsen and Martin Broszat have been the most articulate and insistent structuralists, though Karl A. Schleunes was one of the position's important early advocates. See Schleunes, *The Twisted Road to Auschwitz: Nazi Policy toward German Jews, 1933–1939*

(1970; reprint, Urbana: University of Illinois Press, 1990). Leading intentionalists include Karl Dietrich Bracher, Eberhard Jäckel, and Klaus Hildebrand. Once again, readers are directed to the discussion and references in Kershaw, *The Nazi Dictatorship*, 59–79. For defenses of the structuralist and intentionalist positions, respectively, see Mason, "Intention and Explanation: A Current Controversy about the Interpretation of National Socialism," in *Nazism, Fascism and the Working Class*, 212–30; and Lucy S. Dawidowicz, *The War against the Jews, 1933–1945* (1976; reprint, New York: Bantam, 1986), xix–xxxiii. For a more recent response to this debate, see Christopher Browning, "Beyond 'Intentionalism' and 'Functionalism': The Decision for the Final Solution Reconsidered," in *The Path to Genocide: Essays on Launching the Final Solution* (Cambridge: Cambridge University Press, 1992), 86–121.

79. Max Seydewitz, "Die Ueberwindung der faschistischen Diktatur," *Zeitschrift für Sozialismus* 1, no. 6 (1934): 198.

80. Seydewitz (1892–1987) had been a Social Democrat until 1931, but he broke with the party over its "toleration" of the Brüning cabinet. He then became a joint founder and leader of the Socialist Workers' Party (Sozialistische Arbeiterpartei— SAP) during late Weimar. He was a member of the Revolutionary Socialists (Arbeitskreis revolutionärer Sozialisten) during the war and eventually joined forces with the Communists. Along with his wife, Ruth Lewy Seydewitz (born 1905), he became a postwar stalwart of the Socialist Unity Party of Germany (Sozialistische Einheitspartei Deutschlands, the official name of the "coalition" dominated by the Communist Party in the German Democratic Republic—SED). He served on the executive committee of the SED and also as prime minister of Saxony from 1947 to 1952. See Max Seydewitz, *Es hat sich gelohnt zu leben: Lebenserinnerungen eines alten Arbeiterfunktionärs*, 2 vols. (Berlin: Dietz, 1976–78). For references to his career, see Foitzik, *Zwischen den Fronten*, 323–24; Edinger, *German Exile Politics*, 144, 155, 163, 284, note 5; Morgan, *The Socialist Left and the German Revolution*, 441–42; and Benz and Pehle, eds., *Encyclopedia of German Resistance to the Nazi Movement*, 320.

81. The historian Allan Merson has also noted the broad exculpatory potential of the totalitarianism thesis, for which he chides Richard Löwenthal (whom he labels "the Social-Democratic ideologist"), and which he surely means to discredit. Merson's book, with its claims for the KPD's "moral heritage" and "great constructive achievement," strikes me as no less "ideological" than Löwenthal's writings on non-Communist resistance, however. Nevertheless, Merson's work in recalling the courageous and spontaneous grassroots working-class resistance of German Communists to the National Socialist state goes far to rescue this significant legacy from neglect. See Allan Merson, *Communist Resistance in Nazi Germany* (London: Lawrence and Wishart, 1985), 5. On the KPD's resistance to Nazism, see also Duhnke, *Die KPD von 1933 bis 1945;* Detlev Peukert, *Die KPD im Widerstand: Verfolgung und Untergrundarbeit an Rhein und Ruhr, 1933 bis 1945* (Wuppertal: Peter Hammer, 1980); and Martin Broszat, "A Social and Historical Typology of the German Opposition to Hitler," in *Contending with Hitler*, ed. Large, 25–33. Peter Hoffman's *German Resistance to Hitler* (Cambridge, Mass.: Harvard University Press,

1988) remains a useful brief survey. See also Peter Hoffman, *The History of the German Resistance, 1933–1945,* trans. Richard Barry (Montreal: McGill-Queen's University Press, 1996).

82. Seydewitz's drift into the camp of the KPD and SED also points to the existence, rarely discussed, of a Communist version of the intentionalist argument. See the extensive discussions of these issues, with references to the pertinent literature, in Kershaw, *The Nazi Dictatorship,* 59–79.

83. See Liebich, "Marxism and Totalitarianism." For a look at the cold war career of Menshevism in exile, see also André Liebich, "Mensheviks Wage the Cold War," *Journal of Contemporary History* 30, no. 2 (1995): 247–64; and Liebich, *From the Other Shore.*

84. Wippermann has discovered a number of these, and he discusses them in his *Faschismustheorien,* 32, 96–101. See also Wippermann, *Zur Analyse des Faschismus,* 44–50.

85. Ceplair, *Under the Shadow of War,* 123–42.

86. "Protokoll vom 4.5.36," 4 May 1936, Neu Beginnen Archiv, 13, IISH, Amsterdam.

87. See "Protokoll," 5 August 1936, Neu Beginnen Archiv, 13, IISH, Amsterdam; and "Zur Beurteilung der Erschiessungen der 16 Angeklagten des Mosk. Proz.," 3 October 1936, Neu Beginnen Archiv, 33, IISH, Amsterdam.

88. See untitled essay on the Soviet Union, 26 January 1937, Neu Beginnen Archiv, 33, IISH, Amsterdam. Max Blatt (born 1905) was a typical member of ORG/Neu Beginnen in terms of his age and previous political involvement, having joined the KPD in his teens and left it by 1928. He joined the ORG in 1932 and used the names Maxim and Landau. He moved to Australia at the end of the war. See Foitzik, *Zwischen den Fronten,* 253.

89. Anderson (1909–77), originally Leonore Seligmann, left the KPD in 1929, as had Löwenthal. Having earned her doctoral degree in economics and sociology in 1932, she joined the ORG in 1933 (code name Mary) and became a leading member of the Neu Beginnen faction in London, along with her husband, Paul Anderson (1908–72). During the war, both Andersons began successful careers in newspaper and broadcast journalism. The dynamic British journalist, Labour activist, and politician Aneurin Bevan appointed Evelyn Anderson to an important editorial position at the *Tribune* in London. One of the writers she worked with at the *Tribune* was George Orwell, who became a good personal friend. See Foitzik, *Zwischen den Fronten,* 248; Michael Foot, *Aneurin Bevan: A Biography,* vol. 1 (New York: Atheneum, 1963), 302; and George Orwell, *The Collected Essays, Journalism, and Letters,* ed. Sonia Orwell and Ian Angus, vol. 4, *In Front of Your Nose, 1945–1950* (New York: Harcourt Brace Jovanovich, 1968), 509 note 1.

90. For this exchange, see the documents of 26 January 1937, 21 April 1937, and Landau [Blatt] to Ernst [Richard Löwenthal] and Mary [Evelyn Anderson], n.d., Neu Beginnen Archiv, 33, IISH, Amsterdam.

91. An example of the kind of criticism of the Comintern's role in the Spanish

civil war that Neu Beginnen routinely articulated is contained in "Probleme und Perspektiven der spanischen Revolution," 1937, Neu Beginnen Archiv, 18, IISH, Amsterdam. The author mentions the "great achievement" of the Comintern and the Soviet Union in intensifying their "party dictatorship." "It is now clear," continues the document, "that the socialist forces cannot win. They have proven their incapacity. They are already defeated."

92. Otto Bauer (1881–1938) was an important leader and theoretician in the Austrian Social Democratic Party from the early 1900s through the interwar years. Among his most important writings of this period are *Zwischen zwei Weltkriegen? Die Krise der Weltwirtschaft, der Demokratie und des Sozialismus* (Bratislava: Eugen Prager, 1936); and the posthumously published *Die illegale Partei* (Paris: Éditions de la lutte socialiste, 1939).

93. The book on philosophy, completed in 1932 but delayed in print because of the Nazi takeover, was Franz Borkenau, *Der Übergang vom feudalen zum bürgerlichen Weltbild* (Paris: Alcan, 1934). On Borkenau's continuing contacts with Austrian socialists just before the February 1934 action, see Rabinbach, *The Crisis of Austrian Socialism*, 116. The articles Borkenau published in response to current political crises included "Zur Soziologie des Faschismus," *Archiv für Sozialwissenschaft und Sozialpolitik* 68, no. 5 (1933): 513–43; "Fascisme et syndicalisme," *Annales d'histoire économique et sociale* 6 (1934): 337–50; and "La crise des parties socialistes dans l'Europe contemporaine," *Annales d'histoire économique et sociale* 7 (1935): 337–52.

94. For a succinct and deftly argued study of the importance of Pareto and other antidemocratic theorists to the political debates of this century, see Robert A. Nye, *The Anti-Democratic Sources of Elite Theory: Pareto, Mosca, Michels* (London: Sage Publications, 1977). Another possible factor that might explain Borkenau's interest in Pareto was that Pareto's *Mind and Society* had just been translated into English in 1935, and the increased access to his ideas might have influenced Borkenau or his editors to select Pareto as a worthy subject to include in the series on sociologists. Karl Korsch's *Karl Marx* (London: Chapman and Hall, 1938) was a later volume in this same series.

95. Franz Borkenau, *Pareto* (London: Chapman and Hall, 1936), 72–77, 88–90.

96. Ibid., 127–29, 161–63.

97. Ibid., 168.

98. Ibid., 151–56, 171–73; Vilfredo Pareto, *The Mind and Society*, trans. Andrew Bongiorno and Arthur Livingstone (1935; reprint, New York: Dover, 1963), vol. 3, 973–76; vol. 4, 1515–41, 1912.

99. The sociologist T. H. Marshall's review of *Pareto* rightly pointed out that Borkenau appeared less interested in a presentation of Pareto's model than in the appropriation of parts of it in the service of his own critical pursuits. See Marshall's review in *Political Quarterly* 7, no. 3 (1936): 459–61.

100. Borkenau, *Pareto*, 198.

101. Ibid., 202–3.

102. Ibid., 203.

103. Ibid., 176.

104. Ibid., 181–82.

105. Ibid., 180.

106. Ibid., 209.

107. Ibid., 115, 179–89.

108. Ibid., 193–94. In this passage, Borkenau set Lenin's circle and methods of leadership at a clear distance from Stalin's style of personal, autocratic rule.

109. Ibid., 211.

110. Ibid., 184–95, 203–10, passim.

111. Ibid., 196.

112. The literature on the Spanish civil war is voluminous. The standard English-language study of the war remains Hugh Thomas, *The Spanish Civil War* (Harmondsworth, England: Penguin Books, 1986). See also Gabriel Jackson, *A Concise History of the Spanish Civil War* (London: Thames and Hudson, 1980); Paul Preston, *The Coming of the Spanish Civil War: Reform, Reaction, and Revolution in the Second Republic, 1931–1936* (New York: Barnes and Noble Books, 1978); Raymond Carr, ed., *The Republic and the Civil War in Spain* (London: Macmillan, 1971); and Gabriel Jackson, ed. *The Spanish Civil War* (New York: Quadrangle Books, 1972).

The best and most comprehensive study of the subject of the German Left's involvement in the war is Patrik von zur Mühlen, *Spanien war ihre Hoffnung: Die deutsche Linke im Spanischen Bürgerkrieg, 1936 bis 1939* (Berlin: Dietz, 1985). For a vivid memoir and photographic account of the first days of the war as seen by two young left-wing German exiles, see Hans Namuth and Georg Reisner, *Spanisches Tagebuch, 1936: Fotografien und Texte aus den ersten Monaten des Bürgerkriegs* (Berlin: Dirk Nishen, 1986). In their travels across the countryside, Reisner and Namuth, socialist activists and photojournalists, were for a time accompanied by a scholarly writer: Franz Borkenau. Namuth pursued a highly successful career in photography in the United States and later completed a well-known film of the American artist Jackson Pollock at work.

113. On the effort to create a broad leftist alliance in Spain, see Gabriel Jackson, "The Spanish Popular Front, 1934–7," *Journal of Contemporary History* 5, no. 3 (1970): 21–35. Gerd-Rainer Horn shows clearly that, in this coalition as in other popular front alliances, the socialists quickly became the political captives of the more moderate Spanish republicans, giving ground on issue after issue. See Horn, *European Socialists Respond to Fascism,* 105–6.

114. Henri Rabasseire [Henry Pachter], *Espagne: Creuset politique* (Paris: Éditions Fustier, 1938), 54–55, 179–80, 185. In an introduction to a 1965 Spanish translation of the book, *España crisol político,* Pachter acknowledged some changes in his view of the international significance and consequences of the war but did not retreat from his earlier position that the twin goals of war and revolution were both essential. For the English translation of this introduction, see Pachter, "Reflections on the Spanish Civil War," in *Socialism in History,* 147–57.

115. Korsch had an informant on the scene, his friend and student Paul Partos, who participated on the republican side as part of the propaganda section of the CNT (Confederación Nacional del Trabajo). See Kellner, ed., *Karl Korsch,* 196; and von zur Mühlen, *Spanien war ihre Hoffnung,* 91ff., 100ff., 110, 238.

116. Kellner, ed., *Karl Korsch,* 196. The articles, somewhat delayed in publication, were "Economics and Politics in Revolutionary Spain," *Living Marxism* 4, no. 3 (1938): 76–82; and "Collectivisation in Spain," *Living Marxism* 4, no. 6 (1939): 178–82. Korsch did, however, publish a book review on collectivization in Spain in the institute's journal: review of *Collectivisations: L'oeuvre constructive de la Révolution Espagnole; Receuil de documents, Zeitschrift für Sozialforschung* 7, no. 3 (1938): 469–74. On the issue of collectivization in Catalonia, see Michael Seidman, "Work and Revolution: Workers' Control in Barcelona in the Spanish Civil War, 1936–38," *Journal of Contemporary History* 17, no. 3 (1982): 409–33.

117. Quoted in Kellner, ed., *Karl Korsch,* 242.

118. In the editorial introductions and summaries that appear in his *Karl Korsch,* Kellner ably discusses the tensions in the political and theoretical outlook of Korsch's various projects in the late 1930s. See especially 73–113, 270–74.

119. Jay, *The Dialectical Imagination,* 113–218, passim.

120. Herbert Marcuse, *Kultur und Gesellschaft* (Frankfurt am Main: Suhrkamp, 1965), 11.

121. Helmut Dubiel asserts that "the literary and theoretical reconsiderations of the Show Trials and the Pact in the émigré circles began for the most part first in the 1940s." See Dubiel, *Wissenschaftsorganisation und politische Erfahrung: Studien zur frühen Kritischen Theorie* (Frankfurt am Main: Suhrkamp, 1978), 91. This statement is partly inaccurate, as evidence from the writings of Korsch, Neu Beginnen, and Borkenau during the period 1936–39 demonstrates. The error is repeated and worsened somewhat by the omission of the phrase "for the most part" in the English translation of the book. See Dubiel, *Theory and Politics: Studies in the Development of Critical Theory,* trans. Benjamin Gregg (Cambridge, Mass.: MIT Press, 1985), 73. Dubiel supports his claim by stating that, for example, "Borkenau's *The Spanish Cockpit* . . . appeared at the end of 1939" (73)—indicating that the book was published after the Hitler-Stalin Pact and the invasion of Poland. This statement is also incorrect. The book was published in mid-1937. The timing of the left-wing émigrés' criticism of the Soviet Union and the Comintern is certainly far more important for my argument than it is for Dubiel's, so the correct dates of publication for these writings deserve mention here. These minor errors do not, however, diminish the value of Dubiel's book.

For a discussion of intellectuals' responses to the war that includes a section on Borkenau, see James Wilkinson, "Truth and Delusion," *Salmagundi* 76/77 (1987–88): 3–52. See also Wilkinson's *The Intellectual Resistance in Europe* (Cambridge, Mass: Harvard University Press, 1981); and Lewis Coser, "Remembering the Spanish Revolution," *Dissent* 33 (Winter 1986): 53–58.

122. Franz Borkenau, *The Spanish Cockpit: An Eye-Witness Account of the Political and Social Conflicts of the Spanish Civil War* (London: Faber and Faber, 1937), 254.

123. The NKVD became the successor organization to the GPU in 1934, but most writers discussed here continued to use the earlier acronym. On the changes in the names attached to the Soviet secret political police, see Nicholas Riasanovsky, *A History of Russia* (New York: Oxford University Press, 1993), 503. For discussions generally sympathetic to the POUM and anarchist perspectives on the civil war and highly critical of the role of the PCE and the NKVD, see Victor Alba and Stephen Schwartz, *Spanish Marxism versus Soviet Communism: A History of the P.O.U.M.* (New Brunswick, N.J.: Transaction Books, 1988), 212–18; E. H. Carr, *The Comintern and the Spanish Civil War* (New York: Pantheon, 1984), 25, 30–32; and two books by Burnett Bolloten, *The Grand Camouflage: The Communist Conspiracy in the Spanish Civil War* (New York: Praeger, 1961) and *The Spanish Revolution: The Left and the Struggle for Power during the Civil War* (Chapel Hill: University of North Carolina Press, 1978). A classic study of the war's background written by someone who had a good deal of contact with Borkenau is Gerald Brenan, *The Spanish Labyrinth: An Account of the Social and Political Background of the Civil War* (Cambridge: Cambridge University Press, 1943). Brenan's acerbic autobiography includes several vignettes of Borkenau that offer his mixed view of the Austrian-German intellectual. See Brenan, *Personal Record, 1920–1972* (New York: Knopf, 1975).

124. Borkenau, *The Spanish Cockpit*, 289.

125. Two key anarchist groups were the CNT and the FAI: Confederación Nacional del Trabajo (a trade union group) and Federación Anarquista Ibérica (a collective of anarchist groups). For perspectives of the members of these and a variety of other organizations, see Ronald Fraser's superb *Blood of Spain: An Oral History of the Spanish Civil War* (New York: Pantheon, 1979).

126. Orwell, *The Collected Essays, Journalism, and Letters*, vol. 1, *An Age Like This*, 276–82, 297, 299. For an alternative perspective, see Michael Seidman, "The Unorwellian Barcelona," *European History Quarterly* 20 (April 1990): 163–80.

127. Franz Borkenau to George Orwell, 6 August 1937, George Orwell Archive, University College, London. See also George Orwell, *Homage to Catalonia* (1938; reprint, New York: Harcourt Brace Jovanovich, 1952).

128. Franz Borkenau to George Orwell, 11 June 1938, George Orwell Archive, University College, London.

129. Bernard Crick, *George Orwell: A Life* (Harmondsworth, England: Penguin Books, 1980), 340–41, 446. Crick mentions that Eileen Blair also helped the Neu Beginnen activist Evelyn Anderson edit her wartime study of the German Left, *Hammer or Anvil: The Story of the German Working-class Movement* (London: Gollancz, 1945). Anderson and Borkenau had been friends on the German left during the Weimar years.

130. Nonetheless, at the time Borkenau found the speeches and persona of La Pasionaria (Dolores Ibarruri), the Communists' most important public figure,

moving and authentic expressions of the traditional Spanish revolutionary spirit. See Borkenau, *The Spanish Cockpit*, 1. He repeated his praise for her in *The Communist International*, 405. After he learned of her self-serving behavior during the years of Moscow exile, however, he would "explicitly revoke" his positive discussions of her in his later *European Communism* (London: Faber and Faber, 1953), 164, note 1.

131. Borkenau, *The Spanish Cockpit*, 259, 268.

132. Ibid., 278.

133. Franz Borkenau, "State and Revolution in the Paris Commune, the Russian Revolution, and the Spanish Civil War," *Sociological Review* 29, no. 1 (1937): 41–75. Without reference to Borkenau's article, Karl Korsch would make a similar argument the following year in his article on "Economics and Politics in Revolutionary Spain." Korsch, however, saw Spain as one more lesson for the revolutionary working class, while Borkenau concluded that the war should end all Marxist illusions about the inherently revolutionary character of working-class politics.

134. Franz Borkenau, "A Program for Counter-Revolution," in *After Peace, What?* (Norman, Okla.: Cooperative Books, 1941), 1–10.

135. See Memo on the Case of the Disappearance of Mark Rein, 12 November 1937, Neu Beginnen Archiv, 14, 1–14, IISH, Amsterdam. See also "Willi Müller" [Karl Frank] to Otto Bauer, 18 December 1937, Neu Beginnen Archiv, 16, IISH, Amsterdam. The letter lists Willy Brandt as a friend of Rein. Brandt himself described meeting with Rein in Barcelona and his subsequent anger and dismay at Rein's disappearance in *My Life in Politics* (New York: Viking, 1992), 104–5.

136. "Walter" [Walter Ulbricht] to Neu Beginnen, 24 September 1937, Neu Beginnen Archiv, 14, IISH, Amsterdam.

137. Heinrich Brandler, a friend of August Thalheimer and a former leader of the KPD, became involved with the attempt to discover Rein's fate. He wrote to Neu Beginnen that likely "ihn [Rein] die GPU um die Ecke gebracht habe" (The GPU took him around the corner—that is, killed him). See Heinrich Brandler to "Karl" [Frank], 13 July 1937, Neu Beginnen Archiv, 17, IISH, Amsterdam. For a more extended account of the Mark Rein episode, see von zur Mühlen, *Spanien war ihre Hoffnung*, 192–99; and Liebich, *From the Other Shore*, 261–63. Von zur Mühlen mentions the scenario Deutsch offered. Willy Brandt echoed Deutsch's hypothesis in *My Life in Politics*, 105. Liebich's account emphasizes the sadly desperate and persistent efforts by Abramovitsch to learn the details of his son's death.

138. Richard Löwenthal, interview with author, Berlin, 3 August 1987.

139. "Die Sozialisten und der deutsche-russische Pakt," late August 1939, Neu Beginnen Archiv, 34, IISH, Amsterdam. For an authoritative account of the key military events leading up to and immediately following the German and Soviet invasions of Poland, see Gerhard Weinberg, *A World at Arms: A Global History of World War II* (Cambridge: Cambridge University Press, 1994), 54–62.

140. Some historians have argued persuasively that, despite the official position of leading Communists, many rank-and-file German Communists continued to agitate against the Nazis even during the months when the Hitler-Stalin Pact

was in force. Allan Merson admits that German Communists were unsettled and disoriented, but his evidence shows that they were not without their own organized efforts at resistance in 1939-41. See Merson, *Communist Resistance in Nazi Germany*, 211-32, 309-10.

141. Sering [Richard Löwenthal], "Zur Einschätzung der deutsch-russischen Zusammenarbeit," 1 October 1939, Neu Beginnen Archiv, 41, IISH, Amsterdam.

142. Ibid., 4, 8.

143. Karl Frank, "War Aims of the German Opposition," 15 October 1939, Neu Beginnen Archiv, 27, IISH, Amsterdam. See also Richard Löwenthal, *Die Widerstandsgruppe "Neu Beginnen,"* 13-14.

144. Richard Löwenthal, interview with author, Berlin, 3 August 1987; Richard Löwenthal, *Die Widerstandsgruppe "Neu Beginnen,"* 14; Foitzik, *Zwischen den Fronten*, 130-40, 270-71.

145. Richard Löwenthal, *Die Widerstandsgruppe "Neu Beginnen,"* 15-17.

146. One of those who remained a radical and a consistent cold war opponent was Wolfgang Abendroth (1906-85), the Marburg political scientist. He had always been on the group's left during his time with Neu Beginnen. See his iconoclastic and valuable personal reminiscences, Wolfgang Abendroth, *Ein Leben in der Arbeiterbewegung: Gespräche, aufgezeichnet und herausgegeben von Barbara Dietrich und Joachim Perels* (Frankfurt am Main: Suhrkamp, 1981). For a brief summary of Abendroth's career on the left, see Foitzik, *Zwischen den Fronten*, 246.

147. The most recent major study of German resistance that focuses on the movement behind the failed July 1944 attempt to assassinate Hitler is Theodore Hamerow's detailed and thoughtfully critical *On The Road to the Wolf's Lair: German Resistance to Hitler* (Cambridge, Mass.: Harvard University Press, 1997). The Rote Kapelle (Red Orchestra), whose membership included a number of Communists, was another of the larger and relatively diverse groups of the anti-Nazi resistance and therefore also merits a reference here. For recent accounts that include source listings on both groups, see Hans Mommsen, "Bourgeois (National-Conservative) Resistance," and Hans Coppi, "Red Orchestra," in *Encyclopedia of German Resisance*, ed. Belz and Pehle, 35-44, 223-26.

Chapter 3: Varieties of Antitotalitarianism

1. Helmut Dubiel has made a similar point about the diversity of conceptions of state-party dictatorship on the left, but he focuses on separating the writings of the Frankfurt Circle, Horkheimer, Adorno, and Pollock, from those that explicitly formulated the kind of comparison or equation of the Soviet Union and Nazi Germany that would be a hallmark of the cold war versions of the totalitarianism thesis, such as American political scientist Carl J. Friedrich's. I do not dispute Dubiel's conclusion that the Frankfurt theorists' writings on dictatorship stand apart from most others. I simply want to frame the issue differently: Friedrich's model is not the only totalitarianism concept, so I am exploring what directions other writers took in generating such concepts before the cold war. See Dubiel, *Wissenschaftsorganisation und politische Erfahrung*, 93-94.

2. The best single-volume accounts of World War II in English are Gordon Wright, *The Ordeal of Total War, 1939–1945* (New York: Harper and Row, 1969); John Keegan, *The Second World War* (New York: Viking, 1990); and Weinberg, *A World at Arms.*

3. Ruth Fischer, *Stalin and German Communism,* 7.

4. On Rühle (1874–1943), see Henry Jacoby and Ingrid Herbst, *Otto Rühle zur Einführung* (Hamburg: Junius, 1984); Foitzik, *Zwischen den Fronten,* 315–16; Gottfried Mergner, "Zum Verständnis der Texte," in Otto Rühle, *Schriften: Perspektiven einer Revolution in hochindustrialisierten Ländern,* ed. Gottfried Mergner (Reinbek: Rowohlt Taschenbuch, 1971), 206–13; Ruth Fischer, *Stalin and German Communism,* 7, 13, 77; and Fowkes, *Communism in Germany under the Weimar Republic,* 10–12, 46, 51. A discussion of Rühle's role in SPD education policy during the late Imperial period appears in Stanley Pierson, *Marxist Intellectuals and the Working-Class Mentality in Germany, 1887–1912* (Cambridge, Mass.: Harvard University Press, 1993), 193–204. References to Rühle's activities in the left-wing party upheavals of the World War I period and its aftermath are in Morgan, *The Socialist Left and the German Revolution,* 44, 170, 177, 208, note 98. Rühle's "Brauner und Roter Faschismus" was written in 1939 but not published until 1971. See Rühle, "Brauner und Roter Faschismus," in *Schriften,* 7–71, 190.

5. Mergner, "Zum Verständnis der Texte," 214–15; Henry Jacoby and Herbst, *Rühle zur Einfuhrung,* passim; Foitzik, *Zwischen den Fronten,* 315–16.

6. Rühle, "Brauner und Roter Faschimus," 7.

7. Ibid., 8. Rühle was yet another advocate of the term *state capitalism* to describe the Soviet economy.

8. Ibid., 11.

9. Ibid., 17.

10. Ibid., 18.

11. Borkenau, *The Communist International,* 134–60; Rosenberg, *Entstehung und Geschichte der Weimarer Republik,* 241–42.

12. Rühle, "Brauner und Roter Faschismus," 23.

13. Ibid., 25.

14. Ibid., 27, 34, 39–41.

15. Ibid., 35.

16. Ibid., 63.

17. Ibid., 68.

18. Ibid., 71. Rühle's hostile pairing of Nazism and Soviet Communism would later have an audience very different from the one he apparently wanted. The gradual emergence of the "red fascism" argument in the United States is examined in Les K. Adler and Thomas G. Paterson, "Red Fascism: The Merger of Nazi Germany and Soviet Russia in the American Image of Totalitarianism, 1930s-1950s," *American Historical Review* 75, no. 4 (1970): 1046–64.

19. See John Day Co. to Carmen Haider Phillips, 11 December 1939, and Max Eastman to Otto Rühle, 25 May 1940, Nachlaß Otto Rühle, 79, 82, IISH, Amsterdam.

Phillips and Eastman had made inquiries to publishers in Rühle's behalf. Mattick, who was born in Germany, was one of Korsch's close friends and intellectual collaborators in the United States. He established a strong reputation in his own right as an independent Marxist. For pertinent examples of his postwar theoretical and historical writings, see Paul Mattick, *Marx and Keynes: The Limits of the Mixed Economy* (Boston: Extending Horizons Books, 1969); and "Anti-Bolshevist Communism in Germany," *Telos,* no. 26 (Winter 1975–76): 57–69.

20. Karl Korsch to Paul Mattick, 25 June 1940, Nachlaß Karl Korsch, 32/96, IISH, Amsterdam.

21. Sering [Richard Löwenthal], "Zur Einschätzung der deutsch-russischen Zusammenarbeit," 1 October 1939, Neu Beginnen Archiv, 41, 1–2, IISH, Amsterdam.

22. Ibid., 4.

23. Ibid., 9.

24. "Russland und die deutsche Revolution," n.d., Neu Beginnen Archiv, 41, 1–9, IISH, Amsterdam. No author is provided on the document, but its style and the various specific arguments indicate that Richard Löwenthal was almost certainly the author or coauthor. The date is also impossible to state with precision. It is not clear whether the paper was written before or after the beginning of Operation Barbarossa—the German invasion of the Soviet Union on 22 June 1941.

25. Ibid., 1.

26. Ibid.

27. See, for instance, Richard Löwenthal, "Letter to the Editor of the *Frankfurter Allgemeine Zeitung,*" 29 November 1986, in *Forever in the Shadow of Hitler?* 199–201.

28. "Russland und die deutsche Revolution," 2–5.

29. Ibid., 6–7.

30. Paul Sering, [Richard Löwenthal], "Unsere Taktik gegenüber den Kommunisten," 6 June 1942, Neu Beginnen Archiv, 40, 1, IISH, Amsterdam.

31. Ibid., 1.

32. Ibid., 2.

33. Franz Borkenau, *The Totalitarian Enemy* (London: Faber and Faber, 1940), 7.

34. Ibid., 13.

35. Ibid., 7.

36. Franz Borkenau to Geoffrey Faber, 3 October 1939, Faber and Faber Archive, London.

37. This is at best an approximation. One of Borkenau's acquaintances, Gerald Brenan, later claimed that Borkenau never made a very good liberal and instead labeled him a "Nietzschean romantic." See Brenan, foreword to *The Spanish Cockpit,* by Franz Borkenau (reprint, London: Pluto, 1986), viii.

38. Borkenau, *The Totalitarian Enemy,* 101.

39. Ibid., 30.

40. Ibid., 66.

41. Ibid., 8, 67–68. The similarity between these views and those that Richard Löwenthal had expressed in his articles on fascism a few years earlier in *Zeitschrift*

für Sozialismus is no coincidence. Borkenau acknowledged his debt to Löwenthal's essays in the preface.

42. Borkenau, *The Totalitarian Enemy*, 68.

43. Ibid., 69–74, 100. There are broad and suggestive similarities between Borkenau's outlook in the wartime period and that of another ex-Communist, James Burnham, author of *The Managerial Revolution* (New York: John Day, 1941). Borkenau had not and would not move quite so far to the right as Burnham would, but their parallel development deserves study. Christopher Hitchens offers a shrewd account of Burnham's influence in the United States in "How Neo-conservatives Perish," in *For the Sake of Argument*, 143–45.

44. Borkenau, *The Totalitarian Enemy*, 76, 102.

45. Borkenau's judgment followed in part the response of an "orthodox" Marxist that Korsch had sarcastically described in "The Fascist Counter-Revolution": "Our orthodox Marxist might not be willing, for the present, to go so far as to acknowledge the fascist allies of Stalin as the genuine promoters of socialism in our time. He would then content himself with feeling that the victory of fascism, planned economy, state capitalism, and the weeding out of all ideas and institutions of traditional 'bourgeois democracy' will bring us to the very threshold of the genuine social revolution and proletarian dictatorship" (quoted in Kellner, ed., *Karl Korsch*, 245). Borkenau, however, foresaw no revolution, and he certainly held no hope for a positive result emerging from the "victory of fascism."

46. Borkenau, *The Totalitarian Enemy*, 78–79.

47. See, for example, Friedrich A. Hayek, *The Road to Serfdom* (Chicago: University of Chicago Press, 1944). Interestingly, however, Hayek cited favorably Borkenau's *Socialism: National or International* (141, note 1).

48. Borkenau, *The Totalitarian Enemy*, 146.

49. Ibid., 164.

50. Ibid., 161–63.

51. Ibid., 182–83.

52. Ibid., 229.

53. Ibid., 225.

54. Ibid., 225–26.

55. Ibid., 213–20.

56. Ibid., 227–34, 246–47.

57. Ibid., 254.

58. George Orwell, "War-time Diary: 1940," in *The Collected Essays, Journalism, and Letters*, vol. 2, *My Country Right or Left*, 341, 344–45.

59. John E. Tashjean, "Franz Borkenau: A Study of His Social and Political Ideas" (Ph.D. diss., Georgetown University, 1962), 15, note 43; Richard Löwenthal, interview with author, Berlin, 3 August 1987; Karl Korsch, review of *The New German Empire*, by Franz Borkenau, *Living Marxism* 5, no. 2 (1940): 63.

60. Karl Korsch to Max Horkheimer, 14 September 1939, Max-Horkheimer-

Archiv, I, 14, 74, Stadt- und Universitätsbibliothek Frankfurt am Main (hereafter SUBF), Frankfurt am Main.

61. These articles were originally published during the early war years: "State and Counter-Revolution," *Modern Quarterly* 11, no. 2 (1939): 60–67, "The Fascist Counter-Revolution," *Living Marxism* 5, no. 2 (1940): 29–37; and "The Workers' Fight against Fascism," *Living Marxism* 5, no. 3 (1941): 36–49.

62. Quoted in Keller, ed., *Karl Korsch,* 238.

63. Ibid., 238–39. As Kellner contends, "Korsch's critique of the Soviet Union takes its most radical form in this context" (235).

64. Ibid., 240.

65. Ibid., 241–42.

66. Ibid., 44–45, 141–45, 153–57.

67. Ibid., 243–44.

68. Quoted in Kellner, ed., *Karl Korsch,* 248.

69. This is Marx's well-known, brilliantly provocative, and much contested passage of 1859 on the conditions for and the process of socialist revolution: "At a certain stage of their development, the material productive forces of society come in conflict with the existing relations of production. . . . From forms of development of the productive forces these relations turn into their fetters. Then begins an epoch of social revolution." See Karl Marx, "Marx on the History of His Opinions," in *The Marx-Engels Reader,* ed. Robert Tucker (New York: Norton, 1972), 4–5.

70. Quoted in Kellner, ed., *Karl Korsch,* 249.

71. Ibid., 249–52.

72. Ibid., 253.

73. Quoted in Kellner, ed., *Karl Korsch,* 254.

74. Ibid.

75. Ibid., 255–56.

76. Ibid., 258. Korsch might have been referring to the title of a well-known book by the Austrian émigré and later U.S. business and managerial theorist Peter Drucker, *The End of Economic Man: A Study of the New Totalitarianism* (New York: John Day, 1939), though that is not necessarily the case.

77. Quoted in Kellner, ed., *Karl Korsch,* 267.

78. Götz Langkau of the International Institute for Social History in Amsterdam suggested the "Kondratieff Wave" analogy to me a decade ago in a conversation about the nature and political thrust of Korsch's antitotalitarian writings.

79. Karl Korsch to Max Horkheimer, 26 May 1940, Max-Horkheimer-Archiv, I, 14, 58, SUBF, Frankfurt am Main. On the date of the original version of the "Autoritärer Staat" essay, see Horkheimer, *Gesammelte Schriften,* vol. 5, 460.

80. The published writings of Walter Benjamin (1892–1940) and the secondary literature on his life and work constitute a large and growing archive. The essays collected in Walter Benjamin, *Illuminations,* ed. Hannah Arendt, trans. Harry Zohn (New York: Schocken, 1969), are a reasonable starting point for readers unfamiliar

with Benjamin. On the move of some of the institute's operations to Santa Monica, California—which was not completed until 1941—and its consequences, see Wiggershaus, *Die Frankfurter Schule*, 327–38. On the "Autoritärer Staat" essay, see Jay, *The Dialectical Imagination*, 156–58, 256, 259; Russell Jacoby, "Postscript to Horkheimer's 'The Authoritarian State,'" *Telos*, no. 15 (Spring 1973): 21–24; Russell Jacoby, *Dialectic of Defeat*, 113–14; and Wiggershaus, *Die Frankfurter Schule*, 316. Wiggershaus rather uncharitably characterizes the first appearance of the essay as an effort "more to hide it than to publish it." Jay gives the essay more thoughtful attention and perceives the latent Luxemburgist component of Horkheimer's thought as well as the rationale for a retreat from praxis to theory. In *Dialectic of Defeat*, Jacoby writes of "two Horkheimers"—the scholarly organization man and the radical theorist—and uses the essay to ward off those critics who see Horkheimer in constant retreat from politics and praxis and to insist that for Horkheimer to emphasize theory over practice in his California exile of the early 1940s was to dispense with illusions about the political possibilities of that time and that place.

81. Max Horkheimer, "Autoritärer Staat," in *Gesammelte Schriften*, vol. 5, 300. Helmut Dubiel discusses the terminological distinctions briefly in *Wissensschaftsorganisation und politische Erfahrung*, 94.

82. Horkheimer, "Autoritärer Staat," 294. I have also consulted the translation of "The Authoritarian State" that appears in *The Essential Frankfurt School Reader*, ed. Andrew Arato and Eike Gebhardt (New York: Continuum, 1993), 95–117. I have made a few changes in terminology.

83. Horkheimer, "Autoritärer Staat," 295–97.

84. Ibid., 297.

85. Ibid., 300.

86. Ibid.

87. Ibid., 301.

88. Ibid.

89. Ibid., 304.

90. Ibid., 318.

91. Ibid., 319.

92. Benjamin, *Illuminations*, 264.

93. Liebich, "Marxism and Totalitarianism." Liebich has continued his exploration of the crucial intellectual relationship between Hilferding and the exiled Mensheviks in *From the Other Shore*.

94. Rudolf Hilferding, ["State Capitalism or Totalitarian State Economy?"], *Sotsialisticheskii Vestnik* (April 1940): 118–20. Translated as "State Capitalism or Totalitarian State Economy," *Modern Review* 1 (1947): 266–71. See also Smaldone, *Rudolf Hilferding*, 196–200.

95. Quoted in Liebich, "Marxism and Totalitarianism," 239.

96. Ibid., 238.

97. Hilferding, "State Capitalism or Totalitarian State Economy," 266. See also Hilferding, quoted in Franz Neumann, *Behemoth*, 223.

98. Quoted in Liebich, "Marxism and Totalitarianism," 239.

99. Ibid., 239.

100. Rudolf Hilferding, "Das historische Problem," *Zeitschrift für Politik* 1, no. 4 (1954): 293–324. Interestingly, however, William Smaldone's biography of Hilferding indicates that his new theoretical and practical positions generated other controversies: one of Hilferding's colleagues, Paul Hertz (1888–1961), broke with Hilferding and SOPADE in 1938. He soon linked up with Karl Frank and Neu Beginnen. See Smaldone, *Rudolf Hilferding*, 191–200. On Hertz, see Foitzik, *Zwischen den Fronten*, 280–81; and Ursula Langkau-Alex, "Paul Hertz," in *Vor dem Vergessen bewahren: Lebenswege Weimarer Sozialdemokraten*, ed. Peter Lösche, Michael Scholing, and Franz Walter (Berlin: Colloquium, 1988), 145–69. Smaldone also argues persuasively that in his increasing wartime pessimism, Hilferding often failed to see that the mechanistic element in his own theories, rather than those in Marx's work, was a fundamental source of analytical weaknesses. In *Zur Analyse des Faschismus*, Wippermann argues that Hilferding's reliance on Bonapartism theory in his assessment of the collapse of the Weimar Republic underlay his assertion of the "primacy of the political" (44–45).

101. Liebich, "Marxism and Totalitarianism," 239–40. William Smaldone's account indicates that Hilferding took his own life. Smaldone cites Masaaki Kurotake, "Zur Todesursache Rudolf Hilferdings," *Beiträge der Miyagi-Gakuin Frauenhochschule* 61 (December 1984): 1–21. On the subject of the posthumous publication in English of Hilferding's late writings, Liebich notes that *Modern Review*'s other editors were Lewis Coser, the sociologist later associated with the democratic socialist journal *Dissent*, and Travers Clement.

102. See the discussion of the institute's opposition to the Soviet Union in Slater, *Origin and Significance of the Frankfurt School*, 58–63; and Held, *Introduction to Critical Theory*, 45–52.

103. Dubiel, *Wissenschaftsorganisation und politische Erfahrung*, 96–97.

104. One of the best discussions of Friedrich Pollock's and Franz Neumann's positions in this debate—and their relative strengths and weaknesses—is in Kellner, *Critical Theory, Marxism, and Modernity*, 55–63, 77–80. See also Jay, *The Dialectical Imagination*, 143–72; Dubiel, *Wissenschaftsorganisation und politische Erfahrung*, 94–100; Erd, ed., *Reform und Resignation*, 115–25; Alfons Söllner, *Geschichte und Herrschaft: Studien zur materialistischen Sozialwissenschaft, 1929–1942* (Frankfurt am Main: Suhrkamp, 1979), 156–62; Alfons Söllner, "Franz Neumann," *Telos*, no. 50 (Winter 1981–82): 171–79; Wiggershaus, *Die Frankfurter Schule*, 314–27; and Held, *Introduction to Critical Theory*, 52–65.

105. Pollock (1894–1970) published very little during the institute's hectic exile years. For a chronological summary of Pollock's career, see Gunzelin Schmid Noerr and Willem van Reijen, "Friedrich Pollock," in *Grand Hotel Abgrund*, ed. Schmid Noerr and van Reijen, 112–15. See also Jay, *The Dialectical Imagination*, 6–8.

106. Friedrich Pollock, "State Capitalism: Its Possibilities and Limitations," *Studies in Philosophy and Social Science* 9, no. 2 (1941): 201. See also Friedrich Pol-

lock, "Is National Socialism a New Order?" *Studies in Philosophy and Social Science* 9, no. 3 (1941): 440–55. For a discussion of Pollock's analysis and its consequences, see Moishe Postone and Barbara Brick, "Critical Theory and Political Economy," in *On Max Horkheimer*, ed. Benhabib, Bonß, and McCole, 215–56.

107. Pollock had also paid close attention to Soviet economic developments for years. His *Die planwirtschaftlichen Versuche in der Sowjetunion, 1917–1927* (Leipzig: Hirschfeld, 1929) was a study of the extent to which the Soviet state had been able to institute socialism. Jay indicates that Pollock's earlier studies of the Soviet economy had been part of the basis for the "state capitalism" article. See Jay, *The Dialectical Imagination*, 152–53. That Pollock's empirical research had focused primarily on the Soviet Union while Neumann's focused on Nazi Germany may in part explain the incompatibility of their views.

108. Pollock, "State Capitalism," 202.

109. Ibid., 204–7.

110. Ibid., 208.

111. See Hilferding, "State Capitalism or Totalitarian State Economy," 266–67. Helmut Dubiel states that Pollock's essay is simply "the application of the theory of state capitalism to the circumstances of National Socialism" (Dubiel, *Wissenschafts-organisation und politische Erfahrung*, 98).

112. Franz Neumann to Max Horkheimer, 23 July 1941, Max-Horkheimer-Archiv, VI, 30, 54–57, SUBF, Frankfurt am Main. In this letter, Neumann also bracketed Pollock's outlook with that of Karl Mannheim, who had expressed a similar notion of the new role of the state in the economy and arrived at Pollock's question: who plans the planner? Neumann dismissed both formulations of the state capitalist dilemma as departures from a class-based theory of contradiction and crisis. Since Mannheim's views were anathema to Horkheimer and several other leading members of the institute, Neumann's comparison must have been particularly annoying. See Horkheimer, "A New Concept of Ideology?" in *Between Philosophy and Social Science*, 129–49. On the institute and Karl Mannheim, see Jay, "The Frankfurt School's Critique of Karl Mannheim and the Sociology of Knowledge," in *Permanent Exiles*, 62–78; and David Frisby, *The Alienated Mind: The Sociology of Knowledge in Germany, 1918–1933* (London: Heinemann, 1983), 217–27, passim.

113. Franz Neumann, *Behemoth*, 224.

114. Ibid., 223. The reference to Pollock (500, note 1) lumped his article on state capitalism with the writings of thinkers of the "end of economic man" school, Peter Drucker and James Burnham, as well as with those of the leftist Dwight Macdonald.

115. Ibid., 226.

116. Ibid., 228–34.

117. Ibid., 240.

118. Ibid., 261.

119. Ibid., 467.

120. Borkenau, *The Totalitarian Enemy*, 69–104.

121. Dubiel, *Wissenschaftsorganisation und politische Erfahrung*, 99–100.

122. Franz Neumann, *Behemoth*, 216–18, 470–76.

123. In addition to Söllner, "Franz Neumann—Skizzen zu einer intellektuellen und politischen Biographie," 7–57, see the sympathetic portrait of Neumann offered in H. Stuart Hughes, "Franz Neumann between Marxism and Liberal Democracy," in *The Intellectual Migration: Europe and America, 1930–1960,* ed. Donald Fleming and Bernard Bailyn (Cambridge, Mass.: Harvard University Press, Belknap Press, 1969), 446–62.

124. Wiggershaus, *Die Frankfurter Schule,* 324.

125. Franz Neumann to Max Horkheimer, 13 August 1941, Max-Horkheimer-Archiv, VI, 30, 38–39, SUBF, Frankfurt am Main. See also Wiggershaus, *Die Frankfurter Schule,* 286–87.

126. Otto Kirchheimer, for instance, also offered his assessment of the National Socialist legal system in 1941, "The Legal Order of National Socialism," *Studies in Philosophy and Social Science* 9, no. 3 (1941): 456–75.

127. Ernst Fraenkel, *The Dual State: A Contribution to the Theory of Dictatorship,* trans. E. A. Shils et al. (New York: Oxford University Press, 1941), xiii.

128. Ibid., 59–60.

129. Ibid., 59.

130. Ibid., 60.

131. Quoted in ibid., 61.

132. Ibid., 59–61. See also Kennedy, "Carl Schmitt and the Frankfurt School," 37–38, note 2.

133. Fraenkel, *The Dual State,* 61, 97–101, 184–87.

134. Ibid., 208.

135. See Kershaw, *The Nazi Dictatorship,* 63.

136. Fraenkel, *The Dual State,* 3, 57. For a helpful discussion of Fraenkel's use of this distinction, see Gleason, *Totalitarianism,* 57.

137. Fraenkel, *The Dual State,* 72–73.

138. For a broad sampling of these debates, see Kershaw, *The Nazi Dictatorship,* 40–58.

139. Otto Kirchheimer, *Political Justice: The Use of Legal Procedure for Political Ends* (Princeton, N.J.: Princeton University Press, 1961).

140. Ernst Fraenkel, "Vorwort zur deutschen Ausgabe (1974)," in *Der Doppelstaat: Recht und Justiz im "Dritten Reich"* (1974; reprint, Frankfurt am Main: Fischer Taschenbuch, 1984), 11–18.

141. As William Scheuerman has noted, however, the relative level of interest in the two books would shift over the decades, with Horkheimer and Adorno's *Dialectic of Enlightenment* now enjoying a broad and interdisciplinary (even if rather quarrelsome) readership—and Neumann's *Behemoth* now reaching only academics and more diligent students dealing with National Socialism. Likewise, Marcuse's *Reason and Revolution* remains perhaps his least-visited major work. See Scheuerman, *Between the Norm and the Exception,* 149–55. On Neumann's sojourn

in England, where he earned a doctorate in political science at the London School of Economics under Laski's direction, see Erd, ed., *Reform und Resignation,* 58–70. Neumann's dissertation, *The Governance of the Rule of Law,* was completed in 1936. It was published fifty years later as *The Rule of Law: Political Theory and the Legal System in Modern Society,* with a foreword by Martin Jay and an introduction by Matthias Ruete (Berg: Leamington Spa, 1986).

142. Friedrich knew Neumann personally. In the introduction to Bracher's magisterial study, *Die Auflösung der Weimarer Republik,* yet another early postwar Berlin scholar, Hans Herzfeld, testified to the insistence of the "unforgettable Franz Neumann, so tragically torn from life," on the need to connect historical and political studies in the postwar Institut für politische Wissenschaft in Berlin, where Bracher taught for several years (xvii).

143. Kühnl, "'Linke' Totalitarismusversionen," 97–119; Hennig, *Bürgerliche Gesellschaft und Faschismus in Deutschland,* 56.

144. Söllner, *Geschichte und Herrschaft,* 202–8. For another example of such analysis, see Gleason, *Totalitarianism,* 35.

145. Franz Neumann, *Behemoth,* vii.

146. Ibid., 440–58. Neumann recommended Fraenkel's book even as he disputed some of its findings (516, note 63).

147. Ibid., 11–12, 478, note 19.

148. Ibid., 14.

149. Ibid., 47.

150. Ibid., 48.

151. Ibid., 49.

152. This perspective on the uses of totalitarian ideology approached some of Borkenau's arguments in *Pareto.*

153. Franz Neumann, *Behemoth,* 50–51.

154. Ibid., 53.

155. Ibid., 221–22.

156. Ibid., 82.

157. Ibid., 470.

158. Arthur Rosenberg, Review of *Behemoth,* by Franz Neumann, *Studies in Philosophy and Social Science* 9, no. 3 (1941): 526–27.

159. Gert Schäfer's excellent afterword to the German-language edition of *Behemoth* emphasizes this point about the superiority of Neumann's book to those of his contemporaries. See Schäfer, afterword in *Behemoth: Struktur und Praxis des Nationalsozialismus 1933–1944,* trans. Hedda Wagner and Gert Schäfer (Frankfurt am Main: Fischer Taschenbuch, 1984), 665. Ayçoberry also singles out *Behemoth* for special praise, calling it "the first of the classics" on the Nazi regime (*The Nazi Question,* 92–97).

160. Sigmund Neumann, *Permanent Revolution: The Total State in a World at War* (New York: Harper and Brothers, 1942). Sigmund Neumann (1904–62) was not related to Franz Neumann, but their writings reveal similar interests. Sigmund

Neumann had been a Weimar-era liberal, whose earlier study, *Die Parteien der Weimarer Republik* (Berlin: Verlag Junker und Dünnhaupt, 1932), also ranks as an essential text on politics in Germany during this period. For a recent discussion of Sigmund Neumann's contribution to the totalitarianism debate, see Alfons Söllner, "Sigmund Neumann's 'Permanent Revolution': Ein vergessener Klassiker der vergleichenden Diktaturforschung," in *Totalitarismus,* ed. Söllner, Walkenhaus, and Wieland, 53–76.

161. Karl Korsch, "A Social Democrat Looks at Totalitarianism," Nachlaß Karl Korsch, 96/4, IISH, Amsterdam.

162. Ibid., 4–6.

163. Ibid., 7–8. I have changed this passage to include several corrections handwritten by Korsch on the original typed manuscript.

164. Ibid., 11–12.

165. Ibid., 12.

166. Karl Korsch to Paul Mattick, 20 October 1938, Nachlaß Karl Korsch, 32/39–40, IISH, Amsterdam. In this letter, Korsch offered his blunt and often negative appraisals of the various individual members of the institute. For the group as a whole, Korsch cherished little regard: "They talk a lot and work little. They call this 'collectivity.'" See also Karl Korsch to Paul Mattick, 6 May 1941, Nachlaß Karl Korsch, 32/127, IISH, Amsterdam. Korsch complained to Mattick that the Institute of Social Research had approached him for an article to be published in their issue on state capitalism: "However, they withdrew from their proposition, and I have only wasted my time and given away some important new ideas that had occurred to me during the discussion of the problem that I was going to discuss in my contribution. . . . These people keep on disappointing even the most modest hopes one may set on them!"

167. Karl Korsch, "The Structure and Practice of Totalitarianism," *New Essays* 6, no. 2 (1942): 43–49.

168. Karl Korsch, "Germany Today," Nachlaß Karl Korsch, 101, 10–15, IISH, Amsterdam.

169. Franz Neumann, *Behemoth,* 382.

170. Karl Korsch, "Germany Today," 101, 13.

171. Ibid., 15.

172. Ibid., 5–11, 14. See Fritz Fischer, *Germany's Aims in the First World War* (1961; reprint, New York: Norton, 1967).

173. Lukács, 1967 preface to *History and Class Consciousness,* xxx.

174. For an exception to this neglect of Korsch's wartime writings, see Kornder, *Konterrevolution und Faschismus.*

175. Karl Korsch to Herbert Levy, 29 October 1941, Nachlaß Karl Korsch, 26/3, IISH, Amsterdam. Interestingly, these grudgingly positive remarks were inspired by Korsch's reading of the Institute's issue on National Socialism, whose pages were dominated by the articles of Gurland, Adorno, Horkheimer, and Kirchheimer. Korsch singled out only Pollock's article on "state capitalism" for criticism.

176. See Jay, *The Dialectical Imagination*, 5, 235, 284–85, 363–64; and Wiggershaus, *Die Frankfurter Schule*, 254–58, 309–13, 327–38. Massing's book was published in New York in 1949. On the scholarly work and the anti-Communism of both the Massings and Wittfogel, who became professor of history at the University of Washington in 1947, see Ulmen, *The Science of Society*, 179, 211, 240–41, 243, 265–94, 513–17; and Hede Massing, *This Deception* (New York: Duell, Sloan and Pearce, 1951). The institute's project on anti-Semitism was announced and outlined in *Studies in Philosophy and Social Science* 9, no. 1 (1941): 124–43. On Pachter's wartime years, see Stephen Eric Bronner, introduction to *Socialism in History*, by Pachter, xx.

177. An exception to this general rule in the secondary literature on totalitarianism is Abbott Gleason's interesting discussion of Horkheimer and Adorno's development of a critique of totalitarianism in *Dialectic of Enlightenment*. See Gleason, *Totalitarianism*, 35–36. Adorno's use of the philosophical category of "totality," however, has generally received more attention. See Jay, *Marxism and Totality*, 241–75; Susan Buck-Morss, *The Origin of Negative Dialectics: Theodor W. Adorno, Walter Benjamin, and the Frankfurt Institute* (New York: Free Press, 1977); and Christel Beier, *Zum Verhältnis von Gesellschaftstheorie und Erkenntnistheorie: Untersuchungen zum Totalitätsbegriff in der kritischen Theorie Adornos* (Frankfurt am Main: Suhrkamp, 1977).

178. Arendt, for instance, criticized Adorno for dropping the name of his Jewish father (Wiesengrund) as well as for his role in slowing the academic career of Arendt's first husband, Günter Stern, in Germany during the early 1930s. They also diverged sharply in their interpretations of Walter Benjamin. See Carol Brightman, ed., *Between Friends: The Correspondence of Hannah Arendt and Mary McCarthy, 1949–1975* (New York: Harcourt, Brace, 1995), 205–6, note 2. Martin Jay gently disputes the idea that there were ulterior political motives in Adorno's choice of names in his biography, *Adorno* (Cambridge, Mass.: Harvard University Press, 1984), 34.

179. For a brief, introductory survey of the life and writings of Adorno (1903–69), see Martin Jay's sympathetic biographical chapter, "A Damaged Life," in *Adorno*, 24–55. See also the useful discussion of Adorno in Wiggershaus, *Die Frankfurter Schule*, 82–113; and Rolf Wiggershaus, *Theodor W. Adorno* (Munich: Beck, 1987). Both Jay's and Wiggerhaus's biographies of Adorno offer substantial bibliographies of writings by and about Adorno. On Adorno's involvement in cultural modernism, see Lunn, *Marxism and Modernism*. For discussions of Adorno's friendship with Kracauer (1889–1966) and Kracauer's own intellectual contributions, see Jay, "The Extraterritorial Life of Siegfried Kracauer" and "Adorno and Kracauer: Notes on a Troubled Friendship," in *Permanent Exiles*, 152–97, 217–36.

180. Marcuse, *Reason and Revolution*, 403–19. Marcuse's book made several references to the element of totalitarianism in fascist appropriations and (mis)interpretations of Hegel, notably in the work of Giovanni Gentile, Alfred Rosenberg, and Carl Schmitt.

181. Max Horkheimer and Theodor W. Adorno, *Dialectic of Enlightenment*, trans. John Cumming (New York: Continuum, 1986), 6. The original German text

reads just as simply: "Aufklärung ist totalitär." The definitive version of *Dialektik der Aufklärung* appears in Horkheimer, *Gesammelte Schriften*, vol. 5, 11–290. On the circumstances of the book's writing and eventual publication, see Wiggershaus, *Die Frankfurter Schule*, 349–64; Willem van Reijen and Gunzelin Schmid Noerr, eds., *Vierzig Jahre Flaschenpost: "Dialektik der Aufklärung," 1947 bis 1987* (Frankfurt am Main: Fischer, 1987); Christopher Rocco, "Between Modernity and Postmodernity: Reading *Dialectic of Enlightenment* against the Grain," *Political Theory* 22, no. 1 (1994): 71–97; and Anson Rabinbach, "The Cunning of Unreason: Mimesis and the Construction of Anti-Semitism in Horkheimer and Adorno's *Dialectic of Enlightenment*," in *In the Shadow of Catastrophe: German Intellectuals between Apocalypse and Enlightenment* (Berkeley: University of California Press, 1997), 166–98.

182. Jay, *The Dialectical Imagination*, 256. Offering a slightly different perspective on the Frankfurt School and the waning of its Marxism, Susan Buck-Morss emphasizes Adorno's focus on the Marxian notions of labor—the human-Nature relationship that was central to Marx's *Economic and Philosophical Manuscripts of 1844*—rather than the idea of class that Marx elaborated more fully in his later economic and political writings. Buck-Morss's appraisal of Adorno's use of Marxian concepts does not, however, seem to lessen the accuracy of Jay's remarks about the group's increasing distance from "orthodox Marxism." See Buck-Morss, *Origin of Negative Dialectics*, 61–62.

183. On Hegelian "identity theory" and Adorno and Horkheimer's critical response to it, see Jay, *Marxism and Totality*, 54–60, 213–19, 240–42, 260–75.

184. Ibid., 219.

185. Horkheimer and Adorno, *Dialectic of Enlightenment*, 224.

186. Ibid., 185.

187. Ibid., 186. In this section of the book, Horkheimer argued that the proscription of mimesis in Jewish religious life operated as a temptation to the kinds of perverse and violent pseudoreligious mimesis that characterized Nazi public display. In his detailed and subtly argued essay "The Cunning of Unreason," the historian Anson Rabinbach offers a compelling interpretation of the ways Horkheimer and Adorno reconsidered and attended to the problem of Nazi anti-Semitism in *Dialectic of Enlightenment*.

188. Wilhelm Reich, *The Mass Psychology of Fascism*, trans. Theodor P. Wolfe (New York: Orgone Institute, 1946); Erich Fromm, *Fear of Freedom* (New York: Rinehart, 1941). Fromm had once been Horkheimer's colleague at the Institute of Social Research, several of whose members made use of Freudian concepts in analyzing society. On Fromm and his increasingly troubled relationship with the institute's key figures, see Jay, *The Dialectical Imagination*, 88–106; and Bronner, *Of Critical Theory and Its Theorists*, 209–33.

189. This assertion of the persistent and essentially murderous character of German anti-Semitism appears most sharply in Daniel Jonah Goldhagen, *Hitler's Willing Executioners: Ordinary Germans and the Holocaust* (New York: Vintage Books/ Random House, 1997). For more persuasive historical discussions of the origins and

development of Nazi policies of genocide, see Friedländer, *Nazi Germany and the Jews,* vol. 1, passim; Kershaw, *The Nazi Dictatorship,* 90–107; Fritzsche, *Germans into Nazis,* 227–35; and Browning, "Beyond 'Intentionalism' and 'Functionalism,'" 86–121.

190. Max Horkheimer, "Die Juden und Europa," *Zeitschrift für Sozialforschung* 8, nos. 1/2 (1939): 115–37. Marx's essay, "On the Jewish Question," written in 1843, continues to generate controversy. For reconsiderations of "Marx's anti-Semitism," see Pachter, "Marx and the Jews," in *Socialism in History,* 219–55; and Albert S. Lindemann, *Esau's Tears: Modern Anti-Semitism and the Rise of the Jews* (Cambridge: Cambridge University Press, 1997), 162–66. For carefully argued accounts of the increasing scope and intensity of the policy of genocide against Jews carried out by the Nazis and their accomplices, see Browning, *The Path to Genocide;* Christopher R. Browning, *Ordinary Men: Reserve Police Battalion 101 and the Final Solution in Poland* (New York: Harper Collins, 1992); and Richard Breitman, *The Architect of Genocide: Himmler and the Final Solution* (New York: Knopf, 1991). See also Raul Hilberg's influential study, *The Destruction of the European Jews* (Chicago: Quadrangle Books, 1961), as well as his more recent book, *Perpetrators, Victims, Bystanders: The Jewish Catastrophe, 1933–1945* (New York: Harper Collins, 1992). In attempting to clarify the shifting emphasis of Horkheimer's critique of anti-Semitism, I have relied on Dan Diner's essay "Reason and the 'Other': Horkheimer's Reflections on Anti-Semitism and Mass Annihilation," in *On Max Horkheimer,* ed. Benhabib, Bonß, and McCole, 335–63.

191. This rather abstract and "objectively" dispassionate way of seeing anti-Semitism shows how much a certain kind of Marxist-influenced macroeconomic perspective could miss in sheer human terms what Marx's own writings on capitalism often did not neglect: a recounting of the outrageous violence carried out against the victims of economic policies. A study of Nazi policies from 1933 to 1939 that gave attention to the perspective of German Jews who had been driven from their own businesses, jobs, and homes, who had lost their property through confiscations, who were sent forcibly to concentration camps, or whose legal, economic, and political rights had been effectively abolished would have had quite a different focus and effect. This is precisely the project of Friedländer's compelling recent book, *Nazi Germany and the Jews.* For numerous examples of Marx's attention to the particular fates of those victimized by the processes of economic capital accumulation and technological innovation, see Karl Marx, *Capital,* vol. 1, ed. Frederick Engels, (New York: International, 1967), 612–712.

192. See Jay, "The Jews and the Frankfurt School: Critical Theory's Analysis of Anti-Semitism," in *Permanent Exiles,* 90–100. As Jay mentions, Franz Neumann also began to revise his own judgment on the significance of Nazi anti-Semitism in the second edition of *Behemoth,* published in 1944. But Neumann still viewed the issue largely in terms of the Nazis' antiliberalism, terrorist methods, and desire for accomplices. See Franz Neumann, *Behemoth,* 2d ed. (New York: Oxford University Press, 1944), 550–52.

193. As Jay notes, Leo Lowenthal also contributed to this section of the book. See Jay, *Adorno*, 39.

194. Horkheimer and Adorno, *Dialectic of Enlightenment*, 208. On the "rescue operation" discernible in this passage, see Rabinbach, "The Cunning of Unreason."

195. Some interpreters of the writings of Horkheimer and Adorno situate their work in close proximity to existentialism. See, for instance, Tar, *The Frankfurt School*, 205–6; and Kolakowski, *Main Currents of Marxism*, vol. 3, 369–72. There are certainly some biographical and theoretical connections, such as the Nietzchean element of a shared skepticism about the universally beneficial effects of rationality and social modernism. Some members of the Frankfurt group were for a time personally close to important existentialist thinkers, Heidegger chief among them. But one has to ignore the frequent and deeply hostile criticism of existentialism produced by the Frankfurt critics, such as Adorno's *The Jargon of Authenticity*, trans. Kurt Tarnowsky and Frederic Will (Evanston, Ill.: Northwestern University Press, 1973), which is a sustained polemic *against* Heideggerian existentialism, to reach the conclusion that their work fits neatly within its boundaries.

196. Adorno, cited by Leo Lowenthal in *An Unmastered Past*, 148. But as Leo Lowenthal joked, the later reception of the writings of Horkheimer and Adorno showed that the bottle was soon opened, with a quite a pop.

197. Jay, *The Dialectical Imagination*, 297.

198. See the cogent and yet generous discussions of Howard, *The Marxian Legacy*, 53–79; Bronner, *Of Critical Theory and Its Theorists*, 72–101, 180–208; and Slater, *Origin and Significance of the Frankfurt School*, 87–89.

199. Bronner, *Of Critical Theory and Its Theorists*, 84. The image of a comprehended (subjectively) and yet implacable (objectively) social totality in *Dialectic of Enlightenment* offered a preview of Adorno's argument and imagery in his later book *Negative Dialectics*, trans. E. B. Ashton (New York: Continuum, 1973).

200. Horkheimer and Adorno, *Dialectic of Enlightenment*, 85. Again, note the unhelpful conflation of "bourgeois" and "liberal" that Eley and Blackbourn have rightly criticized.

201. See Jürgen Habermas, "Remarks on the Development of Horkheimer's Work," in *On Max Horkheimer*, ed. Benhabib, Bonß, and McCole, 49–65.

202. Jay, *Adorno*, 44–45.

203. Herbert Marcuse to Max Horkheimer, 18 October 1946, Max-Horkheimer-Archiv, VI, 27A, 270–71, SUBF, Frankfurt am Main. The letter indicates that Richard Löwenthal, Karl Mannheim, and Raymond Aron were among those who, during encounters in postwar London and Paris, urged Marcuse to renew publication of the *Zeitschrift*. On Marcuse's early postwar years, see Katz, *Herbert Marcuse and the Art of Liberation*, 129–35; Kellner, *Herbert Marcuse and the Crisis of Marxism*, 149–53, 199–200; and Alfons Söllner, "'The Philosopher Not as King': La théorie politique de Herbert Marcuse dans les années quarante et cinquante," *Archives de philosophie* 52, no. 3 (1989): 427–42.

204. On Borkenau's work in postwar Europe, see Franz Borkenau to Geoffrey

Faber, 22 October 1945, Faber and Faber Archive, London; and Richard Löwenthal, editor's introduction to *End and Beginning,* by Borkenau, 6. Fraenkel's book was entitled *Military Occupation and the Rule of Law: Occupation Government in the Rhineland, 1918-1923* (London: Oxford University Press, 1944). On Neumann, Kirchheimer, and Marcuse, see Barry Katz, "The Criticism of Arms: The Frankfurt School Goes to War," *Journal of Modern History* 59 (September 1987): 437-78; Jay, *The Dialectical Imagination;* and Wiggershaus, *Die Frankfurter Schule.* A noteworthy collection of wartime and early postwar texts produced by German émigrés—including several of the intellectuals discussed in this book—working for the U.S. government or supplying it with information has been edited by Alfons Söllner: *Zur Archäologie der Demokratie in Deutschland,* 2 vols. (Frankfurt am Main: Fischer, 1986).

Chapter 4: Totalitarianism's Temptations

1. This cold war controversy between the two wartime friends—both important figures on the French intellectual left—was sparked by differences in their attitudes toward Communism and the Soviet Union. Camus had left the Algerian Communist Party after a few years of activism and remained hostile toward Communism thereafter. Sartre was a quintessential "fellow traveler" for a number of years, though he never joined the French Communist Party. The sharply critical response of Sartre's journal, *Les temps modernes,* to the publication of Camus' book, *L'homme révolté (The Rebel),* in 1951, brought their differences into the open. Brief accounts of this episode and the intellectual scene of the postwar French Left are in H. Stuart Hughes, *The Obstructed Path: French Social Thought in the Years of Desperation, 1930-1960* (New York: Harper and Row, 1969), 228-47; and Herbert R. Lottman, *The Left Bank: Writers, Artists, and Politics from the Popular Front to the Cold War* (Boston: Houghton Mifflin, 1982), 256-88, passim.

2. On the developing cold war and its impact on the democratic Left, see the cogent analysis in Stephen Eric Bronner, *Moments of Decision: Political History and the Crises of Radicalism* (New York: Routledge, 1992), 77-100. See also Judt, *Marxism and the French Left,* 169-238.

3. On Gurland and Massing, see Jay, *The Dialectical Imagination,* 150, 170-71. On Gurland, see Dieter Emig and Rüdiger Zimmermann, "Arkadij Gurland (1904-1979)," in *Vor dem Vergessen bewahren,* ed. Lösche, Scholing, and Walter, 81-98. Before his exile and involvement with the Institute of Social Research, Gurland had been the author of a pair of books that placed him squarely in the tradition of left socialist radicalism: *Marxismus und Diktatur* (Leipzig: Leipziger Buchdruckerei, 1930); and *Das Heute der proletarischen Aktion: Hemmnisse und Wandlungen im Klassenkampf* (Berlin: Laubsche Verlagsbuchhandlung, 1931)

4. "Discussion Re: German Labor Movement on September 12, 1947," 12 September 1947, Max-Horkheimer-Archiv, 23, 20, 305, Stadt- und Universitätsbibliothek, Frankfurt-am-Main.

5. Franz Borkenau, *Socialism: National or International* (London: Routledge and Sons, 1942).

6. Kurt Schumacher's personal courage was beyond question, but his occasional ideological and political inflexibility in the early postwar years, perhaps more than the moralism that Neumann criticized, was certainly helpful to the political cause of the Christian Democratic Union and its leader, Konrad Adenauer. See Lewis Edinger, *Kurt Schumacher: A Study in Personality and Political Behavior* (Stanford, Calif.: Stanford University Press, 1965).

7. Kurotake, "Zur Todesursache Rudolf Hilferdings," 1–21; David Beetham, "Biographical Notes," in *Marxists in Face of Fascism*, ed. Beetham, 359–60; Foitzik, *Zwischen den Fronten*, 314–16.

8. See Jay, "Remembering Henry Pachter," in *Permanent Exiles*, 257–61; and Bronner, introduction to *Socialism in History*, by Pachter, xi–xxx. See also Henry Pachter, *Weimar Études*, ed. Stephen Eric Bronner (New York: Columbia University Press, 1982). *Dissent*, founded in 1954, has provided a vital forum for the leftist antitotalitarian outlook in the United States.

9. Franz Neumann, "German Democracy 1950," *International Conciliation*, no. 461 (May 1950): 291.

10. See, for example, Max Horkheimer's blistering attack on "totalitarian bureaucracy" and the "pseudorevolutionary" youth of the New Left in *Critical Theory: Selected Essays of Max Horkheimer*, trans. Matthew J. O'Connell et al. (New York: Continuum, 1986), viii–ix. One of the best critical commentaries on Horkheimer's later career appears in Bronner, *Of Critical Theory and Its Theorists*, 73–101.

11. On Neumann's and Kirchheimer's important postwar contributions to political and legal theory, see Scheuerman, *Between the Norm and the Exception.* The dilemmas shared by such former Communist Party members as Borkenau and Löwenthal are reconsidered in Ignazio Silone, *Emergency Exit,* ed. Ruth Nanda Anshen (New York: Harper and Row, 1968). See, in particular, the essays "Emergency Exit" and "The Situation of the 'Ex.'"

12. Gunzelin Schmid Noerr and Willem van Reijen, "Karl Korsch," in *Grand Hotel Abgrund,* ed. Schmid Noerr and van Reijen, 80.

13. See the Fischer-Korsch correspondence in Nachlaß Karl Korsch, 9, IISH, Amsterdam. See especially Ruth Fischer to Karl Korsch, 2 May 1949, 9/1; Karl Korsch to Ruth Fischer, 10 May 1949, 9/2–3; Karl Korsch to Ruth Fischer, 27 May 1950, 9/5; Karl Korsch to Ruth Fischer, 10 February 1952, 9/18; Karl Korsch to Ruth Fischer, 5 November 1952, 9/20–21; Ruth Fischer to Karl Korsch, 18 November 1952, 9/24, and Karl Korsch to Ruth Fischer, 26 November 1952, 9/26–28. In the letter dated 27 May 1950, Korsch thanked Fischer for the clippings she had sent of articles about her from *Life, Time,* and *Fortune* magazines. Other letters from their correspondence are gathered in Fischer and Maslow, *Abtrünnig wider Willen,* 318–21. See also Milovan Djilas, *The New Class: An Analysis of the Communist System* (New York: Praeger, 1957); and Milovan Djilas, *The Unperfect Society: Beyond the New Class,* trans. Dorian Cooke (New York: Harcourt Brace Jovanovich, 1969).

14. Karl Korsch to Hayden Carruth, 9 September 1952, Nachlaß Karl Korsch, 6/15–17, IISH, Amsterdam.

15. Kellner, ed., *Karl Korsch*, 289ff.

16. Ibid., 281–83. The "Ten Theses" appeared first in the French journal *Arguments* in 1959.

17. Fischer and Maslow, *Abtrünnig wider Willen*, 320–21.

18. See the discussions of this point by Erd and others in *Reform und Resignation*, 185–236, passim.

19. Franz Neumann, "Wandlungen des Marxismus," 6–8, and "Marxismus und Intelligenz," 2–6, in "Vorträge der "RIAS Funk-Universität," gehalten im V. Sendeabschnitt, "Mensch, Gesellschaft und Kultur," 20 and 28 November 1950. Franz Borkenau gave the inaugural lecture in this series, "Mensch und Gesellschaft bei Karl Marx," 6 November 1950. RIAS stands for Radio in the American Sector (of Berlin). On the complex role of the SPD and the unions as agents of both change and conformism, see the instructive discussion in Richard Breitman, "Negative Integration and Parliamentary Politics: Literature on German Social Democracy, 1890–1933," *Central European History* 13, no. 2 (1980): 175–97.

20. Franz Neumann, "Economics and Politics in the Twentieth Century," in *The Democratic and the Authoritarian State*, 266.

21. See the remarks of Alfons Söllner in Erd, ed., *Reform und Resignation*, 217–20.

22. Judith Shklar, *After Utopia: The Decline of Political Faith* (Princeton, N.J.: Princeton University Press, 1957), 263.

23. Mason, "The Primacy of Politics," 53–76.

24. On the reception of Neumann's postwar work, see Hughes, "Franz Neumann between Marxism and Liberal Democracy," 446–62. Hughes makes the point that Neumann's scholarship exerted greater influence among historians than among political scientists. Scheuerman's *Between the Norm and the Exception* constitutes a significant attempt to restore Neumann's and Kirchheimer's writings—including their less influential postwar studies—as a radical, albeit non-Marxist, defense of the rule of law, which Scheuerman fears is once again under attack.

25. Franz Neumann, "Anxiety and Politics," in *The Democratic and the Authoritarian State*, 294.

26. Franz Borkenau, "Praxis und Utopie," in *Karl Marx*, ed. Franz Borkenau (Frankfurt am Main: Fischer Bucherei, 1956), 7–37.

27. Franz Borkenau to Geoffrey Faber, 30 March 1946, Faber and Faber Archive, London.

28. Richard Löwenthal, editor's introduction to *End and Beginning*, by Borkenau, 6–8. See also Tashjean, "Franz Borkenau," 17–18. Borkenau took the rather derisive term *Kreml-Astrologie* as his own and published an article explaining his interests in Soviet studies and his methods: "Was ist Kreml-Astrologie?" *Der Monat* 7, no. 79 (1955): 32–39. See also Leopold Labedz, *The Use and Abuse of Sovietology* (New Brunswick, N.J.: Transaction, 1989).

29. The most complete bibliography of Borkenau's publications appears in Jean-Pierre Chrétien-Goni, Iskender Gokalp, Danièle Guillerm, Christian Lazzeri,

and Dominique Wolton, eds., *L'ésprit du mécanisme: Science et société chez Franz Borkenau,* Cahiers S.T.S., Science-Technologie-Société, no. 7 (Paris: Éditions du Centre National de la Recherche Scientifique, 1985), 12–20. Even this list, however, omits a few items.

30. For a brief account of the case (but one that does not mention Borkenau), see Caute, *The Great Fear,* 323. I have also examined copies of U.S. government documents regarding Borkenau's testimony. Permission to study these documents was granted by the late Kay Boyle and her lawyer, Jerome Garchik, who received them under the provisions of the Freedom of Information Act.

31. For an account of this meeting and Borkenau's role in it, see Peter Coleman, *The Liberal Conspiracy: The Congress for Cultural Freedom and the Struggle for the Mind of Postwar Europe* (New York: Free Press, 1989), 15, 21, 29–31. See also Hugh Trevor-Roper, "Ex-Communist v. Communist," *Manchester Guardian,* July 10, 1950.

32. The Stalinization thesis argued that developments in the KPD were controlled and conditioned by decisions made by the Soviet leadership, particularly Stalin. Such a position is not without foundation, but as Eric D. Weitz has argued, indigenous German social, political, and economic factors often drop out of analyses based on the Stalinization thesis, and he cites Borkenau and Fischer as key figures in the postwar history of this argument. See Weitz, *Creating German Communism,* 12, note 15. Weitz does not dispute the fact that the Soviet Union was a factor in German Communist developments. Indeed, he states elsewhere in his book that "in the course of the Weimar Republic, the Soviet Union came to exert increasing authority over the KPD. Moscow set overall strategy and broke and made KPD leaderships. Paul Levi, Ernst Reuter, Ernst Meyer, Heinrich Brandler, and Ruth Fischer—party leaders between 1919 and 1925—all foundered when, for various reasons, they lost the backing of the Russian Communist Party . . ." (234). What Weitz argues with great effectiveness is that the course of the KPD and the postwar German Democratic Republic (DDR) should not be understood at every stage in the terms of such a deterministic model. The KPD's development as well as the history of the DDR emerged from a more complex and varying set of factors than the Stalinization thesis acknowledges. In short, Weitz persuasively disputes the claim that "the entire history of the DDR can really be characterized as 'Stalinist'" (392). He makes a similarly clear objection to the use of the "totalitarian thesis" to explain the DDR, noting that equating the Communist East German government with Nazi Germany remains primarily "political," not "analytical" (392–93).

33. Borkenau, *End and Beginning.* Borkenau's various historical writings are the subject of Volker Reinecke, *Kultur und Todesantinomie: Die Geschichtsphilosophie Franz Borkenaus* (Vienna: Passagen, 1992).

34. Ruth Fischer, *Stalin and German Communism,* 663.

35. Ibid., 644–45.

36. Heinrich Brandler to Ruth Fischer, 6 October 1948; Curt Geyer to Ruth Fischer, 24 October 1948 and 2 November 1948; George Orwell to Ruth Fischer, 21 April 1949, all in Fischer and Maslow, *Abtrünnig wider Willen,* 225–45, 256–57.

37. On the events surrounding the publication of *Oriental Despotism*, see Ulmen, *The Science of Society*, 306–24. Useful and divergent accounts of Wittfogel's testimony before Congress and its related consequences appear in Ulmen, *The Science of Society*, 275–94; Jay, *The Dialectical Imagination*, 284–85; and Heilbut, *Exiled in Paradise*, 379–81, 316–21, 415.

38. See especially Donald Worster, *Rivers of Empire: Water, Aridity, and the Growth of the American West* (New York: Oxford University Press, 1985). Worster cannot be regarded as a Wittfogel disciple, but he argues that the "grand theory" notions of Wittfogel—despite their occasionally distracting antitotalitarian polemics—are still useful tools with which to clarify historical issues and offer benchmark models of change in society and in state policy. Worster also mentions the influence of Adorno and Horkheimer's *Dialectic of Enlightenment* and Horkheimer's *Eclipse of Reason* on his interpretations of the human domination of nature in the American Southwest. See Worster, *Under Western Skies: Nature and History in the American West* (New York: Oxford University Press, 1992), 55–56, 71, 73–74, 262, note 7.

39. Wittfogel, *Oriental Despotism*, 7.

40. See, for example, ibid., 137–60, 369–412.

41. Max Horkheimer, *The Eclipse of Reason* (1947; reprint, New York: Continuum, 1974), 164.

42. See in particular Hannah Arendt, *Essays in Understanding, 1930–1954*, ed. Jerome Kern (New York: Harcourt, Brace, 1994); Hannah Arendt, *The Life of the Mind*, 2 vols. (New York: Harcourt Brace Jovanovich), 1978; Leo Strauss, *Persecution and the Art of Writing* (Glencoe, Ill.: Free Press, 1952); Leo Strauss, *Natural Right and History* (Chicago: University of Chicago Press, 1953); Leo Strauss, *On Tyranny*, rev. ed., ed. Victor Gourevitch and Michael S. Roth (New York: Free Press, 1991); Dante Germino, *Beyond Ideology: The Revival of Political Theory* (New York: Harper and Row, 1967); Dante Germino, *Political Philosophy and the Open Society* (Baton Rouge: Louisiana State University Press, 1982); and Michael Oakeshott, *Rationalism in Politics and Other Essays* (Indianapolis: Liberty, 1991); and Michael Oakeshott, *Morality and Politics in Europe: The Harvard Lectures*, ed. Shirley Robin Letwin (New Haven, Conn.: Yale University Press, 1993). See also Peter Graf Kielmansegg et al., eds. *Hannah Arendt and Leo Strauss: German Émigrés and American Political Thought after World War II* (Cambridge: German Historical Institute and Cambridge University Press, 1995).

43. See Slater, *Origin and Significance of the Frankfurt School;* and Tar, *The Frankfurt School.*

44. Horkheimer, *Critical Theory*, viii–ix.

45. For discussions of Horkheimer's later, more openly anti-Communist political stance, see Douglas Kellner, "The Frankfurt School Revisited," *New German Critique* 4 (Winter 1975): 131–52.

46. See Richard T. Bernstein, "Herbert Marcuse: An Immanent Critique," *Social Theory and Practice* 1, no. 4 (1971): 97–111.

47. In the 1961 preface to the paperback edition of *Soviet Marxism*, Marcuse

maintained that he had been at least "relatively objective" in his analysis because he had managed to irritate both American conservatives and orthodox Soviet commentators. See Herbert Marcuse, *Soviet Marxism: A Critical Analysis* (1958; reprint, with new preface, New York: Knopf/Vintage, 1961), v. See also the instructive discussion of *Soviet Marxism* in Kellner, *Herbert Marcuse and the Crisis of Marxism*, 197–228.

48. Marcuse, *Soviet Marxism*, 206.

49. Ibid., 105–20, 233–52. This argument could be read as a more hopeful version of Borkenau's critique of Soviet irrationalism stated in *Pareto* twenty years earlier.

50. Herbert Marcuse, *Eros and Civilization: A Philosophical Inquiry into Freud* (1955; reprint, with new preface, Boston: Beacon, 1966), 93–94.

51. Dutschke quoted in Herbert Marcuse, *Das Ende der Utopie: Vorträge und Diskussionen in Berlin 1967* (Frankfurt am Main: Verlag Neue Kritik, 1980), 100; Kühnl, "'Linke' Totalitarismusversionen."

52. Herbert Marcuse, *One-Dimensional Man: Studies in the Ideology of Advanced Industrial Society* (Boston: Beacon, 1964), 225, 257.

53. Marcuse managed to offend a remarkable variety of thinkers. Among the most systematically hostile attacks against his position is Alasdair MacIntyre, *Herbert Marcuse: An Exposition and a Polemic* (New York: Viking, 1970). See also Kolakowski, *Main Currents of Marxism*, vol. 3, 396–420. A critical Marxist perspective appears in Paul Mattick, *Critique of Marcuse: One-Dimensional Man in Class Society* (New York: Herder and Herder, 1972). Marcuse's postwar role receives a more sympathetic appraisal in Bernstein, "Herbert Marcuse."

54. For the example among his writings that is most often criticized for its alleged political vanguardism, see Herbert Marcuse, "Repressive Tolerance," in *A Critique of Pure Tolerance*, by Robert Paul Wolff, Barrington Moore Jr., and Herbert Marcuse (Boston: Beacon, 1969), 81–123. Given the context of its appearance in 1965, however, the enraged tone of Marcuse's article is not so surprising. In 1964, the Democratic Party elite had torpedoed the work of the Mississippi Freedom Democratic Party delegation at its presidential nominating convention, precipitating further splits in the civil rights movement. In 1965, the U.S. military buildup in Vietnam had increased swiftly, and it was clear by the end of summer that—despite the passage of the Voting Rights Act that year—race relations had already shifted gears, as evidenced by the violence in the Watts district of Los Angeles. Even so, in a somewhat chastened "Postscript 1968," Marcuse cautioned specifically against the emergence of a revolutionary, intellectual elite, inviting instead "the struggle for a real democracy" (ibid., 122). See also Kellner, *Herbert Marcuse and the Crisis of Marxism*, 276–90.

55. See Jay, *The Dialectical Imagination*, 285–99; and Wiggershaus, *Die Frankfurter Schule*, 479–501, 519–34, 597–730, passim.

56. The fortieth anniversary of the Free University in 1988 generated numerous accounts of that embattled institution. The best narrative of the university's

rough journey through the cold war period is James F. Tent's lively and thorough study, *The Free University of Berlin: A Political History* (Bloomington: Indiana University Press, 1988). On Friedrich's role in establishing the Free University, see 110–12. Tent mentions that another American scholar involved with the Free University in its early years, who had also authored an important book on totalitarianism, was Sigmund Neumann (210, 232, 238, 284–85). Sigmund Neumann's brilliant study of modern dictatorship, first published in 1942, *The Permanent Revolution,* is familiar to many readers.

57. Ossip K. Flechtheim, interview with author, Berlin, 18 July 1989. See also Foitzik, *Zwischen den Fronten,* 270. While still working as an attorney for the U.S. war crimes prosecutor in Berlin, Flechtheim had been assigned to interview Carl Schmitt, who was still being interned there in March 1947. See Joseph W. Bendersky, ed. and trans., "Interrogation of Carl Schmitt by Robert Kempner," *Telos,* no. 72 (Summer 1987): 97–98, note 3. For a more extensive analysis of the role of totalitarian theory in the early years of the Free University, see Hubertus Buchstein, "Totalitarismustheorie und empirische Politikforschung—die Wandlung der Totalitarismuskonzeption in der frühen Berliner Politikforschung," in *Totalitarismus,* ed. Söllner, Walkenhaus, and Wieland, 239–66.

58. Kirchheimer became the master of an understated sarcastic wit in some of his later essays on postwar politics and sociology. For an example of this element of his underappreciated postwar work, see Kirchheimer, "Private Man and Society," in *Politics, Law, and Social Change,* 453–77.

59. For information on Fraenkel, Neumann, and Friedrich and the early years of the Free University, see Tent, *The Free University of Berlin.* See also Ernst Fraenkel, *Reformismus und Pluralismus: Materialen zu einer ungeschriebenen politischen Autobiographie,* ed. Jalk Esche and Frank Grube (Hamburg: Hoffman und Campe, 1973).

60. Sering [Richard Löwenthal], *Jenseits des Kapitalismus.* See the discussion of the book's impact in William David Graf, *The German Left since 1945: Socialism and Social Democracy in the German Federal Republic* (Cambridge: Oleander, 1976), 72–75; and Ossip K. Flechtheim's characteristically dissenting and optimistic epilogue in Graf's book (280–91).

61. Richard Löwenthal, interview with author, Berlin, 3 August 1987; Foitzik, *Zwischen den Fronten,* 298.

62. Tent mentions, however, that some years after the younger man's death, Löwenthal still judged Dutschke an estimable student and public disputant. See Tent, *The Free University of Berlin,* 480, note 98.

63. See the description of Dutschke's role during 1967–68 in ibid., 327–29. Dutschke's health was wrecked by the shooting, and he died just eleven years later. It is all the more remarkable that he completed *Ein Versuch Lenin auf die Füße zu stellen: Über den halbasiatischen und den westeuropäischen Weg zum Sozialismus; Lenin, Lukács und die Dritte Internationale* (Berlin: Verlag Klaus Wagenbach, 1974). For an account of both generations of German student leftism, see Hans Manfred

Bock, *Geschichte des "linken Radicalismus" in Deutschland: Ein Versuch* (Frankfurt am Main: Suhrkamp, 1976). On the character and membership of the German SDS (as opposed to the U.S. version of the SDS), see the excellent and concise discussion in Andrei Markovitz and Philip S. Gorski, *The German Left: Red, Green and Beyond* (New York: Oxford University Press, 1993), 49–58.

64. Quoted in Marcuse, *Das Ende der Utopie,* 100.

65. This debate of July 1967 is transcribed in ibid., 87–123. In the course of informal "recruitment" of possible associates in the event of a revival of the *Zeitschrift für Sozialforschung* that took place in the early postwar period, Marcuse offered a negative appraisal of Richard Löwenthal. See Herbert Marcuse to Max Horkheimer, 15 November 1946, Max-Horkheimer-Archiv, 27A, 268–68A, SUBF, Frankfurt am Main.

66. Richard Löwenthal, *World Communism: The Disintegration of a Secular Faith* (New York: Oxford University Press, 1964).

67. Richard Löwenthal, "Totalitarianism Reconsidered," *Commentary* 29 (June 1960): 504–12.

68. Richard Löwenthal, "Beyond Totalitarianism", in *1984 Revisited: Totalitarianism in Our Century,* ed. Irving Howe (New York: Harper and Row, 1983), 209–67. Walter Laqueur, another scholar of modern dictatorship, rejected Löwenthal's revisionism regarding the phenomenon of totalitarianism, and the two exchanged letters on the subject in the pages of *Commentary.* See *Commentary* 81, no. 1 (1986): 2–6. For another instance of Löwenthal's revisionist view of totalitarianism, which attended to the changing performance of Communist regimes and parties, see Richard Löwenthal, "The 'Missing Revolution' in Industrial Societies: Comparative Reflections on a German Problem," in *Germany in the Age of Total War: Essays in Honor of Francis Carsten,* ed. Volker R. Berghahn and Martin Kitchen (Totowa, N.J.: Barnes and Noble Books, 1981), 240–57.

Even into the 1970s and 1980s, Löwenthal actively served the SPD, taking a key role in discussions of party ideology and arguing in behalf of the party's conservative wing during the debates regarding possible coalitions with the Greens and the impact such a move might have on the SPD's connection to its working-class political base. Several essays from this period of his career are gathered in Richard Löwenthal, *Social Change and Cultural Crisis* (New York: Columbia University Press, 1984). See also Markovits and Gorski, *The German Left,* 199, 348 note 23; and Gerald Braunthal, *The German Social Democrats since 1969: A Party in Power and Opposition* (Boulder, Colo.: Westview, 1993), 195–202, 233–34. Braunthal mentions that when the SPD considered establishing a new institute for democratic socialism in 1973, the party's leftists put forth Habermas as a candidate for the directorship, while the rightists supported Löwenthal. No compromise was reached, and the idea came to naught (199–200).

69. The author was present at this lecture on 30 November 1988 and witnessed the events described.

70. One of the best and most thoughtfully critical appraisals of the stultifying

effects on both scholarship and policy that the totalitarian model emphasizing the implacable character of dictatorships could exert appears in Stephen Cohen, *Rethinking the Soviet Experience: Politics and History since 1917* (New York: Oxford University Press, 1985), 3–37.

71. Howard, *The Marxian Legacy,* 339, note 1.

72. The "end of history debate," with its roots in the writings of Hegel, Marx, Alexandre Kojève, and Leo Strauss, gained renewed attention with the publication of Francis Fukuyama's *The End of History and the Last Man* (New York: Free Press, 1992). Fukuyama argued that the victories of liberal democracy and capitalism over Communism were now total and that a happy "end of history" was at hand. For two of the most knowledgeable and telling critical responses to Fukuyama's book, see Michael S. Roth, *The Ironist's Cage: Memory, Trauma, and the Construction of History* (New York: Columbia University Press, 1995), 163–74; and Peter Fritzsche's review of *The End of History and the Last Man* in *American Historical Review* 97, no. 3 (1992): 817–19. Roth concluded that Fukuyama endorsed not so much a criticism of the present but a self-serving and nostalgic retreat from it. Fritzsche argued that the happy ending to the twentieth century scripted by Fukuyama in the light of the events of 1989 and 1991 should not so easily overlook the troublesome and persisting relationship between liberal democracy and both fascism and Marxism, ideologies that still linger on the historical stage.

73. Jürgen Habermas, *The New Conservatism: Cultural Criticism and the Historians' Debate,* ed. and trans. Shierry Weber Nicholsen (Cambridge, Mass.: MIT Press, 1989), 226–27. I was reminded of this passage by Michael Roth's use of it in his introduction to *The Ironist's Cage,* 14.

74. Arendt, *The Origins of Totalitarianism,* 395. One of the most thoughtfully critical reviews of *Origins* to appear in the 1950s was written by Raymond Aron. It has been edited and reprinted as "The Essence of Totalitarianism according to Hannah Arendt," *Partisan Review* 60, no. 3 (1993): 366–76. See also Stephen J. Whitfield's thorough and well-argued study, *Into the Dark: Hannah Arendt and Totalitarianism* (Philadelphia: Temple University Press, 1980).

75. See Elisabeth Young-Bruehl, *For Love of the World* (New Haven, Conn.: Yale University Press, 1982), 97–105, 124–48; and Jeffrey C. Isaac, *Arendt, Camus, and Modern Rebellion* (New Haven, Conn.: Yale University Press, 1992), 28.

76. Hannah Arendt, *On Revolution* (1965; reprint, Harmondsworth, England: York: Penguin Books, 1990), 257–67. See the illuminating and critical discussions of Arendt's favorable view of council democracy (also rightly called "council communism" in the cases of St. Petersburg in 1905 and Munich in 1918–19, which Arendt cited) in Wolin, *Labyrinths,* 168–70. Wolin questions attributing a democratic cast to Arendt's valorization of the councils, arguing that she saw them more as the arena for the emergence of vital new political elites. See also John F. Sitton, "Hannah Arendt's Argument for Council Democracy," in *Hannah Arendt: Critical Essays,* ed. Lewis Hinchman and Sandra Hinchman (Albany: State University of New York Press, 1993), 307–34; and Arendt, *Men in Dark Times,* 33–56.

77. Benhabib, *The Reluctant Modernism of Hannah Arendt*, 77–82, 130–37. See also the comparative discussion of Arendt's and Albert Camus' critiques of Marxism in Isaac, *Arendt, Camus, and Modern Rebellion*, 80–92.

78. George Orwell, *Homage to Catalonia* (New York: Harcourt Brace Jovanovich, 1952), 57, note 2. See also Franz Borkenau to George Orwell, 11 June 1938, George Orwell Archive, University College, London. One standard and generally authoritative biography, Crick's *George Orwell*, unfortunately offers erroneous assertions about Borkenau: he was "an Australian Communist who had worked for the Comintern in Moscow" and then "studied at Frankfurt under Adorno," and so on (341). In fact, Borkenau was born and reared in Austria and later became a KPD member (never an Austrian Communist Party member). He was interned in Australia briefly during the war. He had worked for the Comintern in Berlin, not Moscow. I have found no evidence that Adorno was ever Borkenau's teacher.

79. Karl Korsch, "Notes on History: The Ambiguities of Totalitarian Ideologies," *New Essays* 6, no. 2 (1942): 3.

80. See for instance, Arendt, *The Origins of Totalitarianism*, 185–86. Arendt put the issue of the totalitarian and imperial violence of "civilization" almost as bluntly as Korsch had—but with a slightly different focus: "Even the emergence of totalitarian governments is a phenomenon within, not outside, our civilization. The danger is that a global, universally interrelated civilization may produce barbarians from its own midst by forcing millions of people into conditions which, despite all appearances, are the conditions of savages" (302). The case of Orwell is equally revealing on this point. Alok Rai shows painstaking thoroughness in revealing how some of Orwell's most radical articles have been carefully truncated (and, in the case of one scathingly anti-imperialist column, omitted entirely) in the commonly used edition of Orwell's *Collected Essays, Journalism, and Letters*. See Alok Rai, *Orwell and the Politics of Despair: A Critical Study of the Writings of George Orwell* (Cambridge: Cambridge University Press, 1988), 159, 162–64. I would argue along with Rai that the "tamer" social democratic Orwell, so useful to cold war anti-Communism, needs to be juxtaposed with the blunter, bolder, more radically socialist and internationalist Orwell.

81. In addition to her opposition to the Soviet Union, Arendt also opposed the McCarthy hearings and despised those ex-Communists who claimed a place of privilege on the basis of their recantations. See Isaac, *Arendt, Camus, and Modern Rebellion*, 188–89. As for Orwell, the revelations in 1996 about the "list of names" he generated for use by the British secret service mostly underscore his anti-Stalinism. His socialist outlook is not in doubt. Moreover, some of the facts about Orwell's willingness to draw up a list of Communist "sympathizers" and potential collaborators revealed in his recently published correspondence with Celia Kirwan have been known for years. See, for instance, Crick, *George Orwell*, 556, 637–38, note 49; and Rai, *Orwell and the Politics of Despair*, 156, 182, note 19. The most interesting and reasonable defense of Orwell's actions is in an article by Christopher Hitchens, "Orwell on Trial," *Vanity Fair* 59 (October 1996): 142–49.

82. See, for example, Horkheimer's sensitive discussion in *The Eclipse of Reason,* 128–61.

83. Marcuse, *Das Ende der Utopie,* 111–17. Abbott Gleason mentions a similar encounter in the United States in 1963, with the generational victory reversed: the older leftist Irving Howe silenced the New Left SDS leader Tom Hayden by mocking his unwillingness to characterize the Eastern European nations as "totalitarian." See Gleason, *Totalitarianism,* 130.

84. Helmut Dubiel develops some important distinctions between the original critical theory of Horkheimer and Adorno and the later theoretical efforts of Habermas in "Domination or Emancipation? The Debate over the Heritage of Critical Theory," in *Cultural-Political Interventions in the Unfinished Project of Enlightenment,* ed. Honneth et al., 3–16. Dubiel emphasizes the differences in the historical origins of prewar and postwar critical theory: "One is a theory of late totalitarian capitalism, the other a theory of the welfare state in a postfascist mass democracy" (5). While this is neither the only nor the most essential distinction Dubiel draws between these variants of critical theory, it serves to limit the range of application and the kind of critique each branch of this philosophical tradition merits. Dubiel indicates in his concluding remarks that a critical theory of civilization may be impossible but that by indicating the "fragility of the status quo," critical theory—in a variety of its expressions—achieved more than its initiators might have imagined possible.

85. Some of the important books by Habermas in which he took up these issues fairly early in his career include *The Structural Transformation of the Public Sphere: An Inquiry into a Category of Bourgeois Society,* trans. Thomas Burger and Frederick Lawrence (Cambridge, Mass.: MIT Press, 1989); *Knowledge and Human Interests,* trans. Jeremy J. Shapiro (Boston: Beacon, 1971); *Theory and Practice,* trans. John Viertel (Boston: Beacon, 1973); *Legitimation Crisis,* trans. Thomas McCarthy (Boston: Beacon, 1973); and *The Theory of Communicative Action,* 2 vols. (Boston: Beacon, 1985). A sardonically critical review of *Legitimation Crisis* appears in Richard Löwenthal, *Social Change and Cultural Crisis,* 42–69. Löwenthal took Habermas to task for, among other things, the utopian impracticality of his "ideal speech situation" in politics. The best historical critique of Habermas's notion of the public sphere is Geoff Eley, "Nations, Publics, and Political Cultures: Placing Habermas in the Nineteenth Century," in *Culture/Power/History: A Reader in Contemporary Social Theory,* ed. Nicholas B. Dirks, Geoff Eley, and Sherry B. Ortner (Princeton, N.J.: Princeton University Press, 1994), 297–335.

86. For analyses of Habermas, the poststructuralist critique of his work, and the postwar philosophical influence of Adorno and Horkheimer in Germany and France, see Jay, *Marxism and Totality,* 462–537, passim.

87. Jean-François Lyotard, *The Postmodern Condition: A Report on Knowledge,* trans. Geoff Bennington and Brian Massumi (Minneapolis: University of Minnesota Press, 1984), 65–73. Lyotard concludes his "Report" with a call to "wage a war

on totality" (82). Years earlier, Lyotard had also been a member of the radical French Marxist Socialisme ou Barbarie group, along with Lefort and Castoriadis.

88. Lefort, *The Political Forms of Modern Society*. For Lefort's assessment of the weaknesses of Marx's critique of human rights and his analysis of Arendt, see Lefort, *Democracy and Political Theory*, 21–55.

89. Quoted in Richard J. Bernstein, "Foucault: Critique as a Philosophical Ethos," in *Critique and Power: Recasting the Foucault/Habermas Debate*, ed. Michael Kelly (Cambridge, Mass.: MIT Press, 1994), 235.

90. See, for example, Andrew Arato and Jean Cohen, *Civil Society and Political Theory* (Cambridge, Mass.: MIT Press, 1992); Andrew Arato and Jean Cohen, "Politics and the Reconstruction of the Concept of Civil Society," in *Cultural-Political Interventions in the Unfinished Project of Enlightenment*, ed. Honneth et al., 121–42; Isaac, *Arendt, Camus, and Modern Rebellion;* and Seyla Benhabib, *Situating the Self: Gender, Community and Postmodernism in Contemporary Ethics* (New York: Routledge, 1992). See, in particular, the analysis of Habermas's and Arendt's thinking about public discussion in Lisa Jane Disch, *Hannah Arendt and the Limits of Philosophy* (Ithaca, N.Y.: Cornell University Press, 1994), 87–92. In addition to their debate with such poststructuralists as Foucault and Lyotard, thinkers allied with the Habermasian critical theory tradition have taken up the issues of democratic participation and social justice with liberal pragmatists as well as so-called communitarian theorists, an even more diverse group. For some of the more influential statements in this debate, see Michael Walzer, *Spheres of Justice: A Defense of Pluralism and Equality* (New York: Basic Books, 1983); Charles Taylor, *Sources of the Self: The Making of the Modern Identity* (Cambridge, Mass.: Harvard University Press, 1992); and Richard Rorty, *Contingency, Irony, and Solidarity* (Cambridge: Cambridge University Press, 1989). More recently, Habermas has offered a magisterial summary of his considerations on the issues of political democracy, rights, and legal theory in *Between Facts and Norms: Contributions to a Discourse Theory of Law and Democracy*, trans. William Rehg (Cambridge, Mass.: MIT Press, 1998).

91. Michel Foucault, *Discipline and Punish: The Birth of the Prison*, trans. Alan Sheridan (New York: Vintage, 1977), 293–308. For his rejection of the cold war totalitarianism disputes, see Michel Foucault, *Power/Knowledge: Selected Interviews and Other Writings, 1972–1977*, ed. Colin Gordon (New York: Pantheon, 1980), 115–16.

92. In spite of his philosophical disagreements with Foucault, Jacques Derrida is also frequently labeled a poststructuralist. Derrida historicizes the emergence of his particular philosophical approach, deconstruction, as partly a response to "what we had known or what some of us for quite some time no longer hid from concerning totalitarian terror in all the Eastern countries, all the socio-economic disasters of Soviet bureaucracy, the Stalinism of the past and the neo-Stalinism in process (roughly speaking, from the Moscow trials to the repression in Hungary, to take only these minimal indices). Such was no doubt the element in which what is called deconstruction developed—and one can understand nothing of this period of deconstruction, notably in France, unless one takes this historical entangle-

ment into account." See Derrida, *Specters of Marx: The State of the Debt, the Work of Mourning, and the New International,* trans. Peggy Kamuf (New York: Routledge, 1994), 15. Martin Jay argues that one of the links joining Foucault, Derrida, Gilles Deleuze, Jean-François Lyotard, and others was their common hostility to the notion of totality. See Jay, *Marxism and Totality,* 515.

93. See, for example, the collection of articles—including essays by Habermas and Foucault—in Kelly, ed., *Critique and Power.* See also Michael Roth's reconsideration of Foucault in *The Ironist's Cage,* 71–95; and Axel Honneth's extensive commentaries on the Habermas-Foucault debate in *The Critique of Power: Reflective States in a Critical Social Theory,* trans. Kenneth Baynes (Cambridge, Mass.: MIT Press, 1991). Lyotard has also felt the need to defend himself against related charges that his philosophy was insufficient to the task of resisting totalitarianism. See Jean-François Lyotard, *The Postmodern Explained: Correspondence, 1982–1985,* trans. Don Barry, Bernadette Maher, Julian Pefanis, Virginia Spate, and Morgan Thomas, ed. Julian Pefanis and Morgan Thomas (Minneapolis: University of Minnesota Press, 1993), 61–66. The French "New Philosophers," led by Bernard-Henri Lévy and André Glucksmann, were mostly former Marxists (including some erstwhile Maoists) who were shocked into a rejection of Marxism during the late 1970s by Solzhenitsyn's *Gulag Archipelago.* For a brief discussion of this strikingly belated but nonetheless influential recognition of the scope and oppressiveness of the Soviet prison system, see Gleason, *Totalitarianism,* 154–55.

94. On the weaknesses of council Marxism, see also Martin Jay, *Cultural Semantics: Keywords of Our Time* (Amherst: University of Massachusetts Press, 1998), 79–84.

95. Martin Jay cites the statement of the Hungarian philosopher Mihály Vajda that the "totalitarian forms of domination of 'existing socialism'"—that is, Eastern European Communism—were not simply a result of Marxism. But Vajda argued that it was equally impossible to pretend that "this totalitarian form of domination had nothing to do with the ideas of Marx." See Jay, *Marxism and Totality,* 533. The original source of the quoted passage is Mihály Vajda, *The State and Socialism: Political Essays* (London: Allison and Busby, 1981), 107.

One of the most thorough and persuasive books produced during the past two decades that attempts to reassess and recover "what is living" in Marxian thinking is Dick Howard's *Marxian Legacy.* Howard is particularly attentive to the various critiques of totalitarianism on the left and offers a systematic analysis of the Marxian elements—or the departures from Marxism—in the theories of Luxemburg, Horkheimer, Lukács, Marcuse, Korsch, Bloch, Lefort, Habermas, and Castoriadis, among others.

96. Lefort does not embrace any and all uses of totalitarian theory, however. He has strongly criticized images of totalitarianism as permanently successful systems of oppression. Likewise, he engages the ideas and practices of human rights as problems to be considered and debated publicly rather than as "givens." See

Lefort, *Democracy and Political Theory,* 21–44; and Lefort, *The Political Forms of Modern Society,* 239–72, 307–19.

Several writers on totalitarianism see the concept as similar to the notion advanced here in connection with Lefort's approach—that is, as an "ideal type" that actual regimes may approach but not realize. This may be the most reasonable way to retain the concept. See, for example, Michael Walzer, quoted in Gleason, *Totalitarianism,* 204.

97. Bracher, *Turning Points in Modern Times,* 302–5.

98. Ibid. It could also be argued, though Bracher understandably does not do so, that whatever hope there might be for the renewal of peace and tolerance in the Balkans rests on the ideal of internationalism that is also at least partly attributable to the "Communist legacy." On Bosnia's complex and tragic recent history, see Robert J. Donia and John V. A. Fine, *Bosnia and Hercegovina: A Tradition Betrayed* (New York: Columbia University Press, 1994).

99. Bracher, *Turning Points in Modern Times,* 191–92. Bracher also states that the horrible consequences of the German dictatorship "surpass everything that has gone before in human history" 191–92. The contrast between such a statement as this and the equivocations and obfuscations of Nolte could hardly be stronger. But I must add one further cautionary note regarding Bracher's recent considerations on the future of Europe: if the policies of "economic cooperation and political integration" that Bracher championed for Europe should entrench themselves before effective mechanisms for the guarantee of rights have been established, then the kind of "one-dimensional" society Herbert Marcuse criticized over three decades ago might well be realized in an even larger sphere. On the timeliness of some elements of Marcuse's critique, see Douglas Kellner, introduction to *One-Dimensional Man,* by Herbert Marcuse, 2d ed. (Boston: Beacon, 1991), xi–xxxix.

100. Of course, nations must occasionally make difficult policy choices between support for one objectionable dictatorship or support for another, a choice that might have to be faced under some of the most appallingly dangerous and complex historical conditions, such as World War II. On the dangers of a version of totalitarian theory that posits an "unchanging" Soviet Union, see Cohen, *Rethinking the Soviet Experience,* passim; Lefort, *The Political Forms of Modern Society,* 315–19; and Hitchens, "How Neo-conservatives Perish," in *For the Sake of Argument,* 143–48. Hitchens in particular emphasized and sharply criticized the tone of despair that has so often characterized writings on totalitarian dictatorship. Robert V. Daniels, a cautious defender of the cold war totalitarian theory, acknowledges that the theory's unhistorical categories sap its analytic force. See Daniels, *The End of the Communist Revolution* (London: Routledge, 1993), 77–78.

101. For recent examples of significant historical scholarship that examines state violence against citizens or civilians of foreign nations without any systematic use of or reliance on a concept of totalitarianism, see Burleigh and Wippermann, *The Racial State;* Friedländer, *Nazi Germany and the Jews;* Browning, *The Path*

to Genocide; Orlando Figes, *A People's Tragedy: A History of the Russian Revolution* (New York: Viking, 1997); Robert Thurston, *Life and Terror in Stalinist Russia, 1934–1941* (New Haven, Conn.: Yale University Press, 1996); and Kershaw and Lewin, eds., *Stalinism and Nazism.* As mentioned previously, Klaus Fischer invokes the Friedrich-Brzezinski totalitarianism model in *Nazi Germany,* but he makes little use of this model after having introduced it—which does not detract at all from the quality of his exhaustive and thoughtful study. A recent analysis of German anti-Semitism that dismisses totalitarian theory but replicates its tendency toward insufficient attention to contingent and proximate historical factors in the political success of the Nazi Party and the Nazi regime's policy of race murder is Goldhagen's *Hitler's Willing Executioners.* Goldhagen criticizes totalitarian theory's potential to overrate the pervasive control of the Nazi regime and thereby to ex-culpate Germans who helped perpetrate the Holocaust (491, note 32). This is a valid and important point, but he also insists (in the same reference note) on "the sub-stantial freedom and pluralism that actually existed" under the Nazis. One won-ders how extensive a pluralism Goldhagen means to assert here. Even as he argues that anti-Semitism in pre-Nazi Germany was in "flux" and "evolution," Goldhagen posits an overriding German "antisemitic cultural cognitive model" that generated an "eliminationist mind-set" (64–79). Goldhagen admits the compressed and se-lective nature of his historical account of nineteenth-century anti-Semitism, but ultimately the "flux" he occasionally refers to gives way to the "underlying con-stancy" of the "cognitive model" that he emphasizes far more strongly. For a sys-tematic critique of Goldhagen's claims and use of evidence—albeit laced with broad polemics against "Holocaust literature"—see Norman G. Finkelstein and Ruth Bettina Birn, *A Nation on Trial: The Goldhagen Thesis and Historical Truth* (New York: Henry Holt, 1998). Readers should also consult Robert R. Shandley, ed., *Un-willing Germans? The Goldhagen Debate,* trans. Jeremiah Riemer (Minneapolis: University of Minnesota Press, 1998). Pulzer's *Rise of Political Anti-Semitism in Ger-many and Austria,* Lindemann's *Esau's Tears,* and Fritzsche's books on the Weimar Republic, especially *Germans into Nazis,* offer far better historical arguments on the politics of anti-Semitism than Goldhagen does. Fritzsche, for example, offers this assessment in conclusion: "That so many ordinary Germans were complicit in the murder of Jews and other so-called undesirables was not so much the function of a genocidal anti-Semitism which they shared in uncomplicated fashion with Nazi leaders; rather, over the course of the twelve-year Reich, more and more Germans came to play active and generally congenial parts in the Nazi revolution and then subsequently came to accept the uncompromising terms of Nazi racism" (*Germans into Nazis,* 230).

102. The best recent reconsideration of the interpretive problems attending the comparative totalitarianism model is Kershaw, "Totalitarianism Revisited." For an excellent critical discussion of the domestic political and juridical use and abuse of antitotalitarianism in postwar Germany, see Alf Lüdtke, "'Coming to Terms with the Past': Illusions of Remembering, Ways of Forgetting Nazism in West Germany,"

Journal of Modern History 65 (September 1993): 542–72. See also the books and articles by Barber, Mommsen, and Wippermann cited in the introduction.

103. Mason, "Intention and Explanation," in *Nazism, Fascism and the Working Class,* 230.

104. As the historians Geoff Eley and David Blackbourn have convincingly shown in *The Peculiarities of German History,* the application of this Western (and largely Anglo-American) model of liberal success as the measure of nineteenth-century Germany's performance avoids or deftly smooths over as many crucial questions about the actual historical development of modern European (and American) regimes as it answers.

105. A forcefully argued critique of how the totalitarianism notion functioned with mixed effects in the critique of imperialism and the democratic socialism of one of its most important exponents, George Orwell, appears in Rai, *Orwell and the Politics of Despair,* 63–67, 151–66.

106. For discussions of the uses of the terms *totalitarian* and *authoritarian* by President Ronald Reagan and Jeane Kirkpatrick, see Gleason, *Totalitarianism,* 197–205.

107. See, for example, Franz Neumann's "Notes on the Theory of Dictatorship," in *The Democratic and the Authoritarian State,"* 250–51.

108. Marcuse, *One-Dimensional Man,* 1964, 19–48. Hannah Arendt argued a similar point but from a somewhat different perspective. In her view, the working class was disappearing into mass society and therefore could no longer claim to represent "the people." She made this claim during the 1950s, when such arguments were perhaps easier to sustain than they might be today. See Arendt, *The Human Condition* (Chicago: University of Chicago Press, 1958), 218–20.

109. See, for example, Klaus Fischer, *Nazi Germany,* 215–17, 225–26, 252–62. Fischer's most attentive discussions of class occur at the macro- and microhistorical levels: first, when he describes the gross inequalities of wealth in the United States and, second, when he explains the ideological conflict between Hitler and the "leftist" Nazi Otto Strasser. Fischer does mention the class-related issues of the conservative elite's choice of Hitler and the high degree of upper-class electoral support for Hitler, but he offers little analysis of what these facts imply—or ought to—for the study of class and other economic factors in Nazism's political success. Despite my criticism of some of its claims and omissions, however, I must also mention that Fischer's *Nazi Germany* is a skillfully written and impressively comprehensive work. It also acknowledges some of the recent and significant work on issues related to social history, the construction of gender roles, and sexual identity under modern dictatorial regimes. Excellent examples of the great value of a social historical approach to the study of dictatorship are the books and articles by Victoria de Grazia, Atina Grossman, Renate Bridenthal, Robert Thurston, Claudia Koonz, Detlev Peukert, and Jill Stephenson listed in the bibliography. See also David Schoenbaum's path-breaking study, *Hitler's Social Revolution: Class and Status in Nazi Germany, 1933–1945* (New York: Doubleday, 1966). On the need for

continued attention to the issue of class in historical scholarship on modern dictatorships, see Mason, "Whatever Happened to Fascism," 323–31.

110. The best accounts of the events that precipitated the *Historikerstreit* are in Charles S. Maier, *The Unmasterable Past: History, Holocaust, and German National Identity* (Cambridge, Mass.: Harvard University Press, 1988); and Richard J. Evans, *In Hitler's Shadow: West German Historians and the Attempt to Escape from the Nazi Past* (New York: Pantheon, 1989). Evans is particularly good at explaining in detail Nolte's developing attraction to the ideas that set off the *Historikerstreit* and his often specious modes of historical argumentation.

111. Nolte had been referring to the necessity to "deepen" the concept of totalitarianism (albeit in his usual abstract and elliptical style) roughly a decade before the outbreak of the *Historikerstreit*. In a paper given at a conference of the American Historical Association in 1977, he made a dubious comparison between "self-critical" and "self-praising states," citing the Soviet Union as an unadulterated version of the latter. Nolte argued for a renewal of the totalitarian concept as a bulwark for an overly "self-critical," Western, liberal civilization. In retrospect, it is clear that Nolte's argument was not so far from the call by conservative politicians and scholars in the 1980s for a more self-assertive Germany—the very arguments that gave the *Historikerstreit* its strongly political cast. See Ernst Nolte, "Despotism—Totalitarianism—Freedom-Oriented Society," in *Totalitarianism Reconsidered*, ed. Menze, 167–78.

112. See, for example, Michael Stürmer, ed., *Dissonanzen des Fortschritts: Essays über Geschichte und Politik in Deutschland* (Munich: Piper, 1986); and Andreas Hillgruber, *Zweierlei Untergang: Die Zerschlagung des deutschen Reiches und das Ende des europäischen Judentums* (Berlin: Corso bei Siedler, 1986).

113. The key articles in this controversy are gathered in *"Historikerstreit"* and translated into English as *Forever in the Shadow of Hitler?* See also Dan Diner, ed., *Ist der Nationalsozialismus Geschichte? Zu Historisierung und Historikerstreit* (Frankfurt am Main: Fischer, 1987); Maier, *The Unmasterable Past;* Hans-Ulrich Wehler, *Entsorgung der deutschen Vergangenheit? Ein polemischer Essay zum "Historikerstreit"* (Munich: Beck, 1988); Hennig, *Zum Historikerstreit;* Imanuel Geiss, *Die Habermas-Kontroverse: Ein deutscher Streit* (Berlin: Siedler, 1988); Evans, *In Hitler's Shadow;* Peter Baldwin, ed., *Reworking the Past: Hitler, the Holocaust, and the Historians' Debate* (Boston: Beacon, 1990); Saul Friedländer, ed., *Probing the Limits of Representation* (Cambridge, Mass.: Harvard University Press, 1992); and Deborah Lipstadt, *Denying the Holocaust: The Growing Assault on Truth and Memory* (New York: Free Press, 1993), 110–11, 211–15. Most of these writers sharply criticized Nolte's conclusions as well as his singular use of totalitarian theory. Lipstadt did not accuse Nolte of denying the historical fact of the Holocaust, but she criticized the effect that his recent work had in relativizing the issues of guilt and responsibility for violence in the Holocaust. Nolte offered his version of the episode in *Das Vergehen der Vergangenheit*. He has described his studies with Heidegger in his book *Martin Heidegger: Politik und Geschichte im Leben und Denken* (Berlin: Propyläen, 1992), 7–8.

114. Karl Dietrich Bracher, "Letter to the Editor of the *Frankfurter Allgemeine Zeitung*, September 6, 1986," in *Forever in the Shadow of Hitler?* 72–73. See also Bracher, *Turning Points in Modern Times*, 35–36, 140–41, 143, 200. Bracher's predecessor in the matter of defending *Totalitarismustheorie*, Carl J. Friedrich, had stated his distrust of Nolte's conclusions and his "phenomenological" approach to the study of fascist dictatorship years earlier. See Friedrich, "Fascism versus Totalitarianism: Ernst Nolte's Views Reexamined," *Central European History* 4, no. 3 (1971): 271–84. In 1990, Nolte continued to defend his approach and his conclusions and to accuse his opponents (chiefly Ian Kershaw, Hans Mommsen, and Hans-Ulrich Wehler, in this case) of misquoting him. See Ernst Nolte, *Lehrstück oder Tragödie? Beiträge zur Interpretation der Geschichte des 20. Jahrhunderts* (Cologne: Böhlau, 1991), 225–49. See also Hans Mommsen, *Der Nationalsozialismus und die deutsche Gesellschaft: Ausgewählte Aufsätze*, ed. Lutz Niethammer and Bernd Weisbrod (Reinbeck: Rowohlt, 1991).

115. See Weitz, *Creating German Communism*, 391–93; and Kershaw, *The Nazi Dictatorship*, 206–09.

116. Kershaw, "Totalitarianism Revisited," 39.

117. Ibid., 39–40.

118. Kershaw, "Working towards the Führer," in *Stalinism and Nazism*, ed. Kershaw and Lewin, 89, 106. Kershaw also criticizes "Stalinism" as a historical approach to the history of the post-Stalin Soviet Union and other postwar Communist regimes because it presents the same oversimplification and unhistorical comparison that the totalitarian concept does.

The most widely cited English-language studies of Stalin and Stalinism are still useful, though they are now over two decades old: Robert Tucker, ed. *Stalinism: Essays in Historical Interpretation* (New York: Norton, 1977); and Adam B. Ulam, *Stalin: The Man and His Era* (New York: Viking, 1973). More recent books that offer historical perspectives on the totalitarianism paradigm as well as Stalinism include Alec Nove, ed., *The Stalin Phenomenon* (New York: St. Martin's, 1993); and J. Arch Getty and Roberta A. Manning, eds., *Stalinist Terror: New Perspectives* (Cambridge: Cambridge University Press, 1993). Recently published biographies or personal papers of Stalin and Lenin have reignited old debates about the degree of continuity between the ideas and policies of these two Soviet leaders. See, in particular, Dimitrii Volkogonov, *Lenin: A New Biography,* ed. and trans. Harold Shukman (New York: Free Press, 1994), which reprises the argument that the origins of the violent extremes characteristic of Stalin's rule are found in the policies begun during Lenin's years of power. Partly because of Volgonokov's status as a former military "insider," his conclusions have been subject to both intense support and condemnation.

119. See the books cited in note 101.

120. See the reflections on the term and its different uses in Kershaw, "Totalitarianism Revisited"; Kershaw and Lewin, eds., *Stalinism and Nazism;* Gleason, *Totalitarianism;* and Söllner, "Das Totalitarismuskonzept in der Ideengeschichte des 20. Jahrhunderts," 10–21.

121. In addition to the writings of Mason, Peukert, and Kershaw already cited, see Jane Caplan, *Government without Administration: State and Civil Service in Weimar and Nazi Germany* (Oxford: Clarendon Press/Oxford University Press, 1988). Caplan's superb study of the workings of the German bureaucracy can be reasonably situated in proximity to the Marxian tradition of scholarship on the Weimar Republic and Nazi Germany established by Franz Neumann and Ernst Fraenkel (though in the detail and scope of her study she moves far beyond their exploratory analyses) as well as to the work of such later structuralist historians as Hans Mommsen and Martin Broszat. In her introduction to the collected essays of Tim Mason, Caplan also emphasizes his reliance on Neumann's writings, especially *Behemoth*. See Caplan, introduction to *Nazism, Fascism and the Working Class*, by Mason, 3–4.

122. Even the more ardently anti-Communist, anti–New Left, and antitotalitarian scholars, such as Richard Löwenthal and Ernst Fraenkel, continued to resist encroachments on the political and programmatic gains of the working class in the welfare state of the Federal Republic. The most famous and successful of their political counterparts, Willy Brandt, embraced the heritage of socialist radicalism even more openly, prodding his Social Democratic Party to "risk more democracy" years after it had officially abandoned Marxism. Brandt, quoted in Richard Löwenthal, *Social Change and Cultural Crisis*, 120. Likewise, Brandt's policy of engagement with East European Communist regimes—Ostpolitik—bore an interesting resemblance to the wartime efforts of Neu Beginnen. See Richard Löwenthal, "Vom kalten Krieg zur Ostpolitik," in *Die zweite Republik—25 Jahre Bundesrepublik Deutschland—eine Bilanz,* ed. Richard Löwenthal and Hans-Peter Schwarz (Stuttgart: Seewald, 1974), 604–99.

BIBLIOGRAPHY

Collected Papers and Correspondence

Internationaal Instituut voor Sociale Geschiedenis (Amsterdam)

    Nachlaß Otto Bauer

    Nachlaß Karl Kautsky

    Nachlaß Karl Korsch

    Nachlaß Otto Rühle

    Neu Beginnen Archiv

Faber and Faber Publishers, Archive (London)

    Franz Borkenau—Faber and Faber Correspondence

Stadt- und Universitätsbibliothek Frankfurt am Main

    Max-Horkheimer-Archiv

George Orwell Archive—University College (London)

Interviews

Richard Löwenthal, Berlin, 3 August 1987

Ossip K. Flechtheim, Berlin, 18 July 1989

Journals

Die Gesellschaft. 1928–33.

Living Marxism. 1938–42.

New Essays. 1942–43.

Zeitschrift für Sozialforschung (also published as *Studies in Philosophy and Social Science*). 1932–41.

Zeitschrift für Sozialismus (also published as *Sozialistische Revolution*). 1933–36.

Selected Writings by Individuals and Groups Discussed

Adorno, Theodor W. *Gesammelte Schriften*. Edited by Rolf Tiedemann. Frankfurt am Main: Suhrkamp, 1970–86.

———. *The Jargon of Authenticity*. Translated by Knut Tarnowski and Frederic Will. Evanston, Ill.: Northwestern University Press, 1973. Originally published as *Jargon der Eigentlichkeit: Zur deutschen Ideologie* (Frankfurt am Main: Suhrkamp, 1964).

———. *Negative Dialectics*. Translated by E. B. Ashton. New York: Continuum, 1973. Originally published as *Negative Dialektik* (Frankfurt am Main: Suhrkamp, 1966).

Adorno, Theodor W., et al. *The Authoritarian Personality*. New York: Harper, 1950.

Arato, Andrew, and Eike Gebhardt, eds. *The Essential Frankfurt School Reader*. With an introduction by Paul Piccone. New York: Continuum, 1993.

Beetham, David, ed. *Marxists in Face of Fascism: Writings by Marxists on Fascism from the Inter-War Period*. Totowa, N.J.: Barnes and Noble Books, 1984.

Biehahn, Walter. "Zur Geschichte des Bolschewismus." *Die Gesellschaft* 10, no. 1 (1933): 36–52.

Bienstock, Gregor. *Europa und die Weltpolitik*. Karlsbad: Graphia, 1936.

———. "Die Umgruppierung der Komintern." *Zeitschrift für Sozialismus* 2, nos. 24/25 (1935): 787–92.

Borkenau, Franz. *Austria and After*. London: Faber and Faber, 1938.

———. *The Communist International*. London: Faber and Faber, 1938.

———. "La crise des partis socialistes dans l'Europe contemporaine." *Annales d'histoire économique et sociale* 7 (1935): 337–52.

———. *End and Beginning: On the Generations of Cultures and the Origins of the West*. Edited by Richard Löwenthal. New York: Columbia University Press, 1981.

———. *European Communism*. London: Faber and Faber, 1953. Originally published as *Der Europäische Kommunismus: Seine Geschichte von 1917 bis zur Gegenwart* (Bern: Francke, 1952).

———. "Fascisme et syndicalisme." *Annales d'histoire économique et sociale* 6 (1934): 337–50.

——— [Ludwig Neureither, pseud.]. "Klassenbewußtsein." *Zeitschrift für Sozialismus* 1, no. 5 (1934): 152–59.

———. "Mensch und Gesellschaft bei Karl Marx." In "Vorträge der 'RIAS Funk-Universität,'" 6 November 1950. Typed transcript of radio broadcasts. Library, Free University of Berlin.

———. *The New German Empire*. New York: Viking, 1939.

——— [Ludwig Neureither, pseud.]. "Noch einmal 'Klassenbewußtsein.'" *Zeitschrift für Sozialismus* 1, no. 10 (1934): 325–29.

———. *Pareto*. London: Chapman and Hall, 1936.

———. "A Program for Counter-Revolution." In *After Peace, What?* 1–10. Norman, Okla.: Cooperative Books, 1941.

———. Review of *Karl Marx*, by Karl Korsch. *Sociological Review* 31, no. 1 (1939): 117–18.

———. *Socialism: National or International*. London: Routledge and Sons, 1942.

———. *The Spanish Cockpit: An Eye-Witness Account of the Political and Social Conflicts of the Spanish Civil War*. London: Faber and Faber, 1937.

——— [Ludwig Neureither, pseud.]. "Staat und Revolution." *Zeitschrift für Sozialismus* 1, no. 6 (1934): 181–85.

———. "State and Revolution in the Paris Commune, the Russian Revolution, and the Spanish Civil War." *Sociological Review* 29, no. 1 (1937): 41–75.

———. *The Totalitarian Enemy*. London: Faber and Faber, 1940.

———. "Was ist Kreml-Astrologie?" *Der Monat* 7, no. 79 (1955): 32–39.

———. *Der Übergang vom feudalen zum bürgerlichen Weltbild: Studien zur Geschichte der Philosophie der Manufakturperiode*. Paris: Alcan, 1934.

———. "Zur Soziologie des Faschismus." *Archiv für Sozialwissenschaft und Sozialpolitik* 68, no. 5 (1933): 513–43.

———. ed. *Karl Marx*. Frankfurt am Main: Fischer Bucherei, 1956.

Denicke, Iurii [Georg Decker, pseud.]. "Antikapitalismus." *Zeitschrift für Sozialismus* 1, no. 3 (1933): 91–96.

———. "Die Dynamik der Koalitionspolitik." *Die Gesellschaft* 2 (1929): 16–23.

———. "Das Jahr der Wahlen." *Die Gesellschaft* 1 (1928): 1–14.

———. "Der Kampf um die Demokratie." *Die Gesellschaft* 1 (1929): 293–312.

———. "Nicht Radikal Genug!" *Sozialistische Revolution* 1, no. 1 (1933): 20–24.

———. "Offenbarungen der Tat." *Die Gesellschaft* 2 (1929): 224–35.

———. "Die Reichstagswahlen." *Die Gesellschaft* 1 (1928): 481–84.

———. "Die Tod einer Partei." *Die Gesellschaft* 1 (1928): 385–99.

———. "Wahlrechtsreform oder Reform der Politik?" *Die Gesellschaft* 2 (1928): 385–99.

———. "Zur Soziologie der Reichstagswahlen." *Die Gesellschaft* 2 (1928): 1–12.

Deutschland-Berichte der Sozialdemokratischen Partei Deutschlands (Sopade), 1934–40. 7 vols. Edited by Klaus Behnken. Frankfurt am Main: Verlag Petra Nettelbeck, 1980.

Fischer, Ruth. *Stalin and German Communism: A Study in the Origins of the State Party*. 1948. Reprint, New Brunswick, N.J.: Transaction Books, 1982.

Fisher, Ruth, and Arkadij Maslow. *Abtrünnig wider Willen: Aus Briefen und Manuskripten des Exils*. With a foreword by Hermann Weber. Edited by Peter Lübbe. Munich: R. Oldenbourg, 1990.

Fraenkel, Ernst. *The Dual State: A Contribution to the Theory of Dictatorship*. Translated by Edward A. Shils et al. New York: Oxford University Press, 1941. Translated from the English as *Der Doppelstaat: Recht und Justiz im "Dritten Reich"* (1974; reprint, Frankfurt am Main: Fischer Tascherbuch, 1984).

———. *Military Occupation and the Rule of Law: Occupation Government in the Rhineland, 1918–1923*. London: Oxford University Press, 1944.

———. *Reformismus und Pluralismus: Materialen zu einer ungeschriebenen politischen*

Autobiographie. Edited by Jalk Esche and Frank Grube. Hamburg: Hoffmann und Campe, 1973.

Gurland, Arkadij [Arcadius]. *Das Heute der proletarischen Aktion: Hemmnisse und Wandlungen im Klassenkampf.* Berlin: E. Laubsche Verlagsbuchhandlung, 1931.

———. *Marxismus und Diktatur.* Leipzig: Leipziger Buchdruckerei, 1930.

———. "Technological Trends and Economic Structure under National Socialism." *Studies in Philosophy and Social Science* 9, no. 2 (1941): 226–63.

Hilferding, Rudolf. "Aufbau des Rätesystems." *Die Freiheit,* 5 February 1919.

———. *Das Finanzkapital: Eine Studie über die jüngste Entwicklung des Kapitalismus.* 1910. Reprint, Vienna: Wiener Volksbuchandlung, 1920. Translated and edited by Tom Bottomore as *Finance Capital: A Study of the Latest Phase of Capitalist Development* (London: Routledge and Kegan Paul, 1981).

———. "Das historische Problem." *Zeitschrift für Politik* 1, no. 4 (1954): 293–324.

———. "In die Gefahrenzone." *Die Gesellschaft* 7, no. 2 (1930): 289–97.

———. "Kampf und Ziel des revolutionären Sozialismus: Die Politik der Sozialdemokratischen Partei Deutschlands." *Neuer Vorwärts,* 28 January 1934.

———. "Das Londoner Abkommen." *Zeitschrift für Sozialismus* 2, no. 18 (1934–35): 561–68.

———. "The Modern Totalitarian State." *Modern Review* 1 (1947): 597–605.

———. "Parlamentarismus und Massenstreik." *Die Neue Zeit* 23, no. 2 (1904–5): 804–16.

———. "Revolutionärer Sozialismus." *Zeitschrift für Sozialismus* 1, no. 5 (1933–34): 145–52.

———. "Revolutionäres Vertrauen!" *Die Freiheit,* 18 November 1918.

———. "State Capitalism or Totalitarian State Economy." *Modern Review* 1 (1947): 266–71.

———. "Um die Zukunft der deutschen Arbeiterbewegung." *Die Neue Zeit* 34, no. 2 (1916): 167–75.

———. "Die Zeit und die Aufgabe." *Sozialistische Revolution* 1, no. 1 (1933): 1–11.

———. "Zur Frage des Generalstreiks." *Die Neue Zeit* 22, no. 1 (1903–4): 134–42.

———. "Zwischen den Entscheidungen." *Die Gesellschaft* 10, no. 1 (1933): 1–9.

Horkheimer, Max. *Between Philosophy and Social Science: Selected Early Writings.* With an introduction by G. Frederick Hunter. Translated by G. Frederick Hunter, Matthew S. Kramer, and John Torpey. Cambridge, Mass.: MIT Press, 1993.

———. *Critical Theory: Selected Essays.* Translated by Matthew J. O'Connell et al. New York: Continuum, 1986.

——— [Heinrich Regius, pseud.]. *Dämmerung: Notizen in Deutschland.* Zurich: Oprecht und Heibling, 1934.

———. *The Eclipse of Reason.* 1947. Reprint, New York: Continuum, 1974.

———. "The End of Reason." *Studies in Philosophy and Social Science* 9, no. 3 (1941): 366–88.

———. *Gesammelte Schriften.* 18 vols. Edited by Alfred Schmidt and Gunzelin Schmid Noerr. Frankfurt am Main: Fischer, 1987-96.

———. "Die Juden und Europa." *Zeitschrift für Sozialforschung* 8, nos. 1/2 (1939): 115-37.

———, ed. *Studien über Autorität und Familie.* Paris: Alcan, 1936.

Horkheimer, Max, and Theodor W. Adorno. *Dialectic of Enlightenment.* Translated by John Cumming. New York: Continuum, 1986. Originally published as *Dialektik der Aufklärung* (New York: Social Studies Association, 1944).

Kirchheimer, Otto. "Franz Neumann: An Appreciation." *Dissent* 4 (Fall 1957): 382-86.

———. *Funktionen des Staats und der Verfassung: 10 Analysen.* Frankfurt am Main: Suhrkamp, 1972.

———. "Legalität und Legitimität." *Die Gesellschaft* 9 (1932): 8-20.

———. "The Legal Order of National Socialism." *Studies in Philosophy and Social Science* 9, no. 3 (1941): 456-75.

———. "Marxismus, Diktatur, und Organisationsformen des Proletariats." *Die Gesellschaft* 10 (1933): 230-39.

———. *Political Justice: The Use of Legal Procedure for Political Ends.* Princeton, N.J.: Princeton University Press, 1961.

———. *Politics, Law, and Social Change: Selected Essays of Otto Kirchheimer.* Edited by Frederic S. Burin and Kurt L. Shell. New York: Columbia University Press, 1969.

———. *Politik und Verfassung.* Frankfurt am Main: Suhrkamp, 1981.

———. *Politische Herrschaft: Fünf Beiträge zur Lehre vom Staat.* Frankfurt am Main: Suhrkamp, 1981.

———. *Staatsgefüge und Recht des Dritten Reiches.* Hamburg: Hanseatische Verlagsanstalt, 1935.

———. "Die Verfassungslehre des Preußenkonfliktes." *Die Gesellschaft* 9 (1932): 194-209.

———. "Verfassungsreaktion 1932." *Die Gesellschaft* 9 (1932): 415-27.

———. "Verfassungsreform und Sozialdemokratie." *Die Gesellschaft* 10 (1933): 20-35.

———. *Von der Weimarer Republik zum Faschismus: Die Auflösung der demokratischen Rechtsordnung.* Edited by Wolfgang Luthardt. Frankfurt am Main: Suhrkamp, 1981.

———. *Weimar—und Was Dann? Entstehung und Gegenwart der Weimarer Verfassung.* Berlin: Laubverlag, 1930.

———. "Zur Staatslehre des Sozialismus und Bolschewismus." *Zeitschrift für Politik* 17 (1928): 593-611.

Kirchheimer, Otto, and Franz Neumann. *Social Democracy and the Rule of Law.* Edited by Keith Tribe. Translated by Leena Tanner and Keith Tribe. London: Allen and Unwin, 1987.

Kirchheimer, Otto, and Georg Rusche. *Punishment and Social Structure.* 1939. Reprint, New York: Russell and Russell, 1968.

Korsch, Karl. "Blutiger Mai in Berlin." *Die Aktion* 19, nos. 3/4 (1929): 92–94.

——. "Collectivisation in Spain." *Living Marxism* 4, no. 6 (1939): 178–82.

——. "Economics and Politics in Revolutionary Spain." *Living Marxism* 4, no. 3 (1938): 76–82.

——. "The Fascist Counter-Revolution." *Living Marxism* 5, no. 2 (1940): 29–37.

—— [Beta, pseud.]. "The Fight for Britain, the Fight for Democracy, and War Aims of the Working Class." *Living Marxism* 5, no. 4 (1941): 1–6.

——. *Gesamtausgabe.* 2 vols. Edited by Michael Buckmiller. Frankfurt: Europäische Verlags-Anstalt, 1980.

——. *Karl Marx.* New York: Chapman and Hall, 1938.

——. *Marxism and Philosophy.* Translated and with an introduction by Fred Halliday. New York: Monthly Review Press, 1970. Originally published as *Marxismus und Philosophie* (1923; reprint, Frankfurt am Main: Europäische Verlagsanstalt, 1966).

——. "Notes on History: The Ambiguities of Totalitarian Ideologies." *New Essays* 6, no. 2 (1942): 1–9.

——. Review of *Collectivisations: L'oeuvre constructive de la Révolution Espagnole; Receuil de documents. Zeitschrift für Sozialforschung* 7, no. 3 (1938): 469–74.

——. Review of *The New German Empire,* by Franz Borkenau. *Living Marxism* 5, no. 2 (1940): 61–63.

——. "State and Counter-Revolution." *Modern Quarterly* 11, no. 2 (1939): 60–67.

——. "The Structure and Practice of Totalitarianism." *New Essays* 6, no. 2 (1942): 43–49.

——. *Three Essays on Marxism.* With an introduction by Paul Breines. New York: Monthly Review Press, 1971.

——. "The Workers' Fight against Fascism." *Living Marxism* 5, no. 3 (1941): 36–49.

——. "Zur Geschichte der marxistischen Ideologie in Russland." *Der Gegner,* 5 February 1932.

Löwenheim, Walter. *Geschichte der Org (Neu Beginnen), 1929–1935: Eine zeitgenössische Analyse.* Edited and with an introduction by Jan Foitzik. Berlin: Edition Hentrich, 1995.

—— [Miles, pseud.]. *Neu beginnen: Faschismus oder Sozialismus Als Diskussionsgrundlage der Sozialisten Deutschlands.* Karlsbad: Graphia, 1933. Translated as *Socialism's New Start: A Secret German Manifesto,* with a preface by H. N. Brailsford (London: Allen and Unwin, 1934).

Löwenthal, Richard [Paul Sering, pseud.]. "Die Aufgraben der deutschen Revolution." *Zeitschrift für Sozialismus* 3, no. 33 (1936): 1041–49.

——. "Beyond Totalitarianism." In *1984 Revisited: Totalitarianism in Our Century,* edited by Irving Howe, 209–67. New York: Harper and Row, 1983.

——. "The Bolshevisation of the Spartacus League." In *International Communism,* St. Antony's Papers, no. 9, edited by David Footman, 23–71. London: Chatto and Windus, 1960.

———. "Democratic Socialism as an International Force." *Social Research* 47 (Spring 1980): 63–92.

——— [Paul Sering, pseud.]. "Der Faschismus." *Zeitschrift für Sozialismus* 2, nos. 24/25 (1935): 765–87.

——— [Paul Sering, pseud.]. "Der Faschismus." *Zeitschrift für Sozialismus* 2, nos. 25/26 (1935): 839–56.

———. "The German Question Transformed." *Foreign Affairs* 63, no. 2 (1984/85): 303–15.

——— [Paul Sering, pseud.]. "Historische Voraussetzungen des deutschen Nationalsozialismus." *Zeitschrift für Sozialismus* 3, no. 30 (1936): 959–75.

———. "In Memoriam Franz Borkenau." *Der Monat* 9, no. 106 (1957): 57–60.

——— [Paul Sering, pseud.]. *Jenseits des Kapitalismus: Ein Beitrag zur sozialistischen Neuorientierung.* Nuremburg: Nest, 1946.

———. "Letter to the Editor of the *Frankfurter Allgemeine Zeitung*," 29 November 1986. In *Forever in the Shadow of Hitler? Original Documents of the Historikerstreit, the Controversy concerning the Singularity of the Holocaust,* translated by James Knowlton and Truett Cates, 199–201. Atlantic Highlands, N.J.: Humanities, 1993.

———. "The 'Missing Revolution' in Industrial Societies: Comparative Reflections on a German Problem." In *Germany in the Age of Total War: Essays in Honor of Francis Carsten,* edited by Volker R. Berghahn and Martin Kitchen, 240–57. Totowa, N.J.: Barnes and Noble Books, 1981.

———. Preface and editor's introduction to *End and Beginning,* by Franz Borkenau. New York: Columbia University Press, 1981.

———. *Social Change and Cultural Crisis.* New York: Columbia University Press, 1984.

———. *Sozialismus und aktive Demokratie: Essays zu ihren Voraussetzungen in Deutschland.* Frankfurt am Main: Fischer, 1974.

———. "Totalitarianism Reconsidered." *Commentary* 29 (June 1960): 504–12.

——— [Paul Sering, pseud.]. "Die Wandlungen des Kapitalismus." *Zeitschrift für Sozialismus* 2, nos. 22/23 (1935): 704–25.

——— [Paul Sering, pseud.]. "Was ist der Volkssozialismus?" *Zeitschrift für Sozialismus* 3, no. 36 (1936): 1105–36. Translated and edited by Harriet Young and Mary Fox as *What is Folksocialism?* (pamphlet), with an introduction by Sidney Hook (New York: League for Industrial Democracy, 1937).

———. *Die Widerstandsgruppe "Neu Beginnen."* Beiträge zum Thema Widerstand, 20. Berlin: Informationszentrum Berlin, 1982.

———. *World Communism: The Disintegration of a Secular Faith.* New York: Oxford University Press, 1964.

Löwenthal, Richard, and Patrick von zur Mühlen. *Widerstand und Verweigerung in Deutschland, 1933 bis 1945.* Berlin: Dietz, 1982.

Löwenthal, Richard, and Hans-Peter Schwarz, eds. *Die zweite Republik—25 Jahre Bundesrepublik Deutschland—eine Bilanz.* Stuttgart: Seewald, 1974.

Marcuse, Herbert. *Das Ende der Utopie: Vorträge und Diskussionen in Berlin 1967.* Frankfurt am Main: Verlag Neue Kritik, 1980.

———. *Eros and Civilization: A Philosophical Inquiry into Freud.* 1955. Reprint, with new preface, Boston: Beacon, 1966.

———. *An Essay on Liberation.* Boston: Beacon, 1969.

———. *Hegel's Ontology and the Theory of Historicity.* Translated by Seyla Benhabib. Cambridge, Mass.: MIT Press, 1987. Originally published as *Hegels Ontologie und die Grundlegung einer Theorie der Geschichtlichkeit* (Frankfurt am Main: Klostermann, 1932).

———. *Ideen zu einer kritischen Theorie der Gesellschaft.* Frankfurt am Main: Suhrkamp, 1969.

———. *Kultur und Gesellschaft.* 2 vols. Frankfurt am Main: Suhrkamp, 1965.

———. *Negations: Essays in Critical Theory.* Translated by Jeremy J. Shapiro. Boston: Beacon, 1968.

———. *One-Dimensional Man.* 2d ed. With an introduction by Douglas Kellner. Boston: Beacon, 1991.

———. *One-Dimensional Man: Studies in the Ideology of Advanced Industrial Society.* Boston: Beacon, 1964.

———. *Reason and Revolution: Hegel and the Rise of Social Theory.* 1941. Reprint, Boston: Beacon, 1960.

———. "Repressive Tolerance." In *A Critique of Pure Tolerance,* by Robert Paul Wolff, Barrington Moore Jr., and Herbert Marcuse, 81–123. Boston: Beacon, 1969.

———. *Soviet Marxism: A Critical Analysis.* 1958. Reprint, with new preface, New York: Knopf/Vintage, 1961.

———. "Zur Wahrheitsproblematik der soziologischen Methode: Karl Mannheim, *Ideologie und Utopie.*" *Die Gesellschaft* 2 (1929): 356–69.

Neumann, Franz. *Behemoth: The Structure and Practice of National Socialism.* New York: Oxford University Press, 1942. 2d ed., 1944. Translated by Hedda Wagner and Gert Schäfer as *Behemoth: Struktur und Praxis des Nationalsozialismus, 1933–1944* (Frankfurt am Main: Fischer Taschenbuch, 1984).

———. "The Decay of German Democracy." *Political Quarterly* 4, no. 4 (1933): 525–43.

———. *The Democratic and the Authoritarian State: Essays in Political and Legal Theory.* Edited and with a preface by Herbert Marcuse. Glencoe, Ill.: Free Press, 1957. Translated by Alfred Schmidt as *Demokratischer und autoritärer Staat,* with an introduction by Helge Pross (Frankfurt am Main: Fischer, 1986).

———. "German Democracy 1950." *International Conciliation,* no. 461 (May 1950): 249–96.

———. "Marxismus und Intelligenz." In "Vorträge der 'RIAS Funk-Universität,'" 28 November 1950. Typed transcript of radio broadcasts. Library, Free University of Berlin.

———. *The Rule of Law: Political Theory and the Legal System in Modern Society.* With a foreword by Martin Jay and an introduction by Matthias Ruete. Berg: Lea-mington Spa, 1986. Originally appeared as "The Governance of the Rule of Law" (Ph.D. diss., Oxford University, 1936).

———. "Wandlungen des Marxismus." In "Vorträge der 'RIAS Funk-Universität,'" 20 November 1950. Typed transcript of radio broadcasts. Library, Free University of Berlin.

———. *Wirtschaft, Staat, Demokratie: Aufsätze, 1930–1954.* Edited by Alfons Söllner. Frankfurt am Main: Suhrkamp, 1978.

Neumann, Franz, and Kirchheimer, Otto. *The Rule of Law under Siege: Selected Essays of Franz L. Neumann and Otto Kirchheimer.* Edited by William E. Scheuerman. Berkeley: University of California Press, 1996.

Pachter, Henry [Henri Rabasseire, pseud.]. *Espagne: Creuset politique.* Paris: Éditions Fustier, 1938.

———. *The Fall and Rise of Europe: A Political, Social, and Cultural History of the Twentieth Century.* New York: Praeger, 1975.

——— [Henri Rabasseire, pseud.]. "Kellner on Korsch." *Telos,* no. 28 (Summer 1976): 195–98.

———. "On Being an Exile." In *The Legacy of the German Refugee Intellectuals,* edited by Robert Boyers, 12–51. New York: Schocken, 1972.

———. *Socialism in History: Political Essays of Henry Pachter.* Edited and with an introduction by Stephen Eric Bronner. New York: Columbia University Press, 1984.

———. *Weimar Etudes.* Edited by Stephen Eric Bronner. New York: Columbia University Press, 1982.

Pollock, Friedrich. "Is National Socialism a New Order?" *Studies in Philosophy and Social Science* 9, no. 3 (1941): 440–55.

———. *Die planwirtschaftlichen Versuche in der Sowjetunion, 1917–1927.* Leipzig: Hirschfeld, 1929.

———. "State Capitalism: Its Possibilities and Limitations." *Studies in Philosophy and Social Science* 9, no. 2 (1941): 200–225.

Rosenberg, Arthur. *Demokratie und Klassenkampf: Ausgewählte Studien.* Edited and with an introduction by Hans-Ulrich Wehler. Frankfurt am Main: Verlag Ullstein, 1974.

———. *Demokratie und Sozialismus.* 1938. Reprint, Frankfurt am Main: Athenäum, 1988. Translated by George Rosen as *Democracy and Socialism* (New York: Knopf, 1939).

———. *Die Entstehung der Deutschen Republik.* Berlin: Rowohlt, 1928.

———. *Entstehung und Geschichte der Weimarer Republik.* Frankfurt am Main: Europäische Verlagsanstalt, 1984.

——— [Historicus, pseud.]. *Der Faschismus als Massenbewegung: Sein Aüfstieg und seine Zersetzung.* Karlsbad: Verlagsanstalt Graphia, 1934.

———. *Geschichte der Deutschen Republik.* Karlsbad: Graphia, 1935.

———. *Geschichte des Bolschewismus.* 1932. Reprint, Frankfurt am Main: Athenäum, 1987. Translated by Ian F. D. Morrow as *A History of Bolshevism* (London: Oxford University Press, 1934).

———. Review of *Behemoth*, by Franz Neumann. *Studies in Philosophy and Social Science* 9, no. 3 (1941): 526–27.

———. "Treitschke und die Juden: Zur Soziologie der deutschen akademischen Reaktion." *Die Gesellschaft* 2 (1930): 78–83.

Rühle, Otto. "Brauner und Roter Faschismus." In *Schriften: Perspektiven einer Revolution in Hochindustrialisierten Ländern.* Edited by Gottfried Mergner. Reinbek: Rowohlt Taschenbuch, 1971.

———. *Karl Marx: His Life and Work.* Translated by Eden and Cedar Paul. New York: New Home Library, 1943.

Schifrin, Alexander. "Wege aus der Spaltung." *Die Gesellschaft* 10, no. 1 (1933): 10–19.

Seydewitz, Max. "Die Ueberwindung der faschistischen Diktatur." *Zeitschrift für Sozialismus* 1, no. 6 (1934): 198–207.

Thalheimer, August. "So-called Social-fascism." In *Marxists in Face of Fascism: Writings by Marxists on Fascism from the Inter-War Period,* edited by David Beetham, 195–97. Totowa, N.J.: Barnes and Noble Books, 1984.

———. "Ueber den Faschismus," parts 1–4. *Gegen den Strom,* parts 1/2, 11 January 1930: 32–33; part 3, 18 January 1930: 48–49; part 4, 25 January 1930: 66–67.

Wegner, Franz. "Koporativstaat." *Zeitschrift für Sozialismus* 1, no. 2 (1933): 101–6.

Wittfogel, Karl August. *Das erwachende China: Ein Abriss der Geschichte und der gegenwärtige Probleme Chinas.* Vienna: Agis, 1926.

———. "The Monolithic Party." Review of *Stalin and German Communism: A Study in the Origins of the State Party,* by Ruth Fischer. *New Leader* 31 (October 23, 1948): 10–12.

———. *Oriental Despotism: A Comparative Study of Total Power.* New Haven, Conn.: Yale University Press, 1957.

———. *Staatliches Konzentrationslager VII: Eine "Erziehungsanstalt" im Dritten Reich.* London: Malik, 1936.

———. *Wirtschaft und Gesellschaft Chinas: Versuch der wissenschaftlichen Analyse einer grossen asiatischen Agrargesellschaft.* Leipzig: Hirschfeld, 1931.

Selected Writings by Key Contemporaries and Other Theorists

Abendroth, Wolfgang. *Ein Leben in der Arbeiterbewegung: Gespräche, aufgezeichnet und herausgegeben von Barbara Dietrich und Joachim Perels.* Edited by Barbara Dietrich and Joachim Perels. Frankfurt am Main: Suhrkamp, 1981.

———. ed. *Faschismus und Kapitalismus.* Frankfurt: Europäische Verlags-Anstalt, 1967.

Anderson, Evelyn. *Hammer or Anvil: The Story of the German Working-class Movement.* London: Gollancz, 1945.

Arendt, Hannah. "The Cold War and the West." *Partisan Review* 29, no. 1 (1962): 10–20.

———. *Eichmann in Jerusalem: A Report on the Banality of Evil.* New York: Viking, 1963. Rev. and enlarged ed., Harmondsworth, England: Penguin Books, 1965.

———. *Essays in Understanding, 1930–1954.* Edited by Jerome Kern. New York: Harcourt, Brace, 1994.

———. "The Ex-Communists." *Commonweal* 57, no. 24 (1953): 595–99.

———. *The Human Condition.* Chicago: University of Chicago Press, 1958.

———. *The Life of the Mind.* 2 vols. New York: Harcourt Brace Jovanovich, 1978.

———. *Men in Dark Times.* New York: Harcourt, Brace and World, 1968.

———. *On Revolution.* 1965. Reprint, Harmondsworth, England: Penguin Books, 1990.

———. *On Violence.* New York: Harcourt, Brace and World, 1970.

———. *The Origins of Totalitarianism.* 1951. Reprint, New York: Harcourt Brace Jovanovich, 1979.

———. "Philosophie und Soziologie: Anlässlich Karl Mannheim, *Ideologie und Utopie.*" *Die Gesellschaft* 7 (1930): 163–76.

———. "Totalitarian Imperialism: Reflections on the Hungarian Revolution." *Journal of Politics* 20, no. 1 (1958): 5–43.

———. *Die ungarische Revolution und der totalitäre Imperialismus.* Munich: Piper, 1958.

Aron, Raymond. *Démocratie et totalitarisme.* Paris: Gallimard, 1965.

———. "The Essence of Totalitarianism according to Hannah Arendt." *Partisan Review* 60, no. 3 (1993): 366–76.

———. Introduction to *World Communism: A History of the Communist International,* by Franz Borkenau. Ann Arbor: University of Michigan Press, 1962.

———. *L'opium des intellectuels.* Paris: Calmann-Lévy, 1955.

Bauer, Otto. *Der Faschismus.* Bratislava: Eugen Prager, 1936.

———. *Die illegale Partei.* Paris: Éditions de la lutte socialiste, 1939.

———. *Zwischen zwei Weltkriegen? Die Krise der Weltwirtschaft, der Demokratie und des Sozialismus.* Bratislava: Eugen Prager, 1936.

Benjamin, Walter. *Gesammelte Schriften.* Edited by Rolf Tiedemann and Hermann Schweppenhäuser. Frankfurt am Main: Suhrkamp, 1974–89.

———. *Illuminations.* Edited and with an introduction by Hannah Arendt. Translated by Harry Zohn. New York: Schocken, 1969.

———. *Moskauer Tagebuch.* Edited by Gary Smith. Frankfurt am Main: Suhrkamp, 1980. Translated by Richard Sieburth as *Moscow Diary,* with a preface by Gershom Scholem and an afterword by Gary Smith (Cambridge, Mass.: Harvard University Press, 1986).

Bloch, Ernst. *Erbschaft dieser Zeit.* 1962. Reprint, Frankfurt am Main: Suhrkamp, 1973. Translated by Neville Plaice and Stephen Plaice as *Heritage of Our Times* (Cambridge: Polity, 1990).

———. *Geist der Utopie.* Berlin: Cassirer, 1923.

Brandt, Willy. *My Life in Politics.* New York: Viking, 1992.

Brenan, Gerald. *Personal Record, 1920–1972.* New York: Knopf, 1975.

———. *The Spanish Labyrinth: An Account of the Social and Political Background of the Civil War.* Cambridge: Cambridge University Press, 1943.

Bry, Gerhard. *Resistance: Recollections from the Nazi Years.* Shady Glen, West Orange, N.J.: Published by author, 1979.

Buber-Neumann, Margarete. *Als Gefangene bei Stalin und Hitler.* Stuttgart: Seewald, 1968.

Burnham, James. *The Managerial Revolution.* New York: John Day, 1941.

Camus, Albert. *L'homme révolté.* Paris: Gallimard, 1951. Translated by Anthony Bower as *The Rebel* (New York: Knopf, 1954).

Chiaromonte, Nicola. *The Worm of Consciousness and Other Essays.* With a preface by Mary McCarthy. Edited by Miriam Chiaromonte. New York: Harcourt Brace Jovanovich, 1976.

Coser, Lewis. "Remembering the Spanish Revolution: A Memoir of What Happened in 1936." *Dissent* 33 (Winter 1986): 53–58.

Crossman, Richard. Review of *European Communism,* by Franz Borkenau. *New Statesman* 45 (June 6, 1953): 674.

———, ed. *The God That Failed.* New York: Harper, 1950.

Djilas, Milovan. *The New Class: An Analysis of the Communist System.* New York: Praeger, 1957.

———. *The Unperfect Society: Beyond the New Class.* Translated by Dorian Cooke. New York: Harcourt Brace Jovanovich, 1969.

Drucker, Peter. *The End of Economic Man: A Study of the New Totalitarianism.* New York: John Day, 1939.

Flechtheim, Ossip K. Introduction to *Geschichte des Bolschewismus,* by Arthur Rosenberg. Frankfurt: Athenäum, 1987.

———. *Die KPD in der Weimarer Republik.* 1948. Reprint, Hamburg: Junius, 1986.

———. *Rosa Luxemburg: Zur Einführung.* Hamburg: Junius, 1986.

———. *Von Marx bis Kolakowski: Sozialismus oder Untergang in der Barbarei?* Cologne: Europäische Verlagsanstalt, 1978.

———. *Weltkommunismus im Wandel.* 1965. Reprint, Berlin: Verlag europäische ideen, 1977.

Foot, Michael. *Aneurin Bevan: A Biography.* 2 vols. New York: Atheneum, 1963–74.

Fromm, Erich. *Escape from Freedom.* New York: Rinehart, 1941.

Germino, Dante. *Beyond Ideology: The Revival of Political Theory.* New York: Harper and Row, 1967.

———. *The Italian Fascist Party in Power.* Minneapolis: University of Minnesota Press, 1959.

———. *Political Philosophy and the Open Society.* Baton Rouge: Louisiana State University Press, 1982.

Geyer, Curt. *Die Partei der Freiheit.* Paris: Graphia, 1939.

———. *Die revolutionäre Illusion: Zur Geschichte des linken Flügels der USPD; Erinnerungen von Curt Geyer.* Edited by Wolfgang Benz and Hermann Graml. Stuttgart: Deutsche Verlagsanstalt, 1976.

———— [Max Klinger, pseud.]. "Der Rückfall in den Machtstaat." *Sozialistische Revolution* 1, no. 1 (1933): 14–20.

Goldmann, Lucien. *Das Denken Herbert Marcuses: Kritik und Interpretation der kritischen Theorie*. Munich: TWA Reprints, 1970.

Gramsci, Antonio. *Letters from Prison*. 2 vols. Edited by Frank Rosengarten. Translated by Raymond Rosenthal. New York: Columbia University Press, 1994.

————. *Quaderni del carcere: Edizione critica*. 4 vols. Edited by Valentino Gerratana. Turin: Giulio Einaudi Editore, 1975.

————. *Selections from the Prison Notebooks of Antonio Gramsci*. Edited and translated by Quintin Hoare and Geoffrey Nowell Smith. New York: International, 1971.

Hayek, Friedrich A. *The Road to Serfdom*. Chicago: University of Chicago Press, 1944.

Hegel, G. W. F. *Phenomenology of Mind*. With an introduction by George Lichtheim. Translated by J. B. Baillie. New York: Harper and Row, 1967.

————. *The Philosophy of History*. With an introduction by C. J. Friedrich. Translated by J. Sibree. New York: Dover, 1956.

————. *Philosophy of Right*. Translated by T. M. Knox. Oxford: Clarendon, 1942.

Heidegger, Martin. *Sein und Zeit*. Tübingen: Niemeyer, 1927.

————. *Die Selbstbehauptung der deutschen Universität: Rede, gehalten bei der feierlichen Übernahme des Rektorats der Universität Freiburg i. Br. am 27.5.1933*. Freiburger Universitätsreden, 11. Breslau: Korn, 1933.

Heller, Hermann. *Europa und der Faschismus*. Berlin: W. de Gruyter, 1931.

Heym, Stefan. *Radek*. Munich: Bertelsmann, 1995.

James, C. L. R. *World Revolution, 1917–1936: The Rise and Fall of the Communist International*. New York: Pioneer, 1937.

Kahn-Freund, Otto. *Labour Law and Politics in the Weimar Republic*. Edited by Roy Lewis and Jon Clark. Oxford: Blackwell, 1981.

Kautsky, Karl. "Eine Diskussionsgrundlage." *Zeitschrift für Sozialismus* 1, no. 2 (1933): 50–58.

Koestler, Arthur. *Arrival and Departure*. New York: Macmillan, 1943.

————. *Arrow in the Blue*. 1952. Reprint, New York: Macmillan, 1970.

————. *Darkness at Noon*. New York: Macmillan, 1941.

————. *The Scum of the Earth*. New York: Macmillan, 1941.

————. *Spanish Testament*. With an introduction by the Duchess of Atholl. London: Gollancz, 1937.

————. *The Yogi and the Commissar*. New York: Macmillan, 1945.

Kojève, Alexandre. *Introduction to the Reading of Hegel*. Edited by Allan Bloom. Translated by James. H. Nichols. Ithaca, N.Y.: Cornell University Press, 1980.

Korsch, Hedda. "Memories of Karl Korsch." *New Left Review*, no. 76 (November/December 1972): 35–45.

Lederer, Emil. *State of the Masses: The Threat of the Classless Society*. New York: Norton, 1940.

Lichtheim, George. *The Concept of Ideology*. New York: Praeger, 1967.

————. *George Lukács*. New York: Viking, 1970.

————. *Marxism: An Historical and Critical Study.* New York: Praeger, 1961.

Lowenthal, Leo. *An Unmastered Past: The Autobiographical Reflections of Leo Lowenthal.* Edited and with an introduction by Martin Jay. Berkeley: University of California Press, 1987. Originally published as *Mitmachen wollte ich nie: Ein autobiographisches Gespräch mit Hulmut Dubiel* (Frankfurt am Main: Suhrkamp, 1980).

Lukács, Georg. *Briefwechsel, 1902–1917.* Edited by Éva Karádi and Éva Fekete. Stuttgart: Metzler, 1982.

————. *History and Class Consciousness.* Translated by Rodney Livingstone. Cambridge, Mass.: MIT Press, 1971. Originally published as *Geschichte und Klassenbewußtsein* (Berlin: Malik, 1923).

————. *Political Writings, 1919–1929.* Edited by Rodney Livingstone. Translated by Michael McColgan. London: New Left Books, 1972.

————. *Record of a Life: An Autobiographical Sketch.* Edited by István Eörsi. Translated by Rodney Livingstone. London: Verso, 1983.

————. *Werke.* Darmstadt-Neuwied: Hermann Luchterhand, 1968.

————. *Die Zerstörung der Vernunft.* Berlin: Aufbau-Verlag, 1954.

Luxemburg, Rosa. *The Accumulation of Capital.* Translated by Agnes Schwarzschild. New York: Monthly Review Press, 1968.

————. *The Letters of Rosa Luxemburg.* Edited and translated and with an introduction by Stephen Eric Bronner. Atlantic Highlands, N.J.: Humanities, 1993.

————. *Politische Schriften.* 3 vols. Edited and with an introduction by Ossip Flechtheim. Frankfurt am Main: Athenäum, 1966.

————. *The Russian Revolution, and Leninism or Marxism?* Translated and with an introduction by Bertram Wolfe. Ann Arbor: University of Michigan Press, 1961.

Macdonald, Dwight. "The End of Capitalism in Germany." *Partisan Review* 8, no. 3 (1941): 198–220.

Mannheim, Karl. *Ideologie und Utopie.* Bonn: Cohen, 1929. Translated by Louis Wirth and Edward Shils as *Ideology and Utopia: An Introduction to the Sociology of Knowledge* (New York: Harcourt, Brace, 1936).

Manuilski, Dmitrii. "On Fascism." In *Marxists in Face of Fascism: Writings by Marxists on Fascism from the Inter-War Period,* edited by David Beetham, 157–61. Totowa, N.J.: Barnes and Noble Books, 1984.

Marshall, T. H. Review of *Pareto,* by Franz Borkenau. *Political Quarterly* 7, no. 3 (1936): 459–61.

Marx, Karl. *Capital.* 3 vols. Edited by Frederick Engels. New York: International, 1967.

Marx, Karl, and Friedrich Engels. *Collected Works.* New York: International, 1975–.

————. *The Marx-Engels Reader.* Edited by Robert C. Tucker. New York: Norton, 1972.

————. *Werke.* Berlin: Dietz, 1984.

Massing, Hede. *This Deception.* New York: Duell, Sloan and Pearce, 1951. Translated as *Die Grosse Täuschung. Geschichte einer Sowjetagentin* (Freiburg: Herder, 1967).

Massing, Paul. *Rehearsal for Destruction: A Study of Political Anti-Semitism in Imperial Germany.* New York: Harper and Brothers, 1949.

———— [Karl Billinger, pseud.]. *Schutzhäftling 880: Aus einem deutschen Konzentrationslager.* Paris: Éditions du Carrefour, 1935. Translated as *Fatherland,* with a foreward by Lincoln Steffens (New York: International, 1935).

Mattick, Paul. "Anti-Bolshevist Communism in Germany." *Telos,* no. 26 (Winter 1975–76): 57–69.

————. *Critique of Marcuse: One-Dimensional Man in Class Society.* New York: Herder and Herder, 1972.

————. *Marx and Keynes: The Limits of the Mixed Economy.* Boston: Extending Horizons Books, 1969.

Merleau-Ponty, Maurice. *Humanism and Terror: An Essay on the Communist Problem.* Translated by John O'Neill. Boston: Beacon, 1969.

Michels, Robert. *Political Parties.* Translated by Eden and Cedar Paul. New York: Dover, 1959.

Milosz, Czeslaw. *The Captive Mind.* Translated by Jane Zielonko. New York: Knopf, 1953.

Mises, Ludwig von. *Omnipotent Government: The Rise of the Total State and Total War.* New Haven, Conn.: Yale University Press, 1948.

————. *Planned Chaos.* Irvington-on-Hudson: Foundation for Economic Education, 1947.

Nenni, Pietro. *Six ans de guerre civile en Italie.* Paris: Valois, 1930.

————. *Storia di quattro anni, 1919–1922.* Rome: Einaudi, 1946.

Neumann, Sigmund. *Die Parteien der Weimarer Republik.* Berlin: Verlag Junker und Dünnhaupt, 1932.

————. *Permanent Revolution: The Total State in a World at War.* New York: Harper and Brothers, 1942.

Oakeshott, Michael. *Morality and Politics in Europe: The Harvard Lectures.* Edited by Shirley Robin Letwin. New Haven, Conn.: Yale University Press, 1993.

————. *Rationalism in Politics and Other Essays.* Indianapolis: Liberty, 1991.

Orwell, George. *Animal Farm.* London: Secker and Warburg, 1945.

————. *The Collected Essays, Journalism, and Letters of George Orwell.* 4 vols. Edited by Sonia Orwell and Ian Angus. New York: Harcourt Brace Jovanovich, 1968.

————. *Homage to Catalonia.* 1938. Reprint, New York: Harcourt Brace Jovanovich, 1952.

————. *Inside the Whale and Other Essays.* Harmondworth, England: Penguin Books, 1982.

————. *Nineteen Eighty-Four.* London: Secker and Warburg, 1949.

Pareto, Vilfredo. *The Mind and Society.* 4 vols. Translated by Andrew Bongiorno and Arthur Livingston. 1935. Reprint, New York: Dover, 1963. Originally published as *Trattato di sociologia generale* (Florence: G. Barbéra, 1916–23).

————. *Les systèmes socialistes.* 2 vols. 2d ed. Paris: Giard, 1926.

Reich, Wilhelm. *The Mass Psychology of Fascism.* Translated by Theodor P. Wolfe. New York: Orgone Institute, 1946.

Rousset, David. *Les jours de nôtre mort.* Paris: Éditions du Pavois, 1947.

———. *L'univers concentrationnaire.* Paris: Édition du Pavois, 1946. Translated by Ramon Guthrie as *The Other Kingdom* (1946; reprint, New York: Fertig, 1982).

Salvemini, Gaetano. *Under the Axe of Fascism.* New York: Viking, 1936.

Sas, Gyula. "The Nature and Historical Significance of Fascism." In *Marxists in Face of Fascism: Writings by Marxists on Fascism from the Inter-War Period,* edited by David Beetham, 113–21. Totowa, N.J.: Barnes and Noble Books, 1984.

Schmitt, Carl. *Der Begriff des Politischen.* Berlin: Duncker und Humblot, 1932. Translated by George Schwab as *The Concept of the Political,* with a foreward by Tracy B. Strong (Chicago: University of Chicago Press, 1996).

———. *Der Hüter der Verfassung.* Tübingen: Mohr, 1931.

———. *Legalität und Legitimität.* Munich: Duncker und Humblot, 1932.

———. *Political Theology.* Translated by George Schwab. Cambridge, Mass.: MIT Press, 1985. Originally published as *Politische Theologie* (Munich: Duncker und Humblot, 1922).

———. *Staat, Bewegung, Volk.* Hamburg: Hanseatische Verlagsanstalt, 1935.

Serge, Victor. *Memoires d'un révolutionaire, 1901–1941.* Paris: Éditions du Seuil, 1978.

———. *Les révolutionnaires.* Paris: Éditions du Seuil, 1967.

———. *Russia Twenty Years After.* Edited by Susan Weissman. Translated by Max Schachtman. Atlantic Highlands, N.J.: Humanities, 1996.

Seydewitz, Max. *Es hat sich gelohnt zu leben: Lebenserinnerungen eines alten Arbeiterfunktionärs.* 2 vols. Berlin: Dietz, 1976–78.

Silone, Ignazio. *Bread and Wine.* Rev. ed. With an afterword by Marx Slonim. Translated by Harvey Fergusson II. New York: New American Library, 1963.

———. *Emergency Exit.* Edited by Ruth Nanda Anshen. New York: Harper and Row, 1968.

———. *Der Faczismus: Seine Entstehung und seine Entwicklung.* Zurich: Europaverlag, 1934.

———. *Fontamara.* With an introduction by Irving Howe. Translated by Eric Mosbacher. New York: New American Library, 1981.

———. *The School for Dictators.* Translated by Gwenda David and Eric Mosbacher. New York: Harper and Brothers, 1938.

Speier, Hans. *German White-Collar Workers and the Rise of Hitler.* New Haven, Conn.: Yale University Press, 1986.

Stalin, Joseph. "The Period of Bourgeois-Democratic Pacifism." In *Marxists in Face of Fascism: Writings by Marxists on Fascism from the Inter-War Period,* edited by David Beetham, 153–54. Totowa, N.J.: Barnes and Noble Books, 1984.

Strauss, Leo. *Natural Right and History.* Chicago: University of Chicago, 1953.

———. *On Tyranny.* Rev. ed. including the Strauss-Kojève Correspondence. Edited and with an introduction by Victor Gourevitch and Michael S. Roth. New York: Free Press, 1991.

———. *Persecution and the Art of Writing*. Glencoe, Ill.: Free Press, 1952.

Trevor-Roper, Hugh. "Ex-Communist v. Communist." *Manchester Guardian*, July 10, 1950.

Trotsky, Leon. *Fascism: What It Is, How to Fight It*. New York: Pioneer Publishers, 1944.

———. "For a Workers' United Front against Fascism." In *Marxists in Face of Fascism: Writings by Marxists on Fascism from the Inter-War Period*, edited by David Beetham, 208–11. Totowa, N.J.: Barnes and Noble Books, 1984.

———. *My Life*. New York: Pathfinder, 1970.

———. *The Revolution Betrayed: What Is the Soviet Union and Where Is It Going?* Translated by Max Eastman. 1937. Reprint, New York: Pathfinder, 1972.

———. *The Struggle against Fascism in Germany (1930–40)*. With an introduction by Ernest Mandel. Edited by George Breitman and Merry Maisel. New York: Pathfinder, 1971.

———. *Writings of Leon Trotsky (1936–37)*. Edited by Naomi Allen and George Breitman. New York: Pathfinder, 1978.

Zetkin, Clara. "The Struggle against Fascism." In *Marxists in Face of Fascism: Writings by Marxists on Fascism from the Inter-War Period*, edited by David Beetham, 102–13. Totowa, N.J.: Barnes and Noble Books, 1984.

———. *Trotzkis Verbannung und die Sozialdemokratie*. Berlin: Internationaler Arbeiter, 1928.

Selected Writings about Key Individuals and Groups Discussed

Adler, Frank. "Thalheimer, Bonapartism and Fascism." *Telos*, no. 40 (Summer 1979): 95–108.

Anderson, Perry. *Considerations on Western Marxism*. London: New Left Books, 1976.

Arato, Andrew, and Paul Breines. *The Young Lukács and the Origins of Western Marxism*. New York: Seabury, 1979.

Beier, Christel. *Zum Verhältnis von Gesellschaftstheorie und Erkenntnistheorie: Untersuchungen zum Totalitätsbegriff in der kritischen Theorie Adornos*. Frankfurt am Main: Suhrkamp, 1977.

Bendersky, Joseph W. *Carl Schmitt: Theorist for the Reich*. Princeton, N.J.: Princeton University Press, 1983.

———, ed. and trans. "Interrogation of Carl Schmitt by Robert Kempner." *Telos*, no. 72 (Summer 1987): 97–107.

Benhabib, Seyla. *Critique, Norm, and Utopia: A Study of the Foundations of Critical Theory*. New York: Columbia University Press, 1986.

———. *The Reluctant Modernism of Hannah Arendt*. Thousand Oaks, Calif.: Sage Publications, 1996.

———. *Situating the Self: Gender, Community and Postmodernism in Contemporary Ethics*. New York: Routledge, 1992.

Benhabib, Seyla, Wolfgang Bonß, and John McCole, eds. *On Max Horkheimer: New Perspectives*. Cambridge, Mass.: MIT Press, 1993.

Berding, Helmut. "Arthur Rosenberg." In *Deutsche Historiker,* vol. 4, edited by Hans-Ulrich Wehler, 81–96. Göttingen: Vandenhoeck und Ruprecht, 1972.

Bernstein, Richard T. "Herbert Marcuse: An Immanent Critique." *Social Theory and Practice* 1, no. 4 (1971): 97–111.

Bonß, Wolfgang, and Axel Honneth, eds. *Sozialforschung als Kritik: Zum sozialwissenschaftlichen Potential der Kritischen Theorie.* Frankfurt am Main: Suhrkamp, 1982.

Bottomore, Thomas. *The Frankfurt School.* Sussex: Ellis Horwood, 1984.

Bottomore, Thomas, and Patrick Goode, eds. and trans. *Austro-Marxism.* With an introduction by Tom Bottomore. Oxford: Oxford University Press, 1978.

Breines, Paul. "Korsch's Road to Marx." *Telos,* no. 26 (Winter 1975–76): 42–56.

———. "Praxis and Its Theorists: The Impact of Lukács and Korsch in the 1920s." *Telos,* no. 11 (Spring 1972): 67–103.

Brightman, Carol, ed. *Between Friends: The Correspondence of Hannah Arendt and Mary McCarthy, 1949–1975.* New York: Harcourt, Brace, 1995.

Bronner, Stephen Eric. *Moments of Decision: Political History and the Crises of Radicalism.* New York: Routledge, 1992.

———. *Of Critical Theory and Its Theorists.* Cambridge, Mass.: Blackwell, 1994.

———. *Rosa Luxemburg: A Revolutionary for Our Times.* New York: Columbia University Press, 1987.

———, ed. and trans. *The Letters of Rosa Luxemburg.* Atlantic Highlands, N.J.: Humanities, 1993.

Buchstein, Hubertus. "Totalitarismustheorie und empirische Politikforschung—die Wandlung der Totalitarismuskonzeption in der frühen Berliner Politikforschung." In *Totalitarismus: Eine Ideengeschichte des 20. Jahrhunderts,* edited by Alfons Söllner, Ralf Walkenhaus, and Karin Wieland, 239–66. Berlin: Akademie, 1997.

Buckmiller, Michael. "Die 'Marxistische Arbeitswoche' 1923 und die Gründung des 'Instituts für Sozialforschung.'" In *Grand Hotel Abgrund: Eine Photobiographie der Kritischen Theorie,* edited by Gunzelin Schmid Noerr and Willem van Reijen, 141–82. Hamburg: Junius, 1988.

———, ed. *Zur Aktualität von Karl Korsch.* Frankfurt am Main: Europäische Verlagsanstalt, 1981.

Buck-Morss, Susan. *The Origin of Negative Dialectics: Theodor Adorno, Walter Benjamin, and the Frankfurt Institute.* New York: Free Press, 1977.

Campbell, Stuart L. "The Four Paretos of Raymond Aron." *Journal of the History of Ideas* 47, no. 2 (1986): 287–98.

Carsten, Francis. "Arthur Rosenberg: Ancient Historian into Leading Communist." *Journal of Contemporary History* 8, no. 1 (1973): 63–75.

Chrétien-Goni, Jean-Pierre, Iskender Gokalp, Danièle Guillerm, Christian Lazzeri, and Dominique Wolton, eds. *L'ésprit du mécanisme: Science et société chez Franz Borkenau.* Cahiers S.T.S., Science-Technologie-Société, no. 7. Paris: Éditions du Centre National de la Recherche Scientifique, 1985.

Coleman, Peter. *The Liberal Conspiracy: The Congress for Cultural Freedom and the Struggle for the Mind of Postwar Europe.* New York: Free Press, 1989.

Congdon, Lee. *The Young Lukács.* Chapel Hill: University of North Carolina Press, 1983.

Connerton, Paul. *The Tragedy of Enlightenment: An Essay on the Frankfurt School.* Cambridge: Cambridge University Press, 1980.

Crick, Bernard. *George Orwell: A Life.* Harmondworth, England: Penguin Books, 1980.

Dubiel, Helmut. "Domination or Emancipation? The Debate over the Heritage of Critical Theory." In *Cultural-Political Interventions in the Unfinished Project of Enlightenment,* edited by Axel Honneth et al., 3–16. Cambridge, Mass.: MIT Press, 1992.

———. *Wissenschaftsorganisation und politische Erfahrung: Studien zur frühen Kritischen Theorie.* Frankfurt am Main: Suhrkamp, 1978. Translated by Benjamin Gregg as *Theory and Politics: Studies in the Development of Critical Theory,* with an introduction by Martin Jay (Cambridge, Mass.: MIT Press, 1985).

Erd, Rainer, ed. *Reform und Resignation: Gespräche über Franz L. Neumann.* Frankfurt am Main: Suhrkamp, 1985.

Fleming, Donald, and Bernard Bailyn, eds. *The Intellectual Migration: Europe and America, 1930–1960.* Cambridge, Mass.: Harvard University Press, Belknap Press, 1969.

Foitzik, Jan. *Zwischen den Fronten: Zur Politik, Organization und Funktion linker politischer Kleinorganisationen im Widerstand, 1933 bis 1939/40.* Bonn: Verlag Neue Gesellschaft, 1986.

Geras, Norman. *The Legacy of Rosa Luxemburg.* London: New Left Books, 1976.

Goode, Patrick. *Karl Korsch: A Study in Western Marxism.* London: Macmillan, 1979.

Gottschalch, Wilhelm. *Strukturveränderungen der Gesellschaft und politisches Handeln in der Lehre von Rudolf Hilferding.* Berlin: Duncker und Humblot, 1962.

Habermas, Jürgen. "Remarks on the Development of Horkheimer's Work." In *On Max Horkheimer: New Perspectives,* edited by Seyla Benhabib, Wolfgang Bonß, and John McCole, 49–65. Cambridge, Mass.: MIT Press, 1993.

Haupt, Heinz-Gerhard. "Rudolf Hilferding." In *Deutsche Historiker,* vol. 8, edited by Hans-Ulrich Wehler, 56–77. Göttingen: Vandenhoeck und Ruprecht, 1982.

Held, David. *Introduction to Critical Theory: Horkheimer to Habermas.* Berkeley: University of California Press, 1980.

Heller, Agnes, ed. *Lukács Reappraised.* New York: Columbia University Press, 1983.

Hering, Sabine, and Kurt Schilde. *Kampfname Ruth Fischer: Wandlungen einer deutschen Kommunistin.* Frankfurt am Main: Dipa, 1995.

Heym, Stefan. *Radek.* Munich: Bertelsmann, 1995.

Hinchman, Lewis, and Sandra Hinchman, eds. *Hannah Arendt: Critical Essays.* Albany: State University of New York Press, 1993.

Honeycutt, Karen. "Clara Zetkin: A Socialist Approach to the Problem of Women's Oppression." *Feminist Studies* 3, nos. 3/4 (1976): 131–44.

————. "Clara Zetkin and the Women's Social Democratic Movement in Germany." Ph.D. diss., Columbia University, 1976.

Hughes, H. Stuart. "Franz Neumann between Marxism and Liberal Democracy." In *The Intellectual Migration: Europe and America, 1930–1960,* edited by Donald Fleming and Bernard Bailyn, 446–62. Cambridge, Mass.: Harvard University Press, Belknap Press, 1969.

Jacoby, Henry, and Ingrid Herbst. *Otto Rühle zur Einführung.* Hamburg: Junius, 1984.

Jacoby, Russell. *Dialectic of Defeat: Contours of Western Marxism.* Cambridge: Cambridge University Press, 1981.

————. "Postscript to Horkheimer's 'The Authoritarian State.'" *Telos,* no. 15 (Spring 1973): 21–24

Jay, Martin. *Adorno.* Cambridge, Mass.: Harvard University Press, 1984.

————. *Cultural Semantics: Keywords of Our Time.* Amherst: University of Massachusetts Press, 1998.

————. *The Dialectical Imagination: A History of the Frankfurt School and the Institute of Social Research, 1923–1950.* Boston: Little, Brown, 1973.

————. *Marxism and Totality: The Adventures of a Concept from Lukács to Habermas.* Berkeley: University of California Press, 1984.

————. *Permanent Exiles: Essays on the Intellectual Migration from Germany to America.* New York: Columbia University Press, 1986.

————. "Reconciling the Irreconcilable? Rejoinder to Kennedy." *Telos,* no. 71 (Spring 1987): 67–80.

————. Review of *Weimar's Left-Wing Intellectuals,* by Istvan Deak. *Commentary* 48, no. 4 (1969): 94–98.

Jones, William David. "The Path from Weimar Communism to the Cold War: Franz Borkenau and *The Totalitarian Enemy.*" In *Totalitarismus: Eine Ideengeschichte des 20. Jahrhunderts,* edited by Alfons Söllner, Ralf Walkenhaus, and Karin Wieland, 35–52. Berlin: Akademie, 1997.

————. "Toward a Theory of Totalitarianism: Franz Borkenau's *Pareto.*" *Journal of the History of Ideas* 53, no. 3 (1992): 455–66.

Katz, Barry. "The Criticism of Arms: The Frankfurt School Goes to War." *Journal of Modern History* 59 (September 1987): 437–78.

————. *Herbert Marcuse and the Art of Liberation: An Intellectual Biography.* London: Verso, 1982.

Kellner, Douglas. *Critical Theory, Marxism, and Modernity.* Baltimore: Johns Hopkins University Press, 1989.

————. "The Frankfurt School Revisited." *New German Critique* 4 (Winter 1975): 131–52.

————. *Herbert Marcuse and the Crisis of Marxism.* Berkeley: University of California Press, 1984.

————. "Korsch's Revolutionary Historicism." *Telos,* no. 26 (Winter 1975–76): 70–93.

————, ed. *Karl Korsch: Revolutionary Theory.* Austin: University of Texas Press, 1977.

Kennedy, Ellen. "Carl Schmitt and the Frankfurt School." *Telos,* no. 71 (Spring 1987): 37–66.

———. "Carl Schmitt and the Frankfurt School: A Rejoinder." *Telos,* no. 73 (Fall 1987): 101–16.

Kielmansegg, Peter Graf, Horst Mewes, and Elisabeth Glaser-Schmidt, eds. *Hannah Arendt and Leo Strauss: German Émigrés and American Political Thought after World War II.* Cambridge: German Historical Institute and Cambridge University Press, 1995.

Kitchen, Martin. "August Thalheimer's Theory of Fascism." *Journal of the History of Ideas* 34, no. 1 (1973): 67–78.

Kliem, Kurt. "Der sozialistische Widerstand gegen das Dritte Reich, dargestellt an der Gruppe 'Neu Beginnen.'" Ph.D. diss., Marburg, 1957.

Kolakowski, Leszek. *Main Currents of Marxism.* 3 vols. Oxford: Oxford University Press, 1978.

Kornder, Hans-Jürgen. *Konterrevolution und Faschismus: Zur Analyse von National-sozialismus, Faschismus und Totalitarismus im Werk von Karl Korsch.* Frankfurt am Main: Peter Lang, 1987.

Kurotake, Masaaki. "Zur Todesursache Rudolf Hilferdings." *Beiträge der Miyagi-Gakuin Frauenhochschule* 61 (December 1984): 1–21.

Liebich, André. *From the Other Shore: Russian Social Democracy after 1921.* Cambridge, Mass.: Harvard University Press, 1997.

———. "Marxism and Totalitarianism: Rudolf Hilferding and the Mensheviks." *Dissent* 34 (Spring 1987): 223–40.

———. *Marxism and Totalitarianism: Rudolf Hilferding and the Mensheviks.* Occasional Paper 217. Washington, D.C.: Kennan Institute of Advanced Russian Studies, 1987.

———. "Mensheviks Wage the Cold War." *Journal of Contemporary History* 30, no. 2 (1995): 247–64.

Linz, Juan. "Totalitarianism and Authoritarianism: My Recollections on the Development of Comparative Politics." In *Totalitarismus: Eine Ideengeschichte des 20. Jahrhunderts,* edited by Alfons Söllner, Ralf Walkenhaus, and Karin Wieland, 141–57. Berlin: Akademie, 1997.

Löwy, Michael. *Georg Lukács: From Romanticism to Bolshevism.* Translated by Patrick Camiller. London: New Left Books, 1979.

———. "Partisan Truth: Knowledge and Social Classes in Critical Theory." In *Foundations of the Frankfurt School of Social Research,* edited by Judith Marcus and Zoltán Tar, 289–304. New Brunswick, N.J.: Transaction Books, 1984.

Lunn, Eugene. *Marxism and Modernism: An Historical Study of Lukács, Brecht, Benjamin, and Adorno.* Berkeley: University of California Press, 1984.

MacIntyre, Alasdair. *Herbert Marcuse: An Exposition and a Polemic.* New York: Viking, 1970.

Marcus, Judith, and Zoltán Tar, eds. *Foundations of the Frankfurt School of Social Research.* New Brunswick, N.J.: Transaction Books, 1984.

Mehringer, Hartmut. *Waldemar von Knoeringen: Der Weg vom revolutionären Sozialismus zur sozialen Demokratie.* Munich: Saur, 1989.

Möller, Dietrich. *Revolutionär, Intrigant, Diplomat: Karl Radek in Deutschland.* Cologne: Verlag Wissenschaft und Politik, 1976.

Müller, Rudolf Wolfgang, and Gert Schäfer, eds. *Arthur Rosenberg zwischen Alter Geschichte und Zeitgeschichte, Politk und politischer Bildung.* Göttingen: Muster-Schmidt, 1986.

Nettl, J. P. *Rosa Luxemburg.* 2 vols. New York: Oxford University Press, 1966.

Perels, Joachim, ed. *Recht, Demokratie und Kapitalismus: Aktualität und Probleme der Theorie Franz L. Neumanns.* Baden-Baden: Nomos, 1984.

Preuss, Ulrich K. "The Critique of German Liberalism: Reply to Kennedy." *Telos,* no. 71 (Spring 1987): 97–109.

Pross, Helge. *Die deutsche akademische Emigration nach den Vereinigten Staaten, 1933–41.* Berlin: Duncker und Humblot, 1955.

Quataert, Jean. *Reluctant Feminists in German Social Democracy, 1885–1917.* Princeton, N.J.: Princeton University Press, 1979.

Rabinbach, Anson. *In the Shadow of Catastrophe: German Intellectuals between Apocalypse and Enlightenment.* Berkeley: University of California Press, 1997.

Rai, Alok. *Orwell and the Politics of Despair: A Critical Study of the Writings of George Orwell.* Cambridge: Cambridge University Press, 1988.

Reijen, Willem van, and Gunzelin Schmid Noerr, eds. *Vierzig Jahre Flaschenpost: "Dialektik der Aufklärung," 1947 bis 1987.* Frankfurt am Main: Fischer, 1987.

Reinecke, Volker. *Kultur und Todesantinomie: Die Geschichtsphilosophie Franz Borkenaus.* Vienna: Passagen, 1992.

Rocco, Christopher. "Between Modernity and Postmodernity: Reading *Dialectic of Enlightenment* against the Grain." *Political Theory* 22, no. 1 (1994): 71–97.

Rusconi, Gian Enrico. "Korsch's Political Development." *Telos,* no. 27 (Spring 1976): 61–78.

Russo, Valeria E. "Franz Borkenau e l'origine del moderno." *La politica* 1 (June 1985): 110–14.

———. "Henryk Grossmann and Franz Borkenau: A Bio-Bibliography." *Science in Context* 1, no. 1 (1987): 181–91.

———. "Profilo di Franz Borkenau." *Rivista di filosofia* 20 (June 1981): 291–316.

———. "A Proposito di un'interpretazione sociologica del fascismo." *Dimensioni* 20 (September 1981): 39–46.

———. "Les transformations de l'image du monde: Notes sur Franz Borkenau." In *L'ésprit du mécanisme: Science et société chez Franz Borkenau,* edited by Jean-Pierre Chrétien-Goni et al., 133–54. Cahiers S.T.S., Science-Technologie-Société, no. 7. Paris: Éditions du Centre National de la Recherche Scientifique, 1985.

Schäfer, Gert. "Geschichtsschreibung und politische Erfahrung bei Arthur Rosenberg." In *Arthur Rosenberg zwischen Alter Geschichte und Zeitgeschichte, Politk und politischer Bildung,* edited by Rudolf Wolfgang Müller and Gert Schäfer, 115–34. Göttingen: Muster-Schmidt, 1986.

Scheuerman, William. *Between the Norm and the Exception: The Frankfurt School and the Rule of Law*. Cambridge, Mass.: MIT Press, 1994.

———. "Legal Indeterminacy and the Origins of Nazi Legal Thought: The Case of Carl Schmitt." *History of Political Thought* 17, no. 4 (1996): 571–90.

Schmid Noerr, Gunzelin, and Willem van Reijen, eds. *Grand Hotel Abgrund: Eine Photobiographie der Kritischen Theorie*. Hamburg: Junius, 1988.

Schneeberger, Guido. *Nachlese zu Heidegger: Dokumenten zu seinem Leben und Denken*. Bern: Suhr, 1962.

Sitton, John F. "Hannah Arendt's Argument for Council Democracy." In *Hannah Arendt: Critical Essays*, edited by Lewis Hinchman and Sandra Hinchman, 307–34. Albany: State University of New York Press, 1993.

Slater, Phil. *Origin and Significance of the Frankfurt School: A Marxist Perspective*. London: Routledge and Kegan Paul, 1977.

Smaldone, William. *Rudolf Hilferding: The Tragedy of a German Social Democrat*. De Kalb: Northern Illinois University Press, 1998.

———. "Rudolf Hilferding and the Theoretical Foundations of German Social Democracy, 1902–33." *Central European History* 21, no. 3 (1988): 267–99.

———. "Rudolf Hilferding and the Total State." *Historian* 57 (August 1994): 97–112.

Söllner, Alfons. "Beyond Carl Schmitt: Political Theory in the Frankfurt School." *Telos,* no. 71 (Spring 1987): 81–96.

———. "Franz Neumann." *Telos,* no. 50 (Winter 1981–82): 171–79.

———. "Franz L. Neumann—Skizzen zu einer intellektuellen und politischen Biographie." In *Wirtschaft, Staat, Demokratie: Aufsätze, 1930–1954*, by Franz L. Neumann, 7–56. Frankfurt am Main: Suhrkamp, 1978.

———. *Geschichte und Herrschaft: Studien zur materialistischen Sozialwissenschaft, 1929–1942*. Frankfurt am Main: Suhrkamp, 1979.

———. "Leftist Students of the Conservative Revolution: Neumann, Kirchheimer and Marcuse." *Telos,* no. 61 (Fall 1984): 55–70.

———. *Neumann zur Einführung*. Hamburg: Junius, 1982.

———. "'The Philosopher Not as King': La théorie politique de Herbert Marcuse dans les années quarante et cinquante." *Archives de philosophie* 52, no. 3 (1989): 427–42.

———. "Das Totalitarismuskonzept in der Ideengeschichte des 20. Jahrhunderts." In *Totalitarismus: Eine Ideengeschichte des 20. Jahrhunderts*, edited by Alfons Söllner, Ralf Walkenhaus, and Karin Wieland, 10–21. Berlin: Akademie, 1997.

———, ed. *Zur Archäologie der Demokratie in Deutschland*. 2 vols. Frankfurt am Main: Fischer, 1986.

Söllner, Alfons, Ralf Walkenhaus, and Karin Wieland, eds. *Totalitarismus: Eine Ideengeschichte des 20. Jahrhunderts*. Berlin: Akademie, 1997.

Tar, Zoltán. *The Frankfurt School: The Critical Theories of Max Horkheimer and Theodor W. Adorno*. New York: John Wiley and Sons, 1977.

Tashjean, John E. "Borkenau: The Rediscovery of a Thinker." *Partisan Review* 51, no. 2 (1984): 289–300.

———. "Borkenau on Marx: An Intellectual Biography." *Wiseman Review*, no. 235 (Summer 1961): 149–57.

———. "Franz Borkenau: A Study of His Social and Political Ideas." Ph.D. diss., Georgetown University, 1962.

Ulmen, G. L. *The Science of Society: Toward an Understanding of the Life and Work of Karl August Wittfogel*. The Hague: Mouton, 1978.

Wagner, F. Peter. *Rudolf Hilferding: Theory and Politics of Democratic Socialism*. Atlantic Highlands, N.J.: Humanities, 1996.

Weitz, Eric D. "'Rosa Luxemburg Belongs to Us!': German Communism and the Luxemburg Legacy." *Central European History* 27, no. 1 (1994): 27–64.

Wieland, Karin. "'Totalitarismus' als Rache: Ruth Fischer und ihr Buch 'Stalin and German Communism.'" In *TotalitarismusIn Totalitarismus: Eine Ideengeschichte des 20. Jahrhunderts,* edited by Alfons Söllner, Ralf Walkenhaus, and Karin Wieland, 117–38. Berlin: Akademie, 1997.

Wiggershaus, Rolf. *Die Frankfurter Schule: Geschichte, Theoretische Entwicklung, Politische Bedeutung*. Munich: Deutscher Taschenbuch, 1988. Translated by Michael Robertson as *The Frankfurt School: Its History, Theories, and Political Significance* (Cambridge, Mass.: MIT Press, 1994).

———. *Theodor W. Adorno*. Munich: Beck, 1987.

Wilson, Michael. *Das Institut für Sozialforschung und seine Faschismusanalysen*. Frankfurt am Main: Campus, 1982.

Wolin, Richard. "Carl Schmitt, Political Existentialism, and the Total State." *Theory and Society* 19, no. 4 (1990): 389–416.

———. *Labyrinths: Explorations in the Critical History of Ideas*. Amherst: University of Massachusetts Press, 1995.

———. *The Terms of Cultural Criticism: The Frankfurt School, Existentialism, Poststructuralism*. New York: Columbia University Press, 1992.

———, ed. *The Heidegger Controversy: A Critical Reader*. Cambridge, Mass.: MIT Press, 1993.

Worster, Donald. *Rivers of Empire: Water, Aridity, and the Growth of the American West*. New York: Oxford University Press, 1985.

———. *Under Western Skies: Nature and History in the American West*. New York: Oxford University Press, 1992.

Young-Bruehl, Elisabeth. *Hannah Arendt: For Love of the World*. New Haven, Conn.: Yale University Press, 1982.

Selected Writings on Political Theory and Twentieth-Century European History

Abraham, David. *The Collapse of the Weimar Republic*. 2d ed. Princeton, N.J.: Princeton University Press, 1987.

Adler, Les K., and Thomas G. Paterson. "Red Fascism: The Merger of Nazi Germany and Soviet Russia in the American Image of Totalitarianism, 1930s-1950s." *American Historical Review* 75, no. 4 (1970): 1046–64.

Alba, Victor, and Stephen Schwartz. *Spanish Marxism versus Soviet Communism: A History of the P.O.U.M.* New Brunswick, N.J.: Transaction Books, 1988.

Allardyce, Gilbert. "What Fascism Is Not: Thoughts on the Deflation of a Concept." *American Historical Review* 84, no. 2 (1979): 367–88.

Angress, Werner. *Stillborn Revolution: The Communist Bid for Power in Germany, 1921–1923.* Princeton, N.J.: Princeton University Press, 1963.

Arato, Andrew, and Jean Cohen. *Civil Society and Political Theory.* Cambridge, Mass.: MIT Press, 1992.

———. "Politics and the Reconstruction of the Concept of Civil Society." In *Cultural-Political Interventions in the Unfinished Project of Enlightenment,* edited by Axel Honneth et al., 121–42. Cambridge, Mass.: MIT Press, 1992.

Atwood, Margaret. *The Handmaid's Tale.* Boston: Houghton Mifflin, 1986.

Ayçoberry, Pierre. *The Nazi Question: An Essay on the Interpretations of National Socialism (1922–1975).* Translated by Robert Hurley. London: Routledge and Kegan Paul, 1981. Originally published as *La question nazi* (Paris: Seuil, 1979).

Baldwin, Peter, ed. *Reworking the Past: Hitler, the Holocaust, and the Historians' Debate.* Boston: Beacon, 1990.

Benz, Wolfgang, and Walter H. Pehle, eds. *Encyclopedia of German Resistance to the Nazi Movement.* New York: Continuum, 1997.

Berghahn, Volker. *Modern Germany: Society, Economy and Politics in the Twentieth Century.* Cambridge: Cambridge University Press, 1987.

Berghahn, Volker, and Martin Kitchen, eds. *Germany in the Age of Total War: Essays in Honor of Francis Carsten.* Totowa, N.J.: Barnes and Noble Books, 1981.

Bernstein, Richard J. "Foucault: Critique as a Philosophical Ethos." In *Critique and Power: Recasting the Foucault/Habermas Debate,* edited by Michael Kelly, 211–41. Cambridge, Mass.: MIT Press, 1994.

Bessel, Richard, ed. *Fascist Italy and Nazi Germany: Comparisons and Contrasts.* Cambridge: Cambridge University Press, 1996.

Blinkhorn, Martin, ed. *Fascists and Conservatives.* London: Unwin Hyman, 1990.

Bock, Hans Manfred. *Geschichte des "linken Radikalismus" in Deutschland: Ein Versuch.* Frankfurt am Main: Suhrkamp, 1976.

Bolloten, Burnett. *The Grand Camouflage: The Communist Conspiracy in the Spanish Civil War.* New York: Praeger, 1961.

———. *The Spanish Revolution: The Left and the Struggle for Power during the Civil War.* Chapel Hill: University of North Carolina Press, 1979.

Bracher, Karl Dietrich. *Die Auflösung der Weimarer Republik: Eine Studie zum Problem des Machtverfalls in der Demokratie.* Stuttgart: Ring, 1955.

———. *Die deutsche Diktatur: Entstehung, Struktur, Folgen des Nationalsozialismus.* Berlin: Kiepenheuer und Witsch, 1969. Translated by Jean Steinberg as *The German Dictatorship: The Origins, Structure, and Effects of National Socialism* (New York: Praeger, 1970).

———. "Letter to the Editor of the *Frankfurter Allgemeine Zeitung,* September 6, 1986." In *Forever in the Shadow of Hitler? Original Documents of the Historikerstreit, the Controversy concerning the Singularity of the Holocaust,* translated by James Knowlton and Truett Cates, 72–73. Atlantic Highlands, N.J.: Humanities, 1993.

———. *Die totalitäre Erfahrung.* Munich: Piper, 1987.

———. "Totalitarianism." In *Dictionary of the History of Ideas,* vol. 4, edited by Philip P. Wiener, 406–11. New York: Scribner, 1974.

———. *Turning Points in Modern Times: Essays on German and European History.* With a foreword by Abbott Gleason. Translated by Thomas Dunlap. Cambridge, Mass.: Harvard University Press, 1995. Originally published as *Wendezeiten der Geschichte: Historisch-politische Essays 1987–1992* (Stuttgart: Deutsche Verlagsanstalt, 1992).

———. *Zeitgeschichtliche Kontroversen: Um Faschismus, Totalitarismus, Demokratie.* Munich: Piper, 1984.

Bracher, Karl Dietrich, Wolfgang Sauer, and Gerhard Schulz. *Die nationalsozialistische Machtergreifung: Studien zur Errichtung des totalitären Herrschaftssystems in Deutschland, 1933/34.* Cologne: Westdeutscher, 1962.

Braunthal, Gerard. *The German Social Democrats since 1969: A Party in Power and Opposition.* Boulder, Colo.: Westview, 1993.

Breitman, Richard. *The Architect of Genocide: Himmler and the Final Solution.* New York: Knopf, 1991.

———. *German Socialism and Weimar Democracy.* Chapel Hill: University of North Carolina Press, 1981.

———. "Negative Integration and Parliamentary Politics: Literature on German Social Democracy, 1890–1933." *Central European History* 13, no. 2 (1980): 175–97.

Bridenthal, Renate, Atina Grossmann, and Marion Kaplan, eds. *When Biology Became Destiny: Women in Weimar and Nazi Germany.* New York: Monthly Review Press, 1984.

Broszat, Martin. *Hitler and the Collapse of Weimar Germany.* Translated by V. R. Berghahn. Leamington Spa: Berg, 1987. Originally published as *Die Machtergreifung: Der Aufstieg der NSDAP und die Zerstörung der Weimarer Republik* (Munich: Deutscher Taschenbuch, 1984).

———. *The Hitler State: The Foundation and Development of the Internal Structure of the Third Reich.* Translated by John Hiden. London: Longman, 1981. Originally published as *Der Staat Hitlers: Grundlegung und Entwicklung seiner inneren Verfassung* (Munich: Deutscher Taschenbuch, 1969).

———. *Nach Hitler: Der Schwierige Umgang mit unserer Geschichte.* Munich: Deutscher Taschenbuch, 1988.

Browning, Christopher R. *Ordinary Men: Reserve Police Battalion 101 and the Final Solution in Poland.* New York: Harper Collins, 1992.

———. *The Path to Genocide: Essays on Launching the Final Solution.* Cambridge: Cambridge University Press, 1992.

Brzezinski, Zbigniew. "The Soviet Political System: Transformation or Degeneration?" *Problems of Communism* 15, no. 1 (1966): 1–15.

Buchheim, Hans. *Totalitäre Herrschaft: Wesen und Merkmale.* Munich: Kösel, 1962.

Translated by Ruth Hein as *Totalitarian Rule: Its Nature and Characteristics* (Middletown, Conn.: Wesleyan University Press, 1968).

Burleigh, Michael, and Wolfgang Wippermann. *The Racial State: Germany, 1933–1945.* Cambridge: Cambridge University Press, 1991.

Caplan, Jane. *Government without Administration: State and Civil Service in Weimar and Nazi Germany.* Oxford: Clarendon Press/Oxford University Press, 1988.

———. "Theories of Fascism: Nicos Poulantzas as Historian." *History Workshop Journal,* no. 3 (Spring 1977): 83–100.

Carr, E. H. *The Comintern and the Spanish Civil War.* Edited by Tamara Deutscher. New York: Pantheon, 1984.

Carr, Raymond, ed. *The Republic and the Civil War in Spain.* London: Macmillan, 1971.

Carsten, Francis. *The German Workers and the Nazis.* Aldershot, England: Scolar, 1995.

———. *Revolution in Central Europe, 1918–1919.* Berkeley: University of California Press, 1972.

———. *The Rise of Fascism.* Berkeley: University of California Press, 1982.

Castoriadis, Cornelius. *Capitalisme moderne et révolution.* Paris: Union générale d'éditions, 1979.

———. *The Castoriadis Reader.* Translated by David Ames Curtis. Oxford: Blackwell, 1997.

———. *L'experience du mouvement ouvrier.* 2 vols. Paris: Union générale d'éditions, 1974.

———. *L'institution imaginare de la société.* Paris: Seuil, 1975.

———. *Philosophy, Politics, Autonomy: Essays in Political Philosophy.* Edited by David Ames Curtis. New York: Oxford University Press, 1991.

———. *Political and Social Writings.* 2 vols. Edited and translated by David Ames Curtis. Minneapolis: University of Minnesota Press, 1988.

———. "Power, Politics, Autonomy." In *Cultural-Political Interventions in the Unfinished Project of Enlightenment,* edited by Axel Honneth et al., 269–97. Cambridge, Mass.: MIT Press, 1992.

———. *La société bureaucratique.* Paris: Union générale d'éditions, 1973.

———. *La société française* (Paris: Union générale d'éditions, 1979).

Caute, David. *The Fellow-Travellers: A Postscript to the Enlightenment.* New York: Macmillan, 1973.

———. *The Great Fear: The Anti-Communist Purge under Truman and Eisenhower.* New York: Touchstone Books, 1979.

Ceplair, Larry. *Under the Shadow of War: Fascism, Anti-Fascism, and Marxists, 1918–1939.* New York: Columbia University Press, 1987.

Childers, Thomas. *The Nazi Voter: The Social Foundations of Fascism in Germany, 1919–1933.* Chapel Hill: University of North Carolina Press, 1983.

———, ed. *The Formation of the Nazi Constituency, 1919–1933.* Totowa, N.J.: Barnes and Noble Books, 1986.

Childers, Thomas, and Jane Caplan, eds. *Reevaluating the Third Reich.* With a fore-word by Charles S. Maier. New York: Holmes and Meier, 1993.

Cohen, Stephen F. *Rethinking the Soviet Experience: Politics and History since 1917.* New York: Oxford University Press, 1985.

Craig, Gordon. *Germany, 1866–1945.* Oxford: Oxford University Press, 1978.

———. *The Politics of the Prussian Army, 1640–1945.* Oxford: Oxford University Press, 1955.

Curtis, Michael. *Totalitarianism.* New Brunswick, N.J.: Transaction Books, 1979.

Dahrendorf, Ralf. "Totalitarianism Revisited." *Partisan Review* 55, no. 4 (1988): 541–54.

Daniels, Robert V. *The End of the Communist Revolution,* London: Routledge, 1993.

Dawidowicz, Lucy S. *The War against the Jews, 1933–1945.* 1976. Reprint, New York: Bantam, 1986.

De Felice, Renzo. *Interpretations of Fascism.* Translated by Brenda Huff Everett. Cambridge, Mass.: Harvard University Press, 1977.

De Grazia, Victoria. *The Culture of Consent: The Mass Organization of Leisure in Fascist Italy.* Cambridge and New York: Cambridge University Press, 1981.

———. *How Fascism Ruled Women: Italy, 1922–1945.* Berkeley: University of California Press, 1992.

Derrida, Jacques. *Specters of Marx: The State of the Debt, the Work of Mourning, and the New International.* Translated by Peggy Kamuf. New York: Routledge, 1994.

Diner, Dan, ed. *Ist der Nationalsozialismus Geschichte? Zu Historisierung und Historikerstreit.* Frankfurt am Main: Fischer, 1987.

Dirks, Nicholas B., Geoff Eley, and Sherry B. Ortner, eds. *Culture/Power/History: A Reader in Contemporary Social Theory.* Princeton, N.J.: Princeton University Press, 1994.

Disch, Lisa Jane. *Hannah Arendt and the Limits of Philosophy.* Ithaca, N.Y.: Cornell University Press, 1994.

Donia, Robert J., and John V. A. Fine. *Bosnia and Hercegovina: A Tradition Betrayed.* New York: Columbia University Press, 1994.

Duhnke, Horst. *Die KPD von 1933 bis 1945.* Cologne: Kiepenheuer und Witsch, 1972.

Dülffer, Jost. "Bonapartism, Fascism and National Socialism." *Journal of Contemporary History* 11, no. 4 (1976): 109–28.

Dutschke, Rudi. *Ein Versuch Lenin auf die Füße zu stellen: Über den halbasiatischen und den westeuropäischen Weg zum Sozialismus; Lenin, Lukács und die Dritte Internationale.* Berlin: Verlag Klaus Wagenbach, 1974.

Eatwell, Roger. *Fascism: A History.* New York: Penguin Books, 1996.

Edinger, Lewis J. *German Exile Politics: The Social Democratic Executive Commitee in the Nazi Era.* Berkeley: University of California Press, 1956.

———. *Kurt Schumacher: A Study in Personality and Political Behavior.* Stanford, Calif.: Stanford University Press, 1965.

Eley, Geoff. "Nations, Publics, and Political Cultures: Placing Habermas in the

Nineteenth Century." In *Culture/Power/History: A Reader in Contemporary Social Theory,* edited by Nicholas B. Dirks, Geoff Eley, and Sherry B. Ortner, 297–335. Princeton, N.J.: Princeton University Press, 1994.

Eley, Geoff, and David Blackbourn. *The Peculiarities of German History: Bourgeois Society and Politics in Nineteenth-Century Germany.* Oxford: Oxford University Press, 1984.

Escher, Felix. *Neukölln.* Berlin: Colloquium, 1988.

Evans, Richard J. *In Hitler's Shadow: West German Historians and the Attempt to Escape the Nazi Past.* New York: Pantheon, 1989.

———. *Rethinking German History: Nineteenth-Century Germany and the Origins of the Third Reich.* London: Unwin and Hyman, 1987.

Falter, Jürgen. "The Two Hindenburg Elections of 1925 and 1932: A Total Reversal of Voter Coalitions." *Central European History* 23, nos. 2/3 (1990): 225–41.

Figes, Orlando. *A People's Tragedy: A History of the Russian Revolution.* New York: Viking, 1997.

Finkelstein, Norman G., and Ruth Bettina Birn. *A Nation on Trial: The Goldhagen Thesis and Historical Truth.* New York: Henry Holt, 1998.

Fischer, Fritz. *Germany's Aims in the First World War.* 1961. Reprint, New York: Norton, 1967.

Fischer, Klaus P. *Nazi Germany: A New History.* New York: Continuum, 1995.

Fleming, Donald, and Bernard Bailyn. *The Intellectual Migration: Europe and America, 1930–1950.* Cambridge, Mass.: Harvard University Press, 1969.

Forever in the Shadow of Hitler? Original Documents of the Historikerstreit, the Controversy concerning the Singularity of the Holocaust. Translated by James Knowlton and Truett Cates (Atlantic Highlands, N.J.: Humanities, 1993). Originally published as *"Historikerstreit": Die Dokumentation der Kontroverse um die Einzigartigkeit der nationalsozialistischen Judenvernichtung* (Munich: Piper, 1989).

Foucault, Michel. *Discipline and Punish: The Birth of the Prison.* Translated by Alan Sheridan. New York: Vintage, 1977. Originally published as *Surveiller et Punir: Naissance de la prison* (Paris: Éditions Gallimard, 1975).

———. *Power/Knowledge: Selected Interviews and Other Writings, 1972–1977.* Edited by Colin Gordon. New York: Pantheon, 1980.

Fowkes, Ben. *Communism in Germany under the Weimar Republic.* London: Macmillan, 1984.

Fraser, Ronald. *Blood of Spain: An Oral History of the Spanish Civil War.* New York: Pantheon, 1979.

Friedländer, Saul, *Nazi Germany and the Jews.* Vol. 1, *The Years of Persecution, 1933–1939.* New York: Harper Collins, 1997.

———, ed. *Probing the Limits of Representation: Nazism and the "Final Solution."* Cambridge, Mass.: Harvard University Press, 1992.

Friedrich, Carl J. "Fascism versus Totalitarianism: Ernst Nolte's Views Reexamined." *Central European History* 4, no. 3 (1971): 271–84.

————, ed. *Totalitarianism: Proceedings of a Conference Held at the American Academy of Arts and Sciences, March 1953.* With an introduction by Carl J. Friedrich. Cambridge, Mass.: Harvard University Press, 1954.

Friedrich, Carl J., and Zbigniew Brzezinski. *Totalitarian Dictatorship and Autocracy.* Cambridge, Mass.: Harvard University Press, 1956; 2d ed., 1965.

Friedrich, Carl J., Michael Curtis, and Benjamin R. Barber. *Totalitarianism in Perspective: Three Views.* New York: Praeger, 1969.

Frisby, David. *The Alienated Mind: The Sociology of Knowledge in Germany, 1918–1933.* London: Heinemann, 1983.

Fritzsche, Peter. "Did Weimar Fail?" *Journal of Modern History* 68 (September 1996): 629–56.

————. *Germans into Nazis.* Cambridge, Mass.: Harvard University Press, 1998.

————. *Rehearsals for Fascism: Populism and Political Mobilization in Weimar Germany.* New York: Oxford University Press, 1990.

————. Review of *The End of History and the Last Man,* by Francis Fukuyama. *American Historical Review* 97, no. 3 (1992): 817–19.

Fukuyama, Francis. *The End of History and the Last Man.* New York: Free Press, 1992.

Funke, Manfred, ed. *Totalitarismus: Ein Studien-Reader zur Herrschaftsanalyse modernen Diktaturen.* Düsseldorf: Droste, 1978.

Furet, François. *Le passé d'une illusion: Essai sur l'idée communiste au XXe siècle.* Paris: Laffont/Calmann-Lévy, 1995.

Gates, Robert A. "German Socialism and the Crisis of 1929–33." *Central European History* 7, no. 4 (1974): 332–59.

Gay, Peter. *Weimar Culture: The Outsider as Insider.* New York: Harper and Row, 1968.

Geiss, Imanuel. *Die Habermas-Kontroverse: Ein deutscher Streit.* Berlin: Siedler, 1988.

Gentile, Emilio. "Fascism in Italian Historiography: In Search of an Individual Historical Identity." *Journal of Contemporary History* 21, no. 2 (1986): 179–208.

————. *Le origini dell'ideologia fascista.* Cremona: Cremona Nuova, 1975.

Getty, J. Arch, and Roberta A. Manning, eds. *Stalinist Terror: New Perspectives.* Cambridge: Cambridge University Press, 1993.

Gillingham, John R. *Industry and Politics in the Third Reich: Ruhr Coal, Hitler and Europe.* New York: Columbia University Press, 1985.

Gleason, Abbott. *Totalitarianism: The Inner History of the Cold War.* New York: Oxford University Press, 1995.

Goldhagen, Daniel Johah. *Hitler's Willing Executioners: Ordinary Germans and the Holocaust.* New York: Vintage Books/Random House, 1997.

Graf, William David. *The German Left since 1945: Socialism and Social Democracy in the German Federal Republic.* Cambridge: Oleander, 1976.

Gregor, A. James. *The Ideology of Fascism: The Rationale of Totalitarianism.* New York: Free Press, 1969.

————. *Interpretations of Fascism.* New Brunswick, N.J.: Transaction, 1997.

————. *Italian Fascism and Developmental Dictatorship.* Princeton, N.J.: Princeton University Press, 1979.

Greiffenhagen, Martin, R. Kühnl, and J. B. Müller, eds. *Totalitarismus: Zur Problematik eines politischen Begriffs*. Munich: List, 1972.

Griffin, Roger. *The Nature of Fascism*. New York: St. Martin's, 1991.

Grossman, Atina. "Abortion and Economic Crisis: The 1931 Campaign against §218 in Germany." *New German Critique* 14 (Spring 1978): 119–38.

Guttsman, W. L. *The German Social Democratic Party, 1875–1933: From Ghetto to Government*. London: Allen and Unwin, 1981.

Habermas, Jürgen. *Eine Art Schadensabwicklung*. Frankfurt am Main: Suhrkamp, 1987.

———. *A Berlin Republic: Writings on Germany*. With an introduction by Peter Uwe Hohendahl. Translated by Steven Rendall. Lincoln: University of Nebraska Press, 1997. Originally published as *Die Normalität einer Berliner Republik* (Frankfurt am Main: Suhrkamp, 1995).

———. *Between Facts and Norms: Contributions to a Discourse Theory of Law and Democracy*. Translated and with an introduction by William Rehg. Cambridge, Mass.: MIT Press, 1998. Originally published as *Faktizität und Geltung: Beiträge zur Diskurstheorie des Rechts und des demokratischen Rechtsstaats* (Frankfurt am Main: Suhrkamp, 1992).

———. *Knowledge and Human Interests*. Translated by Jeremy J. Shapiro. Boston: Beacon, 1971. Originally published as *Erkenntnis und Interesse* (Frankfurt am Main: Suhrkamp, 1968).

———. *Legitimation Crisis*. Translated by Thomas McCarthy. Boston: Beacon, 1975. Originally published as *Legitimationsprobleme im Spätkapitalismus*. Frankfurt am Main: Suhrkamp, 1973.

———. *Die Neue Unübersichtlichkeit*. Frankfurt am Main: Suhrkamp, 1985.

———. *The New Conservatism: Cultural Criticism and the Historians' Debate*. With an introduction by Richard Wolin. Edited and translated by Shierry Weber Nicholsen. Cambridge, Mass.: MIT Press, 1989.

———. *The Past as Future*. With a foreword by Peter Hohendahl. Translated by Max Pensky. Lincoln: University of Nebraska Press, 1994.

———. *Philosophical-Political Profiles*. Translated by Frederick Lawrence. Cambridge, Mass.: MIT Press, 1983. Originally published as *Philosophisch-politische Profile* (Frankfurt am Main: Suhrkamp, 1971).

———. *The Structural Transformation of the Public Sphere: An Inquiry into a Category of Bourgeois Society*. Translated by Thomas Burger and Frederick Lawrence. Cambridge, Mass.: MIT Press, 1989. Originally published as *Strukturwandel der Offentlichkeit* (Darmstadt: Hermann Luchterhand, 1962).

———. *Theory and Practice*. Translated by John Viertel. Boston: Beacon, 1973. Originally published as *Theorie und Praxis* (Frankfurt am Main: Suhrkamp, 1971).

———. *The Theory of Communicative Action*. 2 vols. Boston: Beacon, 1985.

Hagtvet, Bernt, and Reinhard Kühnl. "Contemporary Approaches to Fascism: A Survey of Paradigms." In *Who Were the Fascists? Social Roots of European Fascism*, edited by Stein Ugelvik Larsen, Bernt Hagtvet, and Jan Petter Myklebust, 26–51. Bergen: Universitetsforlaget, 1980.

Hamerow, Theodore S. *On The Road to the Wolf's Lair: German Resistance to Hitler.* Cambridge, Mass.: Harvard University Press, 1997.

Hamilton, Richard F. *Who Voted for Hitler?* Princeton, N.J.: Princeton University Press, 1982.

Harsch, Donna. *German Social Democracy and the Rise of Nazism.* Chapel Hill: University of North Carolina Press, 1993.

Havel, Václav. "The Velvet Hangover." Translated by Káca Poláčková Henley. *Harper's* 281 (October 1990): 18–21.

Hazareesingh, Sudhir. *Intellectuals and the French Communist Party: Disillusion and Decline.* New York: Oxford University Press, 1992.

Heilbut, Anthony. *Exiled in Paradise: German Refugee Artists and Intellectuals in America from the 1930's to the Present.* New York: Viking, 1983.

Hennig, Eike. *Bürgerliche Gesellschaft und Faschismus in Deutschland: Ein Forschungsbericht.* Frankfurt am Main: Suhrkamp, 1982.

———. *Thesen zur deutschen Sozial- und Wirtschaftsgeschichte, 1933 bis 1938.* Frankfurt am Main: Suhrkamp, 1973.

———. *Zum Historikerstreit: Was heißt und zu welchem Ende studiert man Faschismus?* Frankfurt am Main: Athenäum, 1988.

———. "Zur Theorie der Totalitarismustheorien oder Anmerkungen zum Nimbus eines politischen Begriffs." *Neue Politische Literatur* 21, no. 1 (1976): 1–25.

Herf, Jeffrey. *Reactionary Modernism: Technology, Culture, and Politics in Weimar and the Third Reich.* Cambridge: Cambridge University Press, 1984.

Hilberg, Raul. *The Destruction of the European Jews.* Chicago: Quadrangle Books, 1961.

———. *Perpetrators, Victims, Bystanders: The Jewish Catastrophe, 1933–1945.* New York: Harper Collins, 1992.

Hildebrand, Klaus. *Das Dritte Reich.* Munich: Oldenbourg, 1980.

Hillgruber, Andreas. *Zweierlei Untergang: Die Zerschlagung des deutschen Reiches und das Ende des europäischen Judentums.* Berlin: Corso bei Siedler, 1986.

Hitchens, Christopher. *For the Sake of Argument: Essays and Minority Reports.* London: Verso, 1993.

———. "Orwell on Trial." *Vanity Fair* 59 (October 1996): 142–49.

———. *Prepared for the Worst: Selected Essays and Minority Reports.* New York: Hill and Wang, 1988.

Hoffman, Peter. *German Resistance to Hitler.* Cambridge, Mass.: Harvard University Press, 1988.

———. *The History of the German Resistance, 1933–1945.* Translated by Richard Barry. Montreal: McGill–Queen's University Press, 1996.

Honneth, Axel. *The Critique of Power: Reflective Stages in a Critical Social Theory.* Translated by Kenneth Baynes. Cambridge, Mass.: MIT Press, 1991. Originally published as *Kritik Der Macht. Reflexionsstufen einer kritischen Gesellschaftstheorie* (Frankfurt am Main: Suhrkamp, 1985).

Honneth, Axel, Thomas McCarthy, Claus Offe, and Albrecht Wellmer, eds. *Cul-*

tural-Political Interventions in the Unfinished Project of Enlightenment. Translated by Barbara Fultner. Cambridge, Mass.: MIT Press, 1992.

Horn, Gerd-Rainer. *European Socialists Respond to Fascism: Ideology, Activism and Contingency in the 1930s.* New York: Oxford University Press, 1996.

Howard, Dick. *The Marxian Legacy.* 2d ed. Minneapolis: University of Minnesota Press, 1988.

Howe, Irving, ed. *1984 Revisited: Totalitarianism in Our Century.* New York: Harper and Row, 1983.

Hughes, H. Stuart. *The Obstructed Path: French Social Thought in the Years of Desperation, 1930–1960.* New York: Harper and Row, 1969.

———. *The Sea Change: The Migration of Social Thought, 1930–1965.* New York: Harper and Row, 1975.

Isaac, Jeffrey C. *Arendt, Camus, and Modern Rebellion.* New Haven, Conn.: Yale University Press, 1992.

Jäckel, Eberhard. *Hitler's Weltanschauung: Entwurf einer Herrschaft.* Stuttgart: Deutsche Verlags-Anstalt, 1983.

Jackson, Gabriel. *A Concise History of the Spanish Civil War.* London: Thames and Hudson, 1980.

———. "The Spanish Popular Front, 1934–7." *Journal of Contemporary History* 5, no. 3 (1970): 21–35.

———, ed. *The Spanish Civil War.* Chicago: Quadrangle Books, 1972.

Jänicke, Martin. *Totalitäre Herrschaft: Anatomie eines politischen Begriffs.* Berlin: Duncker und Humblot, 1971.

Jarausch, Konrad. *Students, Society, and Politics in Imperial Germany: The Rise of Academic Illiberalism.* Princeton, N.J.: Princeton University Press, 1982.

Jones, Larry Eugene. *German Liberalism and the Dissolution of the Weimar Party System, 1918–1933.* Chapel Hill: University of North Carolina Press, 1988.

Judt, Tony. *Marxism and the French Left: Studies on Labour and Politics in France, 1830–1981.* Oxford: Clarendon, 1989.

———. *Past Imperfect: French Intellectuals, 1944–1956.* Berkeley: University of California Press, 1992.

Kaes, Anton, Martin Jay, and Edward Dimendberg, eds. *The Weimar Republic Sourcebook.* Berkeley: University of California Press, 1994.

Keegan, John. *The Second World War.* New York: Viking, 1990.

Kelly, Michael, ed. *Critique and Power: Recasting the Foucault/Habermas Debate.* Cambridge, Mass.: MIT Press, 1994.

Kershaw, Ian. *The "Hitler" Myth: Image and Reality in the Third Reich.* Oxford: Oxford University Press, 1987.

———. *The Nazi Dictatorship: Problems and Perspectives of Interpretation.* 3d ed. London: Edward Arnold, 1993.

———. "Nazisme et stalinisme: Limites d'une comparaison." *Le débat,* no. 89 (March–April 1996): 177–89.

———. "Totalitarianism Revisited: Nazism and Stalinism in Comparative Perspective." In *Tel Aviver Jahrbuch für deutsche Geschichte,* vol. 23, 23–40. Gerlingen: Bleicher, 1994.

———. "'Working towards the Führer': Reflections on the Nature of the Hitler Dictatorship." *Contemporary European History* 2, no. 2 (1993): 103–18.

Kershaw, Ian, and Moshe Lewin, eds. *Stalinism and Nazism: Dictatorships in Comparison.* Cambridge: Cambridge University Press, 1997.

Kirkpatrick, Jeane. *Dictatorships and Double Standards: Rationalism and Reason in Politics.* New York: American Enterprise Institute, 1982.

———. *The Withering Away of the Totalitarian State and Other Surprises.* New York: American Enterprise Institute, 1991.

Kis, Danilo. *Garden, Ashes.* Translated by William J. Hannaher. New York: Harcourt Brace Jovanovich, 1975.

———. *A Tomb for Boris Davidovich.* Translated by Duska Mikic-Mitchell. New York: Harcourt Brace Jovanovich, 1978.

Kitchen, Martin. *The Coming of Austrian Fascism.* London: Croom Helm, 1980.

———. *Fascism.* London: Macmillan, 1976.

Klemperer, Klemens von. *German Resistance against Hitler: The Search for Allies Abroad, 1938–1945.* New York: Oxford University Press, 1992.

Klotz, Johannes. *Das "kommende Deutschland": Vorstellungen und Konzeptionen des sozialistischen Parteivorstandes im Exil 1933–1945 zu Staat und Wirtschaft.* Cologne: Pahl Rugenstein, 1983.

Kolb, Eberhard. *The Weimar Republic.* Translated by P. S. Falla. London: Routledge, 1992.

Koonz, Claudia. *Mothers in the Fatherland: Women, the Family, and Nazi Politics.* New York: St. Martin's, 1987.

Koshar, Rudy. *Social Life, Local Politics, and Nazism: Marburg, 1880–1935.* Chapel Hill: University of North Carolina Press, 1986.

Kühnl, Reinhard. *Formen bürgerlichen Herrschaft: Liberalismus-Faschismus.* Reinbek: Rowohlt, 1974.

———. "'Linke' Totalitarismusversionen." In *Totalitarismus: Zur Problematik eines politischen Begriffs,* edited by M. Greiffenhagen, R. Kühnl, and J. B. Müller, 97–119. Munich: List, 1972.

———. "Zur politischen Funktion der Totalitarismustheorien in der BRD." In *Totalitarismus: Zur Problematik eines politischen Begriffs,* edited by M. Greiffenhagen, R. Kühnl, and J. B. Müller, 7–21. Munich: List, 1972.

———, ed. *Vergangenheit, die nicht vergeht: Die "Historiker-Debatte"; Darstellung, Dokumentation, Kritik.* Cologne: Pahl-Rugenstein, 1987.

Kundera, Milan. *The Book of Laughter and Forgetting.* Translated by Michael Henry Heim. New York: Knopf, 1981.

———. *The Unbearable Lightness of Being.* Translated by Michael Henry Heim. New York: Harper and Row, 1984.

Kurz, Thomas. *"Blutmai": Sozialdemokraten und Kommunisten im Brennpunkt der Berliner Ereignisse von 1929.* Berlin: Dietz, 1988.

Labedz, Leopold. *The Use and Abuse of Sovietology.* With a preface by Zbigniew Brzezinski. Edited by Melvin J. Lasky. New Brunswick, N.J.: Transaction, 1989.

Laqueur, Walter. *The Dream That Failed: Reflections on the Soviet Union.* New York: Oxford University Press, 1994.

———. *Fascism: Past, Present, Future.* New York: Oxford University Press, 1996.

———. *The Fate of the Revolution: Interpretations of Soviet History.* New York: Macmillan, 1967.

———. "Is There Now or Has There Ever Been Such a Thing as Totalitarianism?" *Commentary* 80, no. 4 (1985): 29–35.

———, ed. *Fascism: A Reader's Guide.* Berkeley: University of California Press, 1976.

Large, David Clay. *Between Two Fires: Europe's Path in the 1930s.* New York: Norton, 1990.

———, ed. *Contending with Hitler: Varieties of Resistance in the Third Reich.* Cambridge: Cambridge University Press and the German Historical Institute, 1991.

Larsen, Stein Ugelvik, Bernt Hagtvet, and Jan Petter Myklebust, eds. *Who Were the Fascists? Social Roots of European Fascism.* Bergen: Universitetsforlaget, 1980.

Lefort, Claude. *Éléments d'une critique de la bureaucratie.* Geneva: Droz, 1971.

———. *Essais sur le politique.* Paris: Seuil, 1986. Translated by David Macey as *Democracy and Political Theory* (Minneapolis: University of Minnesota Press, 1988).

———. *L'invention démocratique: Les limites de la domination totalitaire.* Paris: Fayard, 1981.

———. *The Political Forms of Modern Society: Bureaucracy, Democracy, Totalitarianism.* Edited and translated by John B. Thompson. Cambridge, Mass.: MIT Press, 1986.

———. *Un homme en trop: Réflections sur "L'Archipel du Goulag."* Paris: Seuil, 1976.

———. *Sur une colonne absente: Écrits autour de Merleau-Ponty.* Paris: Gallimard, 1978.

Lehmann, Hartmut, and James J. Sheehan, eds. *An Interrupted Past: German-Speaking Refugee Historians in the United States after 1933.* Washington, D.C., and Cambridge: German Historical Institute and Cambridge University Press, 1991.

Lerner, Warren. *Karl Radek: The Last Internationalist.* Stanford, Calif.: Stanford University Press, 1970.

Levi, Primo. *Survival in Auschwitz.* 1958. Reprint, New York: Collier Books, 1993.

Lévy, Bernard-Henri. *La barbarie à visage humain.* Paris: Éditions Grasset and Fasquelle, 1977. Translated by George Holoch as *Barbarism with a Human Face* (New York: Harper and Row, 1979).

Liebersohn, Harry. *Fate and Utopia in German Sociology, 1870–1923.* Cambridge, Mass.: MIT Press, 1988.

Lindemann, Albert S. *Esau's Tears: Modern Anti-Semitism and the Rise of the Jews.* Cambridge: Cambridge University Press, 1997.

———. *A History of European Socialism.* New Haven, Conn.: Yale University Press, 1983.

———. *The "Red Years": European Socialism versus Bolshevism, 1919–1921.* Berkeley: University of California Press, 1974.

Lipstadt, Deborah E. *Denying the Holocaust: The Growing Assault on Truth and Memory.* New York: Free Press, 1993.

Lösche, Peter, Michael Scholing, and Franz Walter, eds. *Vor dem Vergessen bewahren: Lebenswege Weimarer Sozialdemokraten.* Berlin: Colloquium, 1988.

Lottman, Herbert R. *The Left Bank: Writers, Artists, and Politics from the Popular Front to the Cold War.* Boston: Houghton Mifflin, 1982.

Löw, Konrad, ed. *Totalitarismus.* Berlin: Duncker und Humblot, 1988.

Lüdtke, Alf. "'Coming to Terms with the Past': Illusions of Remembering, Ways of Forgetting Nazism in West Germany." *Journal of Modern History* 65 (September 1993): 542–72.

———. "What Happened to the 'Fiery Red Glow?'" In *The History of Everyday Life: Reconstructing Historical Experiences and Ways of Life,* edited by Alf Lüdtke and translated by William Templer, 198–251. Princeton, N.J.: Princeton University Press, 1995.

Luebbert, Gregory. *Liberalism, Fascism, or Social Democracy.* New York: Oxford University Press, 1991.

Luthardt, Wolfgang. *Sozialdemokratische Verfassungstheorie in der Weimarer Republik.* Opladen: Westdeutscher, 1986.

Lyotard, Jean-François. *La condition postmoderne: Rapport sur la savoir.* Paris: Éditions de Minuit, 1979. Translated by Geoff Bennington and Brian Massumi as *The Postmodern Condition: A Report on Knowledge* (Minneapolis: University of Minnesota Press, 1984).

———. *Le postmoderne expliqué aux enfants.* Paris: Éditions Galilée, 1988. Translated by Don Barry, Bernadette Maher, Julian Pefanis, Virginia Spate, and Morgan Thomas as *The Postmodern Explained: Correspondence, 1982–1985* (Minneapolis: University of Minnesota Press, 1993).

Maehl, William Harvey. *The German Socialist Party: Champion of the First Republic, 1918–1933.* Philadelphia: American Philosophical Society, 1986.

Maier, Charles. *Recasting Bourgeois Europe: Stabilization in France, Germany, and Italy in the Decade after World War I.* Princeton, N.J.: Princeton University Press, 1975.

———. *The Unmasterable Past: History, Holocaust, and German National Identity.* Cambridge, Mass.: Harvard University Press, 1988.

Mallmann, Klaus-Michael. *Kommunisten in der Weimarer Republik: Sozialgeschichte einer revolutionären Bewegung.* Damrstadt: Wissenschaftliche Buchgesellschaft, 1996.

Markovits, Andrei, and Philip S. Gorski. *The German Left: Red, Green and Beyond.* New York: Oxford University Press, 1993.

Mason, Tim. *Nazism, Fascism and the Working Class: Essays by Tim Mason.* Edited by Jane Caplan. Cambridge: Cambridge University Press, 1995.

———. *Social Policy in the Third Reich: The Working Class and the National Community.* Providence, R.I.: Berg, 1993.

McCormick, John P. *Carl Schmitt's Critique of Liberalism: Against Politics as Technology.* Cambridge: Cambridge University Press, 1997.

Medvedev, Roy. *Let History Judge: The Origins and Consequences of Stalinism.* Edited and translated by George Shriver. New York: Columbia University Press, 1989.

Menze, Ernest, ed. *Totalitarianism Reconsidered.* Port Washington, N.Y.: Kennikat, 1981.

Merson, Allan. *Communist Resistance in Nazi Germany.* London: Lawrence and Wishart, 1985.

Miller, Susanne. *Die Bürde der Macht: Die deutsche Sozialdemokratie, 1918–1920.* Beiträgre zur Geschichte des Parliamentarismus und der politischen Parteien, vol. 63. Düsseldorf: Droste, 1978.

Mommsen, Hans. "The Concept of Totalitarian Dictatorship vs. the Comparative Theory of Fascism: The Case of National Socialism." In *Totalitarianism Reconsidered,* edited by Ernest Menze, 146–65. Port Washington, N.Y.: Kennikat, 1981.

———. *From Weimar to Auschwitz.* Translated by Philip O'Connor. Princeton, N.J.: Princeton University Press, 1991.

———. *Der Nationalsozialismus und die deutsche Gesellschaft: Ausgewählte Aufsätze.* Edited by Lutz Niethammer and Bernd Weisbrod. Reinbek: Rowohlt, 1991.

———. *The Rise and Fall of Weimar Democracy.* Translated by Elborg Forster and Larry Eugene Jones. Chapel Hill: University of North Carolina Press, 1996.

Morgan, David W. *The Socialist Left and the German Revolution: A History of the German Independent Social Democratic Party, 1917–1922.* Ithaca, N.Y.: Cornell University Press, 1975.

Moore, Barrington. *Social Origins of Dictatorship and Democracy: Lord and Peasant in the Making of the Modern World.* Boston: Beacon, 1967.

Mühlen, Patrick von zur. *Spanien war ihre Hoffnung: Die deutsche Linke im Spanischen Bürgerkrieg, 1936 bis 1939.* Berlin: Dietz, 1985.

Namuth, Hans, and Georg Reisner. *Spanisches Tagebuch, 1936: Fotografien und Texte aus den ersten Wochen des Bürgerkriegs.* Edited and with an introduction by Diethart Krebs. Berlin: Dirk Nishen, 1986.

Neocleous, Mark. *Fascism.* Minneapolis: University of Minnesota Press, 1997.

Nolte, Ernst. "Despotism—Totalitarianism—Freedom-Oriented Society." In *Totalitarianism Reconsidered,* edited by Ernest Menze, 167–78. Port Washington, N.Y.: Kennikat, 1981.

———. *Die Deutschen und ihre Vergangenheiten: Erinnerung und Vergessen von der Reichsgründung Bismarcks bis heute.* Berlin: Propyläen, 1995.

———. *Deutschland und der Kalte Krieg.* Munich: Piper, 1974.

———. *Der europäische Bürgerkrieg: Nationalsozialismus und Bolschewismus.* Frankfurt am Main: Propyläen, 1987.

———. "Die historisch-genetisch Version der Totalitarismustheorie: Ärgernis oder Einsicht?" *Zeitschrift für Politik* 43 (1996): 111–22.

———. *Lehrstück oder Tragödie? Beiträge zur Interpretation der Geschichte des 20. Jahrhunderts.* Cologne: Böhlau, 1991.

———. *Martin Heidegger: Politik und Geschichte im Leben und Denken.* Berlin: Propyläen, 1992.

———. *Marxismus-Faschismus-Kalter Krieg: Vorträge und Aufsätze, 1964–1976.* Stuttgart: Deutsche Verlagsanstalt, 1977. Translated by Lawrence Krader as *Marxism, Fascism, Cold War* (Atlantic Highlands, N.J.: Humanities, 1982).

———. *Streitpunkte: Heutige und künftige Kontroversen um den Nationalsozialismus.* Berlin: Propyläen, 1993.

———. *Three Faces of Fascism.* Translated by Leila Vennewitz. 1963. Reprint, New York: New American Library, 1969. Originally published as *Der Faschismus in seiner Epoche: Die Action française, Der italienische Faschismus, Der Nationalsozialismus* (Munich: Piper, 1963).

———. *Das Vergehen der Vergangheit: Antwort an meine Kritiker im sogenannten Historikerstreit.* Berlin: Verlag Ullstein, 1987.

———, ed. *Theorien über den Faschismus.* Cologne: Kiepenheuer und Witsch, 1967.

Nove, Alec. *The Stalin Phenomenon.* New York: St. Martin's, 1993.

Novick, Robert. *That Noble Dream: The "Objectivity Question" and the American Historical Profession.* Cambridge: Cambridge University Press, 1988.

Nye, Robert A. *The Anti-Democratic Sources of Elite Theory: Pareto, Mosca, Michels.* London: Sage Publications, 1977.

Orlow, Dietrich. *The History of the Nazi Party.* 2 vols. Pittsburgh, Pa.: University of Pittsburgh Press, 1969.

———. *Weimar Prussia.* 2 vols. Pittsburgh, Pa.: University of Pittsburgh Press, 1986–92.

Paul, Ellen Frankel, ed. *Totalitarianism at the Crossroads.* New Brunswick, N.J.: Transaction Books, 1990.

Payne, Stanley G. *Falange: A History of Spanish Fascism.* Stanford, Calif.: Stanford University Press, 1961.

———. *Fascism: Comparison and Definition.* Madison: University of Wisconsin Press, 1980.

———. *A History of Fascism, 1914–1945.* Madison: University of Wisconsin Press, 1995.

———. *The Spanish Revolution.* New York: Norton, 1970.

Peukert, Detlev. *Inside Nazi Germany: Conformity, Opposition, and Racism in Everyday Life.* Translated by Richard Deveson. New Haven, Conn.: Yale University Press, 1987. Originally published as *Volksgenossen und Gemeinschaftsfremde: Anpassung, Ausmerze und Aufbegehren unter dem Nationalsozialismus* (Cologne: Bund, 1982).

———. *Die KPD im Widerstand: Verfolgung und Untergrundarbeit an Rhein und Ruhr, 1933–1945.* Wuppertal: Peter Hammer, 1980.

———. *The Weimar Republic: The Crisis of Classical Modernity.* Translated by Richard Deveson. New York: Hill and Wang, 1992. Originally published as *Die Weimarer Republik* (Frankfurt am Main: Suhrkamp, 1987).

Pierson, Karl. *Marxist Intellectuals and the Working-Class Mentality in Germany, 1887–1912.* Cambridge, Mass.: Harvard University Press, 1993.

Poulantzas, Nicos. *Fascism and Dictatorship: The Third International and the Problem of Fascism.* Translated by Judith White. London: New Left Books, 1974.

———. *Political Power and Social Classes.* London: New Left Books, 1973.

Preston, Paul. *The Coming of the Spanish Civil War: Reform, Reaction, and Revolution in the Second Republic, 1931–1936.* New York: Barnes and Noble Books, 1978.

Prowe, Diethelm. "'Classic' Fascism and the New Radical Right in Western Europe: Comparisons and Contrasts." *Contemporary European History* 3, no. 3 (1994): 289–313.

Pulzer, Peter. *The Rise of Political Anti-Semitism in Germany and Austria.* New York: John Wiley and Sons, 1964.

Pyta, Wolfram. *Gegen Hitler und für die Republik: Die Auseinandersetzung der deutschen Sozialdemokratie mit der NSDAP in Weimarer Republik.* Düsseldorf: Droste, 1989.

Rabinbach, Anson. *The Crisis of Austrian Socialism: From Red Vienna to Civil War, 1927–1934.* Chicago: University of Chicago Press, 1983.

Revel, Jean-François. *La tentation totalitaire.* Paris: Éditions Robert Laffont, 1976. Translated by David Hapgood as *The Totalitarian Temptation* (New York: Doubleday, 1977).

Riasanovsky, Nicholas. *A History of Russia.* New York: Oxford University Press, 1993.

Rogger, Hans. "Was There a Russian Fascism? The Union of Russian People." *Journal of Modern History* 36 (December 1964): 398–415.

Rogger, Hans, and Eugen Weber, eds. *The European Right: A Historical Profile.* Berkeley: University of California Press, 1965.

Rorty, Richard. *Contingency, Irony, and Solidarity.* Cambridge: Cambridge University Press, 1989.

Rosenhaft, Eve. *Beating the Fascists? The German Communists and Political Violence, 1929–1933.* Cambridge: Cambridge University Press, 1983.

———. "The Uses of Remembrance: The Legacy of the Communist Resistance in the German Democratic Republic." In *Germans against Nazism: Nonconformity, Opposition and Resistance in the Third Reich; Essays in Honour of Peter Hoffmann,* edited by Francis R. Nicosia and Lawrence D. Stokes, 369–88. New York: Berg, 1990.

Roth, Guenther. *The Social Democrats in Imperial Germany.* Totowa, N.J.: Bedminster, 1963.

Roth, Michael S. *The Ironist's Cage: Memory, Trauma, and the Construction of History.* New York: Columbia University Press, 1995.

———. *Knowing and History: Appropriations of Hegel in Twentieth-Century France.* Ithaca, N.Y.: Cornell University Press, 1988.

Ryder, A. J. *The German Revolution of 1918: A Study of German Socialism in War and Revolt.* Cambridge: Cambridge University Press, 1967.

Sauer, Wolfgang. "National Socialism: Totalitarianism or Fascism?" *American Historical Review* 73, no. 2 (1967): 404–24.

Schapiro, Leonard. *The Communist Party of the Soviet Union.* New York: Random House, 1960.

————. *The Origin of the Communist Autocracy: Political Opposition in the Soviet State; First Phase, 1917–1922.* New York: Praeger, 1965.

————. *Totalitarianism.* New York: Praeger, 1972.

Schieder, Wolfgang. *Faschismus als soziale Bewegung: Deutschland und Italien im Vergleich.* Göttingen: Vandenhoeck und Ruprecht, 1983.

Schlangen, Walter. *Theorie und Ideologie des Totalitarismus: Möglichkeiten und Grenzen einer liberalen Kritik politischer Herrschaft.* Bonn: Bundeszentrale für politische Bildung, 1972.

————. *Die Totalitarismus-Theorie: Entwicklung und Probleme.* Stuttgart: W. Kohlhammer, 1976.

Schleunes, Karl A. *The Twisted Road to Auschwitz: Nazi Policy toward German Jews, 1933–1939.* 1970. Reprint, Urbana: University of Illinois Press, 1990.

Schöck, Eva Cornelia. *Arbeitslosigkeit und Rationalisierung: Die Lage der Arbeiter und die kommunistische Gewerkschaftspolitik, 1920–1928.* Frankfurt am Main: Campus, 1977.

Schoenbaum, David. *Hitler's Social Revolution: Class and Status in Nazi Germany, 1933–1945.* New York: Doubleday, 1966.

Schorske, Carl. *German Social Democracy, 1905–1917: The Development of the Great Schism.* 1955. Reprint, Cambridge, Mass.: Cambridge University Press, 1983.

————. Review of *Totalitarian Dictatorship and Autocracy,* by Carl J. Friedrich and Zbigniew Brzezinski. *American Historical Review* 63, no. 2 (1957): 367–68.

Seidel, Bruno, and Siegfried Jenker, eds. *Wege der Totalitarismusforschung.* Darmstadt: Wissenschaftliche Buchgesellschaft, 1974.

Seidman, Michael. "The Unorwellian Barcelona." *European History Quarterly* 20 (April 1990): 163–80.

————. "Work and Revolution: Workers' Control in Barcelona in the Spanish Civil War, 1936–38." *Journal of Contemporary History* 17, no. 3 (1982): 409–33.

Semprun, Jorge. *L'écriture ou la vie.* Paris: Gallimard, 1994. Translated by Linda Coverdale as *Literature or Life* (New York: Viking, 1997).

————. *Le grand voyage.* Paris: Galliimard, 1963. Translated by Richard Seaver as *The Long Voyage* (Harmondsworth, England: Penguin Books, 1997).

Shandley, Robert R., ed. *Unwilling Germans? The Goldhagen Debate.* Translated by Jeremiah Riemer. Minneapolis: University of Minnesota Press, 1998.

Shklar, Judith N. *After Utopia: The Decline of Political Faith.* Princeton, N.J.: Princeton University Press, 1957.

Snyder, Tim. "'Coming to Terms with the Charm and Power of Soviet Communism.'" *Contemporary European History* 6, no. 1 (1997): 133–44.

Solzhenitsyn, Aleksandr I. *The Gulag Archipelago.* 3 vols. New York: Harper and Row, 1973–78.

————. *One Day in the Life of Ivan Denisovich.* New York: Praeger, 1963.

Sontheimer, Kurt. *Antidemokratisches Denken in der Weimarer Republik: Die politischen Ideen des deutschen Nationalismus zwischen 1918 und 1933.* Munich: Deutscher Taschenbuch, 1978.

Spiro, Herbert. "Totalitarianism." In *International Encyclopedia of the Social Sciences,* 2d ed., vol. 16, 106–13. New York: Macmillan, 1968.

Stephenson, Jill. *The Nazi Organization of Women.* London: Croom Helm, 1981.

Sternhell, Zeev. "The 'Anti-Materialist' Revision of Marxism as an Aspect of the Rise of Fascist Ideology." *Journal of Contemporary History* 22, no. 3 (1987): 379–400.

———. *Ni droite, ni gauche.* Paris: Édition du Seuil, 1983. Translated as *Neither Right nor Left: Fascist Ideology in France* (Berkeley: University of California Press, 1986).

Sternhell, Zeev, Z. Sznajder, and M. Asheri, eds. *The Birth of Fascist Ideology.* Princeton, N.J.: Princeton University Press, 1994.

Stürmer, Michael, ed. *Dissonanzen des Fortschritts: Essays über Geschichte und Politik in Deutschland.* Munich: Piper, 1986.

Talmon, J. L. *The Origins of Totalitarian Democracy.* Boston: Beacon, 1952.

Taylor, Charles. *Sources of the Self: The Making of the Modern Identity.* Cambridge, Mass.: Harvard University Press, 1992.

Tent, James F. *The Free University of Berlin: A Political History.* Bloomington: Indiana University Press, 1988.

Thomas, Hugh. *The Spanish Civil War.* Harmondworth, England: Penguin Books, 1986.

Thompson, E. P. "Inside *Which* Whale?" In *George Orwell: A Collection of Critical Essays,* edited by Raymond Williams, 80–88. Englewood Cliffs, N.J.: Prentice-Hall, 1974.

Thurston, Robert W. *Life and Terror in Stalin's Russia, 1934–1941.* New Haven, Conn.: Yale University Press, 1996.

Tormey, Simon. *Making Sense of Tyranny: Interpretations of Totalitarianism.* Manchester, England: Manchester University Press, 1995.

Tucker, Robert, ed. *Stalinism: Essays in Historical Interpretation.* New York: Norton, 1977.

Turner, Henry A., Jr. *German Big Business and the Rise of Hitler.* Oxford: Oxford University Press, 1985.

———. *Stresemann and the Politics of the Weimar Republic.* Princeton, N.J.: Princeton University Press, 1963.

———. *The Two Germanies since 1945.* New Haven, Conn.: Yale University Press, 1987.

———, ed. *Reappraisals of Fascism.* New York: New Viewpoints, 1975.

Ulam, Adam B. *Stalin: The Man and His Era.* New York: Viking, 1973.

Unger, Aryeh L. *The Totalitarian Party: Party and People in Nazi Germany and Soviet Russia.* Cambridge: Cambridge University Press, 1974.

Vajda, Mihály. *Fascism as a Mass Movement.* New York: St. Martin's, 1976.

———. *The State and Socialism: Political Essays.* London: Allison and Busby, 1981.

Vivarelli, Roberto. "Interpretations of the Origins of Fascism." *Journal of Modern History* 63 (March 1991): 29–43.

Volkogonov, Dimitrii. *Lenin: A New Biography.* Edited and translated by Harold Shukman. New York: Free Press, 1994.

Walicki, Andrzej. *Marxism and the Leap to the Kingdom of Freedom: The Rise and Fall of the Communist Utopia.* Stanford, Calif.: Stanford University Press, 1995.

Walzer, Michael. *Spheres of Justice: A Defense of Pluralism and Equality.* New York: Basic Books, 1983.

Warren, Scott. *The Emergence of Dialectical Theory.* Chicago: University of Chicago Press, 1984.

Weber, Eugen. *Action Française.* Stanford, Calif.: Stanford University Press, 1962.

———. *Varieties of Fascism: Doctrines of Revolution in the Twentieth Century.* New York: Van Nostrand, 1964.

Weber, Hermann, *Aufbau und Fall einer Diktatur: Kritischen Beiträge zur Geschichte der DDR.* Cologne: Bund, 1991.

———. *Der Gründungsparteitag der KPD: Protokoll und Materialien.* Frankfurt am Main: Europäische Verlagsanstalt, 1969.

———, ed. *Die Wandlung des deutschen Kommunismus.* 2 vols. Frankfurt am Main: Europäische Verlagsanstalt, 1969.

Wehler, Hans-Ulrich. *Entsorgung der deutschen Vergangenheit? Ein polemischer Essay zum "Historikerstreit."* Munich: Beck, 1988.

Weinberg, Gerhard. *A World at Arms: A Global History of World War II.* New York: Cambridge University Press, 1994.

Weitz, Eric D. *Creating German Communism, 1890–1990: From Popular Protests to Socialist State.* Princeton, N.J.: Princeton University Press, 1997.

Whitfield, Stephen J. *The Culture of the Cold War.* Baltimore: Johns Hopkins University Press, 1991.

———. *Into the Dark: Hannah Arendt and Totalitarianism.* Philadelphia: Temple University Press, 1980.

———. "'Totalitarianism' in Eclipse: The Recent Fate of an Idea." In *Images and Ideas in American Culture: Essays in Memory of Philip Rahv,* edited by Arthur Edelstein, 60–95. Hanover, N.H.: University Press of New England, 1979.

Wickham, James. "Social Fascism and the Division of the Working-Class Movement." *Capital and Class* 7, no. 1 (1979): 1–65.

Wiesel, Elie. *Night.* Translated by Stella Rodway. New York: Hill and Wang, 1960.

Wildt, Andreas. "Totalitarian State Capitalism." *Telos,* no. 41 (Fall 1979): 33–57.

Wilkinson, James. *The Intellectual Resistance in Europe.* Cambridge, Mass.: Harvard University Press, 1981.

———. "Truth and Delusion: European Intellectuals in Search of the Spanish Civil War." *Salmagundi* 76/77 (1987–88): 3–52.

Willett, John. *The New Sobriety: Art and Politics in the Weimar Period, 1917–1933.* 1978. Reprint, London: Thames and Hudson, 1987.

Williams, Raymond, ed. *George Orwell: A Collection of Critical Essays.* Englewood Cliffs, N.J.: Prentice-Hall, 1974.

Winkler, Heinrich August. "Choosing the Lesser Evil: The German Social Democrats and the Fall of the Weimar Republic." *Journal of Contemporary History* 25, nos. 2–3 (1990): 205–25.

——. *Der Schein der Normalität: Arbeiter und Arbeiterbewegung in der Weimarer Republik, 1924 bis 1930.* Berlin: J. H. W. Dietz Nachf., 1988.

——. *Der Weg in die Katastrophe: Arbeiter und Arbeiterbewegung in der Weimarer Republik, 1930 bis 1933.* Berlin: J. H. W. Dietz Nachf., 1990.

——. *Weimar, 1918-1933: Die Geschichte der ersten deutschen Demokratie.* Munich: Beck, 1993.

——. *Von der Revolution zur Stabilisierung: Arbeiter und Arbeiterbewegung in der Weimarer Republik, 1918 bis 1924.* Berlin: J. H. W. Dietz Nachf., 1984.

——. ed. *Die Krise des europäischen Sozialismus in der Zwischenkriegszeit.* Göttingen: Vandenhoeck und Ruprecht, 1991.

Wippermann, Wolfgang. *Die Bonapartismustheorie von Marx und Engels.* Stuttgart: Klett-Cotta, 1983.

——. *Europäischer Faschismus im Vergleich (1922-1982).* Frankfurt am Main: Suhrkamp, 1983.

——. "Faschismus—nur ein Schlagwort?" In *Tel Aviver Jahrbuch für deutsche Geschichte,* vol. 16, 346-66. Gerlingen: Bleicher, 1987.

——. *Faschismustheorien: Zum Stand der gegenwärtigen Diskussion.* 5th ed. Darmstadt: Wissenschaftliche Buchgesellschaft, 1989.

——. *Der konsequente Wahn: Ideologie und Politik Adolf Hitlers.* Gutersloh: Bertelsmann Lexicon, 1989.

——. "The Post-War German Left and Fascism." *Journal of Contemporary History* 11, no. 4 (1976): 185-219.

——. *Zur Analyse des Faschismus: Die sozialistischen und kommunistischen Faschusmustheorien, 1921-1945.* Frankfurt am Main: Verlag Moritz Diesterweg, 1981.

Wippermann, Wolfgang, and Michael Burleigh. *The Racial State: Germany, 1933-1945.* Cambridge: Cambridge University Press, 1991.

Wistrich, Robert S. "Leon Trotsky's Theory of Fascism." *Journal of Contemporary History* 11, no. 4 (1976): 157-84.

Wright, Gordon. *The Ordeal of Total War, 1939-1945.* New York: Harper and Row, 1969.

INDEX

Abendroth, Wolfgang, 269n.146
Abraham, David, 243n.65
Abramovitsch, Rafael, 103-4, 136
Adenauer, Konrad, 285n.6
Adorno, Theodor Wiesengrund, 176, 190,
193, 204, 207, 214, 280n.178; back-
ground of, 159-60; *Dialektik der
Aufklärung* (*Dialectic of Enlightenment*),
132, 142, 149, 158-70, 192, 205-6, 277-
78n.141; and Institute of Social Research,
10, 54, 171, 184; *The Jargon of Authenticity,* 283n.195; and Marxism, 161, 178,
281n.182; *Negative Dialectics,* 283n.199
Aktion, Die, 37
Albanians, 211
Anarchists, Spanish. *See* Spanish anarchists
Anderson, Evelyn (Lenore Seligmann), 78-
79, 90, 263n.89, 267n.129
Anderson, Paul, 263n.89
Anti-Communism, 6, 10-11, 172, 176, 192,
203, 212, 231n.40; and antifascism, 96,
101; and Congress for Cultural Freedom,
185-86; former Communists and, 31, 46,
103, 106, 119, 179, 185-86, 197
Anti-Semitism, 143, 176, 187, 212, 281-
82n.189, 282n.191, 297-98n.101;
Horkheimer and Adorno on, 159-60,
162-66, 281n.187; Löwenthal on, 82;

Massing on, 158, 256n.30; Neumann on,
166, 282n.192; Rosenberg on, 73-74; in
Weimar politics, 26, 45. *See also* Jews,
European
Arato, Andrew, 207
Arendt, Hannah, 87, 159, 189, 193, 207, 218;
on Adorno, 280n.178; *The Human Condi-
tion,* 203, 299n.108; on imperialism,
293n.80; *On Revolution,* 202, 292n.76;
The Origins of Totalitarianism, 4, 7, 201-
4; and Pachter, 47
Aron, Raymond, 3, 283n.203
Australia, 124
Austria, 31, 34, 64-65, 96; workers' revolt
in, 65, 91, 96
Austrian Communist Party, 31, 77
Austrian Social Democratic Party, 60, 77,
91, 264n.92
Authoritarianism, 2, 69, 87
Ayçoberry, Pierre, 13, 253n.4, 254-55n.14

Balkans, 210-11. *See also* Bosnia; Yugosla-
via
Bauer, Otto, 52, 91, 252-53n.3, 264n.92
Bebel, August, 165
Belgium, 26
Benhabib, Seyla, 5, 203, 207
Benjamin, Walter, 130, 133, 159
Berlin, 106, 117, 195; and May Day 1929,

35–39; Neu Beginnen in, 76–80; and Weimar leftists, 49, 51, 60, 67, 76, 103
Berlin, Free University of. *See* Free University of Berlin
Berlin blockade and airlift, 3, 174, 178
Berlin Transport Workers' (BVG): strike of, 61, 250n.132
Berlin Wall, 2, 199–200, 213, 216
Bevan, Aneurin, 263n.89
Biehahn, Walter, 61
Bienstock, Gregor, 86
Bismarck, Otto von, 131
Bitburg controversy, 215
Blair, Eileen O'Shaughnessy, 101, 267n.129. *See also* Orwell, George
Blatt, Max, 90, 263n.88
Bloch, Ernst, 159
Blücher, Heinrich, 202. *See also* Arendt, Hannah
Blum, Leon, 39
Bolshevism, 7, 23, 27, 63, 79, 86, 89, 160, 220; Borkenau on, 91–95, 121, 124; Kirchheimer on, 56–60; Korsch on, 39; Luxemburg on, 28, 30–31; Neumann on, 181–82; Rosenberg on, 49–51, 71; Rühle on, 111–13. *See also* Communism; Lenin, Vladimir I.; Leninism; Soviet Union; Stalin, Joseph; Stalinism
Bonapartism: Thalheimer and, 43–45, 243n.65; theory of, 90, 116, 126, 244n.74, 275n.100
Borkenau, Franz, 8, 11, 87, 112, 125, 132, 151, 162, 167, 171, 190, 202, 204, 208, 212, 214, 219, 223–24n.5, 271n.37; anti-Communism of, 47, 177–78, 185–86, 188, 272n.43, 287n.30; background of, 51–52, 293n.78; *The Communist International,* 91, 186; on counterrevolution, 103; *European Communism,* 186; in exile, 253n.4; and Institute of Social Research, 51, 54, 91; and Kautsky on Neu Beginnen, 78–79; and KPD, 76; and Kremlinology, 185, 286n.28; on Luxemburg, 30–31; on Marx and Marxism, 90, 161, 179, 184, 268n.133; and Neu Beginnen, 77; and Orwell, 100–101, 124, 186, 267n.129; *Pareto,* 14, 85, 91–96, 99, 118, 120; *The Spanish Cockpit,* 91, 99–103, 203, 265n.112, 267–68n.130; and Stalinization thesis, 287n.32; "State and Revolution," 103; and state capitalism, 141–42; *The Totalitarian Enemy,* 118–24, 144, 211,

272n.45; "Zur Soziologie des Faschismus," 52–53, 60, 73, 80, 246n.99
Bosnia, 210–11, 297n.98
Boyle, Kay, 185.
Bracher, Karl Dietrich, 14–15, 149, 159, 210–11, 216, 297n.98, 297n.99
Brandler, Heinrich, 27, 43, 110, 186–87, 268n.137, 287n.32
Brandt, Willy, 104, 196, 268n.135, 268n.137, 302n.122
Braun, Otto, 151, 245n.86
BRD. *See* Federal Republic of Germany
Brecht, Bertolt, 37, 159, 180, 187, 240–41n.45
Bronner, Stephen Eric, 28, 168–69
Browning, Christopher, 165
Bruck, Moeller van den, 69
Brüning, Heinrich, 75
Brzezinski, Zbigniew, 4, 224n.6
Buck-Morss, Susan, 281n.182
Bukharin, Nikolai, 25
Bundesrepublik Deutschland. *See* Federal Republic of Germany
Burnham, James, 272n.43, 276n.104

Caesarism, 2, 181,
Camus, Albert, 3, 174, 284n.1
Capitalism, 30, 41, 75, 109, 117, 134–42, 173, 208–9, 213, 282n.191; Borkenau on, 92–93, 121, 123; fascism and, 9; Fraenkel on, 146–48; Horkheimer on, 130, 160, 165; Korsch on, 126–29, 155–56; Löwenthal on, 80–83; Marcuse on, 68–71, 192; Nazi Germany and, 75, 82–83, 140; Neumann on, 82–83, 137, 139–42, 151, 183; New Left critiques of, 204–5. *See also* State capitalism
Caplan, Jane, 218, 302n.121
Castoriadis, Cornelius, 3, 174, 294–95n.87
Catalonia, 97–98
CDU. *See* Christian Democratic Union
Center Party (Zentrum), 30, 46
China, 116, 179, 187, 213–14
Christian Democratic Union (Christlich Demokratische Union Deutschlands—CDU), 285n.6
Christianity: Horkheimer and Adorno on, 163, 165
Christlich Demokratische Union Deutschlands. *See* Christian Democratic Union
Class and class conflict, 75, 81, 83–84, 94,

160, 162, 178, 214–15, 254–55n.14. *See also* Marx, Karl; Marxism; Working class
Clay, Lucius, 195
Cohen, Jean, 207
Cold war, 11–12, 158, 172, 174, 178–79, 185–95, 200, 207, 212–15, 217–20
Comintern (Communist International), 43–45, 80, 86, 89, 100, 105–6, 117, 123; and KPD, 24–28, 30–33; Rosenberg on, 49–51; and social fascism, 38, 45
Communism, 5–6, 8, 73, 79, 84, 118, 188, 198, 205, 208, 210–11, 220, 224–25n.8, 297n.98; as a movement, party, or organization, 9, 36, 114, 157–58, 181, 186, 284n.1; post-1989, 113, 181, 216; in the Soviet Union, 8, 123, 204, 208; as a state regime, 85, 102, 109, 168, 171, 179, 216, 296n.95; in Weimar Germany, 46, 66, 77, 85. *See also* Council Communism
Communist Party, Austrian. *See* Austrian Communist Party
Communist Party, French. *See* French Communist Party
Communist Party, German. *See* German Communist Party; Socialist Unity Party of Germany.
Communist Party, Soviet Union. *See* Soviet Communist Party
Communist Party, Spanish. *See* Spanish Communist Party
Communist Party, U.S.A., 19, 182
Congress for Cultural Freedom, 177–78, 185–86
Conservatism, 17, 106, 167, 208
Coughlin, Charles, 164
Council Communism, 7, 203, 208–9, 292n.76. *See also Räte*
Council for Democracy, 143
Counterrevolution, theories of, 208; Borkenau's, 103; Korsch's, 125–29, 157
Croatia, 211
Cuba, 66, 213
Czechoslovakia, 66, 80, 89, 178

Dan, Fyodor, 59–60
Daniels, Robert V., 297n.100
DDP. *See* German Democratic Party
DDR. *See* German Democratic Republic
Deconstructionism, 207. *See also* Poststructuralism
Denicke, Iurii (George Decker), 86, 89, 136
Derrida, Jacques, 208, 295–96n.92

Deutsch, Julius, 104, 268n.137
Deutsche Demokratische Partei. *See* German Democratic Party
Deutschnationale Volkspartei. *See* German National People's Party
Dewey, John, 110
Diner, Dan, 165–66
Disch, Lisa Jane, 207
Dissent, 177
Djilas, Milovan, 179–80
DNVP. *See* German National People's Party
Drucker, Peter, 114, 276n.114
Dubiel, Helmut, 269n.1, 294n.84
Dutschke, Rudi, 192, 196–97, 199, 204, 290–91n.63

East Germany. *See* German Democratic Republic
Eastman, Max, 114
Ebert, Friedrich, 23, 151
Eisler, Elfriede. *See* Fischer, Ruth
Eisler, Gerhart, 19, 186, 232n.45
Eisler, Hanns, 159, 232n.44, 232n.45
Eisner, Kurt, 67
End of history: idea of, 292,n.72. *See also* Kojève, Alexandre; Fritzsche, Peter; Fukuyama, Francis; Hegel, Georg Friedrich Wilhelm; Marx, Karl; Roth, Michael; Strauss, Leo
Engels, Friedrich, 43
England, 53–54, 66, 86, 100. *See also* Great Britain
Enlightenment, 205; and critique of society, 167–69; and human rights, 206–7; and instrumentalized reason, 161–63, 207–8
Erler, Fritz, 259n.45
Existentialism, 69–70, 189, 283n.195

Fabian Society, 36, 105
Falange, 96
Fascism, 47, 64–66, 100–102, 109, 118, 122–23, 131, 160–65, 167, 171, 209, 211, 220, 224–25n.8; Borkenau on, 51–53, 92–95, 100–102, 118, 122–23; in Germany, 42, 46, 59, 67, 113; Horkheimer on, 131; Horkheimer and Adorno on, 160–65, 167; as ideology, 72, 84, 190, 208; Korsch on, 126–28; Löwenthal on, 80–85; Marcuse on, 68–71, 75; as a movement, party, or organization, 7, 29, 43–45, 60, 75, 92–95; "red and brown," 101, 109,

151, 171, 270n.18; Rosenberg on, 71–76; as a state regime, 3, 5, 63, 71–72, 84–85, 89; Thalheimer on, 43–45; theories of, 2, 6–8, 23, 39–40, 60, 65, 91, 93, 95, 98–99, 107, 214, 216, 251–52n.1, 252–53n.3; Zetkin on, 24–27. *See also Falange,* Fascist Italy; Fascist Party, Italian; Hitler, Adolf; Mussolini, Benito; National Socialism; Nazi Germany; Nazi Party; Neofascism

Fascist Italy, 9, 39, 43, 45, 52–53, 58, 62, 64, 66, 73, 86, 91, 98, 102, 124, 134, 136, 141, 157. *See also* Fascism; Fascist Party, Italian; Mussolini, Benito

Fascist Party, Italian, 6, 52, 72, 74, 94

Federal Republic of Germany (Bundesrepublik Deutschland—BRD), 104, 106, 179, 189, 196, 201, 211, 220; and debates on National Socialism, 215–16; and totalitarian theory, 2, 9–10, 15, 148

First World War. *See* World War I

Fischer, Fritz, 157

Fischer, Klaus P., 299–300n.109

Fischer, Ruth (Elfriede Eisler), 11, 19, 77–78, 158, 179–80; anti-Communism of, 31, 47, 103, 177–79, 185, 232n.44; background of, 31; in exile, 253n.4; Korsch and, 179–80; as KPD leader, 26–27, 31–33, 234n.13, 234–35n.14; on Luxemburg, 31–32, 235n.15, 236–37n.28; *Stalin and German Communism,* 179, 186–87; and Stalinization thesis, 287n.32

Flechtheim, Ossip K., 78, 148, 195, 290n.57

Foucault, Michel, 207–8, 295n.90

Fraenkel, Ernst, 11, 53, 143, 166, 171, 178, 202, 218, 302n.122; background of, 144; *The Dual State,* 144–50, 153–54; and Free University of Berlin, 148, 195, 198

France, 15, 25–26, 43–45, 65–66, 86, 89, 130, 136, 144, 174

Franckenstein, Joseph von, 185

Franco, Francisco, 5, 101–2

Frank, Karl, 77, 79, 105

Franke, Vera, 78

Frankfurt School, 10–11, 161, 281n.182. *See also* Institute of Social Research

Free University of Berlin, 148, 181, 195–99, 289–90n.56, 290n.57

French Communist Party, 174, 182, 284n.1

French Socialist Party, 174

Freudian thought, 192

Frick, Wilhelm, 151

Friedländer, Saul, 282n.191

Friedrich, Carl J., 4, 14, 102, 144, 159, 223–24n.5; and Free University of Berlin, 195, 289–90n.56; Neumann and, 143; on Nolte, 301n.114

Friedrich-Brzezinski model, 4–6, 12, 18, 197, 211–12, 214, 225n.9, 297–98n.101. *See also* Totalitarianism, cold war theories of

Fritzsche, Peter, 256n.32, 292n.72, 297–98n.101

Fromm, Erich, 164, 281n.188

Fukuyama, Francis, 292n.72

Functionalism. *See* Structuralism

Gegen den Strom, 43

Genocide, 165, 215–16

German Communist Party (Kommunistische Partei Deutschlands—KPD), 16, 19, 287n.32; founding of, 24, 110, 234n.8; during Nazi period, 64, 70, 74, 79, 85–86, 250–51n.136, 262–63n.81; Neu Beginnen members and, 76–77, 89–90, 103–6, 116–18; "Schlageter line" of, 25–27; Stalinization thesis and, 217, 238n.36, 287n.32, 301n.118; during Weimar Republic, 8, 22–38, 41–49, 51, 54–56, 60–62, 66, 150–51, 176, 187, 202. *See also* Socialist Unity Party of Germany

German Communist Party Opposition (Kommunistische Partei Deutschlands Opposition—KPDO), 32, 43, 76.

German Democratic Party (Deutsche Demokratische Partei—DDP), 61

German Democratic Republic (Deutsche Demokratische Republik—DDR), 2, 177, 220, 287n.32

German Empire. *See* Imperial Germany

German International Communists (Internationale Kommunisten Deutschlands—IKD), 110

German National People's Party (Deutschnationale Volkspartei—DNVP), 45

German Social Democratic Party. *See* Social Democratic Party of Germany

German-Soviet Pact. *See* Hitler-Stalin Pact

Germany. *See* Federal Republic of Germany; German Democratic Republic; Imperial Germany; Nazi Germany; Weimar Republic

Germany, post-WWII (1945–49), 3, 117, 171,

176, 178, 185; occupation and division
of, 3, 174–75
Germino, Dante, 189
Gesellschaft, Die, 46, 57, 60–61, 80, 85, 135
Geyer, Curt, 66, 87, 187
Glaeßner, Gert-Joachim, 199
Gleason, Abbott, 12, 15–17, 254–55n.14,
280n.177
Goebbels, Joseph, 46, 151, 164
Goldhagen, Daniel Jonah, 281–82n.189,
297–98n.101
GPU, 267n.123, 268n.137. *See also* NKVD
Gramsci, Antonio, 36, 239–40n.43,
246n.99
Great Britain, 53–54, 66, 86, 100, 117, 124,
136
Groener, Wilhelm, 151
Grünberg, Carl, 91
Gruppe Leninistische Organisation (ORG).
See Neu Beginnen
Gurland, Arkadij, 77, 158, 175–76, 284n.1

Habermas, Jürgen, 194, 201, 205–8, 216,
218, 291n.68, 295n.90; discourse theory
and ethics of, 206–8, 294n.85
Hapsburgs, 210
Havel, Václav, 4, 223n.4
Hayden, Tom, 294n.83
Hayek, Friedrich A., 121
Hegel, Georg Wilhelm Friedrich: philoso-
phy of, 36, 162, 206, 239–40n.43,
292n.72
Heidegger, Martin, 167, 283n.195; and
Marcuse, 70–71, 253n.8; and membership in Nazi Party, 255n.23; and Nolte,
215, 300n.113; as rector of Freiburg University under Nazis, 67, 70
Heller, Hermann, 53
Hennig, Eike, 11, 149
Hertz, Paul, 275n.100
Hess, Rudolf, 152
Hilferding, Rudolf, 8, 11, 35, 111, 130, 133,
136–37, 161, 171, 177, 202, 275n.100; background of, 34; *Das Finanzkapital (Finance Capital),* 34; and *Die Gesellschaft,*
46, 60–61, 85; "Das historische Problem," 136; "State Capitalism or Totalitarian State Economy," 134–41, 182; and
"total state," 86–87; and Weimar SPD,
34–35, 60–62; and *Zeitschrift für
Sozialismus,* 85–87, 89, 261n.70

Hillgruber, Andreas, 216
Hindenburg, Paul von, 33, 59, 61–62, 74
Historikerstreit (historians' debate), 11, 215–
16, 300n.111, 300n.113, 301n.114
Hitchens, Christopher, 231n.40, 272n.43,
297n.100
Hitler, Adolf, 27, 31, 35, 39, 74, 106, 123, 127,
156–57, 164, 190, 197, 212; appointment
to chancellorship, 59, 61–62; Heidegger
on, 70; and the Nazi state, 87–88, 94,
151–52, 217
Hitler-Stalin Pact, 65, 89, 98, 109, 111, 125,
158, 187, 268–69n.140; Borkenau on, 119,
123; Neu Beginnen on, 104–5, 114–17
Hitler Youth, 46
Hobbes, Thomas, 150
Horkheimer, Max, 11, 32, 121, 125, 134, 139,
176, 178, 184, 193, 202, 204, 207, 214; on
anti-Semitism, 164–67, 281n.187; "Autoritärer Staat," 129–34, 142, 273–74n.80;
background of, 40; *Critical Theory,* 189–
90; *Dämmerung,* 40–41; *Dialektik der
Aufklärung (Dialectic of Enlightenment),*
142, 149, 158–70, 189, 192, 205–6, 277–
78n.141, 283n.195; *Eclipse of Reason,* 189;
and Institute of Social Research, 10, 40–
42, 54, 89, 91, 98–99, 137–39, 158–60,
189, 194, 241–42n.55; "Die Ohnmacht
der Arbeiterklasse," 40–41; *Studien über
Autorität und Familie,* 98
House Committee on Un-American Activities (HUAC), 19, 232n.44, 232n.45
Howe, Irving, 294n.83
HUAC. *See* House Committee on Un-
American Activities
Hugenberg, Alfred, 45
Hungary: 1956 revolution in, 4, 295–96n.92
Hussein, Saddam, 213
Husserl, Edmund, 47, 67, 159

Ibarruri, Dolores (La Pasionaria), 267–
68n.130
IKD. *See* German International Commu-
nists
Imperial Germany, 71, 74, 211
Imperialism, 203, 213
Independent Social Democratic Party of
Germany (Unabhängige
Sozialdemokratische Partei
Deutschlands—USPD), 29, 32, 34, 36, 87
Institute of Social Research, 10, 51, 53, 70,

77, 89, 158–71, 176, 187–88, 195, 208, 281n.188, 294n.84; in exile, 68, 78, 98–99, 136–38, 144, 158–59, 253n.4; Korsch on, 155, 158, 279n.166, 279n.175; Marxism and, 161, 242n.56, 281n.182; postwar, 188–89, 194, 205; Schmitt and, 248–49n.115; during Weimar, 36–37, 40–42, 241–42n.55. *See also* Adorno, Theodor Wiesengrund; Frankfurt School; Horkheimer, Max; Kirchheimer, Otto; Lowenthal, Leo; Marcuse, Herbert; Neumann, Franz; Pollock, Friedrich

Institut für Sozialforschung. *See* Institute of Social Research

Intentionalism, 88, 213, 215, 261–62n.78, 263n.82

International Brigades, 101

Internationale Kommunisten Deutschlands. *See* German International Communists

Iraq, 213

Isaac, Jeffrey C., 207

Islamic states, 213

Italian fascism. *See* Fascism; Fascist Italy; Fascist Party, Italian; Mussolini, Benito

Italy, 42. *See also* Fascist Italy

Jacoby, Russell, 241n.53, 273–74n.80

James, C. L. R., 252–53n.3

Japan, 109, 116

Jay, Martin, 249–50n.122; on Horkheimer and Adorno, 161–63, 166, 273–74n.80, 281n.182; on Marcuse, 254n.11, 254–55n.14; on Pollock, 276n.107

Jews, European, 16–17, 53, 74, 79, 82, 132, 152, 164–65, 215. *See also* Anti-Semitism

Jünger, Ernst, 145

Kahn-Freund, Otto, 53

Kamenev, Lev, 25

Kant, Immanuel: philosophy of, 69, 159, 169, 181

Kautsky, Karl, 34, 61, 78–79, 112

Kellner, Douglas: on Korsch, 97, 241n.53; on Neumann and Pollock, 275n.104

Kershaw, Ian, 8, 11–12, 216–18, 301n.114, 301n.118

Kirchheimer, Otto, 158, 160, 171, 176–77, 179, 218, 286n.24; background of, 56; and Institute of Social Research, 158–60; and Luxemburg, 32, 58–60; "Marxismus,

Diktatur und Organisationsformen des Proletariats," 59–60; *Political Justice,* 148; postwar writings of, 195, 290n.58; and Schmitt, 56, 230n.36, 248–49n.115, 249n.119; and SPD, 249–50n.122; *Weimar—und Was Dann?* 57–59; "Zur Staatslehre des Sozialismus und Bolschewismus," 56–58

Kirkpatrick, Jeane, 231n.40, 299n.106

Kirwan, Celia, 293n.81

Koestler, Arthur, 4

Kohl, Helmut, 215

Kojève, Alexandre, 239–40n.43, 292n.72

Kolakowski, Leszek, 230n.34, 260n.63

Kollontai, Alexandra, 25

Kommunistische Partei Deutschlands. *See* German Communist Party

Kommunistische Partei Deutschlands Opposition. *See* German Communist Party Opposition

Korean War, 186

Korsch, Hedda, 37

Korsch, Karl, 11, 32, 47, 114, 121, 124, 129–34, 138, 142, 161, 167, 171, 186, 188, 200, 202, 204, 208–9; background of, 36–37; "Blutiger Mai in Berlin," 37; "Economics and Politics in Revolutionary Spain," 97, 268n.133; in exile, 41–42, 253n.4; "The Fascist Counter-Revolution," 126–28, 272n.45; on imperialism, 203; and Institute of Social Research, 97–98, 155, 158, 279n.166, 279n.175; *Karl Marx,* 98; and KPD, 31, 36; on Lenin, 241n.53; *Marxismus und Philosophie,* 239–40n.43; "The Marxist Ideology in Russia," 39–40; on Neumann's *Behemoth,* 154–57; postwar career of, 179–81; and Soviet Union, 240–41n.45; and Spanish civil war, 97–98; "State and Counter-Revolution," 125–26; "The Workers' Fight against Fascism," 127–28

Kosovo, 211

KPD. *See* German Communist Party

KPDO. *See* German Communist Party Opposition

Kracauer, Siegfried, 159

Kreisau Circle, 106

Krenek, Ernst, 159

Kristallnacht pogrom ("Crystal Night"), 74, 165

Kühnl, Reinhard, 9, 11, 149, 192

Labour Party, 116, 120
Laqueur, Walter, 291n.68
Lasch, Christopher, 192–93
Laski, Harold, 53, 277–78n.141
Lasky, Melvin J., 185
Lassalle, Ferdinand, 130
Lederer, Emil, 246n.96
Lefort, Claude, 11–12, 15, 200, 204, 206–7, 209, 218, 295n.88, 296–97n.96; and Socialisme ou Barbarie, 3, 174, 294–95n.87
Lenin, Vladimir I., 25, 31, 43, 50, 190, 196, 212; Borkenau on, 94, 123–24; Fischer on, 187; Korsch on, 241n.53; Neumann on, 181, Rühle on, 112–13. *See also* Bolshevism; Leninism
Leninism, 31, 39, 45, 49, 78, 94, 117, 170, 212; Kirchheimer on, 58–59
Lenya, Lotte, 159
Levi, Paul, 28, 31, 287n.32
Lewin, Moshe, 217
Liberalism, 17, 51, 119, 124, 167, 178–79, 182–83, 207, 209, 213, 299n.104; and the bourgeoisie, 165, 169, 236n.21, 283n.200; and capitalism, 92, 121; fascist attacks on, 71, 82; and rights, 28, 168–69, 176, 209, 213, 254n.11; socialist critiques of, 57, 68–71, 75, 128, 132
Liebknecht, Karl, 30, 39, 67, 109–10
Linz, Juan, 227n.21
Living Marxism, 97, 125
Löwenheim, Walter, 77–79, 175
Lowenthal, Leo, 10, 158, 283n.196
Löwenthal, Richard, 8, 11, 84–85, 121, 124, 135, 141–42, 161–62, 167, 179, 186, 202, 204, 218–19, 283n.203; anti-Communism of, 178, 197–98, 302n.122; background of, 76; "Der Faschismus," 80–84; and Free University of Berlin, 148, 195–99; on Habermas, 294n,85; *Jenseits des Kapitalismus*, 84, 196; and KPD, 51, 54, 76, 116–18; on Marcuse, 254n.12; and Neu Beginnen, 76–80, 90, 104–6, 114–18, 171, 198; and SPD, 76, 84, 104–6, 195–98, 262–63n.81, 291n.68; "Die Wandlungen des Kapitalismus," 80–81
Lukács, Georg, 36–37, 41, 157, 159, 196, 239–40n.43
Luxemburg, Rosa, 24, 27, 34, 39, 67, 109, 112, 190, 202; Borkenau on, 30–31; Fischer on, 31–32, 236–37n.28; Horkheimer on, 32, 190; Kirchheimer on, 32, 58–59; Korsch on, 32; Rosenberg on, 31, 236n.26; on Russian Revolution, 27–28, 190
Lyotard, Jean-François, 3, 206–8, 294–95n.87, 295n.90, 296n.93

Macdonald, Dwight, 276n.114
Mannheim, Karl, 6–7, 276n.112, 283n.203
Marcuse, Herbert, 10–11, 40, 75–76, 80, 84, 121, 146, 171, 176, 178, 202, 204–5, 209, 214; background of, 66–68; and cold war, 178, 190–91, 194; *Eros and Civilization*, 184, 191–92; and Free University of Berlin, 196–97; *Hegel's Ontology and the Theory of Historicity*, 67–68; and Heidegger, 67–68, 70–71, 253n.8; and Institute of Social Research, 54, 68–69, 158, 170, 283n.203; "Der Kampf gegen den Liberalismus," 68–71, 166, 254n.11, 254n.12, 254–55n.14; on liberalism, 255n.21, 255n.22; *One-Dimensional Man*, 184, 193–94, 297n.99; and OSS and State Department, 158, 171; *Reason and Revolution*, 149, 159–60, 255n.22; "Repressive Tolerance," 289n.54; *Soviet Marxism*, 191–92; and Spanish civil war, 98
Martov, Yulii (Yuri), 59–60
Marx, Karl, 15, 43, 58, 76, 83, 110, 113, 121, 184, 187–88, 202, 206, 281n.182; on capitalist crisis, 120–21, 273n.69; *Eighteenth Brumaire of Louis Bonaparte*, 44, 73, 126; on Jews and anti-Semitism, 164, 282n.190, 282n.191
Marxism, 16–17, 41, 56, 65, 75–76, 90, 94–95, 107, 121, 125, 134, 140, 149, 157, 167, 169–70, 174–75, 194, 202, 206–9, 212, 260n.63, 292n.72; and anti-Semitism, 164, 166, 282n.191; and capitalism, 93, 126, 128–30, 208; and class conflict, 56, 73, 157, 215; cold war opposition to, 19, 178; critiques and revisions of, 136, 139, 141–42, 155, 160–63, 178–84, 195–96, 296n.93; and critiques of dictatorship, 80, 82–83, 209, 219–20; Hegel and, 36, 239–40n.43; and revolution, 56; Soviet, 39, 189, 191–92, 296n.95; Western, 39
Marxists, 7, 9, 12, 23–25, 31, 36, 73, 96, 113, 119, 200, 202, 214, 219
Maslow, Arkadij, 33, 253n.4
Mason, Tim, 183, 212–13, 218, 226n.16, 256n.28

Massing, Hede, 158
Massing, Paul, 158, 175
Mattick, Paul, 32, 97, 114, 270–71n.19
May Day violence of 1929, 35–39
Mensheviks, 16, 59–60, 86, 89, 135–36,
    250n.126
Mexico, 66, 110
Milosz, Czeslaw, 4
Mises, Ludwig von, 121
Modernization theory, 52, 73, 83, 101–2,
    246n.99
Modern Quarterly, 125
Modern Review, 136
Mommsen, Hans, 13, 301n.114, 302n.121
Mussolini, Benito, 6–7, 52, 69, 72, 74, 94,
    164; and "March on Rome" coup, 25, 44

Namuth, Hans, 265n.112
Nationalism, 94, 176, 211
National Socialism (Nazism), 48, 62, 65,
    74–75, 88, 164, 174, 183, 186; Borkenau
    on, 92–94, 120–22; and Communism/
    Stalinism, 109, 111, 150, 193, 203, 205,
    209–12, 214–15, 217; and fascism, 8–9, 13,
    42–43, 52, 109; Horkheimer on, 130;
    Horkheimer and Adorno on, 160;
    Korsch on, 128, 154; Neumann on, 150–
    51; and "race," 16, 74. *See also* Fascism;
    Hitler, Adolf; Nazi Germany; Nazi Party
Nationalsozialistische Arbeiterpartei
    Deutschlands. *See* Nazi Party
NATO (North Atlantic Treaty Organiza-
    tion), 19, 177–78
Nazi Germany, 1–2, 5, 8–9, 14, 18, 56, 62,
    64–66, 71, 73, 79, 82–89, 91, 93, 98, 102,
    105–11, 114–19, 123–25, 130, 133–57, 165,
    168, 171–73, 175, 182, 191–92, 199–200,
    211, 215–19, 287n.32; anti-Semitism in,
    16–17, 73–74, 122, 164–66, 216, 281n.187,
    281–82n.189, 297–98n.101; economy of,
    50, 82–84, 119–22, 135–36, 140–41, 147,
    150, 154–56, 260n.62. *See also* National
    Socialism
Nazi Party (Nationalsozialistische
    Arbeiterpartei Deutschlands—NSDAP),
    7–8, 21–22, 29, 35, 38–39, 41–42, 45–46,
    48, 51, 53–56, 59–62, 67, 74–75, 141, 150–
    51, 187; and *Machtergreifung* (seizure of
    power), 51, 60, 62–64, 66, 71, 77, 85, 106,
    152, 165. *See also* Hitler, Adolf; National
    Socialism; Nazi Germany
Nenni, Pietro, 252–53n.3

Neoconservatism, 216
Neofascism, 14, 208
NEP (New Economic Policy), 50
Neu Beginnen, 85, 105–7, 171, 175, 259n.45,
    263n.88, 263n.89; in Germany, 76–80;
    and Hitler-Stalin Pact, 104–5, 114–16;
    and KPD, 89–90, 116–18; postwar roles
    of former members of, 176, 195, 198–99;
    and SOPADE, 259n.52; and Spanish civil
    war, 103–4, 263–64n.91
Neumann, Franz, 8, 11, 60, 88, 144, 146,
    160, 162, 177–78, 195, 198, 202, 204, 218–
    19; on anti-Semitism, 166, 282n.192;
    background of, 53–54; *Behemoth*, 53, 88,
    139–42, 148–57, 159, 183, 202, 217,
    260n.62, 277–78n.141; on capitalism and
    Nazi Germany, 82–83, 130, 140, 151–55,
    260n.62; "The Decay of German De-
    mocracy," 22, 54–56; and Free Univer-
    sity of Berlin, 195; and Institute of Social
    Research, 53–54, 78, 143, 158; and Laski,
    53; and OSS, 158, 171; postwar criticism
    of Marxism, 179, 181–84, 195, 260n.63;
    postwar writings of, 183–84, 214,
    286n.24; and Schmitt, 53, 146, 151–53,
    230n.36, 248–49n.115; and SPD, 53–54,
    85, 151, 175–76, 181–82; and state capital-
    ism, 133, 137, 139–43, 276n.112; on Wei-
    mar Republic, 22, 54–56, 58, 151–52
Neumann, Sigmund, 154, 278–79n.160,
    289–90n.56
New Essays, 155
New Left, 10, 189–92, 214; in Germany,
    148, 196–97, 199, 290–91n.63; in United
    States, 290–91n.63, 294n.83. *See also*
    Dutschke, Rudi; Hayden, Tom; Socialist
    German Students' League; Students for a
    Democratic Society
New Philosophers, 208, 296n.93
New School for Social Research, 144,
    246n.96
Nicaragua, 213
"Night of the Long Knives," 75, 257n.35
Nixon, Richard, 19
NKVD, 100, 104, 267n.123. *See also* GPU
Nolte, Ernst, 198, 201, 223–45n.5,
    301n.114; on fascism, 12–13; and
    Historikerstreit, 215–16, 300n.111,
    300n.113
NSDAP. *See* Nazi Party
Nuremberg Laws, 74. *See also* Anti-
    Semitism; Nazi Germany

Oakeshott, Michael, 189
ORG (Gruppe Leninistische Organisation).
  See Neu Beginnen
Orwell, George, 4, 96, 187, 193, 227n.20,
  263n.89, 293n.81; and Borkenau, 100–
  101, 124, 186, 267n.129; *Homage to
  Catalonia,* 101, 203; on imperialism,
  203, 293n.80; *Nineteen Eighty-Four,* 4,
  187, 201–4
OSS (Office of Strategic Services), 158, 171
Ostpolitik, 302n.122
Ottomans, 210

Pachter, Henry (Heinz Paechter), 54, 158;
  and Arendt, 47; background of, 46–47;
  and *Dissent,* 177; *Espagne,* 96–97;
  "Kommunismus und Klasse," 46–49, 63,
  97; and Korsch, 47, 241n.53; on Marcuse,
  254n.12; and Spanish civil war, 96–97;
  and SPD, 46; and Wittfogel, 47
Panama, 66, 253n.4
Papen, Franz von, 61–62, 74, 245n.86
Pareto, Vilfredo, 85, 91–94, 99
Partido Comunista de España. *See* Spanish
  Communist Party
Partido Obrero de Unificación Marxista.
  See Workers' Party of Marxist
  Unification
Paxmann, Liesel, 78
PCE. *See* Spanish Communist Party
Peukert, Detlev, 218
Pilsudski, Jósef Klemens, 5
Poland, 180–214; invasion of, 105, 109,
  114, 118, 165
Pollock, Friedrich, 10–11, 144, 176, 178;
  background of, 137–38, and Institute of
  Social Research, 91, 98–99, 137–38, 160,
  171, 275n.105; *Die planwirtschaftlichen
  Versuche in der Sowjetunion, 1917–1927,*
  276n.107; "State Capitalism," 137–43,
  146, 276n.107, 276n.112, 276n.114; and
  state capitalism debate with Neumann,
  130, 132–33, 182
Pollock, Jackson, 265n.112
Popular Front, 89, 101
Poststructuralism, 205–8. See also Foucault, Michel; Lyotard, Jean-François
POUM. *See* Workers' Party of Marxist
  Unification
Primacy of the political, theory of the,
  135–37, 140–42, 219; Bonapartism
  theory and, 244n.74; Hilferding's turn

to, 136, 275n.100; Löwenthal and, 83;
  Mason on, 256n.28; Neumann's turn to,
  182–83, 260n.63

Radek, Karl, 25–27, 235n.15, 235n.18
Räte (soldiers' and workers' councils), 131,
  202, 236n.26; Geyer and, 87; Korsch and,
  36; Marcuse and, 67; Rühle and, 110, 112–
  13. *See also* Council Communism
Reagan, Ronald, 215, 299n.106
Red Army Fraction (Rote Armee Fraktion),
  14
Reich, Wilhelm, 164
Reichstag, 27, 36, 49, 54, 109, 152; and elec-
  tion of 1928, 32–33, 45, 55; and election
  of 1930, 38, 46; and election of July 1932,
  51
Rein, Mark, 103–4, 136, 268n.135, 268n.137
Reuter, Ernst, 176, 287n.32
Rights, civil and human, 65, 206–7, 213,
  218; liberalism and, 69, 176, 209,
  254n.11; Luxemburg on, 28
Röhm, Ernst, 152
Rosenberg, Arthur, 11, 47, 80, 84, 177, 202,
  219; on anti-Semitism, 73–74; back-
  ground of, 49; *Demokratie und
  Sozialismus,* 177; in exile, 71; *Der
  Faschismus als Massenbewegung,* 71–76;
  Geschichte der Deutschen Republik, 74;
  Geschichte des Bolschewismus, 49–51, 60–
  61, 134; on Luxemburg, 31, 236n.26; on
  Neumann's *Behemoth,* 142, 153–54
Rote Armee Fraktion. *See* Red Army Faction
Rote Kapelle, 269n.147
Roth, Michael S., 292n.72
Rousset, David, 3
Rühle, Alice Gerstel, 110, 253n.4
Rühle, Otto, 11, 65, 78, 107, 113–15, 118, 123,
  131, 151, 167, 171, 177; background of,
  109–10; "Brauner und Roter
  Faschismus," 14, 110–14; and Council
  Communism, 208–9; in exile, 110,
  253n.4; on Hilferding, 111; Korsch on,
  114; and Trotsky, 110
Russia (post-1991), 113, 180
Russian Revolution, 31, 45; Borkenau on,
  94, 103, 123; Dutschke on, 196; Luxem-
  burg on, 27–28, 190; Rosenberg on, 49–
  51; Rühle on, 112

SA (Sturmabteilung), 54, 75, 152
Salvemini, Gaetano, 252–53n.3

Sartre, Jean-Paul, 174, 284n.1
Sas, Gyula, 234n.11
Schapiro, Leonard, 225n.11
Scheidemann, Philipp, 23
Scheuerman, William, 286n.24
Schifrin, Alexander, 61, 65–66, 86, 89
Schlageter, Leo, 25–27, 67
"Schlageter line" of KPD, 25–27
Schlangen, Walter, 13–14, 17
Schleicher, Kurt von, 62
Schmidt, Erich, 79
Schmitt, Carl, 14, 71, 230n.36, 248–49n.115, 249n.118, 290n.57; Fraenkel on, 145–47; Kirchheimer and, 56–58; and membership in Nazi Party, 53, 255n.23; Neumann and, 53, 151–53
Schoenberg, Arnold, 159
Schorske, Carl E., 5
Schumacher, Kurt, 175–76, 285n.6
Schumann, Edith, 78
Second World War. *See* World War II
SED. *See* Socialist Unity Party of Germany
SDS. *See* Socialist German Students' League; Students for a Democratic Society
Sedov, Leon, 253n.4
Sedova, Natalya, 110, 253n.4
Serbia, 211
Serge, Victor, 252–53n.3
Seydewitz, Max, 88, 262n.80, 263n.82
Seydewitz, Ruth Lewy, 262n.80
Shah of Iran, 196
Shklar, Judith, 183
Show trials, 89–90, 98
Silone, Ignazio, 252–53n.3
Slovenia, 211
Social democracy, 32, 36, 77, 119, 136, 198
Social Democratic Party of Germany (Sozialdemokratische Partei Deutschlands—SPD), 29, 109–10; leftist critiques of, 41, 56–69, 70, 113, 155, 175–76, 181–82, 196–97; during Nazi period, 64, 66, 74, 76, 78–79, 81, 85–87, 89, 103–6, 136; Neu Beginnen members and, 76–79, 81, 89, 106, 117, 291n.68; in postwar period, 11, 175–78, 196–97, 291n.68; during Weimar Republic, 22–24, 27, 29–38, 41–42, 46–48, 53–62, 111, 144, 151, 176, 245n.86, 249–50n.122. *See also* Social democracy; Socialism; Social Democratic Party of Germany in Exile; Independent Social Democratic Party of Germany
Social Democratic Party of Germany in Ex-

ile (Sozialdemokratische Partei Deutschlands im Exil—SOPADE), 79, 117, 259n.52.
Social fascism, 27, 37–38, 51, 66, 76, 105; Brecht on, 240–41n.45; Thalheimer on, 38; Trotsky on, 38
Socialism, 65, 71, 105, 119–20, 124, 139, 168, 175–76, 178–79, 200–201, 209, 220, 224–25n.8
Socialisme ou Barbarie, 3, 174, 294–95n.87
Socialist German Students' League (Sozialistische Deutsche Studenten—SDS), 196–97, 290–91n.63
Socialist Unity Party of Germany (Sozialistische Einheitspartei Deutschlands—SED), 175, 187, 197, 262n.80
Soldiers' and workers' councils. *See* Räte; Council Communism
Solidarity movement, 214
Söllner, Alfons, 12, 150; on Marcuse, 255n.21
Solzhenitsyn, Alexander, 4, 296n.93
SOPADE. *See* Social Democratic Party of Germany in Exile
Sotsialisticheskii Vestnik, 135
Soviet Communism. *See* Bolshevism; Leninism; Soviet Union; Stalinism
Soviet Communist Party, 94, 117, 123, 135, 180, 287n.32. *See also* Bolshevism; Communism; Lenin, Vladimir I.; Leninism; Soviet Union; Stalin, Joseph; Stalinism
Soviet-German Pact. *See* Hitler-Stalin Pact
Soviet Union: and cold war, 2–6, 19, 106, 174, 177–78, 185, 188–89, 191–92, 197, 207–8; economy of, 50, 126–28, 130–31, 134–41, 148, 182; and interwar Left, 25, 28–29, 33, 38–40, 49–51, 57–59, 62, 64–66, 89–91, 97–98, 100, 107, 181–82; as place of exile, 27; and totalitarian theory, 1, 3–5, 8–9, 14–16, 18, 45, 65, 84–86, 91, 93–95, 102, 108–11, 114–19, 123–28, 161, 163, 171, 173, 188, 191–92, 197, 200, 209, 211–12, 215–17; and World War II, 105, 109, 114–18, 297n.100. *See also* Bolshevism; Lenin, Vladimir I.; Leninism; Stalin, Joseph; Stalinism
Sozialdemokratische Partei Deutschlands. *See* Social Democratic Party of Germany
Sozialdemokratische Partei Deutschlands im Exil. *See* Social Democratic Party of Germany in Exile

Sozialistische Einheitspartei Deutschlands. *See* Socialist Unity Party of Germany

Spain, 107, 116, 130, 136; Borkenau and, 96; civil war in, 65, 96–104; fascism in, 64; Korsch and, 97–98; Pachter and, 96–97

Spanish anarchists, 97, 99–101, 103

Spanish civil war, 65, 89–90, 96–104, 107, 203, 263–64n.91

Spanish Communist Party (Partido Comunista de España—PCE), 97, 99–100, 103

Spanish liberals, 99

Spartacist Group (Spartacist League), 24, 30, 43, 110, 202

SPD. *See* Social Democratic Party of Germany

Speier, Hans, 246n.96

Spiro, Herbert, 225n.11

Stalin, Joseph, 7, 19, 25, 50, 80, 105, 112–13, 116, 123–24, 131, 185, 187, 197, 210, 217; and KPD, 33, 187; and Soviet state, 19, 38, 64–65, 94, 123–24, 137, 181, 212, 217. *See also* Soviet Union; Stalinism

Stalinism, 2–3, 63, 75, 174, 191, 193, 200, 203, 214, 217, 220; Derrida on, 295–96n.92; and fascism or Nazism, 79, 109, 172; Fischer on, 19; Hilferding on, 135; Horkheimer on, 190; Korsch on, 39; Rühle on, 113; Trotsky on, 252–53n.3; weaknesses as analytical category, 217, 238n.36, 287n.32, 301n.118. *See also* Stalin; Soviet Union

Stalinization thesis. *See* Stalinism

State capitalism, 50, 129–43, 146, 165, 170; Hilferding on, 135; Institute of Social Research and, 129–34, 137–43, 165; Korsch on, 125, 128; Lenin and, 50; Rosenberg on, 134; Rühle and, 111. *See also* Capitalism

Stern, Günther, 202, 280n.178

Sternhell, Zeev, 226n.16

Strauss, Leo, 189, 292n.72

Stresemann, Gustav, 29–30, 35

Structuralism (functionalism), 88, 213, 215, 261–62n.78

Students for a Democratic Society (SDS), 294n.83

Studies in Philosophy and Social Science. See *Zeitschrift für Sozialforschung*

Stürmer, Michael, 216

Switzerland, 68

Thalheimer, August, 27, 38, 46, 52–53, 110, 243n.65; background of, 43; and Bonapartism theory, 43–45, 90, 126, 244n.74

Thälmann, Ernst, 33, 47, 80

Thompson, E. P., 9, 227n.20

Tito (Josip Broz), 179, 210

Totalitarianism, cold war theories of, 2–4, 13–17, 26, 108–9, 171–72, 195–96, 199–200, 209–18, 251–52n.1, 269n.1; Arendt and, 4, 159, 193; Bracher and, 14–15, 159; criticisms of, 9–11, 196–98, 209–18, 225n.11, 231n.4, 297n.100; Friedrich and, 4–6, 143, 159; Orwell and, 4, 193. *See also* Friedrich-Brzezinski model; Gleason, Abbott

Trevor-Roper, Hugh, 186

Trilling, Lionel, 203

Trotsky, Leon, 25, 43, 95, 112, 114, 123, 190; in exile, 110, 253n.4; on social fascism, 38; on SPD, 241n.49; on Stalinist-fascist comparison, 65–66, 252–53n.3

Trotskyism, 181

Trotskyists, 104

Ulbricht, Walter, 104

Unabhängige Sozialdemokratische Partei Deutschlands. *See* Independent Social Democratic Party of Germany

Unions: trade and labor, 34–35, 55, 61, 91, 152, 176, 214

United Nations, 186, 211

United States of America, 2, 168, 192, 195–96; and cold war, 10, 174, 177–78, 185–87; as place of exile, 53, 66, 78, 105, 124, 144, 155, 157–59, 176, 178–79, 253n.4; and totalitarian theory, 6, 14–15, 200, 203, 213, 216, 218; and World War II, 109, 117

USPD. *See* Independent Social Democratic Party of Germany

Ustasha, Croatian, 211

Varga, Eugen, 51

Vietnam War, 15, 196

Vorwärts, 87

Wandervögel, 46, 67

Wegner, Franz, 87–88

Wehler, Hans-Ulrich, 301n.114

Weill, Kurt, 159

Weimar Constitution, 21–22, 29, 54–58; Article 48 of, 245n.86

Weimar Republic, 16, 23, 26–29, 32, 34–38, 40, 43, 45, 58, 106, 140, 155–56, 220; collapse of, 14, 21–22, 54–56, 61–63, 122, 151, 166, 168, 182, 190, 211

Weitz, Eric. D., 216, 287n.32

Wels, Otto, 259n.52

West Germany. *See* Federal Republic of Germany

White Rose resistance group, 106

Wiggershaus, Rolf, 143, 273–74n.80

Wilhelm II, Kaiser, 34

Wippermann, Wolfgang, 10, 12, 198–99, 244n.74

Wittfogel, Karl August, 103, 180, 244–45n.80, 288n.38; anti-Communism of, 47, 103, 187–88; background of, 47; and Institute of Social Research, 47, 158, 187; and KPD, 47, 158, 187; *Oriental Despotism*, 47, 188

Wolff, Hans J., 69

Wolin, Richard, 292n.76

Workers' Party of Marxist Unification (Partido Obrero de Unificación Marxista—POUM), 96–97, 104

Working class: under capitalism (Weimar, Nazi, and postwar), 40–41, 129, 183, 214, 299n.108; under Communism, 131, 183, 214; under Nazi regime, 70, 75, 106, 142–43, 156–57, 183, 214, 262–63n.81; and socialist parties, 29, 32, 34, 38, 40–41, 48, 60–62, 138, 178, 214; socialist theories of, 40–41, 54, 59–60, 103, 111–12, 127, 134, 166, 208, 214–15, 268n.133

World War I, 22–23, 29, 31, 34, 43, 53, 87, 93, 103, 111, 157, 164, 171, 210

World War II, 3, 18, 32, 90, 109, 118–19, 157, 168, 171, 210, 297n.100

Worster, Donald, 288n.38

Yakovlev, Alexander, 223n.4

Yugoslavia, 113, 179, 210–11. *See also* Balkans; Bosnia

Zeitschrift für Sozialforschung (and *Studies in Philosophy and Social Science*), 37, 67, 97, 155, 159, 283n.203

Zeitschrift für Sozialismus, 80, 84–87, 89, 135, 261n.69, 261n.70

Zentrum. *See* Center Party

Zetkin, Clara, 24, 27, 31; on fascism, 24–26, 28, 110, 234n.11

Zinoviev, Gregory, 27, 33

Zionism, 215

Zörgiebel, Karl, 35

William David Jones is a graduate of Mt. San Antonio College in Walnut, California, and the University of California at Los Angeles. He received his Ph.D. in history from the Claremont Graduate School. He teaches history at Mt. San Antonio College, the Claremont Graduate University, and the California State Polytechnic University, Pomona.

Typeset in 9.5/13 ITC Stone Serif
with display in Copperplate
Designed by Paula Newcomb
Composed by Jim Proefrock
at the University of Illinois Press
Manufactured by Quinn-Woodbine, Inc.